Fractional Differential Equations, Inclusions and Inequalities with Applications II

Fractional Differential Equations, Inclusions and Inequalities with Applications II

Guest Editor

Sotiris K. Ntouyas

MDPI

Basel • Beijing • Wuhan • Barcelona • Belgrade • Novi Sad • Cluj • Manchester

Guest Editor
Sotiris K. Ntouyas
Department of Mathematics
University of Ioannina
Ioannina
Greece

Editorial Office
MDPI AG
Grosspeteranlage 5
4052 Basel, Switzerland

This is a reprint of the Special Issue, published open access by the journal *Mathematics* (ISSN 2227-7390), freely accessible at: https://www.mdpi.com/journal/mathematics/special_issues/Fractional_Differential_Equations_Inclusions_Inequalities_Applications_II.

For citation purposes, cite each article independently as indicated on the article page online and as indicated below:

Lastname, A.A.; Lastname, B.B. Article Title. *Journal Name* **Year**, *Volume Number*, Page Range.

ISBN 978-3-7258-7028-8 (Hbk)
ISBN 978-3-7258-7029-5 (PDF)
https://doi.org/10.3390/books978-3-7258-7029-5

Contents

About the Editor

Sotiris K. Ntouyas

Sotiris K. Ntouyas is Professor Emeritus in the Department of Mathematics of the University of Ioannina, Greece. He received his B.S. and Ph.D. from the University of Ioannina in 1972 and 1980, respectively. His research interests include initial and boundary value problems for differential equations (ordinary, functional, with deviating arguments, neutral, partial, integrodifferential, inclusions, impulsive, fuzzy, stochastic, fractional), inequalities, asymptotic behavior and controllability. He has contributed to more than 825 papers that have been published in refereed journals. He is the co-author of the following books: *Impulsive Differential Equations and Inclusions* (Hindawi), *Controllabibility for Semilinear Functional Differential Equations and Inclusions* (Wydawnictwo Naukowe), *Quantum Calculus: New Concepts, Impulsive IVPs and BVPs, Inequalities* (World Scientific), *Hadamard-Type Fractional Differential Equations, Inclusions and Inequalities* (Springer), *Nonlocal Nonlinear Fractional-Order Boundary Value Problems* (World Scientific) and *Nonlinear Systems of Fractional Differential Equations* (Springer). He is a member of the editorial boards of 21 international journals and a reviewer for many international journals. He appears in the 2018 list of Highly Cited Researchers, published by Clarivate Analytics.

Preface

Fractional calculus extends the principles of classical calculus to non-integer real orders and has emerged as a significant and intriguing domain of research. It focuses on exploring so-called fractional derivatives and integrals across complex domains and their wide-ranging applications. Over the past decade, this field has gained considerable attention. Its relevance has drawn the interest of numerous scholars due to its extensive use in diverse disciplines such as probability theory, biomathematics, image analysis, fluid dynamics, material science, viscoelasticity, and engineering, among others.

In recent years, many mathematicians have employed their own symbols and methodologies to explore various definitions that align with the concept of fractional-order differentiation and integration.

We are delighted to present this Reprint, which features a curated selection of 19 papers highlighting recent progress in the field of fractional differential equations and inclusions. Each contribution underwent thorough peer review by multiple experts and was originally published in the Special Issue titled "Fractional Differential Equations, Inclusions and Inequalities with Applications II" in the journal *Mathematics*. These works offer fresh and valuable insights across various aspects of fractional differential equations, enabling readers to stay abreast of the latest advancements in this area.

We extend our sincere gratitude to the editorial team for their generous support throughout the publication process. Our heartfelt thanks also go to the authors for their outstanding research contributions and to the reviewers for their meticulous evaluation of the submitted manuscripts.

As Guest Editor, I would like to express my gratitude to all of the authors for their contributions to this Special Issue. I would also like to thank all reviewers for their assistance and valuable efforts in improving the quality of the papers. Lastly, I am incredibly grateful to *Mathematics* (ISSN 2227-7390) for all of the support given during the development and publication of the Special Issue "Fractional Differential Equations, Inclusions and Inequalities with Applications II".

Sotiris K. Ntouyas
Guest Editor

mathematics

Editorial

Editorial for the Special Issue of Mathematics "Fractional Differential Equations, Inclusions and Inequalities with Applications II"

Sotiris K. Ntouyas

Department of Mathematics, University of Ioannina, 451 10 Ioannina, Greece; sntouyas@uoi.gr

1. Introduction

Within the field of fractional calculus, defined fractional derivatives and integrals within complex domains and their practical applications are frequently explored, and in recent years, this field has seen a significant rise in research interest. Fractional differential equations, in particular, have garnered widespread attention in academic literature due to their effectiveness in modeling various real-world phenomena across disciplines such as physics, engineering, design, materials science, fluid dynamics, probability theory, image analysis, optimal control, and more. These equations are also considered superior to traditional integer-order differential equations when it comes to representing the hereditary characteristics of different materials and dynamic systems.

2. Special Issue Overview

This Special Issue, entitled "Fractional Differential Equations, Inclusions, and Inequalities with Applications II" emphasizes new developments in both the conceptual basis and applied aspects of fractional differential equations, inclusions, and inequalities, as well as the systems involving these elements. The scope includes, but is not limited to, the following topics:

- Oscillation for fractional-order differential equations, Contribution 1;
- (p,q)-difference equations, Contribution 2;
- q-difference inclusions, Contribution 5;
- Integral inequalities, Contributions 4, 10, 18;
- Fractional integro-differential equations, Contribution 6;
- Sequential fractional differential equations, Contribution 7;
- Sequential fractional differential inclusions, Contribution 3;
- Numerical fractional differential equations, Contribution 8;
- Λ-fractional differential equations, Contribution 9;
- Positive solutions for fractional boundary value problems, Contributions 13, 19;
- Stochastic fractional differential equations, Contribution 14;
- Fractional-order systems, Contribution 17;
- Caputo fractional differential equations, Contributions 12, 15;
- Delay difference equations, Contribution 16;
- Black–Scholes fractional equations, Contribution 11.

A total of eighty manuscripts were received, out of which nineteen papers authored by sixty-eight researchers were accepted for publication. The contributing authors represent twenty-one different countries:

1. Algeria (1)
2. Azerbaijan (1)
3. China (8)
4. Egyp (3)
5. Greece (3)
6. India (2)
7. Indonesia (2)
8. Iraq (2)
9. Iran (7)
10. Jordan (3)
11. Malaysia (2)
12. Pakistan (2)
13. Poland (1)
14. Portugal (1)
15. Romania (1)
16. Saudi Arabia (9)
17. Taiwan (1)
18. Thailand (6)
19. Turkiye (3)
20. UAE (3)
21. USA (7)

This Special Issue features 19 articles spanning various areas within the field of fractional differential equations. The key findings of these contributions are summarized below.

- In Contribution 1, the authors provide an in-depth overview of recent progress in the study of oscillatory behavior associated with fractional difference equations. Various forms of these equations are examined through the application of both nabla and delta operators.
- The existence and uniqueness of solutions for a fractional (p,q)-difference equation with separated local boundary conditions are explored in Contribution 2. Uniqueness is established via Banach's contraction principle, while existence is proven using Krasnosel'skiĭ's fixed point theorem and the Leray–Schauder alternative. Several illustrative examples are included to support the main results.
- In Contribution 3, the authors focus on establishing theoretical existence results for a new class of problems that incorporates a sequential Caputo-type term within a hybrid integro-differential framework. The boundary conditions are expressed as hybrid constraints involving multiple orders of integro-differential operators. The study begins by deriving fundamental inequalities related to the corresponding integral equation. To address the problem, the authors employ recently developed analytical techniques involving product operators in Banach algebras, along with special function-based tools such as $\alpha - \psi$-contractions and α-admissible mappings. These methods are used to establish existence criteria for the proposed class of mixed sequential hybrid boundary value problems. Key properties—including the approximate endpoint property, the C_α-property, and compactness—are essential for the analysis. The paper concludes with two illustrative examples that demonstrate the applicability of the theoretical results.
- In Contribution 4, the authors introduce the notion of (g,h)-convexity, a generalized form of coordinated convexity defined in realtion to a pair of functions on the coordinates. The fundamental properties of this new convexity concept are investigated in detail. Additionally, the study derives new Hermite–Hadamard and Ostrowski-

 https://doi.org/10.3390/math14030424

type inequalities corresponding to this form of coordinated convexity. These results extend and generalize several known inequalities in the existing literature. The paper concludes with various mathematical examples and graphical representations that illustrate and validate the newly developed inequalities.

- In Contribution 5, the authors analyze the existence and topological configuration of the solution set associated with a q-fractional differential inclusion in a Banach space setting. Analytical techniques are drawn from set-valued analysis, the Kuratowski non-compactness measure, and Darbo's fixed point principle. To validate the theoretical results, an illustrative example is presented.
- In Contribution 6, the authors establish sufficient conditions for the existence of both local and global solutions for a general class of nonlinear fractional integro-differential equations in two dimensions. The uniqueness of these solutions is also proven. To enable numerical approximation, the study utilizes operational matrices derived from two-variable shifted Jacobi polynomials within a collocation method framework, thereby converting the original equations into a system that can be efficiently solved. Error estimates for the proposed numerical approach are provided. A set of five test problems is presented, and the corresponding numerical results demonstrate the accuracy, efficiency, and practical effectiveness of the method.
- Contribution 7 introduces and explores a novel class of boundary value problems characterized by a mixed-type fractional differential equation involving both the ψ_1-Hilfer and ψ_2-Caputo fractional derivatives, coupled with non-local integro-differential boundary conditions. The uniqueness of the solutions is demonstrated via the Banach contraction method and ensures existing results via the Leray–Schauder nonlinear alternative approach. Numerical examples are included to illustrate and validate the theoretical results.
- Contribution 8 aims to present a novel numerical method for solving fractional boundary value problems. This method relies on two numerical schemes: A fractional central scheme is considered for approximating the Caputo derivative of order α, along with a newly developed central formula for approximating the Caputo derivative of order 2α, where $0 < \alpha \leq 1$. The first method is re-examined, while the second is derived using the generalized Taylor expansion. The stability of the proposed approach is examined through well-established theoretical frameworks. Additionally, several numerical examples are provided to showcase the method's accuracy and practical utility.
- The study in Contribution 9 investigates wave propagation in solids using the framework of inherently non-local Λ-fractional analysis. Beginning with the fundamental equations of Λ-fractional continuum mechanics, the corresponding Λ-fractional wave equations are formulated. Due to the global nature of the variational formulation in this setting, the analysis allows for the representation of discontinuities in strain or stress. The model is further employed to examine impact-induced phase transitions in composite materials exhibiting both elastic and viscoelastic behavior.
- The central focus of Contribution 10 lies in developing a generalized and original identity related to the Caputo–Fabrizio fractional operator. Building on this new identity, the authors derive a series of fractional integral inequalities related to exponentially convex functions. Moreover, the paper presents applications of these results to specific special means.
- In Contribution 11, the study investigates methods for solving the modified fractional Black–Scholes equation. Given the crucial role of option pricing theory in financial markets, call and put options help investors theoretically determine the optimal times to buy, sell, or hold stocks to maximize returns. However, the classical Black–Scholes model, based on the assumption of normally distributed returns, often yields

https://doi.org/10.3390/math14030424

option pricing formulas that do not accurately capture real market dynamics. Hence, modifying the model is necessary for more realistic option valuations. To solve the modified fractional Black–Scholes equation, this work implements a hybrid technique merging the finite difference method with the fractional differential transformation method. The results indicate that this combined technique offers a highly accurate approximation of the solution.

- As noted in several studies, the equivalence between Caputo-type fractional differential equations and their corresponding integral formulations may fail outside absolutely continuous function spaces, including within certain Hölder spaces. To address this limitation, Contribution 12 introduces a novel fractional integral operator that acts as the right inverse of the Caputo derivative in specific Hölder spaces with critical orders of less than 1. The paper provides multiple illustrative examples and counterexamples to emphasize the importance of this development. As an application, the method is used to analyze the boundary value problem for the Langevin fractional differential equation $\frac{d_{\psi}^{\beta,\mu}}{dt^{\beta}}\left(\frac{d_{\psi}^{\alpha,\mu}}{dt^{\alpha}}+\lambda\right)u(t)=h(t,u(t)), t\in[x_1,y_1], \lambda\in\mathbb{R}$, where $h\in C([x_1,y_1]\times\mathbb{R})$ and the critical fractional orders $\beta,\alpha\in(0,1)$, subject to appropriate initial or boundary conditions. The analysis is further extended to a wider class of ψ -tempered Hilfer problems involving ψ -tempered fractional derivatives. Additionally, boundary value problems for Bagley–Torvik type fractional differential equations are examined.
- The study of Contribution 13 investigates the existence and uniqueness of solutions to boundary fractional difference equations framed within the context of Riemann–Liouville operators. The study begins by revisiting the general solution of the related homogeneous problem involving fractional operators. Next, the Green's function for the fractional boundary value problem is constructed by applying homogeneous boundary conditions to determine the unknown constants. The existence of solutions is then established through fixed-point theorems applied to this Green's function. Moreover, uniqueness results are derived under conditions involving the Lipschitz constant.
- In Contribution 14, a novel numerical method is introduced for fractional stochastic differential equations featuring neutral delays. The method is based on a stepwise collocation technique combined with Jacobi poly-fractonomials to effectively treat the unknown stochastic components. To implement this, the original delay differential equations are transformed into equivalent delay-free systems, making them amenable to the collocation technique. The iterative application of the method leads to a system of nonlinear equations at each step. A comprehensive analysis of the method's convergence is provided. The accuracy and computational efficiency of the proposed technique are validated through a series of numerical experiments.
- Contribution 15 addresses comments on sequential Caputo fractional differential equations governed by fractional initial and boundary conditions.
- Contribution 16 examines a system of inhomogeneous second-order difference equations featuring linear terms with noncommutative matrix coefficients. A closed-form solution is obtained by introducing novel delayed matrix sine and cosine functions, employing the Z-transform alongside a determining function. This framework facilitates the analysis of iterative learning control by integrating suitable update rules and establishing sufficient conditions to guarantee asymptotic convergence in tracking performance.
- Contribution 17 investigates barrier function-based safety control within fractional-order dynamical systems, an area less explored compared to their integer-order counterparts. While barrier functions have been extensively used to guarantee safety in

integer-order systems—including nonlinear, hybrid, and linear models—this study extends their application to fractional-order systems. The authors introduce two novel constructs: the Caputo reciprocal barrier function and the Caputo zeroing barrier function. They establish theorems demonstrating that these functions ensure uniform asymptotic or exponential stability while preserving safety. Furthermore, the paper proposes a new concept of input-to-state safety for Caputo fractional-order systems, accompanied by two criteria derived from the newly introduced barrier functions. These contributions lay a foundational framework for advancing safety control in fractional-order systems.
- In Contribution 18, new theoretical advances concerning the well-posedness and Ulam–Hyers stability of fractional systems are presented, with a focus on Caputo–Katugampola fractional stochastic delay integro-differential equations. The authors develop a generalized version of Grönwall's inequality, which is then used to establish Ulam–Hyers stability in the $\mathcal{L}^p$ space. These results extend existing theories by incorporating the Caputo–Katugampola fractional derivative framework, thereby enriching the mathematical foundation of fractional differential equations. An illustrative example is provided to demonstrate and validate the theoretical findings.
- Contribution 19 examines the positive solution existence and non-existence for a non-linear Riemann–Liouville fractional boundary value problem of order $\alpha + 2n$ where $\alpha \in (m-1, m]$, with $m \geq 3$ and m, n are natural numbers. The boundary conditions are based on Lidstone-type formulations.The non-linear term involves a positive parameter, and the authors establish conditions on this parameter that dictate the existence or non-existence of positive solutions. By convolving the Green functions from a lower-order problem and its conjugate counterpart, a Green's function is constructed and applied along with the Guo–Krasnosel'skiĭ fixed-point theorem. Illustrative examples highlight the parameter values for which solutions exist or fail to exist.

We hope this Special Issue, along with the ideas and publications it contains, will engage readers and inspire further research on fractional differential equations, inclusions, and inequalities.

Funding: This research received no external funding.

Data Availability Statement: Data is contained within the article.

Acknowledgments: Serving as Guest Editor, I wish to express my deep gratitude to all authors for their significant contributions to this Special Issue. I would also like to express my deep appreciation to the reviewers for their efforts in enhancing the quality of the papers. I am deeply grateful to *Mathematics* (ISSN 2227-7390).

Conflicts of Interest: The author declares no conflict of interest.

List of Contributions

1. Alzabut, J.; Agarwal, R.P.; Grace, S.R.; Jonnalagadda, J.M.; Selvam G.M.; Wang C. A Survey on the Oscillation of Solutions for Fractional Difference Equations. *Mathematics* **2022**, *10*, 894. https://doi.org/10.3390/math10060894.
2. Neang, P.; Nonlaopon, K.; Tariboon, J.; Ntouyas, S.K.; Ahmad, B. Existence and Uniqueness Results for Fractional (p, q)-Difference Equations with Separated Boundary Conditions. *Mathematics* **2022**, *10*, 767. https://doi.org/10.3390/math10050767.
3. Etemad, S.; Ntouyas, S.K.; Ahmad, B.; Rezapour, S.; Tariboon, J. Sequential Fractional Hybrid Inclusions: A Theoretical Study via Dhage's Technique and Special Contractions. *Mathematics* **2022**, *10*, 2090. https://doi.org/10.3390/math10122090.

4. Ali, M.A.; Wannalookkhee, F.; Budak, H.; Etemad, S.; Rezapour S. New Hermite–Hadamard and Ostrowski-Type Inequalities for Newly Introduced Co-Ordinated Convexity with Respect to a Pair of Functions. *Mathematics* **2022**, *10*, 3469. https://doi.org/10.3390/math10193469.
5. Rezaiguia, A.; Hassan, T.S. Topological Structure and Existence of Solutions Set for q-Fractional Differential Inclusion in Banach Space. *Mathematics* **2023**, *11*, 683. https://doi.org/10.3390/math11030683.
6. Eftekhari, T.; Rashidinia, J. An Investigation on Existence, Uniqueness, and Approximate Solutions for Two-Dimensional Nonlinear Fractional Integro-Differential Equations. *Mathematics* **2023**, *11*, 824. https://doi.org/10.3390/math11040824.
7. Sitho, S.; Ntouyas, S.K.; Sudprasert, C.; Tariboon, J. Integro-Differential Boundary Conditions to the Sequential ψ_1-Hilfer and ψ_2-Caputo Fractional Differential Equations. *Mathematics* **2023**, *11*, 867. https://doi.org/10.3390/math11040867.
8. Al-Nana, A.; Batiha, I.M.; Momani, S. A Numerical Approach for Dealing with Fractional Boundary Value Problems. *Mathematics* **2023**, *11*, 4082. https://doi.org/10.3390/math11194082.
9. Lazopoulos, K.A; Lazopoulos A.K. On Λ-Fractional Wave Propagation in Solids. *Mathematics* **2023**, *11*, 4183. https://doi.org/10.3390/math11194183.
10. Junjua M.; Qayyum, A.; Munir, A.; Budak, H.; Saleem, M.M.; Supadi, S.S. A Study of Some New Hermite–Hadamard Inequalities via Specific Convex Functions with Applications. *Mathematics* **2024**, *12*, 478. https://doi.org/10.3390/math12030478.
11. Sugandha, A.; Rusyaman, E.; Sukono; Carnia, E. Using a Mix of Finite Difference Methods and Fractional Differential Transformations to Solve Modified Black–Scholes Fractional Equations. *Mathematics* **2024**, *12*, 1077. https://doi.org/10.3390/math12071077.
12. Cichoń, M.; Salem, H.A.H.; Shammakh W. On the Equivalence between Differential and Integral Forms of Caputo-Type Fractional Problems on Hölder Spaces. *Mathematics* **2024**, *12*, 2631. https://doi.org/10.3390/math12172631.
13. Mohammed, P.P.; Agarwal, R.P.; Yousif, M.A.; Al-Sarairah, E.; Lupas, A.A.; Abdelwahed, M. Theoretical Results on Positive Solutions in Delta Riemann–Liouville Setting. *Mathematics* **2024**, *12*, 2864. https://doi.org/10.3390/math12182864.
14. Babaei, A.; Banihashemi, S.; Moghaddam, B.P.; Dabiri, A.; Galhano, A. Efficient Solutions for Stochastic Fractional Differential Equations with a Neutral Delay Using Jacobi Poly-Fractonomials. *Mathematics* **2024**, *12*, 3273. https://doi.org/10.3390/math12203273.
15. Vatsala, A.S.; Sambandham, B. Remarks on Sequential Caputo Fractional Differential Equations with Fractional Initial and Boundary Conditions. *Mathematics* **2024**, *12*, 3970. https://doi.org/10.3390/math12243970.
16. Mahmudov, N.; Awadalla, M.; Arab, M. Explicit Form of Solutions of Second-Order Delayed Difference Equations: Application to Iterative Learning Control. *Mathematics* **2025**, *13*, 916. https://doi.org/10.3390/math13060916.
17. Zhu, Z.Z.; Shen, B.; Yao, L.; Chai, Y.; Song, Z. Caputo Barrier Functions and Their Applications to the Safety, Safety-and-Stability, and Input-to-State Safety of a Class of Fractional-Order Systems. *Mathematics* **2025**, *13*, 1215. https://doi.org/10.3390/math13081215.
18. Djaouti, A.M.; Liaqat, M.I. Generalized Grönwall Inequality and Ulam–Hyers Stability in $\mathcal{L}^p$ Space for Fractional Stochastic Delay Integro-Differential Equations. *Mathematics* **2025**, *13*, 1252. https://doi.org/10.3390/math13081252.
19. Lyons, J.W.; Neugebauer, J.T.; Wingo, A.G. Existence and Nonexistence of Positive Solutions for Fractional Boundary Value Problems with Lidstone-Inspired Fractional Conditions. *Mathematics* **2025**, *13*, 1336. https://doi.org/10.3390/math13081336.

mathematics MDPI

Article

Existence and Nonexistence of Positive Solutions for Fractional Boundary Value Problems with Lidstone-Inspired Fractional Conditions

Jeffrey W. Lyons [1,*], Jeffrey T. Neugebauer [2] and Aaron G. Wingo [3]

[1] Department of Mathematical Sciences, The Citadel, 171 Moultrie Street, Charleston, SC 29409, USA
[2] Department of Mathematics and Statistics, Eastern Kentucky University, 521 Lancaster Avenue, Richmond, KY 40475, USA; jeffrey.neugebauer@eku.edu
[3] Independent Researcher, Marieta, GA 30060, USA; aaron.wingo@yahoo.com
* Correspondence: jlyons3@citadel.edu

Abstract: This paper investigates the existence and nonexistence of positive solutions for a class of nonlinear Riemann–Liouville fractional boundary value problems of order $\alpha + 2n$, where $\alpha \in (m-1, m]$ with $m \geq 3$ and $m, n \in \mathbb{N}$. The conjugate fractional boundary conditions are inspired by Lidstone conditions. The nonlinearity depends on a positive parameter on which we identify constraints that determine the existence or nonexistence of positive solutions. Our method involves constructing Green's function by convolving the Green functions of a lower-order fractional boundary value problem and a conjugate boundary value problem and using properties of this Green function to apply the Guo–Krasnosel'skii fixed-point theorem. Illustrative examples are provided to demonstrate existence and nonexistence intervals.

Keywords: fractional derivative; Lidstone; fixed-point theorem; existence; nonexistence; convolution

MSC: 26A33; 34A08

1. Introduction

Let $m, n \in \mathbb{N}$, $m \geq 3$, with $\alpha \in (m-1, m]$ and $\beta \in [1, m-1]$. Consider a Riemann–Liouville fractional boundary value problem

$$D_{0^+}^{\alpha+2n} u(t) + (-1)^n \lambda g(t) f(u) = 0, \quad 0 < t < 1, \tag{1}$$

subject to the Lidstone-inspired boundary conditions

$$\begin{aligned} u^{(i)}(0) = 0, \quad i = 0, 1, \ldots, m-2, \quad D_{0^+}^{\beta} u(1) = 0, \\ D_{0^+}^{\alpha+2l} u(0) = D_{0^+}^{\alpha+2l} u(1) = 0, \quad l = 0, 1, \ldots, n-1. \end{aligned} \tag{2}$$

Here, $f : [0, \infty) \to [0, \infty)$ and $g : [0, 1] \to [0, \infty)$ are continuous functions with $g(t)$ satisfying the condition $\int_0^1 g(t)\, dt > 0$, and $\lambda > 0$ is a positive parameter. This paper is concerned with the existence and nonexistence of positive solutions to (1) and (2).

To address this, we follow the procedure of Eloe et al. in [1] of constructing the associated Green's function for the given problem by convolving a lower-order Green's function, $G_0(t, s)$, for the equation of a conjugate boundary value problem. We present properties of Green's function, many of which can be found in [2,3]. Then, we deploy those in an application of the Guo–Krasnosel'skii fixed-point theorem.

Our method involves the analysis of the operator defined by

$$Tu(t) = (-1)^n \lambda \int_0^1 G(t,s)g(s)f(u(s))\,ds,$$

which will be shown to have a fixed point under suitable conditions on parameter λ. This fixed point is a positive solution to (1) and (2). We will also give suitable conditions on λ for the nonexistence of solutions to (1) and (2).

This study extends the existing literature on fractional boundary value problems that leverage Guo–Krasnosel'skii's fixed-point theorem. The major impetus of this work is two papers [2,3]. In the former, Lyons and Neugebauer used the convolution of two Green functions to prove existence and nonexistence results for two-point fractional boundary value problems. Recently, the latter work by Neugebauer and Wingo investigated a way to move to an even higher-order two-point boundary value problem using convolution and induction. The novelty here is that repeated convolution with induction leads one to creating arbitrary $\alpha + 2n$-order two-point boundary value problems.

Previous articles have applied various fixed-point theorems to demonstrate the existence of positive solutions for similar problems. For results obtained by employing the Guo–Krasnosel'skii fixed-point theorem similar to that realized in this paper, we cite [4–7]. One may find singular nonlinearity results in [8,9]. A quite recent application for the Guo–Krasnosel'skii fixed-point theorem to fractional boundary value problems was studied by Raghavendran et al. in [10]. Other recent applications of fixed-point theory to fractional boundary value problems were carried out by Zhang et al. in [11,12].

Here, we use the Guo–Krasnosel'skii fixed-point theorem to guarantee the existence of positive solutions by establishing two separate sizing conditions on parameter λ based upon the liminfs and limsups of the nonlinearity. Additionally, we provide nonexistence results determined with the parameter. This approach is based on the properties of Green's function, which plays a critical role in showing the existence of positive solutions.

Section 2 provides definitions for the Riemann–Liousville fractional derivative and suggestions for further study therein and states the Guo–Krasnosel'skii fixed-point theorem. The subsequent sections are devoted to the construction of Green's function and its properties. Then, in Sections 5 and 6, we establish intervals for λ that yield the existence or nonexistence of positive solutions. Finally, we present two examples to illustrate the application of our results.

2. Preliminaries and the Fixed-Point Theorem

We begin by defining the Riemann–Liouville fractional integral, which is used to define the Riemann–Liouville fractional derivative used in this work. Both are widely adopted and commonly used. Then, we present Guo–Krasnosel'skii's fixed-point theorem [13,14].

Definition 1. *Let $\nu > 0$. The Riemann–Liouville fractional integral of a function u of order ν, denoted $I_{0+}^{\nu} u$, is defined as*

$$I_{0+}^{\nu} u(t) = \frac{1}{\Gamma(\nu)} \int_0^t (t-s)^{\nu-1} u(s)ds,$$

provided the right-hand side exists.

Definition 2. *Let n denote a positive integer and assume $n-1<\alpha\le n$. The Riemann–Liouville fractional derivative of order α of the function $u:[0,1]\to\mathbb{R}$, denoted $D^{\alpha}_{0^+}u$, is defined as*

$$D^{\alpha}_{0^+}u(t)=\frac{1}{\Gamma(n-\alpha)}\frac{d^n}{dt^n}\int_0^t (t-s)^{n-\alpha-1}u(s)ds=D^n I^{n-\alpha}_{0^+}u(t),$$

provided the right-hand side exists.

We refer to [15–18] for further study of fractional calculus and fractional differential equations.

Theorem 1 (Guo–Krasnosel'skii fixed-point theorem)**.** *Let $\mathcal{B}$ be a Banach space, and let $\mathcal{P}\subset X$ be a cone in $\mathcal{P}$. Assume that Ω_1 and Ω_2 are open sets with $0\in\Omega_1$, and $\overline{\Omega}_1\subset\Omega_2$. Let $T:\mathcal{P}\cap(\overline{\Omega}_2\backslash\Omega_1)\to\mathcal{P}$ be a completely continuous operator such that either of the following holds:*

1. $\|Tu\|\ge\|u\|,\ u\in\mathcal{P}\cap\partial\Omega_1$, *and* $\|Tu\|\le\|u\|,\ u\in\mathcal{P}\cap\partial\Omega_2$;
2. $\|Tu\|\le\|u\|,\ u\in\mathcal{P}\cap\partial\Omega_1$, *and* $\|Tu\|\ge\|u\|,\ u\in\mathcal{P}\cap\partial\Omega_2$.

Then, T has a fixed point in $\mathcal{P}\cap(\overline{\Omega}_2\backslash\Omega_1)$.

3. Green's Function

Now, we construct Green's function, used for (1) and (2) utilizing induction with a convolution of a lower-order problem and a conjugate problem. The procedure is similar to that found in [3].

First, the conjugate boundary value problem

$$-u''=0,\quad 0<t<1,\quad u(0)=0,\quad u(1)=0,$$

has a well-known Green's function

$$G_{conj}(t,s)=\begin{cases} s(1-t), & 0\le s<t\le 1,\\ t(1-s), & 0\le t<s\le 1.\end{cases}$$

Let $G_0(t,s)$ be Green's function for

$$-D^{\alpha}_{0^+}au=0,\quad 0<t<1,\quad u^{(i)}(0)=0,\ i=0,1,\dots,m-2,\quad D^{\beta}_{0^+}u(1)=0,$$

which is given by [19]

$$G_0(t,s)=\frac{1}{\Gamma(\alpha)}\begin{cases} t^{\alpha-1}(1-s)^{\alpha-1-\beta}-(t-s)^{\alpha-1}, & 0\le s<t\le 1,\\ \\ t^{\alpha-1}(1-s)^{\alpha-1-\beta}, & 0\le t\le s<1.\end{cases}$$

For $k=1,\dots,n-1$, recursively define $G_k(t,s)$ by

$$G_k(t,s)=-\int_0^1 G_{k-1}(t,r)G_{conj}(r,s)dr.$$

Then,

$$G_n(t,s)=-\int_0^1 G_{n-1}(t,r)G_{conj}(r,s)dr,$$

is Green's function for

$$-D^{\alpha+2n}_{0^+}u(t)=0,\quad 0<t<1,$$

with boundary condition (2), and $G_{n-1}(t,s)$ is Green's function for

$$-D_{0^+}^{\alpha+2(n-1)}u(t) = 0, \quad 0 < t < 1,$$

with boundary conditions

$$u^{(i)}(0) = 0,\ i = 0,1,\ldots,m-2, \quad D_{0^+}^{\beta}u(1) = 0,$$

$$D_{0^+}^{\alpha+2l}u(0) = D_{0^+}^{\alpha+2l}u(1) = 0,\ l = 0,1,\ldots,n-2.$$

To see this, for the base case $k = 1$, consider the linear differential equation

$$D_{0^+}^{\alpha+2}u(t) + h(t) = 0, \quad 0 < t < 1,$$

satisfying the boundary conditions

$$u^{(i)}(0) = 0,\ i = 0,1,\ldots,m-2, \quad D_{0^+}^{\beta}u(1) = 0,$$

$$D_{0^+}^{\alpha}u(0) = 0, \quad D_{0^+}^{\alpha}u(1) = 0.$$

Make the change of variable:

$$v(t) = D_{0^+}^{\alpha+2-2}u(t).$$

Then,

$$D^2v(t) = D^2D_{0^+}^{\alpha+2-2}u(t) = D_{0^+}^{\alpha+2}u(t) = -h(t),$$

and since $v(t) = D_{0^+}^{\alpha}u(t)$,

$$v(0) = D_{0^+}^{\alpha}u(0) = 0 \quad \text{and} \quad v(1) = D_{0^+}^{\alpha}u(1) = 0.$$

Thus, v satisfies the Dirichlet boundary value problem:

$$v'' + h(t) = 0, \quad 0 < t < 1,$$

$$v(0) = 0, \quad v(1) = 0.$$

Also, u now satisfies a lower-order boundary value problem:

$$D_{0^+}^{\alpha}u(t) = v(t), \quad 0 < t < 1,$$

$$u^{(i)}(0) = 0,\ i = 0,1,\ldots,m-2, \quad D_{0^+}^{\beta}u(1) = 0.$$

So,

$$\begin{aligned} u(t) &= \int_0^1 G_0(t,s)(-v(s))ds \\ &= \int_0^1 G_0(t,s)\left(-\int_0^1 G_{conj}(s,r)h(r)ds\right)dr \\ &= \int_0^1 \left(\int_0^1 -G_0(t,s)G_{conj}(s,r)ds\right)h(r)dr. \end{aligned}$$

Therefore,

$$u(t) = \int_0^1 G_1(t,s)h(s)ds,$$

where

$$G_1(t,s) = -\int_0^1 G_0(t,r)G_{conj}(r,s)dr.$$

For the inductive step, the argument is similar. Assume that $k = n-1$ is true, and consider the linear differential equation

$$D_{0^+}^{\alpha+2n}u(t) + k(t) = 0, \quad 0 < t < 1,$$

satisfying boundary condition (2).

Make the change of variables

$$v(t) = D_{0^+}^{\alpha+2(n-1)}u(t)$$

so that

$$D^2v(t) = D_{0^+}^{\alpha+2n} = -k(t)$$

and

$$v(0) = D_{0^+}^{\alpha+2(n-1)}u(0) = 0 \quad \text{and} \quad v(1) = D_{0^+}^{\alpha+2(n-1)}v(1) = 0.$$

Similarly to before, $v(t)$ satisfies the Dirichlet boundary value problem

$$v'' + k(t) = 0, \quad 0 < t < 1,$$

$$v(0) = 0, \quad v(1) = 0,$$

while $u(t)$ satisfies the lower-order problem

$$D_{0^+}^{\alpha+2(n-1)}u(t) = v(t), \quad 0 < t < 1,$$

$$u(0) = 0, \quad D_{0^+}^{\beta}u(1) = 0,$$

$$D_{0^+}^{\alpha+2l}u(0) = D_{0^+}^{\alpha+2l}u(1) = 0,\ l = 0,1,\ldots,n-2.$$

By induction,

$$\begin{aligned} u(t) &= \int_0^1 G_{n-1}(t,s)(-v(s))ds \\ &= \int_0^1 \left(-\int_0^1 G_{n-1}(t,s)G_{conj}(s,r)ds\right)k(r)dr \\ &= \int_0^1 G_n(t,s)k(s)ds. \end{aligned}$$

Therefore,

$$u(t) = \int_0^1 G_n(t,s)k(s)ds,$$

where

$$G_n(t,s) = -\int_0^1 G_{n-1}(t,r)G_{conj}(r,s)dr.$$

So, the unique solution to

$$D_{0^+}^{\alpha+2n}u(t) + k(t) = 0, \quad 0 < t < 1,$$

satisfying boundary condition (2) is given by

$$u(t) = \int_0^1 G_n(t,s)k(s)ds.$$

4. Green's Function Properties

We now discuss properties for $G_n(t,s)$ that are inherited from $G_0(t,s)$ and $G_{conj}(t,s)$. The results of the first lemma regarding $G_{conj}(t,s)$ are well known and easily verifiable.

Lemma 1. *For* $(t,s) \in [0,1] \times [0,1]$, $G_{conj}(t,s) \in C^{(1)}$ *and* $G_{conj}(t,s) \geq 0$.

The following lemma regarding $G_0(t,s)$ is Lemma 3.1 proved in [2].

Lemma 2. *The following are true:*

(1) *For* $(t,s) \in [0,1] \times [0,1)$, $G_0(t,s) \in C^{(1)}$.
(2) *For* $(t,s) \in (0,1) \times (0,1)$, $G_0(t,s) > 0$ *and* $\frac{\partial}{\partial t} G_0(t,s) > 0$.
(3) *For* $(t,s) \in [0,1] \times [0,1)$, $t^{\alpha-1} G_0(1,s) \leq G_0(t,s) \leq G_0(1,s)$.

Parts (1) and (2) of the following lemma regarding the convoluted Green's function $G_n(t,s)$ are proved in Lemma 5.1 [3], and part (3) is proven here inductively.

Lemma 3. *The following are true:*

(1) *For* $(t,s) \in [0,1] \times [0,1)$, $G_n(t,s) \in C^{(1)}$.
(2) *For* $(t,s) \in (0,1) \times (0,1)$, $(-1)^n G_n(t,s) > 0$ *and* $(-1)^n \frac{\partial}{\partial t} G_n(t,s) > 0$.
(3) *For* $(t,s) \in [0,1] \times [0,1)$,

$$(-1)^n t^{\alpha-1} G_n(1,s) \leq (-1)^n G_n(t,s) \leq (-1)^n G_n(1,s).$$

Proof. For part (3), we proceed inductively.

For the base case $k = 1$, we use Lemma 2 (3) to find

$$\begin{aligned}
(-1)^1 t^{\alpha-1} G_1(1,s) &= -t^{\alpha-1}\left(-\int_0^1 G_0(1,r) G_{conj}(r,s)dr\right) \\
&= -\left(\int_0^1 -t^{\alpha-1} G_0(1,r) G_{conj}(r,s)dr\right) \\
&\leq -\left(\int_0^1 -G_0(t,r) G_{conj}(r,s)dr\right) \\
&= -\left(-\int_0^1 G_0(t,r) G_{conj}(r,s)dr\right) \\
&= (-1)^1 G_1(t,s),
\end{aligned}$$

and

$$\begin{aligned}
(-1)^1 G_1(t,s) &= -\left(-\int_0^1 G_0(t,r) G_{conj}(r,s)dr\right) \\
&= \int_0^1 G_0(t,r) G_{conj}(r,s)dr \\
&\leq \int_0^1 G_0(1,r) G_{conj}(r,s)dr \\
&= -\left(-\int_0^1 G_0(1,r) G_{conj}(r,s)dr\right) \\
&= (-1)^1 G_1(1,s).
\end{aligned}$$

Now, assume that $k = n - 1$ is true. Then,

$$\begin{aligned}(-1)^n t^{\alpha-1} G_n(1,s) &= (-1)^n t^{\alpha-1}\left(-\int_0^1 G_{n-1}(1,r)G_{conj}(r,s)dr\right)\\ &= (-1)^2\left(\int_0^1 (-1)^{n-1} t^{\alpha-1} G_{n-1}(1,r)G_{conj}(r,s)dr\right)\\ &\leq (-1)^2\left(\int_0^1 (-1)^{n-1} G_{n-1}(t,r)G_{conj}(r,s)dr\right)\\ &= (-1)^n\left(-\int_0^1 G_{n-1}(t,r)G_{conj}(r,s)dr\right)\\ &= (-1)^n G_n(t,s),\end{aligned}$$

and

$$\begin{aligned}(-1)^n G_n(t,s) &= (-1)^n\left(-\int_0^1 G_{n-1}(t,r)G_{conj}(r,s)dr\right)\\ &= (-1)^2\left(\int_0^1 (-1)^{n-1} G_{n-1}(t,r)G_{conj}(r,s)dr\right)\\ &\leq (-1)^2\left(\int_0^1 (-1)^{n-1} G_{n-1}(1,r)G_{conj}(r,s)dr\right)\\ &= (-1)^n\left(-\int_0^1 G_{n-1}(1,r)G_{conj}(r,s)dr\right)\\ &= (-1)^n G_n(1,s).\end{aligned}$$

□

5. Existence of Solutions

We are now in a position to demonstrate the existence of positive solutions to (1) and (2) based upon the parameter λ using the Guo–Krasnosel'skii fixed-point theorem and our constructed Green's function and its properties.

Define the constants

$$A_{G_n} = \int_0^1 (-1)^n s^{\alpha-1} G_n(1,s)g(s)ds, \quad B_{G_n} = \int_0^1 (-1)^n G_n(1,s)g(s)ds,$$

$$F_0 = \limsup_{u\to 0^+} \frac{f(u)}{u}, \quad f_0 = \liminf_{u\to 0^+} \frac{f(u)}{u},$$

$$F_\infty = \limsup_{u\to\infty} \frac{f(u)}{u}, \quad f_\infty = \liminf_{u\to\infty} \frac{f(u)}{u}.$$

Let $\mathcal{B} = C[0,1]$ be a Banach space with norm

$$\|u\| = \max_{t\in[0,1]} |u(t)|.$$

Define the cone:

$$\mathcal{P} = \Big\{u \in \mathcal{B} : u(0) = 0,\ u(t) \text{ is nondecreasing, and } t^{\alpha-1}u(1) \leq u(t) \leq u(1) \text{ on } [0,1]\Big\}.$$

Define the operator $T : \mathcal{P} \to \mathcal{B}$ by

$$Tu(t) = (-1)^n \lambda \int_0^1 G_n(t,s)g(s)f(u(s))ds.$$

Lemma 4. *Operator $T : \mathcal{P} \to \mathcal{P}$ is completely continuous.*

Proof. Let $u \in \mathcal{P}$. Then, by definition,

$$Tu(0) = (-1)^n \lambda \int_0^1 G_n(0,s)g(s)f(u(s))ds = 0.$$

Also, for $t \in (0,1)$ and by Lemma 3 (2),

$$\frac{\partial}{\partial t}[Tu(t)] = (-1)^n \lambda \int_0^1 \frac{\partial}{\partial t} G_n(t,s)g(s)f(u(s))ds > 0$$

which implies that $Tu(t)$ is nondecreasing.

Next, for $t \in [0,1]$ and by Lemma 3 (3),

$$\begin{aligned} t^{\alpha-1}Tu(1) &= t^{\alpha-1}(-1)^n \lambda \int_0^1 G_n(1,s)g(s)f(u(s))ds \\ &\leq (-1)^n \lambda \int_0^1 G_n(t,s)g(s)f(u(s))ds \\ &= Tu(t), \end{aligned}$$

and

$$\begin{aligned} Tu(t) &= (-1)^n \lambda \int_0^1 G_n(t,s)g(s)f(u(s))ds \\ &\leq (-1)^n \lambda \int_0^1 G_n(1,s)g(s)f(u(s))ds \\ &= Tu(1). \end{aligned}$$

Therefore, $Tu \in \mathcal{P}$. A standard application of the Arzela–Ascoli Theorem yields the result that T is completely continuous. □

Theorem 2. *If*

$$\frac{1}{A_{G_n} f_\infty} < \lambda < \frac{1}{B_{G_n} F_0},$$

then (1) *and* (2) *have at least one positive solution.*

Proof. Since $F_0 \lambda B_{G_n} < 1$, there exists an $\epsilon > 0$ such that

$$(F_0 + \epsilon)\lambda B_{G_n} \leq 1.$$

Also, since

$$F_0 = \limsup_{u \to 0^+} \frac{f(u)}{u},$$

there exists an $H_1 > 0$ such that

$$f(u) \leq (F_0 + \epsilon)u \quad \text{for} \quad u \in (0, H_1].$$

Define $\Omega_1 = \{u \in \mathcal{B} : \|u\| < H_1\}$. If $u \in \mathcal{P} \cap \partial\Omega_1$, then $\|u\| = H_1$, and

$$\begin{aligned}
|(Tu)(1)| &= (-1)^n \lambda \int_0^1 G_n(1,s)g(s)f(u(s))ds \\
&\le (-1)^n \lambda \int_0^1 G_n(1,s)g(s)(F_0+\epsilon)u(s)ds \\
&\le (F_0+\epsilon)u(1)\lambda \int_0^1 (-1)^n G_n(1,s)g(s)ds \\
&\le (F_0+\epsilon)\|u\|\lambda B_{G_n} \\
&\le \|u\|.
\end{aligned}$$

Since $Tu \in \mathcal{P}$, $\|Tu\| \le \|u\|$ for $u \in \mathcal{P} \cap \partial\Omega_1$.

Next, since $f_\infty \lambda > \dfrac{1}{A_{G_n}}$, there exists a $c \in (0,1)$ and an $\epsilon > 0$ such that

$$(f_\infty - \epsilon)\lambda > \left((-1)^n \int_c^1 G_n(1,s)g(s)ds\right)^{-1}.$$

Since

$$f_\infty = \liminf_{u\to\infty} \frac{f(u)}{u},$$

there exists an $H_3 > 0$ such that

$$f(u) \ge (f_\infty - \epsilon)u \quad \text{for} \quad u \in [H_3, \infty).$$

Define

$$H_2 = \max\left\{\frac{H_3}{c^{\alpha-1}}, 2H_1\right\},$$

and define $\Omega_2 = \{u \in \mathcal{B} : \|u\| < H_2\}$.

Let $u \in \mathcal{P} \cap \partial\Omega_2$. Then, $\|u\| = H_2$. Notice that for $t \in [c,1]$,

$$u(t) \ge t^{\alpha-1}u(1) \ge c^{\alpha-1}H_2 \ge c^{\alpha-1}\frac{H_3}{c^{\alpha-1}} = H_3.$$

Therefore,

$$\begin{aligned}
|(Tu)(1)| &\ge (-1)^n \lambda \int_c^1 G_n(1,s)g(s)f(u(s))ds \\
&\ge (-1)^n \lambda \int_c^1 G_n(1,s)g(s)(f_\infty-\epsilon)u(s)ds \\
&\ge \lambda(f_\infty-\epsilon)u(1) \int_c^1 (-1)^n s^{\alpha-1} G_n(1,s)g(s)ds \\
&\ge \|u\|.
\end{aligned}$$

Hence, $\|Tu\| \ge \|u\|$ for $u \in \mathcal{P} \cap \partial_2$. Notice that since $H_1 < H_2$, we have $_1 \subset {}_2$. Thus, by Theorem 1 (1), T has a fixed point $u \in \mathcal{P}$. By the definition of T, this fixed point is a positive solution of (1) and (2). □

Theorem 3. *If*

$$\frac{1}{A_{G_n} f_0} < \lambda < \frac{1}{B_{G_n} F_\infty},$$

then (1) *and* (2) *have at least one positive solution.*

Proof. Since $f_0 \lambda A_{G_n} > 1$, there exists an $\epsilon > 0$ such that

$$(f_0 - \epsilon)\lambda A_{G_n} \geq 1.$$

Then, since

$$f_0 = \liminf_{u \to 0^+} \frac{f(u)}{u},$$

there exists an $H_1 > 0$ such that

$$f(u) \geq (f_0 - \epsilon)u, \quad t \in (0, H_1].$$

Define $\Omega_1 = \{u \in \mathcal{B} : \|u\| < H_1\}$. If $u \in \mathcal{P} \cap \partial\Omega_1$, then $u(t) \leq H_1$ for $t \in [0,1]$. So,

$$\begin{aligned}
|(Tu)(1)| &= (-1)^n \lambda \int_0^1 G_n(1,s) g(s) f(u(s)) ds \\
&\geq (-1)^n \lambda \int_0^1 G_n(1,s) g(s) (f_0 - \epsilon) u(s) ds \\
&\geq \lambda (f_0 - \epsilon) u(1) \int_0^1 (-1)^n s^{\alpha-1} G_n(1,s) g(s) ds \\
&\geq \lambda (f_0 - \epsilon) \|u\| A_{G_n} \\
&\geq \|u\|.
\end{aligned}$$

Thus, $\|Tu\| \geq \|u\|$ for $u \in \mathcal{P} \cap \partial\Omega_1$.
Next, since $F_\infty B_{G_n} \lambda < 1$, there exists an $\epsilon \in (0,1)$ such that

$$((F_\infty + \epsilon) B_{G_n} + \epsilon)\lambda \leq 1.$$

Since

$$F_\infty = \limsup_{u \to \infty} \frac{f(u)}{u},$$

there exists an $H_3 > 0$ such that

$$f(u) \leq (F_\infty + \epsilon)u, \quad u \in [H_3, \infty).$$

Define

$$M = \max_{u \in [0, H_3]} f(u).$$

Now, there exists a $k \in (0,1)$ with

$$(-1)^n \int_0^k G_n(1,s) g(s) ds \leq \frac{\epsilon}{M}.$$

Let

$$H_2 = \max\left\{2H_1, \frac{H_3}{k^{\alpha-1}}, 1\right\},$$

and define $\Omega_2 = \{u \in \mathcal{B} : \|u\| < H_2\}$. Let $u \in \mathcal{P} \cap \partial\Omega_2$. Then, $\|u\| = H_2$, and so

$$u(1) = H_2 \geq \frac{H_3}{k^{\alpha-1}} > H_3.$$

Now, $u(0) = 0$. So, by the Intermediate Value Theorem, there exists a $\gamma \in (0,1)$ with $u(\gamma) = H_3$. But for $t \in [k, 1]$, we have

$$u(t) \geq t^{\alpha-1} u(1) = t^{\alpha-1} H_2 \geq k^{\alpha-1} \frac{H_3}{k^{\alpha-1}} = H_3.$$

So, $\gamma \in (0,k]$. Moreover, since $u(t)$ is nondecreasing, this implies that

$$0 \leq u(t) \leq H_3, \quad t \in [0,\gamma)$$

and

$$u(t) \geq H_3, \quad t \in (\gamma,1].$$

Therefore,

$$\begin{aligned}
|(Tu)(1)| &= (-1)^n \lambda \int_0^1 G_n(1,s)g(s)f(u(s))ds \\
&= \lambda\left((-1)^n \int_0^{\gamma} G_n(1,s)g(s)f(u(s))ds + (-1)^n \int_{\gamma}^1 G_n(1,s)g(s)f(u(s))ds\right) \\
&\leq \lambda\left(M \int_0^{\gamma} (-1)^n G_n(1,s)g(s)ds + (-1)^n \int_{\gamma}^1 G_n(1,s)g(s)(F_\infty + \epsilon)u(s)ds\right) \\
&\leq \lambda\left(M\frac{\epsilon}{M} + (F_\infty + \epsilon)u(1) \int_{\gamma}^1 (-1)^n G_n(1,s)g(s)ds\right) \\
&\leq \lambda(\epsilon + (F_\infty + \epsilon)\|u\|\, B_{G_n}) \\
&\leq \lambda(\epsilon\|u\| + (F_\infty + \epsilon)\|u\|\, B_{G_n}) \\
&= \lambda\|u\|(\epsilon + (F_\infty + \epsilon)B_{G_n}) \\
&\leq \|u\|.
\end{aligned}$$

Thus, $\|Tu\| \leq \|u\|$ for $u \in \mathcal{P} \cap \partial\Omega_2$. Notice that since $H_1 < H_2$, we have $\overline{\Omega}_1 \subset \Omega_2$. Thus, by Theorem 1 (2), T has a fixed point $u \in \mathcal{P}$. By the definition of T, this fixed point is a positive solution of (1) and (2). $\square$

6. Nonexistence Results

Penultimately, we provide two nonexistence results of positive solutions based on the size of parameter λ. First, we need the following lemma.

Lemma 5. *Suppose $D_{0^+}^{\alpha+2n}u \in C[0,1]$. If $(-1)^n(-D_{0^+}^{\alpha+2n}u(t)) \geq 0$ for all $t \in [0,1]$ and $u(t)$ satisfies (2). Then, we have the following:*

(1) $u'(t) \geq 0, \quad 0 \leq t \leq 1;$

(2) $t^{\alpha-1}u(1) \leq u(t) \leq u(1), \quad 0 \leq t \leq 1.$

Proof. Let $0 \leq t \leq 1$.

For (1), by Lemma 3 (2),

$$\begin{aligned}
u'(t) &= \int_0^1 \frac{\partial}{\partial t} G_n(t,s)(-D_{0^+}^{\alpha+2n}u(s))ds \\
&= \int_0^1 (-1)^n \frac{\partial}{\partial t} G_n(t,s)(-1)^n(-D_{0^+}^{\alpha+2n}u(s))ds \\
&\geq 0.
\end{aligned}$$

For (2), by Lemma 3 (3),

$$\begin{aligned}
t^{\alpha-1}u(1) &= t^{\alpha-1}\int_0^1 G_n(1,s)(-D_{0^+}^{\alpha+2n}u(s))ds \\
&= \int_0^1 (-1)^n t^{\alpha-1}G_n(1,s)(-1)^n(-D_{0^+}^{\alpha+2n}u(s))ds \\
&\le \int_0^1 (-1)^n G_n(t,s)(-1)^n(-D_{0^+}^{\alpha+2n}u(s))ds \\
&= \int_0^1 G_n(t,s)(-D_{0^+}^{\alpha+2n}u(s))ds \\
&= u(t),
\end{aligned}$$

and

$$\begin{aligned}
u(t) &= \int_0^1 G_n(t,s)(-D_{0^+}^{\alpha+2n}u(s))ds \\
&= \int_0^1 (-1)^n G_n(t,s)(-1)^n(-D_{0^+}^{\alpha+2n}u(s))ds \\
&\le \int_0^1 (-1)^n G_n(1,s)(-1)^n(-D_{0^+}^{\alpha+2n}u(s))ds \\
&= \int_0^1 G_n(1,s)(-D_{0^+}^{\alpha+2n}u(s))ds \\
&= u(1).
\end{aligned}$$

□

Theorem 4. *If*

$$\lambda < \frac{u}{B_{G_n} f(u)}$$

for all $u \in (0,\infty)$*, then no positive solution exists for* (1) *and* (2).

Proof. For contradiction, suppose that $u(t)$ is a positive solution to (1) and (2). Then, $(-1)^n(-D_{0^+}^{\alpha+2n}u(t)) = \lambda g(t)f(u(t)) \ge 0$. So, by Lemma 5,

$$\begin{aligned}
u(1) &= (-1)^n\lambda\int_0^1 G_n(1,s)g(s)f(u(s))ds \\
&< (-1)^n(B_{G_n})^{-1}\int_0^1 G_n(1,s)g(s)u(s)ds \\
&\le u(1)(B_{G_n})^{-1}\int_0^1 (-1)^n G_n(1,s)g(s)ds \\
&= u(1),
\end{aligned}$$

which is a contradiction. □

Theorem 5. *If*

$$\lambda > \frac{u}{A_{G_n} f(u)}$$

for all $u \in (0,\infty)$*, then no positive solution exists for* (1) *and* (2).

Proof. For contradiction, suppose that $u(t)$ is a positive solution to (1) and (2). Then, $(-1)^n(-D_{0^+}^{\alpha+2n}u(t)) = \lambda g(t)f(u(t)) \geq 0$. So, by Lemma 5,

$$\begin{aligned} u(1) &= (-1)^n\lambda \int_0^1 G_n(1,s)g(s)f(u(s))ds \\ &> (-1)^n(A_{G_n})^{-1} \int_0^1 G_n(1,s)g(s)u(s)ds \\ &\geq u(1)(A_{G_n})^{-1} \int_0^1 (-1)^n s^{\alpha-1}G_n(1,s)g(s)ds \\ &= u(1), \end{aligned}$$

which is a contradiction. □

7. An Example

To conclude this paper, we provide an explicit example and calculate approximate bounds of the parameter λ for the existence and nonexistence of positive solutions. We use Theorems 2, 4 and 5. Examples constructed using Theorems 3–5 are found and proved similarly.

Set $n = 2$, $m = 3$, $\alpha = 2.5$, $\beta = 1.5$, and $g(t) = t$. We note that $g(t) \geq 0$ is continuous for $0 \leq t \leq 1$ and $\int_0^1 g(t)dt > 0$. Now, we have that

$$\begin{aligned} G_0(1,s) &= \frac{1}{\Gamma(2.5)}\begin{cases} 1^{1.5}(1-s)^0 - (1-s)^{1.5}, & 0 \leq s < t \leq 1, \\ 1^{1.5}(1-s)^0, & 0 \leq t \leq s < 1 \end{cases} \\ &= \frac{1-(1-s)^{1.5}}{\Gamma(2.5)}, \end{aligned}$$

and we compute

$$\begin{aligned} A_{G_2} &= \int_0^1 (-1)^2 s^{1.5} G_2(1,s)(s)ds \\ &= \int_0^1 \left[-\int_0^1 G_1(1,r_1)G_{conj}(r_1,s)dr_1\right] s^{2.5}ds \\ &= \int_0^1 \left[-\int_0^1 \left(\int_0^1 -G_0(1,r_2)G_{conj}(r_2,r_1)dr_2\right) G_{conj}(r_1,s)dr_1\right] s^{2.5}ds \\ &\approx 0.00095454, \end{aligned}$$

and

$$\begin{aligned} B_{G_2} &= \int_0^1 (-1)^2 G_2(1,s)(s)ds \\ &= \int_0^1 \left[-\int_0^1 G_1(1,r_1)G_{conj}(r_1,s)dr_1\right] sds \\ &= \int_0^1 \left[-\int_0^1 \left(\int_0^1 -G_0(1,r_2)G_{conj}(r_2,r_1)dr_2\right) G_{conj}(r_1,s)dr_1\right] sds \\ &\approx 0.00197039. \end{aligned}$$

Now that we have A_{G_2} and B_{G_2}, applying these Theorems is much simpler as they are based on the liminfs and limsups of choice of $f(u)$.

Example 1. *We demonstrate an example for Theorems 2, 4, and 5. Set $f(u) = u(3u+1)/(u+1)$. We note that $f(u) \geq 0$ is continuous for $u \geq 0$. Thus, the fractional boundary value problem is*

$$D_{0^+}^{6.5}u(t) + \lambda tu\left(\frac{3u+1}{u+1}\right) = 0, \quad 0 < t < 1, \tag{3}$$

subject to

$$\begin{gathered} u(0) = u'(0) = 0, \quad D_{0^+}^{1.5}(1) = 0 \\ D_{0^+}^{2.5}u(0) = D_{0^+}^{4.5}(0) = 0, \quad D_{0^+}^{2.5}(1) = D_{0^+}^{4.5}(1) = 0. \end{gathered} \tag{4}$$

We compute the liminfs and limsups for $f(u)/u = (3u+1)/(u+1)$.

$$f_\infty = \liminf_{u\to\infty} \frac{3u+1}{u+1} = 3, \qquad F_0 = \limsup_{u\to 0^+} \frac{3u+1}{u+1} = 1$$

$$f_0 = \liminf_{u\to 0^+} \frac{3u+1}{u+1} = 1, \qquad F_\infty = \limsup_{u\to\infty} \frac{3u+1}{u+1} = 3$$

Then, we have

$$\frac{1}{A_{G_2} f_\infty} \approx \frac{1}{0.00095454 \cdot 3} \approx 349.28$$

and

$$\frac{1}{B_{G_2} F_0} \approx \frac{1}{0.00197039 \cdot 1} \approx 507.61.$$

Next, for $u \in (0,\infty)$, we investigate

$$\frac{u}{B_{G_2} f(u)} = \frac{u+1}{B_{G_2}(3u+1)}.$$

We calculate

$$\inf_{u\in(0,\infty)} \frac{u+1}{B_{G_2}(3u+1)} = \frac{1}{B_{G_2}} \inf_{u\in(0,\infty)} \frac{u+1}{(3u+1)} \approx \frac{1}{0.00197039}\left(\frac{1}{3}\right) \approx 169.15.$$

Finally, for $u \in (0,\infty)$, we investigate

$$\frac{u}{A_{G_2} f(u)} = \frac{u+1}{A_{G_2}(3u+1)}.$$

We calculate

$$\sup_{u\in(0,\infty)} \frac{u+1}{A_{G_2}(3u+1)} = \frac{1}{A_{G_2}} \sup_{u\in(0,\infty)} \frac{u+1}{(3u+1)} \approx \frac{1}{0.00095454}(1) \approx 1047.17.$$

Therefore, by Theorems 2, 4, and 5, if $349.28 < \lambda < 507.61$, then (3) *and* (4) *have at least one positive solution, and if $\lambda < 169.15$ or $\lambda > 1047.17$, then* (3) *and* (4) *do not have a positive solution.*

8. Conclusions

A Riemann–Liouville fractional derivative with fractional boundary conditions including Lidstone-inspired conditions was studied. With the use of Green's function, convolution, induction, and fixed-point theory, at least one positive solution was proven to exist if parameter λ was within certain bounds. Subsequently, no positive solutions were shown to exist if λ satisfied other bounds. An explicit example was constructed to demonstrate how to utilize the presented theorems.

Future work would aim to investigate the convolution of the fractional boundary value problem with other types of Green functions such as those for right-focal or multipoint problems. Additionally, one could use the convolution with induction approach to find positive solutions for fractional boundary value problems that contain a singularity.

Author Contributions: All authors contributed substantially and in equal proportion to this research. All authors have read and agreed to the published version of the manuscript.

Funding: This research received no external funding.

Data Availability Statement: Data are contained within the article.

Conflicts of Interest: The authors declare no conflicts of interest.

References

1. Eloe, P.W.; Neugebauer, J.T. Convolutions and Green's functions for two families of boundary value problems for fractional differential equations. *Electron. J. Differ. Equ.* **2016**, *2016*, 1–13.
2. Lyons, J.W.; Neugebauer, J.T. Two point fractional boundary value problems with a fractional boundary condition. *Fract. Calc. Appl. Anal.* **2018**, *21*, 442–461. [CrossRef]
3. Neugebauer, J.T.; Wingo, A.G. Positive solutions for a fractional boundary value problem with Lidstone-like boundary conditions. *Kragujev. J. Math.* **2024**, *48*, 309–322. [CrossRef]
4. Bai, Z.; Lü, H. Positive solutions for boundary value problem of nonlinear fractional differential equation. *J. Math. Anal. Appl.* **2005**, *311*, 495–505. [CrossRef]
5. Graef, J.R.; Yang, B. Positive solutions to a three point fourth order focal boundary value problem. *Rocky Mt. J. Math.* **2014**, *4*, 937–951. [CrossRef]
6. Kaufmann, E.R.; Mboumi, E. Positive solutions of a boundary value problem for a nonlinear fractional differential equation. *Electron. J. Qual. Theory Differ. Equ.* **2008**, *2008*, 1–11. [CrossRef]
7. Rehman, M.U.; Khan, R.A.; Eloe, P.W. Positive solutions of nonlocal boundary value problem for higher order fractional differential system. *Dynam. Systems Appl.* **2011**, *20*, 169–182.
8. Agarwal, R.P.; O'Regan, D.; Staněk, S. Positive solutions for Dirichlet problems of singular nonlinear fractional differential equations. *J. Math. Anal. Appl.* **2010**, *371*, 57–68. [CrossRef]
9. Henderson, J.; Luca, R. Existence of positive solutions for a singular fraction boundary value problem. *Nonlinear Anal. Model. Control* **2017**, *22*, 99–114. [CrossRef]
10. Raghavendran, P.; Gunasekar, T.; Santra, S.S.; Baleanu, D.; Majumder, D. Analytical study of existence, uniqueness, and stability in impulsive neutral fractional Volterra-Fredholm equations. *J. Math. Computer. Sci.* **2025**, *38*, 313–329. [CrossRef]
11. Zhang, W.; Fu, X.; Ni, J. Existence of positive solutions for Hadamard-type fractional boundary value problems at resonance on an infinite interval. *J. Nonlinear Math. Phys.* **2024**, *31*, 1–22. [CrossRef]
12. Zhang, Z.; Ni, J. New multiple positive solutions for Hadamard-type fractional differential equations with nonlocal conditions on an infinite interval. *Appl. Math. Lett.* **2021**, *118*, 1–10. [CrossRef]
13. Guo, D.; Lakshmikantham, V. *Problems in Abstract Cones*; Academic Press: New York, NY, USA, 1988.
14. Krasnosel'skii, M.A. *Topological Methods in the Theory of Nonlinear Integral Equations*; The Macmillan Co.: New York, NY, USA, 1964.
15. Diethelm, K. *The Analysis of Fractional Differential Equations: An Application-Oriented Exposition Using Differential Operators of Caputo Type*; Springer: Berlin/Heidelberg, Germany, 2010.
16. Kilbas, A.A.; Srivastava, H.M.; Trujillo, J.J. *Theory and Applications of Fractional Differential Equations*; North-Holland Mathematics Studies 204; Elsevier Science B.V.: Amsterdam, The Netherlands, 2006.
17. Miller, K.S.; Ross, B. *An Introduction to the Fractional Calculus and Fractional Differential Equations*; A Wiley-Interscience Publication; John Wiley & Sons, Inc.: New York, NY, USA, 1993.
18. Podlubny, I. *Fractional Differential Equations*; Academic Press, Inc.: San Diego, CA, USA, 1999.
19. Eloe, P.; Lyons, J.W.; Neugebauer, J.T. An ordering on Green's functions for a family of two-point boundary value problems for fractional differential equations. *Commun. Appl. Anal.* **2015**, *19*, 453–462.

mathematics MDPI

Article

Generalized Grönwall Inequality and Ulam–Hyers Stability in $\mathcal{L}^p$ Space for Fractional Stochastic Delay Integro-Differential Equations

Abdelhamid Mohammed Djaouti [1,*] and Muhammad Imran Liaqat [2]

[1] Department of Mathematics and Statistics, Faculty of Sciences, King Faisal University, Al Hofuf 31982, Saudi Arabia
[2] Department of Mathematics, National College of Business Administration & Economics, Lahore 54000, Pakistan; imranliaqat@ncbae.edu.pk
* Correspondence: adjaout@kfu.edu.sa

Abstract: In this work, we derive novel theoretical results concerning well-posedness and Ulam–Hyers stability. Specifically, we investigate the well-posedness of Caputo–Katugampola fractional stochastic delay integro-differential equations. Additionally, we develop a generalized Grönwall inequality and apply it to prove Ulam–Hyers stability in $\mathcal{L}^p$ space. Our findings generalize existing results for fractional derivatives and space, as we formulate them in the Caputo–Katugampola fractional derivative and $\mathcal{L}^p$ space. To support our theoretical results, we present an illustrative example.

Keywords: well-posedness; Ulam–Hyers stability; generalized Grönwall inequality; Hölder's inequality

MSC: 34A08; 26A24; 26A33

1. Introduction

Fractional derivatives extend integer-order derivatives to non-integer orders and describe both the local and global behavior of functions. Unlike ordinary derivatives, which represent instantaneous rates of change and are not aware of past events, fractional derivatives include memory effects and depend on the entire history of a function.

Different types of fractional operators can be found in the literature [1–4]. Recently, some scholars have incorporated the Caputo–Katugampola fractional derivative (Cap-KFrD) into their research. It interpolates the Caputo fractional derivative (Cap-FrD) and the Caputo–Hadamard fractional derivative (Cap-HFrD). The authors of [5] established an approach to solve for fractional systems using Cap-KFrD. Maa and Chen [6] examined the stability and well-posedness of fractional problems involving Cap-KFrD. Sweilam et al. [7] developed a novel method to solve various problems. Boucenna et al. [8] discussed stability results related to Cap-KFrD. In [9], various inequalities were established using Cap-KFrD. In [10], Hoa et al. explored different concepts regarding the solutions of fuzzy fractional systems with Cap-KFrD. Omaba and Sulaimani [11] presented theoretical results for stochastic problems involving Cap-KFrD. Elbadri [12] found solutions to Burgers' equation using the Laplace transform in the context of Cap-KFrD. Al-Ghafri et al. [13] conducted a qualitative analysis of integro-differential equations and also obtained solutions using the Adomian approach with Cap-KFrD. For more studies related to Cap-KFrD, see [14–16].

Assume that the function ℓ is integrable on $[0,\varpi]$. The Cap-KFrD of orders $0 < \eta < 1$ and $\zeta > 0$ for the function ℓ is given as follows [17]:

$$ {}^{c}\mathfrak{D}^{\eta,\zeta}_{\mathfrak{u}^+}\ell(\mathfrak{c}) = \frac{\zeta^{\eta}}{\Gamma(1-\eta)}\int_{\mathfrak{u}}^{\mathfrak{c}} \frac{\ell^{*}(\mathfrak{u})}{\left(\mathcal{F}(\mathfrak{c})-\mathcal{F}(\mathfrak{u})\right)^{\eta}}d\mathfrak{u}. \tag{1} $$

The Caputo–Katugampola fractional integral is given as follows [18]:

$$ \mathcal{I}^{\eta,\zeta}_{\mathfrak{u}^+}\ell(\mathfrak{c}) = \frac{\zeta^{1-\eta}}{\Gamma(\eta)}\int_{\mathfrak{u}}^{\mathfrak{c}} \frac{\mathcal{F}'(\mathfrak{u})}{\left(\mathcal{F}(\mathfrak{c})-\mathcal{F}(\mathfrak{u})\right)^{1-\eta}}\ell(\mathfrak{u})d\mathfrak{u}. \tag{2} $$

The Cap-FrD and Cap-HFrD can be interpolated using the Cap-KFrD: Cap-FrD ($\zeta = 1$) [19] and Cap-HFrD ($\zeta \to 0^+$) [19]. The following graph (Figure 1) illustrates this phenomenon.

Figure 1. A schematic representation of the limiting behavior of the Cap-KFrD as the parameter ζ approaches 1 and 0^+, recovering the Cap-FrD and Cap-HFrD fractional derivatives, respectively.

Stochastic differential equations are employed to describe systems that are driven by random processes. They are a generalization of classical differential equations with terms describing random noise, usually described by Brownian motion or Wiener processes. These equations have extensive applications in areas such as finance, physics, and biology to model systems that change with time and intrinsic randomness. Fractional differential equations are equations involving derivatives of non-integer order. These equations can be employed to model systems with memory effects or hereditary behavior, where the future state of the system relies on its current and past states. Stochastic fractional differential equations (SFDEs) combine the concept of both stochastic and fractional differential equations to model systems with randomness and memory effects. SFDEs are widely applied in most applications with randomness and memory effects. In biology, SFDEs model anomalous diffusion in cell transport in which molecules exhibit subdiffusive or superdiffusive dynamics due to complex environments. In finance, they model stock price dynamics and interest rate models with long-range dependence in order to enhance the modeling of market memory effects. SFDEs are applied in physics to describe viscoelastic materials in which stress and strain exhibit hereditary characteristics. In hydrology, SFDEs model groundwater flow in porous media with long-term dependence. Additionally, SFDEs are used in engineering for signal processing and control systems. Their ability to account for history-dependent stochasticity makes them effective tools for real-world complex systems.

Fractional stochastic integro-differential equations (FSIDEs) with delay are equations that combine fractional derivatives, stochastic processes, integro-differential terms, and time delays. They are highly suited for modeling intricate systems that display memory dependence, hereditary effects, and randomness. FSIDEs with delay are especially valuable for representing phenomena where retention effects, stochastic dynamics, and inherited characteristics are essential, such as finance, physics, and engineering.

The well-posedness of a fractional-order stochastic system is a fascinating branch of mathematical research. It ensures that such equations have unique solutions that depend continuously on the initial condition. The well-posedness of a fractional-order stochastic system is critical to establishing the equation as a meaningful and reliable mathematical model. Since fractional-order stochastic systems couple both fractional derivatives (which imply memory effects) and stochastic processes (which describe randomness), their solutions must be well defined to remain physically and practically applicable.

Ulam–Hyers stability (UHS) is a crucial principle in the stability analysis of fractional-order stochastic systems, ensuring that small variations in system parameters or initial conditions cause only minimal discrepancies in the solution. This aspect is especially crucial for systems defined by fractional derivatives, which exhibit memory and hereditary properties. Additionally, stochastic effects introducing randomness make stability analysis even more challenging.

In recent years, many scholars have actively worked on various topics related to SFDEs and FSIDEs. In [20], Batiha et al. proposed an innovative approach for solving SFDEs. They formulated a scheme specifically designed to approximate the Riemann–Liouville integral operator, which is subsequently used to obtain approximate solutions for these equations. The authors compared their results with those from the Euler–Maruyama method and the exact solution, highlighting the accuracy and efficiency of their proposed technique. Chen et al. reconstructed a backward equation for SFDEs in [21]. They employed the norm technique to analyze the stability as well as the existence and uniqueness (Ex-Un) of the solution to the backward equation. Moreover, the authors also investigated a simulation case of a European call option using the Euler–Maruyama technique to solve the SFDEs, thus illustrating the applicability of their theoretical results. In [22], Moualkia and Xu conducted a theoretical analysis of variable-order SFDEs. In [23], Ali et al. investigated the coupled system of SFDEs. The article chiefly seeks to find solutions for the coupled system of SFDEs with variable-order derivatives, which will serve as the basis for identifying the necessary conditions for Ex-Un. In this pursuit, the authors utilized the Picard method, which has been shown to work well in this field. The study also serves as the basis for the formulation of Ulam stability conditions for the given model. Li et al. carried out a stability investigation of a system of SFDEs in [24]. The research analyzes the interaction between fractional calculus, stochastic processes, and time delays to provide a better understanding of system stability. It sheds light on the effective solution of these equations via several numerical methods. Moreover, the paper examines both the asymptotic and Lyapunov stability of SFDEs, proposing local stability conditions and examining how delays and fractional orders affect stability characteristics. In [25], Singh et al. investigated the asymptotic stability of SFDEs. The authors of [26] considered a class of SFDEs with variable delay. They employed the Lipschitz condition on the nonlinearity and used the Banach method to obtain their main results. The paper ends with an example showing the theoretical results and exhibiting the applicability of the obtained results in practice. The Euler–Maruyama technique for Caputo SFDEs with coefficients satisfying the linear growth condition and the Lipschitz condition was constructed by Doan et al. in [27]. The authors proved the strong convergence rate of the scheme, especially for time-independent coefficients. Moreover, the article provides findings regarding the convergence and stability of an exponential Euler–Maruyama approach for Caputo SFDEs. Such results further advance the knowledge of numerical solutions for such complicated equations. In [28], the authors conducted an analysis of SFDEs. The Ex-Un of solutions was defined through the Picard scheme. Furthermore, the authors considered the stability of nonlinear SFDEs with Lévy noise, using the Mittag–Leffler function to prove stability. In [29], Li et al. studied Hilfer SFDEs with delay. The Ex-Un of the solutions was then determined by the Picard method and the method of contradiction. Moreover, finite-time stability was investigated using the generalized Grönwall–Bellman inequality. In [30], the authors obtained solutions for FSIDEs using the collocation approach. Cui and Yan [31] discussed the qualitative analysis of FSIDEs. Badr and El-Hoety [32] obtained approximate solutions for FSIDEs using the Galerkin approach. The authors of [33] analyzed the solutions of FSIDEs with the Hilfer fractional operator in $\mathcal{L}^2$ space using the fixed-point approach. For more studies related to SFDEs, see [34–38].

Notable outcomes for FSIDEs with delay concerning Cap-KFrD in $\mathcal{L}^{\mathfrak{p}}$ space are presented in this research work. The Banach fixed-point approach is used to determine the Ex-Un of solutions. By leveraging various inequalities, we derive results concerning the continuous dependence of solutions on initial conditions. In the second part, we formulate a generalized Grönwall inequality for Cap-KFrD and apply it to demonstrate UHS in the $\mathcal{L}^{\mathfrak{p}}$ space. Several fundamental inequalities, including Jensen's inequality [39], the Burkholder–Davis–Gundy inequality [40], and Hölder's inequality [41], play a crucial role in substantiating our findings.

Below are some key contributions of our study:

1. As far as we know, this is the first comprehensive analysis of the well-posedness of the solutions of FSIDEs and UHS concerning Cap-KFrD in the $\mathcal{L}^{\mathfrak{p}}$ space.
2. We prove all results for the Cap-KFrD, which generalizes Cap-FrD and Cap-HFrD, such that our results are consistent with Cap-FrD when $\zeta = 1$ holds and match with Cap-HFrD when $\zeta \to 0^+$ holds.
3. Most results related to FDSDEs and FSIDEs have been established in the $\mathcal{L}^2$ space; however, we establish these results in the $\mathcal{L}^{\mathfrak{p}}$ space.
4. This research work presents a generalized Grönwall inequality regarding Cap-KFrD.

We examine the following FSIDEs with delay:

$$\begin{cases} {}^{c}\mathfrak{D}_{0^+}^{\eta,\zeta}\left(\ell(\mathfrak{c}) - \sum_{\jmath=1}^{\mathfrak{e}} \mathcal{I}_{0^+}^{\mathcal{U}_\jmath,\zeta}\Psi_\jmath(\mathfrak{c},\ell(\mathfrak{c}))\right) = \mathfrak{Z}(\mathfrak{c},\ell(\mathfrak{c}),\ell(\mathfrak{c}-\varrho)) + \mathfrak{B}(\mathfrak{c},\ell(\mathfrak{c}),\ell(\mathfrak{c}-\varrho))\frac{d\mathcal{W}(\mathfrak{c})}{d\mathfrak{c}}, \ \mathfrak{c} \in [0,\varpi], \\ \ell(0) = \varphi, \end{cases} \tag{3}$$

where $\ell(\mathfrak{c})$ is an $\mathbb{R}^{\mathrm{m}}$-valued stochastic process; ${}^{c}\mathfrak{D}_{0^+}^{\eta,\zeta}$ represents the Cap-KFrD with $\eta \in (\frac{1}{2},1)$, $\zeta > 0$; $\mathcal{I}_{0^+}^{\mathcal{U}_\jmath,\zeta}$ is the Caputo–Katugampola fractional integral with $\frac{1}{2} \leq \mathcal{U}_\jmath \leq 1$, $1 \leq \jmath \leq \mathfrak{e}$, and $\varrho \in \mathbb{R}$ the delay time; the functions $\mathfrak{Z} : [0,\varpi] \times \mathbb{R}^{\mathrm{m}} \times \mathbb{R}^{\mathrm{m}} \to \mathbb{R}^{\mathrm{m}}$ and $\mathfrak{B} : [0,\varpi] \times \mathbb{R}^{\mathrm{m}} \times \mathbb{R}^{\mathrm{m}} \to \mathbb{R}^{\mathrm{m}\times\sigma}$ are measurable continuous mappings. The stochastic process $(\mathcal{W}_{\mathfrak{c}})_{\mathfrak{c}\in[0,\infty)}$ follows a standard Brownian trajectory within the σ-dimensional complete filtered probability space $(\Omega, \mathrm{F}, \mathbb{F} = (\mathrm{F}_{\mathfrak{c}})_{\mathfrak{c}\in[0,\infty)}, \mathrm{P})$.

Section 2 defines relevant concepts and presents the fundamental hypothesis that facilitates the basis for the novel results related to well-posedness and UHS of FSIDEs with delay and generalized Grönwall inequality. Section 3 determines the well-posedness of the FSIDEs. Section 4 shows the results of the generalized Grönwall inequality and UHS. Section 5 provides two examples. To conclude, Section 6 outlines our key findings.

2. Preliminaries

This section consists of definition and assumptions that are essentially for establishing important results.

Definition 1. *Suppose* $\mathscr{X}_{\mathfrak{c}}^{\mathfrak{p}} = \mathcal{L}^{\mathfrak{p}}(\Omega, \mathrm{F}_{\mathfrak{c}}, \mathrm{P})$ *represents the* $\mathrm{F}_{\mathfrak{c}}$*-measurable and* $\mathfrak{p}^{th}$ *integrable functions* $\ell = (\ell_1, \ell_2, \cdots, \ell_m)^{\mathbb{T}}$, *then* $\Omega \to \mathbb{R}^m$ *satisfies*

$$\|\ell\|_{\mathfrak{p}} = \left(\sum_{\imath=1}^{m} \mathfrak{E}|\ell_\imath|^{\mathfrak{p}}\right)^{\frac{1}{\mathfrak{p}}}.$$

A process conforming to measurability criteria $\ell : [0,\varpi] \to \mathcal{L}^{\mathfrak{p}}(\Omega, \mathrm{F}_{\mathfrak{c}}, \mathrm{P})$ is referred to as $\mathbb{F}$-adapted subject to $\ell(\mathfrak{c}) \in \mathscr{X}_{\mathfrak{c}}^{\mathfrak{p}}$, $\mathfrak{c} \geq 0$. Over each $\varphi \in \mathscr{X}_0^{\mathfrak{p}}$, the ℓ, which is an $\mathbb{F}$-adapted process, provides the solution of (3) with $\ell(0) = \varphi$, on the condition that the subsequent (4) is satisfied. This is achieved by applying $\mathcal{I}_{0^+}^{\eta,\zeta}$ on (3).

$$\begin{aligned}\ell(\mathfrak{c}) = \varphi + \sum_{j=1}^{\mathfrak{e}} \frac{1}{\Gamma(\mathcal{U}_j)} \int_0^{\mathfrak{c}} (F(\mathfrak{c}) - F(\mathfrak{u}))^{\mathcal{U}_j - 1} F'(\mathfrak{u}) \Psi_j(\mathfrak{u}, \ell(\mathfrak{u})) d\mathfrak{u} \\ + \frac{1}{\Gamma(\eta)} \int_0^{\mathfrak{c}} (F(\mathfrak{c}) - F(\mathfrak{u}))^{\eta-1} F'(\mathfrak{u}) \mathfrak{J}(\mathfrak{u}, \ell(\mathfrak{u}), \ell(\mathfrak{u}-\gamma)) d\mathfrak{u} \\ + \frac{1}{\Gamma(\eta)} \int_0^{\mathfrak{c}} (F(\mathfrak{c}) - F(\mathfrak{u}))^{\eta-1} F'(\mathfrak{u}) \mathfrak{B}(\mathfrak{u}, \ell(\mathfrak{u}), \ell(\mathfrak{u}-\gamma)) d\mathcal{W}(\mathfrak{u}). \end{aligned} \tag{4}$$

For $\mathfrak{J}$ and $\mathfrak{B}$, assume the following:

1. $(\hbar_1)$ $\forall \delta_1, \delta_2, \mathcal{V}_1, \mathcal{V}_2 \in \mathfrak{R}^{\varkappa}$, there is $\mathfrak{T}$ such as

$$\begin{aligned}&\|\Psi_j(\mathfrak{c}, \delta_1) - \Psi_j(\mathfrak{c}, \mathcal{V}_1)\|_{\mathfrak{p}} + \|\mathfrak{J}(\mathfrak{c}, \delta_1, \delta_2) - \mathfrak{J}(\mathfrak{c}, \mathcal{V}_1, \mathcal{V}_2)\|_{\mathfrak{p}} \\ &+ \|\mathfrak{B}(\mathfrak{c}, \delta_1, \delta_2) - \mathfrak{B}(\mathfrak{c}, \mathcal{V}_1, \mathcal{V}_2)\|_{\mathfrak{p}} \\ &\le \mathfrak{T}(\|\delta_1 - \mathcal{V}_1\|_{\mathfrak{p}} + \|\delta_2 - \mathcal{V}_2\|_{\mathfrak{p}}), \ j = 1, 2, \cdots, \mathfrak{e}. \end{aligned} \tag{5}$$

2. $(\hbar_2)$ The $\Psi_j(\mathfrak{c}, 0), j = 1, 2, \cdots, \mathfrak{e}$, $\mathfrak{J}(\mathfrak{c}, 0, 0)$ and $\mathfrak{B}(\mathfrak{c}, 0, 0)$ satisfies

$$\underset{\mathfrak{c}\in[0,\varpi]}{esssup} \|\Psi_j(\mathfrak{c}, 0)\|_{\mathfrak{p}} < \wp, \ \underset{\mathfrak{c}\in[0,\varpi]}{esssup} \|\mathfrak{J}(\mathfrak{c}, 0, 0)\|_{\mathfrak{p}} < \wp, \ \underset{\mathfrak{c}\in[0,\varpi]}{esssup} \|\mathfrak{B}(\mathfrak{c}, 0, 0)\|_{\mathfrak{p}} < \wp. \tag{6}$$

3. Generalized Results

In the $\mathcal{L}^{\mathfrak{p}}$ space, we establish generalized theorems on Ex-Un and consistent dependence for the solution of delay FSIDEs.

Using the Banach fixed-point technique, we first determine the Ex-Un results for the solutions of delay FSIDEs. For this, we postulate that $\mathbb{H}^{\mathfrak{p}}([0, \varpi])$ is the space of all measurable and $\mathbb{F}_{\varpi}$-adapted processes ℓ with $\|\ell\|_{\mathbb{H}^{\mathfrak{p}}} = \underset{\mathfrak{c}\in[0,\varpi]}{esssup} \|\ell(\mathfrak{c})\|_{\mathfrak{p}} < \infty$. It is straightforward to prove that $(\mathbb{H}^{\mathfrak{p}}([0, \varpi]), \|\cdot\|_{\mathbb{H}^{\mathfrak{p}}})$ is a complete normed vector space.

Next, describe an operator $\psi_\varphi : \mathbb{H}^{\mathfrak{p}}([0, \varpi]) \to \mathbb{H}^{\mathfrak{p}}([0, \varpi])$ with $\psi_\varphi(\ell(0)) = \varphi$ and

$$\begin{aligned}\psi_\varphi(\ell(\mathfrak{c})) = \varphi + \sum_{j=1}^{\mathfrak{e}} \frac{\zeta^{1-\mathcal{U}_j}}{\Gamma(\mathcal{U}_j)} \int_0^{\mathfrak{c}} (F(\mathfrak{c}) - F(\mathfrak{u}))^{\mathcal{U}_j - 1} F'(\mathfrak{u}) \Psi_j(\mathfrak{u}, \ell(\mathfrak{u})) d\mathfrak{u} \\ + \frac{\zeta^{1-\eta}}{\Gamma(\eta)} \int_0^{\mathfrak{c}} (F(\mathfrak{c}) - F(\mathfrak{u}))^{\eta-1} F'(\mathfrak{u}) \mathfrak{J}(\mathfrak{u}, \ell(\mathfrak{u}), \ell(\mathfrak{u}-\gamma)) d\mathfrak{u} \\ + \frac{\zeta^{1-\eta}}{\Gamma(\eta)} \int_0^{\mathfrak{c}} (F(\mathfrak{c}) - F(\mathfrak{u}))^{\eta-1} F'(\mathfrak{u}) \mathfrak{B}(\mathfrak{u}, \ell(\mathfrak{u}), \ell(\mathfrak{u}-\gamma)) d\mathcal{W}(\mathfrak{u}). \end{aligned} \tag{7}$$

The lemma below plays a crucial role in proving various results.

$$\|\ell_1 + \ell_2\|_{\mathfrak{p}}^{\mathfrak{p}} \le 2^{\mathfrak{p}-1}(\|\ell_1\|_{\mathfrak{p}}^{\mathfrak{p}} + (\|\ell_2\|_{\mathfrak{p}}^{\mathfrak{p}}), \ \forall \ell_1, \ell_2 \in \mathfrak{R}^{\varkappa}. \tag{8}$$

Lemma 1. *Presume that* $(\hbar_1)$ *and* $(\hbar_2)$ *are valid. Then,* ψ_φ *is well defined.*

Proof. Suppose $\ell(\mathfrak{c}) \in \mathbb{H}^{\mathfrak{p}}[0, \varpi]$ and $\forall \mathfrak{c} \in [0, \varpi]$. Based on (7) and (8), we derive

$$\begin{aligned}&\|\psi_\varphi(\ell(\mathfrak{c}))\|_{\mathfrak{p}}^{\mathfrak{p}} \le 2^{2\mathfrak{p}-2} \|\varphi\|_{\mathfrak{p}}^{\mathfrak{p}} \\ &+ 2^{(\mathfrak{e}+2)\mathfrak{p}-(\mathfrak{e}+2)} \sum_{j=1}^{\mathfrak{e}} \left(\frac{\zeta^{1-\mathcal{U}_j}}{\Gamma(\mathcal{U}_j)}\right)^{\mathfrak{p}} \left\| \int_0^{\mathfrak{c}} (F(\mathfrak{c}) - F(\mathfrak{u}))^{\mathcal{U}_j - 1} F'(\mathfrak{u}) \Psi_j(\mathfrak{u}, \ell(\mathfrak{u})) d\mathfrak{u} \right\|_{\mathfrak{p}}^{\mathfrak{p}}\end{aligned}$$

$$+\frac{2^{2\mathfrak{p}-2}(\zeta^{1-\eta})^{\mathfrak{p}}}{(\Gamma(\eta))^{\mathfrak{p}}}\left\|\int_0^{\mathfrak{c}}(F(\mathfrak{c})-F(\mathfrak{u}))^{\eta-1}\mathfrak{I}(\mathfrak{u},\ell(\mathfrak{u}),\ell(\mathfrak{u}-\gamma))F'(\mathfrak{u})d\mathfrak{u}\right\|_{\mathfrak{p}}^{\mathfrak{p}}$$
$$+\frac{2^{2\mathfrak{p}-2}(\zeta^{1-\eta})^{\mathfrak{p}}}{(\Gamma(\eta))^{\mathfrak{p}}}\left\|\int_0^{\mathfrak{c}}(F(\mathfrak{c})-F(\mathfrak{u}))^{\eta-1}\mathfrak{B}(\mathfrak{u},\ell(\mathfrak{u}),\ell(\mathfrak{u}-\gamma))F'(\mathfrak{u})d\mathcal{W}(\mathfrak{u})\right\|_{\mathfrak{p}}^{\mathfrak{p}}. \quad (9)$$

By Hölder's inequality, we have

$$2^{(\mathfrak{e}+2)\mathfrak{p}-(\mathfrak{e}+2)}\sum_{j=1}^{\mathfrak{e}}\left(\frac{\zeta^{1-\mathcal{U}_j}}{\Gamma(\mathcal{U}_j)}\right)^{\mathfrak{p}}\left\|\int_0^{\mathfrak{c}}(F(\mathfrak{c})-F(\mathfrak{u}))^{\mathcal{U}_i-1}F'(\mathfrak{u})\Psi_j(\mathfrak{u},\ell(\mathfrak{u}))d\mathfrak{u}\right\|_{\mathfrak{p}}^{\mathfrak{p}}$$
$$\leq 2^{(\mathfrak{e}+2)\mathfrak{p}-(\mathfrak{e}+2)}\sum_{j=1}^{\mathfrak{e}}\left(\frac{\zeta^{1-\mathcal{U}_j}}{\Gamma(\mathcal{U}_j)}\right)^{\mathfrak{p}}\sum_{\imath=1}^{m}\mathfrak{E}\left(\int_0^{\mathfrak{c}}(F(\mathfrak{c})-F(\mathfrak{u}))^{\mathcal{U}_j-1}|\Psi_{\imath,j}(\mathfrak{u},\ell(\mathfrak{u}))|F'(\mathfrak{u})d\mathfrak{u}\right)^{\mathfrak{p}}$$
$$\leq 2^{(\mathfrak{e}+2)\mathfrak{p}-(\mathfrak{e}+2)}\sum_{j=1}^{\mathfrak{e}}\left(\frac{\zeta^{1-\mathcal{U}_j}}{\Gamma(\mathcal{U}_j)}\right)^{\mathfrak{p}}\sum_{\imath=1}^{m}\mathfrak{E}\left(\left(\int_0^{\mathfrak{c}}(F(\mathfrak{c})-F(\mathfrak{u}))^{\frac{(\mathcal{U}_j-1)\mathfrak{p}}{(\mathfrak{p}-1)}}(F'(\mathfrak{u}))^{\frac{\mathfrak{p}}{\mathfrak{p}-1}}d\mathfrak{u}\right)^{\mathfrak{p}-1}\int_0^{\mathfrak{c}}|\Psi_{\imath,j}(\mathfrak{u},\ell(\mathfrak{u}))|^{\mathfrak{p}}d\mathfrak{u}\right)$$
$$\leq 2^{(\mathfrak{e}+2)\mathfrak{p}-(\mathfrak{e}+2)}\sum_{j=1}^{\mathfrak{e}}\left(\frac{\zeta^{1-\mathcal{U}_j}}{\Gamma(\mathcal{U}_j)}\right)^{\mathfrak{p}}\sum_{\imath=1}^{m}\mathfrak{E}\left(\left(\sup_{1<\mathfrak{u}\leq\mathfrak{c}}(F'(\mathfrak{u}))^{\frac{1}{\mathfrak{p}-1}}\right)^{\mathfrak{p}-1}\left(\int_0^{\mathfrak{c}}(F(\mathfrak{c})-F(\mathfrak{u}))^{\frac{(\mathcal{U}_j-1)\mathfrak{p}}{(\mathfrak{p}-1)}}F'(\mathfrak{u})d\mathfrak{u}\right)^{\mathfrak{p}-1}\right.$$
$$\left.\int_0^{\mathfrak{c}}|\Psi_{\imath,j}(\mathfrak{u},\ell(\mathfrak{u}))|^{\mathfrak{p}}d\mathfrak{u}\right)$$
$$\leq 2^{(\mathfrak{e}+2)\mathfrak{p}-(\mathfrak{e}+2)}\sum_{j=1}^{\mathfrak{e}}\left(\frac{\zeta^{1-\mathcal{U}_j}}{\Gamma(\mathcal{U}_j)}\right)^{\mathfrak{p}}\mathbb{X}^{\mathfrak{p}-1}\left((\mathfrak{c}^{\zeta})^{\frac{\mathcal{U}_j\mathfrak{p}-1}{\mathfrak{p}-1}}\right)^{\mathfrak{p}-1}\left(\frac{\mathfrak{p}-1}{\mathcal{U}_j\mathfrak{p}-1}\right)^{\mathfrak{p}-1}\int_0^{\mathfrak{c}}\|\Psi_j(\mathfrak{u},\ell(\mathfrak{u}))\|_{\mathfrak{p}}^{\mathfrak{p}}d\mathfrak{u}, \quad (10)$$

where $\mathbb{X}=\sup_{0<\mathfrak{u}\leq\mathfrak{c}}(F'(\mathfrak{u}))^{\frac{1}{\mathfrak{p}-1}}$.

In accordance with $(\hbar_1)$, we have

$$\|\Psi_j(\mathfrak{u},\ell(\mathfrak{u}))\|_{\mathfrak{p}}^{\mathfrak{p}}\leq 2^{\mathfrak{p}-1}\left(\|\Psi_j(\mathfrak{u},\ell(\mathfrak{u}))-\Psi_j(\mathfrak{u},0)\|_{\mathfrak{p}}^{\mathfrak{p}}+\|\Psi_j(\mathfrak{u},0)\|_{\mathfrak{p}}^{\mathfrak{p}}\right)$$
$$\leq 2^{\mathfrak{p}-1}\left(\mathfrak{T}^{\mathfrak{p}}\|\ell(\mathfrak{u})\|_{\mathfrak{p}}^{\mathfrak{p}}+\|\Psi_j(\mathfrak{u},0)\|_{\mathfrak{p}}^{\mathfrak{p}}\right). \quad (11)$$

Hence, we establish

$$\int_0^{\mathfrak{c}}\|\Psi_j(\mathfrak{u},\ell(\mathfrak{u}))\|_{\mathfrak{p}}^{\mathfrak{p}}d\mathfrak{u}\leq 2^{\mathfrak{p}-1}\mathfrak{T}^{\mathfrak{p}}\underset{\mathfrak{u}\in[1,\varpi]}{esssup}\|\ell(\mathfrak{u})\|_{\mathfrak{p}}^{\mathfrak{p}}\int_0^{\mathfrak{c}}1d\mathfrak{u}+2^{\mathfrak{p}-1}\int_0^{\mathfrak{c}}\|\Psi_j(\mathfrak{u},0)\|_{\mathfrak{p}}^{\mathfrak{p}}d\mathfrak{u}$$
$$\leq 2^{\mathfrak{p}-1}\varpi\mathfrak{T}^{\mathfrak{p}}\|\ell(\mathfrak{u})\|_{\mathbb{H}^{\mathfrak{p}}}^{\mathfrak{p}}+2^{\mathfrak{p}-1}\int_0^{\mathfrak{c}}\|\Psi_j(\mathfrak{u},0)\|_{\mathfrak{p}}^{\mathfrak{p}}d\mathfrak{u}. \quad (12)$$

As a result, we accomplish

$$2^{(\mathfrak{e}+2)\mathfrak{p}-(\mathfrak{e}+2)}\sum_{j=1}^{\mathfrak{e}}\left(\frac{\zeta^{1-\mathcal{U}_j}}{\Gamma(\mathcal{U}_j)}\right)^{\mathfrak{p}}\left\|\int_0^{\mathfrak{c}}(F(\mathfrak{c})-F(\mathfrak{u}))^{\mathcal{U}_i-1}F'(\mathfrak{u})\Psi_j(\mathfrak{u},\ell(\mathfrak{u}))d\mathfrak{u}\right\|_{\mathfrak{p}}^{\mathfrak{p}}\leq 2^{(\mathfrak{e}+2)\mathfrak{p}-(\mathfrak{e}+2)}\sum_{j=1}^{\mathfrak{e}}\left(\frac{\zeta^{1-\mathcal{U}_j}}{\Gamma(\mathcal{U}_j)}\right)^{\mathfrak{p}}$$
$$\left(\mathbb{X}^{\mathfrak{p}-1}\left((\mathfrak{c}^{\zeta})^{\frac{\mathcal{U}_j\mathfrak{p}-1}{\mathfrak{p}-1}}\right)^{\mathfrak{p}-1}\left(\frac{\mathfrak{p}-1}{\mathcal{U}_j\mathfrak{p}-1}\right)^{\mathfrak{p}-1}\left(2^{\mathfrak{p}-1}\varpi\mathfrak{T}^{\mathfrak{p}}\|\ell(\mathfrak{u})\|_{\mathbb{H}^{\mathfrak{p}}}^{\mathfrak{p}}+2^{\mathfrak{p}-1}\int_0^{\mathfrak{c}}\|\Psi_j(\mathfrak{u},0)\|_{\mathfrak{p}}^{\mathfrak{p}}d\mathfrak{u}\right)\right). \quad (13)$$

Now, consider the second term of (9). By employing Hölder's inequality, we obtain the following:

$$\left\|\int_0^{\mathfrak{c}}(F(\mathfrak{c})-F(\mathfrak{u}))^{\eta-1}\mathfrak{I}(\mathfrak{u},\ell(\mathfrak{u}),\ell(\mathfrak{u}-\gamma))F'(\mathfrak{u})d\mathfrak{u}\right\|_{\mathfrak{p}}^{\mathfrak{p}}=$$

$$\sum_{\iota=1}^{m}\mathfrak{E}\left|\int_0^{\mathfrak{c}}(F(\mathfrak{c})-F(\mathfrak{u}))^{\eta-1}|\mathfrak{I}_\iota(\mathfrak{u},\ell(\mathfrak{u}),\ell(\mathfrak{u}-\gamma))|F'(\mathfrak{u})d\mathfrak{u}\right|^{\mathfrak{p}}$$
$$\leq \sum_{\iota=1}^{m}\mathfrak{E}\left(\left(\int_0^{\mathfrak{c}}(F(\mathfrak{c})-F(\mathfrak{u}))^{\frac{(\eta-1)\mathfrak{p}}{(\mathfrak{p}-1)}}(F'(\mathfrak{u}))^{\frac{\mathfrak{p}}{\mathfrak{p}-1}}d\mathfrak{u}\right)^{\mathfrak{p}-1}\int_0^{\mathfrak{c}}|\mathfrak{I}_\iota(\mathfrak{u},\ell(\mathfrak{u}),\ell(\mathfrak{u}-\gamma))|^{\mathfrak{p}}d\mathfrak{u}\right)$$
$$\leq \sum_{\iota=1}^{m}\mathfrak{E}\left(\left(\sup_{0<\mathfrak{u}\leq\mathfrak{c}}(F'(\mathfrak{u}))^{\frac{1}{\mathfrak{p}-1}}\right)^{\mathfrak{p}-1}\left(\int_0^{\mathfrak{c}}(F(\mathfrak{c})-F(\mathfrak{u}))^{\frac{(\eta-1)\mathfrak{p}}{(\mathfrak{p}-1)}}F'(\mathfrak{u})d\mathfrak{u}\right)^{\mathfrak{p}-1}\right.$$
$$\left.\int_0^{\mathfrak{c}}|\mathfrak{I}_\iota(\mathfrak{u},\ell(\mathfrak{u}),\ell(\mathfrak{u}-\gamma))|^{\mathfrak{p}}d\mathfrak{u}\right)$$
$$\leq \mathbb{X}^{\mathfrak{p}-1}\left((\mathfrak{c}^{\zeta})^{\frac{\eta\mathfrak{p}-1}{\mathfrak{p}-1}}\right)^{\mathfrak{p}-1}\left(\frac{\mathfrak{p}-1}{\eta\mathfrak{p}-1}\right)^{\mathfrak{p}-1}\int_0^{\mathfrak{c}}\|\mathfrak{I}(\mathfrak{u},\ell(\mathfrak{u}),\ell(\mathfrak{u}-\gamma))\|_{\mathfrak{p}}^{\mathfrak{p}}d\mathfrak{u}. \quad (14)$$

Based on $(\hbar_1)$, we derive

$$\|\mathfrak{I}(\mathfrak{u},\ell(\mathfrak{u}),\ell(\mathfrak{u}-\gamma))\|_{\mathfrak{p}}^{\mathfrak{p}}\leq 2^{\mathfrak{p}-1}\left(\|\mathfrak{I}(\mathfrak{u},\ell(\mathfrak{u}),\ell(\mathfrak{u}-\gamma))-\mathfrak{I}(\mathfrak{u},0,0)\|_{\mathfrak{p}}^{\mathfrak{p}}+\|\mathfrak{I}(\mathfrak{u},0,0)\|_{\mathfrak{p}}^{\mathfrak{p}}\right)$$
$$\leq 2^{\mathfrak{p}-1}\left(2^{\mathfrak{p}-1}\mathfrak{T}^{\mathfrak{p}}\left(\|\ell(\mathfrak{u})\|_{\mathfrak{p}}^{\mathfrak{p}}+\|\ell(\mathfrak{u}-\gamma)\|_{\mathfrak{p}}^{\mathfrak{p}}\right)+\|\mathfrak{I}(\mathfrak{u},0,0)\|_{\mathfrak{p}}^{\mathfrak{p}}\right). \quad (15)$$

Consequently, we achieve the following:

$$\int_0^{\mathfrak{c}}\|\mathfrak{I}(\mathfrak{u},\ell(\mathfrak{u}),\ell(\mathfrak{u}-\gamma))\|_{\mathfrak{p}}^{\mathfrak{p}}d\mathfrak{u}\leq 2^{2\mathfrak{p}-2}\mathfrak{T}^{\mathfrak{p}}\left(\left(\underset{\mathfrak{u}\in[0,\varpi]}{esssup}\|\ell(\mathfrak{u})\|_{\mathfrak{p}}\right)^{\mathfrak{p}}+\left(\underset{\mathfrak{u}\in[0,\varpi]}{esssup}\|\ell(\mathfrak{u}-\gamma)\|_{\mathfrak{p}}\right)^{\mathfrak{p}}\right)$$
$$\int_0^{\mathfrak{c}}1d\mathfrak{u}+2^{\mathfrak{p}-1}\int_0^{\mathfrak{c}}\|\mathfrak{I}(\mathfrak{u},0,0)\|_{\mathfrak{p}}^{\mathfrak{p}}d\mathfrak{u}$$
$$\leq 2^{2\mathfrak{p}-2}\varpi\mathfrak{T}^{\mathfrak{p}}\left(\|\ell(\mathfrak{u})\|_{\mathbb{H}^{\mathfrak{p}}}^{\mathfrak{p}}+\|\ell(\mathfrak{u}-\gamma)\|_{\mathbb{H}^{\mathfrak{p}}}^{\mathfrak{p}}\right)+2^{\mathfrak{p}-1}\int_0^{\mathfrak{c}}\|\mathfrak{I}(\mathfrak{u},0,0)\|_{\mathfrak{p}}^{\mathfrak{p}}d\mathfrak{u}. \quad (16)$$

In light of (14) and (16), we determine

$$\left\|\int_0^{\mathfrak{c}}(F(\mathfrak{c})-F(\mathfrak{u}))^{\eta-1}\mathfrak{I}(\mathfrak{u},\ell(\mathfrak{u}),\ell(\mathfrak{u}-\gamma))F'(\mathfrak{u})d\mathfrak{u}\right\|_{\mathfrak{p}}^{\mathfrak{p}}\leq \mathbb{X}^{\mathfrak{p}-1}\left((\mathfrak{c}^{\zeta})^{\frac{(\eta\mathfrak{p}-1)}{\mathfrak{p}-1}}\right)^{\mathfrak{p}-1}$$
$$\left(\frac{\mathfrak{p}-1}{\eta\mathfrak{p}-1}\right)^{\mathfrak{p}-1}2^{\mathfrak{p}-1}\left(2^{\mathfrak{p}-1}\mathfrak{T}^{\mathfrak{p}}\varpi\left(\|\ell(\mathfrak{u})\|_{\mathbb{H}^{\mathfrak{p}}}^{\mathfrak{p}}+\|\ell(\mathfrak{u}-\gamma)\|_{\mathbb{H}^{\mathfrak{p}}}^{\mathfrak{p}}\right)+\int_0^{\mathfrak{c}}\|\mathfrak{I}(\mathfrak{u},0,0)\|_{\mathfrak{p}}^{\mathfrak{p}}d\mathfrak{u}\right). \quad (17)$$

Based on $(\hbar_2)$, we derive from (17) that

$$\left\|\int_0^{\mathfrak{c}}(F(\mathfrak{c})-F(\mathfrak{u}))^{\eta-1}\mathfrak{I}(\mathfrak{u},\ell(\mathfrak{u}),\ell(\mathfrak{u}-\gamma))F'(\mathfrak{u})d\mathfrak{u}\right\|_{\mathfrak{p}}^{\mathfrak{p}}\leq \mathbb{X}^{\mathfrak{p}-1}\left((\mathfrak{c}^{\zeta})^{\frac{(\eta\mathfrak{p}-1)}{\mathfrak{p}-1}}\right)^{\mathfrak{p}-1}$$
$$\left(\frac{\mathfrak{p}-1}{\eta\mathfrak{p}-1}\right)^{\mathfrak{p}-1}2^{\mathfrak{p}-1}\left(2^{\mathfrak{p}-1}\mathfrak{T}^{\mathfrak{p}}\varpi\left(\|\ell(\mathfrak{u})\|_{\mathbb{H}^{\mathfrak{p}}}^{\mathfrak{p}}+\|\ell(\mathfrak{u}-\gamma)\|_{\mathbb{H}^{\mathfrak{p}}}^{\mathfrak{p}}\right)+\varpi\wp^{\mathfrak{p}}\right). \quad (18)$$

Proceeding to the third term of (9), we employ the Burkholder–Davis–Gundy inequality and Hölder's inequality to obtain the following:

$$\left\|\int_0^{\mathfrak{c}}(\mathfrak{c}^{\zeta}-\mathfrak{u}^{\zeta})^{\eta-1}\mathfrak{B}(\mathfrak{u},\ell(\mathfrak{u}),\ell(\mathfrak{u}-\gamma))F'(\mathfrak{u})d\mathcal{W}(\mathfrak{u})\right\|_{\mathfrak{p}}^{\mathfrak{p}}$$
$$=\sum_{\iota=1}^{m}\mathfrak{E}\left|\int_0^{\mathfrak{c}}(F(\mathfrak{c})-F(\mathfrak{u}))^{\eta-1}(\mathfrak{B}_\iota(\mathfrak{u},\ell(\mathfrak{u}),\ell(\mathfrak{u}-\gamma))F'(\mathfrak{u})d\mathcal{W}(\mathfrak{u})\right|^{\mathfrak{p}}$$

$$\leq \sum_{\imath=1}^{m} \mathcal{C}_{\mathfrak{p}}\mathfrak{E}\left|\int_0^{\mathfrak{c}} (F(\mathfrak{c})-F(\mathfrak{u}))^{2\eta-2}\left|\mathfrak{B}_\imath(\mathfrak{u},\ell(\mathfrak{u}),\ell(\mathfrak{u}-\gamma))\right|^2 (F'(\mathfrak{u}))^2 d\mathfrak{u}\right|^{\frac{\mathfrak{p}}{2}}$$

$$\leq \sum_{\imath=1}^{m} \mathcal{C}_{\mathfrak{p}}\mathfrak{E}\int_0^{\mathfrak{c}} (F(\mathfrak{c})-F(\mathfrak{u}))^{2\eta-2}\left|\mathfrak{B}_\imath(\mathfrak{u},\ell(\mathfrak{u}),\ell(\mathfrak{u}-\gamma))\right|^{\mathfrak{p}} (F'(\mathfrak{u}))^2 d\mathfrak{u}$$

$$\left(\int_0^{\mathfrak{c}} (F(\mathfrak{c})-F(\mathfrak{u}))^{2\eta-2}(F'(\mathfrak{u}))^2 d\mathfrak{u}\right)^{\frac{\mathfrak{p}-2}{2}}$$

$$\leq \sum_{\imath=1}^{m} \mathcal{C}_{\mathfrak{p}}\mathfrak{E}\int_0^{\mathfrak{c}} (F(\mathfrak{c})-F(\mathfrak{u}))^{2\eta-2}\left|\mathfrak{B}_\imath(\mathfrak{u},\ell(\mathfrak{u}),\ell(\mathfrak{u}-\gamma))\right|^{\mathfrak{p}} (F'(\mathfrak{u}))^2 d\mathfrak{u}$$

$$\left(\sup_{0<\mathfrak{u}\leq\mathfrak{c}} F'(\mathfrak{u})\int_0^{\mathfrak{c}} (F(\mathfrak{c})-F(\mathfrak{u}))^{2\eta-2}F'(\mathfrak{u})d\mathfrak{u}\right)^{\frac{\mathfrak{p}-2}{2}}$$

$$\leq \mathbf{G}^{\frac{\mathfrak{p}-2}{2}}\mathcal{C}_{\mathfrak{p}}\left(\frac{(\mathfrak{c}^{\zeta})^{2\eta-1}}{2\eta-1}\right)^{\frac{\mathfrak{p}-2}{2}}\int_0^{\mathfrak{c}} (F(\mathfrak{c})-F(\mathfrak{u}))^{2\eta-2}\|\mathfrak{B}(\mathfrak{u},\ell(\mathfrak{u},\ell(\mathfrak{u}-\gamma))\|_{\mathfrak{p}}^{\mathfrak{p}}(F'(\mathfrak{u}))^2 d\mathfrak{u}, \quad (19)$$

where $\mathbf{G} = \sup_{0<\mathfrak{u}\leq\mathfrak{c}} F'(\mathfrak{u})$ and $\mathcal{C}_{\mathfrak{p}} = \left(\frac{\mathfrak{p}^{\mathfrak{p}+1}}{2(\mathfrak{p}-1)^{\mathfrak{p}-1}}\right)^{\frac{\mathfrak{p}}{2}}$.

Utilizing $(\hbar_1)$ and $(\hbar_2)$, we conclude

$$\begin{aligned}\|\mathfrak{B}(\mathfrak{u},\ell(\mathfrak{u}),\ell(\mathfrak{u}-\gamma))\|_{\mathfrak{p}}^{\mathfrak{p}} &\leq 2^{2\mathfrak{p}-2}\mathfrak{T}^{\mathfrak{p}}\left(\|\ell(\mathfrak{u})\|_{\mathfrak{p}}^{\mathfrak{p}}+\|\ell(\mathfrak{u}-\gamma)\|_{\mathfrak{p}}^{\mathfrak{p}}\right)+2^{\mathfrak{p}-1}\|\mathfrak{B}(\mathfrak{u},0,0)\|_{\mathfrak{p}}^{\mathfrak{p}}\\ &\leq 2^{2\mathfrak{p}-2}\mathfrak{T}^{\mathfrak{p}}\left(\|\ell(\mathfrak{u})\|_{\mathfrak{p}}^{\mathfrak{p}}+\|\ell(\mathfrak{u}-\gamma)\|_{\mathfrak{p}}^{\mathfrak{p}}\right)+2^{\mathfrak{p}-1}\wp^{\mathfrak{p}}. \quad (20)\end{aligned}$$

Accordingly, we obtain

$$\int_0^{\mathfrak{c}} (F(\mathfrak{c})-F(\mathfrak{u}))^{2\eta-2}\|\mathfrak{B}(\mathfrak{u},\ell(\mathfrak{u}),\ell(\mathfrak{u}-\gamma))\|_{\mathfrak{p}}^{\mathfrak{p}}(F'(\mathfrak{u}))^2 d\mathfrak{u} \leq 2^{2\mathfrak{p}-2}\mathfrak{T}^{\mathfrak{p}}$$

$$\int_0^{\mathfrak{c}} (F(\mathfrak{c})-F(\mathfrak{u}))^{2\eta-2}\left(\left(\underset{\mathfrak{u}\in[0,\varpi]}{esssup}\|\ell(\mathfrak{u})\|_{\mathfrak{p}}\right)^{\mathfrak{p}}+\left(\underset{\mathfrak{u}\in[0,\varpi]}{esssup}\|\ell(\mathfrak{u}-\gamma)\|_{\mathfrak{p}}\right)^{\mathfrak{p}}\right)(F'(\mathfrak{u}))^2 d\mathfrak{u}$$

$$+2^{\mathfrak{p}-1}\wp^{\mathfrak{p}}\int_0^{\mathfrak{c}} (F(\mathfrak{c})-F(\mathfrak{u}))^{2\eta-2}(F'(\mathfrak{u}))^2 d\mathfrak{u}$$

$$\leq 2^{2\mathfrak{p}-2}\mathfrak{T}^{\mathfrak{p}}\sup_{0<\mathfrak{u}\leq\mathfrak{c}} F'(\mathfrak{u})\int_0^{\mathfrak{c}} (F(\mathfrak{c})-F(\mathfrak{u}))^{2\eta-2}\left(\left(\underset{\mathfrak{u}\in[0,\varpi]}{esssup}\|\ell(\mathfrak{u})\|_{\mathfrak{p}}\right)^{\mathfrak{p}}\right.$$

$$\left.+\left(\underset{\mathfrak{u}\in[0,\varpi]}{esssup}\|\ell(\mathfrak{u}-\gamma)\|_{\mathfrak{p}}\right)^{\mathfrak{p}}\right)F'(\mathfrak{u})d\mathfrak{u}+2^{\mathfrak{p}-1}\wp^{\mathfrak{p}}\sup_{0<\mathfrak{u}\leq\mathfrak{c}} F'(\mathfrak{u})\int_0^{\mathfrak{c}} (F(\mathfrak{c})-F(\mathfrak{u}))^{2\eta-2}F'(\mathfrak{u})d\mathfrak{u}$$

$$=\mathbf{G}\frac{2^{\mathfrak{p}-1}(\mathfrak{c}^{\zeta})^{(2\eta-1)}}{(2\eta-1)}\left(2^{\mathfrak{p}-1}\mathfrak{T}^{\mathfrak{p}}\left(\|\ell(\mathfrak{u})\|_{\mathbb{H}_{\mathfrak{p}}}^{\mathfrak{p}}+\|\ell(\mathfrak{u}-\gamma)\|_{\mathbb{H}_{\mathfrak{p}}}^{\mathfrak{p}}\right)+\wp^{\mathfrak{p}}\right). \quad (21)$$

Hence, the preceding leads to

$$\begin{aligned}\int_0^{\mathfrak{c}} (F(\mathfrak{c})-F(\mathfrak{u}))^{2\eta-2}\|\mathfrak{B}(\mathfrak{u},\ell(\mathfrak{u}),\ell(\mathfrak{u}-\gamma))\|_{\mathfrak{p}}^{\mathfrak{p}}(F'(\mathfrak{u}))^2 d\mathfrak{u} &\leq \frac{2^{\mathfrak{p}-1}(\mathfrak{c}^{\zeta})^{(2\eta-1)}}{(2\eta-1)}\mathbf{G}\\ &\left(2^{\mathfrak{p}-1}\mathfrak{T}^{\mathfrak{p}}\left(\|\ell(\mathfrak{u})\|_{\mathbb{H}_{\mathfrak{p}}}^{\mathfrak{p}}+\|\ell(\mathfrak{u}-\gamma)\|_{\mathbb{H}_{\mathfrak{p}}}^{\mathfrak{p}}\right)+\wp^{\mathfrak{p}}\right). \quad (22)\end{aligned}$$

From (19) and (22), we conclude

$$\left\|\int_0^{\mathfrak{c}} (F(\mathfrak{c})-F(\mathfrak{u}))^{\eta-1}\mathfrak{B}(\mathfrak{u},\ell(\mathfrak{u}),\ell(\mathfrak{u}-\gamma))F'(\mathfrak{u})d\mathcal{W}(\mathfrak{u})\right\|_{\mathfrak{p}}^{\mathfrak{p}} \leq \mathbf{G}^{\frac{\mathfrak{p}-2}{2}}$$

$$\mathcal{C}_{\mathfrak{p}}\left(\frac{(\mathfrak{c}^{\zeta})^{(2\eta-1)}}{(2\eta-1)}\right)^{\frac{\mathfrak{p}-2}{2}}\frac{2^{\mathfrak{p}-1}(\mathfrak{c}^{\zeta})^{(2\eta-1)}}{(2\eta-1)}$$
$$\mathbf{G}\left(2^{\mathfrak{p}-1}\mathfrak{T}^{\mathfrak{p}}\left(\|\ell(\mathfrak{u})\|^{\mathfrak{p}}_{\mathbb{H}_{\mathfrak{p}}}+\|\ell(\mathfrak{u}-\gamma)\|^{\mathfrak{p}}_{\mathbb{H}_{\mathfrak{p}}}\right)+\wp^{\mathfrak{p}}\right). \tag{23}$$

It follows that $\|\psi(\ell(\mathfrak{c}))\|_{\mathbb{H}\mathfrak{p}}$ is finite, thereby fulfilling the needed result. □

The following lemma is important for Ex-Un.

Lemma 2. *Assume $\eta, \lambda > 0$, and $\mathfrak{c} \in [0, \varpi]$, then*

$$\mathcal{I}^{\eta,\zeta}_{\mathfrak{c}} \exp\left(\lambda(\mathfrak{c}^{\zeta})\right) \leq \frac{\exp\left(\lambda(\mathfrak{c}^{\zeta})\right)}{\lambda^{\eta}}.$$

Proof. It follows from (2) that

$$\mathcal{I}^{\eta,\zeta}_{\mathfrak{c}} \exp\left(\lambda(\mathfrak{c}^{\zeta})\right) = \frac{\zeta^{1-\eta}}{\Gamma(\eta)}\int_0^{\mathfrak{c}}\left(F(\mathfrak{c})-F(\mathfrak{u})\right)^{\eta-1}\exp\left(\lambda(\mathfrak{u}^{\zeta})\right)F'(\mathfrak{u})d\mathfrak{u}.$$

By $\mathbb{K} = \mathfrak{c}^{\zeta} - \mathfrak{u}^{\zeta}$,

$$\mathcal{I}^{\eta,\zeta}_{\mathfrak{c}} \exp\left(\lambda(\mathfrak{c}^{\zeta})\right) = \frac{\zeta^{-\eta}\exp(\lambda(\mathfrak{c}^{\zeta}))}{\Gamma(\eta)}\int_0^{\mathfrak{c}^{\zeta}}\mathbb{K}^{\eta-1}\exp(-\lambda\mathbb{K})d\mathbb{K}. \tag{24}$$

Apply $\mathcal{G} = \lambda\mathbb{K}$ in (24),

$$\begin{aligned}\mathcal{I}^{\eta,\zeta}_{\mathfrak{c}} \exp\left(\lambda(\mathfrak{c}^{\zeta})\right) &= \frac{\zeta^{-\eta}\exp\left(\lambda(\mathfrak{c}^{\zeta})\right)}{\lambda^{\eta}\Gamma(\eta)}\int_0^{\lambda\mathfrak{c}^{\zeta}}\mathcal{G}^{\eta-1}\exp(-\mathcal{G})d\mathcal{G}\\ &\leq \frac{\zeta^{-\eta}\exp\left(\lambda(\mathfrak{c}^{\zeta})\right)}{\lambda^{\eta}\Gamma(\eta)}\int_0^{\infty}\mathcal{G}^{\eta-1}\exp(-\mathcal{G})d\mathcal{G}\\ &= \frac{\zeta^{-\eta}\exp\left(\lambda(\mathfrak{c}^{\zeta})\right)}{\lambda^{\eta}}.\end{aligned}$$

This implies that

$$\frac{1}{\Gamma(\eta)}\int_0^{\mathfrak{c}}\left(F(\mathfrak{c})-F(\mathfrak{u})\right)^{\eta-1}\exp\left(\lambda(\mathfrak{u}^{\zeta})\right)F'(\mathfrak{u})d\mathfrak{u} \leq \frac{\exp\left(\lambda(\mathfrak{c}^{\zeta})\right)}{\zeta\lambda^{\eta}}. \tag{25}$$

□

The next lemma deals with the Ex-Un solution of delay FSIDEs.

Theorem 1. *Let $(\hbar_1)$ and $(\hbar_2)$ be valid; afterward, delay FSIDEs (3) ensure a unique solution.*

Proof. Considering $\|\cdot\|_{\lambda}$, we have

$$\|\ell(\mathfrak{c})\|_{\lambda} = \underset{\mathfrak{c}\in[0,\varpi]}{esssup}\left(\frac{\|\ell(\mathfrak{c})\|^{\mathfrak{p}}_{\mathfrak{p}}}{\Lambda(\mathfrak{c})}\right)^{\frac{1}{\mathfrak{p}}},\ \lambda > 0, \tag{26}$$

where $\Lambda(\mathfrak{c}) = \exp(\lambda(\mathfrak{c}^{\zeta}))$.

It can be easily demonstrated that $\|\cdot\|_{\mathbb{H}\mathfrak{p}}$ and $\|\cdot\|_{\lambda}$ are equivalent. So, $(\mathbb{H}^{\mathfrak{p}}([0,\mathfrak{c}]), \|\cdot\|_{\lambda})$ is also complete and normed.

Take the following into account:

$$\kappa = \left(2^{(\mathfrak{e}+1)\mathfrak{p}-(\mathfrak{e}+1)}\sum_{\jmath=1}^{\mathfrak{e}}\left(\frac{\zeta^{1-\mathcal{U}_\jmath}}{\Gamma(\mathcal{U}_\jmath)}\right)^{\mathfrak{p}}\mathrm{G}\mathfrak{n}^{\mathfrak{p}-1}\frac{\mathfrak{T}^{\mathfrak{p}}(\mathfrak{c}^{\zeta})^{(\mathfrak{p}\mathcal{U}_\jmath-2\mathcal{U}_\jmath+1)}(\mathfrak{p}-1)^{\mathfrak{p}-1}}{(\mathfrak{p}\mathcal{U}_\jmath-2\mathcal{U}_\jmath+1)^{\mathfrak{p}-1}}\frac{\Gamma(2\mathcal{U}_\jmath-1)\zeta}{\lambda^{2\mathcal{U}_\jmath-1}}\right.$$

$$+\frac{2^{2\mathfrak{p}-2}(\zeta^{1-\eta})^{\mathfrak{p}}}{(\Gamma(\eta))^{\mathfrak{p}}}\left(2^{\mathfrak{p}-1}\mathbf{G}\mathfrak{n}^{\mathfrak{p}-1}\frac{\mathfrak{T}^{\mathfrak{p}}(\mathfrak{c}^{\zeta})^{(\mathfrak{p}\eta-2\eta+1)}(\mathfrak{p}-1)^{\mathfrak{p}-1}}{(\mathfrak{p}\eta-2\eta+1)^{\mathfrak{p}-1}}+2^{\mathfrak{p}-1}\mathbf{G}^{\frac{\mathfrak{p}-2}{2}}\left(\frac{(\mathfrak{c}^{\zeta})^{(2\eta-1)}}{(2\eta-1)}\right)^{\frac{\mathfrak{p}-2}{2}}\mathfrak{T}^{\mathfrak{p}}\mathcal{C}_{\mathfrak{p}}\mathbf{G}\right)\frac{2\zeta\Gamma(2\eta-1)}{\lambda^{2\eta-1}}\right)<1. \quad (27)$$

For $\ell(\mathfrak{c}),\ell^*(\mathfrak{c})\in\mathbb{H}^{\mathfrak{p}}([0,\varpi])$, we obtain

$$\begin{aligned}
&\|\psi_\varphi(\ell(\mathfrak{c}))-\psi_\varphi(\ell^*(\mathfrak{c}))\|_{\mathfrak{p}}^{\mathfrak{p}}\le 2^{(\mathfrak{e}+1)\mathfrak{p}-(\mathfrak{e}+1)}\sum_{j=1}^{\mathfrak{e}}\left(\frac{\zeta^{1-\mathcal{U}_j}}{\Gamma(\mathcal{U}_j)}\right)^{\mathfrak{p}}\\
&\left\|\int_0^{\mathfrak{c}}(F(\mathfrak{c})-F(\mathfrak{u}))^{\mathcal{U}_j-1}\Big(\Psi_j(\mathfrak{u},\ell(\mathfrak{u}))-\Psi_j(\mathfrak{u},\ell^*(\mathfrak{u}))\Big)F'(\mathfrak{u})d\mathfrak{u}\right\|_{\mathfrak{p}}^{\mathfrak{p}}\\
&+\frac{2^{2\mathfrak{p}-2}(\zeta^{1-\eta})^{\mathfrak{p}}}{(\Gamma(\eta))^{\mathfrak{p}}}\left\|\int_0^{\mathfrak{c}}(F(\mathfrak{c})-F(\mathfrak{u}))^{\eta-1}\Big(\mathfrak{I}(\mathfrak{u},\ell(\mathfrak{u}),\ell(\mathfrak{u}-\gamma))-\mathfrak{I}(\mathfrak{u},\ell^*(\mathfrak{u}),\ell^*(\mathfrak{u}-\gamma))\Big)F'(\mathfrak{u})d\mathfrak{u}\right\|_{\mathfrak{p}}^{\mathfrak{p}}+\\
&+\frac{2^{2\mathfrak{p}-2}(\zeta^{1-\eta})^{\mathfrak{p}}}{(\Gamma(\eta))^{\mathfrak{p}}}\left\|\int_0^{\mathfrak{c}}(F(\mathfrak{c})-F(\mathfrak{u}))^{\eta-1}\Big(\mathfrak{B}(\mathfrak{u},\ell(\mathfrak{u}),\ell(\mathfrak{u}-\gamma))-\mathfrak{B}(\mathfrak{u},\ell^*(\mathfrak{u}),\ell^*(\mathfrak{u}-\gamma))\Big)F'(\mathfrak{u})d\mathcal{W}(\mathfrak{u})\right\|_{\mathfrak{p}}^{\mathfrak{p}}.
\end{aligned} \quad (28)$$

Through the use of Hölder's inequality and $(\hbar_1)$, we achieve

$$\begin{aligned}
&2^{(\mathfrak{e}+1)\mathfrak{p}-(\mathfrak{e}+1)}\sum_{j=1}^{\mathfrak{e}}\left(\frac{\zeta^{1-\mathcal{U}_j}}{\Gamma(\mathcal{U}_j)}\right)^{\mathfrak{p}}\left\|\int_0^{\mathfrak{c}}(F(\mathfrak{c})-F(\mathfrak{u}))^{\mathcal{U}_j-1}\Big(\Psi_j(\mathfrak{u},\ell(\mathfrak{u}))-\Psi_j(\mathfrak{u},\ell^*(\mathfrak{u}))\Big)F'(\mathfrak{u})d\mathfrak{u}\right\|_{\mathfrak{p}}^{\mathfrak{p}}\\
&=2^{(\mathfrak{e}+1)\mathfrak{p}-(\mathfrak{e}+1)}\sum_{j=1}^{\mathfrak{e}}\left(\frac{\zeta^{1-\mathcal{U}_j}}{\Gamma(\mathcal{U}_j)}\right)^{\mathfrak{p}}\sum_{\imath=1}^{m}\mathfrak{E}\left|\int_0^{\mathfrak{c}}(F(\mathfrak{c})-F(\mathfrak{u}))^{\mathcal{U}_j-1}\Big(\Psi_{\imath,j}(\mathfrak{u},\ell(\mathfrak{u}))-\Psi_{\imath,j}(\mathfrak{u},\ell^*(\mathfrak{u}))\Big)F'(\mathfrak{u})d\mathfrak{u}\right|^{\mathfrak{p}}\\
&\le 2^{(\mathfrak{e}+1)\mathfrak{p}-(\mathfrak{e}+1)}\sum_{j=1}^{\mathfrak{e}}\left(\frac{\zeta^{1-\mathcal{U}_j}}{\Gamma(\mathcal{U}_j)}\right)^{\mathfrak{p}}\sum_{\imath=1}^{m}\mathfrak{E}\left(\left(\int_0^{\mathfrak{c}}(F(\mathfrak{c})-F(\mathfrak{u}))^{\frac{(\mathcal{U}_j-1)(\mathfrak{p}-2)}{\mathfrak{p}-1}}(F'(\mathfrak{u}))^{\frac{\mathfrak{p}-2}{\mathfrak{p}-1}}d\mathfrak{u}\right)^{\mathfrak{p}-1}\right.\\
&\left.\left(\int_0^{\mathfrak{c}}(F(\mathfrak{c})-F(\mathfrak{u}))^{2\mathcal{U}_j-2}|\Psi_{\imath,j}(\mathfrak{u},\ell(\mathfrak{u}))-\Psi_{\imath,j}(\mathfrak{u},\ell^*(\mathfrak{u}))|F'(\mathfrak{u})d\mathfrak{u}\right)\right)\\
&\le 2^{(\mathfrak{e}+1)\mathfrak{p}-(\mathfrak{e}+1)}\sum_{j=1}^{\mathfrak{e}}\left(\frac{\zeta^{1-\mathcal{U}_j}}{\Gamma(\mathcal{U}_j)}\right)^{\mathfrak{p}}\sum_{\imath=1}^{m}\mathfrak{E}\left(\left(\sup_{1<\mathfrak{u}\le\mathfrak{c}}(F'(\mathfrak{u}))^{\frac{1}{1-\mathfrak{p}}}\int_0^{\mathfrak{c}}(F(\mathfrak{c})-F(\mathfrak{u}))^{\frac{(\mathcal{U}_j-1)(\mathfrak{p}-2)}{\mathfrak{p}-1}}F'(\mathfrak{u})d\mathfrak{u}\right)^{\mathfrak{p}-1}\right.\\
&\left.\left(\int_0^{\mathfrak{c}}(F(\mathfrak{c})-F(\mathfrak{u}))^{2\mathcal{U}_j-2}|\Psi_{\imath,j}(\mathfrak{u},\ell(\mathfrak{u}))-\Psi_{\imath,j}(\mathfrak{u},\ell^*(\mathfrak{u}))|(F'(\mathfrak{u}))^2d\mathfrak{u}\right)\right)\\
&\le 2^{(\mathfrak{e}+1)\mathfrak{p}-(\mathfrak{e}+1)}\sum_{j=1}^{\mathfrak{e}}\left(\frac{\zeta^{1-\mathcal{U}_j}}{\Gamma(\mathcal{U}_j)}\right)^{\mathfrak{p}}\mathfrak{n}^{\mathfrak{p}-1}\frac{\mathfrak{T}^{\mathfrak{p}}(\mathfrak{c}^{\zeta})^{(\mathfrak{p}\mathcal{U}_j-2\mathcal{U}_j+1)}(\mathfrak{p}-1)^{\mathfrak{p}-1}}{(\mathfrak{p}\mathcal{U}_j-2\mathcal{U}_j+1)^{\mathfrak{p}-1}}\\
&\sup_{1<\mathfrak{u}\le\mathfrak{c}}F'(\mathfrak{u})\int_0^{\mathfrak{c}}(F(\mathfrak{c})-F(\mathfrak{u}))^{2\mathcal{U}_j-2}\Big(\|\ell(\mathfrak{u})-\ell^*(\mathfrak{u})\|_{\mathfrak{p}}^{\mathfrak{p}}\Big)F'(\mathfrak{u})d\mathfrak{u},
\end{aligned} \quad (29)$$

where $\mathfrak{n}=\sup_{0<\mathfrak{u}\le\mathfrak{c}}(F'(\mathfrak{u}))^{\frac{1}{1-\mathfrak{p}}}$.

Accordingly, we find

$$\begin{aligned}
&2^{(\mathfrak{e}+1)\mathfrak{p}-(\mathfrak{e}+1)}\sum_{j=1}^{\mathfrak{e}}\left(\frac{\zeta^{1-\mathcal{U}_j}}{\Gamma(\mathcal{U}_j)}\right)^{\mathfrak{p}}\left\|\int_0^{\mathfrak{c}}(F(\mathfrak{c})-F(\mathfrak{u}))^{\mathcal{U}_j-1}(\Psi_j(\mathfrak{u},\ell(\mathfrak{u}))-\Psi_j(\mathfrak{u},\ell^*(\mathfrak{u})))F'(\mathfrak{u})d\mathfrak{u}\right\|_{\mathfrak{p}}^{\mathfrak{p}}\\
&\le 2^{(\mathfrak{e}+1)\mathfrak{p}-(\mathfrak{e}+1)}\sum_{j=1}^{\mathfrak{e}}\left(\frac{\zeta^{1-\mathcal{U}_j}}{\Gamma(\mathcal{U}_j)}\right)^{\mathfrak{p}}\mathbf{G}\mathfrak{n}^{\mathfrak{p}-1}\frac{\mathfrak{T}^{\mathfrak{p}}(\mathfrak{c}^{\zeta})^{(\mathfrak{p}\mathcal{U}_j-2\mathcal{U}_j+1)}(\mathfrak{p}-1)^{\mathfrak{p}-1}}{(\mathfrak{p}\mathcal{U}_j-2\mathcal{U}_j+1)^{\mathfrak{p}-1}}\\
&\int_0^{\mathfrak{c}}(F(\mathfrak{c})-F(\mathfrak{u}))^{2\mathcal{U}_j-2}\mathop{esssup}_{\mathfrak{c}\in[0,\varpi]}\left(\frac{\|\ell(\mathfrak{u})-\ell^*(\mathfrak{u})\|_{\mathfrak{p}}^{\mathfrak{p}}}{\exp(\lambda(\mathfrak{u}^{\zeta}))}\right)\exp(\lambda(\mathfrak{u}^{\zeta}))F'(\mathfrak{u})d\mathfrak{u}.
\end{aligned} \quad (30)$$

Following (30), we deduce:

$$2^{(\mathfrak{e}+1)\mathfrak{p}-(\mathfrak{e}+1)}\sum_{j=1}^{\mathfrak{e}}\left(\frac{\zeta^{1-\mathcal{U}_j}}{\Gamma(\mathcal{U}_j)}\right)^{\mathfrak{p}}\left\|\int_0^{\mathfrak{c}}(F(\mathfrak{c})-F(\mathfrak{u}))^{\mathcal{U}_j-1}(\Psi_j(\mathfrak{u},\ell(\mathfrak{u}))-\Psi_j(\mathfrak{u},\ell^*(\mathfrak{u})))\frac{1}{\mathfrak{u}}d\mathfrak{u}\right\|_{\mathfrak{p}}^{\mathfrak{p}}$$

$$\leq 2^{(\mathfrak{e}+1)\mathfrak{p}-(\mathfrak{e}+1)} \sum_{j=1}^{\mathfrak{e}} \left(\frac{\zeta^{1-\mathcal{U}_j}}{\Gamma(\mathcal{U}_j)}\right)^{\mathfrak{p}} \mathbf{G}\mathfrak{n}^{\mathfrak{p}-1} \frac{\mathfrak{T}^{\mathfrak{p}}\left(\mathfrak{c}^{\zeta}\right)^{(\mathfrak{p}\mathcal{U}_j-2\mathcal{U}_j+1)}(\mathfrak{p}-1)^{\mathfrak{p}-1}}{\left(\mathfrak{p}\mathcal{U}_j-2\mathcal{U}_j+1\right)^{\mathfrak{p}-1}}$$
$$\int_0^{\mathfrak{c}} (F(\mathfrak{c})-F(\mathfrak{u}))^{2\mathcal{U}_j-2} \|\ell(\mathfrak{u})-\ell^*(\mathfrak{u})\|_{\lambda}^{\mathfrak{p}} \exp(\lambda(\mathfrak{u}^{\zeta}))F'(\mathfrak{u})d\mathfrak{u}$$
$$\leq 2^{(\mathfrak{e}+1)\mathfrak{p}-(\mathfrak{e}+1)} \sum_{j=1}^{\mathfrak{e}} \left(\frac{\zeta^{1-\mathcal{U}_j}}{\Gamma(\mathcal{U}_j)}\right)^{\mathfrak{p}} \mathbf{G}\mathfrak{n}^{\mathfrak{p}-1} \frac{\mathfrak{T}^{\mathfrak{p}}\left(\mathfrak{c}^{\zeta}\right)^{(\mathfrak{p}\mathcal{U}_j-2\mathcal{U}_j+1)}(\mathfrak{p}-1)^{\mathfrak{p}-1}}{\left(\mathfrak{p}\mathcal{U}_j-2\mathcal{U}_j+1\right)^{\mathfrak{p}-1}} \|\ell(\mathfrak{u})-\ell^*(\mathfrak{u})\|_{\lambda}^{\mathfrak{p}} \frac{\Gamma(2\mathcal{U}_j-1)\zeta\exp(\lambda\mathfrak{c}^{\zeta})}{\lambda^{2\mathcal{U}_j-1}}. \quad (31)$$

Proceeding with the second term of (28) and employing Hölder's inequality and $(\hbar_1)$, we obtain:

$$\left\|\int_0^{\mathfrak{c}} (F(\mathfrak{c})-F(\mathfrak{u}))^{\eta-1}\Big(\mathfrak{J}(\mathfrak{u},\ell(\mathfrak{u}),\ell(\mathfrak{u}-\gamma))-\mathfrak{J}(\mathfrak{u},\ell^*(\mathfrak{u}),\ell^*(\mathfrak{u}-\gamma))\Big)F'(\mathfrak{u})d\mathfrak{u}\right\|_{\mathfrak{p}}^{\mathfrak{p}}$$
$$=\sum_{\imath=1}^{m} \mathfrak{E}\left|\int_0^{\mathfrak{c}} (F(\mathfrak{c})-F(\mathfrak{u}))^{\eta-1}\Big(\mathfrak{J}_\imath(\mathfrak{u},\ell(\mathfrak{u}),\ell(\mathfrak{u}-\gamma))-\mathfrak{J}_\imath(\mathfrak{u},\ell^*(\mathfrak{u}),\ell^*(\mathfrak{u}-\gamma))\Big)F'(\mathfrak{u})d\mathfrak{u}\right|^{\mathfrak{p}}$$
$$\leq \sum_{\imath=1}^{m} \mathfrak{E}\left(\left(\int_0^{\mathfrak{c}} (F(\mathfrak{c})-F(\mathfrak{u}))^{\frac{(\eta-1)(\mathfrak{p}-2)}{\mathfrak{p}-1}} (F'(\mathfrak{u}))^{\frac{\mathfrak{p}-2}{\mathfrak{p}-1}} d\mathfrak{u}\right)^{\mathfrak{p}-1}\right.$$
$$\left.\left(\int_0^{\mathfrak{c}} (F(\mathfrak{c})-F(\mathfrak{u}))^{2\eta-2}|\mathfrak{J}_\imath(\mathfrak{u},\ell(\mathfrak{u}),\ell(\mathfrak{u}-\gamma))-\mathfrak{J}_\imath(\mathfrak{u},\ell^*(\mathfrak{u}),\ell^*(\mathfrak{u}-\gamma))|^{\mathfrak{p}}(F'(\mathfrak{u}))^2 d\mathfrak{u}\right)\right)$$
$$\leq \sum_{\imath=1}^{m} \mathfrak{E}\left(\left(\sup_{0<\mathfrak{u}\leq\mathfrak{c}} (F'(\mathfrak{u}))^{\frac{1}{1-\mathfrak{p}}} \int_0^{\mathfrak{c}} (F(\mathfrak{c})-F(\mathfrak{u}))^{\frac{(\eta-1)(\mathfrak{p}-2)}{\mathfrak{p}-1}} F'(\mathfrak{u})d\mathfrak{u}\right)^{\mathfrak{p}-1}\right.$$
$$\left.\left(\int_0^{\mathfrak{c}} (F(\mathfrak{c})-F(\mathfrak{u}))^{2\eta-2}|\mathfrak{J}_\imath(\mathfrak{u},\ell(\mathfrak{u}),\ell(\mathfrak{u}-\gamma))-\mathfrak{J}_\imath(\mathfrak{u},\ell^*(\mathfrak{u}),\ell^*(\mathfrak{u}-\gamma))|^{\mathfrak{p}}(F'(\mathfrak{u}))^2 d\mathfrak{u}\right)\right)$$
$$\leq 2^{\mathfrak{p}-1}\mathfrak{n}^{\mathfrak{p}-1} \frac{\mathfrak{T}^{\mathfrak{p}}\left(\mathfrak{c}^{\zeta}\right)^{(\mathfrak{p}\eta-2\eta+1)}(\mathfrak{p}-1)^{\mathfrak{p}-1}}{(\mathfrak{p}\eta-2\eta+1)^{\mathfrak{p}-1}}$$
$$\sup_{0<\mathfrak{u}\leq\mathfrak{c}} F'(\mathfrak{u}) \int_0^{\mathfrak{c}} (F(\mathfrak{c})-F(\mathfrak{u}))^{2\eta-2}\Big(\|\ell(\mathfrak{u})-\ell^*(\mathfrak{u})\|_{\mathfrak{p}}^{\mathfrak{p}}+\|\ell(\mathfrak{u}-\gamma)-\ell^*(\mathfrak{u}-\gamma)\|_{\mathfrak{p}}^{\mathfrak{p}}\Big)F'(\mathfrak{u})d\mathfrak{u}. \quad (32)$$

It follows that

$$\left\|\int_0^{\mathfrak{c}} (F(\mathfrak{c})-F(\mathfrak{u}))^{\eta-1}\Big(\mathfrak{J}(\mathfrak{u},\ell(\mathfrak{u}),\ell(\mathfrak{u}-\gamma))-\mathfrak{J}(\mathfrak{u},\ell^*(\mathfrak{u}),\ell^*(\mathfrak{u}-\gamma))\Big)F'(\mathfrak{u})d\mathfrak{u}\right\|_{\mathfrak{p}}^{\mathfrak{p}}$$
$$\leq 2^{\mathfrak{p}-1}\mathbf{G}\mathfrak{n}^{\mathfrak{p}-1} \frac{\mathfrak{T}^{\mathfrak{p}}\left(\mathfrak{c}^{\zeta}\right)^{(\mathfrak{p}\eta-2\eta+1)}(\mathfrak{p}-1)^{\mathfrak{p}-1}}{(\mathfrak{p}\eta-2\eta+1)^{\mathfrak{p}-1}}$$
$$\int_0^{\mathfrak{c}} (F(\mathfrak{c})-F(\mathfrak{u}))^{2\eta-2}\Big(\|\ell(\mathfrak{u})-\ell^*(\mathfrak{u})\|_{\mathfrak{p}}^{\mathfrak{p}}+\|\ell(\mathfrak{u}-\gamma)-\ell^*(\mathfrak{u}-\gamma)\|_{\mathfrak{p}}^{\mathfrak{p}}\Big)F'(\mathfrak{u})d\mathfrak{u}. \quad (33)$$

Continuing with the third term of (28) and applying the Burkholder–Davis–Gundy inequality and $(\hbar_1)$, we derive

$$\left\|\int_0^{\mathfrak{c}} (F(\mathfrak{c})-F(\mathfrak{u}))^{\eta-1}\Big(\mathfrak{B}(\mathfrak{u},\ell(\mathfrak{u}),\ell(\mathfrak{u}-\gamma))-\mathfrak{B}(\mathfrak{u},\ell^*(\mathfrak{u}),\ell^*(\mathfrak{u}-\gamma))\Big)F'(\mathfrak{u})d\mathcal{W}(\mathfrak{u})\right\|_{\mathfrak{p}}^{\mathfrak{p}}$$
$$=\sum_{\imath=1}^{m} \mathfrak{E}\left|\int_0^{\mathfrak{c}} (F(\mathfrak{c})-F(\mathfrak{u}))^{\eta-1}\Big(\mathfrak{B}_\imath(\mathfrak{u},\ell(\mathfrak{u}),\ell(\mathfrak{u}-\gamma))-\mathfrak{B}_\imath(\mathfrak{u},\ell^*(\mathfrak{u}),\ell^*(\mathfrak{u}-\gamma))\Big)F'(\mathfrak{u})d\mathcal{W}(\mathfrak{u})\right|^{\mathfrak{p}}$$
$$\leq \sum_{\imath=1}^{m} \mathcal{C}_{\mathfrak{p}}\mathfrak{E}\left|\int_0^{\mathfrak{c}} (F(\mathfrak{c})-F(\mathfrak{u}))^{2\eta-2}|\mathfrak{B}_\imath(\mathfrak{u},\ell(\mathfrak{u}),\ell(\mathfrak{u}-\gamma))-\mathfrak{B}_\imath(\mathfrak{u},\ell^*(\mathfrak{u}),\ell^*(\mathfrak{u}-\gamma))|^2(F'(\mathfrak{u}))^2 d\mathfrak{u}\right|^{\frac{\mathfrak{p}}{2}}$$
$$\leq \sum_{\imath=1}^{m} \mathcal{C}_{\mathfrak{p}}\mathfrak{E}\int_0^{\mathfrak{c}} (F(\mathfrak{c})-F(\mathfrak{u}))^{2\eta-2}|\mathfrak{B}_\imath(\mathfrak{u},\ell(\mathfrak{u}),\ell(\mathfrak{u}-\gamma))-\mathfrak{B}_\imath(\mathfrak{u},\ell^*(\mathfrak{u}),\ell^*(\mathfrak{u}-\gamma))|^{\mathfrak{p}}(F'(\mathfrak{u}))^2 d\mathfrak{u}$$

$$\left(\int_0^{\mathfrak{c}} \left(F(\mathfrak{c}) - F(\mathfrak{u})\right)^{2\eta-2} \left(F'(\mathfrak{u})\right)^2 d\mathfrak{u}\right)^{\frac{\mathfrak{p}-2}{2}}$$
$$\leq \sum_{\iota=1}^{m} \mathcal{C}_{\mathfrak{p}} \mathfrak{L} \int_0^{\mathfrak{c}} \left(F(\mathfrak{c}) - F(\mathfrak{u})\right)^{2\eta-2} \left|\mathfrak{B}_\iota(\mathfrak{u}, \ell(\mathfrak{u}), \ell(\mathfrak{u}-\gamma)) - \mathfrak{B}_\iota(\mathfrak{u}, \ell^*(\mathfrak{u}), \ell^*(\mathfrak{u}-\gamma))\right|^{\mathfrak{p}} \left(F'(\mathfrak{u})\right)^2 d\mathfrak{u}$$
$$\left(\sup_{0<\mathfrak{u}\leq\mathfrak{c}} \left(F'(\mathfrak{u})\right) \int_0^{\mathfrak{c}} \left(F(\mathfrak{c}) - F(\mathfrak{u})\right)^{2\eta-2} F'(\mathfrak{u}) d\mathfrak{u}\right)^{\frac{\mathfrak{p}-2}{2}}$$
$$\leq 2^{\mathfrak{p}-1} \mathbf{G}^{\frac{\mathfrak{p}-2}{2}} \left(\frac{\left(\mathfrak{c}^{\zeta}\right)^{(2\eta-1)}}{(2\eta-1)}\right)^{\frac{\mathfrak{p}-2}{2}} \mathfrak{T}^{\mathfrak{p}} \mathcal{C}_{\mathfrak{p}} \int_0^{\mathfrak{c}} \left(F(\mathfrak{c}) - F(\mathfrak{u})\right)^{2\eta-2} \left(\|\ell(\mathfrak{u}) - \ell^*(\mathfrak{u})\|_{\mathfrak{p}}^{\mathfrak{p}} + \|\ell(\mathfrak{u}-\gamma) - \ell^*(\mathfrak{u}-\gamma)\|_{\mathfrak{p}}^{\mathfrak{p}}\right)$$
$$\left(F'(\mathfrak{u})\right)^2 d\mathfrak{u}$$
$$\leq 2^{\mathfrak{p}-1} \mathbf{G}^{\frac{\mathfrak{p}-2}{2}} \left(\frac{\left(\mathfrak{c}^{\zeta}\right)^{(2\eta-1)}}{(2\eta-1)}\right)^{\frac{\mathfrak{p}-2}{2}} \mathfrak{T}^{\mathfrak{p}} \mathcal{C}_{\mathfrak{p}} \sup_{0<\mathfrak{u}\leq\mathfrak{c}} F'(\mathfrak{u}) \int_0^{\mathfrak{c}} \left(F(\mathfrak{c}) - F(\mathfrak{u})\right)^{2\eta-2}$$
$$\left(\|\ell(\mathfrak{u}) - \ell^*(\mathfrak{u})\|_{\mathfrak{p}}^{\mathfrak{p}} + \|\ell(\mathfrak{u}-\gamma) - \ell^*(\mathfrak{u}-\gamma)\|_{\mathfrak{p}}^{\mathfrak{p}}\right) F'(\mathfrak{u}) d\mathfrak{u}.$$

Accordingly, we derive

$$\left\| \int_0^{\mathfrak{c}} \left(F(\mathfrak{c}) - F(\mathfrak{u})\right)^{\eta-1} \left(\mathfrak{B}(\mathfrak{u}, \ell(\mathfrak{u}), \ell(\mathfrak{u}-\gamma)) - \mathfrak{B}(\mathfrak{u}, \ell^*(\mathfrak{u}), \ell^*(\mathfrak{u}-\gamma))\right) F'(\mathfrak{u}) d\mathcal{W}(\mathfrak{u}) \right\|_{\mathfrak{p}}^{\mathfrak{p}}$$
$$\leq 2^{\mathfrak{p}-1} \mathbf{G}^{\frac{\mathfrak{p}-2}{2}} \left(\frac{\left(\mathfrak{c}^{\zeta}\right)^{(2\eta-1)}}{(2\eta-1)}\right)^{\frac{\mathfrak{p}-2}{2}} \mathfrak{T}^{\mathfrak{p}} \mathcal{C}_{\mathfrak{p}} \mathbf{G} \int_0^{\mathfrak{c}} \left(F(\mathfrak{c}) - F(\mathfrak{u})\right)^{2\eta-2} \left(\|\ell(\mathfrak{u}) - \ell^*(\mathfrak{u})\|_{\mathfrak{p}}^{\mathfrak{p}} + \|\ell(\mathfrak{u}-\gamma) - \ell^*(\mathfrak{u}-\gamma)\|_{\mathfrak{p}}^{\mathfrak{p}}\right) \quad (34)$$
$$F'(\mathfrak{u}) d\mathfrak{u}.$$

From (28), we arrive at

$$\|\psi_\varphi(\ell(\mathfrak{c})) - \psi_\varphi(\ell^*(\mathfrak{c}))\|_{\mathfrak{p}}^{\mathfrak{p}}$$
$$\leq 2^{(\mathfrak{e}+1)\mathfrak{p}-(\mathfrak{e}+1)} \sum_{\jmath=1}^{\mathfrak{e}} \left(\frac{\zeta^{1-\mathcal{U}_\jmath}}{\Gamma(\mathcal{U}_\jmath)}\right)^{\mathfrak{p}} \mathbf{G}\mathfrak{n}^{\mathfrak{p}-1} \frac{\mathfrak{T}^{\mathfrak{p}} \left(\mathfrak{c}^{\zeta}\right)^{(\mathfrak{p}\mathcal{U}_\jmath - 2\mathcal{U}_\jmath + 1)} (\mathfrak{p}-1)^{\mathfrak{p}-1}}{(\mathfrak{p}\mathcal{U}_\jmath - 2\mathcal{U}_\jmath + 1)^{\mathfrak{p}-1}} \|\ell(\mathfrak{u}) - \ell^*(\mathfrak{u})\|_{\lambda}^{\mathfrak{p}} \frac{\Gamma(2\mathcal{U}_\jmath - 1)\zeta \exp(\lambda \mathfrak{c}^{\zeta})}{\lambda^{2\mathcal{U}_\jmath - 1}}$$
$$+ \frac{2^{2\mathfrak{p}-2}(\zeta^{1-\eta})^{\mathfrak{p}}}{(\Gamma(\eta))^{\mathfrak{p}}} \left(2^{\mathfrak{p}-1} \mathbf{G}\mathfrak{n}^{\mathfrak{p}-1} \frac{\mathfrak{T}^{\mathfrak{p}} \left(\mathfrak{c}^{\zeta}\right)^{(\mathfrak{p}\eta - 2\eta + 1)} (\mathfrak{p}-1)^{\mathfrak{p}-1}}{(\mathfrak{p}\eta - 2\eta + 1)^{\mathfrak{p}-1}} + 2^{\mathfrak{p}-1} \mathbf{G}^{\frac{\mathfrak{p}-2}{2}} \left(\frac{\left(\mathfrak{c}^{\zeta}\right)^{(2\eta-1)}}{(2\eta-1)}\right)^{\frac{\mathfrak{p}-2}{2}} \mathfrak{T}^{\mathfrak{p}} \mathcal{C}_{\mathfrak{p}} \mathbf{G}\right)$$
$$\int_0^{\mathfrak{c}} \left(\|\ell(\mathfrak{u}) - \ell^*(\mathfrak{u})\|_{\mathfrak{p}}^{\mathfrak{p}} + \|\ell(\mathfrak{u}-\gamma) - \ell^*(\mathfrak{u}-\gamma)\|_{\mathfrak{p}}^{\mathfrak{p}}\right) \left(F(\mathfrak{c}) - F(\mathfrak{u})\right)^{2\eta-2} F'(\mathfrak{u}) d\mathfrak{u}. \quad (35)$$

Following (35), we establish

$$\frac{\|\psi_\varphi(\ell(\mathfrak{c})) - \psi_\varphi(\ell^*(\mathfrak{c}))\|_{\mathfrak{p}}^{\mathfrak{p}}}{\exp(\lambda(\mathfrak{c}^{\zeta}))} \leq \frac{1}{\exp(\lambda(\mathfrak{c}^{\zeta}))} 2^{(\mathfrak{e}+1)\mathfrak{p}-(\mathfrak{e}+1)}$$
$$\sum_{\jmath=1}^{\mathfrak{e}} \left(\frac{\zeta^{1-\mathcal{U}_\jmath}}{\Gamma(\mathcal{U}_\jmath)}\right)^{\mathfrak{p}} \mathbf{G}\mathfrak{n}^{\mathfrak{p}-1} \frac{\mathfrak{T}^{\mathfrak{p}} \left(\mathfrak{c}^{\zeta}\right)^{(\mathfrak{p}\mathcal{U}_\jmath - 2\mathcal{U}_\jmath + 1)} (\mathfrak{p}-1)^{\mathfrak{p}-1}}{(\mathfrak{p}\mathcal{U}_\jmath - 2\mathcal{U}_\jmath + 1)^{\mathfrak{p}-1}} \|\ell(\mathfrak{u}) - \ell^*(\mathfrak{u})\|_{\lambda}^{\mathfrak{p}} \frac{\Gamma(2\mathcal{U}_\jmath - 1)\zeta \exp(\lambda \mathfrak{c}^{\zeta})}{\lambda^{2\mathcal{U}_\jmath - 1}}$$
$$+ \frac{1}{\exp(\lambda(\mathfrak{c}^{\zeta}))} \frac{2^{2\mathfrak{p}-2}(\zeta^{1-\eta})^{\mathfrak{p}}}{(\Gamma(\eta))^{\mathfrak{p}}} \left(2^{\mathfrak{p}-1} \mathbf{G}\mathfrak{n}^{\mathfrak{p}-1} \frac{\mathfrak{T}^{\mathfrak{p}} \left(\mathfrak{c}^{\zeta}\right)^{(\mathfrak{p}\eta - 2\eta + 1)} (\mathfrak{p}-1)^{\mathfrak{p}-1}}{(\mathfrak{p}\eta - 2\eta + 1)^{\mathfrak{p}-1}} + 2^{\mathfrak{p}-1} \mathbf{G}^{\frac{\mathfrak{p}-2}{2}} \left(\frac{\left(\mathfrak{c}^{\zeta}\right)^{(2\eta-1)}}{(2\eta-1)}\right)^{\frac{\mathfrak{p}-2}{2}} \mathfrak{T}^{\mathfrak{p}} \mathcal{C}_{\mathfrak{p}} \mathbf{G}\right)$$
$$\int_0^{\mathfrak{c}} \left(\frac{\|\ell(\mathfrak{u}) - \ell^*(\mathfrak{u})\|_{\mathfrak{p}}^{\mathfrak{p}}}{\exp(\lambda(\mathfrak{u}^{\zeta}))} \exp(\lambda(\mathfrak{u}^{\zeta})) + \frac{\|\ell(\mathfrak{u}-\gamma) - \ell^*(\mathfrak{u}-\gamma)\|_{\mathfrak{p}}^{\mathfrak{p}}}{\exp(\lambda(\mathfrak{u}-\gamma)^{\zeta})} \exp(\lambda(\mathfrak{u}-\gamma)^{\zeta})\right) \left(F(\mathfrak{c}) - F(\mathfrak{u})\right)^{2\eta-2} F'(\mathfrak{u}) d\mathfrak{u}$$
$$\leq 2^{(\mathfrak{e}+1)\mathfrak{p}-(\mathfrak{e}+1)} \sum_{\jmath=1}^{\mathfrak{e}} \left(\frac{\zeta^{1-\mathcal{U}_\jmath}}{\Gamma(\mathcal{U}_\jmath)}\right)^{\mathfrak{p}} \mathbf{G}\mathfrak{n}^{\mathfrak{p}-1} \frac{\mathfrak{T}^{\mathfrak{p}} \left(\mathfrak{c}^{\zeta}\right)^{(\mathfrak{p}\mathcal{U}_\jmath - 2\mathcal{U}_\jmath + 1)} (\mathfrak{p}-1)^{\mathfrak{p}-1}}{(\mathfrak{p}\mathcal{U}_\jmath - 2\mathcal{U}_\jmath + 1)^{\mathfrak{p}-1}} \|\ell(\mathfrak{u}) - \ell^*(\mathfrak{u})\|_{\lambda}^{\mathfrak{p}} \frac{\Gamma(2\mathcal{U}_\jmath - 1)\zeta}{\lambda^{2\mathcal{U}_\jmath - 1}}$$

$$+\frac{1}{\exp(\lambda(\mathfrak{c}^{\zeta}))}\frac{2^{2\mathfrak{p}-2}(\zeta^{1-\eta})^{\mathfrak{p}}}{(\Gamma(\eta))^{\mathfrak{p}}}\left(2^{\mathfrak{p}-1}\mathbf{G}\mathfrak{n}^{\mathfrak{p}-1}\frac{\mathfrak{T}^{\mathfrak{p}}(\mathfrak{c}^{\zeta})^{(\mathfrak{p}\eta-2\eta+1)}(\mathfrak{p}-1)^{\mathfrak{p}-1}}{(\mathfrak{p}\eta-2\eta+1)^{\mathfrak{p}-1}}+2^{\mathfrak{p}-1}\mathbf{G}^{\frac{\mathfrak{p}-2}{2}}\left(\frac{(\mathfrak{c}^{\zeta})^{(2\eta-1)}}{(2\eta-1)}\right)^{\frac{\mathfrak{p}-2}{2}}\mathfrak{T}^{\mathfrak{p}}\mathcal{C}_{\mathfrak{p}}\mathbf{G}\right)$$
$$\int_0^{\mathfrak{c}}\left(\exp(\lambda(\mathfrak{c}^{\zeta}))\underset{\mathfrak{u}\in[0,\varpi]}{esssup}\left(\frac{\|\ell(\mathfrak{u})-\ell^*(\mathfrak{u})\|_{\mathfrak{p}}^{\mathfrak{p}}}{\exp(\lambda(\mathfrak{c}^{\zeta}))}\right)+\exp(\lambda(\mathfrak{u}-\gamma)^{\zeta})\underset{\mathfrak{u}\in[0,\varpi]}{esssup}\left(\frac{\|\ell(\mathfrak{u}-\gamma)-\ell^*(\mathfrak{u}-\gamma)\|_{\mathfrak{p}}^{\mathfrak{p}}}{\exp(\lambda(\mathfrak{u}-\gamma)^{\zeta})}\right)\right)$$
$$(F(\mathfrak{c})-F(\mathfrak{u}))^{2\eta-2}F'(\mathfrak{u})d\mathfrak{u}$$
$$\leq 2^{(\mathfrak{e}+1)\mathfrak{p}-(\mathfrak{e}+1)}\sum_{j=1}^{\mathfrak{e}}\left(\frac{\zeta^{1-\mathcal{U}_j}}{\Gamma(\mathcal{U}_j)}\right)^{\mathfrak{p}}\mathbf{G}\mathfrak{n}^{\mathfrak{p}-1}\frac{\mathfrak{T}^{\mathfrak{p}}(\mathfrak{c}^{\zeta})^{(\mathfrak{p}\mathcal{U}_j-2\mathcal{U}_j+1)}(\mathfrak{p}-1)^{\mathfrak{p}-1}}{(\mathfrak{p}\mathcal{U}_j-2\mathcal{U}_j+1)^{\mathfrak{p}-1}}\|\ell(\mathfrak{u})-\ell^*(\mathfrak{u})\|_{\lambda}^{\mathfrak{p}}\frac{\Gamma(2\mathcal{U}_j-1)\zeta\exp(\lambda\mathfrak{c}^{\zeta})}{\lambda^{2\mathcal{U}_j-1}}$$
$$+\frac{1}{\exp(\lambda(\mathfrak{c}^{\zeta}))}\frac{2^{2\mathfrak{p}-2}(\zeta^{1-\eta})^{\mathfrak{p}}}{(\Gamma(\eta))^{\mathfrak{p}}}\left(2^{\mathfrak{p}-1}\mathbf{G}\mathfrak{n}^{\mathfrak{p}-1}\frac{\mathfrak{T}^{\mathfrak{p}}(\mathfrak{c}^{\zeta})^{(\mathfrak{p}\eta-2\eta+1)}(\mathfrak{p}-1)^{\mathfrak{p}-1}}{(\mathfrak{p}\eta-2\eta+1)^{\mathfrak{p}-1}}+2^{\mathfrak{p}-1}\mathbf{G}^{\frac{\mathfrak{p}-2}{2}}\left(\frac{(\mathfrak{c}^{\zeta})^{(2\eta-1)}}{(2\eta-1)}\right)^{\frac{\mathfrak{p}-2}{2}}\mathfrak{T}^{\mathfrak{p}}\mathcal{C}_{\mathfrak{p}}\mathbf{G}\right)$$
$$\|\ell(\mathfrak{c})-\ell^*(\mathfrak{c})\|_{\lambda}^{\mathfrak{p}}\int_0^{\mathfrak{c}}(F(\mathfrak{c})-F(\mathfrak{u}))^{2\eta-2}\left(\exp(\lambda(\mathfrak{u}^{\zeta}))+\exp(\lambda(\mathfrak{u}-\gamma)^{\zeta})\right)F'(\mathfrak{u})d\mathfrak{u}$$
$$\leq 2^{(\mathfrak{e}+1)\mathfrak{p}-(\mathfrak{e}+1)}\sum_{j=1}^{\mathfrak{e}}\left(\frac{\zeta^{1-\mathcal{U}_j}}{\Gamma(\mathcal{U}_j)}\right)^{\mathfrak{p}}\mathbf{G}\mathfrak{n}^{\mathfrak{p}-1}\frac{\mathfrak{T}^{\mathfrak{p}}(\mathfrak{c}^{\zeta})^{(\mathfrak{p}\mathcal{U}_j-2\mathcal{U}_j+1)}(\mathfrak{p}-1)^{\mathfrak{p}-1}}{(\mathfrak{p}\mathcal{U}_j-2\mathcal{U}_j+1)^{\mathfrak{p}-1}}\|\ell(\mathfrak{u})-\ell^*(\mathfrak{u})\|_{\lambda}^{\mathfrak{p}}\frac{\Gamma(2\mathcal{U}_j-1)\zeta}{\lambda^{2\mathcal{U}_j-1}}$$
$$+\frac{1}{\exp(\lambda(\mathfrak{c}^{\zeta}))}\frac{2^{2\mathfrak{p}-2}(\zeta^{1-\eta})^{\mathfrak{p}}}{(\Gamma(\eta))^{\mathfrak{p}}}\left(2^{\mathfrak{p}-1}\mathbf{G}\mathfrak{n}^{\mathfrak{p}-1}\frac{\mathfrak{T}^{\mathfrak{p}}(\mathfrak{c}^{\zeta})^{(\mathfrak{p}\eta-2\eta+1)}(\mathfrak{p}-1)^{\mathfrak{p}-1}}{(\mathfrak{p}\eta-2\eta+1)^{\mathfrak{p}-1}}+2^{\mathfrak{p}-1}\mathbf{G}^{\frac{\mathfrak{p}-2}{2}}\left(\frac{(\mathfrak{c}^{\zeta})^{(2\eta-1)}}{(2\eta-1)}\right)^{\frac{\mathfrak{p}-2}{2}}\mathfrak{T}^{\mathfrak{p}}\mathcal{C}_{\mathfrak{p}}\mathbf{G}\right)$$
$$2\|\ell(\mathfrak{c})-\ell^*(\mathfrak{c})\|_{\lambda}^{\mathfrak{p}}\int_0^{\mathfrak{c}}(F(\mathfrak{c})-F(\mathfrak{u}))^{2\eta-2}F'(\mathfrak{u})\exp(\lambda(\mathfrak{u}^{\zeta}))d\mathfrak{u}$$
$$\leq 2^{(\mathfrak{e}+1)\mathfrak{p}-(\mathfrak{e}+1)}\sum_{j=1}^{\mathfrak{e}}\left(\frac{\zeta^{1-\mathcal{U}_j}}{\Gamma(\mathcal{U}_j)}\right)^{\mathfrak{p}}\mathbf{G}\mathfrak{n}^{\mathfrak{p}-1}\frac{\mathfrak{T}^{\mathfrak{p}}(\mathfrak{c}^{\zeta})^{(\mathfrak{p}\mathcal{U}_j-2\mathcal{U}_j+1)}(\mathfrak{p}-1)^{\mathfrak{p}-1}}{(\mathfrak{p}\mathcal{U}_j-2\mathcal{U}_j+1)^{\mathfrak{p}-1}}\|\ell(\mathfrak{u})-\ell^*(\mathfrak{u})\|_{\lambda}^{\mathfrak{p}}\frac{\Gamma(2\mathcal{U}_j-1)\zeta}{\lambda^{2\mathcal{U}_j-1}}$$
$$+\frac{2^{2\mathfrak{p}-2}(\zeta^{1-\eta})^{\mathfrak{p}}}{(\Gamma(\eta))^{\mathfrak{p}}}\left(2^{\mathfrak{p}-1}\mathbf{G}\mathfrak{n}^{\mathfrak{p}-1}\frac{\mathfrak{T}^{\mathfrak{p}}(\mathfrak{c}^{\zeta})^{(\mathfrak{p}\eta-2\eta+1)}(\mathfrak{p}-1)^{\mathfrak{p}-1}}{(\mathfrak{p}\eta-2\eta+1)^{\mathfrak{p}-1}}+2^{\mathfrak{p}-1}\mathbf{G}^{\frac{\mathfrak{p}-2}{2}}\left(\frac{(\mathfrak{c}^{\zeta})^{(2\eta-1)}}{(2\eta-1)}\right)^{\frac{\mathfrak{p}-2}{2}}\mathfrak{T}^{\mathfrak{p}}\mathcal{C}_{\mathfrak{p}}\mathbf{G}\right)$$
$$2\|\ell(\mathfrak{c})-\ell^*(\mathfrak{c})\|_{\lambda}^{\mathfrak{p}}\frac{\Gamma(2\eta-1)\zeta}{\lambda^{2\eta-1}}. \tag{36}$$

Accordingly, from (36), we get

$$\|\psi_{\varphi}(\ell(\mathfrak{c}))-\psi_{\varphi}(\ell^*(\mathfrak{c}))\|_{\lambda}^{\mathfrak{p}}\leq\left(2^{(\mathfrak{e}+1)\mathfrak{p}-(\mathfrak{e}+1)}\sum_{j=1}^{\mathfrak{e}}\left(\frac{\zeta^{1-\mathcal{U}_j}}{\Gamma(\mathcal{U}_j)}\right)^{\mathfrak{p}}\mathbf{G}\mathfrak{n}^{\mathfrak{p}-1}\frac{\mathfrak{T}^{\mathfrak{p}}(\mathfrak{c}^{\zeta})^{(\mathfrak{p}\mathcal{U}_j-2\mathcal{U}_j+1)}(\mathfrak{p}-1)^{\mathfrak{p}-1}}{(\mathfrak{p}\mathcal{U}_j-2\mathcal{U}_j+1)^{\mathfrak{p}-1}}\frac{\Gamma(2\mathcal{U}_j-1)\zeta}{\lambda^{2\mathcal{U}_j-1}}\right.$$
$$\left.+\frac{2^{2\mathfrak{p}-2}(\zeta^{1-\eta})^{\mathfrak{p}}}{(\Gamma(\eta))^{\mathfrak{p}}}\left(2^{\mathfrak{p}-1}\mathbf{G}\mathfrak{n}^{\mathfrak{p}-1}\frac{\mathfrak{T}^{\mathfrak{p}}(\mathfrak{c}^{\zeta})^{(\mathfrak{p}\eta-2\eta+1)}(\mathfrak{p}-1)^{\mathfrak{p}-1}}{(\mathfrak{p}\eta-2\eta+1)^{\mathfrak{p}-1}}+2^{\mathfrak{p}-1}\mathbf{G}^{\frac{\mathfrak{p}-2}{2}}\left(\frac{(\mathfrak{c}^{\zeta})^{(2\eta-1)}}{(2\eta-1)}\right)^{\frac{\mathfrak{p}-2}{2}}\mathfrak{T}^{\mathfrak{p}}\mathcal{C}_{\mathfrak{p}}\mathbf{G}\right)\frac{2\zeta\Gamma(2\eta-1)}{\lambda^{2\eta-1}}\right)$$
$$\|\ell(\mathfrak{c})-\ell^*(\mathfrak{c})\|_{\lambda}^{\mathfrak{p}}. \tag{37}$$

Consequently, we acquire

$$\|\psi_{\varphi}(\ell(\mathfrak{c}))-\psi_{\varphi}(\ell^*(\mathfrak{c}))\|_{\lambda}\leq\kappa^{\frac{1}{\mathfrak{p}}}\|\ell(\mathfrak{c})-\ell^*(\mathfrak{c})\|_{\lambda}. \tag{38}$$

From (27), we have $\kappa<1$. Therefore, we have demonstrated the required result. □

Theorem 2. *Given any φ, φ', the following statement holds:*

$$\|\mathcal{B}_{\eta}(\mathfrak{c},\varphi)-\mathcal{B}_{\eta}(\mathfrak{c},\varphi')|_{\mathfrak{p}}\leq\mathfrak{T}\|\varphi-\varphi'\|_{\mathfrak{p}},\ \forall\,\mathfrak{c}\in[0,\ \varpi]; \tag{39}$$

here, $\mathcal{B}_{\eta}(\mathfrak{c},\varphi)$ is the solution.

Proof. It follows that

$$\mathcal{B}_{\eta}(\mathfrak{c},\varphi)-\mathcal{B}_{\eta}(\mathfrak{c},\varphi')=\varphi-\varphi'$$

$$+\sum_{j=1}^{\mathfrak{e}}\frac{\zeta^{1-\mathcal{U}_j}}{\Gamma(\mathcal{U}_j)}\int_0^{\mathfrak{c}}(F(\mathfrak{c})-F(\mathfrak{u}))^{\mathcal{U}_j-1}\Big(\Psi_j(\mathfrak{u},\mathcal{B}_\eta(\mathfrak{u},\varphi))-\Psi_j(\mathfrak{u},\mathcal{B}_\eta(\mathfrak{u},\varphi'))\Big)F'(\mathfrak{u})d\mathfrak{u}$$
$$+\frac{1}{\Gamma(\eta)}\int_0^{\mathfrak{c}}(F(\mathfrak{c})-F(\mathfrak{u}))^{\eta-1}\Big(\mathfrak{I}(\mathfrak{u},\mathcal{B}_\eta(\mathfrak{u},\varphi),\mathcal{B}_\eta(\mathfrak{u}-\gamma,\varphi))-\mathfrak{I}(\mathfrak{u},\mathcal{B}_\eta(\mathfrak{u},\varphi'),\mathcal{B}_\eta(\mathfrak{u}-\gamma,\varphi'))\Big)F'(\mathfrak{u})d\mathfrak{u}$$
$$+\frac{1}{\Gamma(\eta)}\int_0^{\mathfrak{c}}(F(\mathfrak{c})-F(\mathfrak{u}))^{\eta-1}(\mathfrak{B}(\mathfrak{u},\mathcal{B}_\eta(\mathfrak{u},\varphi),\mathcal{B}_\eta(\mathfrak{u}-\gamma,\varphi))-\mathfrak{B}(\mathfrak{u},\mathcal{B}_\eta(\mathfrak{u},\varphi'),\mathcal{B}_\eta(\mathfrak{u}-\gamma,\varphi')))F'(\mathfrak{u})d\mathcal{W}(\mathfrak{u}). \quad (40)$$

By applying (8) to (40), we arrive at

$$\|\mathcal{B}_\eta(\mathfrak{c},\varphi)-\mathcal{B}_\eta(\mathfrak{c},\varphi')\|_{\mathfrak{p}}^{\mathfrak{p}}\le 2^{\mathfrak{p}-1}\|\varphi-\varphi'\|_{\mathfrak{p}}^{\mathfrak{p}}+2^{(\mathfrak{e}+2)\mathfrak{p}-(\mathfrak{e}+2)}\sum_{j=1}^{\mathfrak{e}}\left(\frac{\zeta^{1-\mathcal{U}_j}}{\Gamma(\mathcal{U}_j)}\right)^{\mathfrak{p}}$$
$$\left\|\int_0^{\mathfrak{c}}(F(\mathfrak{c})-F(\mathfrak{u}))^{\mathcal{U}_j-1}\Big(\Psi_j(\mathfrak{u},\mathcal{B}(\mathfrak{u},\varphi))-\Psi_j(\mathfrak{u},\mathcal{B}(\mathfrak{u},\varphi'))\Big)F'(\mathfrak{u})d\mathfrak{u}\right\|_{\mathfrak{p}}^{\mathfrak{p}}$$
$$+\frac{2^{3\mathfrak{p}-3}}{(\Gamma(\eta))^{\mathfrak{p}}}\left\|\int_0^{\mathfrak{c}}(F(\mathfrak{c})-F(\mathfrak{u}))^{\eta-1}\Big(\mathfrak{I}(\mathfrak{u},\mathcal{B}_\eta(\mathfrak{u},\varphi),\mathcal{B}_\eta(\mathfrak{u}-\gamma,\varphi))-\mathfrak{I}(\mathfrak{u},\mathcal{B}_\eta(\mathfrak{u},\varphi'),\mathcal{B}_\eta(\mathfrak{u}-\gamma,\varphi'))\Big)F'(\mathfrak{u})d\mathfrak{u}\right\|_{\mathfrak{p}}^{\mathfrak{p}}$$
$$+\frac{2^{3\mathfrak{p}-3}}{(\Gamma(\eta))^{\mathfrak{p}}}\left\|\int_0^{\mathfrak{c}}(F(\mathfrak{c})-F(\mathfrak{u}))^{\eta-1}\Big(\mathfrak{B}(\mathfrak{u},\mathcal{B}_\eta(\mathfrak{u},\varphi),\mathcal{B}_\eta(\mathfrak{u}-\gamma,\varphi)))-\mathfrak{B}(\mathfrak{u},\mathcal{B}_\eta(\mathfrak{u},\varphi'),\mathcal{B}_\eta(\mathfrak{u}-\gamma,\varphi'))\Big)F'(\mathfrak{u})d\mathcal{W}(\mathfrak{u})\right\|_{\mathfrak{p}}^{\mathfrak{p}}. \quad (41)$$

From the Hölder's inequality and $(\hbar_1)$, it follows that

$$2^{(\mathfrak{e}+2)\mathfrak{p}-(\mathfrak{e}+2)}\sum_{j=1}^{\mathfrak{e}}\left(\frac{\zeta^{1-\mathcal{U}_j}}{\Gamma(\mathcal{U}_j)}\right)^{\mathfrak{p}}\left\|\int_0^{\mathfrak{c}}(F(\mathfrak{c})-F(\mathfrak{u}))^{\mathcal{U}_j-1}\Big(\Psi_j(\mathfrak{u},\mathcal{B}(\mathfrak{u},\varphi))-\Psi_j(\mathfrak{u},\mathcal{B}(\mathfrak{u},\varphi'))\Big)F'(\mathfrak{u})d\mathfrak{u}\right\|_{\mathfrak{p}}^{\mathfrak{p}}$$
$$=2^{(\mathfrak{e}+2)\mathfrak{p}-(\mathfrak{e}+2)}\sum_{j=1}^{\mathfrak{e}}\left(\frac{\zeta^{1-\mathcal{U}_j}}{\Gamma(\mathcal{U}_j)}\right)^{\mathfrak{p}}\sum_{\imath=1}^{m}\mathfrak{E}\left|\int_0^{\mathfrak{c}}(F(\mathfrak{c})-F(\mathfrak{u}))^{\mathcal{U}_j-1}\Big(\Psi_{\imath,j}(\mathfrak{u},\mathcal{B}(\mathfrak{u},\varphi))-\Psi_{\imath,j}(\mathfrak{u},\mathcal{B}(\mathfrak{u},\varphi'))\Big)F'(\mathfrak{u})d\mathfrak{u}\right|^{\mathfrak{p}}$$
$$\le 2^{(\mathfrak{e}+2)\mathfrak{p}-(\mathfrak{e}+2)}\sum_{j=1}^{\mathfrak{e}}\left(\frac{\zeta^{1-\mathcal{U}_j}}{\Gamma(\mathcal{U}_j)}\right)^{\mathfrak{p}}\sum_{\imath=1}^{m}\mathfrak{E}\Bigg(\left(\int_0^{\mathfrak{c}}(F(\mathfrak{c})-F(\mathfrak{u}))^{\frac{(\mathcal{U}_j-1)(\mathfrak{p}-2)}{\mathfrak{p}-1}}(F'(\mathfrak{u}))^{\frac{\mathfrak{p}-2}{\mathfrak{p}-1}}d\mathfrak{u}\right)^{\mathfrak{p}-1}$$
$$\left(\int_0^{\mathfrak{c}}(F(\mathfrak{c})-F(\mathfrak{u}))^{2\mathcal{U}_j-2}|\Psi_{\imath,j}(\mathfrak{u},\mathcal{B}(\mathfrak{u},\varphi))-\Psi_{\imath,j}(\mathfrak{u},\mathcal{B}(\mathfrak{u},\varphi'))|F'(\mathfrak{u})d\mathfrak{u}\right)\Bigg)$$
$$\le 2^{(\mathfrak{e}+2)\mathfrak{p}-(\mathfrak{e}+2)}\sum_{j=1}^{\mathfrak{e}}\left(\frac{\zeta^{1-\mathcal{U}_j}}{\Gamma(\mathcal{U}_j)}\right)^{\mathfrak{p}}\sum_{\imath=1}^{m}\mathfrak{E}\Bigg(\left(\sup_{1<\mathfrak{u}\le\mathfrak{c}}(F'(\mathfrak{u}))^{\frac{1}{1-\mathfrak{p}}}\int_0^{\mathfrak{c}}(F(\mathfrak{c})-F(\mathfrak{u}))^{\frac{(\mathcal{U}_j-1)(\mathfrak{p}-2)}{\mathfrak{p}-1}}F'(\mathfrak{u})d\mathfrak{u}\right)^{\mathfrak{p}-1}$$
$$\left(\int_0^{\mathfrak{c}}(F(\mathfrak{c})-F(\mathfrak{u}))^{2\mathcal{U}_j-2}|\Psi_{\imath,j}(\mathfrak{u},\mathcal{B}(\mathfrak{u},\varphi))-\Psi_{\imath,j}(\mathfrak{u},\mathcal{B}(\mathfrak{u},\varphi'))|(F'(\mathfrak{u}))^2d\mathfrak{u}\right)\Bigg)$$
$$\le 2^{(\mathfrak{e}+2)\mathfrak{p}-(\mathfrak{e}+2)}\sum_{j=1}^{\mathfrak{e}}\left(\frac{\zeta^{1-\mathcal{U}_j}}{\Gamma(\mathcal{U}_j)}\right)^{\mathfrak{p}}\mathfrak{n}^{\mathfrak{p}-1}\frac{\mathfrak{T}^{\mathfrak{p}}(\mathfrak{c}^{\zeta})^{(\mathfrak{p}\mathcal{U}_j-2\mathcal{U}_j+1)}(\mathfrak{p}-1)^{\mathfrak{p}-1}}{(\mathfrak{p}\mathcal{U}_j-2\mathcal{U}_j+1)^{\mathfrak{p}-1}}$$
$$\sup_{1<\mathfrak{u}\le\mathfrak{c}}F'(\mathfrak{u})\int_0^{\mathfrak{c}}(F(\mathfrak{c})-F(\mathfrak{u}))^{2\mathcal{U}_j-2}\Big(\|\mathcal{B}(\mathfrak{u},\varphi)-\mathcal{B}(\mathfrak{u},\varphi')\|_{\mathfrak{p}}^{\mathfrak{p}}\Big)F'(\mathfrak{u})d\mathfrak{u}. \quad (42)$$

Consequently, we derive

$$2^{(\mathfrak{e}+2)\mathfrak{p}-(\mathfrak{e}+2)}\sum_{j=1}^{\mathfrak{e}}\left(\frac{\zeta^{1-\mathcal{U}_j}}{\Gamma(\mathcal{U}_j)}\right)^{\mathfrak{p}}\left\|\int_0^{\mathfrak{c}}(F(\mathfrak{c})-F(\mathfrak{u}))^{\mathcal{U}_j-1}(\Psi_j(\mathfrak{u},\mathcal{B}_\eta(\mathfrak{u},\varphi))-\Psi_j(\mathfrak{u},\mathcal{B}(\mathfrak{u},\varphi')))F'(\mathfrak{u})d\mathfrak{u}\right\|_{\mathfrak{p}}^{\mathfrak{p}}$$
$$\le 2^{(\mathfrak{e}+2)\mathfrak{p}-(\mathfrak{e}+2)}\sum_{j=1}^{\mathfrak{e}}\left(\frac{\zeta^{1-\mathcal{U}_j}}{\Gamma(\mathcal{U}_j)}\right)^{\mathfrak{p}}\mathrm{G}\mathfrak{n}^{\mathfrak{p}-1}\frac{\mathfrak{T}^{\mathfrak{p}}(\mathfrak{c}^{\zeta})^{(\mathfrak{p}\mathcal{U}_j-2\mathcal{U}_j+1)}(\mathfrak{p}-1)^{\mathfrak{p}-1}}{(\mathfrak{p}\mathcal{U}_j-2\mathcal{U}_j+1)^{\mathfrak{p}-1}}$$
$$\int_0^{\mathfrak{c}}(F(\mathfrak{c})-F(\mathfrak{u}))^{2\mathcal{U}_j-2}\|\mathcal{B}(\mathfrak{u},\varphi)-\mathcal{B}(\mathfrak{u},\varphi')\|_{\mathfrak{p}}^{\mathfrak{p}}F'(\mathfrak{u})d\mathfrak{u}. \quad (43)$$

By applying Hölder's inequality and $(\hbar_1)$ to the second term of (41), it follows that

$$\left\|\int_0^{\mathfrak{c}}(F(\mathfrak{c})-F(\mathfrak{u}))^{\eta-1}\Big(\mathfrak{I}(\mathfrak{u},\mathcal{B}_\eta(\mathfrak{u},\varphi),\mathcal{B}_\eta(\mathfrak{u}-\gamma,\varphi))-\mathfrak{I}(\mathfrak{u},\mathcal{B}_\eta(\mathfrak{u},\varphi'),\mathcal{B}_\eta(\mathfrak{u}-\gamma,\varphi'))\Big)F'(\mathfrak{u})d\mathfrak{u}\right\|_{\mathfrak{p}}^{\mathfrak{p}}$$

$$
\begin{aligned}
&= \sum_{\imath=1}^{m} \mathfrak{E}\left|\int_0^{\mathfrak{c}} (F(\mathfrak{c})-F(\mathfrak{u}))^{\eta-1}\Big(\mathfrak{I}_\imath(\mathfrak{u},\mathcal{B}_\eta(\mathfrak{u},\varphi),\mathcal{B}_\eta(\mathfrak{u}-\gamma,\varphi))-\mathfrak{I}_\imath(\mathfrak{u},\mathcal{B}_\eta(\mathfrak{u},\varphi'),\mathcal{B}_\eta(\mathfrak{u}-\gamma,\varphi'))\Big)F'(\mathfrak{u})d\mathfrak{u}\right|^{\mathfrak{p}}\\
&\leq \sum_{\imath=1}^{m} \mathfrak{E}\Bigg(\left(\int_0^{\mathfrak{c}} (F(\mathfrak{c})-F(\mathfrak{u}))^{\frac{(\eta-1)(\mathfrak{p}-2)}{\mathfrak{p}-1}}(F'(\mathfrak{u}))^{\frac{\mathfrak{p}-2}{\mathfrak{p}-1}}d\mathfrak{u}\right)^{\mathfrak{p}-1}\\
&\quad\left(\int_0^{\mathfrak{c}} (F(\mathfrak{c})-F(\mathfrak{u}))^{2\eta-2}|\mathfrak{I}_\imath(\mathfrak{u},\mathcal{B}_\eta(\mathfrak{u},\varphi),\mathcal{B}_\eta(\mathfrak{u}-\gamma,\varphi))-\mathfrak{I}_\imath(\mathfrak{u},\mathcal{B}_\eta(\mathfrak{u},\varphi'),\mathcal{B}_\eta(\mathfrak{u}-\gamma,\varphi'))|(F'(\mathfrak{u}))^2d\mathfrak{u}\right)\Bigg)\\
&\leq \sum_{\imath=1}^{m} \mathfrak{E}\Bigg(\left(\sup_{0<\mathfrak{u}\leq\mathfrak{c}}(F'(\mathfrak{u}))^{\frac{1}{1-\mathfrak{p}}}\int_0^{\mathfrak{c}} (F(\mathfrak{c})-F(\mathfrak{u}))^{\frac{(\eta-1)(\mathfrak{p}-2)}{\mathfrak{p}-1}}F'(\mathfrak{u})d\mathfrak{u}\right)^{\mathfrak{p}-1}\\
&\quad\left(\int_0^{\mathfrak{c}} (F(\mathfrak{c})-F(\mathfrak{u}))^{2\eta-2}|\mathfrak{I}_\imath(\mathfrak{u},\mathcal{B}_\eta(\mathfrak{u},\varphi),\mathcal{B}_\eta(\mathfrak{u}-\gamma,\varphi))-\mathfrak{I}_\imath(\mathfrak{u},\mathcal{B}_\eta(\mathfrak{u},\varphi'),\mathcal{B}_\eta(\mathfrak{u}-\gamma,\varphi'))|(F'(\mathfrak{u}))^2d\mathfrak{u}\right)\Bigg)\\
&\leq 2^{\mathfrak{p}-1}n^{\mathfrak{p}-1}\left(\frac{\mathfrak{T}^{\mathfrak{p}}(\mathfrak{c}^{\zeta})^{(\mathfrak{p}\eta-2\eta+1)}(\mathfrak{p}-1)^{\mathfrak{p}-1}}{(\mathfrak{p}\eta-2\eta+1)^{\mathfrak{p}-1}}\right)\int_0^{\mathfrak{c}}(F(\mathfrak{c})-F(\mathfrak{u}))^{2\eta-2}\\
&\quad\left(\|\mathcal{B}_\eta(\mathfrak{u},\varphi)-\mathcal{B}_\eta(\mathfrak{u},\varphi')\|_{\mathfrak{p}}^{\mathfrak{p}}+\|\mathcal{B}_\eta(\mathfrak{u}-\gamma,\varphi)-\mathcal{B}_\eta(\mathfrak{u}-\gamma,\varphi')\|_{\mathfrak{p}}^{\mathfrak{p}}\right)(F'(\mathfrak{u}))^2d\mathfrak{u}.\\
&\leq 2^{\mathfrak{p}-1}n^{\mathfrak{p}-1}\left(\frac{\mathfrak{T}^{\mathfrak{p}}(\mathfrak{c}^{\zeta})^{(\mathfrak{p}\eta-2\eta+1)}(\mathfrak{p}-1)^{\mathfrak{p}-1}}{(\mathfrak{p}\eta-2\eta+1)^{\mathfrak{p}-1}}\right)\sup_{0<\mathfrak{u}\leq\mathfrak{c}}F'(\mathfrak{u})\int_0^{\mathfrak{c}}(F(\mathfrak{c})-F(\mathfrak{u}))^{2\eta-2}\\
&\quad\left(\|\mathcal{B}_\eta(\mathfrak{u},\varphi)-\mathcal{B}_\eta(\mathfrak{u},\varphi')\|_{\mathfrak{p}}^{\mathfrak{p}}+\|\mathcal{B}_\eta(\mathfrak{u}-\gamma,\varphi)-\mathcal{B}_\eta(\mathfrak{u}-\gamma,\varphi')\|_{\mathfrak{p}}^{\mathfrak{p}}\right)F'(\mathfrak{u})d\mathfrak{u}\\
&= 2^{\mathfrak{p}-1}n^{\mathfrak{p}-1}\left(\frac{\mathfrak{T}^{\mathfrak{p}}(\mathfrak{c}^{\zeta})^{(\mathfrak{p}\eta-2\eta+1)}(\mathfrak{p}-1)^{\mathfrak{p}-1}}{(\mathfrak{p}\eta-2\eta+1)^{\mathfrak{p}-1}}\right)\mathbf{G}\int_0^{\mathfrak{c}}(F(\mathfrak{c})-F(\mathfrak{u}))^{2\eta-2}\\
&\quad\left(\|\mathcal{B}_\eta(\mathfrak{u},\varphi)-\mathcal{B}_\eta(\mathfrak{u},\varphi')\|_{\mathfrak{p}}^{\mathfrak{p}}+\|\mathcal{B}_\eta(\mathfrak{u}-\gamma,\varphi)-\mathcal{B}_\eta(\mathfrak{u}-\gamma,\varphi')\|_{\mathfrak{p}}^{\mathfrak{p}}\right)F'(\mathfrak{u})d\mathfrak{u}.
\end{aligned}
\tag{44}
$$

Using the Burkholder–Davis–Gundy inequality and $(\hbar_1)$ for the third term of (41), we conclude that

$$
\begin{aligned}
&\left\|\int_0^{\mathfrak{c}} (F(\mathfrak{c})-F(\mathfrak{u}))^{\eta-1}\Big(\mathfrak{B}(\mathfrak{u},\mathcal{B}_\eta(\mathfrak{u},\varphi),\mathcal{B}_\eta(\mathfrak{u}-\gamma,\varphi))-\mathfrak{B}(\mathfrak{u},\mathcal{B}_\eta(\mathfrak{u},\varphi'),\mathcal{B}_\eta(\mathfrak{u}-\gamma,\varphi'))\Big)F'(\mathfrak{u})d\mathcal{W}(\mathfrak{u})\right\|_{\mathfrak{p}}^{\mathfrak{p}}\\
&= \sum_{\imath=1}^{m} \mathfrak{E}\left|\int_0^{\mathfrak{c}} (F(\mathfrak{c})-F(\mathfrak{u}))^{\eta-1}\Big(\mathfrak{B}_\imath(\mathfrak{u},\mathcal{B}_\eta(\mathfrak{u},\varphi),\mathcal{B}_\eta(\mathfrak{u}-\gamma,\varphi))-\mathfrak{B}_\imath(\mathfrak{u},\mathcal{B}_\eta(\mathfrak{u},\varphi'),\mathcal{B}_\eta(\mathfrak{u}-\gamma,\varphi'))\Big)F'(\mathfrak{u})d\mathcal{W}(\mathfrak{u})\right|^{\mathfrak{p}}\\
&\leq \sum_{\imath=1}^{m} C_{\mathfrak{p}}\mathfrak{E}\left|\int_0^{\mathfrak{c}} (F(\mathfrak{c})-F(\mathfrak{u}))^{2\eta-2}|\mathfrak{B}_\imath(\mathfrak{u},\mathcal{B}_\eta(\mathfrak{u},\varphi),\mathcal{B}_\eta(\mathfrak{u}-\gamma,\varphi))-\mathfrak{B}_\imath(\mathfrak{u},\mathcal{B}_\eta(\mathfrak{u},\varphi'),\mathcal{B}_\eta(\mathfrak{u}-\gamma,\varphi'))|^2(F'(\mathfrak{u}))^2d\mathfrak{u}\right|^{\frac{\mathfrak{p}}{2}}\\
&\leq \sum_{\imath=1}^{m} C_{\mathfrak{p}}\mathfrak{E}\int_0^{\mathfrak{c}} (F(\mathfrak{c})-F(\mathfrak{u}))^{2\eta-2}|\mathfrak{B}_\imath(\mathfrak{u},\mathcal{B}_\eta(\mathfrak{u},\varphi),\mathcal{B}_\eta(\mathfrak{u}-\gamma,\varphi))-\mathfrak{B}_\imath(\mathfrak{u},\mathcal{B}_\eta(\mathfrak{u},\varphi'),\mathcal{B}_\eta(\mathfrak{u}-\gamma,\varphi'))|^{\mathfrak{p}}(F'(\mathfrak{u}))^2d\mathfrak{u}\\
&\quad\left(\int_0^{\mathfrak{c}}(F(\mathfrak{c})-F(\mathfrak{u}))^{2\eta-2}(F'(\mathfrak{u}))^2d\mathfrak{u}\right)^{\frac{\mathfrak{p}-2}{2}}\\
&\leq \sum_{\imath=1}^{m} C_{\mathfrak{p}}\mathfrak{E}\int_0^{\mathfrak{c}} (F(\mathfrak{c})-F(\mathfrak{u}))^{2\eta-2}|\mathfrak{B}_\imath(\mathfrak{u},\mathcal{B}_\eta(\mathfrak{u},\varphi),\mathcal{B}_\eta(\mathfrak{u}-\gamma,\varphi))-\mathfrak{B}_\imath(\mathfrak{u},\mathcal{B}_\eta(\mathfrak{u},\varphi'),\mathcal{B}_\eta(\mathfrak{u}-\gamma,\varphi'))|^{\mathfrak{p}}(F'(\mathfrak{u}))^2d\mathfrak{u}\\
&\quad\left(\sup_{0<\mathfrak{u}\leq\mathfrak{c}}F'(\mathfrak{u})\int_0^{\mathfrak{c}}(F(\mathfrak{c})-F(\mathfrak{u}))^{2\eta-2}F'(\mathfrak{u})d\mathfrak{u}\right)^{\frac{\mathfrak{p}-2}{2}}\\
&\leq 2^{\mathfrak{p}-1}\mathbf{G}^{\frac{\mathfrak{p}-2}{2}}\mathfrak{T}^{\mathfrak{p}}C_{\mathfrak{p}}\left(\frac{(\mathfrak{c}^{\zeta})^{(2\eta-1)}}{(2\eta-1)}\right)^{\frac{\mathfrak{p}-2}{2}}\int_0^{\mathfrak{c}}(F(\mathfrak{c})-F(\mathfrak{u}))^{2\eta-2}\left(\|\mathcal{B}_\eta(\mathfrak{u},\varphi)-\mathcal{B}_\eta(\mathfrak{u},\varphi')\|_{\mathfrak{p}}^{\mathfrak{p}}+\|\mathcal{B}_\eta(\mathfrak{u}-\gamma,\varphi)-\mathcal{B}_\eta(\mathfrak{u}-\gamma,\varphi')\|_{\mathfrak{p}}^{\mathfrak{p}}\right)\\
&\quad(F'(\mathfrak{u}))^2d\mathfrak{u}.\\
&\leq 2^{\mathfrak{p}-1}\mathbf{G}^{\frac{\mathfrak{p}-2}{2}}\mathfrak{T}^{\mathfrak{p}}C_{\mathfrak{p}}\left(\frac{(\mathfrak{c}^{\zeta})^{(2\eta-1)}}{(2\eta-1)}\right)^{\frac{\mathfrak{p}-2}{2}}\sup_{0<\mathfrak{u}\leq\mathfrak{c}}F'(\mathfrak{u})\int_0^{\mathfrak{c}}(F(\mathfrak{c})-F(\mathfrak{u}))^{2\eta-2}
\end{aligned}
$$

$$\left(\|\mathcal{B}_\eta(\mathfrak{u},\varphi)-\mathcal{B}_\eta(\mathfrak{u},\varphi')\|_{\mathfrak{p}}^{\mathfrak{p}}+\|\mathcal{B}_\eta(\mathfrak{u}-\gamma,\varphi)-\mathcal{B}_\eta(\mathfrak{u}-\gamma,\varphi')\|_{\mathfrak{p}}^{\mathfrak{p}}\right)F'(\mathfrak{u})d\mathfrak{u}.$$

$$=2^{\mathfrak{p}-1}\mathbf{G}^{\frac{\mathfrak{p}-2}{2}}\mathfrak{T}^{\mathfrak{p}}\mathcal{C}_{\mathfrak{p}}\left(\frac{(\mathfrak{c}^{\zeta})^{(2\eta-1)}}{(2\eta-1)}\right)^{\frac{\mathfrak{p}-2}{2}}\mathbf{G}\int_0^{\mathfrak{c}}(F(\mathfrak{c})-F(\mathfrak{u}))^{2\eta-2}\left(\|\mathcal{B}_\eta(\mathfrak{u},\varphi)-\mathcal{B}_\eta(\mathfrak{u},\varphi')\|_{\mathfrak{p}}^{\mathfrak{p}}+\|\mathcal{B}_\eta(\mathfrak{u}-\gamma,\varphi)-\mathcal{B}_\eta(\mathfrak{u}-\gamma,\varphi')\|_{\mathfrak{p}}^{\mathfrak{p}}\right)$$
$$F'(\mathfrak{u})d\mathfrak{u}. \quad (45)$$

By considering (41), (43), (44), and (45), we establish

$$\|\mathcal{B}_\eta(\mathfrak{c},\varphi)-\mathcal{B}_\eta(\mathfrak{c},\varphi')\|_{\lambda}^{\mathfrak{p}}\le\frac{2^{\mathfrak{p}-1}}{\exp(\lambda(\mathfrak{c}^{\zeta}))}\|\varphi-\varphi'\|_{\mathfrak{p}}^{\mathfrak{p}}$$
$$+2^{\mathfrak{p}-1}\kappa\|\mathcal{B}_\eta(\mathfrak{u},\varphi)-\mathcal{B}_\eta(\mathfrak{u},\varphi')\|_{\lambda}^{\mathfrak{p}} \quad (46)$$

Accordingly, we conclude

$$\|\mathcal{B}_\eta(\mathfrak{c},\varphi)-\mathcal{B}_\eta(\mathfrak{c},\varphi')\|_{\lambda}^{\mathfrak{p}}(1-2^{\mathfrak{p}-1}\kappa)\le\frac{2^{\mathfrak{p}-1}}{\exp(\lambda(\mathfrak{c}^{\zeta}))}\|\varphi-\varphi'\|_{\mathfrak{p}}^{\mathfrak{p}}$$

Thus, we acquire the following required result:

$$\lim_{\varphi\to\varphi'}\|\mathcal{B}_\eta(\mathfrak{c},\varphi)-\mathcal{B}_\eta(\mathfrak{c},\varphi')\|_{\lambda}^{\mathfrak{p}}=0.$$

□

4. Stability Results

In this section, we first establish a generalized Grönwall inequality concerning Cap-KFrD and then demonstrate the UHS of the FSIDEs in $\mathcal{L}^{\mathfrak{p}}$ space.

Lemma 3. *Assume the functions $\mathbb{M}(\mathfrak{c})>0$ and $\mathbb{L}(\mathfrak{c})>0$ are locally integrable on $\mathfrak{c}\in[\mathfrak{m},\varpi)$ ($\mathfrak{m}\ge 0,\varpi\le+\infty$), and further, consider the continuous and nondecreasing mapping of $\mathbb{Z}:[\mathfrak{m},\varpi)\to[0,\theta]$, $\theta\in\mathrm{R}^+$.*

If the following holds,

$$\mathbb{L}(\mathfrak{c})\le\mathbb{M}(\mathfrak{c})+\frac{\zeta^{1-\eta}\mathbb{Z}(\mathfrak{c})}{\Gamma(\eta)}\int_{\mathfrak{m}}^{\mathfrak{c}}(F(\mathfrak{c})-F(\mathfrak{u}))^{\eta-1}F'(\mathfrak{u})\mathbb{L}(\mathfrak{u})d\mathfrak{u},\ \mathfrak{c}\in[\mathfrak{m},\varpi),$$

then

$$\mathbb{L}(\mathfrak{c})\le\mathbb{M}(\mathfrak{c})+\int_{\mathfrak{m}}^{\mathfrak{c}}\left(\sum_{\mathfrak{r}=0}^{\infty}\frac{(\zeta^{1-\eta}\mathbb{Z}(\mathfrak{c}))^{\mathfrak{r}}}{\Gamma(\mathfrak{r}\eta)}(F(\mathfrak{c})-F(\mathfrak{u}))^{\mathfrak{r}\eta-1}\mathbb{M}(\mathfrak{u})\right)F'(\mathfrak{u})d\mathfrak{u},\ \mathfrak{c}\in[\mathfrak{m},\varpi).$$

Proof. For locally integrable function ϱ, assume

$$\rho\varrho(\mathfrak{c})=\frac{\zeta^{1-\eta}\mathbb{Z}(\mathfrak{c})}{\Gamma(\eta)}\int_{\mathfrak{m}}^{\mathfrak{c}}(F(\mathfrak{c})-F(\mathfrak{u}))^{\eta-1}F'(\mathfrak{u})\varrho(\mathfrak{u})d\mathfrak{u}.$$

So, we obtain

$$\mathbb{L}(\mathfrak{c})\le\mathbb{M}(\mathfrak{c})+\rho\mathbb{L}(\mathfrak{c});$$

therefore,

$$\mathbb{L}(\mathfrak{c})\le\sum_{\iota=0}^{\mathfrak{r}-1}\rho^{\iota}\mathbb{M}(\mathfrak{c})+\rho\mathbb{L}^{\mathfrak{r}}(\mathfrak{c}).$$

We need to prove that

$$\rho^{\mathfrak{r}}\mathbb{L}(\mathfrak{c})\le\int_0^{\mathfrak{c}}\frac{(\zeta^{1-\eta}\mathbb{Z}(\mathfrak{c}))^{\eta}}{\Gamma(\mathfrak{r}\eta)}(F(\mathfrak{c})-F(\mathfrak{u}))^{\mathfrak{r}\eta-1}F'(\mathfrak{u})\mathbb{L}(\mathfrak{u})d\mathfrak{u} \quad (47)$$

and $\rho^{\mathfrak{r}}\mathbb{L}(\mathfrak{c})\to 0$ when $\mathfrak{r}\to\infty$ $\forall\mathfrak{c}\in[\mathfrak{m},\varpi)$.

Inequality (47) holds when $\mathfrak{r} = 1$. Suppose it is also for $\mathfrak{r} = \iota$. Now, we will prove that it is true for $\mathfrak{r} = \iota + 1$

$$\begin{aligned}\rho^{\iota+1}\mathbb{L}(\mathfrak{c}) =& \rho(\rho^{\iota}\mathbb{L}(\mathfrak{c})) \leq \frac{\zeta^{1-\eta}\mathbb{Z}(\mathfrak{c})}{\Gamma(\eta)} \int_0^{\mathfrak{c}} (\mathcal{F}(\mathfrak{c}) - \mathcal{F}(\mathfrak{u}))^{\eta-1} \mathcal{F}'(\mathfrak{u}) \\ & \left(\int_0^{\mathfrak{u}} \frac{(\zeta^{1-\eta}\mathbb{Z}(\mathfrak{c}))^{\iota}}{\Gamma(\iota\eta)} (\mathfrak{u}^{\zeta} - \mathfrak{c}^{\zeta})^{\iota\eta-1}\mathfrak{c}^{\zeta-1}\mathbb{L}(\mathfrak{c})d\mathfrak{c} \right) d\mathfrak{u} \\ \leq & \frac{(\mathbb{Z}(\mathfrak{c}))^{\iota+1}}{\Gamma(\eta)} \int_0^{\mathfrak{c}} (\mathcal{F}(\mathfrak{c}) - \mathcal{F}(\mathfrak{u}))^{\eta-1} \mathcal{F}'(\mathfrak{u}) \\ & \left(\int_0^{\mathfrak{u}} \frac{(\zeta^{1-\eta})^{\iota}}{\Gamma(\iota\eta)} (\mathfrak{u}^{\zeta} - \mathfrak{c}^{\zeta})^{\iota\eta-1}\mathfrak{c}^{\zeta-1}\mathbb{L}(\mathfrak{c})d\mathfrak{c} \right) d\mathfrak{u}. \end{aligned} \tag{48}$$

It follows that we have the following:

$$\rho^{\iota+1}\mathbb{L}(\mathfrak{c}) \leq \int_0^{\mathfrak{c}} \frac{(\mathbb{Z}(\mathfrak{c})\zeta^{1-\eta})^{\iota+1}}{\Gamma((\iota+1)\eta)} (\mathcal{F}(\mathfrak{c}) - \mathcal{F}(\mathfrak{u}))^{(\iota+1)\eta-1} \mathcal{F}'(\mathfrak{u})\mathbb{L}(\mathfrak{u})d\mathfrak{u}.$$

Accordingly, inequality (47) is verified. Proceeding further, from inequality (47), we arrive at the following:

$$\rho^{\mathfrak{r}}\mathbb{L}(\mathfrak{c}) \leq \int_0^{\mathfrak{c}} \frac{(\zeta^{1-\eta}\varpi)^{\mathfrak{r}}}{\Gamma(\mathfrak{r}\eta)} (\mathcal{F}(\mathfrak{c}) - \mathcal{F}(\mathfrak{u}))^{\mathfrak{r}\eta-1} \mathcal{F}'(\mathfrak{u})\mathbb{L}(\mathfrak{u})d\mathfrak{u} \to 0$$

when $\mathfrak{r} \to +\infty$ for $\mathfrak{c} \in [\mathfrak{m}, \varpi)$; this finalizes the proof. □

In the case of $\mathbb{Z}(\mathfrak{c}) = \mathrm{b}$ in Lemma 3, we deduce the following inequality.

Corollary 1. *Assume that* $\mathrm{b} \geq 0$, $\eta > 0$, *and* $\mathbb{M}(\mathfrak{c})$ *is a locally integrable non-negative mapping with* $0 \leq \mathfrak{c} < \varpi$, $(\varpi \leq +\infty)$. *Further, let* $\mathbb{L}(\mathfrak{c})$ *be a locally integrable and non-negative mapping for* $0 \leq \mathfrak{c} < \varpi$. *Then, we have*

$$\mathbb{L}(\mathfrak{c}) \leq \mathbb{M}(\mathfrak{c}) + \mathrm{b}\int_0^{\mathfrak{c}} (\mathcal{F}(\mathfrak{c}) - \mathcal{F}(\mathfrak{u}))^{\eta-1} \mathcal{F}'(\mathfrak{u})\mathbb{L}(\mathfrak{u})d\mathfrak{u},$$

and then,

$$\mathbb{L}(\mathfrak{c}) \leq \mathbb{M}(\mathfrak{c}) + \int_0^{\mathfrak{c}} \left(\sum_{\mathfrak{r}=0}^{\infty} \frac{(\mathrm{b}\Gamma(\eta))^{\mathfrak{r}}}{\Gamma(\mathfrak{r}\eta)} (\mathcal{F}(\mathfrak{c}) - \mathcal{F}(\mathfrak{u}))^{\mathfrak{r}\eta-1} \mathbb{M}(\mathfrak{u}) \right) \mathcal{F}'(\mathfrak{u})d\mathfrak{u},\ 0 \leq \mathfrak{c} < \varpi.$$

□

Corollary 2. *Under the same conditions of Lemma 3, assume* $\mathbb{M}(\mathfrak{c})$ *is a nondecreasing mapping with* $[0, \varpi)$. *Then, we get the following:*

$$\mathbb{L}(\mathfrak{c}) \leq \mathbb{M}(\mathfrak{c})\mathbb{E}_{\eta}(\mathbb{Z}(\mathfrak{c})\Gamma(\eta)(\mathfrak{c}^{\zeta})^{\eta});$$

where $\mathbb{E}_{\eta}$ *is the Mittag-Leffler function defined by* $\mathbb{E}_{\eta}(\mathfrak{c}) = \sum_{\iota=0}^{\infty} \frac{\mathfrak{c}^{\iota}}{\Gamma(\iota\eta+1)}$.

Proof. By the hypotheses

$$\begin{aligned}\mathbb{L}(\mathfrak{c}) &\leq \mathbb{M}(\mathfrak{c})\left(1 + \int_0^{\mathfrak{c}} \sum_{\mathfrak{r}=1}^{\infty} \frac{(\mathbb{Z}(\mathfrak{c})\Gamma(\eta))^{\mathfrak{r}}}{\Gamma(\mathfrak{r}\eta)} (\mathcal{F}(\mathfrak{c}) - \mathcal{F}(\mathfrak{u}))^{\mathfrak{r}\eta-1} \mathcal{F}'(\mathfrak{u})d\mathfrak{u}\right) \\ &= \mathbb{M}(\mathfrak{c}) \sum_{\mathfrak{r}=0}^{\infty} \frac{(\mathbb{Z}(\mathfrak{c})\Gamma(\eta)(\mathfrak{c}^{\zeta})^{\eta})^{\mathfrak{r}}}{\Gamma(\mathfrak{r}\eta+1)} \\ &= \mathbb{M}(\mathfrak{c})\mathbb{E}_{\eta}(\mathbb{Z}(\mathfrak{c})\Gamma(\eta)(\mathfrak{c}^{\zeta})^{\eta}).\end{aligned}$$

This concludes the proof. □

Definition 2. (3) *is UHS with respect to* ε *if there exists* $\mathbb{V} > 0$ *so that for all* $\varepsilon > 0$ *and for all* $\mathbb{G} \in \mathbb{H}^{\mathfrak{p}}(0,\varpi)$, *with* $\mathbb{G}(0) = \mathbb{G}_0$, *of*

$$\mathfrak{E}\Bigg(\Bigg\|\mathbb{G}(\mathfrak{c}) - \mathbb{G}(0) - \Bigg(\sum_{\jmath=1}^{\mathfrak{e}} \frac{\zeta^{1-\mathcal{U}_\jmath}}{\Gamma(\mathcal{U}_\jmath)} \int_0^{\mathfrak{c}} (F(\mathfrak{c}) - F(\mathfrak{u}))^{\mathcal{U}_\jmath - 1} F'(\mathfrak{u}) \Psi_\jmath(\mathfrak{u}, \mathbb{G}(\mathfrak{u}))d\mathfrak{u}$$
$$+ \frac{\zeta^{1-\eta}}{\Gamma(\eta)} \int_0^{\mathfrak{c}} (F(\mathfrak{c}) - F(\mathfrak{u}))^{\eta-1} F'(\mathfrak{u}) \mathfrak{J}(\mathfrak{u}, \mathbb{G}(\mathfrak{u}), \mathbb{G}(\mathfrak{u}-\gamma))d\mathfrak{u}$$
$$+ \frac{\zeta^{1-\eta}}{\Gamma(\eta)} \int_0^{\mathfrak{c}} (F(\mathfrak{c}) - F(\mathfrak{u}))^{\eta-1} F'(\mathfrak{u}) \mathfrak{B}(\mathfrak{u}, \mathbb{G}(\mathfrak{u}), \mathbb{G}(\mathfrak{u}-\gamma))d\mathcal{W}(\mathfrak{u})\Bigg)\Bigg\|_{\mathfrak{p}}^{\mathfrak{p}}\Bigg) < \varepsilon, \ \mathfrak{c} \in [0, \varpi], \tag{49}$$

there exists a solution $\mathbb{U} \in \mathbb{H}^{\mathfrak{p}}(0,\varpi)$ *of* (3), *with* $\mathbb{U}(\mathfrak{c}) = \mathbb{G}_0$ *when* $\mathfrak{c} \in [0,\varpi]$, *and satisfies the following:*

$$\mathfrak{E}(\|\mathbb{G}(\mathfrak{c}) - \mathbb{U}(\mathfrak{c})\|_{\mathfrak{p}}^{\mathfrak{p}}) \le \mathbb{V}\varepsilon, \ \forall \mathfrak{c} \in [0,\varpi].$$

In the following theorem, we establish UHS for the FSIDEs with delay.

Theorem 3. *Suppose* $(\hbar_1)$ *and* $(\hbar_2)$ *hold, then system* (3) *is UHS on* $[0,\varpi]$.

Proof. Assume $\varepsilon > 0$ and $\mathbb{G} \in \mathbb{H}^{\mathfrak{p}}(0,\varpi)$ is the solution of (49), and assume $\mathbb{U} \in \mathbb{H}^{\mathfrak{p}}(0,\varpi)$ is the solution of (3) with initial condition $\mathbb{U}(0) = \mathbb{G}_0$; then, we have

$$\mathbb{U}(\mathfrak{c}) = \mathbb{G}(0) + \sum_{\jmath=1}^{\mathfrak{e}} \frac{\zeta^{1-\mathcal{U}_\jmath}}{\Gamma(\mathcal{U}_\jmath)} \int_0^{\mathfrak{c}} (F(\mathfrak{c}) - F(\mathfrak{u}))^{\mathcal{U}_\jmath - 1} F'(\mathfrak{u}) \Psi_\jmath(\mathfrak{u}, \mathbb{U}(\mathfrak{u}))d\mathfrak{u}$$
$$+ \frac{\zeta^{1-\eta}}{\Gamma(\eta)} \int_0^{\mathfrak{c}} (F(\mathfrak{c}) - F(\mathfrak{u}))^{\eta-1} F'(\mathfrak{u}) \mathfrak{J}(\mathfrak{u}, \mathbb{U}(\mathfrak{u}), \mathbb{U}(\mathfrak{u}-\gamma))d\mathfrak{u}$$
$$+ \frac{\zeta^{1-\eta}}{\Gamma(\eta)} \int_0^{\mathfrak{c}} (F(\mathfrak{c}) - F(\mathfrak{u}))^{\eta-1} F'(\mathfrak{u}) \mathfrak{B}(\mathfrak{u}, \mathbb{U}(\mathfrak{u}), \mathbb{U}(\mathfrak{u}-\gamma))d\mathcal{W}(\mathfrak{u}). \tag{50}$$

So, we obtain

$$\mathbb{G}(\mathfrak{c}) - \mathbb{U}(\mathfrak{c}) = \mathbb{G}(\mathfrak{c}) - \mathbb{G}(0) - \Bigg(\sum_{\jmath=1}^{\mathfrak{e}} \frac{\zeta^{1-\mathcal{U}_\jmath}}{\Gamma(\mathcal{U}_\jmath)} \int_0^{\mathfrak{c}} (F(\mathfrak{c}) - F(\mathfrak{u}))^{\mathcal{U}_\jmath - 1} F'(\mathfrak{u}) \Psi_\jmath(\mathfrak{u}, \mathbb{G}(\mathfrak{u}))d\mathfrak{u}$$
$$+ \frac{\zeta^{1-\eta}}{\Gamma(\eta)} \int_0^{\mathfrak{c}} (F(\mathfrak{c}) - F(\mathfrak{u}))^{\eta-1} F'(\mathfrak{u}) \mathfrak{J}(\mathfrak{u}, \mathbb{G}(\mathfrak{u}), \mathbb{G}(\mathfrak{u}-\gamma))d\mathfrak{u}$$
$$+ \frac{\zeta^{1-\eta}}{\Gamma(\eta)} \int_0^{\mathfrak{c}} (F(\mathfrak{c}) - F(\mathfrak{u}))^{\eta-1} F'(\mathfrak{u}) \mathfrak{B}(\mathfrak{u}, \mathbb{G}(\mathfrak{u}), \mathbb{G}(\mathfrak{u}-\gamma))d\mathcal{W}(\mathfrak{u})\Bigg)$$
$$+ \sum_{\jmath=1}^{\mathfrak{e}} \frac{\zeta^{1-\mathcal{U}_\jmath}}{\Gamma(\mathcal{U}_\jmath)} \int_0^{\mathfrak{c}} (F(\mathfrak{c}) - F(\mathfrak{u}))^{\mathcal{U}_\jmath - 1} F'(\mathfrak{u}) (\Psi_\jmath(\mathfrak{u}, \mathbb{G}(\mathfrak{u})) - \Psi_\jmath(\mathfrak{u}, \mathbb{U}(\mathfrak{u})))d\mathfrak{u}$$
$$- \frac{\zeta^{1-\eta}}{\Gamma(\eta)} \int_0^{\mathfrak{c}} (F(\mathfrak{c}) - F(\mathfrak{u}))^{\eta-1} F'(\mathfrak{u}) (\mathfrak{J}(\mathfrak{u}, \mathbb{G}(\mathfrak{u}), \mathbb{G}(\mathfrak{u}-\gamma)) - \mathfrak{J}(\mathfrak{u}, \mathbb{U}(\mathfrak{u}), \mathbb{U}(\mathfrak{u}-\gamma)))d\mathfrak{u}$$
$$- \frac{\zeta^{1-\eta}}{\Gamma(\eta)} \int_0^{\mathfrak{c}} (F(\mathfrak{c}) - F(\mathfrak{u}))^{\eta-1} F'(\mathfrak{u}) (\mathfrak{B}(\mathfrak{u}, \mathbb{G}(\mathfrak{u}), \mathbb{G}(\mathfrak{u}-\gamma)) - \mathfrak{B}(\mathfrak{u}, \mathbb{U}(\mathfrak{u}), \mathbb{U}(\mathfrak{u}-\gamma)))d\mathcal{W}(\mathfrak{u}). \tag{51}$$

Making use of Jensen's inequality, Hölder's inequality, and the Burkholder–Davis–Gundy inequality, we deduce the following:

$$\mathfrak{E}(\|\mathbb{G}(\mathfrak{c}) - \mathbb{U}(\mathfrak{c})\|_{\mathfrak{p}}^{\mathfrak{p}}) \le 2^{\mathfrak{p}-1}\mathfrak{E}\Bigg(\Bigg\|\mathbb{G}(\mathfrak{c}) - \mathbb{G}(0) - \Bigg(\sum_{\jmath=1}^{\mathfrak{e}} \frac{\zeta^{1-\mathcal{U}_\jmath}}{\Gamma(\mathcal{U}_\jmath)} \int_0^{\mathfrak{c}} (F(\mathfrak{c}) - F(\mathfrak{u}))^{\mathcal{U}_\jmath - 1} F'(\mathfrak{u}) \Psi_\jmath(\mathfrak{u}, \mathbb{G}(\mathfrak{u}))d\mathfrak{u}$$
$$+ \frac{\zeta^{1-\eta}}{\Gamma(\eta)} \int_0^{\mathfrak{c}} (F(\mathfrak{c}) - F(\mathfrak{u}))^{\eta-1} F'(\mathfrak{u}) \mathfrak{J}(\mathfrak{u}, \mathbb{G}(\mathfrak{u}), \mathbb{G}(\mathfrak{u}-\gamma))d\mathfrak{u}$$

$$+\frac{\zeta^{1-\eta}}{\Gamma(\eta)}\int_0^{\mathfrak{c}}(F(\mathfrak{c})-F(\mathfrak{u}))^{\eta-1}F'(\mathfrak{u})\mathfrak{B}(\mathfrak{u},\mathbb{G}(\mathfrak{u}),\mathbb{G}(\mathfrak{u}-\gamma))d\mathcal{W}(\mathfrak{u})\Big)\Big\|_{\mathfrak{p}}^{\mathfrak{p}}\Big)$$

$$+2^{\mathfrak{p}-1}\mathfrak{E}\Big(\Big\|\sum_{\jmath=1}^{\mathfrak{e}}\frac{\zeta^{1-\mathcal{U}_\jmath}}{\Gamma(\mathcal{U}_\jmath)}\int_0^{\mathfrak{c}}(F(\mathfrak{c})-F(\mathfrak{u}))^{\mathcal{U}_\jmath-1}F'(\mathfrak{u})(\Psi_\jmath(\mathfrak{u},\mathbb{G}(\mathfrak{u}))-\Psi_\jmath(\mathfrak{u},\mathbb{U}(\mathfrak{u})))d\mathfrak{u}$$

$$-\frac{\zeta^{1-\eta}}{\Gamma(\eta)}\int_0^{\mathfrak{c}}(F(\mathfrak{c})-F(\mathfrak{u}))^{\eta-1}F'(\mathfrak{u})(\mathfrak{I}(\mathfrak{u},\mathbb{G}(\mathfrak{u}),\mathbb{G}(\mathfrak{u}-\gamma))-\mathfrak{I}(\mathfrak{u},\mathbb{U}(\mathfrak{u}),\mathbb{U}(\mathfrak{u}-\gamma)))d\mathfrak{u}$$

$$-\frac{\zeta^{1-\eta}}{\Gamma(\eta)}\int_0^{\mathfrak{c}}(F(\mathfrak{c})-F(\mathfrak{u}))^{\eta-1}F'(\mathfrak{u})(\mathfrak{B}(\mathfrak{u},\mathbb{G}(\mathfrak{u}),\mathbb{G}(\mathfrak{u}-\gamma))-\mathfrak{B}(\mathfrak{u},\mathbb{U}(\mathfrak{u}),\mathbb{U}(\mathfrak{u}-\gamma)))d\mathcal{W}(\mathfrak{u})\Big)\Big\|_{\mathfrak{p}}^{\mathfrak{p}}$$

$$\leq 2^{\mathfrak{p}-1}\varepsilon+2^{(\mathfrak{e}+2)\mathfrak{p}-(\mathfrak{e}+2)}\mathfrak{E}\Big(\Big\|\sum_{\jmath=1}^{\mathfrak{e}}\frac{\zeta^{1-\mathcal{U}_\jmath}}{\Gamma(\mathcal{U}_\jmath)}\int_0^{\mathfrak{c}}(F(\mathfrak{c})-F(\mathfrak{u}))^{\mathcal{U}_\jmath-1}F'(\mathfrak{u})(\Psi_\jmath(\mathfrak{u},\mathbb{G}(\mathfrak{u}))-\Psi_\jmath(\mathfrak{u},\mathbb{U}(\mathfrak{u})))d\mathfrak{u}\Big\|_{\mathfrak{p}}^{\mathfrak{p}}\Big)$$

$$+6^{\mathfrak{p}-1}\mathfrak{E}\Big(\Big\|\frac{\zeta^{1-\eta}}{\Gamma(\eta)}\int_0^{\mathfrak{c}}(F(\mathfrak{c})-F(\mathfrak{u}))^{\eta-1}F'(\mathfrak{u})(\mathfrak{I}(\mathfrak{u},\mathbb{G}(\mathfrak{u}),\mathbb{G}(\mathfrak{u}-\gamma))-\mathfrak{I}(\mathfrak{u},\mathbb{U}(\mathfrak{u}),\mathbb{U}(\mathfrak{u}-\gamma)))d\mathfrak{u}\Big\|_{\mathfrak{p}}^{\mathfrak{p}}\Big)$$

$$+6^{\mathfrak{p}-1}\mathfrak{E}\Big(\Big\|\frac{\zeta^{1-\eta}}{\Gamma(\eta)}\int_0^{\mathfrak{c}}(F(\mathfrak{c})-F(\mathfrak{u}))^{\eta-1}F'(\mathfrak{u})(\mathfrak{B}(\mathfrak{u},\mathbb{G}(\mathfrak{u}),\mathbb{G}(\mathfrak{u}-\gamma))-\mathfrak{B}(\mathfrak{u},\mathbb{U}(\mathfrak{u}),\mathbb{U}(\mathfrak{u}-\gamma)))d\mathcal{W}(\mathfrak{u})\Big\|_{\mathfrak{p}}^{\mathfrak{p}}\Big)$$

$$\leq 2^{\mathfrak{p}-1}\varepsilon+2^{(\mathfrak{e}+2)\mathfrak{p}-(\mathfrak{e}+2)}\sum_{\jmath=1}^{\mathfrak{e}}\left(\frac{\zeta^{1-\mathcal{U}_\jmath}}{\Gamma(\mathcal{U}_\jmath)}\right)^{\mathfrak{p}}\mathbb{X}^{\mathfrak{p}-1}\left((\mathfrak{c}^{\zeta})^{\frac{\mathcal{U}_\jmath\mathfrak{p}-1}{\mathfrak{p}-1}}\right)^{\mathfrak{p}-1}\left(\frac{\mathfrak{p}-1}{\mathcal{U}_\jmath\mathfrak{p}-1}\right)^{\mathfrak{p}-1}\int_0^{\mathfrak{c}}\|\Psi_\jmath(\mathfrak{u},\mathbb{G}(\mathfrak{u})-\Psi_\jmath(\mathfrak{u},\mathbb{U}(\mathfrak{u}))\|_{\mathfrak{p}}^{\mathfrak{p}}d\mathfrak{u}$$

$$+6^{\mathfrak{p}-1}\mathfrak{I}^{\mathfrak{p}-1}\left((\mathfrak{c}^{\zeta})^{\frac{\eta\mathfrak{p}-1}{\mathfrak{p}-1}}\right)^{\mathfrak{p}-1}\left(\frac{\mathfrak{p}-1}{\eta\mathfrak{p}-1}\right)^{\mathfrak{p}-1}\int_0^{\mathfrak{c}}\|\mathfrak{I}(\mathfrak{u},\mathbb{G}(\mathfrak{u}),\mathbb{G}(\mathfrak{u}-\gamma))-\mathfrak{I}(\mathfrak{u},\mathbb{U}(\mathfrak{u}),\mathbb{U}(\mathfrak{u}-\gamma))\|_{\mathfrak{p}}^{\mathfrak{p}}d\mathfrak{u}$$

$$+6^{\mathfrak{p}-1}\mathbf{G}^{\frac{\mathfrak{p}-2}{2}}C_{\mathfrak{p}}\left(\frac{(\mathfrak{c}^{\zeta})^{2\eta-1}}{2\eta-1}\right)^{\frac{\mathfrak{p}-2}{2}}$$

$$\int_0^{\mathfrak{c}}(F(\mathfrak{c})-F(\mathfrak{u}))^{2\eta-2}\|\mathfrak{B}(\mathfrak{u},\mathbb{G}(\mathfrak{u},\mathbb{G}(\mathfrak{u}-\gamma))-\mathfrak{B}(\mathfrak{u},\mathbb{U}(\mathfrak{u},\mathbb{U}(\mathfrak{u}-\gamma))\|_{\mathfrak{p}}^{\mathfrak{p}}(F'(\mathfrak{u}))^2d\mathfrak{u}$$

$$\leq 2^{\mathfrak{p}-1}\varepsilon+2^{(\mathfrak{e}+2)\mathfrak{p}-(\mathfrak{e}+2)}\mathfrak{T}^{\mathfrak{p}}\sum_{\jmath=1}^{\mathfrak{e}}\left(\frac{\zeta^{1-\mathcal{U}_\jmath}}{\Gamma(\mathcal{U}_\jmath)}\right)^{\mathfrak{p}}\mathbb{X}^{\mathfrak{p}-1}\left((\mathfrak{c}^{\zeta})^{\frac{\mathcal{U}_\jmath\mathfrak{p}-1}{\mathfrak{p}-1}}\right)^{\mathfrak{p}-1}\left(\frac{\mathfrak{p}-1}{\mathcal{U}_\jmath\mathfrak{p}-1}\right)^{\mathfrak{p}-1}\int_0^{\mathfrak{c}}\|\mathbb{G}(\mathfrak{u})-\mathbb{U}(\mathfrak{u})\|_{\mathfrak{p}}^{\mathfrak{p}}d\mathfrak{u}$$

$$+12^{\mathfrak{p}-1}\mathfrak{T}^{\mathfrak{p}}\mathfrak{I}^{\mathfrak{p}-1}\left((\mathfrak{c}^{\zeta})^{\frac{\eta\mathfrak{p}-1}{\mathfrak{p}-1}}\right)^{\mathfrak{p}-1}\left(\frac{\mathfrak{p}-1}{\eta\mathfrak{p}-1}\right)^{\mathfrak{p}-1}\int_0^{\mathfrak{c}}\left(\|\mathbb{G}(\mathfrak{u})-\mathbb{U}(\mathfrak{u})\|_{\mathfrak{p}}^{\mathfrak{p}}+\|\mathbb{U}(\mathfrak{u}-\gamma)-\mathbb{U}(\mathfrak{u}-\gamma)\|_{\mathfrak{p}}^{\mathfrak{p}}\right)d\mathfrak{u}$$

$$+12^{\mathfrak{p}-1}\mathfrak{T}^{\mathfrak{p}}\mathbf{G}^{\frac{\mathfrak{p}-2}{2}}C_{\mathfrak{p}}\left(\frac{(\mathfrak{c}^{\zeta})^{2\eta-1}}{2\eta-1}\right)^{\frac{\mathfrak{p}-2}{2}}$$

$$\sup_{1<\mathfrak{u}\leq\mathfrak{c}}F'(\mathfrak{u})\int_0^{\mathfrak{c}}(F(\mathfrak{c})-F(\mathfrak{u}))^{2\eta-2}\left(\|\mathbb{G}(\mathfrak{u})-\mathbb{U}(\mathfrak{u})\|_{\mathfrak{p}}^{\mathfrak{p}}+\|\mathbb{U}(\mathfrak{u}-\gamma)-\mathbb{U}(\mathfrak{u}-\gamma)\|_{\mathfrak{p}}^{\mathfrak{p}}\right)F'(\mathfrak{u})d\mathfrak{u}. \tag{52}$$

Assume that

$$\Theta(\mathfrak{c})=\underset{\mathfrak{c}\in[0,\varpi]}{esssup}\,\mathfrak{E}(\|\mathbb{G}(\mathfrak{c})-\mathbb{U}(\mathfrak{c})\|_{\mathfrak{p}}^{\mathfrak{p}}),\ \mathfrak{c}\in[0,\varpi],$$

we get $\mathfrak{E}(\|\mathbb{G}(\mathfrak{c})-\mathbb{U}(\mathfrak{c})\|_{\mathfrak{p}}^{\mathfrak{p}})\leq\Theta(\mathfrak{c})$ and $\mathfrak{E}(\|\mathbb{G}(\mathfrak{c}-\gamma)-\mathbb{U}(\mathfrak{c}-\gamma)\|_{\mathfrak{p}}^{\mathfrak{p}})\leq\Theta(\mathfrak{c})$ when $\mathfrak{c}\in[0,\varpi]$. Accordingly, we derive the following:

$$\mathfrak{E}(\|\mathbb{G}(\mathfrak{c})-\mathbb{U}(\mathfrak{c})\|_{\mathfrak{p}}^{\mathfrak{p}})$$

$$\leq 2^{\mathfrak{p}-1}\varepsilon+2^{(\mathfrak{e}+2)\mathfrak{p}-(\mathfrak{e}+2)}\mathfrak{T}^{\mathfrak{p}}\sum_{\jmath=1}^{\mathfrak{e}}\left(\frac{\zeta^{1-\mathcal{U}_\jmath}}{\Gamma(\mathcal{U}_\jmath)}\right)^{\mathfrak{p}}\mathbb{X}^{\mathfrak{p}-1}\left((\mathfrak{c}^{\zeta})^{\frac{\mathcal{U}_\jmath\mathfrak{p}-1}{\mathfrak{p}-1}}\right)^{\mathfrak{p}-1}\left(\frac{\mathfrak{p}-1}{\mathcal{U}_\jmath\mathfrak{p}-1}\right)^{\mathfrak{p}-1}\int_0^{\mathfrak{c}}\Theta(\mathfrak{u})d\mathfrak{u}$$

$$+12^{\mathfrak{p}-1}\mathfrak{T}^{\mathfrak{p}}\mathfrak{I}^{\mathfrak{p}-1}\left((\mathfrak{c}^{\zeta})^{\frac{\eta\mathfrak{p}-1}{\mathfrak{p}-1}}\right)^{\mathfrak{p}-1}\left(\frac{\mathfrak{p}-1}{\eta\mathfrak{p}-1}\right)^{\mathfrak{p}-1}2\int_0^{\mathfrak{c}}\Theta(\mathfrak{u})d\mathfrak{u}$$

$$+12^{\mathfrak{p}-1}\mathfrak{T}^{\mathfrak{p}}\mathbf{G}^{\frac{\mathfrak{p}-2}{2}}C_{\mathfrak{p}}\left(\frac{(\mathfrak{c}^{\zeta})^{2\eta-1}}{2\eta-1}\right)^{\frac{\mathfrak{p}-2}{2}}$$

$$2\mathbf{G}\int_0^{\mathfrak{c}}(F(\mathfrak{c})-F(\mathfrak{u}))^{2\eta-2}\Theta(\mathfrak{u})F'(\mathfrak{u})d\mathfrak{u}. \tag{53}$$

From (53), we derive the following:

$$\Theta(\mathfrak{c}) \leq \left(2^{\mathfrak{p}-1}\varepsilon + 2^{(\mathfrak{e}+2)\mathfrak{p}-(\mathfrak{e}+2)}\mathfrak{T}^{\mathfrak{p}} \sum_{j=1}^{\mathfrak{e}} \left(\frac{\zeta^{1-\mathcal{U}_j}}{\Gamma(\mathcal{U}_j)}\right)^{\mathfrak{p}} \mathbb{X}^{\mathfrak{p}-1}\left(\left(\mathfrak{c}^{\zeta}\right)^{\frac{\mathcal{U}_j\mathfrak{p}-1}{\mathfrak{p}-1}}\right)^{\mathfrak{p}-1}\left(\frac{\mathfrak{p}-1}{\mathcal{U}_j\mathfrak{p}-1}\right)^{\mathfrak{p}-1}\right.$$
$$+12^{\mathfrak{p}-1}\mathfrak{T}^{\mathfrak{p}}\mathfrak{Z}^{\mathfrak{p}-1}\left(\left(\mathfrak{c}^{\zeta}\right)^{\frac{\eta\mathfrak{p}-1}{\mathfrak{p}-1}}\right)^{\mathfrak{p}-1}\left.\left(\frac{\mathfrak{p}-1}{\eta\mathfrak{p}-1}\right)^{\mathfrak{p}-1} 2\right)\int_0^{\mathfrak{c}}\Theta(\mathfrak{u})d\mathfrak{u}$$
$$+12^{\mathfrak{p}-1}\mathfrak{T}^{\mathfrak{p}}\mathbf{G}^{\frac{\mathfrak{p}-2}{2}}\mathcal{C}_{\mathfrak{p}}\left(\frac{\left(\mathfrak{c}^{\zeta}\right)^{2\eta-1}}{2\eta-1}\right)^{\frac{\mathfrak{p}-2}{2}} 2\mathbf{G}\int_0^{\mathfrak{c}}\left(F(\mathfrak{c})-F(\mathfrak{u})\right)^{2\eta-2}\Theta(\mathfrak{u})F'(\mathfrak{u})d\mathfrak{u}. \tag{54}$$

With the help of the generalized Grönwall inequality, we deduce from (54)

$$\Theta(\mathfrak{c}) \leq \left\{2^{\mathfrak{p}-1}\varepsilon + \left(2^{(\mathfrak{e}+2)\mathfrak{p}-(\mathfrak{e}+2)}\mathfrak{T}^{\mathfrak{p}} \sum_{j=1}^{\mathfrak{e}} \left(\frac{\zeta^{1-\mathcal{U}_j}}{\Gamma(\mathcal{U}_j)}\right)^{\mathfrak{p}} \mathbb{X}^{\mathfrak{p}-1}\left(\left(\mathfrak{c}^{\zeta}\right)^{\frac{\mathcal{U}_j\mathfrak{p}-1}{\mathfrak{p}-1}}\right)^{\mathfrak{p}-1}\left(\frac{\mathfrak{p}-1}{\mathcal{U}_j\mathfrak{p}-1}\right)^{\mathfrak{p}-1}\right.\right.$$
$$\left.\left.+12^{\mathfrak{p}-1}\mathfrak{T}^{\mathfrak{p}}\mathfrak{Z}^{\mathfrak{p}-1}\left(\left(\mathfrak{c}^{\zeta}\right)^{\frac{\eta\mathfrak{p}-1}{\mathfrak{p}-1}}\right)^{\mathfrak{p}-1}\left(\frac{\mathfrak{p}-1}{\eta\mathfrak{p}-1}\right)^{\mathfrak{p}-1} 2\right)\int_0^{\mathfrak{c}}\Theta(\mathfrak{u})d\mathfrak{u}\right\}$$
$$\times\,\mathbb{E}_{2\eta-1,1}\left(12^{\mathfrak{p}-1}\mathfrak{T}^{\mathfrak{p}}\mathbf{G}^{\frac{\mathfrak{p}-2}{2}}\mathcal{C}_{\mathfrak{p}}\left(\frac{\left(\mathfrak{c}^{\zeta}\right)^{2\eta-1}}{2\eta-1}\right)^{\frac{\mathfrak{p}-2}{2}} 2\mathbf{G}\Gamma(2\eta-1)\left(\mathfrak{c}^{\zeta}\right)^{(2\eta-1)}\right)$$
$$= \mathrm{Y}_1\varepsilon + \mathrm{Y}_2\int_0^{\mathfrak{c}}\Theta(\mathfrak{u})d\mathfrak{u},\ \mathfrak{c}\in[0,\varpi],$$

where

$$\mathrm{Y}_1 = 2^{\mathfrak{p}-1}\mathbb{E}_{2\eta-1,1}\left(12^{\mathfrak{p}-1}\mathfrak{T}^{\mathfrak{p}}\mathbf{G}^{\frac{\mathfrak{p}-2}{2}}\mathcal{C}_{\mathfrak{p}}\left(\frac{\left(\mathfrak{c}^{\zeta}\right)^{2\eta-1}}{2\eta-1}\right)^{\frac{\mathfrak{p}-2}{2}} 2\mathbf{G}\Gamma(2\eta-1)\left(\mathfrak{c}^{\zeta}\right)^{(2\eta-1)}\right),$$

and

$$\mathrm{Y}_2 = \left(12^{\mathfrak{p}-1}\mathfrak{T}^{\mathfrak{p}}\mathfrak{Z}^{\mathfrak{p}-1}\left(\left(\mathfrak{c}^{\zeta}\right)^{\frac{\eta\mathfrak{p}-1}{\mathfrak{p}-1}}\right)^{\mathfrak{p}-1}\left(\frac{\mathfrak{p}-1}{\eta\mathfrak{p}-1}\right)^{\mathfrak{p}-1} 2\right)\Bigg)$$
$$\times\,\mathbb{E}_{2\eta-1,1}\left(12^{\mathfrak{p}-1}\mathfrak{T}^{\mathfrak{p}}\mathbf{G}^{\frac{\mathfrak{p}-2}{2}}\mathcal{C}_{\mathfrak{p}}\left(\frac{\left(\mathfrak{c}^{\zeta}\right)^{2\eta-1}}{2\eta-1}\right)^{\frac{\mathfrak{p}-2}{2}} 2\mathbf{G}\Gamma(2\eta-1)\left(\mathfrak{c}^{\zeta}\right)^{(2\eta-1)}\right).$$

By utilizing Grönwall inequality, we arrive at

$$\begin{aligned}\Theta(\mathfrak{c}) &\leq \mathrm{Y}_1\varepsilon\exp(\mathrm{Y}_2\mathfrak{c})\\ &\leq \mathrm{Y}_1\varepsilon\exp(\mathrm{Y}_2\varpi)\\ &= \mathbb{V}\varepsilon.\end{aligned}$$

Consequently, the final expression is

$$\mathfrak{E}\left(\|\mathbb{G}(\mathfrak{c})-\mathbb{U}(\mathfrak{c})\|_{\mathfrak{p}}^{\mathfrak{p}}\right) \leq \mathbb{V}\varepsilon,\ \ \mathfrak{c}\in[0,\varpi].$$

This implies that (3) is UHS with ε. □

Remark 1. *The convergence order for UHS is linear, as the power of ε in the stability bound is one.*

Remark 2. *When the model contains small delays, UHS becomes more likely to hold. However, the stability properties fundamentally depend on the magnitude of the delay and the specific characteristics of the problem. For a comprehensive analysis of how delays affect UHS, see [42,43].*

5. Example

In this section, we provide an example to demonstrate our theoretical results.

Example 1. *Examine the following:*

$$\begin{cases} {}^{c}\mathfrak{D}_{0^+}^{\eta,\zeta}\left(\ell(\mathfrak{c}) - \mathcal{I}_{0^+}^{\mathcal{U}_1,\zeta} 5\mathfrak{c}\sin(\ell(\mathfrak{c})) - \mathcal{I}_{0^+}^{\mathcal{U}_2,\zeta} 4\cos(\ell(\mathfrak{c}))\right) = 3\cos(\ell(\mathfrak{c}))\sin(\ell(\mathfrak{c}-\frac{1}{5})) + \\ 4\sin(\ell(\mathfrak{c}))\cos(\ell(\mathfrak{c}-\frac{1}{5}))\frac{d\mathcal{W}(\mathfrak{c})}{d\mathfrak{c}}, \ \mathfrak{c} \in [0,6], \\ \ell(0) = \varphi, \end{cases} \tag{55}$$

where $\mathfrak{e} = 2$, $\varpi = 6$, $\Psi_1(\mathfrak{c}, \ell(\mathfrak{c})) = 5\mathfrak{c}\sin(\ell(\mathfrak{c}))$, $\Psi_2(\mathfrak{c}, \ell(\mathfrak{c})) = 4\cos(\ell(\mathfrak{c}))$, $\mathfrak{I}(\mathfrak{c}, \ell(\mathfrak{c}), \ell(\mathfrak{c}-\varrho)) = 3\cos(\ell(\mathfrak{c}))\sin(\ell(\mathfrak{c}-\frac{1}{5}))$, $\mathfrak{B}(\mathfrak{c}, \ell(\mathfrak{c}), \ell(\mathfrak{c}-\varrho)) = 4\sin(\ell(\mathfrak{c}))\cos(\ell(\mathfrak{c}-\frac{1}{5}))$.

We compute the following:

$$\|\Psi_1(\mathfrak{c}, \Phi_1'(\mathfrak{c})) - \Psi_1(\mathfrak{c}, \Phi_2'(\mathfrak{c}))\| \le 5\|\Phi_1'(\mathfrak{c})) - \Phi_2'(\mathfrak{c}))\|,$$

$$\|\Psi_2(\mathfrak{c}, \Phi_1'(\mathfrak{c})) - \Psi_2(\mathfrak{c}, \Phi_2'(\mathfrak{c}))\| \le 4\|\Phi_1'(\mathfrak{c})) - \Phi_2'(\mathfrak{c}))\|,$$

$$\|\mathfrak{I}(\mathfrak{c}, \Phi_1'(\mathfrak{c}), \Phi_1'(\mathfrak{c}-\varrho)) - \mathfrak{I}(\mathfrak{c}, \Phi_2'(\mathfrak{c}), \Phi_2'(\mathfrak{c}-\varrho))\| \le 3(\|\Phi_1'(\mathfrak{c})) - \Phi_2'(\mathfrak{c}))\| + \|\Phi_1'(\mathfrak{c}-\varrho) - \Phi_2'(\mathfrak{c}-\varrho)\|),$$

$$\|\mathfrak{B}(\mathfrak{c}, \Phi_1'(\mathfrak{c}), \Phi_1'(\mathfrak{c}-\varrho)) - \mathfrak{B}(\mathfrak{c}, \Phi_2'(\mathfrak{c}), \Phi_2'(\mathfrak{c}-\varrho))\| \le 4(\|\Phi_1'(\mathfrak{c})) - \Phi_2'(\mathfrak{c}))\| + \|\Phi_1'(\mathfrak{c}-\varrho) - \Phi_2'(\mathfrak{c}-\varrho)\|).$$

Accordingly, condition $(\hbar_1)$ *is achieved with* $\mathfrak{T} = 5$. *Likewise, for* $\jmath = 1, 2$, *we achieve* $\underset{\mathfrak{c}\in[0,6]}{essup}\|\Psi_\jmath(\mathfrak{c}, 0)\|_{\mathfrak{p}} < 5$, $\underset{\mathfrak{c}\in[0,6]}{essup}\|\mathfrak{I}(\mathfrak{c}, 0, 0)\|_{\mathfrak{p}} < 5$, *and* $\underset{\mathfrak{c}\in[0,6]}{essup}\|\mathfrak{B}(\mathfrak{c}, 0, 0)\|_{\mathfrak{p}} < 5$. *Consequently, Theorem 1 guarantees the Ex-Un of the solution for System* (55). *Furthermore, by Theorem 3, System* (55) *is UHS, as we have demonstrated that conditions* $(\hbar_1)$ *and* $(\hbar_2)$ *are satisfied.*

6. Conclusions

This study introduces new findings on the solution's Ex-Un and its persistent dependence on the initial value for FSIDEs with delay. Additionally, we derive a generalized Grönwall inequality and prove UHS. All these results are presented in the $\mathcal{L}^{\mathfrak{p}}$ space and the context of Cap-KFrD. In this way, we make significant contributions to the literature. Applying several important inequalities, such as Jensen's inequality, the Burkholder–Davis–Gundy inequality, and Hölder's inequality, is a key tool used to prove the theorems and lemmas. In the future, we will develop a financial model using SFDEs that incorporate both fractional Brownian motion and standard Brownian motion.

Author Contributions: Conceptualization, A.M.D. and M.I.L.; methodology, A.M.D. and M.I.L.; software, A.M.D. and M.I.L.; validation, A.M.D. and M.I.L.; formal analysis, A.M.D. and M.I.L.; investigation, A.M.D. and M.I.L.; resources, A.M.D.; writing—original draft preparation, A.M.D. and M.I.L.; writing—review and editing, A.M.D. and M.I.L.; visualization, A.M.D. and M.I.L.; funding acquisition, A.M.D. All authors have read and agreed to the published version of the manuscript.

Funding: This work was supported by the Deanship of Scientific Research, Vice Presidency for Graduate Studies and Scientific Research, King Faisal University, Saudi Arabia (Project No. KFU251299).

Data Availability Statement: No data were generated or analyzed during the current study.

Conflicts of Interest: The authors declare no conflicts of interest.

Abbreviations

The following abbreviations are used in this manuscript:

Cap-KFrD	Caputo–Katugampola fractional derivative
Cap-FrD	Caputo fractional derivative
Cap-HFrD	Caputo–Hadamard fractional derivative
Ex-Un	Existence and uniqueness
SFDEs	Stochastic fractional differential equations
FSIDEs	Fractional stochastic integro-differential equations
UHS	Ulam–Hyers stability

References

1. Subramanian, M.; Manigandan, M.; Zada, A.; Gopal, T.N. Existence and Hyers-Ulam stability of solutions for nonlinear three fractional sequential differential equations with nonlocal boundary conditions. *Int. J. Nonlinear Sci. Numer. Simul.* **2024**, *24*, 3071–3099. [CrossRef]
2. Mohammed Djaouti, A.; Khan, Z.A.; Imran Liaqat, M.; Al-Quran, A. A novel technique for solving the nonlinear fractional-order smoking model. *Fractal Fract.* **2024**, *8*, 286. [CrossRef]
3. Gunasekar, T.; Raghavendran, P.; Santra, S.S.; Majumder, D.; Baleanu, D.; Balasundaram, H. Application of Laplace transform to solve fractional integro-differential equations. *J. Math. Comput. Sci.* **2024**, *33*, 225–237. [CrossRef]
4. Din, A.; Li, Y.; Khan, F.M.; Khan, Z.U.; Liu, P. On Analysis of fractional order mathematical model of Hepatitis B using Atangana–Baleanu Caputo (ABC) derivative. *Fractals* **2022**, *30*, 2240017. [CrossRef]
5. Zeng, S.; Baleanu, D.; Bai, Y.; Wu, G. Fractional differential equations of Caputo-Katugampola type and numerical solutions. *Appl. Math. Comput.* **2017**, *315*, 549–554. [CrossRef]
6. Ma, L.; Chen, Y. Analysis of Caputo–Katugampola fractional differential system. *Eur. Phys. J. Plus* **2024**, *139*, 171. [CrossRef]
7. Sweilam, N.H.; Nagy, A.M.; Al-Ajami, T.M. Numerical solutions of fractional optimal control with Caputo–Katugampola derivative. *Adv. Differ. Equ.* **2021**, *2021*, 425. [CrossRef]
8. Boucenna, D.; Ben Makhlouf, A.; Naifar, O.; Guezane-Lakoud, A.; Hammami, M.A. Linearized stability analysis of Caputo-Katugampola fractional-order nonlinear systems. *J. Nonlinear Funct. Anal.* **2018**, *2018*, 27.
9. Nazeer, N.; Asjad, M.I.; Azam, M.K.; Akgül, A. Study of results of katugampola fractional derivative and chebyshev inequailities. *Int. J. Appl. Comput. Math.* **2022**, *8*, 225. [CrossRef]
10. Van Hoa, N.; Vu, H.; Duc, T.M. Fuzzy fractional differential equations under Caputo–Katugampola fractional derivative approach. *Fuzzy Sets Syst.* **2019**, *375*, 70–99.
11. Omaba, M.E.; Sulaimani, H.A. On Caputo–Katugampola fractional stochastic differential equation. *Mathematics* **2022**, *10*, 2086. [CrossRef]
12. Elbadri, M. An approximate solution of a time fractional Burgers' equation involving the Caputo-Katugampola fractional derivative. *Partial. Differ. Equations Appl. Math.* **2023**, *8*, 100560. [CrossRef]
13. Al-Ghafri, K.S.; Alabdala, A.T.; Redhwan, S.S.; Bazighifan, O.; Ali, A.H.; Iambor, L.F. Symmetrical solutions for non-local fractional integro-differential equations via caputo–katugampola derivatives. *Symmetry* **2023**, *15*, 662. [CrossRef]
14. Sadek, L.; Jarad, F. The general Caputo–Katugampola fractional derivative and numerical approach for solving the fractional differential equations. *Alex. Eng. J.* **2025**, *121*, 539–557. [CrossRef]
15. Nagy, A.M.; Issa, K. An accurate numerical technique for solving fractional advection–diffusion equation with generalized Caputo derivative. *Z. Angew. Math. Phys.* **2024**, *75*, 164. [CrossRef]
16. Dai, Q.; Zhang, Y. Stability of nonlinear implicit differential equations with Caputo–Katugampola fractional derivative. *Mathematics* **2023**, *11*, 3082. [CrossRef]
17. Tran, M.D.; Ho, V.; Van, H.N. On the stability of fractional differential equations involving generalized Caputo fractional derivative. *Math. Probl. Eng.* **2020**, *2020*, 1680761. [CrossRef]
18. Singh, J.; Agrawal, R.; Baleanu, D. Dynamical analysis of fractional order biological population model with carrying capacity under Caputo-Katugampola memory. *Alex. Eng. J.* **2024**, *91*, 394–402. [CrossRef]
19. Oliveira, D.S.; Capelas de Oliveira, E. On a Caputo-type fractional derivative. *Adv. Pure Appl. Math.* **2019**, *10*, 81–91. [CrossRef]
20. Batiha, I.M.; Abubaker, A.A.; Jebril, I.H.; Al-Shaikh, S.B.; Matarneh, K. A numerical approach of handling fractional stochastic differential equations. *Axioms* **2023**, *12*, 388. [CrossRef]
21. Chen, J.; Ke, S.; Li, X.; Liu, W. Existence, uniqueness and stability of solutions to fractional backward stochastic differential equations. *Appl. Math. Sci. Eng.* **2022**, *30*, 811–829. [CrossRef]
22. Moualkia, S.; Xu, Y. On the existence and uniqueness of solutions for multidimensional fractional stochastic differential equations with variable order. *Mathematics* **2021**, *9*, 2106. [CrossRef]
23. Ali, A.; Hayat, K.; Zahir, A.; Shah, K.; Abdeljawad, T. Qualitative analysis of fractional stochastic differential equations with variable order fractional derivative. *Qual. Theory Dyn. Syst.* **2024**, *23*, 120. [CrossRef]

24. Li, S.; Khan, S.U.; Riaz, M.B.; AlQahtani, S.A.; Alamri, A.M. Numerical simulation of a fractional stochastic delay differential equations using spectral scheme: A comprehensive stability analysis. *Sci. Rep.* **2024**, *14*, 6930. [CrossRef] [PubMed]
25. Singh, A.; Vijayakumar, V.; Shukla, A.; Chauhan, S. A note on asymptotic stability of semilinear thermoelastic system. *Qual. Theory Dyn. Syst.* **2022**, *21*, 75. [CrossRef]
26. Abouagwa, M.; Bantan, R.A.; Almutiry, W.; Khalaf, A.D.; Elgarhy, M. Mixed Caputo fractional neutral stochastic differential equations with impulses and variable delay. *Fractal Fract.* **2021**, *5*, 239. [CrossRef]
27. Doan, T.S.; Huong, P.T.; Kloeden, P.E.; Vu, A.M. Euler-Maruyama scheme for Caputo stochastic fractional differential equations. *J. Comput. Appl. Math.* **2020**, *380*, 112989. [CrossRef]
28. Umamaheswari, P.; Balachandran, K.; Annapoorani, N. Existence and stability results for Caputo fractional stochastic differential equations with Lévy noise. *Filomat* **2020**, *34*, 1739–1751. [CrossRef]
29. Li, M.; Niu, Y.; Zou, J. A result regarding finite-time stability for Hilfer fractional stochastic differential equations with delay. *Fractal Fract.* **2023**, *7*, 622. [CrossRef]
30. Mirzaee, F.; Samadyar, N. On the numerical solution of fractional stochastic integro-differential equations via meshless discrete collocation method based on radial basis functions. *Eng. Anal. Bound. Elem.* **2019**, *100*, 246–255. [CrossRef]
31. Cui, J.; Yan, L. Existence result for fractional neutral stochastic integro-differential equations with infinite delay. *J. Phys. A Math. Theor.* **2011**, *44*, 335201. [CrossRef]
32. Badr, A.A.; El-Hoety, H.S. Monte-Carlo Galerkin Approximation of Fractional Stochastic Integro-Differential Equation. *Math. Probl. Eng.* **2012**, *2012*, 709106. [CrossRef]
33. Ahmed, H.M.; El-Borai, M.M. Hilfer fractional stochastic integro-differential equations. *Appl. Math. Comput.* **2018**, *331*, 182–189. [CrossRef]
34. Kamrani, M. Numerical solution of stochastic fractional differential equations. *Numer. Algorithms* **2015**, *68*, 81–93. [CrossRef]
35. Ramkumar, K.; Ravikumar, K.; Varshini, S. Fractional neutral stochastic differential equations with Caputo fractional derivative: Fractional Brownian motion, Poisson jumps, and optimal control. *Stoch. Anal. Appl.* **2021**, *39*, 157–176. [CrossRef]
36. Zou, J.; Luo, D. A new result on averaging principle for Caputo-type fractional delay stochastic differential equations with Brownian motion. *Appl. Anal.* **2024**, *103*, 1397–1417. [CrossRef]
37. Liu, J.; Zhang, H.; Wang, J.; Jin, C.; Li, J.; Xu, W. A note on averaging principles for fractional stochastic differential equations. *Fractal Fract.* **2024**, *8*, 216. [CrossRef]
38. Luo, D.; Wang, X.; Caraballo, T.; Zhu, Q. Ulam–Hyers stability of Caputo-type fractional fuzzy stochastic differential equations with delay. *Commun. Nonlinear Sci. Numer. Simul.* **2023**, *121*, 107229. [CrossRef]
39. Zou, J.; Luo, D. On the averaging principle of Caputo type neutral fractional stochastic differential equations. *Qual. Theory Dyn. Syst.* **2024**, *23*, 82. [CrossRef]
40. Wang, Z.; Lin, P. Averaging principle for fractional stochastic differential equations with Lp convergence. *Appl. Math. Lett.* **2022**, *130*, 108024. [CrossRef]
41. Djaouti, A.M.; Liaqat, M.I. Theoretical Results on the pth Moment of ϕ-Hilfer Stochastic Fractional Differential Equations with a Pantograph Term. *Fractal Fract.* **2025**, *9*, 134. [CrossRef]
42. Otrocol, D.; Ilea, V. Ulam stability for a delay differential equation. *Open Math.* **2013**, *11*, 1296–1303. [CrossRef]
43. Chen, C.; Dong, Q. Existence and Hyers–Ulam stability for a multi-term fractional differential equation with infinite delay. *Mathematics* **2022**, *10*, 1013. [CrossRef]

mathematics

MDPI

Article

Caputo Barrier Functions and Their Applications to the Safety, Safety-and-Stability, and Input-to-State Safety of a Class of Fractional-Order Systems

Zheren Zhu [1], Bingbing Shen [1], Le Yao [1,*], Yi Chai [2] and Zhihuan Song [3]

[1] School of Mathematics, Hangzhou Normal University, Hangzhou 311121, China; drzzr@hznu.edu.cn (Z.Z.); shenbingbing@hznu.edu.cn (B.S.)
[2] School of Automation, Chongqing University, Chongqing 400044, China; chaiyi@cqu.edu.cn
[3] State Key Laboratory of Industrial Control Technology, College of Control Science and Engineering, Zhejiang University, Hangzhou 310028, China; songzhihuan@zju.edu.cn
* Correspondence: yaole@hznu.edu.cn; Tel.: +86-1806-942-1456

Abstract: Safety control based on barrier functions has gradually become one of the emerging and more important directions in the field of safety. Scholars are attempting to apply barrier functions to integer-order dynamical systems, such as general nonlinear systems, hybrid systems, linear systems, etc. Moreover, the introduction of barrier functions has even expanded the research approaches on safe reinforcement learning. However, there is very little research on the safety control problem of fractional-order dynamical systems. Based on our previous work, this article further explores, in depth, the problem of the transfer and adaptability of barrier functions for integer-order systems in fractional-order systems, and it also proposes the Caputo reciprocal barrier function and Caputo zeroing barrier function. And we established two theorems, which proved that we can also achieve uniform asymptotic stability or exponential stability with guaranteed safety. In the end, we created a new description for the definition of input-to-state safety under Caputo's fractional-order systems, and we used this description and the above two Caputo barrier functions to construct two criteria of the Caputo input-to-state safety. Thus, we, finally, established the embryonic form of the theoretical framework of safety control based on barrier functions for fractional-order systems.

Keywords: Caputo barrier function; Caputo's fractional-order system; stability with guaranteed safety; Caputo input-to-state safety

MSC: 93C99

1. Introduction

1.1. Motivation

Safety control is one of the fundamental problems for many kinds of dynamical systems, especially large-scale and complex systems. Recently, in the last two decades, many scholars have verified that (control) barrier functions are effective for realizing safety control.

The research on safety control based on barrier functions can be roughly divided into three categories. The first category is the research on pure barrier functions for safety criteria. A number of prevalent barrier functions have emerged, which were contributed to by Prajna [1], Kong [2], Zhu [3], Dai [4], Ames [5,6], and Xu [7]. In addition, there are many other interesting works about barrier functions, such as vector barrier functions [8],

https://doi.org/10.3390/math13081215

extreme-point barrier functions [9,10], and barrier functions with converse theorems [11,12]. The second category is the research on safety-derived theories based on barrier functions, which mainly consider issues such as the synchronization of safety and stability [13] and the safety robustness and input-to-state safety (ISSf) issues [7,14,15]. The third category is the research on the application of safety control based on barrier functions [16–22].

The abovementioned barrier functions have realized the construction and application of safety control theories for general nonlinear systems, hybrid systems, stochastic systems, and multi-agent systems. Their remarkable common feature is that all these studies are carried out around integer-order systems. Therefore, the theory of fractional-order safety control is still a virgin land and has great research potential.

Fractional-order systems (FOSs) represent a unique class of systems characterized by their distinct integration and differentiation laws. Unlike traditional integer-order systems (IOSs), FOSs are defined by fractional-order differential equations, which have been demonstrated to provide more accurate descriptions of complex systems compared to their integer-order counterparts [23,24]. A notable feature of FOSs is their inherent infinite memory and hereditary properties, which fundamentally differentiate them from classical IOSs. As a result, the well-established theories of integer-order systems may not be directly applicable to the analysis and design of fractional-order systems. Factually, the modeling and control of FOSs has emerged as a significant research direction in the field of control theory. The stability theories of FOSs have been well established, as demonstrated in several studies [25–27]. Additionally, there has been growing interest in fault estimation and accommodation for FOSs [23]. However, the fundamental theories and practical applications of safety control for FOSs remain largely unexplored. Due to the special differential rules of fractional-order systems, such as memory effects, barrier functions are applicable under integer-order differentiation, but they may not be fully applicable in the case of fractional orders. In this regard, by comparing them with our previous work, it can be found that there are differences in details between the two theorems in [3,28]. With the abovementioned challenges, this article aims to extend and adapt the state safety theories based on barrier functions, which have been widely adopted for integer-order systems (IOSs), to the realm of FOSs. Given the increasing demand for robust safety mechanisms in complex dynamic systems, this endeavor is both timely and necessary.

In the past, our prior work [28,29] involved an initial attempt to demonstrate that certain special barrier functions can be employed to ensure the safety of Caputo's fractional-order systems (FOSs). In these two articles, we proposed Caputo less-zero barrier function and Caputo exponential barrier function, as well as a theorem of asymptotic stability with guaranteed safety. However, these two articles have not yet established a comprehensive fundamental theoretical framework for fractional-order barrier functions. This article devotes more efforts to exploring the issues of uniform asymptotic stability with guaranteed safety, exponential stability with guaranteed safety, and the ISSf, so as to effectively supplement the theoretical framework of safety control for fractional-order systems.

1.2. Contributions

Our main contributions in this article are as follows.

(1) We demonstrate the possibility of transferring the reciprocal barrier function (RBF) and the zeroing barrier function (ZBF) to Caputo fractional-order systems (CFOS), and we also propose Caputo RBF and Caputo ZBF. Based on two innovative Caputo BFs, we systematically derive the state safety criteria for fractional-order nonlinear dynamic systems. Our established state-safety theorems provide rigorous guarantees that all system states will remain within an known available state set, given that the initial conditions adhere to the set constraint.

(2) On the basis of the theorem of asymptotical stability with guaranteed safety for CFOSs [29], we further propose the theorems of uniformly asymptotical stability with guaranteed safety and exponential stability with guaranteed safety for CFOSs. These two theorems demonstrate the possibility and solvability of achieving the synchronization of safety and uniformly asymptotical stability (or exponential stability).
(3) We constructed a new description for the definition of Caupto input-to-state safety. The inspiration for this new description comes from the final product of the Caputo reciprocal barrier function proof process. The core inequality of our proposed definition of the Caputo input-to-state safety not only provides a unified representation of safety and ISSf for CFOSs, but it also facilitates the design and derivation of ISSf controllers. Then, under the definition of Caputo ISSf, using Caputo reciprocal barrier function and Caputo zeroing barrier function, we establish two ISSf criteria that can be directly applied to design Caputo ISSf controllers.

1.3. Organizations

This article is structured as follows. It consists of five sections that systematically unfold the research on fractional-order system safety control. Section 1 serves as the introduction, where the motivation and contributions of this study are presented. In Section 2, we introduce a class of Caputo fractional-order systems (CFOSs) and construct two Caputo barrier functions. These functions lay a solid theoretical foundation for subsequent analyses. Section 3 is devoted to a thorough exploration of the synchronous Caputo safety and stability theorems. Through meticulous mathematical derivations and in-depth discussions, we elucidate the compatibility between safety and stability within the framework of CFOSs. In Section 4, we shift our focus to the input-to-state safety and the corresponding ISSf barrier functions of CFOSs. This section offers the relationship between external inputs and the safety performance of CFOSs. In the end, Section 5 presents the conclusions, summarizing the key findings, contributions, and potential directions for future research.

2. Caputo Barrier Functions

This section focuses on extending safety theories for CFOSs with order $\alpha \in (0,1)$ using barrier functions. The objective is to transform the RBF and the ZBF into the Caputo RBF and the Caputo ZBF so as to be suitable for the CFOS. Specifically, we analyze a CFOS governed by Caputo fractional derivatives [26], which is defined as

$$^{C}D^{\alpha}x(t) = f(x(t)), \tag{1}$$

where $\alpha \in (0,1)$, $x \in \mathbb{R}^n$, $t \geq t_0 \in [0,+\infty)$, and $f : \mathbb{R}^n \to \mathbb{R}^n$ are locally Lipschitz. And there is a safe zone $\mathcal{C}$ for CFOS (1), which can be defined by the following (2)–(4):

$$\mathcal{C} = \{x \in \mathbb{R}^n : h(x) \geq 0\}, \tag{2}$$

$$\partial\mathcal{C} = \{x \in \mathbb{R}^n : h(x) = 0\}, \tag{3}$$

$$\mathrm{Int}(\mathcal{C}) = \{x \in \mathbb{R}^n : h(x) > 0\}, \tag{4}$$

with a smooth function $h : \mathbb{R}^n \to \mathbb{R}$. And other states have $\forall x \in \mathbb{R}^n \setminus \mathcal{C}, h(x) < 0$. In addition, we can call CFOS (1) safe, if all the states beginning from $x(t_0) = x_0$ are in the set $\mathcal{C}$.

2.1. Caputo RBF

For IOSs, RBFs have proven to be highly effective in designing state-safety controllers, offering less restrictive constraints compared to the first generation barrier functions [1] and exponential barrier functions [2,3]. This naturally raises the question: can a RBF be developed to ensure the safety of CFOSs?

Definition 1. *For CFOS (1) having a set C defined by (2)–(4) with some continuously differentiable function $h : \mathbb{R}^n \to \mathbb{R}$, we can consider a function $B : C \to \mathbb{R}$ as a Caputo reciprocal barrier function for the set C if there exist locally Lipschitz class $\mathcal{K}$ functions. (A continuous function $\alpha : [0, a) \to [0, \infty)$ is said to belong to class $\mathcal{K}$ if it is strictly increasing and $\alpha(0) = 0$ [30]) $\beta_1, \beta_2, \beta_3$, for all $x \in \text{Int}(C)$, has*

$$\frac{1}{\beta_1(h(x))} \leq B(x) \leq \frac{1}{\beta_2(h(x))}, \tag{5}$$

$$^{C}D^{\alpha}B(x(t)) \leq \beta_3(h(x)). \tag{6}$$

Theorem 1. *Given a set $C \subseteq \mathbb{R}^n$ for CFOS (1) with Conditions (2)–(4), if there exists a Caputo reciprocal barrier function $B : C \to \mathbb{R}$, it can be defined by Definition 1. In addition, we can guarantee the set C is forward-invariant and that CFOS (1) can be said to be safe for any $x_0 \in \text{Int}(C)$.*

Proof of Theorem 1. Let $^{C}D^{\alpha}y = \beta_3\left(\beta_2^{-1}\left(\frac{1}{y}\right)\right) \overset{def}{=} \beta\left(\frac{1}{y}\right)$; hence, β belongs to Class $\mathcal{K}$. By the comparison theorem for fractional-order System [26], we have $\inf y(t) \geq B(x(t))$. According to Caputo's fractional derivative [26], there is

$$^{C}D^{\alpha}y = \frac{1}{\Gamma(1-\alpha)} \int_{t_0}^{t} \frac{y'(\tau)}{(t-\tau)^{\alpha}} d\tau. \tag{7}$$

Then, let $z = \frac{1}{y}$, which means

$$^{C}D^{\alpha}z = \frac{1}{\Gamma(1-\alpha)} \int_{t_0}^{t} \frac{-\frac{y'(\tau)}{y^2}}{(t-\tau)^{\alpha}} d\tau. \tag{8}$$

By the Generalized First Mean Value Theorem for Integrals, there exists some point $\xi \in [t_0, t]$ satisfying

$$\int_{t_0}^{t} \frac{-\frac{y'(\tau)}{y^2}}{(t-\tau)^{\alpha}} d\tau = \frac{-1}{y^2(\xi)} \int_{t_0}^{t} \frac{y'(\tau)}{(t-\tau)^{\alpha}} d\tau.$$

Hence, (8) has

$$\begin{aligned} ^{C}D^{\alpha}z &= \frac{1}{\Gamma(1-\alpha)} \frac{-1}{y^2(\xi)} \int_{t_0}^{t} \frac{y'(\tau)}{(t-\tau)^{\alpha}} d\tau \\ &= -\frac{1}{y^2(\xi)} {}^{C}D^{\alpha}y = -\frac{1}{y^2(\xi)} \beta\left(\frac{1}{y}\right) \\ &= -z^2(\xi)\beta(z) \overset{def}{=} -\bar{\beta}(z). \end{aligned} \tag{9}$$

It is not difficult to find that $\bar{\beta}$ is also a class $\mathcal{K}$ function. By the equivalent Volterra Integral [26] and Bihari's Inequality [31], we can obtain

$$z(t) \leq \eta^{-1}\left[\eta(z(t_0)) + \frac{(t-t_0)^{\alpha}}{\Gamma(\alpha+1)}\right].$$

Following the proof methodology detailed in Theorem 3.1 of reference [26], we have

$$z(t) \leq \sigma(z(t_0), t - t_0), \tag{10}$$

where σ belongs to class $\mathcal{KL}$ function (A continuous function $\beta : [0,a) \times [0,\infty) \to [0,\infty)$ is said to belong to class $\mathcal{KL}$ if, when s is fixed, $\beta(r,s)$ belongs to class $\mathcal{K}$ with respect to r, and—when r is fixed—$\beta(r,s)$ is decreasing with respect to s and $\beta(r,s) \to 0$ as $s \to \infty$ [30]). As $y = \frac{1}{z}$ and $B(x(t)) \leq \inf y(t)$, then, by comparison theorem for fractional-order System [26], we can obtain

$$\frac{1}{\sigma\left(\frac{1}{B(x(t_0))}, t - t_0\right)} \geq B(x(t)).$$

With (5), then, we have

$$h(x(t)) \geq \beta_1^{-1}\left(\sigma\left(\frac{1}{B(x(t_0))}, t - t_0\right)\right) \tag{11}$$

for all $t \in I(x(t_0))$. In Equation (11), β_1^{-1} is the inverse of β_1 and belongs to class $\mathcal{K}$. As $x(t_0) \in C$, then we have $B(x(t_0)) > 0$. This means that $h(x(t)) \geq 0$ for all $t \in I(x(t_0))$. Thus, C is forward-invariant and CFOS (1) is then safe. □

Remark 1. *For integer-order systems with $n = 1$ ([5], Theorem 1), the dynamics are governed by $\dot{z} = -\frac{\dot{y}}{y^2} = -\beta(z)z^2 \overset{def}{=} \bar{\beta}(z)$, where β is a class $\mathcal{K}$ function. However, for fractional-order systems with $\alpha \in (0,1)$, the analysis becomes significantly more complex. In this case, the Generalized First Mean Value Theorem for Integrals must be employed to establish the relationship ${}^{C}D^{\alpha}z = -z^2(\xi)\beta(z) \overset{def}{=} \bar{\beta}(z)$. A key distinction between the two cases lies in the nature of the nonlinear term. For the integer-order case, z^2 is a class $\mathcal{K}$ function. In contrast, for the fractional-order case, $z^2(\xi)$ represents a real positive value, which introduces additional challenges in the analysis. Consequently, the verification of safety theorems under Caputo's fractional-order framework is more intricate compared to their integer-order counterparts.*

2.2. Caputo ZBF

The ZBF is widely utilized in the analysis and control of input-to-state safety, serving as a critical quantitative framework for robust safety analysis. Consequently, transitioning from integer-order to fractional-order systems, it is imperative to verify whether a ZBF can be adapted into a Caputo ZBF.

Definition 2. *For CFOS (1) having a set C defined by (2)–(4) with some smooth function $h : \mathbb{R}^n \to \mathbb{R}$, we can consider h as a Caputo zeroing barrier function for the set C, if there exists a locally Lipschitz class $\mathcal{K}$ function β for all $x \in \mathrm{Int}(C)$, we have*

$${}^{C}D^{\alpha}h(x(t)) \geq -\beta(h(x)). \tag{12}$$

Theorem 2. *Given a set $C \subseteq \mathbb{R}^n$ for CFOS (1) with Conditions (2)–(4), there exists a Caputo zeroing barrier function $h : C \to \mathbb{R}$ defined by Definition 2. If so, we can guarantee the set C is forward-invariant and that CFOS (1) is safe for any $x_0 \in \mathrm{Int}(C)$.*

Proof of Theorem 2. Let $B(x) = \frac{1}{h(x)}$. Then, substitute it into (9); hence, $\exists \xi \in [t_0, t]$, such that

$${}^{C}D^{\alpha}\frac{1}{h} = \frac{1}{\Gamma(1-\alpha)}\int_{t_0}^{t}\frac{-\frac{h'(\tau)}{h^2}}{(t-\tau)^{\alpha}}d\tau = \frac{-1}{h^2(\xi)}\int_{t_0}^{t}\frac{h'(\tau)}{(t-\tau)^{\alpha}}d\tau = -h^2(\xi){}^{C}D^{\alpha}h.$$

Thus, with (12) and the proof of Theorem 1, the set C is forward-invariant. And then CFOS (1) is safe. □

In fact, the ZBF is employed to address the robustness of safety. Based on Theorem 2, we need to redefine the safe zone $\mathcal{C}$ by [7]. For any $\forall\delta \geq 0$, there exists a nonempty closed set $\mathcal{C}_\delta$, which is defined as

$$\mathcal{C}_\delta = \{x \in \mathbb{R}^n : h(x) \geq -\delta\}, \tag{13}$$

$$\partial\mathcal{C}_\delta = \{x \in \mathbb{R}^n : h(x) = -\delta\}, \tag{14}$$

$$\text{Int}(\mathcal{C}_\delta) = \{x \in \mathbb{R}^n : h(x) > -\delta\}, \tag{15}$$

where $h : \mathbb{R}^n \to \mathbb{R}$ is continuously differentiable.

Definition 3. *For CFOS* (1) *having a set $\mathcal{C}_\delta$ defined by* (13)–(15) *with some smooth $h : \mathbb{R}^n \to \mathbb{R}$, we can consider h as an extended Caputo zeroing barrier function for the set $\mathcal{C}_\delta$ if there exists a locally Lipschitz extended class $\mathcal{K}$ function (A continuous function $\beta : (-b, a) \to (-\infty, \infty)$ for some $a, b > 0$ is said to belong to* extended class $\mathcal{K}$ *if it is strictly increasing and $\beta(0) = 0$ [7]) γ. Then, for all $x \in \text{Int}(\mathcal{C}_\delta)$, we have*

$$^{C}D^{\alpha}h(x(t)) \geq -\gamma(h(x)). \tag{16}$$

Theorem 3. *Given a set $\mathcal{C}_\delta \subseteq \mathbb{R}^n$ for CFOS* (1) *with Conditions* (13)–(15), *if there exists an extended Caputo zeroing barrier function $h : \mathcal{C}_\delta \to \mathbb{R}$, which is defined by Definition 3, we can guarantee the set $\mathcal{C}_\delta$ is forward-invariant and that CFOS* (1) *can be said to be safe for any $x_0 \in \text{Int}(\mathcal{C}_\delta)$.*

Proof of Theorem 3. Let $l(x) = h(x) + \delta$. Then, the set $\mathcal{C}_\delta$ can transform into the set $\mathcal{C}$. By (16) and leveraging the properties of the extended class $\mathcal{K}$ function, we can obtain

$$^{C}D^{\alpha}l(x(t)) = {}^{C}D^{\alpha}h(x(t)) \geq -\gamma(h(x)) = -\gamma(l(x) - \delta) \geq -\gamma(l(x)).$$

By Theorem 2, we can easily ensure the safe zone $\mathcal{C}_\delta$ with the function is forward-invariant. Hence, CFOS (1) is safe. □

2.3. Comparison

In this study, we introduce two novel concepts of Caputo barrier functions: the Caputo ZBF (CZBF) and the Caputo RBF (CRBF). While the CZBF offers advantages in system safety analysis and controller design due to its computational tractability in practical scenarios, CRBF encounters limitations in real-world applications. Specifically, the derivative calculations required for CRBF implementation demand advanced fractional-order differentiation techniques, which significantly reduce their practical precedence compared to CZBF and other barrier function methodologies [28,29]. This observation highlights that, under fractional-order dynamics, the inherent computational complexity of reciprocal barrier functions is amplified, thereby compromising their operational efficiency relative to alternative safety control approaches.

3. Caputo Stability with Guaranteed Caputo Safety

For dynamic systems across engineering disciplines, safety control plays a fundamental role in ensuring operational integrity. Notwithstanding its importance, safety alone cannot guarantee other desirable properties such as stability, which is particularly critical for industrial systems where stability directly influences product quality consistency. Consequently, this study aims to develop control methodologies that simultaneously maintain both safety and stability for fractional-order systems. To this end, we first established Assumption 1, which provides the foundational conditions for subsequent analysis.

Assumption 1. *Assume the safe-state set $\mathcal{C}$ is a compact and closed (The word "closed" means that the boundary of the set is a closed curve, surface, etc., in a geometric sense) set, and the point $x = 0 \in \mathcal{C}$ is farthest from $\partial\mathcal{C}$.*

In stability theory, the equilibrium point at the origin often serves as a canonical form through the translation of nonzero equilibria or system solutions [30]. In this context, we consider $x_e = 0$ as the point farthest from $\partial\mathcal{C}$, implying $h(0) = \max_{x\in\mathcal{C}} h(x)$. For some systems with $x_e \neq 0$, define $p = x - x_e$. The transformed function $h(x) = h(p + x_e) \triangleq q(p)$ then satisfies $q(0) = \max_{p\in\mathcal{C}_p} q(p)$, where $\mathcal{C} = \{p|p + x_e \in \mathcal{C}\}$. This transformation allows the origin $x = 0$ to act simultaneously as both the equilibrium point and the farthest point relative to the set boundary.

3.1. Uniformly Asymptotic Stability with Guaranteed Caputo Safety

Theorem 4. *For CFOS* (1) *with a set $\mathcal{C}$ satisfying Assumption 1, and which is well defined by* (2)–(4) *for some some function $h : \mathbb{R}^n \to \mathbb{R}$, then, for all $x \in \mathrm{Int}(\mathcal{C}) \setminus \{0\}$, there exists a Caputo barrier function $B : \mathcal{C} \to \mathbb{R}$ satisfying*

$$-\beta_1(h(x)) \leq B(x(t)) \leq -\beta_2(h(x)), \tag{17}$$

$$^{C}D^{\alpha}B(x(t)) \leq \lambda\beta_3(h(x)), \tag{18}$$

with $\beta_1, \beta_2, \beta_3$ being locally Lipschitz class $\mathcal{K}$ functions and $\lambda < 0$. Meanwhile, $x = 0$ also satisfies (17) *but does not satisfy* (18)*, then the set $\mathcal{C}$ is forward-invariant. Hence, CFOS* (1) *is safe and the origin of* (1) *is uniformly asymptotically stable with $x(t_0) = x_0 \in \mathrm{Int}(\mathcal{C}) \setminus \{0\}$.*

Proof of Theorem 4. The proof can be divided by two parts: one to prove the safety and the other to prove stability.

(1) For safety. From (18), set

$$^{C}D^{\alpha}y = \beta_3\left(\beta_2^{-1}(-y)\right) \overset{def}{=} \beta(-y).$$

Hence, by the comparison theorem for fractional-order System [26], we have

$$\inf y(t) \geq B(x(t)).$$

Let $z = -y$, according to Caputo's fractional derivative [26], then we can easily obtain

$$^{C}D^{\alpha}z = {}^{C}D^{\alpha} - y = -\beta(z).$$

This is very similar to Equation (9) in the proof of Theorem 1. Hence, we can also obtain Inequality (10), which is

$$z(t) \leq \sigma(z(t_0), t - t_0)$$

with σ a class $\mathcal{KL}$ function. As $y = -z$, we have

$$\inf y = -\sigma(z(t_0), t - t_0).$$

Due to $B(x(t)) \leq \inf y(t)$, by the comparison theorem for fractional-order System [26], we can obtain

$$B(x(t)) \leq -\sigma(-B(x(t_0)), t - t_0).$$

By (17), then, we have

$$h(x(t)) \geq \beta_1^{-1}(\sigma(-B(x(t_0)), t - t_0))$$

for all $t \in I(x(t_0))$. Moreover, β_1^{-1} is the inverse of β_1 and belongs to class $\mathcal{K}$. As $x(t_0) \in \mathcal{C}$, we have$B(x(t_0)) < 0$. This means that $h(x(t)) \geq 0$ for all $t \in I(x(t_0))$. Thus, $\mathcal{C}$ is forward-invariant and then CFOS (1) is safe.

(2) For stability. By Assumption 1 and (17), $B(x) \geq B(0)$, there hence exists a real constant $b < 0$, such that $b = \operatorname{ess\,inf} B(x) = B(0)$. According to [26], the Lapunov function V needs to be nonnegative; hence, we can set $V(x) = B(x) - b$. Thus, we have

$$^{C}D^{\alpha}V(x(t)) = {}^{C}D^{\alpha}B(x(t)).$$

By (17) and (18), we have

$$-\beta_1(h(x)) - b \leq V \leq -\beta_2(h(x)) - b \tag{19}$$

$$^{C}D^{\alpha}V(x(t)) \leq -\mu\beta_3(h(x)) \tag{20}$$

with $\mu = -\lambda > 0$. Let $W_1(x) = -\beta_1(h(x)) - b$, $W_2(x) = -\beta_2(h(x)) - b$ and $W_3(x) = \mu\beta_3(h(x))$. We can then easily confirm that $W_1(x)$, $W_2(x)$, and $W_3(x)$ are continuous positive definite functions. Now, we can rewrite Inequalities (19) and (20) as follows:

$$W_1(x) \leq V(x(t)) \leq W_2(x) \tag{21}$$

$$^{C}D^{\alpha}V \leq -W_3(x). \tag{22}$$

By Theorem 3.1 ([26]), we can confirm that $x = 0$ is uniformly asymptotical stable.

Together with (1) and (2), Theorem 4 is established. □

3.2. Exponential Stability with Guaranteed Caputo Safety

Theorem 5. *For CFOS* (1) *with a set $\mathcal{C}$ satisfying Assumption 1 and being defined by* (2)–(4) *for some smooth function $h : \mathbb{R}^n \to \mathbb{R}$, for all $x \in \operatorname{Int}(\mathcal{C}) \setminus \{0\}$ and if there exists a lower-bounded Caputo barrier function $B : \mathcal{C} \to \mathbb{R}$ satisfying*

$$-\beta_1(h(x)) \leq B(x(t)) \leq -\beta_2(h(x)), \tag{23}$$

$$^{C}D^{\alpha}B(x(t)) \leq \lambda(c - B(x(t))), \tag{24}$$

where $\beta_1, \beta_2, \beta_3$ are locally Lipschitz class $\mathcal{K}$ functions, c is a constant with $c = \operatorname{ess\,inf} B(x)$, and $\lambda > 0$, then, the set $\mathcal{C}$ is forward-invariant. Hence, CFOS (1) *is safe and the origin of* (1) *is exponentially stable with $x(t_0) = x_0 \in \operatorname{Int}(\mathcal{C}) \setminus \{0\}$.*

Proof of the Theorem 5. The proof also has two parts: first for safety, and then for stability.

(1) For safety. As $c = \operatorname{ess\,inf} B(x)$, then we have $c - B < 0$. According to our previous work ([29], Theorem 1), it can be easily proved that the set $\mathcal{C}$ is forward-invariant and hence CFOS (1) is safe.

(2) For stability. Let $V(x) = B(x) - c.$, then $|V| \leq -c$ is implied. Hence, there exists positive constants c_1, c_2 such that V satisfies $c_1\|x\|^2 \leq V \leq c_2\|x\|^2 < -c$. Then, we have

$$^{C}D^{\alpha}V(x(t)) = {}^{C}D^{\alpha}B(x(t)).$$

Thus, we can obtain

$$\begin{aligned} ^{C}D^{\alpha}V(x(t)) &= {}^{C}D^{\alpha}B(x(t)) \leq \lambda(c - B) \\ &\leq -\lambda V. \end{aligned} \tag{25}$$

Furthermore, (25) is more like Inequality (39) in the proof of Lemma 3.1 [26]. Hence, we can use the Gronwall–Bellman Inequality [32] and obtain the following inequality, which is similar with Inequality (42) in the proof of Lemma 3.1 [26]:

$$\begin{aligned}V(x(t)) &\leq V(x_0) + \frac{-\lambda}{\Gamma(\alpha)}\int_{t_0}^{t}(t-\tau)^{\alpha-1}V(x(t))d\tau \\ &\leq V(x(t_0))\exp\left(\frac{-\lambda(t-t_0)^{\alpha}}{\Gamma(\alpha+1)}\right).\end{aligned}$$

Thus, we have

$$\begin{aligned}\|x\| &\leq \left[\frac{V(x(t))}{c_1}\right]^{\frac{1}{2}} \\ &\leq \left[\frac{V(x(t_0))}{c_1}\exp\left(\frac{-\lambda(t-t_0)^{\alpha}}{\Gamma(\alpha+1)}\right)\right]^{\frac{1}{2}} \\ &\leq \left[\frac{c_2\|x(t_0)\|^2}{c_1}\exp\left(\frac{-\lambda(t-t_0)^{\alpha}}{\Gamma(\alpha+1)}\right)\right]^{\frac{1}{2}} \\ &= \left(\frac{c_2}{c_1}\right)^{\frac{1}{2}}\|x(t_0)\|\exp\left(\frac{-\lambda(t-t_0)^{\alpha}}{2\Gamma(\alpha+1)}\right).\end{aligned} \tag{26}$$

Therefore, the origin $x = 0$ is exponentially stable.

By all of the above, Theorem 5 is proved. □

Remark 2. *The abovementioned two kinds of synchronous Caputo safety and stability are all infinite-time stable. Since the proof of finite time stability under the fractional order is more difficult, we did not conduct in-depth research on synchronous Caputo safety and finite-time stability.*

4. Caputo Input-to-State Safety

For integer-order systems, like the stability, the safety also needs to consider the robustness. And the concept of safety robustness was first discussed in [7]. Following this, M. Z. Romdlony [14] first proposed ISSf to describe the robustness of safety. He mainly established a notion of ISSf under the description of the distance from a point in the safe set to the unsafe set by *less-zero barrier function*. Meanwhile, Shishir Kolathaya [15] used the description function h of the set $\mathcal{C}$ to propose a different notion of ISSf via *zeroing barrier function*. In this section, we will list our latest theoretical research results using Caputo barrier function with respect to Caputo input-to-state safety, and we will then put forward some new notions of ISSf with different descriptions and different barrier functions.

Here, we consider a dynamic system with an additional disturbance:

$${}^{C}D^{\alpha}x = f(x) + g(x)d(t), \tag{27}$$

with disturbance $d \in \mathbb{L}_{\infty}^{m}$. If we involve forward-invariant sets, further interesting conclusions can be made. Here, there is a set $\mathcal{C}$ defined by (2)–(4) for System (1), which is System (27) without disturbance. In addition, there is a slightly larger set $\mathcal{C}_d \supseteq \mathcal{C}$ following the definition in [15] satisfying

$$\mathcal{C}_d = \{x \in \mathbb{R}^n : h(x) + \delta(\|d\|_{\infty}) \geq 0\}, \tag{28}$$

$$\partial\mathcal{C}_d = \{x \in \mathbb{R}^n : h(x) + \delta(\|d\|_{\infty}) = 0\}, \tag{29}$$

$$\text{Int}(\mathcal{C}_d) = \{x \in \mathbb{R}^n : h(x) + \delta(\|d\|_{\infty}) > 0\}, \tag{30}$$

with a class $\mathcal{K}$ function δ in $[0,a)$, $\|d\|_\infty \leq \bar{d} \in [0,a)$. By [15], the set C is called an ISSf set if the set C_d, which depends on d, is forward-invariant. Hence, on the basis of this aforementioned cognition, learning from Definition 4.7 (in [32]), we can obtain the following.

Definition 4. *System (27) with the set C defined by (2)–(4) and the C_d defined by (28)–(30) is said to be Caputo input-to-state safe if there exist a class $\mathcal{KL}$ function σ and a class $\mathcal{K}$ function δ such that, for any initial state $x(t_0)$ and any bounded disturbance $d(t)$, the solution $x(t)$ for all $t \geq t_0$ satisfies*

$$h(x(t)) \geq \sigma(\eta(x(t_0),d), t-t_0) - \delta(\|d\|_\infty), \tag{31}$$

with $\eta(x(t_0),d) = h(x(t_0)) + \delta(\|d\|_\infty)$.

Remark 3. *In addition to the difference between fractional-order and integer-order systems, Definition 4 uses a new way to describe the input-to-state safety. This description is useful to the proofs of the following two theorems.*

When $t \to \infty$, for Inequality (31) and function $\sigma \to 0$, then we have $h(x) \geq -\delta(\|d\|_\infty)$, which produces $h(x) + \delta(\|d\|_\infty) \geq 0$, meaning the solution $x(t)$ is still in set C_d. Hence, Inequality (31) guarantees that, for any bounded disturbance, the set C_d will be forward-invariant all of the time. If $d(t) \equiv 0$, then (31) has

$$h(x(t)) \geq \sigma(h(x(t_0)), t-t_0).$$

This confirms that input-to-state safety implies the set C for the unforced autonomous System (1) without any disturbance is forward-invariant. It is a necessary condition or prerequisite for the establishment of (Caputo) ISSf.

The new question is how to use Definition 4 and how to judge the Caputo ISSf conveniently. We tried to use the Caputo reciprocal barrier function to explore some sufficient conditions for the Caputo ISSf.

Theorem 6. *System (27) is System (1) with the input of bounded disturbance $d(t)$. There are sets C defined by (2)–(4) and C_d defined by (28)–(30) satisfying $C \subseteq C_d$ and their continuously differentiable function $h : \mathbb{R}^n \to \mathbb{R}$. If there exists a Caputo reciprocal barrier function $B : C_d \to \mathbb{R}$, locally Lipschitz class $\mathcal{K}$ functions $\beta_1, \beta_2, \beta_3$, and a class $\mathcal{K}$ function δ, with $\lim_{r \to a} \delta(r) = b$ and b a finite-large real positive constant, such that for all $x(t_0) \in \mathrm{Int}(C_d)$, then the following applies:*

$$\eta(x,d) = h(x) + \delta(\|d\|_\infty), \tag{32}$$

$$\frac{1}{\beta_1(\eta(x,d))} \leq B(x,d) \leq \frac{1}{\beta_2(\eta(x,d))}, \tag{33}$$

$${}^{C}D^{\alpha} B(x,d) \leq \beta_3(\eta(x,d)), \tag{34}$$

where $\|d\|_\infty \in [0,\bar{d}]$. Moreover, with a real positive and finite-large constant $\bar{d}$, System (27) can be said to be (locally) Caputo input-to-state safe, and the function B can be said to be a Caputo input-to-state safe reciprocal barrier function (Caputo ISSf-RBF).

Proof of Theorem 6. First, we need to prove the set C for System (1) is forward-invariant. As such, set $d(t) \equiv 0$; hence, the set C_d is equal to C, and we thus have $\eta(x,d) = h(x)$. By Theorem 1, it can proved that, in this case, the set C is forward-invariant.

Now, we can rewrite (34) as

$${}^{C}D^{\alpha} B \leq \beta_3\left(\beta_2^{-1}\left(\frac{1}{B}\right)\right).$$

By the proof of Theorem 1, we can obtain

$$\eta(x(t), d) \geq \beta_1^{-1}(\phi(\eta(x(t_0), d), t - t_0)) \tag{35}$$

for all $t \in I(x(t_0))$, where ϕ is a class $\mathcal{KL}$ and $I(x(t_0))$ is a maximum time interval. As β_1^{-1} also belongs to class $\mathcal{K}$, then $\beta_1^{-1} \circ \phi$ belongs to class $\mathcal{KL}$. Let $\sigma = \beta_1^{-1} \circ \phi$. Thus, finally, Inequality (35) implies

$$h(x(t)) \geq \sigma(\eta(x(t_0), d), t - t_0) - \delta(\|d\|_\infty).$$

Therefore, this satisfies Inequality (31). By Definition 4, System (27) is input-to-state safe. □

If we use a *Caputo zeroing barrier function*, can we also obtain Inequality (31) in Definition 4?

Theorem 7. *System* (27) *is System* (1) *with the input of bounded disturbance $d(t)$. There are sets C defined by* (2)–(4), *and C_d is defined by* (28)–(30), *satisfying $C \subseteq C_d$. If a continuously differentiable function $h : \mathbb{R}^n \to \mathbb{R}$ for the set C is a zeroing barrier function and there exists a locally Lipschitz class $\mathcal{K}$ function β and a class $\mathcal{K}$ function δ, then, with $\lim_{r \to a} \delta(r) = b$ and b a finite-large real positive constant, there is the following such that, for all $x(t_0) \in \mathrm{Int}(C_d)$, we have*

$$\eta(x, d) = h(x) + \delta(\|d\|_\infty), \tag{36}$$

$$^{C}D^{\alpha}\eta(x, d) \geq -\beta(\eta(x, d)), \tag{37}$$

where $\|d\|_\infty \in [0, \bar{d}]$ has a real positive and finite-large constant $\bar{d}$, and System (27) *can be said to be (locally) Caputo ISSf and the function h can be said to be a Caputo ISSf-ZBF.*

Proof of Theorem 7. Let $B(x, d) = \frac{1}{\eta(x,d)}$. According to the proof of Theorem 2, we have $^{C}D^{\alpha}B(x, d) = -k^{C}D^{\alpha}\eta(x, d)$ with a constant $k > 0$. Thus, (37) can be rewritten as $^{C}D^{\alpha}B(x, d) \leq k\beta(\eta(x, d))$. As such, this satisfies Theorem 6. Then, we can obtain that the following Inequality (38) by (35) is

$$\eta(x(t), d) \geq \sigma(\eta(x(t_0)), t - t_0), \tag{38}$$

where σ belongs to class $\mathcal{KL}$. Substituting (36) into (38), we can obtain

$$h(x(t)) + \delta(\|d\|_\infty) \geq \sigma(h(x(t_0)) + \delta(\|d\|_\infty), t - t_0)$$
$$\Rightarrow h(x(t)) \geq \sigma(h(x(t_0)) + \delta(\|d\|_\infty), t - t_0) - \delta(\|d\|_\infty).$$

Therefore, by Definition 4, System (27) is Caputo input-to-state safe. □

5. Conclusions

This article established two novel Caputo barrier functions and employed them to derive corresponding safety criteria for a class of Caputo fractional-order systems (CFOSs). Additionally, synchronous safety-stability theorems were proposed for CFOSs under these barrier function frameworks. Finally, the concept of Caputo input-to-state safe barrier functions was introduced to analyze input-to-state safety properties. The key contributions and considerations are summarized as follows.

(1) While CRBFs ensure the forward invariance of the set C for CFOSs, thereby guaranteeing system safety, a significant limitation arises: the computational complexity inherent in fractional-order differentiation makes CRBFs less tractable for real-world safety control applications compared to their integer-order counterparts. This short-

coming stems from the nonlocal nature of fractional derivatives, which complicates barrier function implementation under Caputo dynamics.

(2) We renewed the description of ISSf based on [15] and then established two theorems of ISSf via using Caputo RBF and Caputo ZBF, respectively, which can be used to more conveniently achieve the analysis and control of Caputo ISSf.

Since this article and our two previous works [28,29] jointly established a theoretical framework of Caputo safety for CFOSs, future work will focus on the applications of the proposed methods to practical cases.

Author Contributions: Direction, Z.Z., Y.C. and Z.S.; methodology, Z.Z., B.S. and L.Y.; writing—original draft preparation, Z.Z.; writing—review and editing, L.Y. All authors have read and agreed to the published version of the manuscript.

Funding: This work was supported by the National Natural Science Foundation of China (Grant Nos. 62403416, 61933013, and U2034209).

Data Availability Statement: The original contributions presented in the study are included in the article, further inquiries can be directed to the corresponding author.

Conflicts of Interest: There are no conflicts of interest for this article.

References

1. Prajna, S.; Rantzer, A. On the necessity of barrier certificates. *IFAC Proc. Vol.* **2005**, *38*, 526–531. [CrossRef]
2. Kong, H.; Song, X.; Han, D.; Gu, M.; Sun J. A New Barrier Certificate for safety verification of hybrid systems. *Comput. J.* **2014**, *57*, 1033–1045.
3. Zhu, Z.; Chai, Y.; Yang, Z.; Huang C. Exponential-alpha safety criteria of a class of dynamic systems with barrier functions. *IEEE-CAA J. Autom. Sin.* **2022**, *9*, 1939–1951.
4. Dai, L.; Gan, T.; Xia, B.; Zhan, N. Barrier certificates revisited. *J. Symb. Comput.* **2017**, *80*, 62–86.
5. Ames, A.; Grizzle J.; Tabuada, P. Control barrier function based quadratic programs with application to adaptive cruise control. In Proceedings of the 2014 IEEE 53rd Annual Conference on Decision and Control (CDC), Los Angeles, CA, USA, 15–17 December 2014.
6. Ames, A.; Xu, X.; Grizzle J.; Tabuada, P. Control barrier function based quadratic programs for safety critical systems. *IEEE Trans. Autom. Control* **2017**, *62*, 3861–3876.
7. Xu, X.; Tabuada, P.; Grizzle, J.; Ames A. Robustness of control barrier functions for safety critical control. *IFAC Pap. Online* **2015**, *48*, 54–61.
8. Sogokon, A.; Ghorbal, K.; Tan, Y.; Platzer, A. Vector barrier certificates and comparison systems *Lect. Notes Comput. Sci.* **2018**, *10951*, 418–437.
9. Zhu, Z.; Chai, Y.; Yang, Z. A novel kind of sufficient conditions for safety criterion based on control barrier function. *Sci. China Inf. Sci.* **2021**, *64*, 199205.
10. Zhu, Z.; Chai, Y.; Yang, Z.; Huang, C. Safety criteria based on barrier function under the framework of boundedness for some dynamic systems. *Sci. China Inf. Sci.* **2022**, *65*, 122203.
11. Wisniewski, R.; Sloth, C. Converse Barrier Certificate Theorems. *IEEE Trans. Autom. Control* **2016**, *61*, 1356–1361.
12. Ratschan, S. Converse Theorems for Safety and Barrier Certificates. *IEEE Trans. Autom. Control* **2018**, *63*, 2628–2632.
13. Romdlony, M.; Jayawardhana, B. Stabilization with guaranteed safety using control lyapunov-barrier function. *Automatica* **2016**, *66*, 39–47.
14. Romdlony, M.; Jayawardhana, B. On the new notion of Input-to-State Safety. In Proceedings of the 2016 IEEE 55th Conference on Decision and Control (CDC), Las Vegas, NV, USA, 12–14 December 2016.
15. Kolathaya, S.; Ames, A. Input-to-State Safety With Control Barrier Functions. *IEEE Control Syst. Lett.* **2019**, *3*, 108–113.
16. Prajna, S.; Jadbabaie, A.; Pappas, G. Stochastic safety verification using barrier certificates. In Proceedings of the 2004 43rd IEEE Conference on Decision and Control (CDC) (IEEE Cat. No. 04CH37601), Nassau, Bahamas, 14–17 December 2004.
17. Glotfelter, P.; Cortés, J.; Egerstedt, M. Nonsmooth barrier functions with applications to multi-robot systems. *IEEE Control Syst. Lett.* **2017**, *1*, 310–315.
18. Borrmann, U.; Wang, L.; Ames, A.; Egerstedt, M. Control barrier certificates for safe swarm behavior. *IFAC Pap. Online* **2015**, *48*, 68–73.
19. Wang, L.; Ames, A.; Egerstedt, M. Safety barrier certificates for collisions-free multirobot systems. *IEEE Trans. Robot.* **2017**, *33*, 661–674.

20. Wang, L.; Ames, A.; Egerstedt, M. Safety barrier certificates for heterogeneous multi-robot systems. In Proceedings of the 2016 American Control Conference (ACC), Boston, MA, USA, 6–8 July 2016.
21. Ma, H.; Ren, H.; Zhou, Q.; Li, H.; Wang, Z. Observer-based neural control of n-link flexible-joint robots. *IEEE Trans. Neural Netw. Learn. Syst.* **2024**, *35*, 5295–5305.
22. Ren, H.; Zhang, C.; Ma, H.; Li, H. Cloud-based distributed group asynchronous consensus for switched nonlinear cyber-physical systems. *IEEE Trans. Ind. Inform.* **2025**, *21*, 693–702.
23. Zhang, C.; Yang, H.; Jiang, B. Fault Estimation and Accommodation of Fractional-Order Nonlinear, Switched, and Interconnected Systems. *IEEE Trans. Cybern.* **2022**, *52*, 1443–1453.
24. Makhlouf, A.B.; Naifar, O. On the Barbalat lemma extension for the generalized conformable fractional integrals: Application to adaptive observer design. *Asian J. Control* **2023**, *25*, 563–569.
25. Yu, J.; Hu, C.; Jiang, H. α-stability and α-synchronization for fractional-order neural networks. *Neural Netw.* **2012**, *35*, 82–87. [CrossRef]
26. Delavari, H.; Baleanu, D.; Sadati, J. Stability analysis of Caputo fractional-order nonlinear systems revisited. *Nonlinear Dyn.* **2012**, *67*, 2433–2439. [CrossRef]
27. Kilbas, A.; Srivastava, H.; Trujillo, J. *Theory and Applications of Fractional Differentiable Equations;* Elsevier: Amsterdam, The Netherlands, 2006.
28. Zhu, Z.; Huang, P.; Zhang, X.; Chai, Y.; Song, Z. First attempt of barrier functions for Caputo's fractional-order nonlinear dynamical systems. *Sci. China Inf. Sci.* **2022**, *66*, 179205. [CrossRef]
29. Zhu, Z.; Liu, N.; Zhang, X.; Song, Z.; Chai, Y. A Novel Attempt of Barrier Function to the Safety of Caputo's fractional-order systems. In Proceedings of the 2022 8th International Conference on Control, Decision and Information Technologies (CoDIT 22), Istanbul, Turkey, 17–20 May 2022.
30. Khalil, H. *Nonlinear Systems*, 3rd ed.; Prentice Hall: Englewood Cliffs, NJ, USA, 2002.
31. Bihari, I. A generalization of a lemma of bellman and its application to uniqueness problems of differentiable equations. *Acta Math. Acad. Sci. Hung.* **1956**, *7*, 81–94. [CrossRef]
32. Slotine, J.; Li, W. *Applied Nonlinear Control;* Prentice Hall: Englewood Cliffs, NJ, USA, 1991.

mathematics MDPI

Article

Explicit Form of Solutions of Second-Order Delayed Difference Equations: Application to Iterative Learning Control

Nazim I. Mahmudov [1,2,*], Muath Awadalla [3,*] and Meraa Arab [3]

1 Department of Mathematics, Eastern Mediterranean University, T.R. North Cyprus Mersin 10, Famagusta 99628, Turkey
2 Research Center of Econophysics, Azerbaijan State University of Economics (UNEC), Istiqlaliyyat Str. 6, Baku 1001, Azerbaijan
3 Department of Mathematics and Statistics, College of Science, King Faisal University, Hofuf 31982, Al Ahsa, Saudi Arabia; marab@kfu.edu.sa
* Correspondence: nazim.mahmudov@emu.edu.tr (N.I.M.); mawadalla@kfu.edu.sa (M.A.)

Abstract: A system of inhomogeneous second-order difference equations with linear parts given by noncommutative matrix coefficients are considered. The closed form of its solution is derived by means of a newly defined delayed matrix sine/cosine using the $\mathcal{Z}$ transform and determining function. This representation helps with analyzing iterative learning control by applying appropriate updating laws and ensuring sufficient conditions for achieving asymptotic convergence in tracking.

Keywords: second-order difference; $\mathcal{Z}$ transform; iterative learning control

MSC: 39A06; 93C55; 93C40

1. Introduction

Second-order delayed difference equations are crucial in real-world applications because they model dynamic systems where the future state depends not only on the current and past states but also on delayed interactions. These equations arise in various domains, including population dynamics, where they are used to model species growth with delayed responses due to gestation or maturation periods; economic systems, being applied in financial markets and supply chain modeling where past fluctuations influence current trends; engineering and control systems, where they are found in signal processing, vibration analysis, and control systems where delays affect stability and performance; epidemiology, being used to model the spread of diseases where incubation periods and immunity delays play a role.

The proposed method improves upon existing techniques in several ways:

Enhanced stability analysis—it provides new stability criteria that better capture the effects of delays, reducing uncertainties in predictions; Higher computational efficiency—the method optimizes numerical computations, allowing for faster simulations and real-time applications; Broader applicability—it extends to more complex and nonlinear systems, making it useful for modeling real-world phenomena with varying delay structures; Improved accuracy—by refining approximation methods or incorporating machine learning techniques, the approach yields more precise solutions. These advancements contribute to more reliable modeling, better decision making, and improved system performance across multiple disciplines.

The proposed method may face significant challenges when dealing with singular matrices or nonpermutable coefficients due to the following reasons:

Limitations exist in handling singular matrices. Singular matrices lack an inverse, which can hinder solving linear systems directly. Many numerical techniques, including those used for stability analysis and iterative solutions, rely on matrix inversion or decomposition, which fails in the singular case. This limitation restricts the method's applicability to systems where the coefficient matrices are nonsingular or can be regularized (e.g., by perturbation methods or pseudo-inverses). There are limitations with nonpermutable coefficients. If the system involves coefficients that do not commute under multiplication (e.g., in noncommutative algebra or certain coupled systems), traditional solution techniques may not directly apply. Many iterative or closed-form solutions assume a structure that allows for the reordering of terms, which may not hold in these cases. This constraint affects applications in quantum mechanics, advanced control systems, and coupled network dynamics where nonpermutable interactions are essential. The method remains effective for a broad class of second-order delayed difference equations with well-conditioned coefficient structures. For singular matrices, alternative techniques like regularization, generalized inverses, or alternative formulations may be necessary. For nonpermutable coefficients, more advanced algebraic methods or computational techniques may need to be incorporated, potentially requiring significant modifications to the proposed approach. If these extensions are not currently feasible, it should be explicitly stated that the method is best suited for nonsingular, permutable coefficient systems, and potential workarounds or future research directions should be proposed.

The proposed method can be highly beneficial in ILC systems, where tasks are performed repeatedly, and performance is improved over iterations by learning from past errors. Below are concrete examples where the method could be applied:

- Trajectory tracking in robotics: in robotic arms used for precision tasks (e.g., surgical robots, automated welding arms), trajectory tracking is critical.
- ILC is often used to refine movement paths over successive iterations, compensating for dynamic disturbances and model inaccuracies.
- The second-order delayed difference equation framework models the system's response more accurately, accounting for actuator delays and sensor latencies.
- The improved stability analysis ensures better convergence of the learning process, reducing oscillations or divergence issues in robot movements.
- Compared to traditional ILC methods, this approach can handle systems with more complex dynamics and variable delays, leading to faster convergence and smoother trajectory tracking.

By leveraging the proposed method, industries relying on precision control, automation, and iterative improvements can achieve higher accuracy, efficiency, and adaptability, making it a significant advancement in ILC applications.

In what follows, we use the following notations:

- Θ is a zero matrix, and I is an identity matrix;
- $Z_a^b := \{a, a+1, ..., b\}$ for $a, b \in Z \cup \{\pm\infty\}$, $a \leq b$;
- $\mathbb{M}_{r\times p}$ is the space of $r \times p$ matrices;
- An empty sum $\sum\limits_{i=a}^{b} z(i) = 0$, and an empty product $\prod\limits_{i=a}^{b} z(i) = 1$ for integers $a < b$, where $z(i)$ is a given function that does not have to be defined for each $i \in Z_b^a$ in this case;
- $x(t+1) - x(t) =: \Delta x(t)$ is the forward difference operator;
- $x(t+2) - 2x(t+1) + x(t) =: \Delta^2 x(t)$.

Iterative learning control (ILC) is a control strategy used for systems that perform the same task repeatedly. It improves performance over iterations by learning from previous executions. The idea is to adjust the control input based on errors from past trials, refining it until the desired performance is achieved.

Key Concepts of ILC

- Repetitive tasks: ILC is useful in systems where the same task is performed multiple times, such as robotic arms, industrial automation, and medical rehabilitation devices.
- Error correction: the controller updates the input signal for the next iteration based on the difference between the desired and actual output from the previous iteration.
- Feedforward control: unlike traditional feedback control, ILC predicts and compensates for errors before they occur in future iterations.
- Convergence: a well-designed ILC algorithm ensures that the system output approaches the desired output over iterations.

General ILC Algorithm

The control input for iteration $k+1$ is updated as

$$u_{k+1}(t) = u_k(t) + Le_k(t)$$

where $u_k(t)$ is the control input at iteration k, $e_k(t)$ is the error at iteration k (the difference between the desired and actual output), and L is the learning filter or gain.

Applications of ILC

- Robotics: improving precision in repetitive tasks.
- Industrial automation: enhancing accuracy in machining and assembly lines.
- Medical applications: assisting in rehabilitation by improving repetitive movements.
- Motion control: used in servo systems to improve trajectory tracking.

ILC is a powerful control strategy designed for dynamic systems that operate repetitively over a finite time interval. It has been successfully implemented in various practical applications, including robotics, chemical batch processes, and hard disk drive systems, as highlighted in References [1–4] and the works cited therein.

In recent years, considerable attention has been given to the iterative learning control and robust control of discrete systems by many researchers. Notably, Li et al. [5] investigated ILC for linear continuous systems with time delays using two-dimensional system theory. Similarly, Wan [6] studied ILC for two-dimensional discrete systems under a general model. Extensive research on ILC for discrete systems has often been carried out by analyzing a constructed Roesser model, as demonstrated in References [5–8]. To the best of our knowledge, the application of the Roesser model to ILC for discrete systems was initially explored in Reference [2].

Approximately two decades ago, Diblik and Khusainov [9,10] introduced explicit representations for solutions to discrete linear systems with a single pure delay using delayed discrete exponential matrices. Later, Khusainov et al. [11] extended this approach to derive analytical solutions for oscillatory second-order systems with pure delays by introducing delayed discrete sine and cosine matrices. These pioneering contributions spurred significant advancements in the analytical solutions of retarded integer and fractional differential equations, as well as delayed discrete systems, as seen in References [12–15]. Building on these results, Diblik and Morçivkova [16,17] extended the analysis to discrete linear systems with two pure delays, while Pospişil [18] applied the $\mathcal{Z}$ transform to address multi-delayed systems with linear components represented by permutable matrix coefficients. In 2018, Mahmudov [19] provided explicit solutions for discrete linear delayed systems with nonconstant coefficients and nonpermutable matrices, including first-order differences. Mahmudov [20] later generalized these findings, removing the singularity condition on the non-delayed coefficient matrix and deriving explicit solutions using the $\mathcal{Z}$

transform. Furthermore, Diblik and Mencakova [12] presented closed-form solutions for purely delayed discrete linear systems with second-order differences, while Elshenhab and Wang [21] recently addressed explicit representations for second-order difference systems with multiple pure delays and noncommutative coefficient matrices.

These studies have yielded numerous insights into the qualitative theory of discrete delay systems, encompassing stability analysis, optimal control theory, and iterative learning control, as highlighted in References [22–27].

Although significant progress has been made in studying linear discrete systems and linear delayed discrete systems, research on iterative learning control for delayed linear discrete systems with higher-order differences remains limited. Notable examples include References [6,7], with only a few works addressing delayed linear discrete systems with higher-order differences through the construction of delayed discrete matrix functions.

Therefore, motivated by [12,19,21], we consider an explicit representation of solutions of the following discrete second-order systems with a single delay:

$$\Delta^2 y(t) + Ay(t) + By(t-m) = f(t), \quad t \in \mathbb{Z}_0^\infty, \ m \in \mathbb{Z}_1^\infty \tag{1}$$

where m is a delay, $A, B \in \mathbb{M}_{d\times d}$, $y : \mathbb{Z}_{-m}^\infty \to \mathbb{R}^d$ is a solution, and $f : \mathbb{Z}_0^\infty \to \mathbb{R}^d$ is a function.

Let $\varphi : \mathbb{Z}_{-m}^1 \to \mathbb{R}^d$ be a function. We attach to (1) the following initial conditions:

$$y(t) = \varphi(t), \quad t \in \mathbb{Z}_{-m}^1. \tag{2}$$

It is well known that the initial value problem (1) and (2) has a unique solution in $\mathbb{Z}_{-m}^\infty$.

More precisely, we study the iterative learning control problem for delayed linear discrete systems with a second-order difference as follows:

$$\begin{cases} \Delta^2 y_k(t) + Ay_k(t) + By_k(t-m) = Fu_k(t), & t \in \mathbb{Z}_0^T, \ k \in \mathbb{Z}_1^\infty, \\ y_k(t) = \varphi(t), & t \in \mathbb{Z}_{-m}^1, \\ z_k(t) = Cy_k(t) + Du_k(t), \end{cases} \tag{3}$$

where k denotes the kth iteration, T is a given fixed positive integer, $y_k(\cdot) : \mathbb{Z}_{-m}^T \to \mathbb{R}^d$ denotes the state, $u_k(\cdot) : \mathbb{Z}_0^T \to \mathbb{R}^r$ denotes the dominant input, and $z_k(\cdot) : \mathbb{Z}_0^T \to \mathbb{R}^p$ denotes the output. $A, B \in \mathbb{M}_{d\times d}$, $F \in \mathbb{M}_{r\times d}$, $C \in \mathbb{M}_{d\times p}$, $D \in \mathbb{M}_{r\times p}$ are constant matrices.

Here is a summary of the key contributions:

- This work introduces new delayed discrete matrix functions, which are regarded as extensions of the sine and cosine functions.
- New representation of solutions: This work proposes a new representation for the solutions for the second-order delay difference equations with noncommutative matrices. This representation is likely used in various aspects of this paper, including deriving the prior estimation of the state. This representation is new even for the second-order difference equations with commutative matrices.
- Application to convergence laws and iterative learning control: the new solution representations are applied to derive convergence laws for ILC systems, providing insights into the convergence behavior of the system via the proposed iterative learning control updating laws.
- Extension of ILC problems: this work extends iterative learning control to address problems involving second-order delay difference equations with noncommutative matrices, potentially presenting new methods or solutions for ILC in these contexts.

2. Delayed Discrete Matrix Sine/Cosine

One of the tools in this study is the $\mathcal{Z}$ transform, defined as

$$\mathcal{Z}\{f(t)\}(z) = \sum_{t=0}^{\infty} \frac{f(t)}{z^t} \quad \text{for} z \in \mathbb{R}.$$

$\mathcal{Z}$ transform is considered component-wisely, i.e., the $\mathcal{Z}$ transform of a vector-valued function is a vector of $\mathcal{Z}$-transformed coordinates.

Definition 1. *We say that the function $f : \mathbb{Z}_0^\infty \to \mathbb{R}^d$ is exponentially bounded if there exists $b_1, b_2 > 0$ such that*

$$\|f(t)\| \le b_1 b_2^t \quad \text{for} \ t \in \mathbb{Z}_0^\infty.$$

Lemma 1. *The $\mathcal{Z}$ transform $\mathcal{Z}\{f(t)\}(z)$ of exponentially bounded function $f : \mathbb{Z}_0^\infty \to \mathbb{R}^d$ exists for all sufficiently large z.*

The next lemma provides some features of the $\mathcal{Z}$ transform.

Lemma 2. *Assume that $f_1, f_2 : \mathbb{Z}_0^\infty \to \mathbb{R}^d$ are exponentially bounded functions. Then, for sufficiently large $z \in \mathbb{R}$, we have*

1. $\mathcal{Z}\{af_1(t) + bf_2(t)\} = a\mathcal{Z}\{f_1(t)\} + b\mathcal{Z}\{f_2(t)\}, \quad a, b \in \mathbb{R};$
2. $\mathcal{Z}^{-1}\left\{z^{-l}\right\}(t) = \delta(l, t)$ *for* $l \in Z_0^\infty$, *where δ is the Kroneker delta,*

$$\delta(l,t) = \begin{cases} 1, & t = l, \\ 0, & t \neq l. \end{cases}$$

3. $\mathcal{Z}^{-1}\{F_1(z)F_2(z)\}(t) = (f_1 * f_2)(t)$. *Here, the convolution operation $*$ is defined by*

$$(f * g)(t) = \sum_{j=0}^{t} f(j)g(t-j);$$

4. $\mathcal{Z}^{-1}\{\frac{z}{z-1}\}(t) = \sigma(t)$ *for $z > 1$; here, σ is the step function, defined as*

$$\sigma(t) = \begin{cases} 1, & t \ge 0, \\ 0, & t < 0. \end{cases}$$

5. $\mathcal{Z}^{-1}\left\{\frac{1}{(z-1)^l}\right\}(t) = \begin{pmatrix} t-1 \\ l-1 \end{pmatrix} \sigma(t-l), l \in \mathbb{Z}_0^\infty.$
6. $\mathcal{Z}\{f_1(t+n)\} = z^n \mathcal{Z}\{f_1(t)\} - \sum_{j=0}^{n-1} f_1(j) z^{n-j}, n \in \mathbb{Z}_0^\infty.$

We introduce the determining matrix equation for $Q(t;s), t = 1, 2, \ldots$

$$Q(t+1;s) = AQ(t;s) + BQ(t;s-1),$$
$$Q(0;s) = \begin{pmatrix} 0 & 0 \\ 0 & 0 \end{pmatrix}, \ Q(1;0) = \begin{pmatrix} 1 & 0 \\ 0 & 1 \end{pmatrix},$$
$$t = 1, 2, \ldots 10, \ s = 1, 2, ..10.$$

where I is an identity matrix; Θ is a zero matrix.

Remark 1. *1. Simple calculations show that*

	$s=0$	$s=1$	$s=2$	$s=3$	$\cdots$	$s=p$
$Q(1;s)$	I	Θ	Θ	Θ	$\cdots$	Θ
$Q(2;s)$	A	B	Θ	Θ	$\cdots$	Θ
$Q(3;s)$	A^2	$AB+BA$	B^2	Θ	$\cdots$	Θ
$Q(4;s)$	A^3	$A(AB+BA)+BA^2$	$AB^2+B(AB+BA)$	B^3	$\cdots$	
$\cdots$	$\cdots$	$\cdots$	$\cdots$		$\cdots$	Θ
$Q(p+1;s)$	A^p	$\cdots$	$\cdots$	$\cdots$	$\cdots$	B^p
$\vdots$	$\vdots$	$\vdots$	$\vdots$	$\vdots$	$\vdots$	$\ddots$

(4)

2. *If A and B are commutative, that is, $AB = BA$, we have*

$$Q(t+1;j) = \binom{t}{j} A^{t-j} B^j \sigma(t-j).$$

3. *If $A = \Theta$, then*

$$Q(t+1;j) = \begin{cases} \Theta, & t+1 \neq j, \\ B^j, & t+1 = j. \end{cases}.$$

Definition 2. *The delayed discrete matrix $M_c(t,A,m)$ is defined as*

$$M_c(t,A,m) := \begin{cases} \Theta, & \text{if } t \in \mathbb{Z}_{-\infty}^{-m-1}, \\ I, & \text{if } t \in \mathbb{Z}_{-m}^{1}, \\ I - A\binom{t}{2} + A^2\binom{t-m}{4} - \cdots + (-1)^l A^l \binom{t-(l-1)m}{2l}, & \text{if } t \in \mathbb{Z}_{(l-1)(m+2)+2}^{l(m+2)+1}, \; l = 0,1,2,\ldots. \end{cases}$$

Here,

- *Θ represents the zero matrix.*
- *I is the identity matrix.*
- *$\binom{a}{b}$ denotes the binomial coefficient, defined as $\binom{a}{b} = \frac{a!}{b!(a-b)!}$, with $\binom{a}{b} = 0$ if $b > a$ or $a < 0$.*

Definition 3 ([12]). *The delayed discrete matrix $M_s(t,A,m)$ is defined as*

$$M_s(t,A,m) := \begin{cases} \Theta, & \text{if } t \in \mathbb{Z}_{-\infty}^{-m}, \\ I\binom{t+m}{1}, & \text{if } t \in \mathbb{Z}_{-m+1}^{2}, \\ I\binom{t+m}{1} - A\binom{t}{3} + A^2\binom{t-m}{5} - \cdots + (-1)^l A^l \binom{t-(l-1)m}{2l+1}, & \text{if } t \in \mathbb{Z}_{(l-1)(m+2)+3}^{l(m+2)+2}, \; l = 0,1,2,\ldots. \end{cases}$$

Definition 4 ([12]). *The delayed discrete matrix sine/cosine is defined as follows:*

$$Sin^{A,B}(t) := \sum_{l=0}^{\lfloor \frac{t-1}{m+2} \rfloor} \sum_{0 \le i \le l} (-1)^l \binom{t-im}{2l+1} Q(l+1;i) : \mathbb{Z}_0^{\infty} \to \mathbb{M}_{n\times n},$$

$$Cos^{A,B}(t) := \sum_{l=0}^{\lfloor \frac{t}{m+2} \rfloor} \sum_{0 \le i \le l} (-1)^l \binom{t-im}{2l} Q(l+1;i) : \mathbb{Z}_0^{\infty} \to \mathbb{M}_{n\times n}.$$

Remark 2. *If $A = \Theta$, then*

$$Sin^{\Theta,B}(t+m) := \sum_{l=0}^{\lfloor \frac{t+m-1}{m+2} \rfloor} (-1)^l \begin{pmatrix} t+m-lm \\ 2l+1 \end{pmatrix} B^l = M_s(t,B,m),$$

$$Cos^{\Theta,B}(t+m) := \sum_{l=0}^{\lfloor \frac{t+m}{m+2} \rfloor} (-1)^l \begin{pmatrix} t+m-lm \\ 2l \end{pmatrix} B^l = M_c(t,B,m).$$

Lemma 3 (Binomial formula for noncommutative matrices). *Let $A, B \in \mathbb{M}_{d\times d}$ be two non-commutative matrices. Then, for any $t \in \mathbb{Z}_0^\infty$, we have*

$$(A+B)^t = \sum_{i=0}^{t} Q(t+1;i). \tag{5}$$

Proof. From Equation (4), it can be easily seen that for $t = 0,1,2$ the identity (5) is true. Now, we use induction; assuming that (5) is true for $t = n$, we prove it for $t = n+1$:

$$\begin{aligned}
(A+B)^{n+1} &= (A+B)\sum_{i=0}^{n} Q(n+1;i) \\
&= \sum_{i=0}^{n} AQ(n+1;i) + \sum_{i=0}^{n} BQ(n+1;i) \\
&= \sum_{i=0}^{n} AQ(n+1;i) + \sum_{i=1}^{n+1} BQ(n+1;i-1) \\
&= \sum_{i=0}^{n+1} A[Q(n+1;i) + BQ(n+1;i-1)] \\
&= \sum_{i=0}^{n+1} Q(n+2;i).
\end{aligned}$$

Here, we used the property $Q(n+1;n+1) = \Theta = Q(n+1;-1)$. □

Lemma 4 (Gronwall inequality [28]). *Let*

$$y(t) \le b(t) + a(t)\sum_{j=0}^{t-1} f(j)y(j), \quad t \in \mathbb{Z}_0^\infty.$$

Then,

$$y(t) \le b(t) + a(t)\sum_{j=0}^{t-1} b(j)f(j) \prod_{i=j+1}^{t-1} (1 + a(j)f(i)), \quad t \in \mathbb{Z}_0^\infty.$$

Lemma 5. *For any $t \in \mathbb{Z}_0^\infty$, we have the following identities:*

$$(A + B\sigma^{-m})^t = \sum_{\substack{i(m+1)\leq t\\ i\geq 0}} Q(t+1-im;i),$$

$$(A + Bz^{-m})^t = \sum_{\substack{i(m+1)\leq t\\ i\geq 0}} z^{-im} Q(t+1;i).$$

$$\mathcal{Z}^{-1}\left\{\left((z-1)^2 + A + \frac{B}{z^m}\right)^{-1}\right\} = \sum_{l=0}^{\infty}\sum_{0\leq i\leq l} (-1)^l \binom{t-im-1}{2l+1} Q(l+1;i),$$

$$\mathcal{Z}^{-1}\left\{\frac{1}{z^{j+m}}\left((z-1)^2 + A + \frac{B}{z^m}\right)^{-1}\right\} = \sum_{l=0}^{\infty}\sum_{0\leq i\leq l} (-1)^l \binom{t-j-m-im-1}{2l+1} Q(l+1;i),$$

$$\mathcal{Z}^{-1}\left\{z(z-1)\left((z-1)^2 + A + \frac{B}{z^m}\right)^{-1}\right\} = \sum_{l=0}^{\infty}\sum_{0\leq i\leq l} (-1)^l \binom{t-im}{2l} Q(l+1;i).$$

Proof. The first two identities follow from Lemma 3. We start with the identity

$$(I-C)^j \sum_{t=0}^{\infty} \binom{t+j-1}{j-1} C^t = I, \quad \text{where } \|C\| < 1.$$

For sufficiently large $z \in \mathbb{R}$, such that

$$\left\|\frac{A}{(z-1)^2} + \frac{B}{z^m(z-1)^2}\right\| < 1,$$

we derive

$$\begin{aligned}
\left(z^2 - 2z + 1 + A + \frac{B}{z^m}\right)^{-1} &= \frac{1}{(z-1)^2}\left(I + \frac{A}{(z-1)^2} + \frac{B}{z^m(z-1)^2}\right)^{-1} \\
&= \frac{1}{(z-1)^2}\sum_{j=0}^{\infty}(-1)^j\left(\frac{A}{(z-1)^2} + \frac{B}{z^m(z-1)^2}\right)^j \\
&= \frac{1}{(z-1)^2}\sum_{t=0}^{\infty}\frac{(-1)^t}{(z-1)^{2t}}\left(A + \frac{1}{z^m}B\right)^t.
\end{aligned}$$

Next, we use the formulas

$$(A + Bz^{-m})^t = \sum_{0\leq i\leq t} z^{-im} Q(t+1;i),$$

$$\sum_{j=0}^{t} \delta(im,j)\binom{t-j-1}{2l+1} = \binom{t-im-1}{2l+1},$$

and

$$\delta(j+m+im,t) * \binom{t-1}{2l-1} = \binom{t-j-m-im-1}{2l-1}.$$

Now, consider the inverse $\mathcal{Z}$ transform of the original series:

$$\begin{aligned}\mathcal{Z}^{-1}\left\{\frac{1}{(z-1)^2}\sum_{l=0}^{\infty}\frac{(-1)^l}{(z-1)^{2l}}\left(A+\frac{1}{z^m}B\right)^l\right\} &= \sum_{l=0}^{\infty}\mathcal{Z}^{-1}\left\{\frac{(-1)^l}{(z-1)^{2l+2}}\left(A+\frac{1}{z^m}B\right)^l\right\}\\ &= \sum_{l=0}^{\infty}\mathcal{Z}^{-1}\left\{\sum_{0\le i\le l}\frac{(-1)^l}{z^{im}(z-1)^{2l+2}}Q(l+1;i)\right\}\\ &= \sum_{l=0}^{\infty}\sum_{0\le i\le l}(-1)^t\delta(im,t)*\binom{t-1}{2l+1}Q(l+1;i)\\ &= \sum_{l=0}^{\infty}\sum_{0\le i\le l}(-1)^l\binom{t-im-1}{2l+1}Q(l+1;i).\end{aligned}$$

Using similar steps for $A_j(t)$, we find

$$\begin{aligned}A_j(t) &= \mathcal{Z}^{-1}\left\{\frac{1}{z^{j+m}}\left((z-1)^2+A+\frac{B}{z^m}\right)^{-1}\right\}\\ &= \sum_{l=0}^{\infty}\sum_{0\le i\le l}(-1)^l\delta(j+m+im,t)*\binom{t-1}{2l+1}Q(l+1;i)\\ &= \sum_{l=0}^{\infty}\sum_{0\le i\le l}(-1)^l\binom{t-j-m-im-1}{2l+1}Q(l+1;i).\end{aligned}$$

For the third $\mathcal{Z}^{-1}$ transform, we have

$$\begin{aligned}\mathcal{Z}^{-1}\left\{\frac{z}{z-1}\sum_{l=0}^{\infty}\frac{(-1)^l}{(z-1)^{2l}}\left(A+\frac{1}{z^m}B\right)^l\right\} &= \sum_{l=0}^{\infty}\mathcal{Z}^{-1}\left\{\frac{(-1)^l}{(z-1)^{2l+1}}\left(A+\frac{1}{z^m}B\right)^l\right\}\\ &= \sum_{l=0}^{\infty}\sum_{0\le i\le l}(-1)^l\mathcal{Z}^{-1}\left\{\frac{1}{z^{im-1}(z-1)^{2l+1}}\right\}Q(l+1;i)\\ &= \sum_{l=0}^{\infty}\sum_{0\le i\le l}(-1)^l\delta(im-1,t)*\binom{t-1}{2l}Q(l+1;i)\\ &= \sum_{l=0}^{\infty}\sum_{0\le i\le l}(-1)^l\binom{t-im}{2l}Q(l+1;i).\end{aligned}$$

□

Definition 5. *The delayed discrete matrix sine/cosine is defined as follows:*

$$Sin^{A,B}(t) := \sum_{l=0}^{\infty}\sum_{0\le i\le l}(-1)^l\binom{t-im}{2l+1}Q(l+1;i) : \mathbb{Z}_0^{\infty}\to\mathbb{M}_{n\times n},$$
$$Cos^{A,B}(t) := \sum_{l=0}^{\infty}\sum_{0\le i\le l}(-1)^l\binom{t-im}{2l}Q(l+1;i) : \mathbb{Z}_0^{\infty}\to\mathbb{M}_{n\times n}$$

Lemma 6. *For all $t\in\mathbb{Z}_0^{\infty}$, one has*

$$\left\|Sin^{A,B}(t)\right\|\le l_s(t),\quad \left\|Cos^{A,B}(t)\right\|\le l_c(t). \tag{6}$$

where

$$l_s(t) := \sum_{l=0}^{\lfloor\frac{t-m-1}{m+2}\rfloor}\binom{t}{2l+1}(\|A\|+\|B\|)^l,\quad l_c(t) := \sum_{l=0}^{\lfloor\frac{t-m-1}{m+2}\rfloor}\binom{t}{2l}(\|A\|+\|B\|)^l$$

Proof. We only have the first inequality:

$$\begin{aligned}\left\|\operatorname{Sin}^{A,B}(t)\right\| &\leq \sum_{l=0}^{\lfloor\frac{t-m-1}{m+2}\rfloor} \sum_{0\leq i\leq l} \binom{t-im}{2l+1} \|Q(l+1;i)\| \\ &\leq \sum_{l=0}^{\lfloor\frac{t-m-1}{m+2}\rfloor} \sum_{0\leq i\leq l} \binom{t-im}{2l+1} \binom{l}{i} \|A\|^{l-i} \|B\|^{i} \\ &\leq \sum_{l=0}^{\lfloor\frac{t-m-1}{m+2}\rfloor} \binom{t}{2l+1} (\|A\|+\|B\|)^{l}.\end{aligned}$$

□

Lemma 7. *Under the exponential boundedness of* $f:\mathbb{Z}_0^\infty\to\mathbb{R}^d$*, a solution of (1), (2) has the same property; that is, it is exponentially bounded.*

Proof.

$$\begin{aligned}\sum \Delta y(t+1) &= \Delta y(t) - Ay(t) - By(t-m) + f(t) \\ \sum_{j=0}^{r-1} \Delta y(j+1) &= \sum_{j=0}^{r-1} \Delta y(j) - \sum_{j=0}^{r-1} Ay(j) - \sum_{j=0}^{r-1} By(j-m) + \sum_{j=0}^{r-1} f(j) \\ \Delta y(r) &= \Delta\varphi(0) - \sum_{j=0}^{r-1} Ay(j) - \sum_{j=0}^{r-1} By(j-m) + \sum_{j=0}^{r-1} f(j)\end{aligned}$$

Summing the above equality from 0 to $t-1$, we obtain

$$\sum_{r=0}^{t-1} \Delta y(r) = \sum_{r=0}^{t-1} \Delta\varphi(0) - \sum_{r=0}^{t-1}\sum_{j=0}^{r-1} Ay(j) - \sum_{r=0}^{t-1}\sum_{j=0}^{r-1} By(j-m) + \sum_{r=0}^{t-1}\sum_{j=0}^{r-1} f(j)$$

equivalently

$$y(t) = \varphi(0) + t\Delta\varphi(0) - \sum_{j=0}^{t-1}(t-j)Ay(j) - \sum_{j=0}^{t-1}(t-j)By(j-m) + \sum_{j=0}^{t-1}(t-j)f(j).$$

Taking the norm and applying the triangle inequality, we have

$$\begin{aligned}\|y(t)\| &\leq \|\varphi(0)\| + t\|\Delta\varphi(0)\| + \sum_{j=0}^{t-1}(t-j)\|A\|\|y(j)\| \\ &\quad + \sum_{j=0}^{t-1}(t-j)\|B\|\|y(j-m)\| + \sum_{j=0}^{t-1}(t-j)\|f(j)\| \\ &\leq \|\varphi(0)\| + t\|\Delta\varphi(0)\| + \sum_{j=-m}^{-1}(t-m-j)\|B\|\|\varphi(j)\| \\ &\quad + \sum_{j=0}^{t-1}(t-j)\|A\|\|y(j)\| + \sum_{j=0}^{t-m-1}(t-m-j)\|B\|\|y(j)\| \\ &\quad + \sum_{j=0}^{t-1}(t-j)\|f(j)\|.\end{aligned}$$

In this stage, without losing generality, it is assumed that $b_2 > 1$. Then,

$$\sum_{j=0}^{t-1}(t-j)\|f(j)\| \leq \sum_{j=0}^{t-1}(t-j)b_1 b_2^j \leq \frac{t(t+1)}{2}b_1 b_2^t.$$

Thus,

$$\|y(t)\| \leq a(t) + t(\|A\| + \|B\|)\sum_{j=0}^{t-1}\|y(j)\|.$$

$$\begin{aligned} b(t) &:= \|\varphi(0)\| + t\|\Delta\varphi(0)\| + \sum_{j=-m}^{-1}(t-m-j)\|B\|\|\varphi(j)\| \\ &+ \frac{t(t+1)}{2}b_1 b_2^t \end{aligned}$$

From the Gronwall inequality,

$$\begin{aligned} \|y(t)\| &\leq b(t) + t(\|A\| + \|B\|)\sum_{j=0}^{t-1}b(j)\prod_{i=j+1}^{t-1}(1 + j(\|A\| + \|B\|)) \\ &\leq b(t) + t(\|A\| + \|B\|)\sum_{j=0}^{t-1}b(j)(1 + t(\|A\| + \|B\|))^t \\ &\leq b(t)\Big(1 + t^2(\|A\| + \|B\|)(1 + t(\|A\| + \|B\|))^t\Big). \end{aligned}$$

Therefore, one can easily see that there exists constants $\widehat{b}_1, \widehat{b}_2 > 0$ such that

$$\|y(t)\| \leq \widehat{b}_1 \widehat{b}_2^t, \quad t \in \mathbb{Z}_0^\infty.$$

□

3. Explicit Solutions

Below, we state and prove the main theorem of this paper. The main instrument used is the $\mathcal{Z}$ transform. We give a closed analytical form of the solution of problem (1), (2) in terms of the delayed discrete matrix sine/cosine.

Theorem 1. *Let $f : \mathbb{Z}_0^\infty \to \mathbb{R}^d$ be an exponentially bounded function. The solution $y(t)$ of the IVP problem (1), (2) has the following form:*

$$\begin{aligned} y(t) &= Cos^{A,B}(t)\varphi(0) + Sin^{A,B}(t)\Delta\varphi(0) \\ &+ \sum_{i=-m}^{-1} Sin^{A,B}(t-i-m-1)B\varphi(i) + \sum_{j=0}^{t-2} Sin^{A,B}(t-j-1)f(j), \end{aligned} \tag{7}$$

for $t \in Z_2^\infty$.

Proof. We recall that Lemma 7 says that the $\mathcal{Z}$ transform of the solution of (1) exists. Therefore, one can apply the $\mathcal{Z}$ transform to both sides of the delayed system (1) to obtain

$$\sum_{t=0}^{\infty}\frac{y(t+2)}{z^t}-2\sum_{t=0}^{\infty}\frac{y(t+1)}{z^t}+\sum_{t=0}^{\infty}\frac{y(t)}{z^t}+A\sum_{t=0}^{\infty}\frac{y(t)}{z^t}+B\sum_{t=0}^{\infty}\frac{y(t-m)}{z^t}=\sum_{t=0}^{\infty}\frac{f(t)}{z^t},$$

$$z^2\left(\sum_{t=0}^{\infty}\frac{y(t)}{z^t}-\varphi(0)-\frac{1}{z}\varphi(1)\right)-2z\left(\sum_{t=0}^{\infty}\frac{y(t)}{z^t}-\varphi(0)\right)$$

$$+\sum_{t=0}^{\infty}\frac{y(t)}{z^t}+A\sum_{t=0}^{\infty}\frac{y(t)}{z^t}+\frac{B}{z^m}\left(X(z)+\sum_{t=-m}^{-1}\frac{\varphi(t)}{z^t}\right)=\sum_{t=0}^{\infty}\frac{f(t)}{z^t},$$

$$\left((z-1)^2+A+\frac{B}{z^m}\right)X(z)=z(z-1)\varphi(0)+z\Delta\varphi(0)-\frac{B}{z^m}\sum_{t=-m}^{-1}\frac{\varphi(t)}{z^t}+F(z).$$

This implies

$$X(z)=z(z-1)\left((z-1)^2+A+\frac{B}{z^m}\right)^{-1}\varphi(0)+z\left((z-1)^2+A+\frac{B}{z^m}\right)^{-1}\Delta\varphi(0)$$

$$-\left((z-1)^2+A+\frac{B}{z^m}\right)^{-1}\sum_{t=-m}^{-1}B\frac{\varphi(t)}{z^{t+m}}+\left((z-1)^2+A+\frac{B}{z^m}\right)^{-1}F(z).$$

In order to obtain an explicit form of $y(t)$, we take the inverse $\mathcal{Z}$ transform to have

$$\begin{aligned}
y(t)&=A_0(t)+A_1(t)-\sum_{j=-m}^{-1}A_j(t)+A_f(t),\\
A_j(t)&=\mathcal{Z}^{-1}\left\{\frac{1}{z^{j+m}}\left((z-1)^2+A+\frac{B}{z^m}\right)^{-1}B\varphi(j)\right\}(t)\\
&=\sin(t-j-m-1)B\varphi(j)
\end{aligned}$$

where

$$\begin{aligned}
A_0(t)&=\mathcal{Z}^{-1}\left\{z(z-1)\left((z-1)^2+A+\frac{B}{z^m}\right)^{-1}\varphi(0)\right\}(t),\\
A_1(t)&=\mathcal{Z}^{-1}\left\{z\left((z-1)^2+A+\frac{B}{z^m}\right)^{-1}\Delta\varphi(0)\right\}(t),\\
A_j(t)&=\mathcal{Z}^{-1}\left\{\frac{1}{z^{j+m}}\left((z-1)^2+A+\frac{B}{z^m}\right)^{-1}B\varphi(j)\right\}(t),\ j\in\mathcal{Z}_{-m}^{-1},\\
A_f(t)&=\mathcal{Z}^{-1}\left\{\left((z-1)^2+A+\frac{B}{z^m}\right)^{-1}F(z)\right\}(t).
\end{aligned}$$

Using Lemma 5, we obtain the desired representation (7). □

Lemma 8. *$Cos^{A,B}(t)$ and $Sin^{A,B}(t)$ satisfy the following equations:*

$$\Delta\, Cos^{A,B}(t)=-A\,Sin^{A,B}(t)-B\,Sin^{A,B}(t-m),\tag{8}$$

$$\Delta\, Sin^{A,B}(t)=Cos^{A,B}(t),\tag{9}$$

$$\Delta^2\, Cos^{A,B}(t)=-A\,Cos^{A,B}(t-1)-B\,Cos^{A,B}(t-1-m),\tag{10}$$

$$\Delta^2\, Sin^{A,B}(t)=-A\,Sin^{A,B}(t)-B\,Sin^{A,B}(t-m).\tag{11}$$

Proof. First, we prove identity (8). It is a consequence of the definition of the determining function $Q(l+1;i)$:

$$\begin{aligned}
\Delta\,\mathrm{Cos}^{A,B}(t) &= \mathrm{Cos}^{A,B}(t+1) - \mathrm{Cos}^{A,B}(t) \\
&= \sum_{l=1}^{\infty}\sum_{0\le i\le l}(-1)^l\left[\binom{t+1-im}{2l} - \binom{t-im}{2l}\right]Q(l+1;i) \\
&= \sum_{l=1}^{\infty}\sum_{0\le i\le l}(-1)^l\left[\binom{t-im}{2l-1}\right]Q(l+1;i) \\
&= A\sum_{l=1}^{\infty}\sum_{0\le i\le l}(-1)^l\left[\binom{t-im}{2l-1}\right]Q(l;i) \\
&+ B\sum_{l=1}^{\infty}\sum_{0\le i\le l}(-1)^l\left[\binom{t-im}{2l-1}\right]Q(l;i-1) \\
&= -A\sum_{l=0}^{\infty}\sum_{0\le i\le l}(-1)^l\left[\binom{t-im}{2l+1}\right]Q(l+1;i) \\
&- B\sum_{l=0}^{\infty}\sum_{0\le i\le l}(-1)^l\left[\binom{t-m-im}{2l+1}\right]Q(l+1;i) \\
&= -A\,\mathrm{Sin}^{A,B}(t) - B\,\mathrm{Sin}^{A,B}(t-m).
\end{aligned}$$

The proof of identity (9) is much more simple:

$$\begin{aligned}
\Delta\,\mathrm{Sin}^{A,B}(t) &= \mathrm{Sin}^{A,B}(t+1) - \mathrm{Sin}^{A,B}(t) \\
&= \sum_{l=0}^{\infty}\sum_{0\le i\le l}(-1)^l\left[\binom{t+1-im}{2l+1} - \binom{t-im}{2l+1}\right]Q(l+1;i) \\
&= \sum_{l=0}^{\infty}\sum_{0\le i\le l}(-1)^l\binom{t-im}{2l}Q(l+1;i) \\
&= \mathrm{Cos}^{A,B}(t).
\end{aligned}$$

Equations (10) and (11) can be proved by applying (9) and (8). □

The condition $f:\mathbb{Z}_0^{\infty}\to\mathbb{R}^d$ is an exponentially bounded can be eliminated through direct verification, that is why the proof of the following theorem is not included.

Theorem 2. *The solution of IVP (1), (2) can be rewritten in the following form:*

$$\begin{aligned}
y(t) &= \mathrm{Cos}^{A,B}(t)\varphi(0) + Sin^{A,B}(t)\Delta\varphi(0) + \sum_{j=-m}^{-1} Sin^{A,B}(t-j-m-1)B\varphi(j) \\
&+ \sum_{j=0}^{t-2} Sin^{A,B}(t-j-1)f(j).
\end{aligned} \tag{12}$$

4. Convergence Results

Lemma 9 ([29] Chapter 5.6). *For a matrix $A\in\mathbb{R}^{d\times d}$ and $\forall\varepsilon>0$, there exists a matrix norm $\|\cdot\|$ such that*

$$\|A\| \le \rho(A) + \varepsilon,$$

where $\rho(A)$ denotes the spectral radius of matrix A.

The proof provided is a detailed and rigorous mathematical argument demonstrating the convergence of the error sequence e_k in the λ norm under the given conditions. Below are some clarifications and highlights for better understanding:

- Key assumption: the inequality
$$\rho(I - DL_1) < 1$$
ensures that the spectral radius of matrix $I - DL_1$ is less than 1, which is a critical condition for the contraction and convergence of the error sequence.
- Iterative relation: the proof builds upon the iterative equation that expresses the evolution of error $e_k(t)$ as a combination of the previous error and additional terms influenced by C, F, and L_1.
- Norm bound: by bounding the λ-norm of the error, the proof systematically shows that the error decreases geometrically is controlled by choosing an appropriate λ within the specified range.
- Choice of λ : the selection of λ is crucial.
- Convergence: the result
$$||e_{k+1}||_\lambda < \psi||e_k||_\lambda,$$
with $\psi < 1$ implies that the sequence $||e_k||_\lambda$ converges to 0 as $k \to \infty$.

From (7), one can see that the state $y_k(t)$ of (3) has the following form:

$$\begin{aligned} y_k(t) = {} & \mathrm{Cos}^{A,B}(t)\varphi(0) + \mathrm{Sin}^{A,B}(t)\Delta\varphi(0) + \sum_{i=-m}^{-1} \mathrm{Sin}^{A,B}(t-i-m-1)B\varphi(i) \\ & + \sum_{j=0}^{t-2} \mathrm{Sin}^{A,B}(t-j-1)Fu_k(j). \end{aligned} \tag{13}$$

Consider

$$\begin{aligned} \tilde{y}_k(t) = {} & \mathrm{Cos}^{A,B}(t)\varphi(0) + \mathrm{Sin}^{A,B}(t)\Delta\varphi(0) + \sum_{i=-m}^{-1} \mathrm{Sin}^{A,B}(t-i-m-1)B\varphi(i) \\ & + \sum_{j=0}^{t-2} \mathrm{Sin}^{A,B}(t-j-1)Fu_k(j). \end{aligned} \tag{14}$$

Let z_d be a desired reference trajectory, and

$$e_k(t) := z_d(t) - z_k(t), \tag{15}$$
$$\tilde{e}_k(t) := z_k(t) - z_d(t). \tag{16}$$

Here, $e_k(t)$ and $\tilde{e}_k(t)$ represent the kth iteration error.

Introduce $\delta y_k(t) := y_{k+1}(t) - y_k(t)$ and $\delta u_k(t) := u_{k+1}(t) - u_k(t)$. We construct the following P-type learning law:

$$\delta u_k(t) = L_1 e_k(t). \tag{17}$$

When $D = \Theta$, we set

$$\delta u_k(t) = L_2 \tilde{e}_k(t+2), \tag{18}$$

where L_1 and L_2 are $r \times p$ learning gain parameter matrices determined in (21) and (27), respectively. Thus, from (3),

$$\delta y_k(t) = \sum_{j=0}^{t-2} \mathrm{Sin}^{A,B}(t-j-1)F\delta u_k(j), \tag{19}$$

$$\delta \widetilde{y}_k(t) = -\sum_{j=0}^{t-2} \mathrm{Sin}^{A,B}(t-j-1)F\delta u_k(j). \tag{20}$$

Taking account of (3) together with (15) and (17), separately, we are ready to give the convergence analysis for $\|e_k\|_\lambda$ in the following two theorems.

Theorem 3. *Assume that $z_d(t) = z_k(t)$ ($t \in \mathbb{Z}_{-m}^{1}$). Consider (3) with the P-type learning law (17). For arbitrary initial input $u_1(t)$, if*

$$\rho(I - DL_1) < 1, \tag{21}$$

then we have

$$\lim_{k\to\infty} \|e_k\|_\lambda = 0.$$

Proof. For (3) with $t \in \mathbb{Z}_0^T$, according to (15), we can obtain the relation between the kth error and the $(k+1)$th error:

$$\begin{aligned} e_{k+1}(t) - e_k(t) &= z_k(t) - z_{k+1}(t) \\ &= -C\delta y_k(t) - D\delta u_k(t). \end{aligned}$$

According to (17), we have

$$e_{k+1}(t) = (I - DL_1)e_k(t) - C\delta y_k(t). \tag{22}$$

Taking norm $\|\cdot\|$ on $\mathbb{R}^n$ for (22) and from Lemma 9, we have

$$|e_{k+1}(t)| \le (\rho(I - DL_1) + \varepsilon)|e_k(t)| + \|C\||\delta y_k(t)|, \tag{23}$$

where ε is an arbitrary positive number.

When $0 \le t \le 2$, obviously, $\delta y_k(0)$, $\delta y_k(1)$, and $\delta y_k(2)$ become d-dimensional zero vectors. According to (21) and (23), it is easy to obtain

$$\lim_{k\to\infty} |e_k(t)| = 0.$$

When $t \in \mathbb{Z}_3^T$, multiplying both sides of (23) by λ^t and then taking the λ norm, we have

$$\|e_{k+1}\|_\lambda \le (\rho(I - DL_1) + \varepsilon)\|e_k\|_\lambda + \|C\|\|\delta y_k\|_\lambda. \tag{24}$$

Now, we estimate the value of $\lambda^t|\delta y_k(t)|$. According to (6), (17), and (19), we have

$$\begin{aligned}
\lambda^t|\delta y_k(t)| &= \lambda^t \sum_{j=0}^{t-2} \|\mathrm{Sin}^{A,B}(t-j-1)\|\|F\||\delta u_k(j)| \\
&\leq \lambda^t l_s(t)\|F\| \sum_{j=0}^{t-2} |\delta u_k(j)| \\
&\leq \lambda^t l_s(t)\|F\|\|L_1\| \sum_{j=0}^{t-2} |e_k(j)| \\
&\leq \lambda^t l_s(t)\|F\|\|L_1\| \sum_{j=0}^{t-2} \lambda^{-j}\lambda^j|e_k(j)| \\
&\leq \lambda^t l_s(t)\|F\|\|L_1\|\|e_k\|_\lambda \sum_{j=0}^{t-2} \lambda^{t-j} \\
&\leq \lambda^2(T-1)l_s(t)\|F\|\|L_1\|\|e_k\|_\lambda.
\end{aligned} \tag{25}$$

Taking the supremum norm for both sides of (25), we obtain

$$\|\delta y_k\|_\lambda = \sup_{t\in\mathbb{Z}_0^T}\{\lambda^t|\delta y_k(t)|\} \leq \lambda^2(T-1)l_s(T)\|F\|\|L_1\|\|e_k\|_\lambda. \tag{26}$$

Now linking (24) and (26), we have

$$\|e_{k+1}\|_\lambda \leq ((\rho(I-DL_1)+\varepsilon)+\mu_\lambda)\|e_k\|_\lambda,$$

where

$$\mu_\lambda := \|C\|\lambda^2(T-1)l_s(T)\|F\|\|L_1\|.$$

By (21), one derives

$$\rho(I-DL_1)+\varepsilon+\mu_\lambda < 1$$

when

$$0 < \lambda < \min\left(1, \sqrt{\frac{1-\rho(I-DL_1)-\varepsilon}{\|C\|(T-1)l_s(T)\|F\|\|L_1\|}}\right).$$

Finally, we obtain

$$\|e_{k+1}\|_\lambda < ((\rho(I-DL_1)+\varepsilon)+\mu_\lambda)\|e_k\|_\lambda,$$

which implies

$$\lim_{k\to\infty}\|e_k\|_\lambda = 0.$$

□

Theorem 4. *Assume that* $y_d(t) = y_k(t)$ $(t \in \mathbb{Z}_{-m}^1)$. *Consider (3) with* $D = \Theta$ *and (18). For arbitrary initial input* $u_1(t)$, *if*

$$\rho(I-CBL_2) < 1, \quad CB \neq 0, \tag{27}$$

then

$$\lim_{k\to\infty}\|e_k\|_\lambda = 0,$$

on $\mathbb{Z}_3^T$.

Proof. For (3) with $D = \Theta$ and $t \in \mathbb{Z}_3^T$, we can obtain the relation between the kth error and the $(k+1)$th error via (16):

$$e_{k+1}(t) - e_k(t) = z_{k+1}(t) - z_k(t) = C\delta\widetilde{y}_k(t). \tag{28}$$

Substituting (20) into (28), we obtain

$$\begin{aligned}
e_{k+1}(t) &= e_k(t) + C\delta\widetilde{y}_k(t) \\
&= e_k(t) - C\sum_{j=0}^{t-2} \mathrm{Sin}^{A,B}(t-j-1)F\delta u_k(j) \\
&= e_k(t) - C\mathrm{Sin}^{A,B}(1)F\delta u_k(t-2) - C\sum_{j=0}^{t-3} \mathrm{Sin}^{A,B}(t-j-1)F\delta u_k(j) \\
&= e_k(t) - CF\delta u_k(t-2) - C\sum_{j=0}^{t-3} \mathrm{Sin}^{A,B}(t-j-1)F\delta u_k(j).
\end{aligned}$$

Due to (15) and (18), we have

$$e_{k+1}(t) = (I - CFL_2)e_k(t) - C\sum_{j=0}^{t-3} \mathrm{Sin}^{A,B}(t-j-1)FL_2e_k(j+2). \tag{29}$$

Taking norm $\|\cdot\|$ for (29) and from Lemma 9, we have

$$|e_{k+1}(3)| \leq (\rho(I - CFL_2) + \varepsilon)|e_k(3)|,$$

for $t = 3$. From (27), it is easy to obtain

$$\lim_{k\to\infty} |e_k(3)| = 0.$$

When $t \in \mathbb{Z}_3^T$, we have

$$\begin{aligned}
|e_{k+1}(t)| &\leq (\rho(I - CFL_2) + \varepsilon)|e_k(t)| \\
&\quad + \|C\|\sum_{j=0}^{t-3} \|\mathrm{Sin}^{A,B}(t-j-1)\|\|F\|\|L_2\||e_k(j+2)| \\
&\leq (\rho(I - CFL_2) + \varepsilon)|e_k(t)| \\
&\quad + \|C\|\left\|\mathrm{Sin}^{A,B}(t)\right\|\|F\|\|L_2\|\sum_{j=0}^{t-3} |e_k(j+2)| \\
&\leq (\rho(I - CFL_2) + \varepsilon)|e_k(t)| \\
&\quad + \|C\|l_s(t)\|F\|\|L_2\|\|e_k\|_\lambda \sum_{j=0}^{t-3} \lambda^{-(j+2)}.
\end{aligned}$$

Then, by taking the λ norm, we obtain

$$\begin{aligned}
\|e_{k+1}\|_\lambda &\leq (\rho(I - CFL_2) + \varepsilon)\|e_k\|_\lambda \\
&\quad + \|C\|l_s(T)\|F\|\|L_2\|\|e_k\|_\lambda \sum_{j=0}^{t-3} \lambda^{t-(j+2)} \\
&\leq (\rho(I - CFL_2) + \varepsilon)\|e_k\|_\lambda \\
&\quad + \lambda(T-2)\|C\|l_s(T)\|F\|\|L_2\|\|e_k\|_\lambda \\
&\leq (\rho(I - CFL_2) + \varepsilon + \gamma_\lambda)\|e_k\|_\lambda,
\end{aligned} \tag{30}$$

where $0 < \lambda < 1$ and

$$\gamma_\lambda = \lambda(T-2)\|C\|l_s(T)\|F\|\|L_2\|.$$

We choose λ from the set

$$0 < \lambda < \min\left(1, \frac{1 - \rho(I - CBL_2) - \varepsilon}{(T-2)\|C\| l_s(T) \|F\| \|L_2\|}\right),$$

and, according to (30), we have

$$\|e_{k+1}\|_\lambda < (\rho(I - CBL_2) + \varepsilon + \gamma_\lambda)\|e_k\|_\lambda,$$

which means that

$$\lim_{k\to\infty} \|e_k\|_\lambda = 0.$$

Thus, the proof is completed. □

5. Applicaitons

5.1. Example 1

We consider the discrete-time system:

$$y_{k+1}(t) = Ay_k(t) + Fu_k(t), \tag{31}$$

where

$$A = \begin{bmatrix} 0.8 & 0.2 \\ 0.1 & 0.9 \end{bmatrix}, \quad F = \begin{bmatrix} 0.5 & 0 \\ 0 & 0.3 \end{bmatrix}.$$

The goal is to track a desired trajectory $y_d(t)$ by iteratively updating the control input. We apply a P-type ILC update:

$$u_{k+1}(t) = u_k(t) + Le_k(t), \tag{32}$$

where $e_k(t) = y_d(t) - y_k(t)$ is the tracking error, and L is the learning gain matrix:

$$L = \begin{bmatrix} 0.7 & 0 \\ 0 & 0.6 \end{bmatrix}.$$

The error propagation follows:

$$e_{k+1}(t) = (I - LB)e_k(t). \tag{33}$$

Compute $I - LB$

$$I - LB = \begin{bmatrix} 1 & 0 \\ 0 & 1 \end{bmatrix} - \begin{bmatrix} 0.7 & 0 \\ 0 & 0.6 \end{bmatrix} \begin{bmatrix} 0.5 & 0 \\ 0 & 0.3 \end{bmatrix}$$

$$= \begin{bmatrix} 1 - (0.7 \times 0.5) & 0 \\ 0 & 1 - (0.6 \times 0.3) \end{bmatrix} = \begin{bmatrix} 0.65 & 0 \\ 0 & 0.82 \end{bmatrix}.$$

Since $\|I - LB\| < 1$, the error decreases over iterations, ensuring convergence. Assume initial error

$$e_0(t) = \begin{bmatrix} 1 \\ 1 \end{bmatrix}.$$

and error evolution (Figure 1)

$$e_k(t) = (I - LB)^k e_0(t).$$

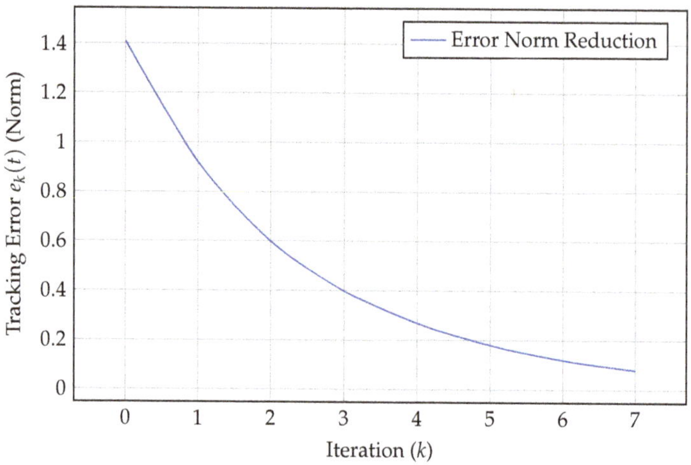

Figure 1. Tracking error norm reduction over iterations.

5.2. Perturbed System Model

We introduce small perturbations to matrices A and B:

$$A_\delta = A + \Delta A, \quad B_\delta = B + \Delta B.$$

Assume that

$$\Delta A = \begin{bmatrix} 0.05 & -0.02 \\ -0.01 & 0.03 \end{bmatrix}, \quad \Delta B = \begin{bmatrix} 0.02 & 0 \\ 0 & -0.01 \end{bmatrix}.$$

Thus, the perturbed system is

$$A_\delta = \begin{bmatrix} 0.85 & 0.18 \\ 0.09 & 0.93 \end{bmatrix}, \quad B_\delta = \begin{bmatrix} 0.52 & 0 \\ 0 & 0.29 \end{bmatrix}.$$

With this uncertainty, the new error propagation becomes

$$e_{k+1}(t) = (I - LB_\delta)e_k(t).$$

Compute $I - LB_\delta$:

$$I - LB_\delta = \begin{bmatrix} 1 - 0.7 \times 0.52 & 0 \\ 0 & 1 - 0.6 \times 0.29 \end{bmatrix} = \begin{bmatrix} 0.636 & 0 \\ 0 & 0.826 \end{bmatrix}.$$

The perturbed system still converges but more slowly due to increased error propagation (Figure 2):

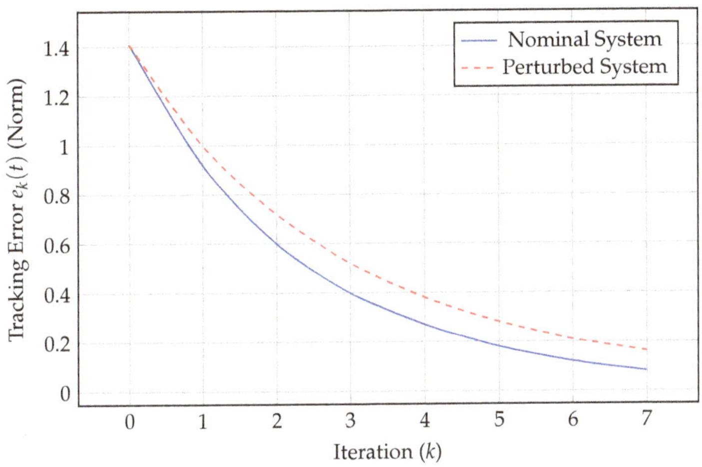

Figure 2. Tracking error norm over iterations for nominal and perturbed systems.

5.3. Example 2

We consider a discrete-time second-order linear system in two dimensions:

$$\begin{aligned} y_k(t+2) &= 2y_k(t+1) + \begin{bmatrix} 1 & 0 \\ 0 & 1 \end{bmatrix} y_k(t) + \begin{bmatrix} 0.3 & 0.1 \\ 0.2 & 0.3 \end{bmatrix} y_k(t-3) + \begin{bmatrix} 1 \\ 2 \end{bmatrix} u_k(t), \\ z_k(t) &= [0.2 \;\; 0.3] y_k(t) + 2u_k(t), \end{aligned}$$

The control input is updated iteratively as

$$\begin{aligned} u_{k+1}(t) &= u_k(t) + Le_k(t), \\ L &= 1/2000 \end{aligned}$$

where the tracking error is given by

$$e_k(t) = z_d(t) - z_k(t) = 2t \sin t + 8 - z_k(t).$$

$$I - LF = \begin{bmatrix} 1 \\ 1 \end{bmatrix} - \frac{1}{2000} \begin{bmatrix} 1 \\ 2 \end{bmatrix}.$$

Since $\|I - LF\| < 1$, the error decreases over iterations, ensuring convergence.

Figure 3 illustrates the system output compared to the desired trajectory over different iterations. The system aims to align with the desired trajectory as the iterations increase.

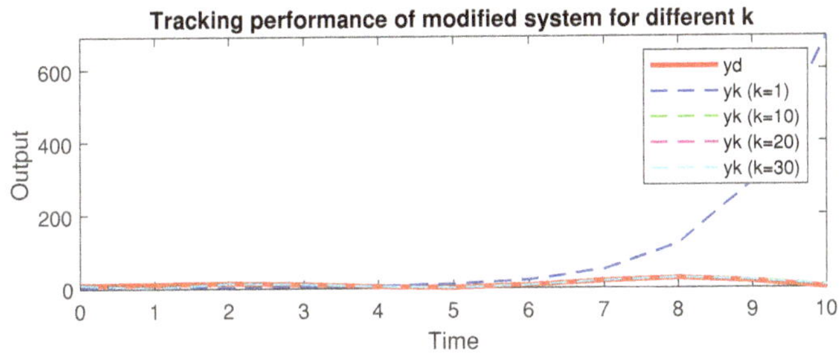

Figure 3. System output trajectory over multiple iterations.

Figure 4 shows the error norm decreasing over time, demonstrating the convergence of the ILC process.

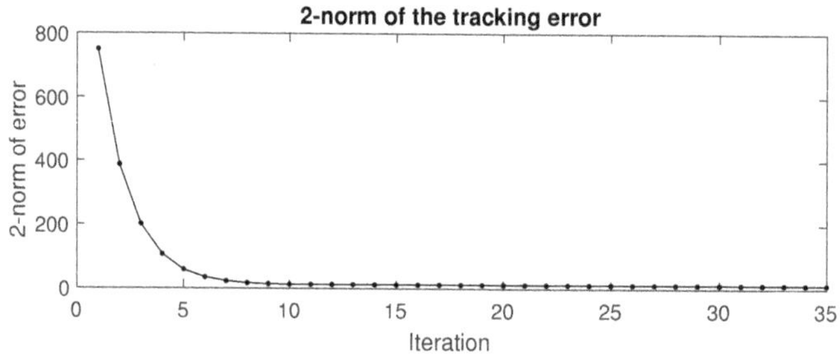

Figure 4. Error norm over time steps.

The ILC approach effectively refines the control input to improve trajectory tracking. The figures demonstrate the system's convergence as errors reduce over iterations (Figure 5).

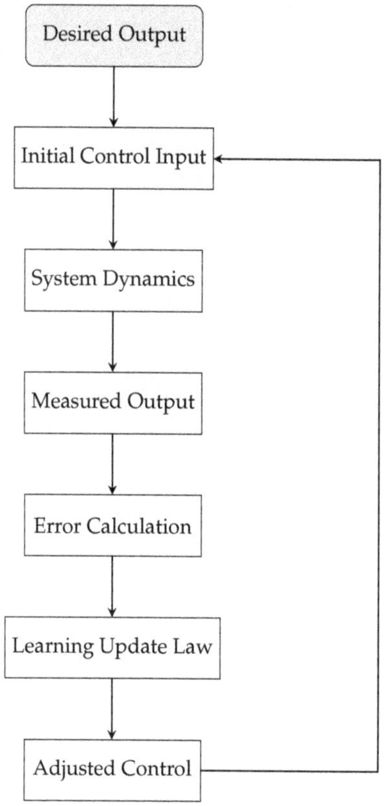

Figure 5. Flowchart of an iterative learning control.

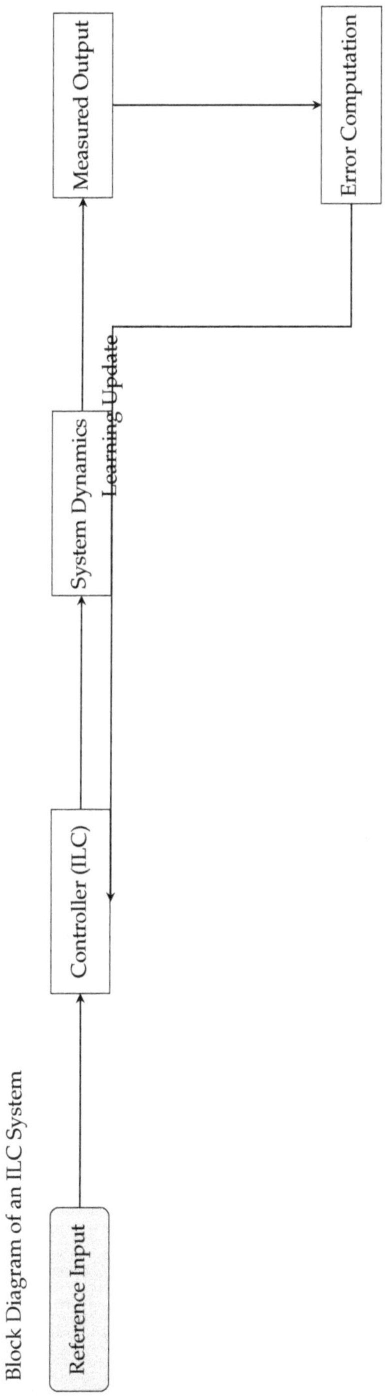
Block Diagram of an ILC System
Reference Input
Controller (ILC)
System Dynamics
Measured Output
Error Computation
Learning Update

6. Conclusions

A system of inhomogeneous second-order difference equations with linear parts given by noncommutative matrix coefficients was considered. The closed-form solution was derived using newly defined delayed matrix sine/cosine functions via the Z transform and determining function. This representation helped analyze iterative learning control by applying appropriate updating laws and ensuring sufficient conditions for achieving asymptotic convergence in tracking.

Future work may focus on controllability, stability, existence and uniqueness problems of multiple delayed discrete semilinear/linear systems.

Author Contributions: Conceptualization, N.I.M. and M.A. (Muath Awadalla); methodology, N.I.M.; validation, N.I.M., M.A. (Muath Awadalla) and M.A. (Meraa Arab); investigation, N.I.M., M.A. (Muath Awadalla) and M.A. (Meraa Arab); writing—original draft preparation, N.I.M. and M.A. (Muath Awadalla); writing—review and editing, N.I.M., M.A. (Muath Awadalla) and M.A. (Meraa Arab). All authors have read and agreed to the published version of this manuscript.

Funding: This work was supported by the Deanship of Scientific Research, Vice Presidency for Graduate Studies and Scientific Research, King Faisal University, Saudi Arabia [Grant No. KFU250955].

Data Availability Statement: Data are contained within this article.

Acknowledgments: This work was supported by the Deanship of Scientific Research, Vice Presidency for Graduate Studies and Scientific Research, King Faisal University, Saudi Arabia [Grant No. KFU250955].

Conflicts of Interest: The authors declare no conflicts of interest.

References

1. Arimoto, S.; Kawamura, S.; Miyazaki, F. Bettering operation of robots by learning. *J. Robot. Syst.* **1984**, *1*, 123–140. [CrossRef]
2. Sun, M.X.; Huang, B.J. *Iterative Learning Control*; National Defense Industry Press: Beijing, China, 1999.
3. Bristow, D.A.; Tharayil, M.; Alleyne, A.G. A survey of iterative learning control. *IEEE Control Syst. Mag.* **2006**, *26*, 96–114.
4. Ahn, H.S.; Chen, Y.Q.; Moore, K.L. Iterative learning control: Brief survey and categorization. *IEEE Trans. Syst. Man Cybern. C Appl. Rev.* **2007**, *37*, 1099–1121. [CrossRef]
5. Li, X.D.; Chow, T.W.S.; Ho, J.K.L. 2-D system theory based iterative learning control for linear continuous systems with time delays. *IEEE Trans Circuits Syst. I Regul. Pap.* **2005**, *52*, 1421–1430.
6. Wan, K. Iterative learning control of two-dimensional discrete systems in general model. *Nonlinear Dyn.* **2021**, *104*, 1315–1327. [CrossRef]
7. Zhu, Q.; Xu, J.; Huang, D.; Hu, G. Iterative learning control design for linear discrete-time systems with multiple high-order internal models. *Automatica* **2015**, *62*, 65–76. [CrossRef]
8. Wei, Y.S.; Li, X.D. Iterative learning control for linear discrete-time systems with high relative degree under initial state vibration. *IET Control Theory Appl.* **2016**, *10*, 1115–1126. [CrossRef]
9. Diblík, J.; Khusainov, D.Y. Representation of solutions of discrete delayed system $y(k+1) = Ay(k) + By(k-m) + f(k)$ with commutative matrices. *J. Math. Anal. Appl.* **2006**, *318*, 63–76. [CrossRef]
10. Diblík, J.; Khusainov, D.Y. Representation of solutions of linear discrete systems with constant coefficients and pure delay. *Adv. Differ. Equ.* **2006**, *2006*, 1–13. [CrossRef]
11. Khusainov, D.Y.; Diblík, J.; Růžičková, M.; Lukáčová, J. Representation of a solution of the Cauchy problem for an oscillating system with pure delay. *Nonlinear Oscil.* **2008**, *11*, 276–285. [CrossRef]
12. Diblík, J.; Mencáková, K. Representation of solutions to delayed linear discrete systems with constant coefficients and with second-order differences. *Appl. Math. Lett.* **2020**, *105*, 106309. [CrossRef]
13. Elshenhab, A.M.; Wang, X.T. Representation of solutions for linear fractional systems with pure delay and multiple delays. *Math. Methods Appl. Sci.* **2021**, *44*, 12835–12860. [CrossRef]
14. Elshenhab, A.M.; Wang, X.T. Representation of solutions of linear differential systems with pure delay and multiple delays with linear parts given by non-permutable matrices. *Appl. Math. Comput.* **2021**, *410*, 126443. [CrossRef]
15. Pospíšil, M. Representation of solutions of systems of linear differential equations with multiple delays and nonpermutable variable coefficients. *Math. Model. Anal.* **2020**, *25*, 303–322. [CrossRef]

16. Diblík, J.; Morávková, B. Discrete matriy delayed eyponential for two delays and its property. *Adv. Differ. Equ.* **2013**, *2013*, 139. [CrossRef]
17. Diblík, J.; Morávková, B. Representation of the solutions of linear discrete systems with constant coefficients and two delays. *Abstr. Appl. Anal.* **2014**, *2014*, 320476. [CrossRef]
18. Pospíšil, M. Representation of solutions of delayed difference equations with linear parts given by pairwise permutable matrices via $\mathcal{Z}$-transform. *Appl. Math. Comput.* **2017**, *294*, 180–194. [CrossRef]
19. Mahmudov, N.I. Representation of solutions of discrete linear delay systems with non permutable matrices. *Appl. Math. Lett.* **2018**, *85*, 8–14. [CrossRef]
20. Mahmudov, N.I. Delayed linear difference equations: The method of $\mathcal{Z}$-transform. Electron. *J. Qual. Theory Differ. Equ.* **2020**, *2020*, 1–12. [CrossRef]
21. Elshenhab, A.M.; Wang, X.T. Representation of solutions of delayed linear discrete systems with permutable or nonpermutable matrices and second-order differences. *Rev. Real Acad. Cienc. Exactas Físicas Nat. Ser. A Matemáticas* **2022**, *116*, 58. [CrossRef]
22. Diblík, J. Relative and trajectory controllability of linear discrete systems with constant coefficients and a single delay. *IEEE Trans. Autom. Control* **2019**, *64*, 2158–2165. [CrossRef]
23. Diblík, J.; Mencáková, K. A note on relative controllability of higher-order linear delayed discrete systems. *IEEE Trans. Autom. Control* **2020**, *65*, 5472–5479. [CrossRef]
24. Liang, C.; Wang, J.; Fečkan, M. A study on ILC for linear discrete systems with single delay. *J. Differ. Equ. Appl.* **2018**, *24*, 358–374. [CrossRef]
25. Liang, C.; Wang, J.; Shen, D. Iterative learning control for linear discrete delay systems via discrete matriy delayed eyponential function approach. *J. Differ. Equ. Appl.* **2018**, *24*, 1756–1776. [CrossRef]
26. Medved,M.; Škripková, L. Sufficient conditions for the eyponential stability of delay difference equations with linear parts defined by permutable matrices. *Electron. J. Qual. Theory Differ. Equ.* **2012**, *2012*, 1–13. [CrossRef]
27. Pospíšil, M. Relative controllability of delayed difference equations to multiple consecutive states. *AIP Conf. Proc.* **2017**, *1863*, 480002. [CrossRef]
28. Agarwal, R.P. *Difference Equations and Inequalities: Theory, Methods, and Applications*, 2nd ed.; Marcel Dekker Inc.: New York, NY, USA, 2000.
29. Horn, R.A.; Johnson, C.R. *Matrix Analysis*; Cambridge University Press: Cambridge, UK, 2012.

mathematics

MDPI

Article

Remarks on Sequential Caputo Fractional Differential Equations with Fractional Initial and Boundary Conditions

Aghalaya S. Vatsala [1,*] and Bhuvaneswari Sambandham [2]

[1] Department of Mathematics, University of Louisiana at Lafayette, Lafayette, LA 70504, USA
[2] Department of Mathematics, Utah Tech University, Saint George, UT 84790, USA; buna.sambandham@utahtech.edu
* Correspondence: vatsala@louisiana.edu

Abstract: In the literature so far, for Caputo fractional boundary value problems of order $2q$ when $1 < 2q < 2$, the problems use the same boundary conditions of the integer-order differential equation of order '2'. In addition, they only use the left Caputo derivative in computing the solution of the Caputo boundary value problem of order $2q$. Further, even the initial conditions for a Caputo fractional differential equation of order nq use the corresponding integer-order initial conditions of order 'n'. In this work, we establish that it is more appropriate to use the Caputo fractional initial conditions and Caputo fractional boundary conditions for sequential initial value problems and sequential boundary value problems, respectively. It is to be noted that the solution of a Caputo fractional initial value problem or Caputo fractional boundary value problem of order 'nq' will only be a C^{nq} solution and not a C^n solution on its interval. In this work, we present a methodology to compute the solutions of linear sequential Caputo fractional differential equations using initial and boundary conditions of fractional order $kq, k = 0, 1, \dots (n-1)$ when the order of the fractional derivative involved in the differential equation is nq. The Caputo left derivative can be computed only when the function can be expressed as $f(x-a)$. Then the Caputo right derivative of the same function will be computed for the function $f(b-x)$. Further, we establish that the relation between the Caputo left derivative and the Caputo right derivative is very essential for the study of Caputo fractional boundary value problems. We present a few numerical examples to justify that the Caputo left derivative and the Caputo right derivative are equal at any point on the Caputo function's interval. The solution of the linear sequential Caputo fractional initial value problems and linear sequential Caputo fractional boundary value problems with fractional initial conditions and fractional boundary conditions reduces to the corresponding integer initial and boundary value problems, respectively, when $q = 1$. Thus, we can use the value of q as a parameter to enhance the mathematical model with realistic data.

Keywords: sequential Caputo fractional derivative; fractional initial value problem; fractional boundary value problem; Mittag–Leffler function

MSC: 34A08; 34A12

1. Introduction

The study and analysis of fractional differential equations with initial and boundary conditions has taken an important role in mathematical modeling in terms of its application to various branches of science and engineering. See [1–12] for the analysis and the references therein for applications. Furthermore, see [13–27] for some more applications of fractional differential equations. Among the several types of fractional derivatives, the most used fractional derivatives are the Riemann–Liouville derivative and the Caputo fractional derivative. Differential equations involving Caputo derivatives have an advantage over differential equations of an integer order. The solution of Caputo fractional differential equations with initial and boundary conditions reduces to the solution of the corresponding integer. Essentially, one can use the value of 'q' as a parameter to enhance the mathematical model that fits the data compared with the solution of the integer-order model. See [28] where they used the appropriate value of 'q' as a parameter to fit the realistic data. In order to achieve this, one needs to compute the solution of the Caputo fractional differential equation with initial and boundary conditions analytically and/or numerically. However, in the literature so far, the initial and/or boundary conditions assumed for a Caputo fractional differential equation of order 'q' when $(n-1) < q < n$ are those of the integer order 'n'. See [3,7] where they used the initial conditions of the nth-order-integer differential equations. Furthermore, the boundary conditions for Caputo fractional boundary conditions for $1 < q < 2$ are those of second-order differential equations. See [29–32] for some of the Caputo fractional boundary value problems. These methods do yield the corresponding integer results as a special case. The main reason for using the initial and boundary conditions of the integer order 'n' for the Caputo fractional differential equation of order 'q' when $(n-1) < q < n$ is that the assumption that the solution is a C^n function is a sufficient condition for the Caputo derivative to exist. In spite of this strong assumption, the solution obtained is only a C^q function. See the solution of the Cauchy problem (4.158) and (4.1.9) in [3]. In particular, when $0 < q < 1$, then the solution of ${}^cD^q_{a+}u = \lambda u,\ u(a) = u_a$ is given by $u(t) = u_a E_{q,1}(\lambda(t-a))^q$. This solution is certainly not a C^1 solution. Similarly, the solution of the homogeneous Caputo differential equation of order nq when $(n-1) < nq < n$ will not be a C^n solution.

The work of this article is related to the fact that the solution of the differential equation of order nq will be a C^{nq} solution. Further, without loss of generality, we can assume the Caputo differential operator of order nq is a sequential operator of order q. The advantages of assuming the Caputo fractional differential operator of order nq is a sequential operator of order 'q' are many:

1. We can now seek C^q solutions instead of $C^{(nq)}$ solutions.
2. We can have Caputo fractional derivative terms of lower-order $kq, k = 1,2,3,\ldots(n-1)$ in the Caputo fractional differential equation provided the initial conditions are of a fractional order. In this case, we can solve a linear Caputo fractional differential equation of the form $\sum_{k=1}^{n} a_k\, {}^cD^{kq}_{a+}(u(t)) = h(t)$ with fractional initial conditions. In addition, when $q = 1$, it yields the solution of the corresponding nth-order linear differential equation with constant coefficients.
3. In sequential boundary value problems, we can use fractional boundary conditions instead of the corresponding integer-order boundary conditions.
4. We can reduce an nq-order sequential Caputo fractional differential equation with fractional initial conditions to an n system of Caputo fractional differential equations with initial conditions.
5. Finally, from a modeling point of view, the value of 'q' as a parameter plays a role in the initial and boundary conditions.

Traditional methods like the variation of parameters and the fundamental matrix method commonly used for solving non-homogeneous-integer differential equations and systems are not applicable to Caputo fractional differential equations with fractional initial conditions. However, the Laplace transform method has been used effectively (see [33–35] for scalar sequential Caputo fractional differential equations with initial conditions). Additionally, see references [36,37] for applications of the Laplace transform for linear systems of Caputo fractional differential equations with constant coefficients. See [29–32,38–40] for Caputo fractional boundary value problems with the corresponding integer boundary conditions. Notably, only in [40] have fractional boundary conditions been used. While Green's functions incorporating both fractional and integer-order derivatives appear in [39], they are limited to the basis functions to be $1, (x-a), (x-a)^2$. In the majority of the Caputo fractional boundary value problems with integer boundary conditions, the Caputo left derivative alone has been used.

In this work, we modify Theorem 2.2 from Kilbas (p. 93) to show that the Caputo left and right derivatives of a function are equal at every point on (a, b), including the points $x = a$ and $x = b$. Observe that the Caputo left derivative starting from $a+$ of any function can be computed as a continuous function only when the function can be expressed as a function of $(x-a)^\lambda$ for $\lambda \geq q$, where q is the order of the derivative. Then the Caputo right derivative of the same function can be obtained by computing the right derivative of the function of $(b-x)^\lambda$.

Similarly, we show that the Caputo right derivative starting from $b-$ of any function can be computed as a continuous function only when the function can be expressed as a function of $(b-x)^\lambda$ for $\lambda \geq q$, where q is the order of the derivative. Then the left Caputo derivative of the same function can be computed by using the function of $(x-a)^\lambda$.

For instance, the following relationship holds:

$$^cD^q_{a+}((x-a)^q) = {^cD^q_{b-}}((b-x)^q) = \Gamma(q+1) \neq {^cD^q_{b-}}((x-a)^q).$$

This proves that the Caputo left derivative of $f(x) = (x-a)^q$ is equal to the Caputo right derivative of $f(x) = (b-x)^q$ at every point on (a, b) including the points a and b. In addition, when $q = 1$, we obtain $\dfrac{d(x-a)}{dx} = 1$ from the left derivative and $-\dfrac{d(b-x)}{dx} = 1$ from the right derivative, which satisfies part (b) of Theorem 2.2 in [3] (p. 93). It should be noted that the Caputo left derivative of $f(x) = (b-x)^q$ and the Caputo right derivative of $f(x) = (x-a)^q$ cannot be obtained in closed form. This addresses the issues raised in reference [41] about the relation of the Caputo left and right derivatives. For that purpose, we present several examples, including numerical examples.

The organization of this work is as follows: In Section 2, we recall definitions and known results which are needed for our main result. In Section 3, we have our main results with illustrative examples and numerical results. Finally, we have obtained an analytic representation form for linear sequential Caputo boundary value problems in terms of the Green's function.

2. Preliminary Results

In this section, we recall some definitions and known results which play an important role in our main results.

Definition 1. *The basic function in fractional calculus is the Gamma function, defined by the integral*

$$\Gamma(z) = \int_0^\infty e^{-t} t^{z-1} dt \tag{1}$$

which converges in the right half of the complex plane $Re(z) > 0$.

Another function we need more is the β-function.

Definition 2. *The two-variable β function is defined by the integral*

$$\beta(z, w) = \int_0^1 t^{z-1}(1-t)^{w-1} dt, \quad Re(z),\ Re(w) > 0 \tag{2}$$

The Γ and β functions are related by

$$\beta(p, q) = \frac{\Gamma(p)\Gamma(q)}{\Gamma(p+q)}.$$

Definition 3. *The Riemann–Liouville (left) fractional integral of $u(x)$ of order $q > 0$ is defined by*

$$D^{-q}_{a+}u(x) = \frac{1}{\Gamma(q)} \int_a^x (x-s)^{q-1} u(s) ds, \quad x > a \tag{3}$$

where $(n-1) < q \leq n$ *and* $\Gamma(q)$ *is the Gamma function.*

Definition 4. *The Riemann–Liouville (right) fractional integral of* $u(x)$ *of order* q *is defined by*

$$D_{b-}^{-q}u(x) = \frac{1}{\Gamma(q)}\int_x^b (s-x)^{q-1}u(s)ds, \ \ x < b \tag{4}$$

where $(n-1) < q \leq n$ *and* $\Gamma(q)$ *is the Gamma function.*

In particular, the above definition holds when $0 < q < 1$.

Definition 5. *The Riemann–Liouville (left-sided) fractional derivative of* $u(x)$ *of order* nq*, when* $(n-1) < nq < n$*, is defined by*

$$D_{a+}^{q}u(x) = \frac{1}{\Gamma(n-nq)}(\frac{d}{dx})^n \int_a^x (x-s)^{n-nq-1}u(s)ds, \ x > a \tag{5}$$

Definition 6. *The Riemann–Liouville (right-sided) fractional derivative of* $u(x)$ *of order* nq*, when* $(n-1) < nq < n$*, is defined by*

$$D_{b-}^{q}u(x) = \frac{1}{\Gamma(n-nq)}(-1)^n(\frac{d}{dx})^n \int_a^x (x-s)^{n-nq-1}u(s)ds, \ x > a \tag{6}$$

In particular, if $nq = n$, then $D_{a+}^{n}(u(x)) = u^{(n)}(x)$ and $D_{b-}^{n}(u(x)) = (-1)^n u^{(n)}(x)$.

Definition 7. *The Caputo (left-sided) fractional derivative of* $u(x)$ *of order* nq*,* $n-1 \leq nq < n$*, is defined by*

$${}^{c}D_{a+}^{nq}u(x) = \frac{1}{\Gamma(n-nq)}\int_a^x (x-s)^{n-nq-1}u^{(n)}(s)ds, \ x > a \tag{7}$$

where $u^{(n)}(x) = \frac{d^n(u(x))}{dx^n}$.

Definition 8. *The Caputo (right-sided) fractional derivative of* $u(x)$ *of order* nq*,* $n-1 \leq nq < n$*, is defined by*

$${}^{c}D_{b-}^{nq}u(x) = \frac{1}{\Gamma(n-nq)}\int_x^b (x-s)^{n-nq-1}u^{(n)}(s)ds, \ x < b \tag{8}$$

where $u^{(n)}(x) = \frac{d^n(u(x))}{dx^n}$.

See [2,3,7] for more details on Caputo and Riemann–Liouville fractional derivatives.

Definition 9. *The Caputo (left) fractional derivative of* $u(t)$ *of order* q*, when* $0 < q < 1$*, is defined as*

$${}^{c}D_{a+}^{q}u(t) = \frac{1}{\Gamma(1-q)}\int_a^t (t-s)^{-q}u'(s)ds \tag{9}$$

We are just replacing n with 1 in the above definition of a Caputo derivative of order nq.

The next definition is useful in our basic Caputo fractional differential inequalities.

Definition 10. *If the Caputo derivative of a function* $u(t)$ *of order* $q, 0 < q \leq 1$*, exists on an interval* $J = [0,T], T > 0$*, then we say* $u \in C^q[J,R)$*, where* $J = [0,T], T > 0$.

If $u \in C^1[0,T]$, then certainly ${}^cD^q_{a+}u(t)$ exists on $[0,T]$. Note that all C^1 functions on $[0,T]$ are C^q functions on $[0,T]$. However, the converse need to be true. For example, the function $f(t) = (t-a)^\omega$ for any ω is a C^q function when $q \le \omega < 1$. However, it is easy to see $f'(t)$ does not exist at $t = 0$.

Next, we define the two-parameter Mittag–Leffler function, which will be useful in solving the systems of linear Caputo fractional differential equations using the Laplace transform. See [24,42] for more on fractional differential equations with applications.

Definition 11. *The two-parameter Mittag–Leffler function is defined as*

$$E_{q,r}(\lambda t^q) = \sum_{k=0}^{\infty} \frac{(\lambda t^q)^k}{\Gamma(qk+r)} \tag{10}$$

where $q, r > 0$, and λ is a constant. Furthermore, for $r = q$, (10) reduces to

$$E_{q,q}(\lambda t^q) = \sum_{k=0}^{\infty} \frac{(\lambda t^q)^k}{\Gamma(qk+q)} \tag{11}$$

If $r = 1$ in (10), then

$$E_{q,1}(\lambda t^q) = \sum_{k=0}^{\infty} \frac{(\lambda t^q)^k}{\Gamma(qk+1)} \tag{12}$$

If $q = 1$ and $r = 1$ in (10), then we have

$$E_{1,1}(\lambda t) = \sum_{k=0}^{\infty} \frac{(\lambda t)^k}{\Gamma(k+1)} = e^{\lambda t} \tag{13}$$

where $e^{\lambda t}$ is the usual exponential function.

Consider the scalar Caputo fractional linear initial value problem:

$${}^cD^q{}_{a+}u = \lambda u + h(t), \quad u(a) = u_0, \tag{14}$$

with $t \in J$ and $u \in C^q(J)$. Here, $h(t) \in C(J \times \mathbb{R}, \mathbb{R})$, the space of continuous functions from J to $\mathbb{R}$.

As seen in [3,7], if $u \in C^q(J)$, then the solution of (14) can be written as

$$u(t) = u_0 E_{q,1}(\lambda t^q) + \int_0^t (t-s)^{(q-1)} E_{q,q}(\lambda (t-s)^q) h(s) ds. \tag{15}$$

Note that this is a C^q solution on the interval $[0,T]$ for any $T > 0$. Consider the linear Cauchy problem for the Caputo fractional differential equation

$$({}^cD^{nq}_{a+})y(x) = \lambda y(x) + f(x), (a \le x \le b, (n-1) < nq < n; n \in \mathrm{N}, \lambda \in \mathrm{R}) \tag{16}$$

$$y^k(a) = b_k \ (b_k \in \mathrm{R}), k = 0, 1, \ldots . n-1 \tag{17}$$

Then the solution of (16) can be written as

$$y(x) = \sum_{j=0}^{(n-1)} b_j (x-a)^j E_{nq,j+1}(\lambda (x-a)^{nq}) + \int_a^x (x-s)^{nq-1} E_{nq,nq}(\lambda (x-s)^{nq}) f(s) ds. \tag{18}$$

See [3], page 230, formula 4.1.62, for details.

Observe that the solution is a C^q solution on $[a,b]$. However, the initial conditions are the same as those of the integer order when $q = 1$. One of the main reasons is that a sufficient condition for $({}^cD^{nq}_{a+})y(x)$ and $({}^cD^{nq}_{b-})y(x)$ exists when $y^n(x)$ exists on $[a,b]$. In addition, when $q = 1$, then (16) is an nth-order-integer differential equation. Hence, the basis solution will be

$$1, (x-a), (x-a)^2, \dots (x-a)^{n-1}.$$

As such, the initial conditions are those of the corresponding integer problem, which are C^n functions on $[a, b]$. Please note that $({}^cD^{nq}_{a+})y(x)$ can be easily computed when the function $y(x)$ can be expressed as a function of $(x-a)$, say as $y = f(x-a)$. In order to compute $({}^cD^{nq}_{b-})y(x)$, we need to compute it by substituting $(x-a)$ with $(b-x)$, which is $y(x) = f(b-x)$. The converse is also true. That is, $({}^cD^{nq}_{b-})y(x)$ can be computed when $y(x)$ can be expressed as a function of $(b-x)$, say $y(x) = f(b-x)$.

Now consider the solution of (16) when $0 < q < 1$. The solution is given by

$$y(x) = b_0E_{q,1}(\lambda(x-a)^q) + \int_a^x (x-s)^{q-1}E_{q,q}(\lambda(x-s)^q)f(s)ds. \tag{19}$$

It is easy to check when $f(x) = 0$ because then the solution is not C^1 on $[a, b]$. It is just a C^q solution on $[a, b]$.

Definition 12. *The Caputo left fractional derivative of $u(x)$ of order nq for $(n-1) < nq < n$ is said to be a sequential left Caputo fractional derivative of order q if the relation*

$$({}^cD^{nq}_{a+})u(x) = {}^cD^{q}_{a+}({}^cD^{(n-1)q}_{a+})u(x) \tag{20}$$

holds for $n = 2, 3, \dots$. We denote this as $({}^{sc}D^{nq}_{a+})u(x)$.

Definition 13. *The Caputo right fractional derivative of $u(x)$ of order nq for $(n-1) < nq < n$ is said to be a sequential right Caputo fractional derivative of order q if the relation*

$$({}^cD^{nq}_{b-})u(x) = {}^cD^{q}_{b-}({}^cD^{(n-1)q}_{b-})u(x) \tag{21}$$

holds for $n = 2, 3, \dots$. We denote this as $({}^{sc}D^{nq}_{b-})u(x)$.

Note that if the Caputo left fractional derivative of order nq is a sequential derivative of order q, then the basis for the left Caputo sequential fractional differential equation $({}^cD^{nq}_{a+})u(x) = 0$ will be

$$1, (x-a)^q, (x-a)^{2q}, (x-a)^{3q}, \dots (x-a)^{(n-1)q}.$$

Similarly, note that if the Caputo right fractional derivative of order nq is a sequential derivative of order q, then the basis for the right Caputo sequential fractional differential equation $({}^cD^{nq}_{b-})u(x) = 0$ will be

$$1, (b-x)^q, (b-x)^{2q}, (b-x)^{3q}, \dots (b-x)^{(n-1)q}.$$

3. Main Results

In this section, we redefine the left and right Caputo derivatives in such a way that they match the left and right derivatives of the corresponding integer derivative. Furthermore, if both the left and right Caputo derivatives exist for any function $f(x)$, then for any x such that $a < x < b$, the left Caputo derivative will be equal to the right Caputo derivative.

For this purpose, we recall Theorem 2.2 in Kilbas et al. with the following modification. We assume the function under consideration to be a C^{nq} function instead of a C^n function. In order for the Caputo left derivative or Caputo right derivative (of order nq) to exist, it is sufficient for the function to be a C^n function. However, the solution which we compute will only be a C^{nq} solution. In our next result, we also assume that the Caputo fractional derivative of order nq is a sequential derivative of q.

Theorem 1. *Let $\Re(q) \geq 0$ and let $n = [\Re(q)] + 1$. Furthermore, let $u(x) \in C^n[a,b]$. Then the Caputo fractional derivatives $({}^cD^q_{a+})y(x)$ and $({}^cD^q_{b-})y(x)$ are continuous on $[a,b]$, $({}^cD^q_{a+})y(x) \in C[a,b]$, and $({}^cD^q_{b-})y(x) \in C[a,b]$.*

(a) If $q \not\subseteq N_0$, then

$$({}^cD^q_{a+})y(x)|_{x=a} = ({}^cD^q_{b-})y(x)|_{x=b} = 0,$$

(b) If $q \subseteq N_0$, then

$$({}^cD^n_{a+})y(x) = y^{(n)}(x) \text{ and } ({}^cD^n_{b-})y(x) = (-1)^n y^{(n)}(x) \ (n \in N).$$

Proof. The proof is very similar to the proof of Theorem 2.2 from [3]. The above theorem holds true under the weaker condition that the function is a C^{nq} function. The proof using this condition $f \in C^{nq}$ also follows along the same line as in [3]. □

Here, we apply the theorem from the application point of view. The aim is to show that we can compute the solution of sequential Caputo fractional initial value problems and sequential Caputo fractional boundary value problems with ease.

Remark 1. *Please note that in order for the above theorem to hold true and yield the integer result as a special case, we claim the following:*

1. *To compute a left-sided Caputo derivative of any order q, the function $y = f(x)$ should be expressed as a function of $(x-a)$, that is, $y = f(x-a)$.*
2. *Then we can compute the right derivative of the same function by replacing $(x-a)$ with $(b-x)$, that is, $y = f(b-x)$.*
3. *Similarly, in order to compute the right Caputo derivative of any function, the function should be expressed as a function of $(b-x)$, that is, $y = f(b-x)$.*
4. *Then we can compute its left derivative by replacing $(b-x)$ with $(x-a)$, that is, $y = f(x-a)$.*
5. *If the left and the right Caputo derivatives are computed using (1) and (2) or (3) and (4), then the conclusion of Theorem 1 holds true provided the exponent λ of $(x-a)^\lambda$ is $> q$.*
6. *In particular, if $\lambda = q$, then if the function $y(x)$ has a term $k(x-a)^q$ present when computing the Caputo left derivative and/or $k(b-x)^q$ is present when computing the Caputo right derivative of $y(x)$, then part (a) of Theorem 1 will not hold true. In the special case when $0 < q < 1$, then it is easy to see that*

$$({}^cD^q_{a+})((x-a)^q) = \Gamma(q+1) = ({}^cD^q_{b-})((b-x)^q).$$

   This can be easily extended for any q between $(n-1) < nq < n$.
7. *The Caputo left derivative of any function $y = f(x-a)$ at any point x_1 for $a < x_1 < b$ will be equal to the Caputo right derivative of $y = f(b-x)$ at the same point x_1 and vice versa.*

We illustrate our claim with several examples. Initially, we consider examples when $0 < q < 1$.

Example 1. *Let $f(x) = (x-a)$. Note that $f'(x) = 1$ on $[a,b]$.*
Then

$${}^cD^q_{a+}(x-a) = \frac{1}{\Gamma(1-q)} \int_a^x (x-s)^{-q} ds = \frac{(x-a)^{(1-q)}}{\Gamma(2-q)}$$

and

$${}^cD^q_{b-}(x-a) = \frac{-1}{\Gamma(1-q)} \int_x^b (s-x)^{-q} ds = \frac{-(b-x)^{(1-q)}}{\Gamma(2-q)}.$$

Further, ${}^{c}D^{q}_{a+}(x-a)|_{x=a} = 0$*, and* ${}^{c}D^{q}_{b-}(x-a)|_{x=b} = 0$*. However, if* $q = 1$*, then the left-sided integral reduces to* $f'(x) = 1$ *for all* x *on* $[a,b]$*.*

On the other hand, if $q = 1$*, then the right-sided integral reduces to* $f'(x) = -1$ *for all* x *on* $[a,b]$*. This does not verify the second part (b) of Theorem 1.*

However, if we choose $f(x) = b - x$ *for the Caputo right derivative, then*

$$ {}^{c}D^{q}_{b-}(b-x) = \frac{(b-x)^{(1-q)}}{\Gamma(2-q)}. $$

Also, in this case, substituting $q = 1$*, we have* $f'(x) = 1$ *on* $[a,b]$*. In addition,* $-f'(x) = -d/dx(b-x) = 1$*, which verifies the second part (b) of Theorem 1.*

The above example confirms [1] and [2] of the above remark.

In conclusion, we can compute the left derivative of any function $f(x)$ only when we can write $f(x)$ as a function of $x-a$, say $f(x-a)$. Then, we can compute the right derivative of the same function by computing $f(b-x)$.

Example 2. *Let* $f(x) = (b-x)$*. Note that* $f'(x) = -1$ *on* $[a,b]$*. In order to compute the Caputo left derivative of order* q*, such that* $0 < q < 1$*, of* $f(x) = (b-x)$*, we write* $f(x) = (b-a) - (x-a)$*. In order to compute the Caputo right derivative, we need to write* $f(x) = (b-a) - (b-x)$*. Then we can show that*

$$ {}^{c}D^{q}_{a+}((b-a)-(x-a)) = -\frac{(x-a)^{(1-q)}}{\Gamma(2-q)}, $$

and

$$ {}^{c}D^{q}_{b-}((b-a)-(b-x)) = -\frac{(b-x)^{(1-q)}}{\Gamma(2-q)}. $$

In addition,

$$ {}^{c}D^{q}_{a+}((b-a)-(x-a))|_{x=a} = 0 = {}^{c}D^{q}_{b-}((b-a)-(b-x))|_{x=b}. $$

It is easy to see ${}^{c}D^{q}_{a+}(b-x)|_{x=a} = 0$ *and* ${}^{c}D^{q}_{b-}(x-a)|_{x=b} = 0$*.*

Furthermore, when $q = 1$*, then* $-\dfrac{(x-a)^{(1-q)}}{\Gamma(2-q)}$ *reduces to* $f'(x) = -1$*. Similarly, when* $q = 1$*, then* $-\dfrac{(b-x)^{(1-q)}}{\Gamma(2-q)}$ *reduces to* $f'(x) = -1$*.*

The above example confirms [1] and [2] of the above remark.

Example 3. *Let* $f(x) = (x-a)^{\omega}$*.*

It is easy to see the left Caputo derivative of order q *of* $f(x) = (x-a)^{\omega}$ *is*

$$ {}^{c}D^{q}_{a+}(x-a)^{\omega} = \frac{\Gamma(\omega+1)(x-a)^{(\omega-q)}}{\Gamma(\omega-q+1)}. $$

Similarly, the right derivative of $(b-x)^{\omega}$ *is*

$$ {}^{c}D^{q}_{b-}(b-x)^{\omega} = \frac{\Gamma(\omega+1)(b-x)^{(\omega-q)}}{\Gamma(\omega-q+1)}. $$

Observe that $(x-a)^{\omega}$ *is not* C^1 *at* $x = a$*, and* $(b-x)^{\omega}$ *is not* C^1 *at* $x = b$ *when* $\omega < 1$*. However, part (a) of Theorem 1 holds true when* $q < \omega$*. In addition, if* $q = \omega = 1$*, then part (b) also holds true.*

Remark 2. *(i) If $\omega = 1, n = 1$, then our example will yield Example 1 as a special case.*
(ii) If $\omega = q$, then $f(x) \notin C^1$ on $[a,b]$. In this case, we obtain

$$ {}^{c}D^{q}_{a^+}(x-a)^q = \Gamma(q+1) = {}^{c}D^{q}_{b^-}(b-x)^q. $$

If $q = 1$, it satisfies part (b) of Theorem 1. Further, it illustrates that

$$ {}^{c}D^{q}_{a^+}(x-a)^q = {}^{c}D^{q}_{b^-}(b-x)^q $$

for all $x \in [a,b]$.
(iii) Observe that the left derivative at any point $x = x_1$ can be written $x_1 = a + \alpha$, and for the right derivative $x_1 = b - \alpha$, $\alpha \in (0,(b-a))$. Then the left derivative at any x_1 will be equal to $\dfrac{\Gamma(\omega+1)(\alpha)^{(\omega-q)}}{\Gamma(\omega-q+1)}$. Similarly, the right derivative will be equal to $\dfrac{\Gamma(\omega+1)(\alpha)^{(\omega-q)}}{\Gamma(\omega-q+1)}$.

Next, we present some numerical results for Example 3. We observe that both the left and right derivative graphs are one and the same for $a = 1$, $b = 2$, $\omega = 2$, and $q = 0.7, 0.8, 0.9, 1.0$ where the left derivative at any point $x = x_1$ can be written $x_1 = 1 + \alpha$, and for the right derivative $x_1 = 2 - \alpha$, $\alpha \in (0,1)$.

Let $f(x) = (x-1)^2$. The left Caputo derivative of order q of $f(x) = (x-1)^2$ is

$$ {}^{c}D^{q}_{1^+}(x-1)^2 = \frac{\Gamma(3)(x-1)^{(2-q)}}{\Gamma(3-q)}. $$

The right derivative of $(2-x)^2$ is

$$ {}^{c}D^{q}_{2^-}(2-x)^2 = \frac{\Gamma(3)(2-x)^{(2-q)}}{\Gamma(3-q)}. $$

In particular, if $x_1 = 1.4$, then $\alpha = 0.4$. Then the Caputo left derivative and the Caputo right derivative will be as below.

$$ {}^{c}D^{q}_{1^+}(x-1)^2|_{x=x_1} = 1 + 0.4 = \frac{\Gamma(3)(0.4)^{(2-q)}}{\Gamma(3-q)}, $$

$$ {}^{c}D^{q}_{2^-}(2-x)^2|_{x=x_1} = 2 - 0.4 = \frac{\Gamma(3)(0.4)^{(2-q)}}{\Gamma(3-q)}. $$

This shows that the Caputo left derivative equals the Caputo right derivative at $x_1 = 1.4$. Similarly, we can show this for every point.

We used MATLAB 9.14 to draw all our numerical results (see Figure 1).

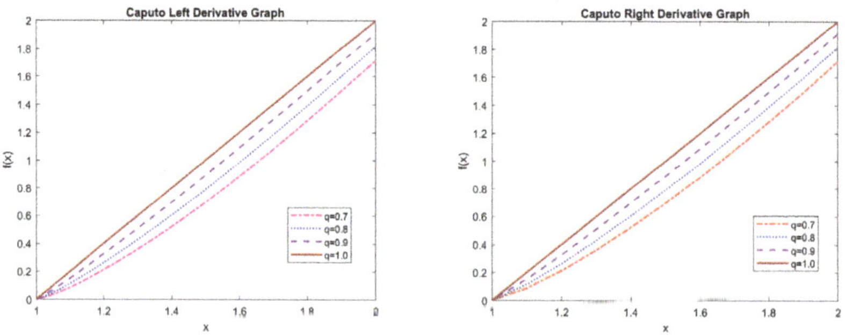

(**a**) (**b**)

Figure 1. (**a**) $\omega = 2$, $q = 0.7, 0.8, 0.9, 1.0$. The graph is plotted from the right of 'a' to the left of 'b'. (**b**) $\omega = 2$, $q = 0.7, 0.8, 0.9, 1.0$. The graph is plotted from the left of 'b' to the right of 'a'.

If $a = 1$, $b = 2$, $\omega = 1$, and $q = 0.7, 0.8, 0.9, 1.0$ where the left derivative at any point $x = x_1$ can be written $x_1 = 1 + \alpha$, and for the right derivative $x_1 = 2 - \alpha$, $\alpha \in (0, 1)$. Let $f(x) = (x-1)^1$. The left Caputo derivative of order q of $f(x) = (x-1)^1$ is

$$^{c}D^{q}_{1^+}(x-1)^1 = \frac{\Gamma(2)(x-1)^{(1-q)}}{\Gamma(2-q)}$$

The right derivative of $(2-x)^1$ is

$$^{c}D^{q}_{2^-}(2-x)^1 = \frac{\Gamma(2)(2-x)^{(1-q)}}{\Gamma(2-q)}.$$

See (Figure 2).

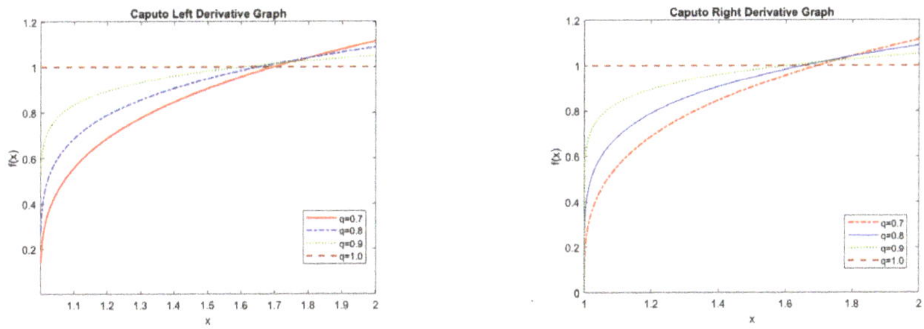

(**a**) (**b**)

Figure 2. (**a**) $\omega = 1$, $q = 0.7, 0.8, 0.9, 1.0$. The graph is plotted from the right of 'a' to the left of 'b'. (**b**) $\omega = 1$, $q = 0.7, 0.8, 0.9, 1.0$. The graph is plotted from the left of 'b' to the right of 'a'.

If $a = 1$, $b = 2$, $\omega = 0.9$, and $q = 0.7, 0.8, 0.9, 1.0$ where the left derivative at any point $x = x_1$ can be written $x_1 = 1 + \alpha$, and for the right derivative $x_1 = 2 - \alpha$, $\alpha \in (0, 1)$.

Let $f(x) = (x-1)^{0.9}$.

The left Caputo derivative of order q of $f(x) = (x-1)^2$ is

$$^{c}D^{q}_{1^+}(x-1)^{0.9} = \frac{\Gamma(1.9)(x-1)^{(0.9-q)}}{\Gamma(1.9-q)}$$

The right derivative of $(2-x)^{0.9}$ is

$$^{c}D^{q}_{2^-}(2-x)^{0.9} = \frac{\Gamma(1.9)(2-x)^{(0.9-q)}}{\Gamma(1.9-q)}$$

See (Figure 3).

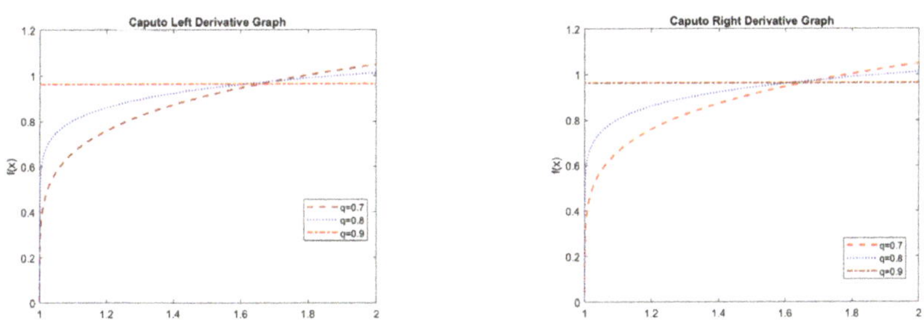

(**a**) (**b**)

Figure 3. (**a**) $\omega = 0.9$, $q = 0.7, 0.8, 0.9$. The graph is plotted from the right of 'a' to the left of 'b'. (**b**) $\omega = 0.9$, $q = 0.7, 0.8, 0.9$. The graph is plotted from the left of 'b' to the right of 'a'.

All our above numerical examples are to justify that the Caputo left derivative and the Caputo right derivative are equal at every point on the interval (a, b).

In the next set of examples, we replace the notation q with nq where $(n-1) < nq < n$.

Example 4. *Let $f(x) = (x-a)^{n\omega}$, where $nq < n\omega < n$. Then one can compute and show that*

$$ {}^{c}D_{a^+}^{nq}(x-a)^{n\omega} = \frac{\Gamma(n\omega+1)(x-a)^{(n\omega-nq)}}{\Gamma(n\omega-nq+1)} $$

Now let $f(x) = (b-x)^{n\omega}$, where $nq < n\omega < n$. Then one can compute and show that

$$ {}^{c}D_{b^-}^{nq}(b-x)^{n\omega} = \frac{\Gamma(n\omega+1)(b-x)^{(n\omega-nq)}}{\Gamma(n\omega-nq+1)} $$

Remark 3. *(i) If $q < \omega \leq n$, then part (a) of Theorem 1 is satisfied.*
(ii) If $\omega = q$, then $f(x) \notin C^1$ on $[a, b]$.

In this case, we obtain

$$ {}^{c}D_{a^+}^{nq}(x-a)^{nq} = \Gamma(nq+1) = {}^{c}D_{b^-}^{nq}(b-x)^{nq}. $$

If $q = 1$, it satisfies part (b) of Theorem 1.

In the next example, we consider the sequential left derivative ${}^{sc}D_{a^+}^{nq}u(x)$, which is a sequential derivative of order q, and the sequential right derivative ${}^{sc}D_{b^-}^{nq}u(x)$, which is a sequential derivative of order q.

Note that when $q = 1$, it is the usual integer derivative which is sequential, unlike computing the Caputo fractional derivative of order nq when it is not sequential, which can be computed at once. However, even in this case, we still need the nth-order-integer derivative of the function $f(x)$ ahead of time, which is sequential.

Example 5. *Let $f(x) = (x-a)^{n\omega}$. Then we can show that*

$$ {}^{sc}D_{a^+}^{nq}(x-a)^{n\omega} = \frac{\Gamma(n\omega+1)(x-a)^{(n\omega-nq)}}{\Gamma(n\omega-nq+1)}, $$

Now let $f(x) = (b-x)^{n\omega}$, where $nq < n\omega < n$. Then one can compute and show that

$$ {}^{sc}D_{b^-}^{nq}(b-x)^{n\omega} = \frac{\Gamma(n\omega+1)(b-x)^{(n\omega-nq)}}{\Gamma(n\omega-nq+1)}. $$

Note that the above relation has to be established by computing the Caputo fractional derivative sequentially.

Remark 4. *It is easy to check that*

$$ {}^{sc}D_{a^+}^{nq}(x-a)^{n\omega} = {}^{c}D_{a^+}^{nq}(x-a)^{n\omega} $$

and

$$ {}^{sc}D_{b^-}^{nq}(b-x)^{n\omega} = {}^{c}D_{b^-}^{nq}(b-x)^{n\omega} $$

when $n\omega > nq$.

In particular, when $\omega = q$, then

$$ {}^{sc}D_{a^+}^{nq}(x-a)^{nq} = {}^{c}D_{a^+}^{nq}(x-a)^{nq} = \Gamma(nq+1), $$

and

$$^{sc}D_{b^-}^{nq}(b-x)^{nq} = {}^{c}D_{b^-}^{nq}(b-x)^{nq} = \Gamma(nq+1).$$

Remark 5. *When we assume the function $u(x) \in C^n[a,b]$, then basis for the solution of the homogeneous equation for ${}^{c}D_{a^+}^{nq}u(x) = 0$ is*

$$1, (x-a), (x-a)^2, \ldots, (x-a)^{(n-1)}.$$

When we assume the function $u(x) \in C^q[a,b]$, then the basis for the solution of the homogeneous equation for ${}^{sc}D_{a^+}^{nq}u(x) = 0$ is

$$1, (x-a)^q, (x-a)^{2q}, \ldots, (x-a)^{(n-1)q}.$$

Similarly, when we assume the function $u(x) \in C^n[a,b]$, then the basis for the solution of the homogeneous equation for ${}^{c}D_{b^-}^{nq}u(x) = 0$ is

$$1, (b-x), (b-x)^2, \ldots, (b-x)^{(n-1)q}.$$

Similarly, when we assume the function $u(x) \in C^q[a,b]$, then the basis for the solution of the homogeneous equation for ${}^{sc}D_{b^-}^{nq}u(x) = 0$ is

$$1, (b-x)^q, (b-x)^{2q}, \ldots, (b-x)^{(n-1)q}.$$

Remark 6. *Irrespective of the Caputo fractional derivative being sequential or not, the Caputo left derivative of the function can be computed only when the function $f(x)$ can be expressed as a function of $(x-a)$, namely, $u(x) = f(x-a)$. Then the Caputo right derivative can be computed by the function $u(x) = f(b-x)$ and vice versa.*

Next we demonstrate that the Caputo left derivative of function $f(x-a)$ at $x = x_1$ such that $a < x_1 < b$ will be equal to the Caputo right derivative of the function $f(b-x)$ at $x = x_1$. Note that any $x = x_1$, such that $a < x_1 < b$, can be expressed as $x_1 = a + \alpha$ for the left derivative and $x_1 = b - \alpha$ for the right derivative.

From Example 3, we have

$${}^{c}D_{a+}^{q}(x-a)^{\omega} = \frac{\Gamma(\omega+1)(x-a)^{(\omega-q)}}{\Gamma(\omega-q+1)},$$

and

$${}^{c}D_{b^-}^{q}(b-x)^{\omega} = \frac{\Gamma(\omega+1)(b-x)^{(\omega-q)}}{\Gamma(\omega-q+1)}.$$

Let $a = 1, b = 2$, and $x_1 = 1 + 0.25$. Then

$${}^{c}D_{1+}^{q}(x-1)^{\omega}|_{x=1+0.25} = \frac{\Gamma(\omega+1)(0.25)^{(\omega-q)}}{\Gamma(\omega-q+1)}$$

and

$${}^{c}D_{2^-}^{q}(2-x)^{\omega}|_{x=2-0.25} = \frac{\Gamma(\omega+1)(0.25)^{(\omega-q)}}{\Gamma(\omega-q+1)}$$

It is easy to see that

$${}^{c}D_{1+}^{q}(x-1)^{\omega}|_{x=1+0.25} = {}^{c}D_{2^-}^{q}(2-x)^{\omega}|_{x=2-0.25}.$$

It is clear from the above examples that

$${}^{c}D_{a+}^{q}f(x-a) = F(x-a)$$

and

$$^{c}D^{q}_{b-}f(b-x) = F(b-x).$$

Then

$$^{c}D^{q}_{a+}f(x-a)|_{x=a+\alpha} = F(\alpha) = {^{c}D^{q}_{b-}}f(b-x)|_{x=b-\alpha}.$$

This proves that the Caputo left derivative is equal to the Caputo right derivative at any point $x = x_1$ on the interval (a,b).

Next we consider a sequential boundary value problem. The advantage of considering sequential boundary value problems is that all the integer results can be obtained as a special case. In the literature, they assume that the solution is a C^2 solution. As a consequence of this, the basis solution of $^{c}D^{2q}_{a+}u(x) = 0$ is taken as in the integer $(x-a),(b-x)$. However, in the sequential boundary value problems $^{sc}D^{2q}_{a+}u(x) = 0$, the basis solution is $1,(x-a)^q$. Instead of the Caputo left derivative, if we use the Caputo right derivative $^{sc}D^{2q}_{b-}u(x) = 0$, then the basis solution is $1,(b-x)^q$. From our examples, it is clear that $^{c}D^{a}_{a+}(x-a)^q = \Gamma(q+1) = {^{c}D^{a}_{b-}}(b-x)^q$. This formula is useful when the fractional derivatives are involved in boundary value problems.

Now consider the linear sequential boundary value problem,

$$^{sc}D^{2q}_{a+}u(x) = h(x) \tag{22}$$

with boundary conditions

$$u(a) = u_a \text{ and } u(b) = u_b.$$

Then the solution of the boundary value problem (22) with Dirichlet boundary conditions is given by

$$u(x) = u_a + \frac{(x-a)^q}{(b-a)^q}(u_b - u_a) + \int_a^b G(x,s)h(s-a)ds,\ a \le s \le x \le b, \tag{23}$$

using the sequential Caputo left derivative. Furthermore, it is given by

$$u(x) = u_b + \frac{(b-x)^q}{(b-a)^q}(u_a - u_b) + \int_a^b G(x,s)h(b-s)ds,\ a \le x \le s \le b, \tag{24}$$

using the sequential Caputo right derivative. The Green's function $G(x,s)$ is given as follows:

$$G(x,s) = \begin{cases} -\dfrac{(x-a)^q(b-s)^{2q-1}}{\Gamma(2q)(b-a)^q} + \dfrac{(x-s)^{(2q-1)}}{\Gamma(2q)} & a \le s \le x \le b \\ -\dfrac{(b-x)^q(s-a)^{2q-1}}{\Gamma(2q)(b-a)^q} + \dfrac{(s-x)^{(2q-1)}}{\Gamma(2q)} & a \le x \le s \le b. \end{cases} \tag{25}$$

Remark 7. *The above solution can be easily obtained by writing the solution as*

$$u(x) = a_0 + a_1(x-a)^q + \frac{1}{\Gamma(2q)}\int_a^x (x-s)^{(2q-1)}h(s-a)ds,\ \ a \le s \le x \le b,$$

and

$$u(x) = b_0 + b_1(b-x)^q + \frac{1}{\Gamma(2q)}\int_x^b (s-x)^{(2q-1)}h(b-s)ds,\ \ a \le x \le s \le b,$$

using the Caputo left and right derivatives, respectively.

Next we present a simple example when $h(s) = 1$ in (22). In this case, the solution can be written as

$$u(x) = u_a + \frac{(x-a)^q}{(b-a)^q}(u_b - u_a) - \frac{(x-a)^q(b-a)^q}{\Gamma(2q+1)} + \frac{(x-a)^{2q}}{\Gamma(2q+1)}.$$

The solution of the boundary value problem

$$^{sc}D^{2q}_{a+}u(x) = h(x) \tag{26}$$

with the following boundary conditions

$$u(a) - \alpha_0 {}^cD^q_{a+}(u(x))|_{x=a} = u_a, \text{ and } u(b) + \beta_0 {}^cD^q_{b-}(u(x))|_{x=b} = u_b,$$

where $\alpha_0 \geq 0, \beta_0 \geq 0$ can easily be computed using our Remark 7.

4. Conclusions

The computation of the left Caputo derivative of a function of order nq for $n = 1, 2, \ldots k-1, k$ starting from the point $x = a$ can be computed when the function $u = f(x)$ can be expressed as a function of $u = f(x-a)$. In addition, the Caputo left derivative exists when the exponent λ of $(x-a)$ should be such that $n\lambda \geq nq$. If $n\lambda < n$ when $(n-1) < q < n$, then it is not a C^n function. In the literature, so far when $(n-1) < nq < n$, they have assumed that $u = f(x-a)$ is a C^n function on $[a,b]$. However, the solution obtained is only a C^{nq} function. This is true for initial value problems. Any function which is a C^{nq} function can be assumed to be a sequential Caputo fractional derivative of order 'q'.

Once we compute the Caputo left fractional derivative of the function $u = f(x-a)$, then we can compute the right Caputo derivative of the same function by computing $f(b-x)$. Further, if we are computing the Caputo fractional derivative at a specific point, say x_1, $a < x_1 < b$, then $x_1 - a = \alpha$ and $b - x_1 = \alpha$. This helps us to prove that the Caputo left derivative at any interior point $x = x_1$ when $a \leq x_1 \leq b$ equals the Caputo right derivative at the same point x_1.

The Caputo right derivative will be useful in computing the solution of linear sequential Caputo fractional boundary value problems with fractional boundary conditions. The study of linear sequential Caputo boundary value problems can also have lower-order Caputo derivatives with fractional boundary conditions, which will not hold true for non-sequential boundary value problems.

The current known integer boundary value problem results can be obtained by substituting $q = 1$. The work of this article is seed work that will give an insight to handle more general types of linear Caputo differential operators with lower-order fractional derivatives and with fractional boundary conditions. Our aim is to seek a C^{nq} solution for sequential Caputo differential equations with Caputo fractional initial and boundary conditions of a lower order. Since these solutions reduce to the solution of the integer order, we can use q as a parameter to enhance the mathematical model.

Author Contributions: Writing—original draft, A.S.V. and B.S. All authors have read and agreed to the published version of the manuscript.

Funding: This research received no external funding.

Data Availability Statement: The original contributions presented in this study are included in the article. Further inquiries can be directed to the corresponding author.

Conflicts of Interest: The authors declare no conflicts of interest.

References

1. Diethelm, K. *The Analysis of Fractional Differential Equations*; Springer: Berlin/Heidelberg, Germany, 2004.
2. Gorenflo, R.; Kilbas, A.A.; Mainardi, F.; Rogosin, S.V *Mittag-Leffler Functions, Related Topic and Applications*; Springer Monographs in Mathematics Series; Springer: Berlin/Heidelberg, Germany, 2014; 443p.
3. Kilbas, A.A.; Srivsatava, H.M.; Trujillo, J.J. *Theory and Apllications of Fractional Differential Equations*; North-Holland Mathematics Studies; Elsevier Science B.V.: Amsterdam, The Netherlands, 2006; Volume 24.

4. Kiryakova, V. *Generalized Fractional Calculus and Applications*; Pitman Research Notes in Mathematics Volume 301; Longman-Wiley: New York, NY, USA, 1994.
5. Lakshmikantham, V.; Leela, S.; Vasundhara, D.J. *Theory of Fractional Dynamic Systems*; Cambridge University Press: Cambridge, UK, 2009.
6. Oldham, B.; Spanier, J. *The Fractional Calculus*; Academic Press: New York, NY, USA; London, UK, 1974.
7. Podlubny, I. *Fractional Differential Equations*; Academic Press: San Diego, CA, USA, 1999.
8. Sambandham, B.; Vatsala, A.S. Numerical Results for Linear Caputo Fractional Differential Equations with Variable Coefficients and Applications. *Neura Parallel Sci. Comput.* **2015**, *23*, 253–266.
9. Sambandham, B.; Vatsala, A.S. Basic results for sequential Caputo fractional differential equations. *Mathematics* **2015**, *3*, 76–91. [CrossRef]
10. Sambandham, B.; Vatsala, A.S.; Chellamuthu, V.K. Numerical Results for Linear Sequential Caputo Fractional Boundary Value Problems. *Mathematics* **2019**, *7*, 910. [CrossRef]
11. Samko, S.G.; Kilbas, A.A.; Marichev, O.I. *Fractional Integrals and Derivatives, Theory and Applications*; Gordon and Breach: Yverdon, Switzerland, 1993.
12. Vatsala, A.S.; Pageni, G. Series Solution Method for Solving Sequential Caputo Fractional Differential Equations. *AppliedMath* **2023**, *3*, 730–740. [CrossRef]
13. Diethelm, K.; Ford, N.J. Analysis of fractional differential equations. *J. Math. Anal. Appl.* **2002**, *265*, 229–248. [CrossRef]
14. Diethelm, K.; Ford, N.J. Multi-order fractional differential equations and their numerical solution. *Appl. Math. Comput.* **2004**, *154*, 621–640. [CrossRef]
15. Diethelm, K.; Freed, A.D. On the solution of nonlinear fractional differential equations used in the modeling of viscoplasticity. In *Scientific Computing in Chemical Engineering II: Computational Fluid Dynamics, Reaction Engineering, and Molecular Properties*; Keil, F., Mackens, W., Vob, H., Werther, J., Eds.; Springer: Berlin/Heidelberg, Germany, 1999; pp. 217–224.
16. Ding, Y.; Yea, H. A fractional-order differential equation model of HIV infection of CD4C T-cells. *Math. Comput. Model.* **2009**, *50*, 386–392. [CrossRef]
17. Fallahgoul, H.; Focardi, S.; Fabozzi, F. *Fractional Calculus and Fractional Processes with Applications to Financial Economics, Theory and Application*; Academic Press: Cambridge, MA, USA, 2016.
18. Garg, V.; Singh, K. An Improved Grunwald-Letnikov Fractional Differential Mask for Image Texture Enhancement. *Int. J. Adv. Comput. Sci. Appl.* **2012**, *3*, 130–135. [CrossRef]
19. Glöckle, W.G.; Nonnenmacher, T.F. A fractional calculus approach to self similar protein dynamics. *Biophy. J.* **1995**, *68*, 46–53. [CrossRef]
20. Haubold, H.J.; Mathai, A.M.; Saxena, R.K. Mittag-Leffler Functions and Their Applications. *J. Appl. Math.* **2011**, *2011*, 298628. [CrossRef]
21. Javidi, M.; Ahmad, B. Dynamic analysis of time fractional order phytoplankton-toxic phytoplankton-zooplankton system. *Ecol. Model.* **2015**, *318*, 8–18. [CrossRef]
22. Huo, J.; Zhao, H.; Zhu, L. The effect of vaccines on backward bifurcation in a fractional order HIV model. *Nonlinear Anal. Real World Appl.* **2015**, *26*, 289–305. [CrossRef]
23. Klimek, M. Fractional Sequential Mechanics—Models with Symmetric Fractional Derivative. *Czechoslov. J. Phys.* **2001**, *51*, 1348–1354. [CrossRef]
24. Lakshmikantham, V.; Vatsala, A.S. Basic theory of fractional differential equations. *Nonlinear Anal. TMAA* **2008**, *69*, 2677–2682. [CrossRef]
25. Vargas De Leon, C. Volterra type Lyapunov functions for fractional order epidemic systems. *Commun. Nonlinear Sci. Numer. Simul.* **2015**, *24*, 75–85. [CrossRef]
26. Metzler, R.; Schick, W.; Kilian, H.G.; Nonnenmacher, T.F. Relaxation in filled polymers: A fractional calculus approach. *J. Chem. Phy.* **1995**, *103*, 7180–7186. [CrossRef]
27. Paredes, G.E. *Fractional-Order Models for Nuclear Reactor Analysis*; Woodhead Publishing: Cambridge, UK, 2020.
28. Almeida, R.; Bastos, N.R.O.; Monteiro, M.T.T. Modeling some real phenomena by fractional differential equations. *Math. Methods Appl. Sci.* **2016**, *39*, 4846–4855. [CrossRef]
29. El-Ajou, A.; Arqub, O.A.; Momani, S. Solving fractional two-point boundary value problems using continuous analytic method. *Ain Shams Eng. J.* **2013**, *4*, 539–547. [CrossRef]
30. Mehandirattaa, V.; Mehraa, M.; Leugering, G. Existence and uniqueness results for a nonlinear Caputo fractional boundary value problem on a star graph. *J. Math. Anal. Appl.* **2019**, *477*, 1243–1264.
31. Fewster-Young, N. Existence Resuts for Caputo Fractional Boundary Value Problems with Unrestricted Growth Conditions. *Differ. Equ. Appl.* **2023**, *15*, 135–146. [CrossRef]
32. Ibrahim, B.H.E.; Dong, Q.; Fan, Z. Existence for boundary value problems of twoterm Caputo fractional differential equations. *J. Nonlinear Sci. Appl.* **2017**, *10*, 511–520. [CrossRef]
33. Vatsala, A.S.; Sowmya, M. Laplace Transform Method for Linear Sequential Riemann-Liouville and Caputo Fractional Differential Equations. *AIP Conf. Proc.* **2017**, *1798*, 020171.
34. Vatsala, A.S.; Sambandham, B. Sequential Caputo versus Nonsequential Caputo Fractional Initial and Boundary Value Problems. *Int. J. Differ. Equ.* **2020**, *15*, 529–544.

35. Vatsala, A.S.; Pageni, G.; Vijesh, V.A. Analysis of sequential Caputo fractional differential equations versus non-sequential Caputo fractional differential equations with applications. *Foundations* **2022**, *2*, 1129–1142. [CrossRef]
36. Pageni, G.; Vatsala, A.S. Study of two system of Caputo fractional differential equations with initial conditions via Laplace transform method. *Neural Parallel Sci. Comput.* **2021**, *29*, 69–83. [CrossRef]
37. Pageni, G.; Vatsala, A.S. Study of Three Systems of non-linear Caputo Fractional Differential Equations with initial conditions and Applications. *Neural Parallel Sci. Comput.* **2021**, *29*, 211–229.
38. Chikrii, A.; Matychyn, I. Riemann–Liouville, Caputo, and sequential fractional derivatives in differential games. In *Advances in Dynamic Games*; Birkhäuser: Boston, MA, USA, 2011; pp. 61–81.
39. Wang, Y.; Li, X.; Huang, Y. The Green's function for Caputo fractional boundary value problem with a convection term. *AIMS Math.* **2022**, *7*, 4887–4897. [CrossRef]
40. Anderson, D. Positive Green's functions for some fractional-order boundary value problems. *arXiv* **2014**, arXiv:1411.5616.
41. Kiskinova, H.; Petkovab, M.; Zahariev, A. Remarks on the Coincidence of the Left-side and Right-side Fractional Derivatives on an Interval and Some Consequences. *AIP Conf. Proc.* **2021**, *2333*, 080003.
42. Ross, B. *Fractional Calculus and its Applications*; Lecture Notes in Mathematics; Dold, A., Eckmann, B., Eds.; Proceedings; Springer: New York, NY, USA, 1974.

mathematics

MDPI

Article

Efficient Solutions for Stochastic Fractional Differential Equations with a Neutral Delay Using Jacobi Poly-Fractonomials

Afshin Babaei [1], Sedigheh Banihashemi [1], Behrouz Parsa Moghaddam [2], Arman Dabiri [3] and Alexandra Galhano [4,*]

[1] Department of Applied Mathematics, University of Mazandaran, Babolsar P.O. Box 47416-95447, Iran; babaei@umz.ac.ir (A.B.); s.banihashemi@stu.umz.ac.ir (S.B.)
[2] Department of Mathematics, Lahijan Branch, Islamic Azad University, Lahijan P.O. Box 44169-39515, Iran; bparsa@iau.ac.ir
[3] Department of Mechanical and Mechatronics, Southern Illinois University, Edwardsville, IL 62026, USA; adabiri@siue.edu
[4] Faculdade de Ciências Naturais, Engenharias e Tecnologias, Universidade Lusófona do Porto, Rua Augusto Rosa 24, 4000-098 Porto, Portugal
* Correspondence: alexandra.galhano@ulusofona.pt

Abstract: This paper introduces a novel numerical technique for solving fractional stochastic differential equations with neutral delays. The method employs a stepwise collocation scheme with Jacobi poly-fractonomials to consider unknown stochastic processes. For this purpose, the delay differential equations are transformed into augmented ones without delays. This transformation makes it possible to use a collocation scheme improved with Jacobi poly-fractonomials to solve the changed equations repeatedly. At each iteration, a system of nonlinear equations is generated. Next, the convergence properties of the proposed method are rigorously analyzed. Afterward, the practical utility of the proposed numerical technique is validated through a series of test examples. These examples illustrate the method's capability to produce accurate and efficient solutions.

Keywords: fractional neutral stochastic differential equations; Caputo fractional derivative; time-varying delay; iterative collocation method; Jacobi poly-fractonomials; numerical solution

MSC: 45J05; 65R20; 26A33; 97N20

1. Introduction

Ordinary differential equations (ODEs) are fundamental mathematical tools used to determine deterministic dynamical systems' evolution by describing a relationship between the state variables and their rates of change [1]. They are essential for understanding phenomena such as motion [2], electrical circuits [3], and structural mechanics [4]. In real-world phenomena, dynamical systems are often influenced by external noise or inherent randomness, typically represented by Brownian motion, making them difficult to model with ordinary differential equations (ODEs). Stochastic differential equations (SDEs) are introduced as an extension to ODEs in order to incorporate random processes and effectively capture random fluctuations. For example, in finance, SDEs model the random behavior of market prices and interest rates, providing insights into pricing financial instruments and managing risk [5–8]. In engineering, SDEs assist in designing systems that can withstand random environmental disturbances [9,10]. In population dynamics, they model the effects of random events on species populations [11,12], and in biology, they describe processes such as gene expression and the spread of diseases [13–16].

Delay differential equations (DDEs) are a class of differential equations used to model dynamical systems that depend on past states, meaning that the current rate of change of the system's state is a function of the current state and its history. The applications of time-delay systems are vast, ranging from engineering [17], where they model network-induced delays in control systems, to economics [18], where they represent the lag between investment and return, and to biology [19], where they can model the spread of diseases or population dynamics. Delays can be constant, time-varying, or distributed, and they are inherent in many real-world processes due to the finite speed of information transmission [20], material transport delays [18,20], or gestation periods in biological systems [19]. Time delays can lead to complex behaviors such as increased oscillatory tendencies, instability, and bifurcations, posing significant challenges in such systems' analysis, control, and stability [21].

Fractional differential equations (FDEs) are developed by the presence of derivatives and integrals of non-integer order, known as fractional calculus, which generalizes the concept of integer-order differentiation and integration to arbitrary order. Fractional derivatives provide an excellent tool for describing memory and the hereditary properties of various materials and processes [22]. Unlike classical derivative operators, fractional derivatives are non-local, encapsulating effects over an interval, which makes them inherently suitable for modeling systems with memory and spatial heterogeneity [23–25]. Non-locality and the ability to capture long-term memory make fractional systems a natural choice for describing complex phenomena in control theory [26,27], biology [28], and finance [29], where processes are influenced by their entire history rather than just their current state. This is particularly useful in fields such as viscoelasticity [24], where materials exhibit both viscous and elastic characteristics, and in anomalous diffusion, where particle trajectories deviate from classical Brownian motion.

Stochastic fractional delay differential equations (SFDDEs) significantly advance the modeling of complex dynamical real-world problems by incorporating the system's past, possible random processes, and hereditary properties. This class of differential equations has garnered substantial attention from researchers due to its potential to capture the intricate interplay of randomness and memory effects in dynamic systems. For instance, recent studies have delved into the uniqueness and solvability of FSDEs with constant delay [30], proposed collocation methods for solving nonlinear fractional SDEs with constant delay [31–33], and considered approximation techniques for solutions of neutral delay fractional SDEs based on the Faedo–Galerkin method [34]. Additionally, the numerical solution of neutral stochastic integro-differential equations with Caputo fractional derivatives has been explored [35], and innovative approaches such as the least squares support vector regression method based on Chelyshkov polynomials have been presented to solve a class of nonlinear SDEs with variable fractional Brownian motion [36]. While the foundational methods are well-established, considerable challenges emerge when *neutral* DDEs are augmented with fractional derivatives and stochastic terms. Even in basic fractional DDEs, the nonlocal nature of fractional operators causes the numerical errors in explicit finite-difference methods to increase exponentially. Nonetheless, as shown in various studies, these challenges can be effectively mitigated using spectral methods [37,38].

This paper proposes a stepwise collocation scheme incorporating Jacobi poly-fractonomials, a more generalized form of Jacobi polynomials, to obtain the numerical solution of a class of stochastic fractional neutral delay differential equations (SFDDEs) containing neutral delays, which is referred to as SFNDEs. Moreover, Jacobi polynomials form a versatile family of orthogonal polynomials from which several well-known polynomials may be derived through the appropriate specification of parameters or limits. Well-known examples are Legendre polynomials with a zero value for both of the parameters, Gegenbauer (ultra-spherical) polynomials for which the parameters are equal, and Chebyshev polynomials of the first and second kinds corresponding to specific values of the parameters. Besides these, Laguerre and Hermite polynomials can also be transformed into Jacobi polynomials, though not as direct examples. Jacobi poly-fractonomials provide a robust structure for representing intricate systems characterized by fractional-order dynamics. The specific features of these models make them a necessary addition to the mathematical toolbox for extending the capability provided to analysts and researchers working in fields where fractional-order models see widespread application. While they entail a bit more complexity relative to the integer-order polynomials, such difficulties are often overshadowed by their potential for much better modeling and for investigating subtle behaviors in fractional-order systems, both of which are shown in this study. The approach begins by transforming the equations into equivalent delay-free forms. Then, the collocation scheme is iteratively applied to generate a set of nonlinear equations at each stage, which can be solved by a common nonlinear solver. The convergence of the proposed method is studied, and its efficiency is shown in a set of test examples. The organization of this paper is as follows: In Section 2, the fundamental definitions and characteristics necessary for understanding the subsequent topics are elaborated upon. The class of SFDDEs of interest in this study is introduced in Section 3. Section 4 discusses the stepwise Jacobi poly-fractonomials collocation scheme. A thorough analysis of the error associated with this scheme is provided in Section 5. The numerical algorithm for two test examples is explained in detail in Section 6. Finally, Section 7 presents the concluding remarks of this article.

2. Preliminaries and Definitions

This section presents essential principles of fractional definitions and the characteristics of Jacobi polynomials, including the definition associated with fractional types.

Definition 1 ([22]). *The Riemann–Liouville fractional integral of order η is a generalization of the classical integral and is defined as*

$$\mathrm{I}_t^{\eta}u(t) = \frac{1}{\Gamma(\eta)}\int_0^t (t-s)^{\eta-1}u(s)\,\mathrm{d}s, \qquad (\eta, t > 0), \tag{1}$$

where $\Gamma(\eta)$ denotes the Gamma function, which is a continuous extension of the factorial function to non-integer values.

Definition 2 ([22]). *The Caputo fractional derivative of order $\eta \in (0,1]$, denoted by ${}^{\mathrm{C}}\mathscr{D}_t^{\eta}[\cdot]$, provides a modification of the traditional derivative by incorporating fractional calculus principles. That is,*

$${}^{\mathrm{C}}\mathscr{D}_t^{\eta}u(t) = \frac{1}{\Gamma(1-\eta)}\int_0^t (t-s)^{-\eta}u'(s)\,\mathrm{d}s, \quad \eta \in (0,1]. \tag{2}$$

Definition 3 ([39]). *The Jacobi polynomial $\phi_i^{(\beta,\gamma)}(t)$ of degree i satisfies the following explicit form:*

$$\phi_i^{(\beta,\gamma)}(t) = \sum_{k=0}^{i} \Pi_{k,i}^{(\beta,\gamma)}\left(\frac{t+1}{2}\right)^k, \qquad (\beta, \gamma > -1), \tag{3}$$

where

$$\Pi_{k,i}^{(\beta,\gamma)} := \frac{(-1)^{i-k}\,\Gamma(i+\gamma+1)\,\Gamma(i+\beta+\gamma+k+1)}{(i-k)!\,k!\,\Gamma(k+\gamma+1)\,\Gamma(i+\beta+\gamma+1)}.$$

Definition 4 ([40,41]). *The Jacobi poly-fractonomial $\theta_i^{\mu}(t)$ over $[-1,1]$ is defined by*

$$\theta_i^{\mu}(t) = (t+1)^{\mu}\phi_{i-1}^{(-\mu,\mu)}(t), \quad i \geq 1, \tag{4}$$

where the Jacobi polynomial $\phi_{i-1}^{(-\mu,\mu)}(t)$ is defined in Equation (3) when $\mu \in (0,1)$.

Lemma 1 ([41]). *The Jacobi poly-fractonomials $\theta_i^{\mu}(t)$ are orthogonal using the weight function*

$$\mathbf{w}(t) = (1-t)^{-\mu}(1+t)^{-\mu}, \tag{5}$$

such that

$$\int_{-1}^{1} \mathbf{w}(t)\theta_i^{(\mu)}(t)\theta_j^{(\mu)}(t)\mathrm{d}t = \varrho_i^{(-\mu,\mu)}\delta_{i,j},$$

and

$$\varrho_i^{(-\mu,\mu)} = \int_{-1}^{1}(1-t)^{-\mu}(1+t)^{\mu}\left(\phi_i^{(-\mu,\mu)}(t)\right)^2 \mathrm{d}t = \frac{2\Gamma(i-\mu)\Gamma(i+\mu)}{(2i-1)(i-1)!\Gamma(i)},$$

where $\delta_{i,j}$ *is the kronecker function.*

Definition 5 ([40]). *The shifted Gauss–Lobatto–Chebyshev (GLC) quadrature nodes over* $[\mathbf{e}_1, \mathbf{e}_2]$ *are*

$$ {}^{\mathbf{e}_2}_{\mathbf{e}_1}\mathbf{t}_i = \frac{\mathbf{e}_2 - \mathbf{e}_1}{2}(z_i + 1) + \mathbf{e}_1, \quad i = 1, \ldots, n+1, \tag{6}$$

where $\mathbf{z}_i = \cos\left(\frac{\pi}{2}\frac{2i-1}{n+1}\right)$, $i = 1, \ldots, n+1$.

Definition 6 ([32]). *The shifted Jacobi poly-fractonomials, denoted as* $\theta_i^{\mu}(t; \mathbf{e}_1, \mathbf{e}_2)$, *are a specific class of polynomials defined over the interval* $[\mathbf{e}_1, \mathbf{e}_2]$. *These polynomials are formulated by shifting the standard Jacobi polynomials to the desired interval. Namely,*

$$\theta_i^{\mu}(t; \mathbf{e}_1, \mathbf{e}_2) = \theta_i^{\mu}\left(\frac{2}{\mathbf{e}_2 - \mathbf{e}_1}(t - \mathbf{e}_1) - 1\right), \quad i \geq 1,$$

where t *is the variable,* $\mathbf{e}_1$ *and* $\mathbf{e}_2$ *represent the endpoints of the interval, and* μ *is a parameter associated with the poly-fractonomials. This transformation effectively maps the interval* $[\mathbf{e}_1, \mathbf{e}_2]$ *to the standard interval* $[-1, 1]$, *facilitating the use of Jacobi polynomials in various applications.*

Lemma 2 ([40]). *Let* $\Omega := [\mathbf{e}_1, \mathbf{e}_2]$ *and the function space* $\mathbf{L}^2_{\gamma,\delta}(\Omega)$ *be defined as follows:*

$$\mathbf{L}^2_{\gamma,\delta}(\Omega) = \left\{g : \ g \text{ is } \textbf{measurable} \text{ and } \|g\|_{\mathbf{L}^2_{\gamma,\delta}(\Omega)} < \infty\right\},$$

where

$$\|g\|_{\mathbf{L}^2_{\gamma,\delta}(\Omega)} = \left(\int_{\Omega} \mathbf{w}^{\gamma,\delta}(\zeta; \mathbf{e}_1, \mathbf{e}_2)\, |g(\zeta)|^2 \,\mathrm{d}\zeta\right)^{\frac{1}{2}},$$

with the weight function $\mathbf{w}^{\gamma,\delta}(t; \mathbf{e}_1, \mathbf{e}_2) = (\mathbf{e}_2 - t)^{\gamma}(t - \mathbf{e}_1)^{\delta}$, $\gamma, \delta > -1$ [40,42]. *In addition, let*

$$\Lambda^m_{\gamma,\delta}(\Omega) := \left\{g : \ \partial_t^r g \in \mathbf{L}^2_{\gamma+r,\delta+r}(\Omega), \ r = 0, 1, \ldots, m\right\},$$
$$\mathbf{B}^q_{\gamma,-\delta}(\Omega) := \left\{g : \ \mathscr{D}_t^{\delta+r} g \in \mathbf{L}^2_{\gamma+\delta+r,r}(\Omega), \ r = 0, 1, \ldots, q\right\}.$$

For $g \in \mathbf{L}^2_{-\mu,-\mu}(\Omega)$, *then the function* $g(t)$ *can be approximated as follows:*

$$g(t) \simeq g_n(t) = \sum_{r=1}^{n+1} c_r \theta_r^{(\mu)}(t; \mathbf{e}_1, \mathbf{e}_2) \triangleq \mathbf{C}^{\mathrm{T}}\, {}^{\mathbf{e}_2}_{\mathbf{e}_1}\Theta(t), \tag{7}$$

where

$$c_r = \frac{1}{\psi_r}\int_{\Omega} g(t)\, \mathbf{w}^{-\mu,-\mu}(t; \mathbf{e}_1, \mathbf{e}_2)\, \theta_r^{(\mu)}(t; \mathbf{e}_1, \mathbf{e}_2)\mathrm{d}t,$$
$$\psi_r := \frac{(\mathbf{e}_2 - \mathbf{e}_1)\Gamma(r - \mu + 1)\Gamma(r + \mu + 1)}{(2r+1)\Gamma^2(r+1)},$$
$$\mathbf{C} := [c_1, c_2, \cdots, c_{n+1}]^{\mathrm{T}},$$

$$ {}^{e_2}_{e_1}\Theta(t) := \left[\theta_1^{(\mu)}(t;e_1,e_2),\cdots,\theta_{n+1}^{(\mu)}(t;e_1,e_2)\right]^{\mathrm{T}}. $$

Lemma 3 ([43]). *If $g(t) \in \mathbf{C}^{2\bar{\mathrm{P}}}(\Omega)$, where $\Omega := [e_1, e_2]$, then an approximate integral of the function $g(t)$ over the interval Ω can be obtained using the Legendre–Gauss quadrature formula:*

$$ \int_{e_1}^{e_2} g(s)\,\mathrm{d}s \simeq \frac{e_2 - e_1}{2} \sum_{i=0}^{\bar{\mathrm{P}}} \omega_i g\left(\frac{e_2 - e_1}{2}\sigma_i + \frac{e_2 + e_1}{2}\right), \tag{8} $$

where $\{\sigma_i : i = 0, \ldots, \bar{\mathrm{P}}\}$ are the zeros of the Legendre polynomial $\phi_{\bar{\mathrm{P}}+1}^{(0,0)}(t)$, and the corresponding Legendre–Gauss weights $\{\omega_i : i = 0, \ldots, \bar{\mathrm{P}}\}$ are given by

$$ \omega_i = \frac{2}{(1-\sigma_i^2)\left(\partial_t[\phi_{\bar{\mathrm{P}}+1}^{(0,0)}](\sigma_i)\right)^2}. $$

Lemma 4 ([44,45]). *Let $g(t)$, for $t \in \Omega$, be a stochastic process. The Itô integral of $g(t)$ over the interval Ω is defined as*

$$ \int_{e_1}^{e_2} g(s)\,\mathrm{d}\mathscr{B}_s = \sum_{i=0}^{\bar{\mathrm{M}}-1} g(\varsigma_i)\{\mathscr{B}(\varsigma_{i+1}) - \mathscr{B}(\varsigma_i)\} + \mathscr{R}_{\text{Itô}}, \tag{9} $$

where the points ς_i are defined by

$$ \varsigma_i = e_1 + \frac{e_2 - e_1}{\bar{\mathrm{M}}} i, \qquad i = 0, 1, \ldots, \bar{\mathrm{M}}. $$

$\mathscr{B}(t)$ denotes the standard Brownian motion, and $\mathscr{R}_{\text{Itô}}$ represents the remainder term of the Itô integral approximation. The remainder term $\mathscr{R}_{\text{Itô}}$ becomes negligible in the mean square sense as the number of subdivisions $\bar{\mathrm{M}}$ approaches infinity. Specifically, the expectation of the squared norm of the remainder term, $\mathbb{E}\left[|\mathscr{R}_{\text{Itô}}|^2\right]$, tends to zero as $\bar{\mathrm{M}} \to \infty$, ensuring that the approximation converges to the true Itô integral.

3. Problem Statement

This paper studies the following stochastic fractional delay differential equation with a natural delay (SFNDE):

$$ \begin{aligned} &{}^{\mathrm{C}}\mathscr{D}_t^{\eta}[u(t) - \mathfrak{f}(u(t-\alpha(t)))] \\ &\quad = \mathscr{P}(u(t), u(t-\alpha(t))) + \mathscr{H}(u(t), u(t-\alpha(t)))\dot{\mathscr{B}}_t, \quad t \in (0, \mathrm{T}], \end{aligned} \tag{10} $$

subject to the initial condition

$$ u(t) = \varphi(t), \qquad t \in [-\tau, 0], \tag{11} $$

where the continuous function $\alpha(t) : [0, \mathrm{T}] \to [0, \tau]$ is a Borel measurable function for the positive constant τ, and $\mathscr{P}$, $\mathscr{H}$, and $\mathfrak{f}$ are Borel measurable functions satisfying in the following Lipschitz conditions:

$$ |\mathfrak{f}(u) - \mathfrak{f}(\bar{u})| \le \hat{\varsigma}|u - \bar{u}|, \tag{12a} $$

$$ |\mathscr{P}(u,v) - \mathscr{P}(\bar{u},\bar{v})| \le \check{\mu}|u - \bar{u}| + \hat{\mu}|v - \bar{v}|, \tag{12b} $$

$$ |\mathscr{H}(u,v) - \mathscr{H}(\bar{u},\bar{v})| \le \check{\delta}|u - \bar{u}| + \hat{\delta}|v - \bar{v}|, \tag{12c} $$

where $\hat{\varsigma}, \check{\mu}, \hat{\mu}, \check{\delta}, \hat{\delta} \in \mathbb{R}^+$, $\mathrm{T} \in (0, +\infty)$, the stochastic process $\mathscr{B}(t)$ on $t \in [0, \mathrm{T}]$ denotes standard Brownian motion on a complete probability space $\left(\Omega, \mathscr{F}, \{\mathscr{F}_t\}_{t\in[0,\mathrm{T}]}, \mathbb{P}\right)$ with a filtration $\{\mathscr{F}_t\}_{t\in[0,\mathrm{T}]}$ satisfying the usual conditions, i.e., $\dot{\mathscr{B}}_t := \frac{\mathrm{d}\mathscr{B}(t)}{\mathrm{d}t}$, and $u(t)$ is an unknown stochastic process to be determined.

According to Definition 1, the stochastic fractional neutral delay differential Equation (SFNDE) given by Equation (10) can be transformed into its equivalent integral form as

$$
\begin{aligned}
u(t) = u_0 + \mathfrak{f}(u(t-\alpha(t))) &+ \frac{1}{\Gamma(\eta)}\int_0^t (t-s)^{\eta-1}\mathscr{P}(u(s), u(s-\alpha(s)))\,\mathrm{d}s \\
&+ \frac{1}{\Gamma(\eta)}\int_0^t (t-s)^{\eta-1}\mathscr{H}(u(s), u(s-\alpha(s)))\,\mathrm{d}\mathscr{B}_s, \qquad (13)
\end{aligned}
$$

where the initial value u_0 is

$$u_0 := \varphi(0) - \mathfrak{f}(\varphi(-\alpha(0))).$$

4. Stepwise Jacobi Poly-Fractonomials Collocation Scheme

To approximate the numerical solution of the integral Equation (13), the first step involves converting this time-varying delay stochastic neutral integral equation into an equivalent non-delay stochastic neutral integral equation. This transformation is achieved using a stepwise method. The approach involves dividing the entire interval $[0,\mathrm{T}]$ into smaller subintervals of length τ. The delay term $\alpha(t)$ is approximated within each subinterval, effectively transforming the original time-varying delay problem into a series of non-delay problems. The collocation method, utilizing Jacobi poly-fractonomials, is then applied to each subinterval Ω_k.

Let $\tau = \max_{t\in[0,\mathrm{T}]}\{\alpha(t)\}$, and let $\mathrm{p} = \lfloor \frac{\mathrm{T}}{\tau} \rfloor$. The goal is to find the numerical solution of Equation (13), subject to the condition (11), within any subinterval $\Omega_k := [(k-1)\tau, k\tau]$, for $k = 1,\ldots,\mathrm{p}$, by employing a collocation technique based on Jacobi poly-fractonomials. Moreover, in the first step, Equation (13) is equivalent to

$$
\begin{aligned}
u^1(t) &= u_0 + \mathfrak{f}\Big(u^0(t-\alpha(t))\Big) \\
&+ \frac{1}{\Gamma(\eta)}\int_0^t (t-s)^{\eta-1}\mathscr{P}(u^1(s), u^0(s-\alpha(s)))\mathrm{d}s \\
&+ \frac{1}{\Gamma(\eta)}\int_0^t (t-s)^{\eta-1}\mathscr{H}(u^1(s), u^0(s-\alpha(s)))\mathrm{d}\mathscr{B}_s, \qquad (14)
\end{aligned}
$$

where $u^0(t) = \varphi(t)$.

An approximate solution of $u(t)$ in the first interval can be derived using the results presented in Lemma 2. That is,

$$u^1(t) \simeq u_n^1(t) = \sum_{r=1}^{n+1} \mathrm{c}_r^1 \theta_r^{(\mu)}(t;0,\tau) \triangleq \mathbf{C}_1^{\mathrm{T}}\,{}_0^{\tau}\Theta(t), \qquad (15)$$

where $\mathbf{c}_1 = \left[\mathrm{c}_1^1, \mathrm{c}_2^1, \ldots, \mathrm{c}_{n+1}^1\right]^{\mathrm{T}}$.

Using this approximation in Equation (14) provides the following result:

$$
\begin{aligned}
\mathbf{C}_1^{\mathrm{T}}\,{}_0^{\tau}\Theta(t) &\simeq u_0 + \mathfrak{f}\Big(u_n^0(t-\alpha(t))\Big) \\
&+ \frac{1}{\Gamma(\eta)}\int_0^t (t-s)^{\eta-1}\mathscr{P}(\mathbf{C}_1^{\mathrm{T}}\,{}_0^{\tau}\Theta(s), u_n^0(s-\alpha(s)))\mathrm{d}s \\
&+ \frac{1}{\Gamma(\eta)}\int_0^t (t-s)^{\eta-1}\mathscr{H}(\mathbf{C}_1^{\mathrm{T}}\,{}_0^{\tau}\Theta(s), u_n^0(s-\alpha(s)))\mathrm{d}\mathscr{B}_s, \qquad (16)
\end{aligned}
$$

where

$$u^0(t) \simeq u_n^0(t) = \sum_{r=1}^{n+1} \mathrm{c}_r^0 \theta_r^{(\mu)}(t;-\tau,0) \triangleq \mathbf{C}_0^{\mathrm{T}}\,{}_{-\tau}^{0}\Theta(t), \qquad (17)$$

$$\mathrm{c}_r^0 = \frac{1}{\psi_r}\int_{\Omega}\varphi(t)\,\mathbf{w}^{-\mu,-\mu}(t;-\tau,0)\,\theta_r^{(\mu)}(t;-\tau,0)\mathrm{d}t.$$

Now, the CGL points $\mathbf{t}_i^1 := {}_0^{\mathrm{T}}\mathbf{t}_i$, as defined in Definition 5, are utilized in Equation (17), which results in

$$\begin{aligned}\mathbf{C}_1^{\mathrm{T}}\,{}_0^{\mathrm{T}}\Theta(\mathbf{t}_i^1) &= u_0 + \mathfrak{f}\Big(u_n^0(\mathbf{t}_i^1 - \alpha(\mathbf{t}_i^1))\Big)\\ &+ \frac{1}{\Gamma(\eta)}\int_0^{\mathbf{t}_i^1}(\mathbf{t}_i^1 - s)^{\eta-1}\mathscr{P}(\mathbf{C}_1^{\mathrm{T}}\,{}_0^{\mathrm{T}}\Theta(s), u_n^0(s-\alpha(s)))\mathrm{d}s\\ &+ \frac{1}{\Gamma(\eta)}\int_0^{\mathbf{t}_i^1}(\mathbf{t}_i^1 - s)^{\eta-1}\mathscr{H}(\mathbf{C}_1^{\mathrm{T}}\,{}_0^{\mathrm{T}}\Theta(s), u_n^0(s-\alpha(s)))\mathrm{d}\mathscr{B}_s.\end{aligned} \tag{18}$$

Utilizing the Legendre–Gauss integration method as described in Lemma 3, along with the Itô approximation detailed in Lemma 4 for the integral components of Equation (18), yields

$$\begin{aligned}&\int_0^{\mathbf{t}_i^1}(\mathbf{t}_i^1 - s)^{\eta-1}\mathscr{P}(\mathbf{C}_1^{\mathrm{T}}\,{}_0^{\mathrm{T}}\Theta(s), u_n^0(s-\alpha(s)))\mathrm{d}s\\ &\quad= \frac{\mathbf{t}_i^1}{2}\sum_{j=0}^{\bar{\mathrm{P}}}\omega_j(\mathbf{t}_i^1 - v_{i,j}^1)^{\eta-1}\mathscr{P}\Big(\mathbf{C}_1^{\mathrm{T}}{}_0^{\mathrm{T}}\Theta(v_{i,j}^1), u_n^0\Big(v_{i,j}^1 - \alpha(v_{i,j}^1)\Big)\Big),\end{aligned} \tag{19}$$

$$\begin{aligned}&\int_0^{\mathbf{t}_i^1}(\mathbf{t}_i^1 - s)^{\eta-1}\mathscr{H}(\mathbf{C}_1^{\mathrm{T}}\,{}_0^{\mathrm{T}}\Theta(s), u_n^0(s-\alpha(s)))\mathrm{d}\mathscr{B}_s\\ &\quad= \sum_{j=0}^{\bar{\mathrm{M}}-1}(\mathbf{t}_i^1 - \varsigma_{i,j}^1)^{\eta-1}\mathscr{H}\Big(\mathbf{C}_1^{\mathrm{T}}{}_0^{\mathrm{T}}\Theta(\varsigma_{i,j}^1), u_n^0(\varsigma_{i,j}^1 - \alpha(\varsigma_{i,j}^1))\Big)\\ &\quad\times\{\mathscr{B}(\varsigma_{i,j+1}^1) - \mathscr{B}(\varsigma_{i,j}^1)\},\end{aligned} \tag{20}$$

where

$$v_{i,j}^1 = \frac{\mathbf{t}_i^1}{2}\sigma_j + \frac{\mathbf{t}_i^1}{2},\; j = 0,1,\ldots,\bar{\mathrm{P}}, \qquad \varsigma_{i,j}^1 = \frac{\mathbf{t}_i^1}{\bar{\mathrm{M}}}j,\; j = 0,1,\ldots,\bar{\mathrm{M}}.$$

Finally, Equations (18)–(20) give the following system of nonlinear equations:

$$\begin{aligned}\mathbf{C}_1^{\mathrm{T}}\,{}_0^{\mathrm{T}}\Theta(\mathbf{t}_i^1) &= u_0 + \mathfrak{f}\Big(u_n^0(\mathbf{t}_i^1 - \alpha(\mathbf{t}_i^1))\Big)\\ &+ \frac{\mathbf{t}_i^1}{2\Gamma(\eta)}\sum_{j=0}^{\bar{\mathrm{P}}}\omega_j(\mathbf{t}_i^1 - v_{i,j}^1)^{\eta-1}\mathscr{P}\Big(\mathbf{C}_1^{\mathrm{T}}{}_0^{\mathrm{T}}\Theta(v_{i,j}^1), u_n^0\Big(v_{i,j}^1 - \alpha(v_{i,j}^1)\Big)\Big)\\ &+ \frac{1}{\Gamma(\eta)}\sum_{j=0}^{\bar{\mathrm{M}}-1}(\mathbf{t}_i^1 - \varsigma_{i,j}^1)^{\eta-1}\mathscr{H}\Big(\mathbf{C}_1^{\mathrm{T}}{}_0^{\mathrm{T}}\Theta(\varsigma_{i,j}^1), u_n^0(\varsigma_{i,j}^1 - \alpha(\varsigma_{i,j}^1))\Big)\\ &\times\{\mathscr{B}(\varsigma_{i,j+1}^1) - \mathscr{B}(\varsigma_{i,j}^1)\},\quad i = 1,\ldots,n+1.\end{aligned} \tag{21}$$

An approximate numerical solution to the original integral Equation (13) is obtained by solving the resulting system of nonlinear algebraic equations within the subinterval. Furthermore, Newton's iterative scheme can be employed to solve the system of nonlinear Equation (21), which depends on the unknown coefficients c_r^1, for $r = 1,\ldots,n+1$. This approach yields an approximate solution $u_n^1(t)$ on the domain Ω_1.

To find a numerical solution of Equation (13) for any subinterval Ω_k, where $k = 2,\ldots,\mathrm{p}$, all the subscripts 0 and 1 in Equations (14)–(21) can be replaced with $k-1$ and k, respectively, to obtain an analogous system of nonlinear equations similar to Equation (21). This stepwise method ensures that the solution is accurately approximated over the entire interval $[0,\mathrm{T}]$, considering the effects of the stochastic process and the fractional derivatives involved.

After applying these numerical method, we obtain $u(t)$ on interval $[0,\mathrm{T}]$ as follows:

$$u(t) \simeq u_n(t) = \begin{cases} u_n^1(t), & t \in [0,\tau], \\ u_n^2(t), & t \in [\tau,2\tau], \\ \vdots & \vdots \\ u_n^{\mathrm{p}}(t), & t \in [(\mathrm{p}-1)\tau,\mathrm{T}]. \end{cases} \tag{22}$$

5. Convergence Analysis

In this section, the convergence properties of the proposed method are studied in detail. For this purpose, the exact delay function $\alpha(t)$ is incorporated in the transformed system. The analysis addresses the errors arising from discretization and solution approximation, with the exact use of $\alpha(t)$ simplifying the process compared to methods that rely on delay function approximations. It is demonstrated that, under appropriate smoothness conditions, the method achieves spectral convergence, with the proofs accounting for the discretization error while utilizing the exact delay function. This approach enhances the method's accuracy and reliability, allowing for a focus on numerical approximation without introducing additional errors. Throughout, rigorous mathematical proofs are provided, highlighting the interplay between the exact delay function and the numerical scheme in producing precise results. Specifically, it is demonstrated that the method exhibits spectral convergence, meaning that the error decreases exponentially with an increasing number of collocation points or basis functions. This high convergence rate is particularly advantageous for solving complex stochastic fractional differential equations, as it ensures that accurate solutions can be obtained with relatively few computational resources.

Theorem 1 ([40,42]). *Assume that $g \in \mathbf{C}(\Omega) \cap \Lambda^1_{-\mu,-\mu}(\Omega) \cap \mathbf{B}^q_{-\mu,-\mu}(\Omega)$ for some positive integer q and $\mu \in (0,1)$. Also, g_n is defined in (7). Thus, a constant $\rho \in \mathbb{R}^+$, that is independent of n, exists such that for $1 < q \leq n+1$, the inequality*

$$\|g - g_n\|_\infty \leq \rho n^{1-q} \|\mathscr{D}_t^{\mu+q} g\|_{\mathbf{L}^2_{q,q}(\Omega)},$$

holds.

Theorem 2. *Suppose that for any subinterval $\Omega_k = [(k-1)\tau, k\tau] \subseteq [0,\mathrm{T}]$, $k = 0,1,\ldots,\mathrm{p}$, $u^k(t) \in \mathbf{L}^2_{-\mu,-\mu}(\Omega_k)$ and $u_n^k(t)$ are the exact and numerical solutions of (13) obtained using the proposed approach, respectively. Then,*

$$\mathbb{E}|u^k(t) - u_n^k(t)|^2 \leq \zeta_k n^{2(1-q)} \|\mathscr{D}_t^{\mu+q} u^0(t)\|^2_{\mathbf{L}^2_{q,q}(\Omega_0)},$$

where ζ_0 and ζ_1 are positive constants independent of n, and for $k = 2,\ldots,\mathrm{p}$

$$\zeta_k = \bar{\zeta}_k \Big[\zeta_{k-1} + \tau \sum_{l=1}^{k-1} (\zeta_l + \zeta_{l-1}) + \tau \zeta_{k-1}\Big].$$

Proof. According to Equation (16), the solution in the first interval is given by

$$\begin{aligned} u_n^1(t) &= u_0 + \mathfrak{f}\Big(u_n^0(t-\alpha(t))\Big) \\ &+ \frac{1}{\Gamma(\eta)} \int_0^t (t-s)^{\eta-1} \mathscr{P}(u_n^1(s), u_n^0(s-\alpha(s)))\mathrm{d}s \\ &+ \frac{1}{\Gamma(\eta)} \int_0^t (t-s)^{\eta-1} \mathscr{H}(u_n^1(s), u_n^0(s-\alpha(s)))\mathrm{d}\mathscr{B}_s, \end{aligned} \tag{23}$$

and the error of the discretization is

$$\mathbf{e}_n^1(t) = \Phi_n^0[\mathfrak{f}](t) + \Phi_n^1[\mathscr{P}](t) + \Phi_n^1[\mathscr{H}](t), \tag{24}$$

where

$$\begin{aligned}
\mathbf{e}_n^1(t) &:= u^1(t) - u_n^1(t), \\
\Phi_n^0[\mathfrak{f}](t) &:= \mathfrak{f}\Big(u^0(t-\alpha(t))\Big) - \mathfrak{f}\Big(u_n^0(t-\alpha(t))\Big), \\
\Phi_n^1[\mathscr{P}](t) &:= \frac{1}{\Gamma(\eta)} \int_0^t (t-s)^{\eta-1} \Big[\mathscr{P}(u^1(s), u^0(s-\alpha(s))) \\
&\quad - \mathscr{P}(u_n^1(s), u_n^0(s-\alpha(s)))\Big] \mathrm{d}s, \qquad (25a) \\
\Phi_n^1[\mathscr{H}](t) &:= \frac{1}{\Gamma(\eta)} \int_0^t (t-s)^{\eta-1} \Big[\mathscr{H}(u^1(s), u^0(s-\alpha(s))) \\
&\quad - \mathscr{H}(u_n^1(s), u_n^0(s-\alpha(s)))\Big] \mathrm{d}\mathscr{B}_s. \qquad (25b)
\end{aligned}$$

Now, using Equation (17) and Theorem 1 for $t \in \Omega_0$ results in

$$\mathbb{E}\|\mathbf{e}_n^0(t)\|_\infty = \mathbb{E}\|u^0(t) - u_n^0(t)\|_\infty \le \rho_0 n^{1-q} \|\mathscr{D}_t^{\mu+q} u^0(t)\|_{\mathbf{L}^2_{q,q}(\Omega_0)}, \tag{26}$$

where $\rho_0 \in \mathbb{R}^+$ is independent of n. Next, incorporating Equation (26) and Lipschitz condition (a) for $t \in \Omega_1$ leads to

$$\begin{aligned}
|\Phi_n^0[\mathfrak{f}](t)| &\le \varsigma |u^0(t-\alpha(t)) - u_n^0(t-\alpha(t))| \\
&\le \varsigma \|u^0(t-\alpha(t)) - u_n^0(t-\alpha(t))\|_\infty \\
&\le \varsigma \rho_0 n^{1-q} \|\mathscr{D}_t^{\mu+q} u^0(t)\|_{\mathbf{L}^2_{q,q}(\Omega_0)},
\end{aligned}$$

thus,

$$\mathbb{E}\Big|\Phi_n^0[\mathfrak{f}](t)\Big|^2 \le \varrho_0 n^{2(1-q)} \|\mathscr{D}_t^{\mu+q} u^0(t)\|^2_{\mathbf{L}^2_{q,q}(\Omega_0)}, \tag{27}$$

in which $\varrho_0 = (\varsigma\rho_0)^2$. Using Equation (25a) and the Cauchy–Schwartz inequality yields

$$\begin{aligned}
\Big|\Phi_n^1[\mathscr{P}](t)\Big|^2 &\le \frac{1}{\Gamma(\eta)^2} \Big(\int_0^t (t-s)^{\eta-1} \Big| \mathscr{P}(u^1(s), u^0(s-\alpha(s))) \\
&\quad - \mathscr{P}(u_n^1(s), u_n^0(s-\alpha(s))) \Big| \mathrm{d}s \Big)^2 \\
&\le \frac{1}{\Gamma(\eta)^2} \int_0^t (t-s)^{2(\eta-1)} \mathrm{d}s \cdot \int_0^t \Big| \mathscr{P}(u^1(s), u^0(s-\alpha(s))) \\
&\quad - \mathscr{P}(u_n^1(s), u_n^0(s-\alpha(s))) \Big|^2 \mathrm{d}s, \\
&\le \varrho_1 \int_0^t \Big| \mathscr{P}(u^1(s), u^0(s-\alpha(s))) - \mathscr{P}(u_n^1(s), u_n^0(s-\alpha(s))) \Big|^2 \mathrm{d}s,
\end{aligned}$$

where $\varrho_1 \in \mathbb{R}^+$ is independent of n and depends on η and τ. So, by Lipschitz condition (b),

$$\Big|\Phi_n^1[\mathscr{P}](t)\Big|^2 \le \hat{\varrho}_1 \int_0^t \Big(|\mathbf{e}_n^1(s)| + |\mathbf{e}_n^0(s-\alpha(s))| \Big)^2 \mathrm{d}s, \tag{28}$$

where $\hat{\varrho}_1 = \max\{\varrho_1 \check{\mu}^2, \varrho_1 \hat{\mu}^2\}$. Thus, by taking the mathematical expectation of Equation (28) and applying Equation (27) to $t \in \Omega_1$,

$$\mathbb{E}\Big|\Phi_n^1[\mathscr{P}](t)\Big|^2 \le \hat{\varrho}_1 \int_0^t \Big(\mathbb{E}|\mathbf{e}_n^1(s)|^2 + \mathbb{E}|\mathbf{e}_n^0(s-\alpha(s))|^2\Big)\mathrm{d}s$$
$$\le \hat{\varrho}_1 \int_0^t \mathbb{E}|\mathbf{e}_n^1(s)|^2 \mathrm{d}s + \check{\varrho}_1 n^{2(1-q)} \|\mathscr{D}_t^{\mu+q} u^0(t)\|^2_{\mathbf{L}^2_{q,q}(\Omega_0)}, \tag{29}$$

in which $\check{\varrho}_1 = \hat{\varrho}_1 \tau \rho_0^2$.

From Equation (25b) and applying Lipschitz condition (a), for $t \in \Omega_1$,

$$\Big|\Phi_n^1[\mathscr{H}](t)\Big|^2 \le \frac{1}{\Gamma(\eta)^2}\Big(\int_0^t (t-s)^{\eta-1}\Big|\mathscr{H}(u^1(s), u^0(s-\alpha(s)))$$
$$- \mathscr{H}(u_n^1(s), u_n^0(s-\alpha(s)))\Big|\mathrm{d}\mathscr{B}_s\Big)^2$$
$$\le \varrho_2\Big\{\int_0^t \Big(\check{\delta}|\mathbf{e}_n^1(s)| + \hat{\delta}|\mathbf{e}_n^0(s-\alpha(s))|\Big)\mathrm{d}\mathscr{B}_s\Big\}^2, \tag{30}$$

where $\varrho_2 \in \mathbb{R}^+$ is independent of n and depends on η and τ. Thus, mathematical expectation of Equation (30) and Itô isometry gives

$$\mathbb{E}\Big|\Phi_n^1[\mathscr{H}](t)\Big|^2 \le \hat{\varrho}_2 \int_0^t \Big(\mathbb{E}|\mathbf{e}_n^1(s)|^2 + \mathbb{E}|\mathbf{e}_n^0(s-\alpha(s))|^2\Big)\mathrm{d}s,$$

where $\hat{\varrho}_2 = \max\{\varrho_2\check{\delta}^2, \varrho_2\hat{\delta}^2\}$. Hence, from Equation (27),

$$\mathbb{E}\Big|\Phi_n^1[\mathscr{H}](t)\Big|^2 \le \hat{\varrho}_2 \int_0^t \mathbb{E}|\mathbf{e}_n^1(s)|^2 \mathrm{d}s + \check{\varrho}_2 n^{2(1-q)} \|\mathscr{D}_t^{\mu+q} u^0(t)\|^2_{\mathbf{L}^2_{q,q}(\Omega_0)}, \tag{31}$$

in which $\check{\varrho}_2 = \hat{\varrho}_2 \tau \rho_0^2$. Therefore, from (24), (27), (29), and (31),

$$\mathbb{E}|\mathbf{e}_n^1(t)|^2 \le \beta_1 \int_0^t \mathbb{E}|\mathbf{e}_n^1(s)|^2 \mathrm{d}s + \bar{\varrho}_1 n^{2(1-q)} \|\mathscr{D}_t^{\mu+q} u^0(t)\|^2_{\mathbf{L}^2_{q,q}(\Omega_0)},$$

where $\beta_1 = \hat{\varrho}_1 + \hat{\varrho}_2$ and $\bar{\varrho}_1 = \varrho_0 + \check{\varrho}_1 + \check{\varrho}_2$. Thus, using the Gronwall inequality (Lemma 4.1 in [46]), we have

$$\mathbb{E}|\mathbf{e}_n^1(t)|^2 \le \mathrm{e}^{\beta_1 t} \bar{\varrho}_1 n^{2(1-q)} \|\mathscr{D}_t^{\mu+q} u^0(t)\|^2_{\mathbf{L}^2_{q,q}(\Omega_0)}. \tag{32}$$

Let $\tilde{\beta}_1 = \max\limits_{t\in\Omega_1}\{\mathrm{e}^{\beta_1 t}\}$. From Equation (32),

$$\mathbb{E}|\mathbf{e}_n^1(t)|^2 \le \zeta_1 n^{2(1-q)} \|\mathscr{D}_t^{\mu+q} u^0(t)\|^2_{\mathbf{L}^2_{q,q}(\Omega_0)}, \tag{33}$$

where $\zeta_1 = \bar{\varrho}_1 \tilde{\beta}_1$. Due to Equation (16), the numerical solution $u_n^k(t)$, $k = 2, \ldots, \mathrm{p}$, satisfies in the equation

$$u_n^k(t) = u_0 + \mathfrak{f}\Big(u_n^{k-1}(t-\alpha(t))\Big)$$
$$+ \frac{1}{\Gamma(\eta)}\Big\{\sum_{l=1}^{k-1}\int_{\Omega_l}(t-s)^{\eta-1}\mathscr{P}(u_n^l(s), u_n^{l-1}(s-\alpha(s)))\mathrm{d}s$$
$$+ \int_{(k-1)\tau}^t (t-s)^{\eta-1}\mathscr{P}(u_n^k(s), u_n^{k-1}(s-\alpha(s)))\mathrm{d}s\Big\}$$
$$+ \frac{1}{\Gamma(\eta)}\Big\{\sum_{l=1}^{k-1}\int_{\Omega_l}(t-s)^{\eta-1}\mathscr{H}(u_n^l(s), u_n^{l-1}(s-\alpha(s)))\mathrm{d}\mathscr{B}_s$$
$$+ \int_{(k-1)\tau}^t (t-s)^{\eta-1}\mathscr{H}(u_n^k(s), u_n^{k-1}(s-\alpha(s)))\mathrm{d}\mathscr{B}_s\Big\}. \tag{34}$$

Thus, Equation (14) leads to

$$\mathbf{e}_n^k(t) = \Phi_n^{k-1}[\mathfrak{f}](t) + \Pi_n^k[\mathscr{P}](t) + \Pi_n^k[\mathscr{H}](t) + \Phi_n^k[\mathscr{P}](t) + \Phi_n^k[\mathscr{H}](t), \tag{35}$$

where $\mathbf{e}_n^k(t) := u^k(t) - u_n^k(t)$,

$$\Phi_n^{k-1}[\mathfrak{f}](t) := \mathfrak{f}\Big(u^{k-1}(t-\alpha(t))\Big) - \mathfrak{f}\Big(u_n^{k-1}(t-\alpha(t))\Big), \tag{36}$$

$$\begin{aligned}\Pi_n^k[\mathscr{P}](t) := \frac{1}{\Gamma(\eta)} \sum_{l=1}^{k-1} \int_{\Omega_l} (t-s)^{\eta-1} \Big[&\mathscr{P}(u^l(s), u^{l-1}(s-\alpha(s))) \\ &- \mathscr{P}(u_n^l(s), u_n^{l-1}(s-\alpha(s)))\Big] \mathrm{d}s,\end{aligned} \tag{37}$$

$$\begin{aligned}\Pi_n^k[\mathscr{H}](t) := \frac{1}{\Gamma(\eta)} \sum_{l=1}^{k-1} \int_{\Omega_l} (t-s)^{\eta-1} \Big[&\mathscr{H}(u^l(s), u^{l-1}(s-\alpha(s))) \\ &- \mathscr{H}(u_n^l(s), u_n^{l-1}(s-\alpha(s)))\Big] \mathrm{d}\mathscr{B}_s,\end{aligned} \tag{38}$$

$$\begin{aligned}\Phi_n^k[\mathscr{P}](t) := \frac{1}{\Gamma(\eta)} \int_{(k-1)\tau}^{t} (t-s)^{\eta-1} \Big[&\mathscr{P}(u^k(s), u^{k-1}(s-\alpha(s))) \\ &- \mathscr{P}(u_n^k(s), u_n^{k-1}(s-\alpha(s)))\Big] \mathrm{d}s,\end{aligned} \tag{39}$$

and

$$\begin{aligned}\Phi_n^k[\mathscr{H}](t) := \frac{1}{\Gamma(\eta)} \int_{(k-1)\tau}^{t} (t-s)^{\eta-1} \Big[&\mathscr{H}(u^k(s), u^{k-1}(s-\alpha(s))) \\ &- \mathscr{H}(u_n^k(s), u_n^{k-1}(s-\alpha(s)))\Big] \mathrm{d}\mathscr{B}_s.\end{aligned} \tag{40}$$

By using Lipschitz condition (a) and Equation (36), for $t \in \Omega_k$,

$$|\Phi_n^k[\mathfrak{f}](t)| \leq \varsigma |\mathbf{e}_n^{k-1}(t-\alpha(t))|,$$

then,

$$\mathbb{E}\Big|\Phi_n^k[\mathfrak{f}](t)\Big|^2 \leq \varsigma^2 \mathbb{E}|\mathbf{e}_n^{k-1}(t-\alpha(t))|^2. \tag{41}$$

From Equations (37) and (39) and by Lipschitz condition (b), for $t \in \Omega_k$,

$$\begin{aligned}\Big|\Pi_n^k[\mathscr{P}](t)\Big|^2 &\leq \frac{1}{\Gamma(\eta)^2}\Big(\sum_{l=1}^{k-1} \int_{\Omega_l} (t-s)^{\eta-1} \Big|\mathscr{P}(u^l(s), u^{l-1}(s-\alpha(s))) \\ &\quad - \mathscr{P}(u_n^l(s), u_n^{l-1}(s-\alpha(s)))\Big| \mathrm{d}s\Big)^2 \\ &\leq \Big\{\sum_{l=1}^{k-1} \tilde{\varrho}_l \int_{\Omega_l} \Big(\check{\mu}|\mathbf{e}_n^l(s)| + \hat{\mu}|\mathbf{e}_n^{l-1}(s-\alpha(s))|\Big) \mathrm{d}s\Big\}^2,\end{aligned} \tag{42}$$

and

$$\begin{aligned}\Big|\Phi_n^k[\mathscr{P}](t)\Big|^2 &\leq \frac{1}{\Gamma(\eta)^2}\Big(\int_{(k-1)\tau}^{t} (t-s)^{\eta-1} \Big|\mathscr{P}(u^k(s), u^{k-1}(s-\alpha(s))) \\ &\quad - \mathscr{P}(u_n^k(s), u_n^{k-1}(s-\alpha(s)))\Big| \mathrm{d}s\Big)^2\end{aligned}$$

$$\leq \tilde{\varrho}_k\Big\{\int_{(k-1)\tau}^{t}\Big(\check{\mu}|\mathbf{e}_n^k(s)|+\hat{\mu}|\mathbf{e}_n^{k-1}(s-\alpha(s))|\Big)\mathrm{d}s\Big\}^2, \tag{43}$$

where $\tilde{\varrho}_l \in \mathbb{R}^+, l = 1,\ldots,k$, are independent of n and depended on η and τ. Thus, by taking the mathematical expectation of (42) and (43), we get

$$\mathbb{E}\Big|\Pi_n^k[\mathscr{P}](t)\Big|^2 \leq \sum_{l=1}^{k-1}\epsilon_l\int_{\Omega_l}\Big(\mathbb{E}|\mathbf{e}_n^l(s)|^2+\mathbb{E}|\mathbf{e}_n^{l-1}(s-\alpha(s))|^2\Big)\mathrm{d}s, \tag{44}$$

$$\mathbb{E}\Big|\Phi_n^k[\mathscr{P}](t)\Big|^2 \leq \epsilon_k\int_{(k-1)\tau}^{t}\Big(\mathbb{E}|\mathbf{e}_n^k(s)|^2+\mathbb{E}|\mathbf{e}_n^{k-1}(s-\alpha(s))|^2\Big)\mathrm{d}s, \tag{45}$$

where $\epsilon_l = \max\{\tilde{\varrho}_l\check{\mu}, \tilde{\varrho}_l\hat{\mu}\}, l = 1,\ldots,k$. In addition, from Equations (38) and (40) and by Lipschitz condition (c), for $t \in \Omega_k$,

$$\begin{aligned}\Big|\Pi_n^k[\mathscr{H}](t)\Big|^2 &\leq \frac{1}{\Gamma(\eta)^2}\Big(\sum_{l=1}^{k-1}\int_{\Omega_l}(t-s)^{\eta-1}\Big|\mathscr{H}(u^l(s),u^{l-1}(s-\alpha(s)))\\&\quad-\mathscr{H}(u_n^l(s),u_n^{l-1}(s-\alpha(s)))\Big|\mathrm{d}\mathscr{B}_s\Big)^2\\&\leq\Big\{\sum_{l=1}^{k-1}\tilde{\varrho}_l\int_{\Omega_l}\Big(\check{\delta}|\mathbf{e}_n^l(s)|+\hat{\delta}|\mathbf{e}_n^{l-1}(s-\alpha(s))|\Big)\mathrm{d}\mathscr{B}_s\Big\}^2,\end{aligned} \tag{46}$$

and

$$\begin{aligned}\Big|\Phi_n^k[\mathscr{H}](t)\Big|^2 &\leq \frac{1}{\Gamma(\eta)^2}\Big(\int_{(k-1)\tau}^{t}(t-s)^{\eta-1}\Big|\mathscr{H}(u^k(s),u^{k-1}(s-\alpha(s)))\\&\quad-\mathscr{H}(u_n^k(s),u_n^{k-1}(s-\alpha(s)))\Big|\mathrm{d}\mathscr{B}_s\Big)^2\\&\leq\tilde{\varrho}_k\Big\{\int_{(k-1)\tau}^{t}\Big(\check{\delta}|\mathbf{e}_n^k(s)|+\hat{\delta}|\mathbf{e}_n^{k-1}(s-\alpha(s))|\Big)\mathrm{d}\mathscr{B}_s\Big\}^2.\end{aligned} \tag{47}$$

Hence, taking the mathematical expectation of Equations (46) and (47) and using Itô isometry lead to

$$\mathbb{E}\Big|\Pi_n^k[\mathscr{H}](t)\Big|^2 \leq \sum_{l=1}^{k-1}\hat{\epsilon}_l\int_{\Omega_l}\Big(\mathbb{E}|\mathbf{e}_n^l(s)|^2+\mathbb{E}|\mathbf{e}_n^{l-1}(s-\alpha(s))|^2\Big)\mathrm{d}s, \tag{48}$$

$$\mathbb{E}\Big|\Phi_n^k[\mathscr{H}](t)\Big|^2 \leq \hat{\epsilon}_k\int_{(k-1)\tau}^{t}\Big(\mathbb{E}|\mathbf{e}_n^k(s)|^2+\mathbb{E}|\mathbf{e}_n^{k-1}(s-\alpha(s))|^2\Big)\mathrm{d}s, \tag{49}$$

where $\hat{\epsilon}_l = \max\{\tilde{\varrho}_l\check{\delta}, \tilde{\varrho}_l\hat{\delta}\}, l = 1,\ldots,k$. Therefore, from Equations (35), (41), (44), (45), (48), and (49),

$$\mathbb{E}|\mathbf{e}_n^k(t)|^2 \leq \Psi_n^{k-1}(t)+\bar{\epsilon}_k\int_{(k-1)\tau}^{t}\mathbb{E}|\mathbf{e}_n^k(s)|^2\mathrm{d}s, \quad t\in\Omega_k,$$

in which $\bar{\epsilon}_l = \epsilon_l + \hat{\epsilon}_l, l = 1,\ldots,k$ and

$$\begin{aligned}\Psi_n^{k-1}(t) &= \varsigma^2\mathbb{E}|\mathbf{e}_n^{k-1}(t-\alpha(t))|^2+\sum_{l=1}^{k-1}\bar{\epsilon}_l\int_{\Omega_l}\Big(\mathbb{E}|\mathbf{e}_n^l(s)|^2+\mathbb{E}|\mathbf{e}_n^{l-1}(s-\alpha(s))|^2\Big)\mathrm{d}s\\&\quad+\bar{\epsilon}_k\int_{(k-1)\tau}^{t}\mathbb{E}|\mathbf{e}_n^{k-1}(s-\alpha(s))|^2\mathrm{d}s.\end{aligned}$$

So, using the Gronwall inequality, we get

$$\mathbb{E}|\mathbf{e}_n^k(t)|^2 \leq \Psi_n^{k-1}(t)\mathrm{e}^{\bar{\epsilon}_k(t-(k-1)\tau)}, \quad t\in\Omega_k. \tag{50}$$

Let $\tilde{\beta}_k = \max_{t\in\Omega_k}\{e^{\bar{\epsilon}_k(t-(k-1)\tau)}\}$ and $\bar{\zeta}_k = \max_{l=1,\ldots,k}\{\tilde{\beta}_k\hat{\varsigma}^2, \tilde{\beta}_k\bar{\epsilon}_l\}$; thus, from Equation (49),

$$\mathbb{E}|\mathbf{e}_n^k(t)|^2 \le \bar{\zeta}_k\Big[\mathbb{E}|\mathbf{e}_n^{k-1}(t-\alpha(t))|^2 + \sum_{l=1}^{k-1}\int_{\Omega_l}\{\mathbb{E}|\mathbf{e}_n^l(s)|^2 + \mathbb{E}|\mathbf{e}_n^{l-1}(s-\alpha(s))|^2\}\mathrm{d}s + \int_{(k-1)\tau}^{t}\mathbb{E}|\mathbf{e}_n^{k-1}(s-\alpha(s))|^2\mathrm{d}s\Big], \quad t\in\Omega_k. \tag{51}$$

Now, from Equations (26), (33), and (51), for $k=2$, and $t\in\Omega_2$,, we can write

$$\begin{aligned}
\mathbb{E}|\mathbf{e}_n^2(t)|^2 &\le \bar{\zeta}_2\Big[\mathbb{E}|\mathbf{e}_n^1(t-\alpha(t))|^2 + \int_{\Omega_1}\Big(\mathbb{E}|\mathbf{e}_n^1(s)|^2 + \mathbb{E}|\mathbf{e}_n^0(s-\alpha(s))|^2\Big)\mathrm{d}s \\
&\quad + \int_{\tau}^{t}\mathbb{E}|\mathbf{e}_n^1(s-\alpha(s))|^2\mathrm{d}s\Big] \\
&\le \bar{\zeta}_2\Big[\zeta_1 + \tau\sum_{l=1}^{1}(\zeta_l+\zeta_{l-1}) + (t-\tau)\zeta_1\Big]n^{2(1-q)}\|\mathscr{D}_t^{\mu+q}u^0(t)\|^2_{\mathbf{L}^2_{q,q}(\Omega_0)} \\
&\le \zeta_2 n^{2(1-q)}\|\mathscr{D}_t^{\mu+q}u^0(t)\|^2_{\mathbf{L}^2_{q,q}(\Omega_0)},
\end{aligned}$$

where $\zeta_2 = \bar{\zeta}_2\Big[\zeta_1 + \tau\sum_{l=1}^{1}(\zeta_l+\zeta_{l-1}) + \tau\zeta_1\Big]$ and $\zeta_0 = \rho_0^2$. Also, for $k=3$, and $t\in\Omega_3$,

$$\begin{aligned}
\mathbb{E}|\mathbf{e}_n^3(t)|^2 &\le \bar{\zeta}_3\Big[\mathbb{E}|\mathbf{e}_n^2(t-\alpha(t))|^2 + \int_{\Omega_1}\Big(\mathbb{E}|\mathbf{e}_n^1(s)|^2 + \mathbb{E}|\mathbf{e}_n^0(s-\alpha(s))|^2\Big)\mathrm{d}s \\
&\quad + \int_{\Omega_2}\Big(\mathbb{E}|\mathbf{e}_n^2(s)|^2 + \mathbb{E}|\mathbf{e}_n^1(s-\alpha(s))|^2\Big)\mathrm{d}s + \int_{2\tau}^{t}\mathbb{E}|\mathbf{e}_n^2(s-\alpha(s))|^2\mathrm{d}s\Big] \\
&\le \bar{\zeta}_3\Big[\zeta_2 + \tau\sum_{l=1}^{2}(\zeta_l+\zeta_{l-1}) + (t-2\tau)\zeta_2\Big]n^{2(1-q)}\|\mathscr{D}_t^{\mu+q}u^0(t)\|^2_{\mathbf{L}^2_{q,q}(\Omega_0)} \\
&\le \zeta_3 n^{2(1-q)}\|\mathscr{D}_t^{\mu+q}u^0(t)\|^2_{\mathbf{L}^2_{q,q}(\Omega_0)},
\end{aligned}$$

where $\zeta_3 = \bar{\zeta}_3\Big[\zeta_2 + \tau\sum_{l=1}^{2}(\zeta_l+\zeta_{l-1}) + \tau\zeta_2\Big]$.

As a result, in the general form, we find

$$\mathbb{E}|\mathbf{e}_n^k(t)|^2 \le \zeta_k n^{2(1-q)}\|\mathscr{D}_t^{\mu+q}u^0(t)\|^2_{\mathbf{L}^2_{q,q}(\Omega_0)},$$

in which

$$\zeta_k = \bar{\zeta}_k\Big[\zeta_{k-1} + \tau\sum_{l=1}^{k-1}(\zeta_l+\zeta_{l-1}) + \tau\zeta_{k-1}\Big].$$

□

6. Numerical Examples

This section describes the proposed methodology for solving stochastic fractional delay differential equations (SFNDEs) with time-varying delay, as described in Equations (10) and (11), is evaluated. The approach involves considering **Bm**-discretized Brownian paths and calculating the numerical approximation of $u(t)$ along these paths. To assess the accuracy of the method, the error concerning the **L**∞-norm is employed, defined as

$$\|\mathscr{E}n\|_\infty = \max_{t\in[0,T]}\mathbb{E}|u(t) - u_n(t)|,$$

where $u(t)$ represents the exact solution, and $u_n(t)$ denotes the numerical approximation. For numerical experiments, Matlab (version 19a) running on an Intel(R) Core(TM) i7-7500U CPU @ 2.70 GHz with a maximum clock speed of 2.90 GHz was used.

Example 1. *Consider the following SFNDE:*

$$
{}^{C}\mathscr{D}_t^{\eta}[u(t) - u^2(t - \alpha(t))] = e^{-u(t)}u(t - \alpha(t)) + \sigma \sin(u(t))u(t - \alpha(t))\dot{\mathscr{B}}_t + f(t),
$$
$$
u(t) = -t, \qquad \text{for} \quad t \in [-\tau, 0],
$$

where ${}^{C}\mathscr{D}_t^{\eta}[\cdot]$ *denotes the Caputo fractional derivative of order* η*,* $\sigma \in \mathbb{R}^+$ *is a constant,* $\alpha(t) = \frac{1}{2}\sin(\pi t)$ *represents the time-varying delay, and* $\dot{\mathscr{B}}_t$ *is the formal derivative of the standard Brownian motion.*

The piecewise function gives the closed-form solution

$$
u(t) = \begin{cases} -t, & t \in [-\tau, 0], \\ 2t^3, & t \in (0, \mathrm{T}], \end{cases}
$$

where $f(t)$ *is the appropriately chosen source term to satisfy this solution.*

Figure 1 presents the solution obtained using the proposed numerical scheme for the SFNDE described in Example 1, alongside its exact solution for parameters $\eta = 0.5$, $n = 5$, $\sigma = 0.01$, $\bar{\mathrm{M}} = 20$, $\bar{\mathrm{P}} = 45$, $\mathbf{Bm} = 250$, and $\mu = 0.3$.

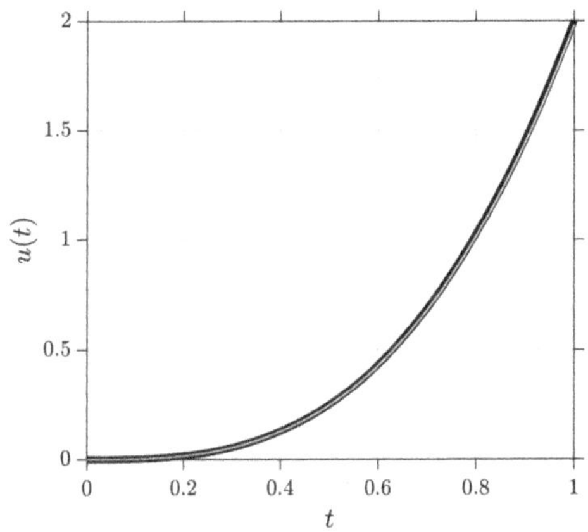

Figure 1. The light blue line represents the numerical solution, while the black line shows the exact solution without noise for Example 1 with the parameters $\eta = 0.5$, $n = 5$, $\sigma = 0.01$, $\bar{\mathrm{M}} = 20$, $\bar{\mathrm{P}} = 45$, $\mathbf{Bm} = 250$, and $\mu = 0.3$.

In addition, Figure 2 presents a logarithmic analysis of the absolute errors $\log_{10}|u(t) - u_n(t)|$ for the solution of the SFNDE in Example 1 plotted against varying noise intensities σ. The numerical scheme was implemented with the following parameters: discretization level $n = 6$, quadrature orders $\bar{\mathrm{M}} = 15$ and $\bar{\mathrm{P}} = 45$, fractional order $\eta = 0.65$, time step $\mu = 0.1$, and $\mathbf{Bm} = 200$ Brownian motion realizations. This semi-log plot elucidates the sensitivity of the numerical approximation to stochastic perturbations of different magnitudes. The divergence of error curves for distinct σ values provides insight into the method's stability and accuracy across a spectrum of noise intensities. This analysis is crucial for assessing the robustness and applicability of our numerical scheme in various stochastic environments, particularly when dealing with fractional-order systems subject to time-varying delays and nonlinear interactions. These results provide strong empirical evidence for the efficacy of our proposed method in approximating solutions to SFNDEs with time-varying delays, even in the presence of nonlinear terms and stochastic perturbations.

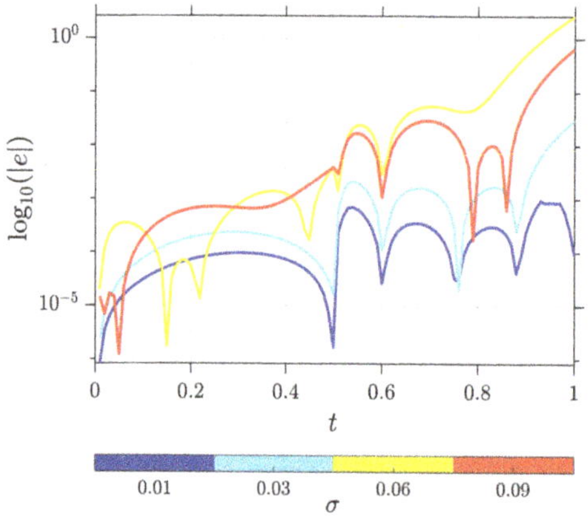

Figure 2. Logarithmic error analysis, $\log_{10}|e(t)|$, i.e., $e(t) = u(t) - u_n(t)$, in Example 1, illustrating the relationship between the error and noise intensity σ for a fractional order of $\eta = 0.65$.

Table 1 provides a detailed analysis of computational efficiency and accuracy for Example 1. It includes $\mathbf{L}_\infty$-norm error values and the CPU time required for various discretization levels (n) with parameters $\eta = 0.65$, $\sigma = 0.01$, $\bar{\mathrm{P}} = 25$, $\bar{\mathrm{M}} = 30$, $\mathrm{T} = 1$, and $\mathbf{Bm} = 200$. The table compares errors for two values of μ (0.1 and 0.2) and lists the CPU time in seconds.

Table 1. Analysis of computational efficiency and accuracy for the numerical solution in Example 1, highlighting the performance of the proposed method.

Discretization Level n	$\mathbf{L}_\infty$-Norm Error ($\mu = 0.1$)	$\mathbf{L}_\infty$-Norm Error ($\mu = 0.2$)	CPU Time (seconds)
3	3.3261×10^{-1}	7.1240×10^{-1}	78.126
6	5.8410×10^{-2}	8.0124×10^{-2}	141.11
9	7.1225×10^{-3}	3.2636×10^{-2}	238.812

Example 2. *Consider the SFDDE*

$$ {}^{c}\mathscr{D}_t^{\eta}[u(t) + u(t-\alpha(t))] = u(t)u(t-\alpha(t)) + \sigma u^2(t-\alpha(t))\dot{\mathscr{B}}_t + f(t), $$
$$ u(t) = 0, \qquad \text{for} \quad t \in [-\tau, 0], $$

where ${}^{c}\mathscr{D}_t^{\eta}[\cdot]$ *denotes the Caputo fractional derivative of order* η, $\sigma \in \mathbb{R}^+$ *is the noise intensity,* $\alpha(t) = 0.5$ *is a constant delay, and* $\dot{\mathscr{B}}_t$ *represents the formal derivative of the standard Brownian motion. The piecewise function gives the analytical solution*

$$ u(t) = \begin{cases} 0, & t \in [-\tau, 0], \\ t\sin(\pi t), & t \in (0, \mathrm{T}], \end{cases} $$

where $f(t)$ *is the appropriately chosen source term to satisfy this solution.*

Figure 3 presents a comparison between the exact solution and the numerical approximation of Example 2 for $\mathbf{Bm} = 300$ Brownian motion realizations and parameters $\eta = 0.5$, $n = 9$, $\sigma = 0.01$, $\bar{\mathrm{P}} = 30$, $\bar{\mathrm{M}} = 20$, and $\mu = 0.2$. In addition, the logarithmic absolute errors $\log_{10}|u(t) - u_n(t)|$ for various values of $\mathbf{Bm} = \{2000, 300, 400\}$ are shown in Figure 4.

Table 2 presents the computational efficiency and accuracy of our numerical scheme, displaying the $\mathbf{L}_\infty$-norm error $\|\mathscr{E}_n\|_\infty = \max_{t\in[0,\mathrm{T}]}|u(t) - u_n(t)|$ and CPU time for varying discretization levels n and time steps μ. The parameters for this analysis are fractional order $\eta = 0.45$, noise intensity $\sigma = 0.005$, quadrature orders $\bar{P} = 30$ and $\bar{M} = 20$, final time $T = 1$, and **Bm** $= 250$ Brownian motion realizations.

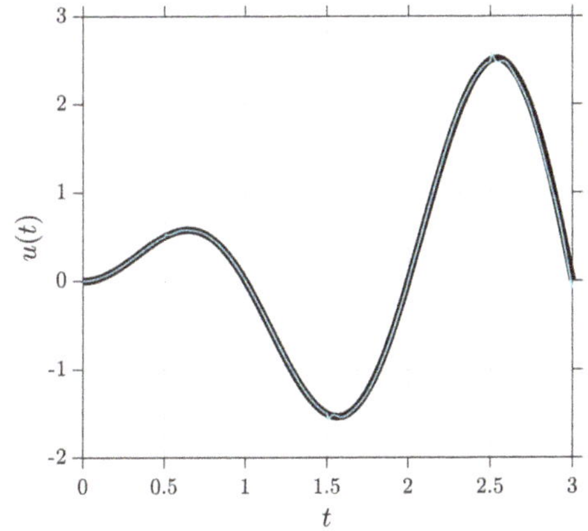

Figure 3. Comparison between the exact solution (black line) and the numerical approximation (light blue line) for Example 2, obtained using the proposed method.

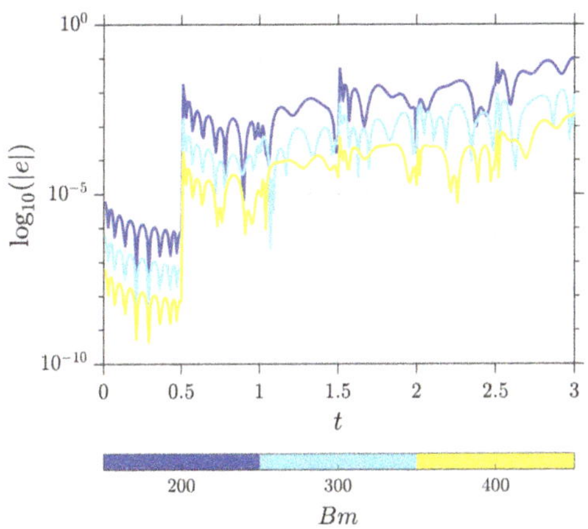

Figure 4. Logarithmic error analysis, $\log_{10}|e(t)|$, i.e., $e(t) = u(t) - u_n(t)$, for Example 2, showing the effect of different numbers of Brownian motion realizations **Bm** with a fractional order of $\eta = 0.5$.

Table 2. Analysis of computational efficiency and accuracy for the numerical solution in Example 2, demonstrating the performance and reliability of the proposed method.

Discretization Level n	L_∞-Norm Error ($\mu = 0.1$)	L_∞-Norm Error ($\mu = 0.2$)	CPU Time (Seconds)
3	4.4310×10^{-2}	7.5463×10^{-1}	42.24
6	3.2467×10^{-3}	5.4505×10^{-2}	73.108
9	4.3311×10^{-4}	2.1173×10^{-2}	164.34

This thorough analysis highlights the proposed numerical scheme's accuracy, stability, and computational efficiency when solving SFDDEs with constant delays. It provides valuable insights into the scheme's performance across different parameter configurations and stochastic realizations.

Example 3. *A comprehensive population growth model for E. coli that demonstrates a prolonged, step-like growth pattern is proposed by NDDE [47]. The proposed model encompasses the following critical features: (i) all cells exhibit identical division times, (ii) cellular division occurs synchronously, (iii) there is an initial period characterized by extended step-like growth, and (iv) the initial population size of E. coli colonies remains indeterminate. That is*

$$ {}^{c}\mathscr{D}_t^{\eta}[u(t) - \rho_2 u(t-\tau)] = \rho_0 u(t) + \rho_1 u(t-\tau) + \sigma \dot{\mathscr{B}}_t, \quad \eta \in (0,1], \tag{52} $$

where $u(t)$ represents the population, and the history function is given by

$$ \phi(t) = u_0 + \beta \Psi(t), \quad t \in [-\tau, 0], $$

where

$$ \Psi(t) = \frac{2u_0\beta\gamma}{\rho_1 \tau} E\left(\frac{2t}{h} + 1\right), $$

and

$$ E(t) = \begin{cases} \exp\left(-\frac{1}{1-t^2}\right), & \text{for } |t| < 1, \\ 0, & \text{otherwise.} \end{cases} $$

where $\rho_0 = 0.004$ is the growth rate parameter, $\rho_1 = 0.004$ is the interaction effect parameter, $\rho_2 = 0.101$ is the delay effect parameter, $\tau = 1.623$ is the delay time in hours, $u_0 = 99$ is the initial population of E. coli cells, $\beta = 0.011$ is a scaling factor, $\gamma = 2.25$ is the growth efficiency, and $h = 1$ is the characteristic time scale. These values are typical and derived from empirical observations in microbial growth studies, providing a solid foundation for modeling E. coli population dynamics.

Figure 5 illustrates the simulation results for various values of η with the numerical algorithm parameters set as $n = 21$, $\sigma = 0.01$, $\bar{\mathrm{P}} = 80$, $\bar{\mathrm{M}} = 2n+1$, and $\mu = 0.5$. The black line corresponds to the integer-order solution based on the approach from [48], showing strong agreement with the proposed model at $\eta = 1$. Moreover, the obtained numerical solutions leverage the Martingale property of the stochastic process, implying that while the solution exhibits random fluctuations, it shows no deterministic trend or drift. Although these fluctuations are more pronounced in the integer-order solution obtained using the approach from [48], they are less visible in the proposed method due to the use of a low-degree interpolating polynomial, which leads to a natural averaging effect. Additionally, as the fractional order decreases, an exponential decline in the growth rate is observed, consistent with the theoretical expectations for such systems.

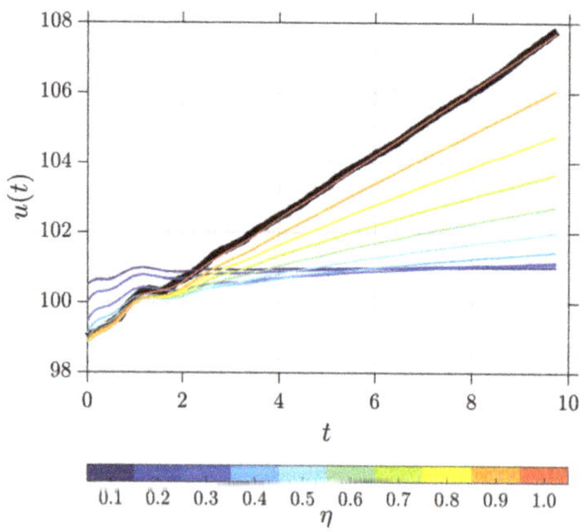

Figure 5. Simulation results of the *E. coli* population growth model for various values of η, and with the parameters set as $n = 21$, $\sigma = 0.01$, $\bar{\mathrm{P}} = 80$, $\bar{\mathrm{M}} = 2n+1$, and $\mu = 0.5$. The black line represents the integer-order solution obtained by the method proposed in [48].

7. Conclusions

This study presented a novel numerical approach for solving fractional neutral stochastic differential equations (SFDDEs) with a neutral delay. The method leveraged Jacobi poly-fractonomials to transform the original problem into a non-delay stochastic neutral integral equation. By applying a collocation scheme based on these poly-fractonomials, the non-delay equations were reduced to systems of nonlinear algebraic equations, which were solved iteratively. The convergence analysis demonstrated that the proposed method exhibits spectral convergence, highlighting its efficiency and accuracy. Numerical examples further validated the robustness and effectiveness of the approach, showing its capability to handle the complexities of SFDDEs with high precision.

Since the fractional operator used in this study is not memoryless and is constrained by the lower terminal of the fractional operator, the need for higher-degree polynomials for extended solution times is inevitable. As the polynomial degree increases, the number of unknowns in the nonlinear augmented algebraic equations also grows, potentially leading to an exponential increase in computation time. This issue could be addressed by using short-memory memory principal [49]. Future work will focus on investigating this approach further.

Author Contributions: A.B. led the investigation, providing expertise in synthesizing and analyzing the literature. S.B. contributed to software development and methodology, creating tools for data analysis and establishing the systematic review protocol. B.P.M. contributed to conceptualization, offering valuable insights into framing the review's scope and objectives. A.D. was responsible for checking for technical errors, for software development, for methodology, for completing a comprehensive review, and for editing to verify the manuscript's clarity and cohesion. A.G. supervised the project, offering guidance on content selection, and contributed to visualizing key findings. All authors have read and agreed to the published version of the manuscript.

Funding: This research received no external funding.

Data Availability Statement: Data sharing is not applicable to this article as no datasets were generated or analyzed during the current study. Data are contained within the article.

Conflicts of Interest: The authors declare no conflicts of interest.

References

1. Dobrushkin, V.A. *Applied Differential Equations with Boundary Value Problems*; Chapman and Hall/CRC: New York, NY, USA, 2017. [CrossRef]
2. Nandakumaran, A.; Datti, P.; George, R. *Ordinary Differential Equations: Principles and Applications*; Cambridge IISc Series; Cambridge University Press: Cambridge, UK, 2017.
3. Nilsson, J.; Riedel, S. *Electric Circuits*; Pearson Education: London, UK, 2014.
4. Chopra, A. *Dynamics of Structures: Theory and Applications to Earthquake Engineering*; Pearson Education: London, UK; Prentice Hall: Upper Saddle River, NJ, USA, 2000.
5. Oksendal, B. *Stochastic Differential Equations, An Introduction with Applications*; Springer: New York, NY, USA, 1998.
6. Chen, X.; Hu, P.; Shum, S.; Zhang, Y. Dynamic stochastic inventory management with reference price effects. *Oper. Res.* **2016**, *64*, 1529–1536. [CrossRef]
7. Huu, A.; Costa-Lima, B. Orbits in a stochastic Goodwin-Lotka-Volterra model. *J. Math. Anal. Appl.* **2014**, *419*, 48–67.
8. Ahmadi, Z.; Mohammad Hosseini, S.; Foroush Bastani, A. A lattice-based approach to option and bond valuation under mean-reverting regime-switching diffusion processes. *J. Comput. Appl. Math.* **2020**, *363*, 156–170. [CrossRef]
9. Bellomo, N.; Brzezniak, Z.; de Socio, L. *Nonlinear Stochastic Evolution Problems in Applied Sciences*; Kluwer Academic Publishers/Springer: Dordrecht, The Netherlands, 1992.
10. Qi, J.; Cui, Q.; Bai, L.; Sun, Y. Investigating exact solutions, sensitivity, and chaotic behavior of multi-fractional order stochastic Davey-Sewartson equations for hydrodynamics research applications. *Chaos Solitons Fractals* **2024**, *180*, 114491. [CrossRef]
11. Singh, S.; Ray, S. Numerical solutions of stochastic Fisher equation to study migration and population behavior in biological invasion. *Int. J. Biomath.* **2017**, *10*, 1750103. [CrossRef]
12. Padgett, W.; Tsokos, C. A new stochastic formulation of a population growth problem. *Math. Biosci.* **1973**, *17*, 105–120. [CrossRef]
13. Aboulaich, R.; Darouichi, A.; Elmouki, I.; Jraifi, A. A Stochastic Optimal Control Model for BCG Immunotherapy in Superficial Bladder Cancer. *Math. Model. Nat. Phenom.* **2017**, *12*, 99–119. [CrossRef]
14. Yang, J.; Tan, Y.; Cheke, R. Thresholds for extinction and proliferation in a stochastic tumour-immune model with pulsed comprehensive therapy. *Commun. Nonlinear Sci. Numer. Simulat.* **2019**, *73*, 363–378. [CrossRef]

15. Jerez, S.; Diaz-Infante, S.; Chen, B. Fluctuating periodic solutions and moment boundedness of a stochastic model for the bone remodeling process. *Math. Biosci.* **2018**, *299*, 153–164. [CrossRef]
16. Babaei, A.; Jafari, H.; Banihashemi, S.; Ahmadi, M. Mathematical analysis of a stochastic model for spread of Coronavirus. *Chaos Solitons Fractals* **2021**, *145*, 110788. [CrossRef]
17. Dabiri, A.; Butcher, E.A.; Poursina, M.; Nazari, M. Optimal periodic-gain fractional delayed state feedback control for linear fractional periodic time-delayed systems. *IEEE Trans. Autom. Control.* **2017**, *63*, 989–1002. [CrossRef]
18. Balachandran, B.; Kalmár-Nagy, T.; Gilsinn, D.E. *Delay Differential Equations*; Springer: New York, NY, USA, 2009.
19. Forde, J.E. *Delay Differential Equation Models in Mathematical Biology*; University of Michigan: Ann Arbor, MI, USA, 2005.
20. Erneux, T. *Applied Delay Differential Equations*; Springer: New York, NY, USA, 2009.
21. Karimi, R.; Dabiri, A.; Cheng, J.; Butcher, E.A. Probabilistic-robust optimal control for uncertain linear time-delay systems by state feedback controllers with memory. In Proceedings of the 2018 Annual American Control Conference (ACC), Wisconsin, MI, USA, 27–29 June 2018; pp. 4183–4188.
22. Podlubny, I. *Fractional Differential Equations: An Introduction to Fractional Derivatives, Fractional Differential Equations, to Methods of Their Solution and Some of Their Applications*; Academic Press: San Diego, CA, USA; London, UK, 1998.
23. Parsa Moghaddam, B.; Dabiri, A.; Mostaghim, Z.S.; Moniri, Z. Numerical solution of fractional dynamical systems with impulsive effects. *Int. J. Mod. Phys. C* **2023**, *34*, 2350013. [CrossRef]
24. Dabiri, A.; Butcher, E.A.; Nazari, M. Coefficient of restitution in fractional viscoelastic compliant impacts using fractional Chebyshev collocation. *J. Sound Vib.* **2017**, *388*, 230–244. [CrossRef]
25. Moghaddam, B.P.; Dabiri, A.; Machado, J.A.T. Application of variable-order fractional calculus in solid mechanics. In *Volume 7 Applications in Engineering, Life and Social Sciences, Part A*; De Gruyter: Berlin, Germany, 2019.
26. Dabiri, A.; Moghaddam, B.; Machado, J.T. Optimal variable-order fractional PID controllers for dynamical systems. *J. Comput. Appl. Math.* **2018**, *339*, 40–48. [CrossRef]
27. Moniri, Z.; Parsa Moghaddam, B.; Zamani Roudbaraki, M. An Efficient and Robust Numerical Solver for Impulsive Control of Fractional Chaotic Systems. *Math. Probl. Eng.* **2023**, *2023*, 9077924. [CrossRef]
28. Ionescu, C.; Lopes, A.; Copot, D.; Machado, J.T.; Bates, J.H. The role of fractional calculus in modeling biological phenomena: A review. *Commun. Nonlinear Sci. Numer. Simul.* **2017**, *51*, 141–159. [CrossRef]
29. Baleanu, D. *Fractional Calculus: Models and Numerical Methods*; World Scientific: Singapore, 2012; Volume 3.
30. Moghaddam, B.P.; Zhang, L.; Lopes, A.M.; Tenreiro Machado, J.A.; Mostaghim, Z.S. Sufficient conditions for existence and uniqueness of fractional stochastic delay differential equations. *Int. J. Probab. Stoch. Process.* **2019**, *92*, 379–396. [CrossRef]
31. Ayazi, N.; Mokhtary, P.; Moghaddam, B.P. Efficiently solving fractional delay differential equations of variable order via an adjusted spectral element approach. *Chaos Solitons Fractals* **2024**, *181*, 114635. [CrossRef]
32. Banihashemi, S.; Jafari, H.; Babaei, A. A novel collocation approach to solve a nonlinear stochastic differential equation of fractional order involving a constant delay. *Discret. Contin. Dyn. Syst. Ser. S* **2021**, *15*, 339–357. [CrossRef]
33. Moghaddam, B.P.; Pishbin, M.; Mostaghim, Z.S.; Iyiola, O.S.; Galhano, A.; Lopes, A.M. A Numerical Algorithm for Solving Nonlocal Nonlinear Stochastic Delayed Systems with Variable-Order Fractional Brownian Noise. *Fractal Fract.* **2023**, *7*, 293. [CrossRef]
34. Chadha, A.; Pandey, D.; Bahuguna, D. Faedo–Galerkin approximate solutions of a neutral stochastic fractional differential equation with finite delay. *J. Comput. Appl. Math.* **2018**, *347*, 238–256. [CrossRef]
35. Chaudhary, R.; Pandey, D.N. Approximation of Solutions to Stochastic Neutral Fractional Integro-Differential Equation with Nonlocal Conditions. *Int. J. Appl. Comput. Math.* **2017**, *3*, 1203–1223. [CrossRef]
36. Rahimkhani, P.; Ordokhani, Y. Chelyshkov least squares support vector regression for nonlinear stochastic differential equations by variable fractional Brownian motion. *Chaos Solitons Fractals* **2022**, *163*, 112570. [CrossRef]
37. Dabiri, A.; Butcher, E.A. Numerical solution of multi-order fractional differential equations with multiple delays via spectral collocation methods. *Appl. Math. Model.* **2018**, *56*, 424–448. [CrossRef]
38. Dabiri, A.; Butcher, E.A. Efficient modified Chebyshev differentiation matrices for fractional differential equations. *Commun. Nonlinear Sci. Numer. Simul.* **2017**, *50*, 284–310. [CrossRef]
39. Kazem, S. An integral operational matrix based on Jacobi polynomials for solving fractional-order differential equations. *Appl. Math. Model.* **2013**, *37*, 1126–1136. [CrossRef]
40. Dastgerdi, M.V.; Bastani, A.F. Solving Parametric Fractional Differential Equations Arising from the Rough Heston Model Using Quasi-Linearization and Spectral Collocation. *SIAM J. Financ. Math.* **2020**, *11*, 1063–1097. [CrossRef]
41. Zayernouri, M.; Karniadakis, G.E. Exponentially accurate spectral and spectral element methods for fractional ODEs. *J. Comput. Phys.* **2014**, *257*, 460–480. [CrossRef]
42. Duan, B.; Zheng, Z.; Cao, W. Spectral approximation methods and error estimates for Caputo fractional derivative with applications to initial-value problems. *J. Comput. Phys.* **2016**, *319*, 108–128. [CrossRef]
43. Hussaini, M.Y.; Zang, T.A. *Spectral Methods in Fluid Dynamics*, Technical report; Springer: Berlin/Heidelberg, Germany, 1986.
44. Choe, G. *Stochastic Analysis for Finance with Simulations*; Springer: Cham, Switzerland, 2016.
45. Aryani, E.; Babaei, A.; Valinejad, A. A numerical technique for solving nonlinear fractional stochastic integro-differential equations with n-dimensional Wiener process. *Comput. Methods Differ. Equ.* **2021**, *10*, 61–76. [CrossRef]
46. Kamrani, M. Numerical solution of stochastic fractional differential equations. *Numer. Algorithms* **2015**, *68*, 81–93. [CrossRef]

47. Jamilla, C.U.; Mendoza, R.G.; Mendoza, V.M.P. Parameter Estimation in Neutral Delay Differential Equations Using Genetic Algorithm With Multi-Parent Crossover. *IEEE Access* **2021**, *9*, 131348–131364. [CrossRef]
48. Shampine, L.F. Dissipative approximations to neutral DDEs. *Appl. Math. Comput.* **2008**, *203*, 641–648. [CrossRef]
49. Deng, W. Short memory principle and a predictor–corrector approach for fractional differential equations. *J. Comput. Appl. Math.* **2007**, *206*, 174–188. [CrossRef]

mathematics

MDPI

Article

Theoretical Results on Positive Solutions in Delta Riemann–Liouville Setting

Pshtiwan Othman Mohammed [1,2,*], Ravi P. Agarwal [3], Majeed A. Yousif [4], Eman Al-Sarairah [5,6], Alina Alb Lupas [7,*] and Mohamed Abdelwahed [8]

1 Department of Mathematics, College of Education, University of Sulaimani, Sulaimani 46001, Iraq
2 Research and Development Center, University of Sulaimani, Sulaimani 46001, Iraq
3 Department of Mathematics and Systems Engineering, Florida Institute of Technology, Melbourne, FL 32901, USA; agarwalr@fit.edu
4 Department of Mathematics, College of Education, University of Zakho, Zakho 42002, Iraq; majeed.yousif@uoz.edu.krd
5 Department of Mathematics, Khalifa University of Science and Technology, Abu Dhabi P.O. Box 127788, United Arab Emirates
6 Department of Mathematics, Al-Hussein Bin Talal University, P.O. Box 20, Ma'an 71111, Jordan
7 Department of Mathematics and Computer Science, University of Oradea, 410087 Oradea, Romania
8 Department of Mathematics, College of Science, King Saud University, P.O. Box 2455, Riyadh 11451, Saudi Arabia
* Correspondence: pshtiwansangawi@gmail.com (P.O.M.); dalb@uoradea.ro (A.A.L.)

Abstract: This article primarily focuses on examining the existence and uniqueness analysis of boundary fractional difference equations in a class of Riemann–Liouville operators. To this end, we firstly recall the general solution of the homogeneous fractional operator problem. Then, the Green function to the corresponding fractional boundary value problems will be reconstructed, and homogeneous boundary conditions are used to find the unknown constants. Next, the existence of solutions will be studied depending on the fixed-point theorems on the constructed Green's function. The uniqueness of the problem is also derived via Lipschitz constant conditions.

Keywords: Riemann–Liouville operators; Green's function (GF); fixed-point theorem; existence and uniqueness solution

MSC: 26A48; 26A51; 33B10; 39A12; 39B62

1. Introduction

The most fundamental and significant notions from integers to fractional difference and differential equations (ordinary or partial) are fractional calculus and discrete fractional calculus [1,2]. In particular, fractional difference models contribute to many work frames with respect to the theory and application in mathematics and physics; see e.g., [3–5]. Furthermore, these models and their associated system of difference equations serve as well-suited mathematical models in various areas, such as physics, ecology, social sciences, chemistry, and biology (cf. [6–10]).

Fractional difference operators have played an indispensable role in shaping our understanding of fractional boundary value problems (FBVPs). These FBVPs provided valuable insights into the importance of convergence analysis in discrete fractional calculus theory and the potential impact of dynamical systems; see for example, Refs. [2,11–14] to be familiar with these operators. In addition, some FBVP models have been proposed and studied in [15–21] and references therein, and the authors mainly focused on Riemann–Liouville- and Liouville–Caputo-type operators. Furthermore, the existence and uniqueness of FBPV solutions are governed by various fractional operators resulting from a variety of continuous and discrete actions involving AB and CF fractional operators (e.g., [14,22–28]).

In addition, the FBVPs have the effect of various parameters on the bandgap and the feasibility of actively adjusting the bandgap of the system [29–31].

In addition, the analysis of the existence/uniqueness of solutions to the fractional difference equations concerning BVPs is paramount in comprehending discrete fractional calculus. These solutions serve as major results in directing and investigating inequalities such as Laypunov-like inequalities. There have been increasing applications of fractional problems in mathematical physics for the existence of positive solutions [32,33]. Recently, Mohammed et al. [34] considered the following FBVP:

$$\begin{cases} -\left({}^{\mathrm{RL}}_{q_0}\Delta^{\theta} g\right)(x) = h(x+\theta), \quad x \in \mathbb{N}(q_0+2;q), \\ g(q_0) = 0, \quad g(q) = 0, \end{cases} \tag{1}$$

and they obtained the existence of its solutions, as discussed in the next section.

Motivated by [34], we aim to examine, in this current study, the uniqueness of a positive solution for the following FBVP:

$$\begin{cases} \left({}^{\mathrm{RL}}_{q_0}\Delta^{\theta} g\right)(x) = -Z(x+\theta-1, g(x+\theta-1)), \\ g(q_0) = C_1, \ g(q) = C_2 \quad x \in \mathbb{N}(q_0+2;q), \end{cases} \tag{2}$$

For $q_0, q, C_1, C_2 \in \mathbb{R}$ with $q - q_0 \in \mathbb{N}(2)$, Z is assumed to be a function from $\mathbb{N}(q_0+2;q) \times \mathbb{R}$ to $\mathbb{R}$. Note that $\mathbb{N}(q_0) = \{q_0, q_0+1, \ldots\}$ and $\mathbb{N}(q_0;q) = \{q_0, q_0+1, \ldots, q\}$.

The remainder of this paper is structured as follows: In the next section, we review the basic theorems about the existence of fractional boundary value problems, focusing on recently published results. In Section 3, we obtain positive solutions in terms of the fundamental systems of solutions on the known fixed-point theorems for solutions of the FBVP and some of their relevant features. Section 4 is devoted to explaining our GF for the corresponding FBVP. Next, in Section 5, the existence of our solutions to the GF formula will be shown by considering the common fixed-point theorems. Two examples are shown in Section 6 as applications of our theoretical results. Finally, our article will end with concluding remarks in Section 7.

2. Review of Results

In this section, we state further results obtained by Mohammed et al. [34].

Theorem 1. *Let $\theta \in (1,2)$, and let q_0 and q be two real numbers such that $q - q_0 \in \mathbb{N}(1)$, and $h : \mathbb{N}(q_0+2;q) \to \mathbb{R}$. Then, FBVP* (1) *has the unique solution*

$$g(x) = \sum_{r=q_0+2}^{q} \mathscr{G}(x,r)h(r), \quad x \in \mathbb{N}(q_0;q), \tag{3}$$

where the GF $\mathscr{G}(x,r)$ is given by

$$\mathscr{G}(x,r) = \begin{cases} \frac{(q+\theta-r-1)^{\underline{\theta-1}}}{(q+\theta-q_0-2)^{\underline{\theta-1}}\Gamma(\theta)}(x+\theta-q_0-2)^{\underline{\theta-1}}, & x \le r-1, \\ \frac{(q+\theta-r-1)^{\underline{\theta-1}}}{(q+\theta-q_0-2)^{\underline{\theta-1}}\Gamma(\theta)}(x+\theta-q_0-2)^{\underline{\theta-1}} - \frac{(x+\theta-r-1)^{\underline{\theta-1}}}{\Gamma(\theta)}, & x \ge r. \end{cases} \tag{4}$$

In the above theorem, for $x \in \mathbb{N}(q_0+\ell-\theta)$ (see [35], (Theorem 2.2)),

$$\left({}^{\mathrm{RL}}_{q_0}\Delta^{\theta} g\right)(x) := \frac{1}{\Gamma(-\theta)} \sum_{r=q_0}^{x+\theta} (x-r-1)^{\underline{-\theta-1}} g(r), \tag{5}$$

is the Riemann–Liouville fractional difference, and its sum formula, for $x \in \mathbb{N}_{q_0+\theta}$ (see [2], (Definition 2.25)),

$$\left({}^{\mathrm{RL}}_{q_0}\Delta^{-\theta} g\right)(x) = \frac{1}{\Gamma(\theta)} \sum_{r=q_0}^{x-\theta} (x-r-1)^{\underline{\theta-1}} g(r), \tag{6}$$

is the Riemann–Liouville fractional sum for the function g on the domain $\mathbb{N}(q_0)$, $\ell - 1 < \theta < \ell$ with $\ell \in \mathbb{N}_1$, and $x^{\underline{\theta}} = \frac{\Gamma(x+1)}{\Gamma(x+1-\theta)}$.

Theorem 2. *Let $\theta \in (1,2)$ in the FBVP:*

$$\begin{aligned} -\left({}^{\mathrm{RL}}_{q_0}\Delta^{\theta} w\right)(x) &= 0, \\ w(q_0) = C_1, \quad w(q) &= C_2. \end{aligned} \tag{7}$$

Then, we have the following:

(a) *For $x \in \mathbb{N}_{q_0+2}$,*

$$w(x) = C_1\left(\frac{q-x}{q-q_0}\right)\frac{(x-q_0+\theta-2)^{\underline{\theta-2}}}{\Gamma(\theta-1)} + C_2\frac{(x-q_0+\theta-2)^{\underline{\theta-1}}}{(q-q_0+\theta-2)^{\underline{\theta-1}}}, \quad x \in \mathbb{N}(q_0;q), \tag{8}$$

is the solution of (7).

(b) *For $x \in \mathbb{N}_{q_0}^{q}$, we have*

$$\mid w(x) \mid \leq 2\max\{|C_1|, |C_2|\}.$$

Theorem 3. *Let $h : \mathbb{N}_{q_0+2}^{q} \to \mathbb{R}$. The FBVP*

$$\begin{aligned} -\left({}^{\mathrm{RL}}_{q_0}\Delta^{\theta} g\right)(x) &= h(x+\theta), \quad x \in \mathbb{N}_{q_0+2}, \\ g(q_0) = C_1, \quad g(q) &= C_2, \end{aligned} \tag{9}$$

has the unique solution

$$g(x) = w(x) + \sum_{r=q_0+2}^{q} \mathcal{G}(x,r)h(r), \quad x \in \mathbb{N}_{q_0}^{q}, \tag{10}$$

where w is as given in the above theorem, and $\mathcal{G}(x,r)$ is as given in Theorem 1.

3. Positive Solution Results

In view of the Guo–Krasnoselskii theorem (see [36]), we examine the existence of positive solutions for FBVP (2) when $C_1 = C_2 = 0$:

$$\begin{cases} \left({}^{\mathrm{RL}}_{q_0}\Delta^{\theta} g\right)(x) = -Z(x+\theta-1, g(x+\theta-1)), \\ g(q_0) = g(q) = 0, \quad x \in \mathbb{N}(q_0+2;q). \end{cases} \tag{11}$$

Definition 1 ([37], (Completely Continuous Operator)). *A bounded linear operator $\mathcal{E} : C \to \bar{C}$, where C and $\bar{C}$ are two Banach spaces (BSs), is completely continuous if it transforms weakly convergent sequences in C to norm-convergent sequences in $\bar{C}$.*

Theorem 4 ([36], (Guo–Krasnoselskii theorem)). *Let $\mathcal{F} \subset C$ be a cone set, and the BS C contains two open sets Ω_1 and Ω_2 such that $\overline{\Omega}_1 \subseteq \Omega_2$ and $0 \in \Omega_1$. Suppose that $\mathcal{E} : \mathcal{F} \cap (\overline{\Omega}_2 \setminus \Omega_1) \to \mathcal{F}$*

is a completely continuous operator. If one of the following properties holds, then $\mathcal{E}$ has at least one fixed point in $\mathcal{F} \cap (\overline{\Omega}_2 \setminus \Omega_1)$:

1. $\|\mathcal{E}g\| \geq \|g\|$ *for* $g \in \mathcal{F} \cap \partial\Omega_2$ *and* $\|\mathcal{E}g\| \leq \|g\|$ *for* $g \in \mathcal{F} \cap \partial\Omega_1$;
2. $\|\mathcal{E}g\| \leq \|g\|$ *for* $g \in \mathcal{F} \cap \partial\Omega_2$ *and* $\|\mathcal{E}g\| \geq \|g\|$ *for* $g \in \mathcal{F} \cap \partial\Omega_1$.

Next, we need a new property of the GF that is as follows.

Theorem 5. *One can have $0 < \gamma < 1$ such that*

$$\min_{x\in\mathbb{N}(q_0+1;q-1)} \mathscr{G}(x,r) \leq \max_{x\in\mathbb{N}(q_0+1;q-1)} \mathscr{G}(x,r) = \gamma \mathscr{G}(r-1,r), \quad r \in \mathbb{N}(q_0+2;q).$$

Proof. In [38], Mohammed et al. showed that $\mathscr{G}(x,r)$ increases from $\mathscr{G}(q_0,r) = 0$ to a positive value in $\mathscr{G}(r-1,r)$ and then decreases to $\mathscr{G}(q,r) = 0$, for fixed $r \in \mathbb{N}(q_0+1;q)$. Now, we define

$$\overline{\mathscr{G}}(x,r) = \frac{\mathscr{G}(x,r)}{\mathscr{G}(r-1,r)}.$$

Then, for $r \in \mathbb{N}(q_0+2;q)$, we consider

$$\overline{\mathscr{G}}(x,r) = \begin{cases} \frac{(x-q_0+\theta-2)^{\overline{\theta-1}}}{(r-q_0+\theta-3)^{\overline{\theta-1}}}, & x \in \mathbb{N}_{q_0+1}^{r-1}, \\ \frac{(x-q_0+\theta-2)^{\overline{\theta-1}}}{(r-q_0+\theta-3)^{\overline{\theta-1}}} - \frac{(x-r+\theta-1)^{\overline{\theta-1}}(q-q_0+\theta-2)^{\overline{\theta-1}}}{(q-r+\theta-1)^{\overline{\theta-1}}(r-q_0+\theta-3)^{\overline{\theta-1}}}, & x \in \mathbb{N}_{r}^{q-1}. \end{cases}$$

Therefore, for $x \in \mathbb{N}(q_0+1;r-1)$ and $r \in \mathbb{N}(q_0+2;q)$, one can have

$$\overline{\mathscr{G}}(x,r) = \frac{(x-q_0+\theta-2)^{\overline{\theta-1}}}{(r-q_0+\theta-3)^{\overline{\theta-1}}} \geq \frac{(\theta-1)^{\overline{\theta-1}}}{(q-q_0+\theta-3)^{\overline{\theta-1}}} = \frac{\Gamma(\theta)}{(q-q_0+\theta-3)^{\overline{\theta-1}}}. \tag{12}$$

Also, for $x \in \mathbb{N}(r;q-1)$ and $r \in \mathbb{N}(q_0+2;q-1)$, we know that $\mathscr{G}(x,r)(\Longrightarrow \overline{\mathscr{G}}(x,r))$ is a decreasing function of x. Then, we obtain

$$\begin{aligned}
\overline{\mathscr{G}}(x,r) &\geq \overline{\mathscr{G}}(q-1,r) \\
&= \frac{(q-q_0+\theta-3)^{\overline{\theta-1}}}{(r-q_0+\theta-3)^{\overline{\theta-1}}} - \frac{(q-r+\theta-2)^{\overline{\theta-1}}(q-q_0+\theta-2)^{\overline{\theta-1}}}{(q-r+\theta-1)^{\overline{\theta-1}}(r-q_0+\theta-3)^{\overline{\theta-1}}} \\
&= \frac{(q-q_0+\theta-3)^{\overline{\theta-1}}}{(r-q_0+\theta-3)^{\overline{\theta-1}}}\left[1 - \frac{(q-r+\theta-2)^{\overline{\theta-1}}(q-q_0+\theta-2)^{\overline{\theta-1}}}{(q-r+\theta-1)^{\overline{\theta-1}}(q-q_0+\theta-3)^{\overline{\theta-1}}}\right] \\
&= \frac{(q-q_0+\theta-3)^{\overline{\theta-1}}}{(r-q_0+\theta-3)^{\overline{\theta-1}}}\left[1 - \left(\frac{q-r}{q-r+\theta-1}\right)\left(\frac{q-q_0+\theta-2}{q-q_0-1}\right)\right] \\
&= \frac{(q-q_0+\theta-3)^{\overline{\theta-2}}}{(r-q_0+\theta-3)^{\overline{\theta-2}}}\left(\frac{\theta-1}{q-q_0+\theta-1}\right) \\
&= \frac{(q-q_0+\theta-3)^{\overline{\theta-2}}}{(\theta-1)^{\overline{\theta-2}}}\left(\frac{\theta-1}{q-q_0+\theta-3}\right) \\
&= \frac{(q-q_0+\theta-3)^{\overline{\theta-2}}}{(q-q_0+\theta-3)\Gamma(\theta-1)}.
\end{aligned} \tag{13}$$

Thus, in view of (12) and (13), we see that

$$\min_{x\in\mathbb{N}(q_0+1;q-1)} \mathscr{G}(x,r) \geq \gamma \mathscr{G}(r-1,r), \quad r \in \mathbb{N}(q_0+2;q),$$

where

$$\gamma = \min\left\{\frac{\Gamma(\theta)}{(q-q_0+\theta-3)^{\overline{\theta-1}}}, \frac{(q-q_0+\theta-3)^{\overline{\theta-2}}}{(q-q_0+\theta-3)\Gamma(\theta-1)}\right\}.$$

It is clear that γ is between 0 and 1. Thus, the proof is complete. □

By considering Theorem 1, we see that g is a solution of (11) **IFF** it is a solution of

$$g(x) = \sum_{r=q_0+2}^{q} Z(r,g(r))\mathcal{G}(x,r), \quad x \in \mathbb{N}(q_0;q). \tag{14}$$

Let us define the operator $\mathcal{E}$ as follows:

$$(\mathcal{E}g)(x) := \sum_{r=q_0+2}^{q} \mathcal{G}(x,r)Z(r,g(r)), \quad x \in \mathbb{N}(q_0;q). \tag{15}$$

We can say that g is a fixed point of $\mathcal{E}$ (according to (14) and (15)) **IFF** it is a solution of (11). In denoting $\mathcal{C}$ by

$$\mathcal{C} = \{g : \mathbb{N}(q_0;q) \to \mathbb{R};\ g(q_0) = g(q) = 0\} \subseteq \mathbb{R}(q-q_0+1).$$

it can be observed that $\mathcal{E} : \mathcal{C} \to \mathcal{C}$ and $\mathcal{C}$ is a BS with the following norm:

$$\|g\| = \max_{x\in\mathbb{N}(q_0;q)} |g(x)|.$$

Now, we define the cone

$$\mathcal{F} : \left\{g \in \mathcal{C} : g(t) \geq 0, \quad \text{for each} \quad x \in \mathbb{N}(q_0;q) \quad \text{and} \quad \min_{\mathbb{N}(q_0+1;q-1)} g(x) \geq \gamma\|g\|\right\}.$$

Now, we try to obtain sufficient conditions for the existence of a fixed point in $\mathcal{E}$. We firstly know that $\mathcal{E}$ is a summation operator defined on a finite set. Therefore, $\mathcal{E}$ is completely continuous. Then, let

$$\eta := \frac{1}{\sum_{r=q_0+2}^{q} \mathcal{G}(r-1,r)} = \frac{\Gamma(\theta)(q-q_0+2\theta-2)^{\overline{2\theta-1}}}{\Gamma(2\theta)(q-q_0+\theta-2)^{\overline{\theta-1}}},$$

and $x_0 \in \mathbb{N}(q_0+1;q-1)$ with

$$\min_{x\in\mathbb{N}(q_0+1;q-1)} \mathcal{G}(x,r) = \mathcal{G}(x_0,r), \quad \text{for all} \quad r \in \mathbb{N}(q_0+2;q).$$

Hence, by making use of Theorem 5, we have

$$\mathcal{G}(r-1,r) \leq \frac{1}{\gamma}\mathcal{G}(x_0,r), \quad r \in \mathbb{N}(q_0+2;q). \tag{16}$$

The following hypotheses will be useful for the next results:

Hypothesis 1 (H1). $Z(x,\xi) \geq 0$, *for* $(x,\xi) \in \mathbb{N}(q_0;q) \times \mathbb{R}^+$.

Hypothesis 2 (H2). *There exists* $a_1 > 0$ *with* $Z(x,g) \leq \eta\, a_1$, *where* $0 \leq g \leq a_1$;

Hypothesis 3 (H3). *There exists* $a_2 > 0$ *with* $Z(x,g) \geq \frac{\eta a_2}{\gamma}$, *where* $\gamma a_2 \leq g \leq a_2$;

Hypothesis 4 (H4). *Suppose that*

$$\lim_{g \to 0^+} \left(\min_{x \in \mathbb{N}(q_0;q)} \frac{Z(x,g)}{g} \right) \to \infty \quad \text{and} \quad \lim_{g \to \infty} \left(\min_{x \in \mathbb{N}(q_0;q)} \frac{Z(x,g)}{g} \right) \to \infty.$$

Hypothesis 5 (H5). *Suppose that*

$$\lim_{g \to 0^+} \left(\min_{x \in \mathbb{N}(q_0;q)} \frac{Z(x,g)}{g} \right) \to 0 \quad \text{and} \quad \lim_{g \to \infty} \left(\min_{x \in \mathbb{N}(q_0;q)} \frac{Z(x,g)}{g} \right) \to 0.$$

Lemma 1. *Let hypothesis* **(H1)** *hold. Then, $\mathcal{E}$ is an operator from $\mathcal{F}$ to $\mathcal{F}$.*

Proof. Let $g \in \mathcal{F}$. It is clear that $(\mathcal{E}g)(x) \geq 0$ for $x \in \mathbb{N}(q_0;q)$. Next, we consider

$$\begin{aligned}
\min_{x \in \mathbb{N}(q_0+1;q-1)} (\mathcal{E}g)(x) &= \min_{x \in \mathbb{N}(q_0+1;q-1)} \left(\sum_{r=q_0+2}^{q} \mathcal{G}(x,r) Z(r,g(r)) \right) \\
&\geq \gamma \sum_{r=q_0+2}^{q} \mathcal{G}(r-1,r) Z(r,g(r)) \\
&= \gamma \sum_{r=q_0+2}^{q} \mathcal{G}(x,r) Z(r,g(r)) \\
&= \gamma \sum_{r=q_0+2}^{q} \mathcal{G}(x,r) Z(r,g(r)) \\
&= \gamma \|\mathcal{E}g\|.
\end{aligned}$$

This leads to $\mathcal{E}g \in \mathcal{F}$. Hence, the proof is complete. □

Theorem 6. *Let* **(H1)–(H3)** *hold on Z. Then, one can find at least one positive solution for* (11).

Proof. It is evident that $\mathcal{E}$ is completely continuous as $\mathcal{E} : \mathcal{F} \to \mathcal{F}$. Let us define

$$\Omega_1 := \{ g \in \mathcal{F} : \|g\| < a_1 \}.$$

It can be said that $\Omega_1 \subseteq C$ is an open set including 0. As $\|g\| = a_1$, for $g \in \partial\Omega_1$, then **(H2)** can hold for each $g \in \partial\Omega_1$. It follows that

$$\begin{aligned}
\|\mathcal{E}g\| = \max_{x \in \mathbb{N}(q_0;q)} \sum_{r=q_0+2}^{q} \mathcal{G}(x_0,r) Z(r,g(r)) \geq \sum_{r=q_0+2}^{q} \mathcal{G}(r-1,r) Z(r,g(r)) \\
\geq \eta a_1 \sum_{r=q_0+2}^{q} \mathcal{G}(r-1,r) = a_1 = \|g\|.
\end{aligned}$$

This implies that $\|\mathcal{E}g\| \geq \|g\|$, where $g \in \mathcal{F} \cap \partial\Omega_1$.
In addition, we define

$$\Omega_2 := \{ g \in \mathcal{F} : \|g\| < a_2 \}.$$

It is evident that $\Omega_2 \subseteq C$ is an open set with $\overline{\Omega}_1 \subseteq \Omega_2$. As $\|g\| = a_2$, for $g \in \partial\Omega_2$, then **(H3)** can hold for each $g \in \partial\Omega_2$. By considering (16), we obtain

$$\begin{aligned}\|\mathcal{E}g\| \geq |\mathcal{E}g(x_0)| = \sum_{r=q_0+2}^{q} \mathcal{G}(x_0,r)Z(r,g(r)) &\geq \gamma \sum_{r=q_0+2}^{q} \mathcal{G}(r-1,r)Z(r,g(r)) \\ &\geq \eta\, a_2 \sum_{r=q_0+2}^{q} \mathcal{G}(r-1,r) = a_2 = \|g\|,\end{aligned}$$

which gives that $\|\mathcal{E}g\| \geq \|g\|$, where $g \in \mathcal{F} \cap \partial\Omega_2$. Therefore, A has at least one fixed point in $\mathcal{F} \cap (\overline{\Omega_2}\,\Omega_1)$ according to Theorem 4. We call this fixed point g_0, which satisfies $a_1 < \|g_0\| < a_2$. This proves our theorem. □

Theorem 7. *Suppose that Z satisfies* **(H1)–(H4)**. *Then, there are at least two positive solutions for* (11).

Proof. Let $M > 0$ and $x_1 \in \mathbb{N}(q_0+1; q-1)$ be fixed with

$$M\gamma \sum_{r=q_0+2}^{q} \mathcal{G}(x_1,r) > 1. \tag{17}$$

Considering **(H4)**, there exists an $a > 0$ such that $a < p$ and $Z(x,g) \geq Mg$ for all $0 \leq g \leq a$ and $x \in \mathbb{N}(q_0;q)$. Define the set

$$\Omega_a := \{g \in \mathcal{F} : \|g\| < a\}.$$

By making use of (17), we obtain

$$\begin{aligned}\|\mathcal{E}g\| \geq |\mathcal{E}g(x_1)| = \sum_{r=q_0+2}^{q} \mathcal{G}(x_1,r)Z(r,g(r)) &\geq M \sum_{r=q_0+2}^{q} \mathcal{G}(x_1,r)|g(r)| \\ &\geq M\gamma\|g\| \sum_{r=q_0+2}^{q} \mathcal{G}(x_1,r) > \|g\|.\end{aligned}$$

This leads to $\|\mathcal{E}g\| > \|g\|$, whenever $g \in \mathcal{F} \cap \partial\Omega_a$. Then, for the same $M > 0$, there is a number $R_1 > 0$ with $Z(x,g) \geq Mg$, for each $g \geq R_1$ and $x \in \mathbb{N}(q_0;q)$. Let us choose R such that

$$R > \max\left\{p, \frac{R_1}{\gamma}\right\}.$$

Now, we define

$$\Omega_R := \{g \in \mathcal{F} : \|g\| < R\}.$$

It is clear that $\|\mathcal{E}g\| > \|g\|$, when $g \in \mathcal{F} \cap \partial\Omega_R$. In the final step, we define

$$\Omega_p := \{g \in \mathcal{F} : \|g\| < p\}.$$

This implies that $\|\mathcal{E}g\| \leq \|g\|$ as $g \in \mathcal{F} \cap \partial\Omega_p$.

Thus, we have found two fixed points g_0 and g_1 for $\mathcal{E}$ with $g_1 \in \Omega_p \backslash \mathring{\Omega}_a$ and $g_2 \in \Omega_R \backslash \mathring{\Omega}_p$, where $\mathring{\Omega}$ refers to the interior of Ω. In particular, we can say that g_0 and g_1 are two positive solutions of (11) that satisfy $0 < \|g_1\|, p < \|g_2\|$. This completes our proof. □

Theorem 8. *Assume that Z satisfies* **(H1)**, **(H3)**, *and* **(H5)**. *Then, there exist at least two positive solutions for* (11).

Proof. For any $\epsilon > 0$, there is an $M > 0$ with $Z(x,g) \geq M + \epsilon g$ according to **(H5)**, for $g \in \mathcal{F}$ and $x \in \mathbb{N}(q_0;q)$. Then, we have

$$|(\mathcal{E}g)| = \sum_{r=q_0+2}^{q} \mathcal{G}(x,r)Z(r,g(r)) \leq \sum_{r=q_0+2}^{q} \mathcal{G}(r-1,r)\left[M + \epsilon g(r)\right].$$

Since $\epsilon > 0$ is arbitrary, we see that

$$|(\mathcal{E}g)| \leq M \sum_{r=q_0+2}^{q} \mathcal{G}(r-1,r) = \frac{M}{\eta}.$$

Taking $R > p$ to be sufficiently large, we have

$$R > \frac{M}{\eta}.$$

Let us define

$$\Omega_R := \{g \in \mathcal{F} : \|g\| < R\}.$$

It follows that $\|\mathcal{E}g\| < R = \|g\|$, whenever $g \in \mathcal{F} \cap \partial\Omega_R$. Again, by considering **(H5)**, we have $a > 0$ such that $a < p$ and $Z(x,g) < \eta g$, for $0 \leq g \leq a, g \in \mathcal{F}$, and $x \in \mathbb{N}(q_0;q)$. Now, we define

$$\Omega_a := \{g \in \mathcal{F} : \|g\| < a\}.$$

Then, we see from this that

$$\|(\mathcal{E}g)\| = \max_{x\in\mathbb{N}(q_0;q)} \sum_{r=q_0+2}^{q} \mathcal{G}(x,r)Z(r,g(r)) \leq \sum_{r=q_0+2}^{q} \mathcal{G}(r-1,r)Z(r,g(r))$$
$$\leq \eta \sum_{r=q_0+2}^{q} \mathcal{G}(r-1,r)|g(r)| \leq \|g\|.$$

This implies that $\|\mathcal{E}g\| < \|g\|$, when $g \in \mathcal{F} \cap \partial\Omega_a$. Lastly, we define

$$\Omega_p := \{g \in \mathcal{F} : \|g\| < p\}.$$

It can be observed that $\|\mathcal{E}g\| > \|g\|$, whereas $g \in \mathcal{F} \cap \partial\Omega_p$.

Thus, we have determined g_1 and g_2, two fixed points of $\mathcal{E}$ with $g_1 \in \Omega_p \backslash \mathring{\Omega}_a$ and $g_2 \in \Omega_R \backslash \mathring{\Omega}_p$. Specifically, we can say that g_1 and g_2 are two positive solutions of (11) that satisfy $0 < \|g_1\|$ and $p < \|g_2\|$. This concludes our result. □

4. Existence Results

Here, we examine the existence of some solutions by considering some known fixed-point theorems. According to Theorem 3, we can define an operator

$$(\mathscr{H}g)(x) := w(x) + \sum_{r=q_0+2}^{q} Z(r,g(r))\,\mathcal{G}(x,r), \quad x \in \mathbb{N}(q_0;q). \tag{18}$$

It follows from (10) and (18) that g is a fixed point of $\mathscr{H}$ **IFF** it is a solution of (2).

Theorem 9 (see [36], (Brouwer theorem)). *Let $\mathbb{R}(n)$ be the set of n-tuples of real numbers, $\emptyset \neq \mathcal{F} \subset \mathbb{R}(n)$ be a compact convex set, and $\mathscr{H} : \mathcal{F} \to \mathcal{F}$ be a continuous function. Then, $\mathscr{H}$ has a fixed point in K.*

Theorem 10 (see [36], (Leray–Schauder theorem)). *Let $\Omega \subset \mathbb{R}(n)$ be an open set with $0 \in \Omega$ and $\mathscr{H} : \overline{\Omega} \to \mathbb{R}(n)$ be a completely continuous function. Note that every $\mathscr{H}$ has at least one of the following properties:*

- *There is $g \in \overline{\Omega}$ such that $\mathscr{H} g = g$.*
- *There are $v \in \partial\Omega$ and $\xi \in (0,1)$ such that $v = \xi \mathscr{H} v$.*

Then, g is a fixed point of $\mathscr{H}$ in Ω.

Theorem 11 (see [36], (Krasnoselskii–Zabreiko theorem)). *Let $\mathscr{H} : \mathbb{R}(n) \to \mathbb{R}(n)$ be a completely continuous function and $\ell : \mathbb{R}(n) \to \mathbb{R}(n)$. If ℓ is a bounded linear function such that 1 is not its eigenvalue and*

$$\lim_{\|g\| \to \infty} \left(\frac{\|\mathscr{H} g - \ell g\|}{\|g\|} \right) = 0,$$

then there exist a fixed point of $\mathscr{H}$ in $\mathbb{R}(n)$.

Now, we know that $\mathbb{R}(q - q_0 + 1)$ is a BS with the following norm:

$$\|g\| := \max_{x \in \mathbb{N}(q_0;q)} |g(x)|.$$

Theorem 12. *Let $Z(x, g)$ be a continuous function with respect to g for all $x \in \mathbb{N}(q_0; q)$. If there exist $\ell, M > 0$ with*

$$\max\{|C_1|, |C_2|\} \leq \ell, \tag{19}$$

$$M = \max_{(x,g) \in \mathbb{N}(q_0;q) \times [-3\ell, 3\ell]} \Big| Z(x + \theta - 1, g(x + \theta - 1)) \Big|, \tag{20}$$

and

$$\delta \leq \frac{\ell}{M}, \tag{21}$$

then, FBVP (2) has a solution.

Proof. Let us define $\mathcal{F}$ as

$$\mathcal{F} := \Big\{ g : \mathbb{N}(q_0; q) \to \mathbb{R} \quad \text{and} \quad \|g\| \leq 3\ell \Big\}.$$

We know that $\emptyset \neq \mathcal{F} \subset \mathbb{R}(q - q_0 + 1)$ is a compact convex set. Now, we claim that

$$\mathscr{H} : \mathcal{F} \to \mathcal{F}.$$

To do this, we suppose that $g \in \mathcal{F}$ and $x \in \mathbb{N}(q_0;q)$. By considering

$$\begin{aligned}|\mathscr{H}g(x)| &= \left|w(x) + \sum_{r=q_0+2}^{q} \mathscr{G}(x,r)Z(r,g(r))\right| \\ &\leq \left|w(x)\right| + \sum_{r=q_0+2}^{q} \mathscr{G}(x,r)\left|Z(r,g(r))\right| \\ &\leq 2\max\{|C_1|,|C_2|\} + M\sum_{r=q_0+2}^{q} \mathscr{G}(x,r) \\ &\leq 2\ell + M\gamma \leq 3\ell,\end{aligned}$$

we obtain $\mathscr{H}g \in \mathcal{F}$. Therefore, $\mathscr{H} : \mathcal{F} \to \mathcal{F}$ as claimed. Moreover, $\mathscr{H}$ is trivially continuous on K because it is a summation operator on a discrete finite set. Hence, we can say that $\mathscr{H}$ has a fixed point according to Theorem 9. This concludes that FBVP (2) has a solution, namely g_0, such that $\|g_0\| \leq 3\ell$. Hence, the proof is complete. □

Theorem 13. *Let $Z(x,g)$ be as in the previous theorem, and it is bounded on $\mathbb{N}(q_0;q) \times \mathbb{R}$. Then, there is a solution for FBVP* (2).

Proof. Let us take

$$P > \sup_{(x,g)\in\mathbb{N}(q_0;q)\times\mathbb{R}} |Z(x,g)|.$$

Choose ℓ to be as large as

$$\max\{|C_1|,|C_2|\} \leq \ell \quad \text{and} \quad \delta \leq \frac{\ell}{M},$$

where M is the same as defined in Theorem 12 and $M \leq P$ so that

$$\delta \leq \frac{\ell}{M}.$$

Thus, FBVP (2) has a solution according to Theorem 12. This completes the proof. □

Theorem 14. *Let Z be as in Theorem 12. If there are two continuous functions ψ and σ such that $\psi : \mathbb{R}^+ \to \mathbb{R}^+$ is non-decreasing, $\sigma : \mathbb{N}(q_0;q) \to \mathbb{R}$, and*

$$|Z(x,g)| \leq \sigma(x)\psi(|g|), \quad (x,g) \in \mathbb{N}(q_0;q) \times \mathbb{R}. \tag{22}$$

Furthermore, if there exists $\gamma > 0$ with

$$\frac{\gamma}{\max\{|C_1|,|C_2|\} + \delta\|\sigma\|\psi(\gamma)} > 1, \tag{23}$$

then FBVP (2) *has a solution.*

Proof. First, we define

$$\Omega := \{g : \mathbb{N}(q_0) \to \mathbb{R} \quad \text{and} \quad \|g\| < \gamma\}.$$

It is obvious that $\Omega \subset \mathbb{R}(q - q_0 + 1)$ is an open set including 0 and $\mathscr{H} : \overline{\Omega} \to \mathbb{R}(q - q_0 + 1)$. So, $\mathscr{H}$ is trivially completely continuous on $\overline{\Omega}$ since $\mathscr{H}$ is as in Theorem 12. On the contrary, we suppose that there are $v \in \Omega$ and $\xi \in (0,1)$ with

$$v = \xi\mathscr{H}v. \tag{24}$$

Using the definition of $\mathscr{H}$ and Theorem 2(b) in (24), we can deduce

$$\begin{aligned}|v(x)| &\leq |w(x)| + \sum_{r=q_0+2}^{q} \mathscr{G}(x,r)|Z(r,v(r))| \\ &\leq 2\max\{|C_1|,|C_2|\} + \sum_{r=q_0+2}^{q} \mathscr{G}(x,r)\sigma(r)\psi(|v(r)|) \\ &\leq 2\max\{|C_1|,|C_2|\} + \|\sigma\|\psi(\|v\|) \sum_{r=q_0+2}^{q} \mathscr{G}(x,r) \\ &\leq 2\max\{|C_1|,|C_2|\} + \delta\|\sigma\|\psi(\gamma).\end{aligned}$$

This leads to

$$\|v\| \leq 2\max\{|C_1|,|C_2|\} + \delta\|\sigma\|\psi(\gamma).$$

Therefore,

$$\frac{\gamma}{2\max\{|C_1|,|C_2|\} + \delta\|\sigma\|\psi(\gamma)} \leq 1.$$

This contradicts (23). As a consequence, by considering Theorem 10, we see that $\mathscr{H}$ has a fixed point in Ω. This tells us that FBVP (2) has a solution, namely g_1, with $\|g_1\| < \gamma$. Thus, our proof is complete. □

Theorem 15. *Let Z be as in Theorem 12. If there exists a continuous function $\phi : \mathbb{N}(q_0;q) \to \mathbb{R}$ with*

$$\lim_{\|g\|\to\infty} \frac{Z(x,g)}{g} = \phi(x), \quad x \in \mathbb{N}(q_0;q), \tag{25}$$

and

$$\|\phi\| < \frac{1}{\delta}, \tag{26}$$

then FBVP (2) *has a solution.*

Proof. It is easy to see that $\mathscr{H} : \mathbb{R}(q-q_0+1) \to \mathbb{R}(q-q_0+1)$. So, $\mathscr{H}$ is trivially completely continuous on $\mathbb{R}(q-q_0+1)$, which is as in Theorem 12. Let us consider a linear bounded mapping ℓ, which is $\ell : \mathbb{R}(q-q_0+1) \to \mathbb{R}(q-q_0+1)$ defined by

$$(\ell g)(x) := \sum_{r=q_0+2}^{q} \mathscr{G}(x,r)\phi(r)g(r), \quad x \in \mathbb{N}(q_0;q). \tag{27}$$

Clearly, $\|\ell g\| < \|g\|$. Then, let $g \in \mathbb{R}(n)$ and $x \in \mathbb{N}(q_0;q)$, and we consider

$$\begin{aligned}(\ell g)(x) &\leq \sum_{r=q_0+2}^{q} \mathscr{G}(x,r)|\phi(r)||g(r)| \\ &\leq \|\phi\|\|g\| \sum_{r=q_0+2}^{q} \mathscr{G}(x,r) \leq \delta\|\phi\|\|g\| < \|g\|.\end{aligned}$$

This implies that $\|\ell g\| < \|g\|$. Thus, 1 is not an eigenvalue of ℓ. By considering (24), we have the following: For every $\epsilon > 0$, there exists a number N with each $x \in \mathbb{N}(q_0;q)$,

$$|Z(x,g(x)) - \phi(x)g(x)| < \epsilon \quad \text{where} \quad \|g\| > N. \tag{28}$$

Next, for each $x \in \mathbb{N}(q_0; q)$, we have

$$
\begin{aligned}
|(\mathscr{H}g)(x) - (\ell g)(x)| \leq & |w(x)| + \sum_{r=q_0+2}^{q} \mathscr{G}(x,r)|Z(r, g(r)) - \phi(r)g(r)| \\
& \leq 2\max\{|C_1|, |C_2|\} + \epsilon \sum_{r=q_0+2}^{q} \mathscr{G}(x,r) \\
& \leq 2\max\{|C_1|, |C_2|\} + \delta\epsilon.
\end{aligned}
$$

This leads to

$$
\frac{\|\mathscr{H}g - \ell g\|}{\|g\|} < \frac{\max\{|C_1|, |C_2|\} + \delta\epsilon}{N}.
$$

As a consequence, we obtain

$$
\lim_{\|g\| \to \infty} \frac{\|\mathscr{H}g - \ell g\|}{\|g\|} = 0.
$$

Thus, $\mathscr{H}$ has a fixed point in $\mathbb{R}(q - q_0 + 1)$ by Theorem 11. Hence, FBVP (2) has a solution, as requested. □

5. Uniqueness Results

This part of our article provides the existence of the unique solution of model (2) by considering the Lipschitz condition.

Theorem 16 (see [36], (Contraction Mapping Theorem)). *Let $S \subset \mathbb{R}(n)$ be closed and $\mathscr{H} : S \to S$ be a contraction function; i.e., $\exists\, \xi \in [0, 1)$ with*

$$
\|\mathscr{H}g - \mathscr{H}v\| \leq \xi \|g - v\|,
$$

for each $g, v \in S$. Then, w is a unique fixed point of $\mathscr{H}$ in S.

Theorem 17. *If $Z(x, g)$ satisfies the Lipschitz condition with respect to g, i.e.,*

$$
\|Z(x, g) - Z(x, v)\| \leq K\|g - v\|, \tag{29}
$$

for each $(x, g), (x, v) \in \mathbb{N}(q_0; q) \times \mathbb{R}$, where K is the Lipschitz constant and if

$$
0 < K\delta < 1, \tag{30}
$$

then there is a unique solution for (2).

Proof. Let $g, v \in \mathbb{R}(q - q_0 + 1)$ and $x \in \mathbb{N}(q_0; q)$. Consider

$$
\begin{aligned}
\left|\mathscr{H}g(x) - \mathscr{H}v(x)\right| \leq & \sum_{r=q_0+2}^{q} \mathscr{G}(x,r)\left|Z(r, g(r)) - Z(r, v(r))\right| \\
& \leq K \sum_{r=q_0+2}^{q} \mathscr{G}(x,r)|g(r) - v(r)| \\
& \leq K\|g - v\| \sum_{r=q_0+2}^{q} \mathscr{G}(x,r) \\
& \leq K\delta\|g - v\|,
\end{aligned}
$$

implying that

$$\|\mathscr{H}g - \mathscr{H}v\| \leq K\delta\|g - v\|,$$

Therefore, $\mathscr{H}$ is a contraction on $\mathbb{R}(q - q_0 + 1)$ according to (30). Thus, $\mathscr{H}$ has a unique fixed point in $\mathbb{R}(q - q_0 + 1)$ by Theorem 17. This implies that (2) has a unique solution. This ends the proof. □

Theorem 18. *Let $\eta, \beta > 0$ with*

$$\|Z(x, g) - Z(x, v)\| \leq \beta\|g - v\|, \tag{31}$$

for each $(x, g), (x, v) \in \mathbb{N}(q_0; q) \times [-\eta, \eta]$. We can choose

$$m_1 = \max_{x \in \mathbb{N}(q_0;q)} |Z(x, 0)|, \tag{32}$$

and

$$m_2 = \max_{(x,g) \in \mathbb{N}(q_0;q) \times [-\eta,\eta]} |Z(x, g)|. \tag{33}$$

Moreover, if

$$0 < \beta\delta < 1, \tag{34}$$

and

$$\eta \geq \frac{m_1\delta + 2\max\{|C_1|, |C_2|\}}{1 - \beta\delta} \implies 2\max\{|C_1|, |C_2|\} + m_2\delta \leq \eta, \tag{35}$$

then (2) *has a unique solution.*

Proof. It can be observed that $\mathscr{H}$ is a contraction on $\mathbb{R}(q - q_0 + 1)$ according to (34). Let us define

$$\mathcal{D} = \left\{g : \mathbb{N}(q_0; q) \to \mathbb{R} \quad \text{and} \quad \|g\| \leq \eta\right\}.$$

It is clear that $\mathcal{D} \subseteq \mathbb{R}(q - q_0 + 1)$. Now, let us claim that $\mathscr{H} : \mathcal{D} \to \mathcal{D}$. To prove this, let $g \in \mathcal{D}$ and $x \in \mathbb{N}(q_0; q)$. We assume that (35) holds, and then we consider

$$\begin{aligned}
|\mathscr{H}(0)(x)| &= \left|w(x) + \sum_{r=q_0+2}^{q} \mathscr{G}(x, r)Z(r, 0)\right| \\
&\leq |w(x)| + \sum_{r=q_0+2}^{q} \mathscr{G}(x, r)|Z(r, 0)| \\
&\leq 2\max\{|C_1|, |C_2|\} + m_1 \sum_{r=q_0+2}^{q} \mathscr{G}(x, r) \\
&\leq 2\max\{|C_1|, |C_2|\} + m_1\delta,
\end{aligned}$$

which leads to

$$\|\mathscr{H}(0)\| \leq 2\max\{|C_1|, |C_2|\} + m_1\delta.$$

Therefore,

$$\begin{aligned}\|\mathscr{H}(g)\| &= \|\mathscr{H}(g)+\mathscr{H}(0)-\mathscr{H}(0)\| \\ &\leq \|\mathscr{H}(g)-\mathscr{H}(0)\| + \|\mathscr{H}(0)\| \\ &\leq \beta\delta\|g-0\| + 2\max\{|C_1|,|C_2|\} + m_1\delta \\ &\leq \beta\delta\eta + 2\max\{|C_1|,|C_2|\} + m_1\delta \leq \eta.\end{aligned}$$

This implies that $\mathscr{H}:\mathcal{D}\to\mathcal{D}$.

On the other hand, let us assume that (35) holds. Let $g\in\mathcal{D}$ and $x\in\mathbb{N}(q_0;q)$. Then, we consider

$$\begin{aligned}|(\mathscr{H}g)(x)| &= \left|w(x) + \sum_{r=q_0+2}^{q}\mathscr{G}(x,r)Z(r,g(r))\right| \\ &\leq |w(x)| + \sum_{r=q_0+2}^{q}\mathscr{G}(x,r)|Z(r,g(r))| \\ &\leq 2\max\{|C_1|,|C_2|\} + m_2\sum_{r=q_0+2}^{q}\mathscr{G}(x,r) \\ &\leq 2\max\{|C_1|,|C_2|\} + m_2\delta \leq \eta,\end{aligned}$$

which leads to

$$\left\|\mathscr{H}g\right\| \leq \eta,$$

which gives $\mathscr{H}:\mathcal{D}\to\mathcal{D}$. As a consequence, $\mathscr{H}$ has a unique fixed point in $\mathbb{R}(q-q_0+1)$ according to Theorem 16. Finally, we see that (2) has a unique solution, namely g_2, and it satisfies $\|g_2\|\leq\eta$. Hence, the proof is complete. □

6. Numerical Examples

The following examples are presented to understand the applicability of the above results.

Example 1. *In the first example, we consider the FBVP*

$$\begin{aligned}&-\left({}^{\mathrm{RL}}_{0}\Delta^{\frac{3}{2}} g\right)(x) = \left(g^2 + \left(x+\frac{1}{2}\right)^2 + 9\right)^{-1}, \quad x\in\mathbb{N}(2;10), \\ &g(0)=1, \quad g(10)=2.\end{aligned} \tag{36}$$

We can observe that

$$q_0=0,\ q=10,\ \theta=1.5, Z(x+\theta-1, g(x+\theta-1)) = \left(g^2+\left(x+\frac{1}{2}\right)^2+9\right)^{-1},$$

$$C_1=1,\ C_2=2,\ \ell\geq 2.$$

Moreover,

$$M = \max_{(x,g)\in\mathbb{N}_0^{10}\times[-3\ell,3\ell]}\left|Z(x+\theta-1, g(x+\theta-1))\right| = \frac{1}{9},$$

and

$$\delta = \frac{9}{(1.5)\Gamma(2.5)}(12+0.5-1)^{\overline{0.5}} = 15.4738,$$

These give that $\delta \leq \frac{\ell}{M}$. *Therefore, FBVP* (36) *has at least one solution (say* g_0*), which satisfies* $|g_0(x) \leq 3\ell|$ *for* $x \in \mathbb{N}(0;10)$, *according to Theorem 12.*

Example 2. *Here, we consider the FBVP*

$$\begin{aligned} &-\left({}^{\text{RL}}_{\rho(0)}\Delta^{\frac{3}{2}} g\right)(x) = x + \frac{1}{20}\sin\big(g(x+0.5)\big), \quad x \in \mathbb{N}(2;10), \\ &g(0) = 1, \quad g(10) = 2. \end{aligned} \tag{37}$$

It is known that $q_0 = 0, q = 10, \theta = 1.5, Z\big(x+\theta-1, g(x+\theta-1)\big) = x + (0.05)\sin g$, $C_1 = 1$, *and* $C_2 = 2$. *It is easy to see that Z satisfies the Lipschitz condition with respect to g on* $\mathbb{N}(2;10) \times \mathbb{R}$; *it has the Lipschitz constant* $K = 0.05$. *Moreover,*

$$\delta = \frac{9}{(1.5)\Gamma(2.5)}(12)^{\overline{0.5}} = 15.4738,$$

which implies that $0 < K\delta < 1$. *Thus, in considering Theorem 17, FBVP* (37) *has a unique solution on* $\mathbb{N}(2;10) \times \mathbb{R}$.

7. Conclusions

We considered the uniqueness of solutions for FBVP (2). We constructed a discrete GF in the sense of Riemann–Liouville operators. In the main results, the minimum value of the GF was found. Furthermore, using five hypotheses **(H1)–(H5)** together with the Guo–Krasnoselskii theorem, we established the positive solutions of (11). Next, by defining the operator (18) together with the theorems of Brouwer, Leray–Schauder, Krasnoselskii–Zabreiko, the existence of solutions for FBVP (2) was derived. In addition, based on the Contraction Mapping Theorem and Lipschitz constant conditions, we obtained the uniqueness of a solution for (2). Finally, the applicability of the main results was confirmed via two special examples.

An important direction of research that has remained unexplored up to now is related to other types of discrete fractional operators that are continuously used over discrete fractional models (see [13,14]). Hence, new discrete fractional operators should be used to prove existence and uniqueness for fractional boundary value problems. Therefore, these will be welcoming lines of thought for future research.

Author Contributions: Conceptualization, A.A.L.; Methodology, M.A.Y.; Software, M.A.; Investigation, R.P.A.; Resources, M.A.Y.; Data curation, E.A.-S.; Writing—original draft, P.O.M.; Writing—review & editing, M.A.; Visualization, P.O.M.; Supervision, E.A.-S.; Project administration, R.P.A.; Funding acquisition, A.A.L. All authors have read and agreed to the published version of the manuscript.

Funding: The publication of this research was supported by the University of Oradea, Romania.

Data Availability Statement: Data are contained within the article.

Acknowledgments: Supporting Project number (RSP2024R136), King Saud University, Riyadh, Saudi Arabia.

Conflicts of Interest: The authors declare no conflicts of interest.

References

1. Hilfer, R. *Applications of Fractional Calculus in Physics*; World Scientific: Singapore, 2000.
2. Agarwal, R.P. *Difference Equations and Inequalities: Theory, Methods, and Applications*; Chapman and Hall/CRC Pure and Applied Mathematics Book: Boca Raton, FL, USA, 2000; Volume 228.
3. Atici, F.; Sengul, S. Modeling with discrete fractional equations. *J. Math. Anal. Appl.* **2010**, *369*, 1–9. [CrossRef]
4. Silem, A.; Wu, H.; Zhang, D.-J. Discrete rogue waves and blow-up from solitons of a nonisospectral semi-discrete nonlinear Schrödinger equation. *Appl. Math. Lett.* **2021**, *116*, 107049. [CrossRef]
5. Cabada, A.; Dimitrov, N. Nontrivial solutions of non-autonomous Dirichlet fractional discrete problems. *Fract. Calc. Appl. Anal.* **2020**, *23*, 980–995. [CrossRef]

6. Wu, G.; Baleanu, D. Discrete chaos in fractional delayed logistic maps. *Nonlinear Dyn.* **2015**, *80*, 1697–1703. [CrossRef]
7. Gholami, Y.; Ghanbari, K. Coupled systems of fractional ∇-difference boundary value problems. *Differ. Eq. Appl.* **2016**, *8*, 459–470. [CrossRef]
8. Atici, F.M.; Eloe, P.W. Initial Value Problems in Discrete Fractional Calculus. *Proc. Am. Math. Soc.* **2009**, *137*, 981–989. [CrossRef]
9. Baleanu, D.; Wu, G.C.; Bai, Y.R.; Chen, F.L. Stability analysis of Caputo-like discrete fractional systems. *Commun. Nonlinear. Sci. Numer. Simul.* **2017**, *48*, 520–530. [CrossRef]
10. Mozyrska, D.; Torres, D.F.M.; Wyrwas, M. Solutions of systems with the Caputo-Fabrizio fractional delta derivative on time scales. *Nonlinear Anal. Hybrid Syst.* **2019**, *32*, 168–176. [CrossRef]
11. Abdeljawad, T. On Riemann and Caputo fractional differences. *Commput. Math. Appl.* **2011**, *62*, 1602–1611. [CrossRef]
12. Atici, F.M.; Eloe, P.W. A transformmethod in discrete fractional calculus. *Int. J. Differ. Equ.* **2007**, *2*, 165–176.
13. Abdeljawad, T. Different type kernel h-fractional differences and their fractional h-sums. *Chaos Solitons Fract.* **2018**, *116*, 146–156. [CrossRef]
14. Mohammed, P.O.; Abdeljawad, T. Discrete generalized fractional operators defined using h-discrete Mittag-Leffler kernels and applications to AB fractional difference systems. *Math. Meth. Appl. Sci.* **2020**, *46*, 7688–7713. [CrossRef]
15. Goodrich, C.S. On discrete sequential fractional boundary value problems. *J. Math. Anal. Appl.* **2012**, *385*, 111–124. [CrossRef]
16. Wang, Z.; Shiri, B.; Baleanu, D. Discrete fractional watermark technique. *Front. Inf. Technol. Electron. Eng.* **2020**, *21*, 880–883. [CrossRef]
17. Ahrendt, K.; Castle, L.; Holm, M.; Yochman, K. Laplace transforms for the nabla-difference operator and a fractional variation of parameters formula. *Commun. Appl. Anal.* **2012**, *16*, 317–347.
18. Wang, M.; Jia, B.; Chen, C.; Zhu, X.; Du, F. Discrete fractional Bihari inequality and uniqueness theorem of solutions of nabla fractional difference equations with non-Lipschitz nonlinearities. *Appl. Math. Comput.* **2020**, *367*, 125118. [CrossRef]
19. Almusawa, M.Y.; Mohammed, P.O. Approximation of sequential fractional systems of Liouville-Caputo type by discrete delta difference operators. *Chaos Soliton. Fract.* **2023**, *176*, 114098. [CrossRef]
20. Baleanu, D.; Mohammed, P.O.; Srivastava, H.M.; Al-Sarairah, E.; Hamed, Y.S. On convexity analysis for discrete delta Riemann-Liouville fractional differences analytically and numerically. *J. Inequal. Appl.* **2023**, *2023*, 4. [CrossRef]
21. Chen, C.R.; Bohner, M.; Jia, B.G. Ulam-Hyers stability of Caputo fractional difference equations. *Math. Meth. Appl. Sci.* **2019**, *42*, 7461–7470. [CrossRef]
22. Brackins, A. Boundary Value Problems of Nabla Fractional Difference Equations. Ph.D. Thesis, The University of Nebraska-Lincoln, Lincoln, NE, USA , 2014.
23. Abdo, M.S.; Abdeljawad, T.; Ali, S.M.; Shah, K. On fractional boundary value problems involving fractional derivatives with Mittag-Leffler kernel and nonlinear integral conditions. *Adv. Differ. Equ.* **2021**, *37*, 2021. [CrossRef]
24. Ma, K.; Li, X.; Sun, S. Boundary value problems of fractional q-difference equations on the half-line. *Bound. Value Probl.* **2019**, *46*, 2019. [CrossRef]
25. Li, X.; Han, Z.; Sun, S. Existence of positive solutions of nonlinear fractional q-difference equation with parameter. *Adv. Differ. Equ.* **2013**, *260*, 2013. [CrossRef]
26. Chen, C.; Bohner, M.; Jia, B. Existence and uniqueness of solutions for nonlinear Caputo fractional difference equations. *Turk. J. Math.* **2020**, *44*, 857–869. [CrossRef]
27. Bekkouche, M.M.; Mansouri, I.; Ahmed, A.A.A. Numerical solution of fractional boundary value problem with caputo-fabrizio and its fractional integral. *J. Appl. Math. Comput.* **2022**, *68*, 4305–4316. [CrossRef] [PubMed]
28. Goodrich, C.S.; Jonnalagadda, J.M. Monotonicity results for CFC nabla fractional differences with negative lower bound. *Analysis* **2021**, *41*, 221–229. [CrossRef]
29. Wang, X.; Wang, G.; Chen, Z.; Lim, C.W.; Li, S.; Li, C. Controllable flexural wave in laminated metabeam with embedded multiple resonators. *JSV* **2024**, *581*, 118386. [CrossRef]
30. Li, C.; Zhu, C.; Lim, C.W.; Li, S. Nonlinear in-plane thermal buckling of rotationally restrained functionally graded carbon nanotube reinforced composite shallow arches under uniform radial loading. *Appl. Math. Mech.-Engl. Ed.* **2022**, *43*, 1821–1840. [CrossRef]
31. Guo, L.M.; Cai, J.W.; Xie, Z.Y.; Li, C. Mechanical Responses of Symmetric Straight and Curved Composite Microbeams. *J. Vib. Eng. Technol.* **2024**, *12*, 1537–1549. [CrossRef]
32. Chu, C.; Liu, H. Existence of positive solutions for a quasilinear Schrödinger equation. *Nonlinear Anal. Real World Appl.* **2018**, *44*, 118–127. [CrossRef]
33. Liu, H.; Zhao, L. Ground-state solution of a nonlinear fractional Schrödinger-Poisson system. *Math. Meth. Appl. Sci.* **2022**, *45*, 1934–1958. [CrossRef]
34. Mohammed, P.O.; Agarwal, R.P.; Baleanu, D.; Sabir, P.O.; Yousif, M.A.; Abdelwahed, M. Uniqueness Results Based on Delta Fractional Operators for Certain Boundary Value Problems. *Fractals* 2024, *accepted*.
35. Guirao, J.L.G.; Mohammed, P.O.; Srivastava, H.M.; Baleanu, D.; Abualrub, M.S. A relationships between the discrete Riemann-Liouville and Liouville-Caputo fractional differences and their associated convexity results. *AIMS Math.* **2022**, *7*, 18127–18141. [CrossRef]
36. Agarwal, R.P.; Meehan, M.; O'Regan, D. *Fixed Point Theory and Applications*; Cambridge Tracts in Mathematics, 141; Cambridge University Press: Cambridge, UK , 2001.

37. Pietsch, A. *History of Banach Spaces and Linear Operators*; Birkhauser: Basel, Switzerland; Springer: Berlin/Heidelberg, Germany, 2007; pp. 49–50.
38. Mohammed, P.O.; Srivastava, H.M.; Muhammad, R.S.; Al-Sarairah, E.; Chorfi, N.; Baleanu, D. On existence of certain delta fractional difference models. *J. King Saud. Univ. Sci.* **2024**, *36*, 103224. [CrossRef]

mathematics

MDPI

Article

On the Equivalence between Differential and Integral Forms of Caputo-Type Fractional Problems on Hölder Spaces

Mieczysław Cichoń [1,*,†], Hussein A. H. Salem [2,†] and Wafa Shammakh [3,†]

1 Faculty of Mathematics and Computer Science, Adam Mickiewicz University, Uniwersytetu Poznańskiego 4, 61-614 Poznań, Poland
2 Department of Mathematics and Computer Science, Faculty of Sciences, Alexandria University, Alexandria 5424041, Egypt; hssdina@alex-sci.edu.eg or hssdina@alexu.edu.eg
3 Department of Mathematics and Statistics, College of Science, University of Jeddah, Jeddah 21493, Saudi Arabia; wmshammakh@uj.edu.sa
* Correspondence: mieczyslaw.cichon@amu.edu.pl
† These authors contributed equally to this work.

Abstract: As claimed in many papers, the equivalence between the Caputo-type fractional differential problem and the corresponding integral forms may fail outside the spaces of absolutely continuous functions, even in Hölder spaces. To avoid such an equivalence problem, we define a "new" appropriate fractional integral operator, which is the right inverse of the Caputo derivative on some Hölder spaces of critical orders less than 1. A series of illustrative examples and counter-examples substantiate the necessity of our research. As an application, we use our method to discuss the BVP for the Langevin fractional differential equation $\frac{d_\psi^{\beta,\mu}}{dt^\beta}\left(\frac{d_\psi^{\alpha,\mu}}{dt^\alpha}+\lambda\right)x(t) = f(t,x(t)),\ t \in [a,b], \lambda \in \mathbb{R}$, for $f \in C([a,b] \times \mathbb{R})$ and some critical orders $\beta, \alpha \in (0,1)$, combined with appropriate initial or boundary conditions, and with general classes of ψ-tempered Hilfer problems with ψ-tempered fractional derivatives. The BVP for fractional differential problems of the Bagley–Torvik type was also studied.

Keywords: fractional calculus; tempered derivative; Hölder space

MSC: 26A33; 26B35; 34A08; 26D10; 34B18; 47H10

1. Introduction

In this paper, we investigate an absolutely fundamental problem arising from the application of the operator method (integral operators) to fractional-order differential problems, namely, the problem of equivalence of differential and integral problems. This problem depends not only on the problem under consideration or on the definition of the solution adopted, but also on the assumptions made about the functions and, therefore, especially about the function spaces in which integral operators operate. This problem has been extensively discussed and commented on in [1].

We will begin by introducing the function spaces on which we will study fractional-order integral operators. We will then discuss a very large class of such operators, examine their properties, and consider the equivalence problem of differential and integral problems, in which the very classes of operators discussed will be useful. We are particularly interested in problems involving operators that depend on two orders of the derivatives. These problems are analogous to those for integral equations involving multiple derivatives of unknown functions of different orders, but in this case, we have a much more complicated problem because successive differentiations and integrations are not the same operations. Of particular importance, then, is the study of how to formulate differential problems in equivalent integral form. When we study fractional differential problems, the key point is to find their equivalent integral forms.

This is an absolutely essential and fundamental step in the study of differential equations of fractional order. Surprisingly, it is sometimes overlooked.

The results of Hardy and Littlewood [2] are the origin of such studies for the Riemann–Liouville operator, and then this research continued in subspaces of the space of continuous functions (cf. [1]). Already the first results of this kind, based on the paper [2], showed clearly that the natural domains of the operators are Hölder spaces (cf. also [1,3–5]). This is because the values of fractional operators always lie in Hölder spaces. For instance, it is known that for $1/p < \alpha < 1 + 1/p$ or $p = 1$ and $1 \leq \alpha < 2$, the fractional Riemann–Liouville integral operator I^α is bounded from $L^p[a,b]$ into $\mathbb{H}^{\alpha-\frac{1}{p}}[a,b]$; hence, for $u \in L^p$, $I^\alpha u$ is Hölder continuous with exponent $\alpha - 1/p$, thus $I^\alpha u$ is continuous.

However, this is not sufficient to study the equivalence problem, since outside the space of absolutely continuous functions, differential and integral problems are not necessarily equivalent. We need to construct Hölder spaces suitable for the problem under consideration and study the properties of integral and differential operators on these spaces. Recall that Hölder spaces are fundamental to studying singular integral operators at all.

The equivalence problem of fractional-order differential and integral problems is much more complicated for operators depending on two different orders (fractional). Such operators, apart from achieving greater generality of considerations, have many natural applications and are, therefore, worth studying. Thus, in this paper, we will deal with the Langevin and Bagley–Torvik equations. Note, that the results for Langevin-type equations are particularly interesting because of the need to study two different orders of fractional derivatives ([6]).

The study of equivalence problems in this paper will, therefore, focus on the equations of the Langevin boundary-value problems with Caputo-type fractional derivatives [3,6]:

$$\frac{d_\psi^{\beta,\mu}}{dt^\beta}\left(\frac{d_\psi^{\alpha,\mu}}{dt^\alpha} + \lambda\right)x(t) = f(t, x(t)),$$

for $t \in [a,b]$, $\lambda \in \mathbb{R}$, $f \in C[a,b] \times \mathbb{R}$ and $\beta, \alpha \in (0,1)$, $\beta + \alpha < 1$, combined with an appropriate initial or boundary condition. It is worth noting that such questions have been studied in $C[a,b]$, an excessively large function space. We do not impose any ordering between α and β (cf. [7–9] and references therein). We study the problems for several classes of tempered fractional-order derivatives obtaining a number of new results and each time establishing Hölder spaces suitable for the equivalence of differential and integral problems. The fractional Langevin equation was used for modeling of single-file diffusion and for a free particle driven by a power law type of noise. Also, the transformation of the Fokker–Planck equation, which corresponds to the Langevin equation with multiplicative white noise, into the Wiener process is made available for any prescription (cf. [10]). Interesting applications of this equation are discussed in detail in [11].

This problem is also related to the Bagley–Torvik equation (with derivatives of order 2 and $3/2$, respectively). This equation can be used to model the motion of a rigid plate immersed in a Newtonian fluid and connected to a fixed point by a massless spring. Moreover, in [12], they also showed applications of this fractional equation to the theory of viscoelasticity. At the same time, it is worth mentioning that the fractional Langevin equation has been used to discuss Brownian motion and anomalous diffusion, which is useful in the study of generalized elastic models and in protein dynamics (see [3] and references therein).

A more complete description of the two types of problems and their interrelationships can be found in [3]. It is worth noting that in the classical fractional-order problem, we have $\alpha + \beta < 1$, and so far, only the operators that are not weakly singular (e.g., for $\alpha = 3$ and $\beta = 3/2$) have been studied. We will cover this case. A study of such problems with a purely mathematical motivation can be found in [13,14], for instance.

The main goal of this paper is to establish equivalence between appropriately defined solutions of a fractional differential boundary value problem and solutions of the corresponding integral equation. This type of equivalence is well known for functions from the space $AC[a,b]$ [3]. However, it is known that solutions of integral equations are Hölder continuous, so this space does not seem to be the best choice. With the results obtained, the paper was able not only to investigate the existence of continuous solutions of the Langevin equation (see [5,15]), but also to demonstrate their existence in Hölder spaces. In this paper, we will identify corresponding differential and integral problems with tempered fractional-order derivatives and study the operators generating such equations on Hölder-type spaces. Due to the completely different norms and their properties, this requires a separate and deeper analysis. In the cases of interest, we will show the equivalence of differential and integral problems by bridging the gap in the current studies.

As an example of the application of the results obtained, the paper will be complemented by results on inhomogeneous Langevin-type problems.

2. Preliminaries

We begin by introducing the function spaces on which we will study fractional-order integral operators. Fractional integrals can improve local properties of functions, but fractional derivatives can have the opposite effect. Therefore, it is necessary to study the mapping properties of fractional integrals in different function spaces. As we have already pointed out, Hölder continuity of solutions is strongly related to fractional-order problems (for example, [1,2,4,5]). This type of space is, therefore, a natural candidate for equivalence studies of differential and integral problems of fractional order. We should start with the Hölder-type spaces. For the convenience of the reader, we will recall the basic concepts and facts.

For $\gamma \in (0,1)$, the Hölder space $\mathcal{H}^\gamma[a,b]$ consists of all functions $f : [a,b] \to \mathbb{R}$ such that for $t,s \in [a,b]$, there exists a constant $M > 0$ (independent on t,s) for which $|f(t) - f(s)| \leq M|t-s|^\gamma$. In addition, if $f(a) = 0$, we consider the so-called little Hölder spaces and we write $f \in \mathcal{H}^\gamma_0[a,b]$. Obviously, $f \in \mathcal{H}^\gamma[a,b]$ if the following seminorm

$$[f]_\gamma := \sup_{t \neq s} \left\{ \frac{|f(t) - f(s)|}{|t-s|^\gamma} \right\}$$

is finite. Also, when $\mathcal{H}^\gamma[a,b]$ equipped with the norm $\|f\|_\gamma := \|f\|_\infty + [f]_\gamma$, it becomes a Banach space (cf. [4,5,15,16]).

It is important to note that there is a relationship between the Hölder space and nowhere differentiable functions. There are functions that are Hölder continuous but not absolutely continuous, such as the Weierstrass function, and functions that are absolutely continuous but not Hölder continuous. For example, the function $f : [0,1] \to \mathbb{R}$ defined by $f(t) := t^\alpha$, $0 < \alpha < \gamma < 1$, is absolutely continuous on $[0,1]$, but $f \notin \mathcal{H}^\gamma[0,1]$. However, for $0 < \gamma_1 < \gamma_2 < 1$, it is not difficult to show that

$$C^1[a,b] \subset \mathcal{H}^1[a,b] \subset \mathcal{H}^{\gamma_2}[a,b] \subset \mathcal{H}^{\gamma_1}[a,b] \subset C[a,b].$$

Obviously all embeddings are strict, e.g., the function $f(x) = 1/\log(x-2)$ for $x \in (0,1]$ and $f(0) = 0$ is continuous, but not in any Hölder space of exponent $\alpha > 0$. It is worth noting at this point that the embeddings between Hölder spaces and their embeddings in $C[a,b]$ are compact (as a consequence of the Arzelá–Ascoli theorem), and so using compactness when studying operators acting between them will be a natural method, where otherwise either the norm contraction property or additional assumptions about the functions under study are needed. The embeddings of different Hölder spaces are not dense.

There are various modifications and generalizations of classical fractional integration operators that are widely used in both theory and applications. The following definition unifies various fractional integrals for integrable functions, allowing for the solution of initial and/or boundary value problems with different types of fractional integrals and derivatives to be solved in a unified way.

For the convenience of the reader, we will now recall all the definitions related to the class of integrals and fractional derivatives of interest. Let $\psi \in C^1[a,b]$ be a positive increasing function such that $\psi'(t) \neq 0$ for all $t \in [a,b]$ with $\psi(a) = 0$. Throughout the paper, we will make these assumptions about the function ψ.

Definition 1 ([17,18]). *(ψ-tempered Riemann–Liouville fractional integral). The tempered ψ-Riemann-Liouville ψ-fractional integral of a given function $f \in L_1[a,b]$ of order $\alpha > 0$ and with parameter $\mu \in \mathbb{R}^+$ is defined by*

$$\mathbb{I}_{\psi}^{\alpha,\mu} f(t) := \frac{1}{\Gamma(\alpha)} \int_a^t e^{-\mu(\psi(t)-\psi(s))} (\psi(t) - \psi(s))^{\alpha-1} f(s) \psi'(s)\, ds. \tag{1}$$

For completeness, we define $\mathbb{I}_{\psi}^{\alpha,\mu} f(a) := 0$. Let us recall that

$$\mathbb{I}_{\psi}^{\alpha,\mu} f(t) = e^{-\mu\psi(t)} \mathbb{I}_{\psi}^{\alpha,0} \left(e^{\mu\psi(t)} f(t) \right), \quad \alpha \in (0,1).$$

If $\mathcal{E}_{\alpha,\beta}(\cdot)$ denotes the Mittag–Leffler function (see [19], then see [20])

$$\mathbb{I}_t^{\alpha,0} \left[t^{\beta-1} \mathcal{E}_{\gamma,\beta}(\lambda t^{\gamma}) \right] = t^{\alpha+\beta-1} \mathcal{E}_{\gamma,\alpha+\beta}(\lambda t^{\gamma}), \quad \alpha, \beta > 0, \lambda \neq 0, \ \gamma \geq 0, \ \ t \in [0,1].$$

We can now define the concept of fractional differentiation [17,21] and list the properties needed to prove the results (see also [22–24]).

Definition 2. *The ψ-tempered Riemann–Liouville fractional derivative of order $n + \alpha$, $\alpha \in (0,1)$, $n \in \mathbb{N} := \{1, 2, \cdots\}$ and with parameter $\mu \in \mathbb{R}^+$ is defined as*

$$\mathfrak{D}_{\psi}^{n+\alpha,\mu} f(t) := \left(\widetilde{\delta}\right)^n \mathfrak{D}_{\psi}^{\alpha,\mu} f(t), \quad \text{where} \ \ \mathfrak{D}_{\psi}^{\alpha,\mu} f(t) := \widetilde{\delta} \mathbb{I}_{\psi}^{1-\alpha,\mu} f(t), \quad f \in L_1[a,b]$$

and where $\widetilde{\delta} := \mu + \frac{1}{\psi'(t)} \frac{d}{dt}$.

Let us recall that

$$\mathfrak{D}_{\psi}^{\alpha,\mu} f(t) = e^{-\mu\psi(t)} \mathfrak{D}_{\psi}^{\alpha,0} \left(e^{\mu\psi(t)} f(t) \right), \quad \alpha \in (0,1).$$

It can easily be seen (see, e.g., [25]) that

$$\mathfrak{D}_t^{\alpha,0} \left[t^{\beta-1} \mathcal{E}_{\gamma,\beta}(\lambda t^{\gamma}) \right] = t^{\beta-\alpha-1} \mathcal{E}_{\gamma,\beta-\alpha}(\lambda t^{\gamma}), \ \ \beta > \alpha > 0, \lambda \neq 0, \ \gamma \geq 0, \ \ t \in [0,1].$$

In this paper, we do not study classical Caputo, as it is not an inverse operator of the generalized integral operators under study, and its definition—although modeled on the Caputo idea—is nevertheless different.

Definition 3 (tempered Caputo fractional derivative). *The ψ-tempered Caputo fractional derivative of order $n + \alpha$, $\alpha \in (0,1)$, $n \in \mathbb{N}$ and with parameter $\mu \in \mathbb{R}^+$ applied to the function $f \in AC[a,b]$ is defined as*

$$\frac{d_{\psi}^{\alpha+n,\mu}}{dt^{\alpha+n}} f(t) := \left(\widetilde{\delta}\right)^n \frac{d_{\psi}^{\alpha,\mu}}{dt^{\alpha}} f(t), \quad \text{where} \ \ \frac{d_{\psi}^{\alpha,\mu}}{dt^{\alpha}} f(t) := \mathbb{I}_{\psi}^{1-\alpha,\mu} \widetilde{\delta} f.$$

The above definition of the derivative is very general and includes many other fractional integral operators which will be considered later. In order not to stray too far from the purpose of the paper, we will limit ourselves to citing the work of [5,15,22], where the interested reader will find a discussion of the special cases covered by our definition.

Let us describe now the acting condition for little Hölder spaces.

Lemma 1 ([5], Lemmas 2 and 3). *Let $\psi \in C^1[a,b]$ be a positive increasing function such that $\psi'(t) \neq 0$ for all $t \in [a,b]$ with $\psi(a) = 0$. For any $\zeta, \alpha \in (0,1)$ such that $\zeta + \alpha < 1$*

$$\mathbb{I}_{\psi}^{\alpha,\mu} : \mathcal{H}_0^{\zeta}[a,b] \to \mathcal{H}_0^{\zeta+\alpha}[a,b] \quad \text{is bijective.}$$

$$\mathfrak{D}_{\psi}^{\alpha,\mu} : \mathcal{H}_0^{\zeta+\alpha}[a,b] \to \mathcal{H}_0^{\zeta}[a,b].$$

Also, according to ([5], Lemma 3), there exists a constant $D_A > 0$ such that

$$\left[\mathfrak{D}_{\psi}^{\alpha,\mu} x\right]_{\zeta} \leq D_A [x]_{\alpha+\zeta},$$

whenever $\alpha + \zeta < 1$.

Recall that for any $f \in C[a,b]$, we have

$$\mathfrak{D}_{\psi}^{\alpha,\mu} \mathbb{I}_{\psi}^{\alpha,\mu} f = \widetilde{\delta} \mathbb{I}_{\psi}^{1-\alpha,\mu} \mathbb{I}_{\psi}^{\alpha,\mu} f = \widetilde{\delta} \mathbb{I}_{\psi}^{1,\mu} f = f.$$

However, we have

Lemma 2 ([5], Theorem 5). *Let $\psi \in C^1[a,b]$ be a positive increasing function such that $\psi'(t) \neq 0$ for all $t \in [a,b]$ with $\psi(a) = 0$. For any $\zeta, \alpha \in (0,1)$ such that $\zeta + \alpha < 1$, $\mathfrak{D}_{\psi}^{\alpha,\mu}$ is continuous left-right inverse to $\mathbb{I}_{\psi}^{\alpha,\mu}$ on $\mathcal{H}_0^{\zeta+\alpha}[a,b]$.*

Interestingly,

$$\mathbb{I}_{\psi}^{1,\mu} \widetilde{\delta} x(t) = x(t) - x(a) e^{-\mu \psi(t)} \quad \text{holds true for any } x \in AC[a,b].$$

3. BVP for Langevin Differential Equations

Let us now describe problems that take advantage of defining equivalent problems. We now turn to the Caputo-type fractional Langevin differential equation. In this section, we will consider the linear case. It is clear that our focus is on a purely fractional problem, i.e., a situation where the sum of the two fractional parameters, α and β, is less than one.

$$\frac{d_{\psi}^{\beta,\mu}}{dt^{\beta}} \left(\frac{d_{\psi}^{\alpha,\mu}}{dt^{\alpha}} + \lambda \right) x(t) = f(t), \tag{2}$$

with $t \in [a,b]$, $\lambda \in \mathbb{R}$, $f \in C[a,b]$, $\beta, \alpha \in (0,1)$, $\beta + \alpha < 1$, combined with an appropriate initial or boundary condition.

As a direct consequence of our previous discussion of tempered derivatives of fractional order, it follows that we will consider the following integral form:

$$\mathbb{I}_{\psi}^{1-\beta,\mu} \widetilde{\delta} \left(\mathbb{I}_{\psi}^{1-\alpha,\mu} \widetilde{\delta} + \lambda \right) x(t) = f(t).$$

We will first study the formal form of the integral problem that is equivalent to the one we are studying. We will then verify the equivalence of these two problems in the spaces studied above. It is important to note that this equivalence depends strongly on the domain of the operators considered. Therefore,

$$\mathbb{I}_{\psi}^{1,\mu} \widetilde{\delta} \left(\mathbb{I}_{\psi}^{1-\alpha,\mu} \widetilde{\delta} + \lambda \right) x(t) = \mathbb{I}_{\psi}^{\beta,\mu} f(t) \quad \Rightarrow \quad \left(\mathbb{I}_{\psi}^{1-\alpha,\mu} \widetilde{\delta} + \lambda \right) x(t) = C_1 e^{-\mu g(t)} + \mathbb{I}_{\psi}^{\beta,\mu} f(t)$$

for some constant C_1. Similarly,

$$\mathbb{I}_{\psi}^{1,\mu}\widetilde{\delta}x(t) + \lambda\mathbb{I}_{\psi}^{\alpha,\mu}x(t) = C_1\frac{e^{-\mu\psi(t)}}{\Gamma(1+\alpha)}(\psi(t))^{\alpha} + \mathbb{I}_{\psi}^{\alpha,\mu}\mathbb{I}_{\psi}^{\beta,\mu}f(t).$$

Then, the formal integral form (of any solution) for (2) has the following form:

$$x(t) = x(a)e^{-\mu\psi(t)} + C_1\frac{e^{-\mu\psi(t)}}{\Gamma(1+\alpha)}(\psi(t))^{\alpha} + \mathbb{I}_{\psi}^{\alpha+\beta,\mu}f(t) - \lambda\mathbb{I}_{\psi}^{\alpha,\mu}x(t), \tag{3}$$

for $t \in [a,b]$ and $C_1 \in \mathbb{R}$.

According to ([15], Lemma 5) and in view of Lemma 1, we see that if $f \in \mathcal{H}_0^{\zeta}[a,b]$ with $\zeta + 2\alpha + \beta < 1$, then (cf. Lemma 1) $\mathbb{I}_{\psi}^{\alpha+\beta,\mu}f \in \mathcal{H}_0^{\zeta+\alpha+\beta}[a,b]$ and (3) admits a Hölder continuous solution $x \in \mathcal{H}_0^{\zeta+\alpha+\beta}[a,b]$.

It is unfortunate that, as shown in [26], the relationship between the left inverse of the function $d_{\psi}^{\alpha,\mu}/dt^{\alpha}$ and $\mathbb{I}_{\psi}^{\alpha,\mu}$ is not as straightforward as one might expect, if not in the space of absolutely continuous functions, then in Hölder spaces.

Therefore, the existence of a Hölder continuous solution to (3) does not guarantee the existence of solutions to (2). Many authors avoided the problem of showing the equivalence between the Caputo-type fractional differential problems and the corresponding integral forms by defining so-called mild-type solutions. Recall, that this type of solution is exactly defined to be a solution to an integral form of a Caputo-type fractional differential problem. Also, some authors avoided the problem of showing the equivalence by redefining the Caputo fractional derivative as

$$\frac{d_{\psi}^{\alpha,\mu}}{dt^{\alpha}}f := \mathfrak{D}_{\psi}^{\alpha,\mu}f - \frac{(\psi(t))^{-\alpha}e^{-\mu\psi(t)}}{\Gamma(1-\alpha)}f(a), \tag{4}$$

for $\alpha \in (0,1)$. Note that the definition (4) of the Caputo fractional derivative coincides with the standard definition (3) on the space of absolutely continuous functions.

Considering spaces other than $AC[a,b]$ leads to mistakes about the equivalence of problems. We will explain this.

Remark 1. *Even if $\alpha,\beta \in (0,1)$, $\alpha+\beta > 1$, the equivalence between (2) and (3) fails outside $AC[a,b]$: Let $\alpha,\beta \in (0,1)$, $\alpha+\beta > 1$, f be Hölder continuous of some order less than 1. In view of the semi-group property of the ψ-tempered Riemann–Liouville fractional integral (see e.g., [5,15]), we can rewrite (3) as*

$$x(t) = x(a)e^{-\mu\psi(t)} + C_1\frac{e^{-\mu\psi(t)}}{\Gamma(1+\alpha)}(\psi(t))^{\alpha} + \mathbb{I}_{\psi}^{1,\mu}\mathbb{I}_{\psi}^{\alpha+\beta-1,\mu}f(t) - \lambda\mathbb{I}_{\psi}^{\alpha,\mu}x(t), \tag{5}$$

for $\alpha,\beta \in (0,1)$, $\alpha+\beta > 1$, $t \in [a,b]$. Lemma 5 in [15], together with our observation that $\mathbb{I}_{\psi}^{\alpha+\beta,\mu}f = \mathbb{I}_{\psi}^{1,\mu}\mathbb{I}_{\psi}^{\alpha+\beta-1,\mu}f$ is in $AC_0[a,b]$, give a reason to believe (5) admits a solution $x \in AC_0[a,b]$. Hence, by ([15], proof of Lemma 4) (see also ([20], Lemma 2.1)), we obtain $\mathbb{I}_{\psi}^{\alpha,\mu}x = \mathbb{I}_{\psi}^{1,\mu}\mathbb{I}_{\psi}^{\alpha,\mu}\widetilde{\delta}x$. Therefore,

$$\widetilde{\delta}x(t) = C_1\frac{e^{-\mu\psi(t)}}{\Gamma(\alpha)}(\psi(t))^{\alpha-1} + \mathbb{I}_{\psi}^{\alpha+\beta-1,\mu}f(t) - \lambda\mathbb{I}_{\psi}^{\alpha,\mu}\widetilde{\delta}x(t).$$

Hence,

$$\begin{aligned}\frac{d_{\psi}^{\alpha,\mu}}{dt^{\alpha}}x(t) &= \mathbb{I}_{\psi}^{1-\alpha,\mu}\widetilde{\delta}x(t) = C_1e^{-\mu\psi(t)} + \mathbb{I}_{\psi}^{\beta,\mu}f(t) - \lambda\mathbb{I}_{\psi}^{1,\mu}\widetilde{\delta}x(t) \\ &= C_1e^{-\mu\psi(t)} + \mathbb{I}_{\psi}^{\beta,\mu}f(t) - \lambda x(t).\end{aligned}$$

So,

$$\frac{d_{\psi}^{\alpha,\mu}}{dt^{\alpha}}x(t)+\lambda x(t)=C_1e^{-\mu\psi(t)}+\mathbb{I}_{\psi}^{\beta,\mu}f(t).$$

Again,

$$\frac{d_{\psi}^{\beta,\mu}}{dt^{\beta}}\left(\frac{d_{\psi}^{\alpha,\mu}}{dt^{\alpha}}+\lambda\right)x=\frac{d_{\psi}^{\beta,\mu}}{dt^{\beta}}\mathbb{I}_{\psi}^{\beta,\mu}f,$$

is meaningless when $f\notin AC[a,b]$.

Remark 2. *Even if* $\alpha\in(0,1)$, $\beta\in(1,2)$, *the equivalence between (2) and (3) fails outside* $AC[a,b]$: *Let* $\alpha(0,1)$, $\beta\in(1,2)$, $f\in C[a,b]$. *Then, (2) takes the form*

$$\widetilde{\delta}\mathbb{I}_{\psi}^{2-\beta,\mu}\widetilde{\delta}\left(\mathbb{I}_{\psi}^{1-\alpha,\mu}\widetilde{\delta}+\lambda\right)x(t)=f(t).$$

So,

$$\mathbb{I}_{\psi}^{2-\beta,\mu}\widetilde{\delta}\left(\mathbb{I}_{\psi}^{1-\alpha,\mu}\widetilde{\delta}+\lambda\right)x(t)=\mathbb{I}_{\psi}^{1,\mu}f(t)+C_0e^{-\mu\psi(t)}.$$

Operation by $\mathbb{I}_{\psi}^{\beta-1,\mu}$ *implies*

$$\mathbb{I}_{\psi}^{1,\mu}\widetilde{\delta}\left(\mathbb{I}_{\psi}^{1-\alpha,\mu}\widetilde{\delta}+\lambda\right)x(t)=\mathbb{I}_{\psi}^{\beta,\mu}f(t)+\frac{e^{-\mu\psi(t)}}{\Gamma(\beta)}(\psi(t))^{\beta-1}.$$

Hence,

$$\left(\mathbb{I}_{\psi}^{1-\alpha,\mu}\widetilde{\delta}+\lambda\right)x(t)=C_1e^{-\mu\psi(t)}+\mathbb{I}_{\psi}^{\beta,\mu}f(t)+\frac{C_0e^{-\mu\psi(t)}}{\Gamma(1+\beta)}(\psi(t))^{\beta-1}.$$

Consequently,

$$\begin{aligned}&\mathbb{I}_{\psi}^{1,\mu}\widetilde{\delta}x(t)+\lambda\mathbb{I}_{\psi}^{\alpha,\mu}x(t)\\&=C_1\frac{e^{-\mu\psi(t)}}{\Gamma(1+\alpha)}(\psi(t))^{\alpha}+\mathbb{I}_{\psi}^{\beta+\alpha,\mu}f(t)+\frac{C_0}{\Gamma(\alpha+\beta)}e^{-\mu\psi(t)}(\psi(t))^{\alpha+\beta-1}.\end{aligned}$$

From the above, we must conclude that

$$\begin{aligned}x(t)&=x(a)e^{-\mu\psi(t)}+C_1\frac{e^{-\mu\psi(t)}}{\Gamma(1+\alpha)}(\psi(t))^{\alpha}+\mathbb{I}_{\psi}^{\beta+\alpha,\mu}f(t)\\&\quad+\frac{C_0}{\Gamma(\alpha+\beta)}e^{-\mu\psi(t)}(\psi(t))^{\alpha+\beta-1}-\lambda\mathbb{I}_{\psi}^{\alpha,\mu}x(t)\end{aligned}\tag{6}$$

Again, ([15], Lemma 5), along with our observation that $\mathbb{I}_{\psi}^{\alpha+\beta,\mu}f=\mathbb{I}_{\psi}^{1,\mu}\mathbb{I}_{\psi}^{\alpha+\beta-1,\mu}f$ *is in* $AC_0[a,b]$, *give reason to believe (5) admits a solution* $x\in AC_0[a,b]$. *Therefore,*

$$\begin{aligned}\widetilde{\delta}x(t)&=C_1\frac{e^{-\mu\psi(t)}}{\Gamma(\alpha)}(\psi(t))^{\alpha-1}+\mathbb{I}_{\psi}^{\beta+\alpha-1,\mu}f(t)\\&+\frac{C_0}{\Gamma(\alpha+\beta-1)}e^{-\mu\psi(t)}(\psi(t))^{\alpha+\beta-2}-\lambda\mathbb{I}_{\psi}^{\alpha,\mu}\widetilde{\delta}x(t).\end{aligned}$$

Hence,

$$\begin{aligned}\frac{d_{\psi}^{\alpha,\mu}}{dt^{\alpha}}x(t)&=\mathbb{I}_{\psi}^{1-\alpha,\mu}\widetilde{\delta}x(t)=C_1e^{-\mu\psi(t)}+\mathbb{I}_{\psi}^{\beta,\mu}f(t)\\&+\frac{C_0}{\Gamma(\beta)}e^{-\mu\psi(t)}(\psi(t))^{\beta-1}-\lambda\mathbb{I}_{\psi}^{1,\mu}\widetilde{\delta}x(t).\end{aligned}$$

So,

$$\mathbb{I}_{\psi}^{2-\beta,\mu}\widetilde{\delta}\left(\frac{d_{\psi}^{\alpha,\mu}}{dt^{\alpha}}+\lambda\right)x(t)=\mathbb{I}_{\psi}^{1,\mu}f(t)+C_0e^{-\mu\psi(t)}.$$

Thus,

$$\frac{d_{\psi}^{\beta,\mu}}{dt^{\beta}}\left(\frac{d_{\psi}^{\alpha,\mu}}{dt^{\alpha}}+\lambda\right)x=f,$$

is meaningful for any continuous function $f\in C[a,b]$.

Remark 3. *When* $\beta\in(0,1)$, $\alpha\in(1,2)$, *the equivalence between (2) and (3) also fails outside* $AC[a,b]$: *Let* $\beta\in(0,1)$, $\alpha\in(1,2)$, $f\in C[a,b]$. *In this case, (2) takes the form*

$$\mathbb{I}_{\psi}^{1-\beta,\mu}\widetilde{\delta}\left(\widetilde{\delta}\mathbb{I}_{\psi}^{2-\alpha,\mu}\widetilde{\delta}+\lambda\right)x(t)=f(t).$$

So,

$$\mathbb{I}_{\psi}^{1,\mu}\widetilde{\delta}\left(\widetilde{\delta}\mathbb{I}_{\psi}^{2-\alpha,\mu}\widetilde{\delta}+\lambda\right)x(t)=\mathbb{I}_{\psi}^{\beta,\mu}f(t)\implies\left(\widetilde{\delta}\mathbb{I}_{\psi}^{2-\alpha,\mu}\widetilde{\delta}+\lambda\right)x(t)=\mathbb{I}_{\psi}^{\beta,\mu}f(t).$$

Hence,

$$\mathbb{I}_{\psi}^{2-\alpha,\mu}\widetilde{\delta}x(t)+\lambda\mathbb{I}_{\psi}^{1,\mu}x(t)=\mathbb{I}_{\psi}^{1+\beta,\mu}f(t)+C_0e^{-\mu\psi(t)}$$

Consequently,

$$\mathbb{I}_{\psi}^{1,\mu}\widetilde{\delta}x(t)+\lambda\mathbb{I}_{\psi}^{\alpha,\mu}x(t)=C_0\frac{e^{-\mu\psi(t)}}{\Gamma(\alpha)}(\psi(t))^{\alpha-1}+\mathbb{I}_{\psi}^{\beta+\alpha,\mu}f(t).$$

This is how we come to

$$x(t)=x(a)e^{-\mu\psi(t)}+C_0\frac{e^{-\mu\psi(t)}}{\Gamma(\alpha)}(\psi(t))^{\alpha-1}+\mathbb{I}_{\psi}^{\beta+\alpha,\mu}f(t)-\lambda\mathbb{I}_{\psi}^{\alpha,\mu}x(t). \tag{7}$$

Again, ([15], Lemma 5) along with our observation that $\mathbb{I}_{\psi}^{\alpha+\beta,\mu}f=\mathbb{I}_{\psi}^{1,\mu}\mathbb{I}_{\psi}^{\alpha+\beta-1,\mu}f\in AC_0[a,b]$, *give reason to believe that (5) admits a solution* $x\in AC_0[a,b]$. *Therefore,*

$$\mathbb{I}_{\psi}^{2-\alpha,\mu}\widetilde{\delta}x(t)=C_0e^{-\mu\psi(t)}+\mathbb{I}_{\psi}^{\beta+1,\mu}f(t)-\lambda\mathbb{I}_{\psi}^{2,\mu}\widetilde{\delta}x(t),$$

$$\widetilde{\delta}\mathbb{I}_{\psi}^{2-\alpha,\mu}\widetilde{\delta}x(t)=\mathbb{I}_{\psi}^{\beta,\mu}f(t)-\lambda\mathbb{I}_{\psi}^{1,\mu}\widetilde{\delta}x(t)=\mathbb{I}_{\psi}^{\beta,\mu}f(t)-\lambda x(t).$$

Hence,

$$\frac{d_{\psi}^{\beta,\mu}}{dt^{\beta}}\left(\frac{d_{\psi}^{\alpha,\mu}}{dt^{\alpha}}+\lambda\right)x=\frac{d_{\psi}^{\beta,\mu}}{dt^{\beta}}\mathbb{I}_{\psi}^{\beta,\mu}f,$$

is meaningless when $f\notin AC[a,b]$.

In what follows, we have avoided the problem by showing the equivalence in a different way, using the following definition:

$$\begin{aligned}\mathrm{I}_{\psi}^{\alpha,\mu}f(t)\;&:=\;\mathbb{I}_{\psi}^{1,\mu}\mathfrak{D}_{\psi}^{1-\alpha,\mu}f(t)=\int_a^t e^{-\mu(\psi(t)-\psi(s))}\mathfrak{D}_{\psi}^{1-\alpha,\mu}f(s)\psi'(s)\,ds\\&=\;e^{-\mu\psi(t)}\mathbb{I}_{\psi}^{1,0}\left(e^{\mu\psi(t)}\mathfrak{D}_{\psi}^{1-\alpha,\mu}f(t)\right).\end{aligned} \tag{8}$$

Remark 4. *Obviously, in view of Lemma 1, the operator* $\mathrm{I}_{\psi}^{\alpha,\mu}$ *is well defined on the space* $\mathcal{H}_0^{\zeta+1-\alpha}[a,b]$ *for any exponent* $\alpha \in (\zeta, 1)$, $\zeta \in (0,1)$. *Also, since (cf. [15]),*

$$\mathfrak{D}_{\psi}^{1-\alpha,\mu} f(t) = e^{-\mu\psi(t)}\mathfrak{D}_{\psi}^{1-\alpha,0}\left(e^{\mu\psi(t)} f(t)\right), \; \mathfrak{D}_{\psi}^{1-\alpha,\mu} f(a) = 0, \;\; \alpha \in (0,1),$$

it follows

$$\mathrm{I}_{\psi}^{\alpha,\mu} f(t) = e^{-\mu\psi(t)}\mathbb{I}_{\psi}^{1,0}\left(\mathfrak{D}_{\psi}^{1-\alpha,0}\left(e^{\mu\psi(t)} f(t)\right)\right) \quad , \quad \mathrm{I}_{\psi}^{\alpha,\mu} f(a) = 0.$$

Let us also remark that, the operators $\mathrm{I}_{\psi}^{\alpha,\mu}$ *coincide with the usual definition of* ψ*-tempered fractional integral operator* $\mathbb{I}_{\psi}^{\alpha,\mu}$ *on the space* $AC[a,b]$: *For any* $f \in AC[a,b]$, *we know that ([15], Lemma 4)* $\mathbb{I}_{\psi}^{\alpha,\mu} f \in AC[a,b]$, *then*

$$\mathrm{I}_{\psi}^{\alpha,\mu} f = \left(\mathbb{I}_{\psi}^{1,\mu}\widetilde{\delta}\right)\mathbb{I}_{\psi}^{\alpha,\mu} f = \mathbb{I}_{\psi}^{\alpha,\mu} f.$$

Since the integrals improve the continuity properties of functions, similarly as in Lemma 1, we can prove the following lemma for little Hölder spaces $\mathcal{H}_0$.

Theorem 1. *Let* $\psi \in C^1[a,b]$ *be a positive increasing function such that* $\psi'(t) \neq 0$ *for all* $t \in [a,b]$ *with* $\psi(a) = 0$. *For arbitrary* $\mu > 0$, $\alpha, \delta, \zeta \in (0,1)$ *such that* $\alpha - \delta \geq \zeta$, *we have*

$$\mathrm{I}_{\psi}^{\alpha,\mu} : \mathcal{H}_0^{\zeta-\alpha+1}[a,b] \to \mathcal{H}_0^{\zeta-\alpha+1+\delta}[a,b].$$

In particular, for any $\alpha, \zeta \in (0,1)$ *with* $\alpha > \zeta$, *the operator* $\mathrm{I}_{\psi}^{\alpha,\mu}$ *maps the Hölder space* $\mathcal{H}_0^{\zeta-\alpha+1}[a,b]$ *into itself.*

Proof. Let $x \in \mathcal{H}_0^{\zeta-\alpha+1}[a,b]$ and define $f := \mathfrak{D}_{\psi}^{1-\alpha,\mu} x$. Since $\alpha > \zeta$ $(\zeta - \alpha + 1 < 1)$, it follows in view of Lemma 1, $f \in \mathcal{H}_0^{\zeta}[a,b]$, for $h > 0$ so that $a \leq t < t+h \leq b$ and note that $|f(t) - f(s)| \leq [f]_{\zeta}|t-s|^{\zeta}$ for any $t, s \in [a,b]$. Therefore,

$$\begin{aligned}
&\mathrm{I}_{\psi}^{\alpha,\mu} x(t+h) - \mathrm{I}_{\psi}^{\alpha,\mu} x(t) = \mathbb{I}_{\psi}^{1,\mu}\mathfrak{D}_{\psi}^{1-\alpha,\mu} x(t+h) - \mathbb{I}_{\psi}^{1,\mu}\mathfrak{D}_{\psi}^{1-\alpha,\mu} x(t) \\
&= \mathbb{I}_{\psi}^{1,\mu} f(t+h) - \mathbb{I}_{\psi}^{1,\mu} f(t) \\
&= \int_a^{t+h} e^{-\mu(\psi(t+h)-\psi(s))} f(s)\psi'(s)\, ds - \int_a^{t} e^{-\mu(\psi(t)-\psi(s))} f(s)\psi'(s)\, ds \\
&= \int_{-h}^{t-a} e^{-\mu(\psi(t+h)-\psi(t-s))} f(t-s)\psi'(t-s)\, ds \\
&\quad - \int_0^{t-a} e^{-\mu(\psi(t+h)-\psi(t-s))} f(t-s)\psi'(t-s)\, ds \\
&= \int_0^{t-a} \left\{e^{-\mu(\psi(t+h)-\psi(t-s))} - e^{-\mu(\psi(t)-\psi(t-s))}\right\} f(t-s)\psi'(t-s)\, ds \\
&\quad + \int_{-h}^{0} e^{-\mu(\psi(t+h)-\psi(t-s))} f(t-s)\psi'(t-s)\, ds \\
&= \int_0^{t-a} \left\{e^{-\mu(\psi(t+h)-\psi(t-s))} - e^{-\mu(\psi(t)-\psi(t-s))}\right\} (f(t-s) - f(t))\psi'(t-s)\, ds \\
&\quad + \int_{-h}^{0} e^{-\mu(\psi(t+h)-\psi(t-s))} (f(t-s) - f(t))\psi'(t-s)\, ds \\
&\quad + \int_{-h}^{t-a} e^{-\mu(\psi(t+h)-\psi(t-s))} (f(t) - f(a))\psi'(t-s)\, ds \\
&\quad - \int_0^{t-a} e^{-\mu(\psi(t)-\psi(t-s))} (f(t) - f(a))\psi'(t-s)\, ds.
\end{aligned}$$

These estimates will, therefore, allow us to examine the Hölder continuity order for $\mathrm{I}_{\psi}^{\alpha,\mu} x$. Our proof will follow the ideas from ([5], proof of Theorem 5), although the estimates must be obtained in the case we are considering and are new. In order not to prolong this paper, we will limit ourselves to the differences in the main steps of the proof, details of which can be found by those interested in [5]. To show in which Hölder space the values of this operator lie, the right side of this estimate can be split and examined separately:

$$\left| \mathrm{I}_{\psi}^{\alpha,\mu} x(t+h) - \mathrm{I}_{\psi}^{\alpha,\mu} x(t) \right| \leq \widetilde{A} + \widetilde{B} + \widetilde{C},$$

where

$$\widetilde{A} := \left| \left\{ \int_{-h}^{t-a} e^{-\mu(\psi(t+h)-\psi(t-s))} - \int_{0}^{t-a} e^{-\mu(\psi(t)-\psi(t-s))} \right\} |f(t) - f(a)| \psi'(t-s)\, ds \right|,$$
$$\widetilde{B} := \int_{-h}^{0} e^{-\mu(\psi(t+h)-\psi(t-s))} |f(t-s) - f(t)| \psi'(t-s)\, ds,$$
$$\widetilde{C} := \int_{0}^{t-a} \left\{ e^{-\mu(\psi(t+h)-\psi(t-s))} - e^{-\mu(\psi(t)-\psi(t-s))} \right\} |f(t-s) - f(t)| \psi'(t-s)\, ds.$$

We will now estimate the order of the Hölder condition for each of the expressions separately.

According to the definition of the Hölder seminorm, and taking into account that $f \in \mathcal{H}_0^{\zeta}[a,b]$ (as claimed above), so $|f(t) - f(a)| \leq [f]_{\zeta}(t-a)^{\zeta}$, $t \in [a,b]$, we come to the following conclusion:

$$\widetilde{A} \leq [f]_{\zeta}(t-a)^{\zeta} \left| \int_{-h}^{t-a} e^{-\mu(\psi(t+h)-\psi(t-s))} - \int_{0}^{t-a} e^{-\mu(\psi(t)-\psi(t-s))} \right| \psi'(t-s)\, ds.$$

Since $\psi \in C^1[a,b]$, using the continuity properties of maps

$$s \mapsto (\psi(t+h) - \psi(t-s)) \quad \text{and} \quad s \mapsto (\psi(t) - \psi(t-s)),$$

and according to the mean value theorem, there exists $\eta_1 \in (t-s, t+h)$ and $\eta_2 \in t-s, t)$ such that

$$\psi(t+h) - \psi(t-s) = \psi'(\eta_1)(h+s), \quad \psi(t) - \psi(t-s) = \psi'(\eta_2)s.$$

This gives us

$$\begin{aligned} \widetilde{A} &\leq [f]_{\zeta}(t-a)^{\zeta} \left| \int_{0}^{\psi(t+h)} e^{-\mu s}\, ds - \int_{0}^{\psi(t)} e^{-\mu s}\, ds \right| \\ &\leq [f]_{\zeta}(t-a)^{\zeta}(-\mu^{-1})|\psi(t+h) - \psi(t)| \leq [f]_{\zeta}\|\psi'\|(t-a)^{\zeta}h \\ &\leq [f]_{\zeta}(-\mu^{-1})h^{\zeta}\|\psi'\|h. \end{aligned}$$

Consequently, taking into account the various possible cases concerning the value of h, we have

$$\begin{aligned} \widetilde{A} &\leq [f]_{\zeta}\|\psi'\|(-\mu^{-1})h^{1+\zeta} = [f]_{\zeta}\|\psi'\|(-\mu^{-1})h^{1+\zeta-(\alpha-\delta)}h^{\alpha-\delta} \\ &\leq [f]_{\zeta}\|\psi'\|(-\mu^{-1})h^{1+\zeta-\alpha+\delta}(b-a)^{\alpha-\delta}, \end{aligned}$$

for $t - a \leq h < b - a$, and

$$\begin{aligned} \widetilde{A} &\leq [f]_{\zeta}\|\psi'\|(-\mu^{-1})(t-a)^{\zeta-\alpha+\delta}(t-a)^{\alpha-\delta}h \leq [f]_{\zeta}\|\psi'\|(-\mu^{-1})h^{\zeta-\alpha+\delta}(b-a)^{\alpha-\delta}h \\ &\leq [f]_{\zeta}\|\psi'\|(-\mu^{-1})h^{1+\zeta-\alpha+\delta}(b-a)^{\alpha-\delta}, \end{aligned}$$

for $h \leq t - a \leq b - a$. We, therefore, obtained the expected estimates for $\widetilde{A}$.

In a similar way, we can also estimate $\widetilde{B}$:

$$\begin{aligned}\widetilde{B} &\leq [f]_\zeta \int_{-h}^{0} e^{-\mu(\psi(t+h)-\psi(t-s))} s^\zeta \psi'(t-s)\, ds = [f]_\zeta \int_0^{\psi(t+h)-\psi(t)} s^\zeta e^{-\mu s}\, ds \\ &\leq \frac{[f]_\zeta}{\mu(1+\zeta)} (\psi(t+h)-\psi(t))^{1+\zeta} \leq \frac{[f]_\zeta \|\psi'\|^{1+\zeta}}{\mu(1+\zeta)} h^{1-\alpha+\zeta+\delta} h^{\alpha-\delta} \\ &\leq \frac{[f]_\zeta \|\psi'\|^{1+\zeta}}{\mu(1+\zeta)} h^{1-\alpha+\zeta+\delta} (b-a)^{\alpha-\delta}.\end{aligned}$$

It remains to estimate:

$$\widetilde{C} \leq [f]_\zeta \|\psi'\| \int_0^{t-a} \left| e^{-\mu(\psi(t+h)-\psi(t-s))} - e^{-\mu(\psi(t)-\psi(t-s))} \right| s^\zeta\, ds.$$

Note again that there exists $\eta_1 \in (t-s, t+h)$ and $\eta_2 \in t-s, t)$ such that $\psi(t+h) - \psi(t-s) = \psi'(\eta_1)(h+s)$, $\psi(t) - \psi(t-s) = \psi'(\eta_2)s$, after the substitution $s \to \frac{s}{h}$, we obtain that

$$\begin{aligned}\widetilde{C} &\leq [f]_\zeta \|\psi'\| \int_0^{t-a} \left|= e^{-\mu\psi'(\eta_1)(h+s)} - e^{-\mu\psi'(\eta_2)s} \right| s^\zeta\, ds \\ &\leq [f]_\zeta \|\psi'\| \int_0^{\frac{t-a}{h}} \left| e^{-\mu\psi'(\eta_1)(s+1)h} - e^{-\mu\psi'(\eta_2)sh} \right| h^{1+\zeta} s^\zeta\, ds.\end{aligned}$$

Hence, if $t-a < h < b-a$, we arrive at

$$\begin{aligned}\widetilde{C} &\leq [f]_\zeta \|\psi'\| \mu^{-1} h^{1+\zeta} \int_0^1 s^\zeta\, ds = \frac{[f]_\zeta \|\psi'\| h^{1+\zeta-\alpha+\delta} h^{\alpha-\delta}}{\mu(1+\zeta)} \\ &\leq \frac{[f]_\zeta \|\psi'\| h^{1+\zeta-\alpha+\delta} (b-a)^{\alpha-\delta}}{\mu(1+\zeta)}.\end{aligned}$$

If $t-a > h$, and by calculating the integrals under consideration, we obtain

$$\begin{aligned}\widetilde{C} &\leq [f]_\zeta \|\psi'\| \mu^{-1} h^{1+\zeta} \int_0^\infty \left| e^{-\psi'(\eta_1)(h+sh)} - e^{-\psi'(\eta_2)sh} \right| s^\zeta\, ds \\ &\leq [f]_\zeta \|\psi'\| \mu^{-1} h^{1+\zeta} \left| \frac{e^{-\psi'(\eta_1)h} \int_0^\infty e^{-s} s^\zeta\, ds}{(\psi'(\eta_1)h)^{1+\zeta}} - \frac{\int_0^\infty e^{-s} s^\zeta\, ds}{(\psi'(\eta_2)h)^{1+\zeta}} \right| \\ &= [f]_\zeta \|\psi'\| \mu^{-1} h^{1-\alpha+\zeta+\delta}\, \Gamma(1+\zeta) \cdot \mathbf{J},\end{aligned}$$

where

$$\mathbf{J} := h^{\alpha-\delta} \left| \frac{e^{-\psi'(\eta_1)h}}{(\psi'(\eta_1)h)^{1+\zeta}} - \frac{1}{(\psi'(\eta_2)h)^{1+\zeta}} \right| = \left| \frac{(\psi'(\eta_1))^{-1-\zeta} e^{-\psi'(\eta_1)h} - (\psi'(\eta_2))^{-1-\zeta}}{h^{1-\alpha+\zeta+\delta}} \right|.$$

Since $\eta_1 \to \eta_2$ (as $h \to 0$), bearing in mind that

$$\lim_{h\to 0} \frac{(\psi'(\eta_1))^{-1-\zeta} e^{-\psi'(\eta_1)h} - (\psi'(\eta_2))^{-1-\zeta}}{h^{1-\alpha+\zeta+\delta}} = \lim_{h\to 0} \frac{-(\psi'(\eta_1))^{-\zeta} e^{-\psi'(\eta_1)h}}{1-\alpha+\zeta+\delta} h^{\alpha-\delta-\zeta} = 0.$$

Therefore, $\mathbf{J} < \infty$, and then there exists a constant $K > 0$ such that

$$\left| \mathrm{I}_\psi^{\alpha,\mu} x(t+h) - \mathrm{I}_\psi^{\alpha,\mu} x(t) \right| \leq K [f]_\zeta h^{1-\alpha+\zeta+\delta}.$$

So if we go back to the function x and remember that $f = \mathfrak{D}_{\psi}^{1-\alpha,\mu}x$, and using the acting properties of $\mathfrak{D}_{\psi}^{1-\alpha,\mu}$, we obtain

$$\left[\mathrm{I}_{\psi}^{\alpha,\mu}x\right]_{1-\alpha+\zeta+\delta} \leq K[f]_{\zeta} = K[\mathfrak{D}_{\psi}^{1-\alpha,\mu}x]_{\zeta} \leq C[x]_{1-\alpha+\zeta}, \tag{9}$$

for $\alpha, \delta, \zeta \in (0,1)$ such that $\alpha - \delta \geq \zeta$ and for some $C > 0$ calculated on the basis of Lemma 1. □

Example 1. Define $x \in \mathcal{H}_0^{\zeta-\alpha+1}[0,1]$ by $x(t) := t^{\zeta-\alpha+1}$, $\zeta < \alpha$. It is easy to calculate that

$$\mathfrak{D}_t^{1-\alpha,0}x(t) = \frac{\Gamma(2+\zeta-\alpha)}{\Gamma(1+\zeta)}t^{\zeta}, \ \mathrm{I}_t^{\alpha,0}x(t) = \frac{\Gamma(2+\zeta-\alpha)}{\Gamma(2+\zeta)}t^{\zeta+1} \in \mathcal{H}_0^{\zeta-\alpha+1}[0,1] :$$

Obviously, without loss of generality, we can assume that $0 \leq s < t$ and set $u = s/t \in [0,1)$. Then, we have

$$\frac{t^{\zeta+1} - s^{\zeta+1}}{(t-s)^{\zeta-\alpha+1}} \leq \frac{1-u^{\zeta+1}}{(1-u)^{\zeta+1}(t-s)^{-\alpha}} \leq \frac{1-u}{(1-u)(t-s)^{-\alpha}} = (t-s)^{\alpha} \leq 1.$$

So $\mathrm{I}_t^{\alpha,0}x \in \mathcal{H}_0^{\zeta-\alpha+1}[0,1]$. Precisely, $\mathrm{I}_t^{\alpha,0}x \in \mathcal{H}_0^{\mu}[0,1] \subseteq \mathcal{H}_0^{\zeta-\alpha+1}[0,1]$, for any $\mu \geq \zeta - \alpha + 1$:

$$\frac{t^{\zeta+1} - s^{\zeta+1}}{(t-s)^{\mu}} \leq \frac{t^{\zeta+1} - s^{\zeta+1}}{(t-s)^{\zeta-\alpha+1}} \leq \frac{1-u^{\zeta+1}}{(1-u)^{\zeta+1}(t-s)^{-\alpha}} \leq \frac{1-u}{(1-u)(t-s)^{-\alpha}} = (t-s)^{\alpha} \leq 1.$$

We will now present a quantitative version of the rather expected fact that the integral operator transforms Hölder spaces into their subspaces, so we should output what is the limiting case. According to (9), we obtain

Corollary 1. *Define* $\mathrm{I}_{\psi}^{n\alpha,\mu} := \underbrace{\mathrm{I}_{\psi}^{\alpha,\mu}\mathrm{I}_{\psi}^{\alpha,\mu}\cdots\mathrm{I}_{\psi}^{\alpha,\mu}}_{n-times}$. *Then, for any* $\alpha, \zeta \in (0,1)$ *with* $\alpha > \zeta$,

$$\left[\mathrm{I}_{\psi}^{n\alpha,\mu}x\right]_{1-\zeta+\alpha} = \left[\mathrm{I}_{\psi}^{\alpha,\mu}\mathrm{I}_{\psi}^{(n-1)\alpha,\mu}x\right]_{\zeta+1-\alpha} \leq C\left[\mathrm{I}_{\psi}^{(n-1)\alpha,\mu}x\right]_{1-\zeta+\alpha} \leq \cdots \leq C^n[x]_{1-\zeta}.$$

Therefore, if in addition $C < 1$, *then for any* $x \in \mathcal{H}_0^{\zeta+1-\alpha}[a,b]$, $\left[\mathrm{I}_{\psi}^{n\alpha,\mu}x\right]_{1-\zeta+\alpha} \to 0$ *as* $n \to \infty$.

Corollary 2. *Let* $\psi \in C^1[a,b]$ *be a positive increasing function such that* $\psi'(t) \neq 0$ *for all* $t \in [a,b]$ *with* $\psi(a) = 0$. *For arbitrary* $\mu > 0, \alpha, \delta, \zeta \in (0,1)$ *such that* $\zeta < \min\{\alpha, \beta\}$, *we have*

$$\mathrm{I}_{\psi}^{\alpha,\mu}\mathrm{I}_{\psi}^{\beta,\mu} : \mathcal{H}_0^{1+\zeta-\beta}[a,b] \to \mathcal{H}_0^{1+\zeta-\alpha}[a,b].$$

Proof. (1) Let $x \in \mathcal{H}_0^{1+\zeta-\beta}[a,b]$, $\beta < \alpha$ and note, in view of the particular case of Theorem 1, $\mathrm{I}_{\psi}^{\beta,\mu}x \in \mathcal{H}_0^{1+\zeta-\beta}[a,b] \subset \mathcal{H}_0^{1+\zeta-\alpha}[a,b]$. Again, by the particular case of Theorem 1, it follows that $\mathrm{I}_{\psi}^{\alpha,\mu}\mathrm{I}_{\psi}^{\beta,\mu}x \in \mathcal{H}_0^{1+\zeta-\alpha}[a,b]$.

(2) Let $x \in \mathcal{H}_0^{1+\zeta-\beta}[a,b]$, $\alpha \leq \beta$ and define a number $\delta := \beta - \alpha$. Since $\beta - \delta = \alpha > \zeta$, from Theorem 1, it follows that $\mathrm{I}_{\psi}^{\beta,\mu}x \in \mathcal{H}_0^{1+\zeta-\beta+\delta}[a,b] \equiv \mathcal{H}_0^{1+\zeta-\alpha}[a,b]$. Again, by the particular case of Theorem 1, we obtain $\mathrm{I}_{\psi}^{\alpha,\mu}\mathrm{I}_{\psi}^{\beta,\mu}x \in \mathcal{H}_0^{1+\zeta-\alpha}[a,b]$.

□

Remark 5. *For any $f \in AC[a,b]$, we have $\mathrm{I}_{\psi}^{\alpha,\mu} f = \mathbb{I}_{\psi}^{1,\mu} \widetilde{\delta \mathbb{I}}_{\psi}^{\alpha,\mu} f$. By [15, Lemma 4] $\mathbb{I}_{\psi}^{\alpha,\mu} f \in AC[a,b]$, $\widetilde{\delta \mathbb{I}}_{\psi}^{\alpha,\mu} f \in L_1[a,b]$ and consequently (see [15], Formula (4))*

$$\mathrm{I}_{\psi}^{\alpha,\mu} f(t) = \mathbb{I}_{\psi}^{\alpha,\mu} f(t) - e^{-\mu\psi(t)} \mathbb{I}_{\psi}^{\alpha,\mu} f(a).$$

We can now study the inhomogeneous integral linear equation, which is the basis for any further study of integral problems of the type studied.

Theorem 2. *If $F \in \mathcal{H}_0^{1-\alpha+\zeta}[a,b]$ with $\alpha > \zeta$, then for sufficiently small $\lambda \in \mathbb{R}$, the linear fractional integral equation*

$$x(t) = F(t) - \lambda \cdot \mathrm{I}_{\psi}^{\alpha,\mu} x(t),\ t \in [a,b], \tag{10}$$

admits a Hölder continuous solution $x \in \mathcal{H}_0^{1-\alpha+\zeta}[a,b]$.

Let us start with an observation. From the properties of the seminorm, we obtain an estimation:

$$[x]_{1-\alpha+\zeta} \le [F]_{1-\alpha+\zeta} + |\lambda| \left[\mathrm{I}_{\psi}^{\alpha,\mu} x\right]_{1-\zeta+\alpha} \le [F]_{1-\alpha+\zeta} + |\lambda| C [x]_{1-\zeta+\alpha}.$$

It follows that

$$[x]_{1-\alpha+\zeta} \le \frac{[F]_{1-\alpha+\zeta}}{1-|\lambda|C} = [F]_{1-\alpha+\zeta} \left(\sum_{n=1}^{\infty} (|\lambda| \cdot C)^n \right).$$

Then, for sufficiently small $\lambda \in \mathbb{R}$, the series is convergent and then any continuous solution x of (10) must lie in the space $\mathcal{H}_0^{1+\zeta-\alpha}[a,b]$ provided that $\|x\|_\infty < \infty$. Next, for any $f \in \mathcal{H}_0^{1-\alpha+\zeta}[a,b]$, we know that (cf. [5], Lemma 3)

$$\begin{aligned} \mathfrak{D}_{\psi}^{1-\alpha,\mu} x(t) &= \frac{1-\alpha}{\Gamma(\alpha)} \int_a^t e^{-\mu(\psi(t)-\psi(s))} (\psi(t)-\psi(s))^{\alpha-2} [x(t)-x(s)] \psi'(s)\, ds \\ &+ \frac{\mu x(t)}{\Gamma(\alpha)} \int_a^t e^{-\mu(\psi(t)-\psi(s))} (\psi(t)-\psi(s))^{\alpha-1} \psi'(s)\, ds. \end{aligned}$$

Hence,

$$\begin{aligned} \left| \mathfrak{D}_{\psi}^{1-\alpha,\mu} x(t) \right| &\le 2\|x\|_\infty \frac{1-\alpha}{\Gamma(\alpha)} \int_a^t e^{-\mu(\psi(t)-\psi(s))} (\psi(t)-\psi(s))^{\alpha-2} \psi'(s)\, ds \\ &+ \frac{\mu \|x\|_\infty}{\Gamma(\alpha)} \int_a^t e^{-\mu(\psi(t)-\psi(s))} (\psi(t)-\psi(s))^{\alpha-1} \psi'(s)\, ds. \end{aligned}$$

It is not difficult to see that

$$
\begin{aligned}
\left|\mathrm{I}_{\psi}^{\alpha,\mu}x(t)\right| &\leq \mathbb{I}_{\psi}^{1,\mu}\left|\mathfrak{D}_{\psi}^{1-\alpha,\mu}x(t)\right| \\
&\leq 2\|x\|_{\infty}\frac{1-\alpha}{\Gamma(\alpha)}\int_a^t e^{-\mu(\psi(t)-\psi(s))}\left(\int_a^s e^{-\mu(\psi(s)-\psi(\theta))}(\psi(s)-\psi(\theta))^{\alpha-2}\psi'(\theta)\,d\theta\right)\psi'(s)\,ds \\
&\quad+\frac{\mu\|x\|_{\infty}}{\Gamma(\alpha)}\int_a^t e^{-\mu(\psi(t)-\psi(s))}\left(\int_a^s e^{-\mu(\psi(s)-\psi(\theta))}(\psi(s)-\psi(\theta))^{\alpha-1}\psi'(\theta)\,d\theta\right)\psi'(s)\,ds \\
&\leq 2\|x\|_{\infty}\frac{1-\alpha}{\Gamma(\alpha)}\int_a^t\int_\theta^t e^{-\mu(\psi(t)-\psi(\theta))}(\psi(s)-\psi(\theta))^{\alpha-2}\psi'(\theta)\,\psi'(s)\,ds\,d\theta \\
&\quad+\frac{\mu\|x\|_{\infty}}{\Gamma(\alpha)}\int_a^t\int_\theta^t e^{-\mu(\psi(t)-\psi(\theta))}(\psi(s)-\psi(\theta))^{\alpha-1}\psi'(\theta)\,\psi'(s)\,ds\,d\theta \\
&\leq 2\|x\|_{\infty}\frac{1}{\Gamma(\alpha)}\int_a^t e^{-\mu(\psi(t)-\psi(\theta))}(\psi(t)-\psi(\theta))^{\alpha-1}\psi'(\theta)\;d\theta \\
&\quad+\frac{\mu\|x\|_{\infty}}{\Gamma(1+\alpha)}\int_a^t e^{-\mu(\psi(t)-\psi(\theta))}(\psi(t)-\psi(\theta))^{\alpha}\psi'(\theta)\;d\theta \\
&\leq \frac{\|\psi\|^{\alpha}\|x\|_{\infty}}{\Gamma(1+\alpha)}\left[2+\frac{\mu\|\psi\|}{\alpha+1}\right].
\end{aligned}
$$

Now, we use the Banach fixed point theorem in order to prove that (10) admits a solution $x \in C[a,b]$. But we also check its regularity, i.e., whether it belongs to the Hölder space with exponent $1-\alpha+\zeta$ with $\alpha > \zeta$.

Proof. Define the linear operator $T : \mathcal{H}_0^{1-\alpha+\zeta}[a,b] \to \mathcal{H}_0^{1-\alpha+\zeta}[a,b]$ by

$$Tx(t) = F(t) - \lambda\mathrm{I}_{\psi}^{\alpha,\mu}x(t) = F(t) - \lambda\mathbb{I}_{\psi}^{1,\mu}\mathfrak{D}_{\psi}^{1-\alpha,\mu}x(t) \quad t \in [a,b], \quad \alpha \in (0,1)$$

Obviously, given Remark 4 and Theorem 1, T is well defined. Since (cf. ([5], Theorem 5)) $\mathfrak{D}_{\psi}^{1-\alpha,\mu}x \in \mathcal{H}_0^{\zeta}[a,b] \subset C_0[a,b]$, then for any $x,y \in \mathcal{H}_0^{1-\alpha+\zeta}[a,b]$, we have (in view of (9))

$$\left[\mathrm{I}_{\psi}^{\alpha,\mu}x - \mathrm{I}_{\psi}^{\alpha,\mu}y\right]_{1-\alpha+\zeta} = \left[\mathrm{I}_{\psi}^{\alpha,\mu}(x-y)\right]_{1-\alpha+\zeta} \leq C[x-y]_{1-\alpha+\zeta},$$

and

$$\left\|\mathrm{I}_{\psi}^{\alpha,\mu}x - \mathrm{I}_{\psi}^{\alpha,\mu}y\right\|_{\infty} := \max_{t\in[a,b]}\left|\mathrm{I}_{\psi}^{\alpha,\mu}\{x(t)-y(t)\}\right| \leq \frac{\|\psi\|^{\alpha}\|x-y\|_{\infty}}{\Gamma(1+\alpha)}\left[2+\frac{\mu\|\psi\|}{\alpha+1}\right].$$

Therefore,

$$\|Tx-Ty\|_{1+\zeta-\alpha} \leq \frac{|\lambda|\|\psi\|^{\alpha}\|x-y\|_{\infty}}{\Gamma(1+\alpha)}\left[2+\frac{\mu\|\psi\|}{\alpha+1}\right] + C|\lambda|[x-y]_{1+\zeta-\alpha} \leq A|\lambda|\|x-y\|_{1+\zeta\alpha},$$

where $A = \max\left\{\frac{\|\psi\|^{\alpha}}{\Gamma(1+\alpha)}\left[2+\frac{\mu\|\psi\|}{\alpha+1}\right], C\right\}$.

Then, for sufficiently small λ, by the Banach contraction principle, T admits a (unique) fixed point $x \in \mathcal{H}_0^{1+\zeta-\alpha}[a,b]$. □

In view of Lemma 1, we have:

Lemma 3. 1. *For any $\zeta,\alpha \in (0,1)$, $\alpha > \zeta$ and $f \in \mathcal{H}_0^{1+\zeta-\alpha}[a,b]$, we have*

$$\frac{d_{\psi}^{\alpha,\mu}}{dt^{\alpha}}\mathrm{I}_{\psi}^{\alpha,\mu}f(t) = \mathbb{I}_{\psi}^{1-\alpha,\mu}\left(\widetilde{\delta\mathbb{I}}_{\psi}^{1,\mu}\right)\mathfrak{D}_{\psi}^{1-\alpha}f(t) = \mathbb{I}_{\psi}^{1-\alpha,\mu}\mathfrak{D}_{\psi}^{1-\alpha}f(t) = f(t).$$

2. *For any $f \in AC[a,b]$,*

$$\begin{aligned} \mathrm{I}_{\psi}^{\alpha,\mu}\frac{d_{\psi}^{\alpha,\mu}}{dt^{\alpha}}f(t) &= \mathbb{I}_{\psi}^{1,\mu}\left(\mathfrak{D}_{\psi}^{1-\alpha,\mu}\mathbb{I}_{\psi}^{1-\alpha,\mu}\widetilde{\delta}\right)f(t) = \mathbb{I}_{\psi}^{1,\mu}\left(\widetilde{\delta}\mathbb{I}_{\psi}^{\alpha,\mu}\mathbb{I}_{\psi}^{1-\alpha,\mu}\widetilde{\delta}\right)f(t) \\ &= \mathbb{I}_{\psi}^{1,\mu}\widetilde{\delta}f(t) = f(t) - f(a)e^{-\mu\psi(t)}. \end{aligned}$$

In this context, we revisit the question raised in the framework of the problem (3): To obtain its formal integral form, we apply the results of Lemma 3. It is essential to consider the need to regulate the exponent of fractional integrals. We note that we can calculate the integral form of the differential equation under consideration: Consider the problem (3) with $f \in \mathcal{H}_0^{1+\zeta-\beta}[a,b]$, $0 < \zeta < \min\{\alpha,\beta\} < 1$, and either $\alpha+\beta < 1$ or $\alpha+\beta > 1$. Then,

$$\begin{aligned} &\mathrm{I}_{\psi}^{\beta,\mu}\frac{d_{\psi}^{\beta,\mu}}{dt^{\beta}}\left(\frac{d_{\psi}^{\alpha,\mu}}{dt^{\alpha}}+\lambda\right)x(t) = \mathrm{I}_{\psi}^{\beta,\mu}f(t) \\ &\left(\frac{d_{\psi}^{\alpha,\mu}}{dt^{\alpha}}+\lambda\right)x(t) = \mathrm{I}_{\psi}^{\beta,\mu}f(t) + C_1e^{-\mu\psi(t)} \\ &\mathrm{I}_{\psi}^{\alpha,\mu}\frac{d_{\psi}^{\alpha,\mu}}{dt^{\alpha}}x(t) = \mathrm{I}_{\psi}^{\alpha,\mu}\mathrm{I}_{\psi}^{\beta,\mu}f(t) - \lambda\mathrm{I}_{\psi}^{\alpha,\mu}x(t) + \frac{C_1e^{-\mu\psi(t)}(\psi(t))^{\alpha}}{\Gamma(1+\alpha)} \\ &x(t) = x(a)e^{-\mu\psi(t)} + \mathrm{I}_{\psi}^{\alpha,\mu}\mathrm{I}_{\psi}^{\beta,\mu}f(t) - \lambda\mathrm{I}_{\psi}^{\alpha,\mu}x(t) + \frac{C_1e^{-\mu\psi(t)}(\psi(t))^{\alpha}}{\Gamma(1+\alpha)}. \end{aligned}$$

Conversely, let $0 < \zeta < \min\{\alpha,\beta\} < 1$ and $f \in \mathcal{H}_0^{1+\zeta-\beta}[a,b]$. By Corollary 2, we know that $\mathrm{I}_{\psi}^{\alpha,\mu}\mathrm{I}_{\psi}^{\beta,\mu}f \in \mathcal{H}_0^{1+\zeta-\alpha}[a,b]$. Then, Theorem 2 shows that, for sufficiently small λ, the above integral form admits a Hölder continuous solution $x \in \mathcal{H}_0^{1+\zeta-\alpha}[a,b]$. Therefore, by Lemma 3, x must satisfy the problem (3): Obviously, as in the proof of corollary 2, we know (given $f \in \mathcal{H}_0^{1+\zeta-\beta}[a,b]$) that $\mathrm{I}_{\psi}^{\beta,\mu}f, \in \mathcal{H}_0^{1+\zeta-\alpha}[a,b]$ and, therefore, by Lemma 3, we have

$$\frac{d_{\psi}^{\alpha,\mu}}{dt^{\alpha}}\mathrm{I}_{\psi}^{\alpha,\mu}\mathrm{I}_{\psi}^{\beta,\mu}f = \mathrm{I}_{\psi}^{\beta,\mu}f \quad\text{and}\quad \frac{d_{\psi}^{\beta,\mu}}{dt^{\beta}}\mathrm{I}_{\psi}^{\beta,\mu}f = f.$$

Hence,

$$\frac{d_{\psi}^{\beta,\mu}}{dt^{\beta}}\left(\frac{d_{\psi}^{\alpha,\mu}}{dt^{\alpha}}+\lambda\right)x(t) = \frac{d_{\psi}^{\beta,\mu}}{dt^{\beta}}\mathrm{I}_{\psi}^{\beta,\mu}f(t) = f(t),$$

as required.

Remark 6. *As already claimed in Remark 3, for $\beta \in (0,1)$, $\alpha \in (1,2)$, the equivalence between (2) and (7) fails outside $AC[a,b]$. Now, using the fractional integral operator defined in (8), we are able to solve such a problem outside $AC[a,b]$: Let $\beta \in (0,1)$, $\alpha \in (1,2)$, $f \in \mathcal{H}_0^{1+\zeta-\beta}[a,b]$, $\zeta < \beta$. Then, (2) takes the form*

$$\begin{aligned} &\mathrm{I}_{\psi}^{\beta,\mu}\frac{d_{\psi}^{\beta,\mu}}{dt^{\beta}}\left(\widetilde{\delta}\mathbb{I}_{\psi}^{2-\alpha,\mu}\widetilde{\delta}+\lambda\right)x(t) = \mathrm{I}_{\psi}^{\beta,\mu}f(t) \\ &\left(\widetilde{\delta}\mathbb{I}_{\psi}^{2-\alpha,\mu}\widetilde{\delta}+\lambda\right)x(t) = \mathrm{I}_{\psi}^{\beta,\mu}f(t) + C_1e^{-\mu\psi(t)} \\ &\mathbb{I}_{\psi}^{2-\alpha,\mu}\widetilde{\delta}x(t) + \lambda\mathbb{I}_{\psi}^{1,\mu}x(t) = \mathbb{I}_{\psi}^{1,\mu}\mathrm{I}_{\psi}^{\beta,\mu}f(t) + C_1\psi(t)e^{-\mu\psi(t)} \\ &\mathbb{I}_{\psi}^{1,\mu}\widetilde{\delta}x(t) + \lambda\mathbb{I}_{\psi}^{\alpha,\mu}x(t) = \mathbb{I}_{\psi}^{\alpha,\mu}\mathrm{I}_{\psi}^{\beta,\mu}f(t) + C_1\frac{(\psi(t)^{\alpha}}{\Gamma(\alpha)}e^{-\mu\psi(t)}. \end{aligned}$$

Hence,

$$x(t) = x(a)e^{-\mu\psi(t)} - \lambda\mathbb{I}_{\psi}^{\alpha,\mu}x(t) + \mathbb{I}_{\psi}^{\alpha,\mu}\mathrm{I}_{\psi}^{\beta,\mu}f(t) + C_1\frac{(\psi(t)^{\alpha}}{\Gamma(\alpha)}e^{-\mu\psi(t)}. \quad (11)$$

Since $\alpha > 1$, ([15], Lemma 5) together with our observation that $\mathbb{I}_{\psi}^{\alpha,\mu}\mathrm{I}_{\psi}^{\beta,\mu} = \mathbb{I}_{\psi}^{1,\mu}\mathbb{I}_{\psi}^{\alpha-1,\mu}\mathrm{I}_{\psi}^{\beta,\mu}f$ is in $AC_0[a,b]$, give a reason to believe that (11) admits a solution $x \in AC_0[a,b]$. Conversely,

$$\widetilde{\delta}x(t) = -\lambda\mathbb{I}_{\psi}^{\alpha-1,\mu}x(t) + \mathbb{I}_{\psi}^{\alpha-1,\mu}\mathrm{I}_{\psi}^{\beta,\mu}f(t) + C_1\frac{(\psi(t)^{\alpha-1}}{\Gamma(\alpha-1)}e^{-\mu\psi(t)}.$$

Hence,

$$\mathbb{I}_{\psi}^{2-\alpha,\mu}\widetilde{\delta}x(t) + \lambda\mathbb{I}_{\psi}^{1,\mu}x(t) = \mathbb{I}_{\psi}^{1,\mu}\mathrm{I}_{\psi}^{\beta,\mu}f(t) + C_0e^{-\mu\psi(t)}.$$

Consequently,

$$\frac{d_{\psi}^{\alpha,\mu}}{dt^{\alpha}}x(t) + \lambda x(t) = \mathbb{I}_{\psi}^{\beta,\mu}f(t).$$

Therefore, since $f \in \mathcal{H}_0^{1+\zeta-\beta}[a,b]$, it follows in view of Lemma 3 that

$$\frac{d_{\psi}^{\beta,\mu}}{dt^{\beta}}\left(\frac{d_{\psi}^{\alpha,\mu}}{dt^{\alpha}} + \lambda\right)x = \frac{d_{\psi}^{\beta,\mu}}{dt^{\beta}}\mathbb{I}_{\psi}^{\beta,\mu}f = f,$$

is meaningful for $f \in \mathcal{H}_0^{1+\zeta-\beta}[a,b]$.

Now, in order to clarify our idea, we will proceed to present the following

Example 2. *Let $\beta, \alpha \in (0,1)$, $\mu = 0$, $\psi(t) = t$, $t \in [0,1]$ and define $f := \mathfrak{D}_t^{\beta,0}\mathfrak{D}_t^{\alpha,0}\omega$, where $\omega(t) := \mathcal{W}(t) - \mathcal{W}(0)$. Here, $\mathcal{W}$ denotes the classical Weierstrass function:*

$$\mathcal{W}(t) := \sum_{n=0}^{\infty}\frac{e^{ib^n t}}{b^n}, \quad b > 1.$$

It is well known that the Weierstrass function is Hölder continuous of any order less than 1 (cf. ([27], Lemma 1)), but nowhere differentiable.

Let $\beta, \alpha, \zeta \in (0,1)$ such that $\alpha + \zeta < 1$, $\zeta < \beta$ and consider ω as a function from $\mathcal{H}_0^{\zeta+\alpha}[0,1]$. Lemma 1 implies $\mathfrak{D}_t^{\alpha,0}\omega \in \mathcal{H}_0^{\zeta}[0,1]$, $f \in \mathcal{H}_0^{\zeta-\beta}[0,1]$ and (cf. Lemma 2) $\mathbb{I}_t^{\alpha,0}\mathbb{I}_t^{\beta,0}f = \omega$.

Consider now the following particular case of (3) with $\mu = \lambda = 0$, $\psi(t) = t$:

$$\frac{d_t^{\beta,0}}{dt^{\beta}}\frac{d_t^{\alpha,0}}{dt^{\alpha}}x(t) = f(t), \ \ t \in [0,1], \ \ \beta, \alpha, \zeta \in (0,1), \ \alpha + \zeta < 1, \ \ \zeta < \beta, \ x(0) = 0. \quad (12)$$

According to our first investigation, outside $AC[a,b]$, the fractional differential problem (12) and the corresponding integral form

$$x(t) = \frac{C_1 t^{\alpha}}{\Gamma(1+\alpha)} + \mathbb{I}_t^{\alpha,0}\mathbb{I}_t^{\beta,0}f(t) = \frac{C_1 t^{\alpha}}{\Gamma(1+\alpha)} + \omega(t), \ \ t \in [0,1]$$

are not necessary equivalent even on the Hölder spaces: Obviously, as already mentioned, W_ζ is nowhere differentiable on $[0,1]$, so $\frac{d_t^{\beta,0}}{dt^{\beta}}\frac{d_t^{\alpha,0}}{dt^{\alpha}}x$ is "meaningless".

Alternatively, as our second investigation shows that

$$x(t) = \mathrm{I}_t^{\alpha,0}\mathrm{I}_t^{\beta,0}f(t) + \frac{C_1 t^{\alpha}}{\Gamma(1+\alpha)}.$$

Since $f \in \mathcal{H}_0^{\zeta-\beta}[0,1]$, *it follows as in the proof of Corollary 2 that* $\mathrm{I}_{\psi}^{\beta,\mu} f, \in \mathcal{H}_0^{\zeta-\alpha}[a,b]$, *and, therefore, by Lemma 3, we have*

$$\frac{d_t^{\beta,0}}{dt^{\beta}}\frac{d_t^{\alpha,0}}{dt^{\alpha}}x = \frac{d_t^{\beta,0}}{dt^{\beta}}\frac{d_t^{\alpha,0}}{dt^{\alpha}}\mathrm{I}_t^{\alpha,0}\mathrm{I}_t^{\beta,0}f = f.$$

3.1. ψ-Tempered Hilfer Fractional Langevin and Bagley–Torvik Problems

In the following, we extend the above discussion by replacing the tempered Caputo fractional derivatives with the most general one, namely,

Definition 4. *(ψ-tempered Hilfer fractional derivative) The ψ-tempered Hilfer fractional derivative of order $n+\alpha$, $\alpha \in (0,1)$, $n \in \mathbb{N} := \{1,2,\cdots\}$ with parameter $\mu > 0$ and type $\beta \in [0,1]$ applied to a function $f \in L_1[a,b]$ is defined as*

$$^{H}\mathbb{D}_{\psi}^{n+\alpha,\beta,\mu} f(t) := \left(\widetilde{\delta}\right)^{n}\, {^{H}\mathbb{D}_{\psi}^{\alpha,\beta,\mu}} f(t), \quad \text{where } {^{H}\mathbb{D}_{\psi}^{\alpha,\beta,\mu}} := \mathbb{I}_{\psi}^{\beta(1-\alpha),\mu}\widetilde{\delta}\mathbb{I}_{\psi}^{(1-\beta)(1-\alpha),\mu}.$$

For completeness, we define $^{H}\mathbb{D}_{\psi}^{0,\beta,\mu} f := \mathbb{I}_{\psi}^{\beta,\mu}\widetilde{\delta}\mathbb{I}_{\psi}^{1-\beta,\mu} f.$

Obviously, when $\beta = 0$, we arrive at the ψ-tempered Riemann–Liouville fractional derivatives where all the following results are well known and standard. So, we concentrate on the most overlapping case when $\beta \in (0,1]$; we start with the following:

Lemma 4. *1. For any $\beta \in (0,1]$ and $\zeta, \alpha \in (0,1)$, $\zeta < \alpha$ and $f \in \mathcal{H}_0^{\zeta+1-\alpha}[a,b]$, we have*

$$\begin{aligned} {^{H}\mathbb{D}_{\psi}^{\alpha,\beta,\mu}}\mathrm{I}_{\psi}^{\alpha,\mu} f(t) &= \mathbb{I}_{\psi}^{\beta(1-\alpha),\mu}\left(\widetilde{\delta}\mathbb{I}_{\psi}^{1+(1-\beta)(1-\alpha),\mu}\right)\mathfrak{D}_{\psi}^{1-\alpha} f(t) \\ &= \mathbb{I}_{\psi}^{\beta(1-\alpha),\mu}\mathbb{I}_{\psi}^{(1-\beta)(1-\alpha),\mu}\mathfrak{D}_{\psi}^{1-\alpha} f(t) = \mathbb{I}_{\psi}^{1-\alpha,\mu}\mathfrak{D}_{\psi}^{1-\alpha} f(t) = f(t). \end{aligned}$$

2. *For any $f \in AC[a,b]$,*

$$\mathrm{I}_{\psi}^{\alpha,\mu}\, {^{H}\mathbb{D}_{\psi}^{\alpha,\beta,\mu}} f(t) = f(t) - f(a)e^{-\mu\psi(t)}.$$

Proof. Let $f \in AC[a,b]$ and note that

$$\begin{aligned} \mathrm{I}_{\psi}^{\alpha,\mu}\, {^{H}\mathbb{D}_{\psi}^{\alpha,\beta,\mu}} f(t) &= \mathbb{I}_{\psi}^{1,\mu}\left(\mathfrak{D}_{\psi}^{1-\alpha,\mu}\mathbb{I}_{\psi}^{\beta(1-\alpha),\mu}\widetilde{\delta}\mathbb{I}_{\psi}^{(1-\beta)(1-\alpha),\mu}\right)f(t) \\ &= \mathbb{I}_{\psi}^{1,\mu}\left(\widetilde{\delta}\mathbb{I}_{\psi}^{\alpha+\beta(1-\alpha),\mu}\widetilde{\delta}\mathbb{I}_{\psi}^{(1-\beta)(1-\alpha),\mu}\right)f(t). \end{aligned}$$

As in [15], (proof of Lemma 4) (see also [20], (Lemma 2.1)), we have

$$\mathbb{I}_{\psi}^{(1-\beta)(1-\alpha),\mu} f(t) = \frac{e^{-\mu\psi(t)}(\psi(t))^{(1-\beta)(1-\alpha)}f(a)}{\Gamma(1+(1-\beta)(1-\alpha))} + \mathbb{I}_{\psi}^{1,\mu}\mathbb{I}_{\psi}^{(1-\beta)(1-\alpha),\mu}\widetilde{\delta}f(t),$$

$$\widetilde{\delta}\mathbb{I}_{\psi}^{(1-\beta)(1-\alpha),\mu} f(t) = \frac{e^{-\mu\psi(t)}(\psi(t))^{(1-\beta)(1-\alpha)-1}f(a)}{\Gamma((1-\beta)(1-\alpha))} + \mathbb{I}_{\psi}^{(1-\beta)(1-\alpha),\mu}\widetilde{\delta}f(t)$$

Hence,

$$\mathbb{I}_{\psi}^{\alpha+\beta(1-\alpha),\mu}\widetilde{\delta}\mathbb{I}_{\psi}^{(1-\beta)(1-\alpha),\mu} f(t) = e^{-\mu\psi(t)}f(a) + \mathbb{I}_{\psi}^{1,\mu}\widetilde{\delta}f(t).$$

Thus,

$$\mathrm{I}_{\psi}^{\alpha,\mu}\, {^{H}\mathbb{D}_{\psi}^{\alpha,\beta,\mu}} f(t) = \mathbb{I}_{\psi}^{1,\mu}\widetilde{\delta}\left[e^{-\mu\psi(t)}f(a) + \mathbb{I}_{\psi}^{1,\mu}\widetilde{\delta}f(t)\right] = \mathbb{I}_{\psi}^{1,\mu}\widetilde{\delta}f(t) = f(t) - f(a)e^{-\mu\psi(t)}.$$

□

We can now apply our results to a Langevin problem with ψ-tempered Hilfer fractional derivatives. Let us consider the ψ-tempered Hilfer fractional Langevin differential equation:

$$ {}^{H}\mathbb{D}_{\psi}^{\alpha_1,\beta,\mu}\left({}^{H}\mathbb{D}_{\psi}^{\alpha_2,\beta,\mu} + \lambda\right)x(t) = f(t), \quad t \in [a,b],\ \beta \in [0,1),\ \alpha_1, \alpha_2, \in (0,1), \tag{13} $$

with $\lambda \in \mathbb{R}$, $f \in C[a,b]$ and $\alpha_1 + \alpha_2 < 1$, combined with appropriate initial or boundary conditions. Of course, (13) and the corresponding "standard" integral form are not equivalent in the space $C[a,b]$. As in the case of $\beta = 0$, the Caputo case, we use our lemmas to formally obtain the "new" corresponding standard integral form:

$$ \mathrm{I}_{\psi}^{\alpha_1,\mu}\ {}^{H}\mathbb{D}_{\psi}^{\alpha_1,\beta,\mu}\left({}^{H}\mathbb{D}_{\psi}^{\alpha_2,\beta,\mu} + \lambda\right)x(t) = \mathrm{I}_{\psi}^{\alpha_1,\mu} f(t) $$
$$ \left({}^{H}\mathbb{D}_{\psi}^{\alpha_2,\beta,\mu} + \lambda\right)x(t) = \mathrm{I}_{\psi}^{\alpha_1,\mu} f(t) + C_1 e^{-\mu\psi(t)} $$
$$ \mathrm{I}_{\psi}^{\alpha_2,\mu}\ {}^{H}\mathbb{D}_{\psi}^{\alpha_2,\beta,\mu}x(t) = \mathrm{I}_{\psi}^{\alpha_2,\mu}\mathrm{I}_{\psi}^{\alpha_1,\mu} f(t) - \lambda \mathrm{I}_{\psi}^{\alpha_2,\mu}x(t) + \frac{C_1 e^{-\mu\psi(t)}(\psi(t))^{\alpha_2}}{\Gamma(1+\alpha_2)} $$
$$ x(t) = x(a)e^{-\mu\psi(t)} + \mathrm{I}_{\psi}^{\alpha_2,\mu}\mathrm{I}_{\psi}^{\alpha_1,\mu} f(t) - \lambda \mathrm{I}_{\psi}^{\alpha_2,\mu}x(t) + \frac{C_1 e^{-\mu\psi(t)}(\psi(t))^{\alpha_2}}{\Gamma(1+\alpha_2)}. $$

Let us examine the inverse relationship again. Let $0 < \zeta < \min\{\alpha_1, \alpha_2\} < 1$ and $f \in \mathcal{H}_0^{1+\zeta-\alpha_1}[a,b]$. By Corollary 2, we know that $\mathrm{I}_{\psi}^{\alpha_2,\mu}\mathrm{I}_{\psi}^{\alpha_1\mu} f \in \mathcal{H}_0^{1+\zeta-\alpha_2}[a,b]$. Then, Theorem 2 shows that, for sufficiently small λ, the above integral form admits a Hölder continuous solution $x \in \mathcal{H}_0^{1+\zeta-\alpha_2}[a,b]$. Therefore, by Lemma 4, x must satisfy the problem (13). In fact, we have

$$ {}^{H}\mathbb{D}_{\psi}^{\alpha_2,\beta,\mu}x(t) = -\lambda\, {}^{H}\mathbb{D}_{\psi}^{\alpha_2,\beta,\mu}\mathrm{I}_{\psi}^{\alpha_2,\mu}x(t) + {}^{H}\mathbb{D}_{\psi}^{\alpha_2,\beta,\mu}\mathrm{I}_{\psi}^{\alpha_2,\mu}\mathrm{I}_{\psi}^{\alpha_1,\mu} f(t) = -\lambda x(t) + \mathrm{I}_{\psi}^{\alpha_1,\mu} f(t). $$

Hence,

$$ {}^{H}\mathbb{D}_{\psi}^{\alpha_1,\beta,\mu}\left({}^{H}\mathbb{D}_{\psi}^{\alpha_2,\beta,\mu} + \lambda\right)x(t) = {}^{H}\mathbb{D}_{\psi}^{\alpha_1,\beta,\mu}\mathrm{I}_{\psi}^{\alpha_1,\mu} f(t) = f(t), $$

as required

All the above results can be obtained for the following fractional differential Bagley–Torvik equation:

$$ {}^{H}\mathbb{D}_{\psi}^{\alpha_1,\beta,\mu}x(t) + \lambda\, {}^{H}\mathbb{D}_{\psi}^{\alpha_2,\beta,\mu}x(t) = f(t), \tag{14} $$

$\beta \in [0,1]$, $\alpha_1, \alpha_2 \in (0,1)$, $\alpha_2 < \alpha_1$, $t \in [a,b]$, combined with appropriate initial/boundary conditions, where $\lambda \in \mathbb{R}$.

The problem (14) has attracted some interest, e.g., [3,15] and some references therein. Unlike [3,15], we consider the most interesting case when $\alpha_1, \alpha_2 \in (0,1)$ with $\alpha_2 \le \alpha_1$. Compared to the results of ([15], Example 6), our result here holds for all $\beta \in [0,1]$ without imposing an absolute continuity condition on f.

Let $\zeta \in (0, \alpha_1 - \alpha_2]$ and assume that $f \in \mathcal{H}_0^{1+\zeta-\alpha_1}[a,b]$.

Standard arguments using ([15], Lemma 8) show that

$$ {}^{H}\mathbb{D}_{\psi}^{\alpha_1,\beta,\mu}\left(\mathbb{I}_{\psi}^{0,\mu} + \lambda\, \mathbb{I}_{\psi}^{\alpha_1-\alpha_2,\mu}\right)x(t) = f(t). $$

By Lemma 4

$$ \mathrm{I}_{\psi}^{\alpha_1,\mu}\ {}^{H}\mathbb{D}_{\psi}^{\alpha_1,\beta,\mu}\left(\mathbb{I}_{\psi}^{0,\mu} + \lambda\, \mathbb{I}_{\psi}^{\alpha_1-\alpha_2,\mu}\right)x(t) = \mathrm{I}_{\psi}^{\alpha_1,\mu} f(t) $$

Then, the formal integral form (any solution) of (14) is the following:

$$ \left(\mathbb{I}_{\psi}^{0,\mu} + \lambda\, \mathbb{I}_{\psi}^{\alpha_1-\alpha_2,\mu}\right)x(t) = \mathrm{I}_{\psi}^{\alpha_1,\mu} f(t) + C_0 e^{-\mu\psi(t)}. \tag{15} $$

Since $f \in \mathcal{H}_0^{1+\zeta-\alpha_1}[a,b]$, Theorem 1 tells us that $\mathrm{I}_\psi^{\alpha_1,\mu} f \in \mathcal{H}_0^{1+\zeta-(\alpha_1-\alpha_2)}[a,b]$. According to Theorem 2, for sufficiently small λ, the linear fractional integral Equation (15) admits a Hölder continuous solution $x \in \mathcal{H}_0^{1+\zeta-\alpha_1+\alpha_2}[a,b]$.

Let us examine the inverse relationship again. Let $f \in \mathcal{H}_0^{1+\zeta-\alpha_1}[a,b]$ and $x \in \mathcal{H}_0^{1+\zeta-\alpha_1+\alpha_2}[a,b]$ solves (15). Therefore,

$$ {}^H\mathbb{D}_\psi^{\alpha_1,\beta,\mu}\left(\mathbb{I}_\psi^{0,\mu} + \lambda\, \mathbb{I}_\psi^{\alpha_1-\alpha_2,\mu}\right)x(t) = {}^H\,\mathbb{D}_\psi^{\alpha_1,\beta,\mu}\mathrm{I}_\psi^{\alpha_1,\mu} f(t) + {}^H\,\mathbb{D}_\psi^{\alpha_1,\beta,\mu}\left[C_0 e^{-\mu\psi(t)}\right] = f. $$

Then, by ([15], Lemma 8), it follows that

$$ {}^H\mathbb{D}_\psi^{\alpha_1,\beta,\mu} x(t) + \lambda\, {}^H\mathbb{D}_\psi^{\alpha_2,\beta,\mu} x(t) = f(t), $$

as expected.

In what follows, we extend the above discussion when replacing the usual differential operators with the most general ones, namely, the proportional (or conformable) derivatives.

3.2. Applications

Let us present a short example of applications of obtained results for the fully nonlinear Langevin boundary value problems. We propose to treat this example also as a set of open problems, still insufficiently studied and solved for equations of fractional order. It turns out that the choice of Hölder spaces suitable for equivalence studies of differential and integral problems leads to questions about the behavior of nonlinear operators in them, in particular, superposition operators.

The study of equations in Hölder spaces is natural and, due to the compact embeddings of these spaces in $C[a,b]$, allows the use of compactness methods. Moreover, it is inefficient to try to formulate assumptions in the language of measures of noncompactness in these spaces (however they are defined), since superposition operators are contractions with respect to classical measures of noncompactness if, and only if, they are Lipschitz operators [28].

Let us consider the following ψ-tempered fractional Langevin nonlinear problem:

$$ \frac{d_\psi^{\beta,\mu}}{dt^\beta}\left(\frac{d_\psi^{\alpha,\mu}}{dt^\alpha} + \lambda\right)x(t) = f(t, x(t)), \tag{16} $$

with boundary-value conditions $x(a) = 0$, $x(b) = x_b$. Let us consider the case $\lambda \in \mathbb{R}$, $\beta, \alpha \in (0,1)$, $\beta + \alpha < 1$, $\zeta, \alpha \in (0,1)$, $\alpha < \zeta$.

The three-point BVP for the Langevin fractional equation with classical Hilfer fractional derivatives has been studied, for example, in [29], but for continuous solutions and a jointly continuous function f satisfying some additional assumptions.

For tempered fractional derivatives, the problem has not yet been investigated. Apart from investigating the problem with a much more general fractional-order derivative, as will be shown below, our result is much deeper in terms of the theory of fractional differential equations and the problem in Hölder spaces is more interesting. The proofs in that paper are based on the properties of the operators for absolutely continuous functions, and in this paper, we simply show how to go beyond that case. In this context (also taking into account the various derivatives), it is worth noting the difference between our Lemma 4 proved in two cases and ([29], Lemma 7). Neither the results nor the proofs from that paper apply to the case of the Hölder space. For the sake of clarity and to highlight the differences, we will restrict ourselves here to the two-point BVP (cf. [9]), as this involves only minor adjustments to the definition of the operator and the fixed point theorem used (cf. [30]).

Proposition 1. *Let $\lambda \in \mathbb{R}$, $\beta, \alpha \in (0,1)$, $\beta + \alpha < 1$, $\zeta, \alpha \in (0,1)$, $\alpha < \zeta$. Moreover, assume that*

(a) $f : [a,b] \times \mathbb{R} \to \mathbb{R}$ *generates the superposition operator* $N(x)(t) = f(t, x(t))$ *such that*

$$N : \mathcal{H}_0^{\max\{1-\zeta+\alpha, 1-\zeta+\beta\}}[a,b] \to \mathcal{H}_0^{\max\{1-\zeta+\alpha, 1-\zeta+\beta\}}[a,b]$$

being bounded and continuous.

(b) *there exists* $r_N > 0$ *such that* $\|N(x)\|_{\max\{1-\zeta+\alpha, 1-\zeta+\beta\}} < r_N$.

If

$$r_N \cdot \left(\frac{\|\psi\|^\beta e^{\mu\|\psi\|}}{\Gamma(\beta)} \left[\frac{2}{\beta} + \frac{\mu\|\psi\|}{\beta+1} \right] \right) \cdot \left(\frac{\|\psi\|^\alpha e^{\mu\|\psi\|}}{\Gamma(\alpha)} \left[\frac{2}{\alpha} + \frac{\mu\|\psi\|}{\alpha+1} \right] \right) + |\lambda| \left(\frac{\|\psi\|^\alpha e^{\mu\|\psi\|}}{\Gamma(\alpha)} \left[\frac{2}{\alpha} + \frac{\mu\|\psi\|}{\alpha+1} \right] \right) < 1,$$

then there exists at least one global solution $x \in \mathcal{H}_0^{1-\zeta}[a,b]$ *of the problem (16) on* $[a,b]$.

Remark 7. *Before starting the proof, we should recall why we chose the abstract form of assumption (a). It is worth remembering this in order to justify the considerable variety of assumptions for problems studied in Hölder spaces.*

In contrast to the situation in $C[a,b]$, *the fact that the superposition operator acts in some Hölder space does not imply its continuity or even boundedness. Even more surprising, in this case, the generating function need not be continuous on* $[a,b] \times \mathbb{R}$. *But it means that it need not be defined on* $C[a,b]$. *Moreover, if this operator is autonomous, it is always bounded, but need not be continuous (cf. ([28], Section 2)). Our condition is, then, more general than for continuous solutions. And this is precisely the reason for proposing studies of nonlinear operators on these spaces. As we have shown, we have sufficient conditions for research, but they are neither optimal nor necessary. Interesting ideas and examples can be found in [31].*

Proof. First of all, we will make use of the equivalence of differential and integral problems, which will allow us to study the integral equation:

$$I_\psi^{\beta,\mu} \frac{d_\psi^{\beta,\mu}}{dt^\beta} \left(\frac{d_\psi^{\alpha,\mu}}{dt^\alpha} + \lambda \right) x(t) = I_\psi^{\beta,\mu} f(t, x(t))$$

$$\left(\frac{d_\psi^{\alpha,\mu}}{dt^\alpha} + \lambda \right) x(t) = I_\psi^{\beta,\mu} f(t, x(t)) + C_1 e^{-\mu\psi(t)}$$

$$I_\psi^{\alpha,\mu} \frac{d_\psi^{\alpha,\mu}}{dt^\alpha} x(t) = I_\psi^{\alpha,\mu} I_\psi^{\beta,\mu} f(t, x(t)) - \lambda I_\psi^{\alpha,\mu} x(t) + \frac{C_1 e^{-\mu\psi(t)} (\psi(t))^\alpha}{\Gamma(1+\alpha)}$$

$$x(t) = x(a) e^{-\mu\psi(t)} + I_\psi^{\alpha,\mu} I_\psi^{\beta,\mu} f(t, x(t)) - \lambda I_\psi^{\alpha,\mu} x(t) + \frac{C_1 e^{-\mu\psi(t)} (\psi(t))^\alpha}{\Gamma(1+\alpha)}.$$

The converse relation between integral and differential forms can be proved again as in Lemma 3.

The fact that in such a general problem, by obtaining an integral form equivalent to the differential problem, it is possible to carry out the classical fixed point theorems is one of the advantages of the present treatment of the subject.

We need to investigate also the superposition operator on Hölder spaces.

$$N(x)(t) = f(t, x(t)).$$

As claimed above, our assumption (a) is very general. We will look for a fixed point of the following operator $T : \mathcal{H}_0^{\max\{1-\zeta+\alpha, 1-\zeta+\beta\}}[a,b] \to \mathcal{H}_0^{\max\{1-\zeta+\alpha, 1-\zeta+\beta\}}[a,b]$ since we are looking for functions from little Hölder spaces, i.e., with $x(a) = 0$ (which is consistent with our assumption). Thus, this operator should be given by

$$Tx(t) = \mathrm{I}_{\psi}^{\alpha,\mu}\mathrm{I}_{\psi}^{\beta,\mu} f(t, x(t)) - \lambda \mathrm{I}_{\psi}^{\alpha,\mu} x(t) + \frac{C_1 e^{-\mu\psi(t)}(\psi(t))^{\alpha}}{\Gamma(1+\alpha)}.$$

defined on the expected space of Hölder continuous functions. The constant C_1 can be calculated from

$$x_b - \mathrm{I}_{\psi}^{\alpha,\mu}\mathrm{I}_{\psi}^{\beta,\mu} f(t, x_b) + \lambda \mathrm{I}_{\psi}^{\alpha,\mu} x_b = \frac{C_1 e^{-\mu\psi(t)}(\psi(t))^{\alpha}}{\Gamma(1+\alpha)},$$

and as $f(\cdot, x_b)$ is Hölder continuous,

$$C_1 = \frac{\Gamma(1+\alpha)}{e^{-\mu\psi(t)}(\psi(t))^{\alpha}} \cdot \left\{ x_b \cdot (1 + \lambda \mathrm{I}_{\psi}^{\alpha,\mu}) - \mathrm{I}_{\psi}^{\alpha,\mu}\mathrm{I}_{\psi}^{\beta,\mu} f(t, x_b) \right\}.$$

For the sake of brevity, let us retain this notation. Now, let us construct an invariant ball for T. By our assumption on N, we obtain $\|N(x)\|_{1-\zeta+\alpha} < r_N$. Let us estimate both parts of the norm on $\mathcal{H}_0^{1-\zeta+\alpha}[a, b]$ separately. Let us suppose that x is a solution of the problem under investigation. It is possible to demonstrate the following "a priori" estimation. First, we need to estimate the supremum norm:

$$\begin{aligned}
\|x\|_{\infty} &= \|T(x)\|_{\infty} \leq |\mathrm{I}_{\psi}^{\alpha,\mu}\mathrm{I}_{\psi}^{\beta,\mu} f(t, x(t))| + |\lambda||\mathrm{I}_{\psi}^{\alpha,\mu} x(t)| + |\frac{C_1 e^{-\mu\psi(t)}(\psi(t))^{\alpha}}{\Gamma(1+\alpha)}| \\
&\leq r_N \cdot \left(\left(\frac{\|\psi\|^{\beta} e^{\mu\|\psi\|}}{\Gamma(\beta)} \left[\frac{2}{\beta} + \frac{\mu\|\psi\|}{\beta+1} \right] \right) \cdot \left(\frac{\|\psi\|^{\alpha} \|x\|_{\infty} e^{\mu\|\psi\|}}{\Gamma(\alpha)} \left[\frac{2}{\alpha} + \frac{\mu\|\psi\|}{\alpha+1} \right] \right) \right) \\
&\quad + |\lambda| \left(\frac{\|\psi\|^{\alpha} \|x\|_{\infty} e^{\mu\|\psi\|}}{\Gamma(\alpha)} \left[\frac{2}{\alpha} + \frac{\mu\|\psi\|}{\alpha+1} \right] \right) + |C_1| \cdot \frac{\|\psi\|^{\alpha}}{\Gamma(1+\alpha)}.
\end{aligned}$$

From this inequality, we obtain an estimation:

$$\begin{aligned}
&\|x\|_{\infty} \\
&\leq \left[\frac{|C_1| \|\psi\|^{\alpha}}{\Gamma(1+\alpha)} \right] / \left[1 - r_N \cdot \left(\left(\frac{\|\psi\|^{\beta} e^{\mu\|\psi\|}}{\Gamma(\beta)} \left[\frac{2}{\beta} + \frac{\mu\|\psi\|}{\beta+1} \right] \right) \cdot \left(\frac{\|\psi\|^{\alpha} e^{\mu\|\psi\|}}{\Gamma(\alpha)} \left[\frac{2}{\alpha} + \frac{\mu\|\psi\|}{\alpha+1} \right] \right) \right) \right. \\
&\quad \left. - |\lambda| \left(\frac{\|\psi\|^{\alpha} e^{\mu\|\psi\|}}{\Gamma(\alpha)} \left[\frac{2}{\alpha} + \frac{\mu\|\psi\|}{\alpha+1} \right] \right) \right] =: R_1.
\end{aligned}$$

Now, we need to estimate the seminorm on the Hölder space:

$$\begin{aligned}
[x]_{\max\{1-\zeta+\alpha, 1-\zeta+\beta\}} &= [T(x)]_{\max\{1-\zeta+\alpha, 1-\zeta+\beta\}} \\
&\leq C \cdot [N(x)]_{\max\{1-\zeta+\alpha, 1-\zeta+\beta\}} + |\lambda| \cdot [x]_{\max\{1-\zeta+\alpha, 1-\zeta+\beta\}}
\end{aligned}$$

and then

$$[x]_{\max\{1-\zeta+\alpha, 1-\zeta+\beta\}} = \frac{CR_N}{1-|\lambda|} = R_2.$$

Thus, $\|x\|_{\max\{1-\zeta+\alpha, 1-\zeta+\beta\}} \leq R_2$. Put $R = R_1 + R_2$. By B_R, denote the ball

$$\{x \in : \|x\|_{\max\{1-\zeta+\alpha, 1-\zeta+\beta\}} \subset \mathcal{H}_0^{\max\{1-\zeta+\alpha, 1-\zeta+\beta\}}[a, b].$$

We just proved that $T : B_R \to B_R$.

Now, we need to discuss the continuity property of the operator T on the ball B_R. Since this operator is a sum and a composition of some operators: $T = \mathrm{I}_{\psi}^{\alpha,\mu}\mathrm{I}_{\psi}^{\beta,\mu} \circ N - \lambda \mathrm{I}_{\psi}^{\alpha,\mu} \circ$

$Id + \Psi$, where $\Psi = \frac{C_1 e^{-\mu\psi(t)}(\psi(t))^{\alpha}}{\Gamma(1+\alpha)}$ is a constant function. By Theorem 1, tempered fractional integral operators are bounded on $\mathcal{H}_0^{\max\{1-\zeta+\alpha,1-\zeta+\beta\}}[a,b]$, then being linear are continuous. From our assumptions, it follows that N is also continuous between the considered Hölder spaces. Thus, all operators composing T are continuous on $\mathcal{H}_0^{\max\{1-\zeta+\alpha,1-\zeta+\beta\}}[a,b]$.

As claimed before, we will apply the Schauder fixed point theorem, so we need to present a compactness argument. Since $\max\{1-\zeta+\alpha, 1-\zeta+\beta\} < 1-\zeta < 1$, the space $\mathcal{H}_0^{\max\{1-\zeta+\alpha,1-\zeta+\beta\}}[a,b]$ is compactly embedded into $\mathcal{H}_0^{1-\zeta}[a,b]$, we have $T(B_R) \subset B_R \subset \mathcal{H}_0^{\max\{1-\zeta+\alpha,1-\zeta+\beta\}}[a,b] \subset \mathcal{H}_0^{1-\zeta}[a,b]$ and then B_R is compact in $\mathcal{H}_0^{1-\zeta}[a,b]$. Thus, we are able to apply the Schauder fixed point theorem in the last space and we are done. □

Remark 8. *It is worth noting that compared to an earlier paper, e.g., [29], with weaker assumptions on the function $f(\cdot,\cdot)$ we obtain more properties of the solutions, e.g., Hölder continuity. Of course, it is possible to obtain an analogous result for multivalued problems, but nevertheless, it is first worthwhile to investigate multivalued superposition operators in Hölder spaces (cf. [16]). We leave this as an open problem for the reader.*

Remark 9. *Arguing similarly as in (16), we can also obtain similar results for the following fractional differential Bagley–Torvik equation:*

$$\frac{d_{\psi}^{\beta,\mu}}{dt^{\beta}}x(t) + \lambda\,\frac{d_{\psi}^{\alpha,\mu}}{dt^{\alpha}}x(t) = f(t,x(t)), \tag{17}$$

with boundary-value conditions $x(a) = 0$, $x(b) = x_b$ in case $\lambda \in \mathbb{R}$, $\beta,\alpha \in (0,1)$, $\alpha < \beta$, $0 < \zeta \leq \beta - \alpha$, $\alpha < \zeta$.

4. Conclusions

In this paper, we prove the equivalence of differential problems with ψ-Hilfer fractional derivatives and integral problems with the corresponding fractional integral operators in Hölder spaces. We also show that such equivalence does not always hold outside the given classes of function spaces. The Hölder continuity of solutions of values of fractional integral operators even acting on Lebesgue spaces is a well-known property, so it should also be checked and proved for all fractional differential problems. Our studies are carried out for the general class of ψ-Caputo fractional derivatives.

We apply the equivalence results to the study of Langevin-type equations: a linear inhomogeneous and boundary value problem that points in the direction of further research, including boundary problems of various kinds.

Author Contributions: Conceptualization, M.C. and H.A.H.S.; Methodology, M.C., H.A.H.S. and W.S.; Software, M.C., H.A.H.S. and W.S.; Validation, M.C., H.A.H.S. and W.S.; Formal analysis, M.C., H.A.H.S. and W.S.; Investigation, M.C., H.A.H.S. and W.S.; Resources, M.C., H.A.H.S. and W.S.; Writing—original draft, M.C., H.A.H.S. and W.S.; Writing—review & editing, M.C. and H.A.H.S.; Visualization, H.A.H.S. and W.S.; Supervision, H.A.H.S.; Project administration, M.C. and H.A.H.S. All authors have read and approved the final manuscript.

Funding: This research received no external funding.

Data Availability Statement: The original contributions presented in the study are included in the article, further inquiries can be directed to the corresponding author.

Conflicts of Interest: The authors declare no conflicts of interest.

References

1. Webb, J.R.L. Initial value problems for Caputo fractional equations with singular nonlinearities. *Electron. J. Differ. Equ.* **2019**, *117*, 1–32.
2. Hardy, G.H.; Littlewood, J.E. Some properties of fractional integrals I. *Math. Z.* **1928**, *27*, 565–606. [CrossRef]

3. Webb, J.R.L.; Lan, K. Fractional differential equations of Bagley-Torvik and Langevin type. *Fract. Calc. Appl. Anal.* **2024**, *27*, 1639–1669.
4. Appell, J.; Dutkiewicz, A.; López, B.; Reinwand, S.; Sadarangani, K. Hölder-type spaces, singular operators, and fixed point theorems. *Fixed Point Theory* **2021**, *22*, 31–58. [CrossRef]
5. Salem, H.A.H.; Cichoń, M. Analysis of tempered fractional calculus in Hölder and Orlicz spaces. *Symmetry* **2022**, *14*, 1581. [CrossRef]
6. Yu, T.; Deng, K.; Luo, M. Existence and uniqueness of solutions of initial value problems for nonlinear Langevin equation involving two fractional orders. *Commun. Nonlin. Sci. Num. Simul.* **2014**, *19*, 1661–1668. [CrossRef]
7. Mainradi, F.; Pironi, P. The fractional Langevin equation: Brownian motion revisited. *Extracta Math.* **1996**, *10*, 140–154.
8. Salem, A.; Azahrani, F.; Almaghamsi, L. Fractional Langevin equations with nonlocal integral boundary conditions. *Mathematics* **2019**, *7*, 402. [CrossRef]
9. Salem, A.; Almaghamsi, L. Existence solution for coupled system of Langevin fractional differential equations of Caputo type with Riemann–Stieltjes integral boundary conditions. *Symmetry* **2021**, *13*, 2123. [CrossRef]
10. Baghani, O. On fractional Langevin equation involving two fractional orders. *Commun. Nonlin. Sci. Num. Simul.* **2017**, *42*, 675–681. [CrossRef]
11. Coffey, W.T.; Kalmykov, Y.P.; Waldron, J.T. *The Langevin Equation: With Applications to Stochastic Problems in Physics, Chemistry and Electrical Engineering*; World Sci.: Singapore, 2004.
12. Bagley, R.L.; Torvik, P.J. A theoretical basis for the application of fractional calculus to viscoelasticity. *J. Rheol.* **1993**, *27*, 201–210.
13. Wongcharoen, A.; Ntouyas, S.K.; Tariboon, J. Nonlocal boundary value problems for Hilfer-type pantograph fractional differential equations and inclusions. *Adv. Differ. Equ.* **2020**, *2020*, 279. [CrossRef]
14. Mali, A.D.; Kucche, K.D. Nonlocal boundary value problem for generalized Hilfer implicit fractional differential equations. *Math. Meth. Appl. Sci.* **2020**, *43*, 8608–8631. [CrossRef]
15. Salem, H.A.H.; Cichoń, M.; Shammakh, W. Existence results for tempered-Hilfer fractional differential problems on Hölder spaces. *Symmetry* **2024**, *16*, 700. [CrossRef]
16. Matkowski, J.; Wróbel, M. Uniformly bounded set-valued Nemytskij operators acting between generalized Hölder function spaces. *Open Math.* **2012**, *10*, 609–618. [CrossRef]
17. Fahad, H.M.; Fernandez, A.; Rehman, M.U.; Siddiqi, M. Tempered and Hadamard-type fractional calculus with respect to functions. *Mediter. J. Math.* **2021**, *18*, 143. [CrossRef]
18. Meerschaert, M.; Sabzikar, F.; Chen, J. Tempered fractional calculus. *J. Comput. Phys.* **2015**, *293*, 14–28.
19. Gorenflo, R.; Kilbas, A.A.; Mainardi, F.; Rogosin, S.V. *Mittag-Leffler Functions, Related Topics and Applications*; Springer: Berlin/Heidelberg, Germany, 2020.
20. Samko, S.; Kilbas, A.; Marichev, O.J. *Fractional Integrals and Derivatives*; Gordon and Breach Science Publisher: London, UK, 1993.
21. Almeida, R. A Caputo fractional derivative of a function with respect to another function. *Commun. Nonlin. Sci. Num. Simul.* **2017**, *44*, 460–481. [CrossRef]
22. Yang, X.-J. *General Fractional Derivatives: Theory, Methods and Applications*; CRC Press: Boca Raton, FL, USA, 2019.
23. Sousa, J.; Vanterler da, C.; Capelas de Oliveira, E. On the ψ-Hilfer fractional derivative. *Commun. Nonlin. Sci. Num. Simul.* **2018**, *60*, 72–91. [CrossRef]
24. Sousa, J.; Vanterler da, C.; Machado, J.A.T.; Capelas de Oliveira, E. The ψ-Hilfer fractional calculus of variable order and its applications. *Comp. Appl. Math.* **2020**, *39*, 296. [CrossRef]
25. Kilbas, A.; Srivastava, H.M.; Trujillo, J.J. *Theory and Applications of Fractional Differential Equations*; Elsevier: Amsterdam, The Netherlands, 2006.
26. Cichoń, M.; Salem, H.A.H. On the lack of equivalence between differential and integral forms of the Caputo-type fractional problems. *J. Pseudo-Differ. Oper. Appl.* **2020**, *11*, 1869–1895. [CrossRef]
27. Ross, B.; Samko, S.G.; Love, E.R. Functions that have no first order derivative might have fractional derivative of all orders less than one. *Real Anal. Exch.* **1994**, *20*, 140–157. [CrossRef]
28. Appell, J.; De Pascale, E. Lipschitz and Darbo conditions for the superposition operator in some non-ideal spaces of smooth functions. *Ann. Mat. Pura Appl.* **1991**, *158*, 205–217. [CrossRef]
29. Wongcharoen, A.; Ahmad, B.; Ntouyas, S.K.; Tariboon, J. Three-point boundary value problems for the Langevin equation with the Hilfer fractional derivative. *Adv. Math. Phys.* **2020**, *2020*, 9606428. [CrossRef]
30. Salem, H.A.H.; Cichoń M.; Shammakh, W. Generalized fractional calculus in Banach spaces and applications to existence results for boundary value problems. *Bound. Value Probl.* **2023**, *2023*, 57. [CrossRef]
31. Appell, J.; Zabrejko, P.P. *Nonlinear Superposition Operators*; Cambridge University Press: Cambridge, UK, 1990.

mathematics

MDPI

Article

Using a Mix of Finite Difference Methods and Fractional Differential Transformations to Solve Modified Black–Scholes Fractional Equations

Agus Sugandha [1,*], Endang Rusyaman [2], Sukono [2] and Ema Carnia [2]

[1] Doctoral Program of Mathematics, Faculty of Mathematics and Natural Sciences, Universitas Padjadjaran, Jatinangor 40132, Indonesia
[2] Department of Mathematics, Faculty of Mathematics and Natural Sciences, Universitas Padjadjaran, Jatinangor 40132, Indonesia; rusyaman@unpad.ac.id (E.R.); sukono@unpad.ac.id (S.); ema.carnia@unpad.ac.id (E.C.)
* Correspondence: agus19011@mail.unpad.ac.id

Abstract: This paper discusses finding solutions to the modified Fractional Black–Scholes equation. As is well known, the options theory is beneficial in the stock market. Using call-and-pull options, investors can theoretically decide when to sell, hold, or buy shares for maximum profits. However, the process of forming the Black–Scholes model uses a normal distribution, where, in reality, the call option formula obtained is less realistic in the stock market. Therefore, it is necessary to modify the model to make the option values obtained more realistic. In this paper, the method used to determine the solution to the modified Fractional Black–Scholes equation is a combination of the finite difference method and the fractional differential transformation method. The results show that the combined method of finite difference and fractional differential transformation is a very good approximation for the solution of the Fractional Black–Scholes equation.

Keywords: modified fractional Black–Scholes; call option; put option; solution; finite difference method; fractional differential transformation method

MSC: 35A01; 35A02; 35R11

1. Introduction

Nowadays, the development and application of mathematics have penetrated almost every area of life, including investment problems. Investment problems are one of the applications of mathematics in financial mathematics. Investors seek to buy or sell assets traded on financial markets to obtain maximum profits. Derivative assets are financial instruments whose value is determined by an underlying asset. One of the purposes of using derivative instruments is to reduce risk by hedging against possible adverse asset price movements. Options are a type of derivative product that is well known to many people.

In 1973, Fisher Black and Myron Scholes built a model for option values called the Black–Scholes model. The problem of determining the option value, which is determined by the value of the underlying asset at a particular time, is not only a problem in economics and finance but also in mathematics. The methods often used to solve the Black–Scholes equation include the Laplace transformation and the Ito integral [1,2]. By using the Stochastic Process, we finally obtain the formula for call-and-put options.

Mathematicians then developed the Black–Scholes equation model into a Fractional Black–Scholes equation. This Fractional Black–Scholes equation model is a generalized form of the Black–Scholes equation. Several methods for solving the Fractional Black–Scholes equation include a combination of homotopy perturbation methods, Sumudu

Transformations, and He's polynomials [3]. The Fractional Black–Scholes equation can be solved using the series decomposition method. It confirms that Sumudu Transformation and fractional calculus are used to solve the Fractional Black–Scholes equation [4]. Meanwhile, the properties of Sumudu Transformation are used to solve partial differential equations [5,6]. The Fractional Black–Scholes equation can be solved using the series decomposition method, asserting that the Sumudu Transformation, combined with fractional calculus, is utilized to solve the Fractional Black–Scholes equation [7].

In the same year, Ref. [8] combined the Laplace transform and radial kernel methods to solve the Fractional Black–Scholes equation. According to several studies on analytical solutions, the Fractional Black–Scholes equation is an endless sequence of Mittag–Lefler functions. Ref. [9] researched the existence and uniqueness of solutions to the Fractional Black–Scholes equation. Banach's fixed point and Arzella Ascoli's fixed point have all been used to discuss the problem's existence and uniqueness. To discuss the numerical solution to the Fractional Black–Scholes issue, the Crank–Nickholson technique is used. Ref. [10] solved Burger's equation using the Modified Laplace Adomian decomposition technique in 2015. Burger's equation was represented using a partial differential equation. The Laplace Adomian decomposition method provides a precise approach for obtaining precise solutions and very speedy convergence of results. Various approaches can be used to solve partial differential equations, including homotopic perturbation, variational iteration, and Adomian decomposition methods. The embedding parameter in the homotopic perturbation method is quite small. It was assumed that the solution to the differential equation would be an infinite series. The Adomian decomposition approach makes use of Adomian polynomials. The absence of the discretization variable is the primary advantage of this strategy. Another advantage is the lack of the necessity for problem linearization, although these approaches were equivalent in terms of the rate of solution convergence.

The topic of European option pricing in the regime-switching model's FMLS (limited log-stable moment) was then investigated [11–13]. The Homotopic Analysis Method (HAM) was used in [14,15] to calculate the European Call Option (ECO) using the Time-Fractional Black–Scholes Equation (TFBSE), where stock prices are supposed to move according to geometric Brownian motion and do not pay dividends. The HAM has discovered a series of solutions for TFBSE. Furthermore, the ECO pricing calculation formula has been obtained. The efficacy, suitability, and correctness of the HAM were demonstratively investigated in the context of Crank Nicolson (CRN), Binomial Model (BM), and Black–Scholes Model (BSM) approaches, using two examples. Because it can converge to analytical results faster, the HAM is judged to be the best alternative instrument for determining ECO prices with fractional orders. Ref. [16] provided a numerical technique for the Time-Fractional Black–Scholes model, which is used in the fractional structural model within financial markets. This method uses an initial discretization based on time and a weighted finite difference spatial approach. Some spatial discretization characteristics are also investigated. A fundamental limitation of this technology is its inability to proceed in time layer by layer.

Common approaches for solving the Fractional Black–Scholes equation include the homotopic perturbation method, He's polynomials, and Adomian decomposition. The numerical operational transformation method is used. However, extreme vigilance is required when modifying time fractional derivatives. Mistakes can occur when using the differential operator after the time inversion techniques have changed. The constructed numerical model employs a variety of methodologies. The discrete, linear, and nonlinear characteristics of European Black–Scholes option pricing models are then captured by [17,18]. To achieve this, this article combines the third-order strong stability of the Runge–Kutta method with a sixth-order finite difference scheme. The findings from the current literature and its precise answers were examined and contrasted. The finite–difference method is a more popular common technique. The key challenge will be to find a more sophisticated model solution with an approach that aligns with precise results. Therefore, the strong stability approach of the third-order Runge–Kutta and the sixth-order finite–difference method must be combined to produce an efficient numerical solution. Asymptotic convergence has been demonstrated through convergence using the norm definition. Ref. [19] provided a numerical technique for the Time-Fractional Black–Scholes model, which is used for the fractional structural model in financial markets. This method uses initial discretization based on time and a weighted finite difference spatial approach. In 2023, Ref. [20] used a simpler method, the Daftardar–Geijji method, to solve the Fractional Black–Scholes equation. It also discusses the problem of existence and the uniqueness of solutions of the Fractional Black–Scholes equation.

2. Formation of the Modified Fractional Black–Scholes Equation

Suppose $V(S,\tau)$ is the option value, while S is the value of the underlying asset, and τ is time. The total flux rate of option value $\overline{Y}(s,\tau)$ per unit of time from time τ to the expiration date T and the option value $V(S,\tau)$ must satisfy:

$$\int_{\tau}^{T} \overline{Y}(s,\tau')d\tau' = S^{d_f-1}\int_{\tau}^{T} H(\tau'-\tau)[V(S,\tau')-V(S,T)]d\tau'$$

where $H(\tau)$ is the transmission function, and d_f is the Haudorff dimension of the fractal transmission system. The equation above is called the conservation equation for the diffusion process of option values in a fractal structure. The transmission function $H(\tau)$ is defined as follows:

$$H(\tau) = m\frac{A_{2\gamma}}{\Gamma(1-2\gamma)t^{2\gamma}} + (1+mk)\frac{B_{\gamma}}{\Gamma(1-\gamma)t^{\gamma}}$$

So, the transmission function $H(\tau)$ is a linear combination of two other transmission functions. In this case, $A_{2\gamma}$ and B_{γ} are constants, while 2γ and γ are transmission exponents. By differentiating the conservation equation above with respect to τ, we obtain:

$$-\overline{Y}(s,\tau') = S^{d_f-1}\frac{d}{dt}\left(\int_{\tau}^{T} H(\tau'-\tau)\left[V(S,\tau')-V(S,T)\right]d\tau'\right).$$

Based on the modified Black–Scholes equation, we obtain:

$$\overline{Y}(s,\tau) = \frac{\partial^2 v}{\partial S^2} + (k-1)\frac{\partial v}{\partial S} - kv \quad (1)$$

Combined with Equation (1), we obtain:

$$A_{2\gamma}S^{d_f-1}m\,\frac{\partial^{2\gamma} v}{\partial \tau^{2\gamma}} + B_{\gamma}S^{d_f-1}(1+mk)\frac{\partial^{\gamma} v}{\partial \tau^{\gamma}} + \frac{\partial^2 v}{\partial S^2} + (k-1)\frac{\partial v}{\partial S} - kv = 0$$

where:

$$\frac{\partial^{\gamma} f}{\partial \tau^{\gamma}} = \frac{1}{\Gamma(n-\alpha)}\frac{\partial^n}{\partial \tau^n}\int_{t}^{T}\frac{f(S,\tau')-f(S,\tau)}{(\tau'-\tau)^{\alpha+1-n}}d\tau'$$

and $\frac{\partial^{2\gamma} f}{\partial \tau^{2\gamma}} = \frac{\partial^{\gamma}}{\partial \tau^{\gamma}}\left(\frac{\partial^{\gamma} f}{\partial \tau^{\gamma}}\right)$. If $A_{2\gamma}S^{d_f-1} = 1$ and $B_{\gamma}S^{d_f-1} = 1$, we obtain the modified Fractional Black–Scholes equation as follows:

$$m\frac{\partial^{2\gamma} v}{\partial \tau^{2\gamma}} + (1+mk_1)\frac{\partial^{\gamma} v}{\partial \gamma} = \frac{\partial^2 v}{\partial S^2} + (k_1-1)\frac{\partial v}{\partial S} - k_1 v \quad (2)$$

with m:: constant
k_1: risk-free interest
S: asset value
Equation (2) is called the modified Fractional Black–Scholes equation.
Based on Equation (2), we obtained:
For m=0, Equation (1) becomes the Fractional Black–Scholes equation.

For ***m*=0** and **γ=1**, Equation (1) becomes the Black–Scholes equation.

So, the Fractional Black–Scholes equation is a special case of the modified Fractional Black–Scholes equation.

3. Fractional Differential Transformation Method

The Fractional Differential Transformation Method is a generalization of the differential transformation method based on the Fractional Taylor formula. The Fractional Taylor series expansion with order α of the function $u(t)$ around the point $t = t_0$ is defined as:

$$u(t) = \sum_{k=0}^{\infty} \frac{(t-t_0)^{k\alpha}}{\Gamma(k\alpha+1)} \left(\frac{d^\alpha}{dt^\alpha}\right)^k u(t);$$

where $\frac{d^\alpha}{dt^\alpha}$ is the Caputo fractional derivative with order α, and $\left(\frac{d^\alpha}{dt^\alpha}\right)^k = \frac{d^\alpha}{dt^\alpha} \cdots \frac{d^\alpha}{dt^\alpha}$ consists of k terms.

The Fractional Differential Transformation with order α of the function $u(t)$ in the neighborhood $t = t_0$ is defined as $U^\alpha(k) = \frac{1}{\Gamma(k\alpha+1)} \left(\frac{d^\alpha}{dt^\alpha}\right)^k u(t)$, and the inverse transformation is $u(t) = \sum_{k=0}^{\infty} U^\alpha(k)(t-t_0)^{k\alpha}$. So, for $t_0 = 0$, we obtain:

$$u(t) = \sum_{k=0}^{\infty} U^\alpha(k) t^{k\alpha} = \sum_{k=0}^{\infty} \varphi_k(t).$$

Theorem 1 ([21]). *If $F^\alpha(k)$ and $G^\alpha(k)$ and $H^\alpha(k)$ are Fractional Differential Transformations of the functions $f(t), g(t)$, and $h(t)$, then this applies:*

(a) *If $f(t) = g(t) \pm h(t)$, then $F^\alpha(k) = G^\alpha(k) \pm H^\alpha(k)$,*

(b) *If $f(t) = (t-t_0)^q$, then $F^\alpha(k) = \delta(k - \frac{q}{\alpha})$ where $\delta = \begin{cases} 1, & if\ k = 0 \\ 0, & if\ k \neq 0 \end{cases}$*

(c) *If $f(t) = g(t)h(t)$, then $F^\alpha(k) = \sum_{l=0}^{k} G^\alpha(k) H^\alpha(k-l)$.*

Theorem 2 ([22]). *If $f(t) = t^\lambda g(t)$ where $\lambda > -1$ and $g(t) = \sum_{n=0}^{\infty} a_n (t-t_0)^{n\alpha}$ with a convergence radius $R > 0$ and $0 < \alpha \leq 1$, then:*

$$D_\alpha^\gamma D_\alpha^\beta = D_\alpha^{\gamma+\beta} f(t).$$

Theorem 3 ([22]). *Suppose $f(t) = D_{t_0}^\gamma g(t)$, $m-1 < \gamma \leq m$, and the function $g(t)$ satisfies the conditions in the theorem above, then:*

$$F^\alpha(k) = \frac{\Gamma(k\alpha+\gamma+1)}{\Gamma(k\alpha+1)} G^\alpha\left(k + \frac{\gamma}{\alpha}\right)$$

for each $t \in (0, R)$, if:

(a) *$\beta < \lambda + 1$, for any α or*

(b) *$\beta \geq \lambda + 1$, for any γ, and $a_k = 0$ for $k = 0, 1, \ldots, m-1$, where $m-1 < \beta \leq m$.*

The following is the convergence theorem to solve the modified Fractional Black–Scholes equation.

Theorem 4. *If, for any $k \in \mathbb{N}_0$ and for each $i \geq k_0$, there exists $0 < \partial_i < 1$ such that $\|\varphi_{i+1}\| < \delta_{i+1}\|\varphi_i\|$, then the series $\sum_{k=0}^{\infty} \varphi_k(t)$ converges to u_t.*

Proof. Suppose there is a Cauchy sequence $u_1, u_2, \ldots,$ where $u_n = \sum_{k=0}^{\infty} \varphi_k(t)$. It will be shown that u_n is a Cauchy sequence. For $0 < \partial_i < 1$, it implies:

$$\|u_i - u_{i-1}\| = \|\varphi_i\| \leq \delta_i\|\varphi_{j-1}\| < \delta_i\delta_{i-1}\ldots\delta_{k_0}\|\varphi_{k_0}\|$$

For $n \geq m \geq k_0$, this is obtained:

$$\|u_n - u_m\| = \sum_{i=m+1}^{n} (s_i - s_{i-1}) \leq \sum_{i=m+1}^{n} \delta_i\delta_{i-1}\ldots\delta_{k_0}\|\varphi_{k_0}\|.$$

Let $\delta = max\left\{\delta_{k_0}, \delta_{k_{0+1}}, \ldots, \delta_n\right\}$. So, it satisfies $\|u_n - u_m\| \leq \frac{1-\delta^{n-m}}{1-\delta}\delta^{m-k_0}\|\varphi_{k_0}\|$. Because for $0 < \partial_i < 1$, it implies $\|u_n - u_m\| \to 0$. Hence, $\{u_n\}$ is a Cauchy sequence. □

a Fractional Differential Transformation Method for solving BSFM

If the second partial derivative of (S,τ) is substituted by $\frac{1}{h^2}(v(S-h,\tau) - 2v(S,\tau) + v(S+h,\tau)) + O(h^2)$ and the first partial derivative on (S,τ) is substituted by $\frac{1}{h}(v(S+h,\tau) - V(S,\tau)$, this is obtained:

$$m\frac{\partial^{2\gamma} v}{\partial \tau^{2\gamma}} + (1+mk)\frac{\partial^{\gamma} v}{\partial \gamma} = \frac{1}{h^2}(v(S-h,\tau) - 2v(S,\tau) + v(S+h,\tau)) + O\left(h^2\right) + \frac{(k-1)}{h}(v(S+h,\tau) - V(S-h,\tau) + O(h) - kv,$$

Then, the interval $[a,b]$ is divided into n subintervals of the same length, denoted by $h = \frac{b-a}{n}$.

So, we obtain *mesh points* $S_i = a + ih$, $i = 1,2,\ldots,n-1$. If the truncation error is removed and $u_i(t)$ is an approximate solution of $v_i(\tau) = v(S_i,\tau)$, then we will obtain a system of ordinary differential equations:

$$\begin{aligned} &m\frac{d^{2\gamma}u_i(\tau)}{d\tau^{2\gamma}} + (1+mk_1)\frac{d^{\gamma}u_i(\tau)}{d\gamma} \\ &= \frac{1}{h^2}(u_{i-1}(\tau) - 2u_i(\tau) + u_{i+1}(\tau)) + \frac{(k_1-1)}{h}((u_{i+1}(\tau) - u_i(\tau)) \\ &-k_1u_i(\tau)),\ i = 1,2,\ldots,n-1. \end{aligned} \quad (3)$$

The system of ordinary differential equations above will be solved using the Fractional Differential Transformation method. Suppose the solution to the system of differential equations above is:

$$u_i(t) = \sum_{k=0}^{\infty} U_i^{\alpha}(k)t^{k\alpha}, \quad (4)$$

where U_i^{α} is the unknown coefficient, i.e., the Fractional Differential Transformation of $u_i(t)$.

Based on Theorem 3, Equation (3) can be written as:

$$\begin{aligned} m\frac{\Gamma(k\alpha+2\gamma+1)}{\Gamma(k\alpha+1)}\ & U_i^{\alpha}\left(k+\tfrac{2\gamma}{\alpha}\right) + (1+mk_1)\frac{\Gamma(k\alpha+\gamma+1)}{\Gamma(k\alpha+1)}U_i^{\alpha}\left(k+\tfrac{\gamma}{\alpha}\right) \\ & = \frac{1}{h^2}\left(U_{i-1}^{\alpha}(k) - 2U_i^{\alpha}(k) + U_{i+1}^{\alpha}(k)\right) + \frac{(k_1-1)}{h}\left(U_{i+1}^{\alpha}(k) - U_i^{\alpha}(k)\right) \\ & -k_1U_i^{\alpha}(k)) \end{aligned} \quad (5)$$

with initial conditions:

$$U_i^{\alpha}(0) = f_1(x_1) \quad (6)$$

$$U_i^{\alpha}\left(\frac{1}{\alpha}\right) = f_2(x_1) \quad (7)$$

and with boundary conditions:

$$U_0^{\alpha}(k) = G_1^{\alpha}(k) \quad (8)$$

$$U_N^{\alpha}(k) = G_2^{\alpha}(k) \tag{9}$$

So, Equations (5)–(9) can be written as the new equation, as follows:

$$\begin{aligned} U_i^{\alpha}\left(k+\frac{2\gamma}{\alpha}\right) &= \frac{\Gamma(k\alpha+1)}{\Gamma(k\alpha+2+1)}\Big(\frac{U_{i-1}^{\alpha}(k)-2U_i^{\alpha}(k)+U_{i+1}^{\alpha}(k)}{mh^2} \\ &+\frac{(k_1-1)}{mh}\left(\left(U_{i+1}^{\alpha}(k)-U_i^{\alpha}(k)\right)-k_1U_i^{\alpha}(k)\right)\Big) \\ &-(1+mk_1)\frac{\Gamma(k\alpha+\gamma+1)}{\Gamma(k\alpha+1)}U_i^{\alpha}\left(k+\frac{\gamma}{\alpha}\right) \end{aligned} \tag{10}$$

with initial conditions:

$$U_i^{\alpha}(0) = f_1(x_1),$$

$$U_i^{\alpha}\left(\frac{1}{\alpha}\right) = f_2(x_1),$$

satisfying the boundary conditions:

$$U_0^{\alpha}(k) = G_1^{\alpha}(k),$$

$$U_N^{\alpha}(k) = G_2^{\alpha}(k).$$

Based on Equation (5) with unknown coefficients $U_i^{\alpha}(1),\ U_i^{\alpha}(2),\ldots,U_i^{\alpha}\left(\frac{2\gamma}{\alpha}-1\right)$, we can satisfy the following equation:

$$U_i^{\alpha}(k) = \begin{cases} \frac{1}{\Gamma(k\alpha+1)} & \left[\frac{d^{k\alpha}}{dt^{k\alpha}}\right]_{t=0} \quad if\ k\alpha \in \mathbb{Z}^+, \\ 0 & \quad if\ k\alpha \notin \mathbb{Z}^+. \end{cases} \tag{11}$$

4. BSFM Solution Using the Fractional Differential Transformation Method

The following will show that the Fractional Differential Transformation method can be used to find solutions to the modified Fractional Black–Scholes equation.

Example 1. *Solve the following modified Fractional Black–Scholes equation:*

$$\frac{\partial^{2\gamma}v}{\partial\tau^{2\gamma}} + 2\frac{\partial^{\gamma}v}{\partial\tau^{\gamma}} = \frac{\partial^2 v}{\partial S^2} + \frac{\partial v}{\partial S} - 2v;\ 0<\gamma<1,\ 0<S<1$$

with initial conditions:

$$v(0,\tau) = e^{-2\tau},\ v(1,\tau) = e^{1-2\tau},\ v(S,0) = \max(e^S-1,0),\ v_\tau(S,0) = 2e^S.$$

Solution:

Given that $\gamma = 0.75$, $\alpha = 0.25$, and $h = 0.1$,

$\frac{\partial^{1.5}v(S,\tau)}{\partial\tau^{1.5}}$ is fractionally differentially transformed into $\frac{\Gamma(k\alpha+2\gamma+1)}{\Gamma(k\alpha+1)}U_i^{0.25}(k+6)$ $= \frac{\Gamma(0.25k+2.5)}{\Gamma(0.25k+1)}U_i^{0.25}(k+6)$,

$\frac{\partial^{0.75}v(S,\tau)}{\partial\tau^{0.75}}$ is fractionally differentially transformed into $\frac{\Gamma(k\alpha+2\gamma+1)}{\Gamma(k\alpha+1)}U_i^{0.25}(k+3)$ $= \frac{\Gamma(0.25k+1.75)}{\Gamma(0.25k+1)}U_i^{0.25}(k+3)$,

$$v(S,\tau) \to U_i^{0.25}(k),$$

$\frac{\partial^2 v}{\partial S^2}$ is fractionally differentially transformed into $\frac{U_{i-1}^{0.25}(k)-2U_i^{0.25}(k)+U_{i+1}^{0.25}(k)}{h^2}$,

$\frac{\partial v}{\partial S}$ is fractionally differentially transformed into $\frac{(U_{i+1}^{0.25}(k)-U_{i-1}^{0.25}(k)}{2h}$,

with initial conditions:

$v(S,0) = \max(e^S - 1, 0)$ is fractionally differentially transformed into $U_i^{0.25}(0) = \max(e^{S_i} - 1, 0)$, for each $i = 0, 1, 2, \ldots, 10$.

Based on Equations (4), (5) and (8) above, we obtain:

$U_i^{0.25}(1) = U_i^{0.25}(2) = U_i^{0.25}(3) = U_i^{0.25}(5) = 0$; for each $i = 0, 1, 2, \ldots, 10$.

Based on Equations (4), (5) and (9), the following system of equations is obtained:

$$v(0,\tau) = e^{-2\tau} \text{ is fractionally differentially transformed into } U_0^{0.25}(k) = \begin{cases} \frac{2.(-2)^{\frac{k}{4}}}{\Gamma\left(\frac{k}{4}+1\right)}, \; if \; \frac{k}{4} \in \mathbb{Z}^+ \\ 0, \; if \; \frac{k}{4} \notin \mathbb{Z}^+ \end{cases},$$

$$v(1,\tau) = e^{1-2\tau} \text{ is fractionally differentially transformed into } U_{10}^{0.25}(k) = \begin{cases} \frac{2.(-2)^{\frac{k}{4}}.e}{\Gamma\left(\frac{k}{4}+1\right)}, \; if \; \frac{k}{4} \in \mathbb{Z}^+ \\ 0, \; if \; \frac{k}{4} \notin \mathbb{Z}^+ \end{cases},$$

$$U_i^{0.25}(k+6) = \frac{1}{m}\left\{\frac{U_{i-1}^{0.25}(k) - 2U_i^{0.25}(k) + U_{i+1}^{0.25}(k)}{h^2} + (k_1 - 1)\frac{\left(U_{i+1}^{0.25}(k) - U_{i-1}^{0.25}(k)\right.}{2h} - k_1 U_i^{0.25}(k)\right\} - (1 + mk_1)\frac{\Gamma(0.25k + 1.75)}{\Gamma(0.25k + 1)} U_i^{0.25}(k+3),$$

$S_0 = 0$, we obtain $u_0(t) = \sum_{k=0}^{\infty} U_0^{0.25}(k)t^{0.25k} = m\sum_{k=0}^{\infty} U_0^{0.25}(k)t^{0.25k} = 2\sum_{k=0}^{\infty} U_0^{0.25}(k)t^{0.25k} = U_0^{0.25}(0) + U_0^{0.25}(1)t^{0.25} + U_0^{0.25}(2)t^{0.5} + U_0^{0.25}(3)t^{0.75} + \cdots = 2 + 0t^{0.25} + 0t^{0.5} + 0t^{0.75} - 4t + 0t^{5.0.25} + 0t^{6.0.25} + 0t^{7.0.25} + 2t^2 - \frac{4}{3}t^3 + \frac{4}{3}t^4 - \frac{32}{120}t^5 + \cdots = \sum_{4m}^{\infty} \frac{(-2)^{\frac{k}{4}}}{\Gamma\left(\frac{k}{4}+1\right)} t^{0.25.k}, m = 0, 1, 2, \ldots$

$$S_0 = 0 - 2t = -2t$$

$S_1 = 0.1$, we obtain $u_1(t) = \sum_{k=0}^{\infty} U_1^{0.25}(k)t^{0.25k} = U_1^{0.25}(0) + U_1^{0.25}(1)t^{0.25} + U_1^{0.25}(2)t^{0.5} + U_1^{0.25}(3)t^{0.75} + \cdots = max\{e^{0.1} - 1, 0\} + 0t^{0.25} + 0t^{0.5} + \cdots - 2e^{0.1}t + \cdots = e^{0.1} - 1 - 2e^{0.1}t + \cdots$

$S_2 = 0.2$ we obtain $u_2(t) = \sum_{k=0}^{\infty} U_2^{0.25}(k)t^{0.25k} = U_2^{0.25}(0) + U_2^{0.25}(1)t^{0.25} + U_2^{0.25}(2)t^{0.5} + U_2^{0.25}(3)t^{0.75} + \cdots = \max(e^{0.2} - 1, 0) + 0t^{0.5} + \cdots - 2e^{0.2}t^{0.75} + \cdots = e^{0.2} - 1 - 2e^{0.2}t + \cdots$

$$S_3 = 0.3 \rightarrow u_3(t) = e^{0.3} - 1 - 2e^{0.3}t + \cdots$$

$$S_4 = 0.4 \rightarrow u_4(t) = e^{0.4} - 1 - 2e^{0.4}t + \cdots$$

$$S_5 = 0.5 \rightarrow u_5(t) = e^{0.5} - 1 - 2e^{0.5}t + \cdots$$

$$S_6 = 0.6 \rightarrow u_5(t) = e^{0.6} - 1 - 2e^{0.6}t + \cdots$$

$$S_7 = 0.7 \rightarrow u_6(t) = e^{0.7} - 1 - 2e^{0.7}t + \cdots$$

$$S_8 = 0.8 \rightarrow u_8(t) = e^{0.8} - 1 - 2e^{0.8}t + \cdots$$

$$S_9 = 0.9 \rightarrow u_9(t) = e^{0.9} - 1 - 2e^{0.9}t + \cdots$$

$S_{10} = 1$, we obtain $u_{10}(t) = \sum_{k=0}^{\infty} U_{10}^{0.25}(k)t^{0.25k} = U_{10}^{0.25}(0) + U_{10}^{0.25}(1)t^{0.25} + U_{10}^{0.25}(2)t^{0.5} + U_{10}^{0.25}(3)t^{0.75} + \cdots S_{10} = 1 \rightarrow u_{10}(t) = e - 1 - 2et + \cdots$

The following is a simulation using the Python program to illustrate the solutions obtained:

Figure 1 shows the graph for solving the modified Black–Scholes fractional equation with $n = 5$ and $t = 0.01$. The resulting graph increases monotonically, but it seems not to be smooth due to a wide interval partition and a few number of sampled points taken. The minimum value is obtained when $S_i = 0$, so $u_i = 0$, while the maximum value is obtained when $S_i = 1.0$, so $u_i = 1.6$. and $t = 0.025$.

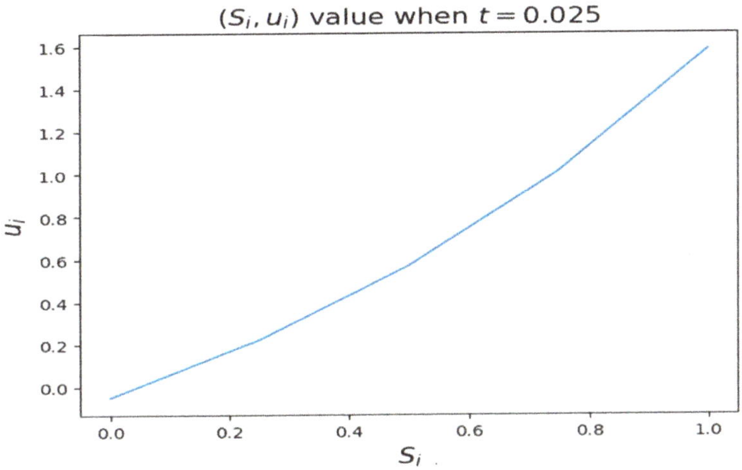

Figure 1. Graph of the solution to the Modified Fractional Black–Scholes equation with $n = 5$ and $t =$ 0.025.

Figure 2 shows a graph of the solution to the modified Fractional Black–Scholes equation, with $n = 25$ and $t = 0.025$. The solution graph obtained is a monotonically increasing function, but it is relatively smooth compared to the graph in Figure 1.

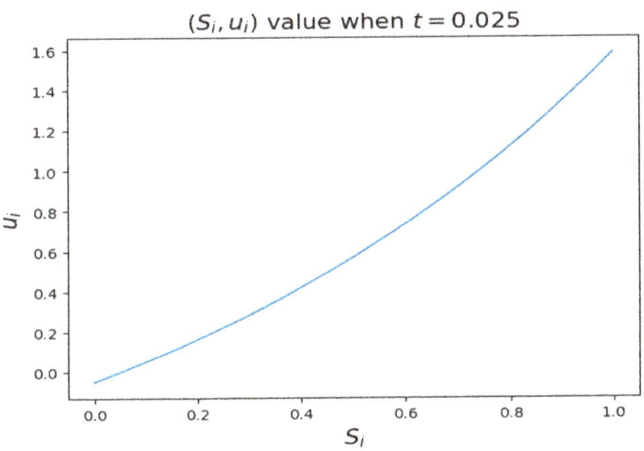

Figure 2. Graph of the solution to the modified Fractional Black–Scholes equation with $n = 25$ and $t = 0.025$.

Example 2. *The following is the procedure for determining the solution of the modified Fractional Black–Scholes equation:*

$$m\frac{\partial^{2\gamma}v}{\partial\tau^{2\gamma}}+(1+mk_1)\frac{\partial^{\gamma}v}{\partial\tau^{\gamma}}=\frac{\partial^2 v}{\partial S^2}+(k_1-1)\frac{\partial v}{\partial S}-k_1 v;$$

with initial conditions:

$$v(S,0)=\frac{e^x-1}{(1+mk_1)}$$

$$v_i(S,0)=\frac{k_1e^x}{(1+mk_1)}$$

$$v(0,\tau)=\frac{\left(1-e^{-k_1\tau}\right)}{(1+mk_1)}$$

$$v(1,\tau)=\frac{\left(2e-e^{1-k_1\tau}-1\right)}{(1+mk_1)}.$$

Suppose we take $\gamma=1.0$ and $\alpha=0.25$, then we obtain the following:
$\frac{\partial^2 v(S,\tau)}{\partial\tau^2}$ is transformed into $\frac{\Gamma(0.25k+3)}{\Gamma(0.25k+1)}U^{0.25}(k+8)$,
$\frac{\partial v}{\partial\tau}$ is transformed into $\frac{\Gamma(0.25k+2)}{\Gamma(0.25k+1)}U^{0.25}(k+4)$,
$\frac{\partial v}{\partial\tau}$ is transformed into $\frac{\left(U_i^{0.25}(k)-U_{i-1}^{0.25}(k)\right)}{2h}$,
$v(S,\tau)$ is transformed into $U_i^{0.25}(k)$. Then, we successively obtain:

$$v(S,0)=\frac{e^S-1}{(1+mk_1)}=U_i^{0.25}(0),$$

for each $i=0,\ 1,\ 2,\ldots,\ 10$:

$$v_i(S,0)=\frac{k_1e^S}{(1+mk_1)}=U_i^{0.25}(4),$$

for each $i=0,\ 1,\ 2,\ldots,\ 10$. Meanwhile, based on Equation (11), the following is obtained:

$$U_i^{0.25}(1)=U_i^{0.25}(2)=U_i^{0.25}(3)=U_i^{0.25}(5)=\cdots=0, v(0,\tau)=\frac{1-e^{-k_1\tau}}{(1+mk_1)},$$

transformed into:

$$U_0^{0.25}(k)=\begin{cases}\frac{1}{1+mk_1}\quad\frac{k_1^{\frac{k}{4}}}{\Gamma\left(\frac{k}{4}+1\right)}, & if\ \frac{k}{4}\in\mathbb{Z}^+\\ 0, & if\ \frac{k}{4}\notin\mathbb{Z}^+\end{cases}.$$

For $S_0=0$, we obtain:

$$\begin{aligned}&u_0(\tau)=\textstyle\sum_{k=0}^{\infty}U_0^{0.25}(k)\tau^{0.25k}\\&=U_0^{0.25}(0)+U_0^{0.25}(1)\tau^{0.25}+U_0^{0.25}(2)\tau^{0.5}+U_0^{0.25}(3)\tau^{0.75}+U_0^{1}(4)\tau^{1}+\cdots\\&=0+0\tau^{0.25}+0\tau^{0.5}+0\tau^{0.75}+\left(\tfrac{k_1}{1+mk_1}\right)\tau=\tfrac{k_1\tau}{1+mk_1}\end{aligned}$$

For $S_1=0.1$, we obtain:

$$\begin{aligned}&u_1(\tau)=\textstyle\sum_{k=0}^{\infty}U_1^{0.25}(k)\tau^{0.25k}\\&=U_1^{0.25}(0)+U_1^{0.25}(1)\tau^{0.25}+U_1^{0.25}(2)\tau^{0.5}+U_1^{0.25}(3)\tau^{0.75}+U_1^{1}(4)\tau^{1}+\cdots\\&=\tfrac{e^{0.1}-1}{1+mk_1}+0\tau^{0.25}+0\tau^{0.5}+0\tau^{0.75}+\tfrac{k_1e^{0.1}}{1+mk_1}\tau\\&=\tfrac{e^{0.1}-1}{1+mk_1}+\tfrac{k_1e^{0.1}}{1+mk_1}\tau\end{aligned}$$

For $S_2 = 0.2$, we obtain:

$$u(\tau) = \sum_{k=0}^{\infty} U_2^{0.25}(k)\tau^{0.25k}$$
$$= U_2^{0.25}(0) + U_2^{0.25}(1)\tau^{0.25} + U_2^{0.25}(2)\tau^{0.5} + U_2^{0.25}(3)\tau^{0.75} + U_2^{1}(4)\tau^{1} + \cdots$$
$$= \frac{e^{0.2}-1}{1+mk_1} + \frac{k_1 e^{0.2}}{1+mk_1}\tau$$

For $S_3 = 0.3$, we obtain

$$u_3(\tau) = \sum_{k=0}^{\infty} U_3^{0.25}(k)\tau^{0.25k}$$
$$= U_3^{0.25}(0) + U_3^{0.25}(1)\tau^{0.25} + U_3^{0.25}(2)\tau^{0.5} + U_3^{0.25}(3)\tau^{0.75} + U_3^{1}(4)\tau^{1} + \cdots$$
$$= \frac{e^{0.3}-1}{1+mk_1} + \frac{k_1 e^{0.3}}{1+mk_1}\tau$$
$$\cdots$$

For $S_{10} = 1$, we obtain $u_{10}(\tau) = \frac{e-1}{1+mk_1} + \frac{k_1 e}{1+mk_1}\tau$. So, we obtain the points (S_i, u_i) for $i = 0, 1, 2, 3, \ldots, 10$. Accordingly, the graph of the solution is as follows.

According to Figure 3, a graph of the solution to the Fractional Black–Scholes equation is obtained, modified with the values $0 \leq m \leq 1$ and $k_1 = 0.05$ in the form of a family of exponential functions. When $m = 0$, the graph is at the bottom. Meanwhile, when $m = 1$, the graph is at the top.

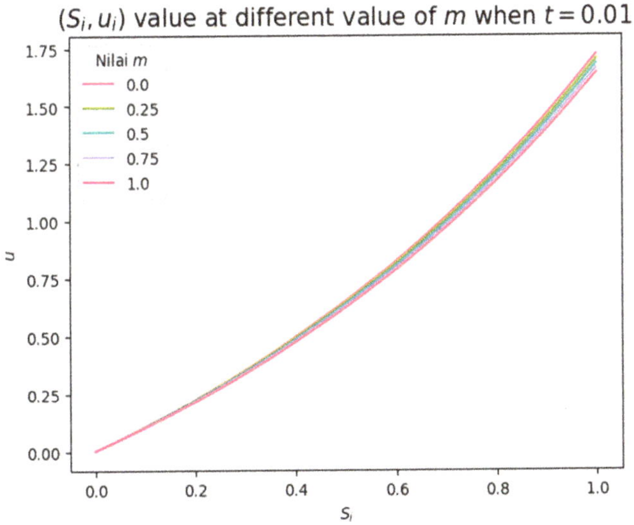

Figure 3. Graph of the solution to the Fractional Black–Scholes equation with $0 \leq m \leq 1$ and $k_1 = 0.05$.

Figure 4 shows that the solution to the Fractional Black–Scholes equation is modified in the form of an exponential function. The minimum value is obtained when $S_i = 0$, with a value of $u_i = 0$. Meanwhile, the maximum value is obtained when $S_i = 1$, with a value of $u_i = 1.75$. Furthermore, based on Equation (2), the Fractional Black–Scholes equation is a special case of the Fractional Black–Scholes equation when the value of $m = 0$.

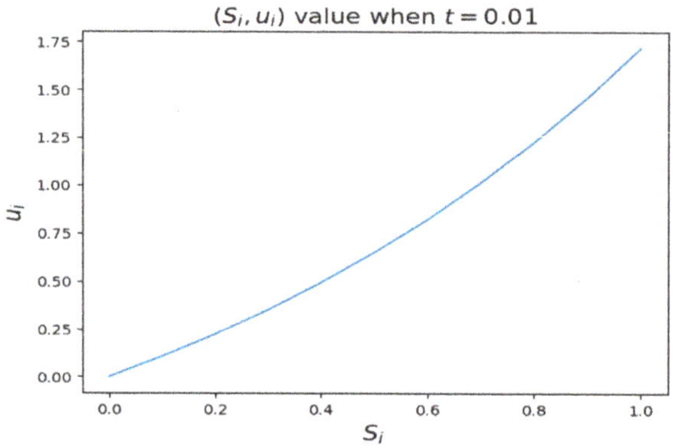

Figure 4. Graph of the solution to the Fractional Black–Scholes equation. modified with $t = 0.01$, $\gamma = 1.0$, $k = 0.05$, $n = 10$, $m = 0$, and $0 \leq S_i \leq 1$.

The general form of the Fractional Black–Scholes equation with a value of $\gamma = 1.0$ is:

$$\frac{\partial v}{\partial \tau} = \frac{\partial^2 v}{\partial S^2} + (k-1)\frac{\partial v}{\partial S} - kv$$

with the initial condition $v(S,0) = \max\{e^x - 1,\ 0\}$. Using the Daftardar–Gejji method, the general solution is:

$v(S,\tau) = \sum_{n=0}^{\infty} v_n(S,\tau) = \max\{e^S - 1,\ 0\}E_{1.0}(-k_1\tau) + \max\{e^x,\ 0\}(1 - E_{1.0}(-k_1\tau)$. If the graph is plotted, it is obtained as follows:

Figure 5 shows that the solution to the Fractional Black–Scholes equation can be approximated using the Fractional Black–Scholes equation solution by taking the value of $m = 0$. This is because, in Figure 5, the pink and blue graphs almost coincide. Thus, the solution error is guaranteed to be very small. The following is the error calculation between the solution of the Fractional Black–Scholes equation and the solution of the modified Fractional Black–Scholes equation:

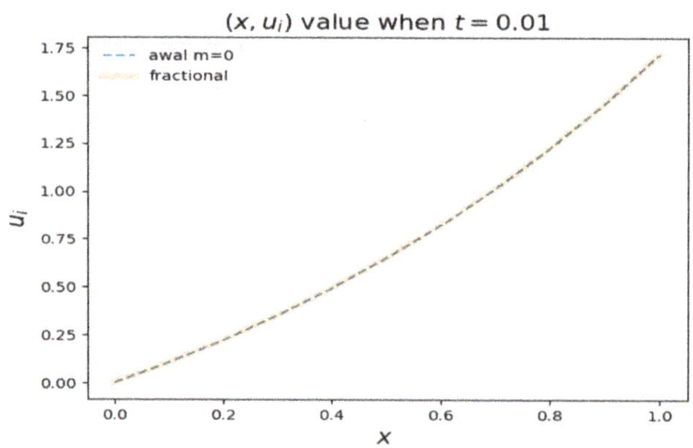

Figure 5. Graph of the solution to the Fractional Black–Scholes equation and the solution to the modified Fractional Black–Scholes equation by taking $k_1 = 0.05$.

Symbol v_i represents the solution to the Fractional Black–Scholes equation, while the symbol u_i represents the solution to the modified Fractional Black–Scholes equation. The values are $k_1 = 0.05$, $\gamma = 1.0$, and $\tau = 0.01$. Table 1 uses the absolute error formula

$= \frac{|v_i - u_i|}{v_i} \times 100\%$ and squared error $= \sum_{i=1}^{n} (v_i - u_i)^2$. Table 1 shows that the squared error and the absolute error for each point is very small. Using Phyton 3.7 software, it is obtained that the mean squared error is $2.1214603575846715 \times 10^{-7}$, and the mean absolute error is 0.049973388247889494%. This means that the solution to the modified Fractional Black–Scholes equation, taking the value s of $m = 0$ and $\gamma = 1.0$, is a very good approximation to the solution to the Fractional Black–Scholes equation with $\gamma = 1.0$. In other words, the Fractional Black–Scholes equation is a special case of the modified Fractional Black–Scholes equation when the value of $m = 0$.

Table 1. Error between v_i and u_i.

No	x_i	v_i	u_i	Squared Error	Abs Error (%)
1	0.100	0.105671	0.105724	2.778390×10^{-9}	0.049882
2	0.109	0.115662	0.115720	3.330000×10^{-9}	0.049892
3	0.118	0.125744	0.125807	3.937190×10^{-9}	0.049901
4	0.127	0.135917	0.135985	4.601382×10^{-9}	0.049908
...	...	...	...	...	...
96	0.964	1.622664	1.623475	6.580569×10^{-7}	0.049992
97	0.973	1.646370	1.647193	6.774279×10^{-7}	0.049992
98	0.982	1.670290	1.671125	6.972588×10^{-7}	0.049993
99	0.991	1.694427	1.695274	7.175589×10^{-7}	0.049993
100	1.000	1.718782	1.719641	7.383379×10^{-7}	0.049993

Moreover, v_i and u_i are compared using the 4th order Rungge–Kutta method. As is known, the Runge–Kutta method is a very accurate method for solving ordinary differential equations numerically. In this paper, the solution to the Fractional Black–Scholes equation, with the value of $\alpha = 1$, will be approached using the 4th order Runge–Kutta method.

Using Python 3.7 software, Figure 6 shows a graph of the solution to the Fractional Black–Scholes equation with $\gamma = 1.0$ using the 4th order Runge–Kutta method in three dimensions with $0 \leq S \leq 1$ and $0 \leq \tau \leq 1$. If the graph in Figure 6 is cut by $\tau = 0.01$, it will obtain Figure 7.

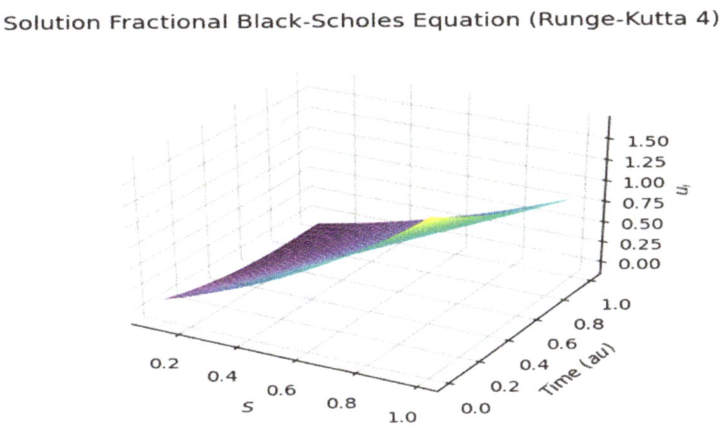

Figure 6. Graph of the solution to the Fractional Black–Scholes Equation with $\gamma = 1.0$ using the 4th order Runge–Kutta method.

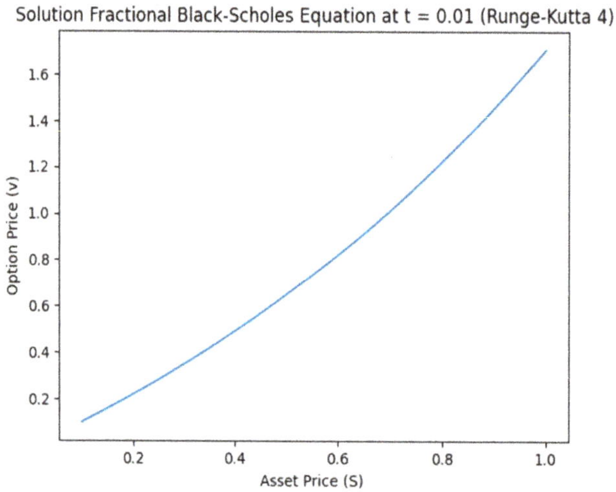

Figure 7. Graph of the solution to the Fractional Black–Scholes equation with $\gamma = 1.0$ using the Runge–Kutta method when $\tau = 0.01$.

Using Python 3.7 software, Figure 7 shows a graph of the solution to the Fractional Black–Scholes equation with $\gamma = 1.0$ when $\tau = 0.01$. The resulting graph is an increasing function graph. Then, if the solution graph for the Fractional Black–Scholes equation with $\gamma = 1.0$, obtained using the combined method of finite difference and fractional differential transformation, along with the graph using the 4th order Runge–Kutta method, are combined into one graph, Figure 8 will be obtained, as shown below.

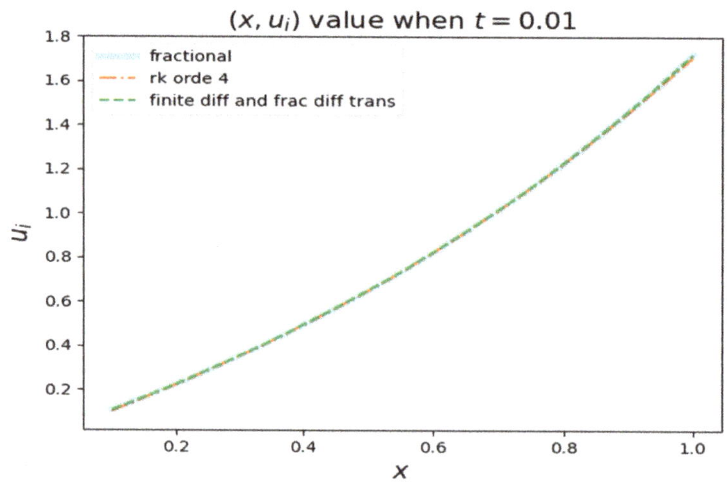

Figure 8. Graph of the combined solution method to the Fractional Black–Scholes equation with $\gamma = 1.0$ when $t = 0.01$.

The graph in blue is a solution to the Fractional Black–Scholes equation, the graph in yellow is an approximate graph of the solution to the Fractional Black–Scholes equation using the 4th order Runge–Kutta method, while the graph in green is an approximation using a combined method of finite difference and fractional differential transformation. Visually, the combined graph between these methods almost coincides. This means that both the 4th order Runge–Kutta method and the combined method of finite difference and fractional differential transformation are good approximations for graphing solutions to the Fractional Black–Scholes equation with $\gamma = 1.0$. Therefore, the error obtained by the 4th order Runge–Kutta method and the combination of finite difference and fractional differential transformation are compared to the solution of the Fractional Black–Scholes equation with $\gamma = 1.0$, as shown in Table 2 below:

Table 2. Error between v_i and RK4.

No	x_i	v_i	RK4	Squared Error	Abs Error (%)
1	0.100	0.105671	0.099972	0.000032	5.700230
2	0.109	0.115662	0.110417	0.000028	4.750148
3	0.118	0.125744	0.120956	0.000023	3.958334
4	0.127	0.135917	0.131507	0.000019	3.353538
...	...	...	...	...	...
96	0.964	1.622664	1.613694	0.000080	0.555898
97	0.973	1.646370	1.636458	0.000098	0.605712
98	0.982	1.670290	1.659431	0.000118	0.654394
99	0.991	1.694427	1.682425	0.000144	0.713348
100	1.000	1.718782	1.705629	0.000173	0.771142

Table 2 shows that the squared error and absolute error for each point are very small. Using Python 3.7 software, the mean squared error was $1.3939683876496377 \times 10^{-5}$, and the mean absolute error was 0.6089656268506086%. Based on the mean squared error and mean absolute error, it can be said that the resulting error is very small, being less than 5%. Therefore, it can be concluded that the 4th order Runge–Kutta method is a very good approximation. When comparing with Table 1, the mean absolute error and mean squared error caused by the combination of the finite difference method and fractional differential transformation are smaller than those of the 4th order Runge–Kutta method. However, both methods are said to be very good for approaching the solution to the Fractional Black–Scholes equation with $\gamma = 1.0$.

5. Conclusions

The combined method of finite difference and fractional differential transformation can be used to solve the modified Fractional Black–Scholes equation. In real financial market conditions, the Black–Scholes equation is more realistic to use for modeling option values compared to the Fractional Black–Scholes equation. This is because the fractional order of the modified Fractional Black–Scholes equation is greater than the order of the Fractional Black–Scholes equation and can vary the value of m.

6. Further Research

There is a lot of research that can be done on the modified Fractional Black–Scholes equation; for example, looking for guarantees of existence and unique solutions. Then, the analytical solution of the Fractional Black–Scholes equation can be modified. Next, conducting error comparisons between the numerical and analytical solutions would be valuable. Other interesting things can also be developed for the Fractional Black–Scholes equation with multiple assets.

Author Contributions: Conceptualization, A.S. and E.R.; methodology, S. and E.C.; soft-ware, A.S. and S.; validation, E.R. and E.C.; formal analysis, A.S.; investigation, E.R., S. and E.C.; resources, A.S.; data curation, E.R.; writing—original draft preparation, A.S. and E.R.; writing—review and editing, E.R., S. and E.C.; visualization, A.S.; supervision, E.R., S. and E.C.; project administration, E.R.; funding acquisition, S. and E.C. All authors have read and agreed to the published version of the manuscript.

Funding: KEMENDIKBUDRISTEKDIKTI PDD2023. No Kontrak Turunan DRPM: 3018/UN6.3.1/PT.00/2023.

Data Availability Statement: Data are contained within the article.

Acknowledgments: The work was supported by Hibah Dikti Year 2023 through Program Doctoral Dissertation Research (PDD 2023) with contract Number 3018/UN6.3.1/PT.00/2023, and the APC was funded by Universitas Padjadjaran.

Conflicts of Interest: The authors declare no conflict of interest.

References

1. Tagliani, A.; Milev, M. Laplace Transform and finite difference methods for the Black–Scholes equation. *Appl. Math. Comput.* **2013**, *220*, 649–658. [CrossRef]
2. Kumar, S.; Yildirim, A.; Khan, Y.; Jafari, H.; Sayevand, K.; Wei, L. Analytical solution of fractional Black-Scholes European option pricing equation by using Laplace transform. *J. Fract. Calc. Appl.* **2012**, *2*, 1–9.
3. Elbeleze, A.A.; Kılıçman, A.; Taib, B.M. Homotopy Perturbation Method for Fractional Black-Scholes European Option Pricing Equations Using Sumudu Transform. *Math. Probl. Eng.* **2013**, *2013*, 524852. [CrossRef]
4. Khan, W.; Ansari, F. European Option Pricing of Fractional Black-Scholes Model Using Sumudu Transform and its Derivatives. *Gen. Lett. Math.* 2016; 1, 74–80. [CrossRef]
5. Kaya, F.; Yilmaz, Y. Basic properties of Sumudu transformation and its application to some partial differential equations. *Sak. Univ. J. Sci.* **2019**, *23*, 509–514. [CrossRef]
6. Ahmed, S.A.; Elzaki, T.M.; Elbadri, M.; Mohamed, M.Z. Solution of partial differential equations by new double integral transform (Laplace—Sumudu transform). *Ain Shams Eng. J.* **2021**, *12*, 4045–4049. [CrossRef]
7. Yavuz, M.; Özdemir, N. A different approach to the European option pricing model with new fractional operator. *Math. Model. Nat. Phenom.* **2018**, *13*, 12. [CrossRef]
8. Uddin, M.; Taufiq, M. Approximation of time fractional Black-Scholes equation via radial kernels and transformations. *Fract. Differ. Calc.* **2011**, *9*, 75–90. [CrossRef]
9. Atangana, A.; Bildik, N. Existence and Numerical Solution of the Volterra Fractional Integral Equations of the Second Kind. *Math. Probl. Eng.* **2013**, *2013*, 981526. [CrossRef]
10. Naghipour, A.; Manafian, J. Application of the Laplace Adomian Decomposition and Implicit Methods for Solving Burgers' equation. *TWMS J. Pure Appl. Math.* **2015**, *6*, 68–77.
11. Lin, S.; He, X.-J. A regime switching fractional Black–Scholes model and European option pricing. *Commun. Nonlinear Sci. Numer. Simul.* **2020**, *85*, 105222. [CrossRef]
12. Fan, C.; Chen, P. Numerical Method for a System of PIDEs Arising in American Contingent Claims under FMLS Model with Jump Diffusion and Regime-Switching Process. *Discret. Dyn. Nat. Soc.* **2021**, *2021*, 8818876. [CrossRef]
13. Hu, Y.; Dong, H.; Fu, L.; Zhai, J. Fractional Stochastic Volatility Pricing of European Option Based on Self-Adaptive Differential Evolution. *J. Math. Finance* **2022**, *12*, 547–565. [CrossRef]
14. Fadugba, S.E.; Edeki, S.O. Homotopy Analysis Method for Fractional Barrier Option PDE. *J. Phys. Conf. Ser.* **2022**, *2199*, 012008. [CrossRef]
15. Fadugba, S.E. Homotopy analysis method and its applications in the valuation of European call options with time-fractional Black-Scholes equation. *Chaos Solitons Fractals* **2020**, *141*, 110351. [CrossRef]
16. Zhou, S.; Li, W.; Wei, Y.; Wen, C. A Positivity-Preserving Numerical Scheme for Nonlinear Option Pricing Models. *J. Appl. Math.* **2012**, *2012*, 205686. [CrossRef]
17. Koleva, M.N. Positivity Preserving Numerical Method for Non-linear Black-Scholes Models. In *Numerical Analysis and Its Applications*; Dimov, I., Faragó, I., Vulkov, L., Eds.; Lecture Notes in Computer Science; Springer: Berlin/Heidelberg, Germany, 2013; Volume 8236, pp. 363–370. [CrossRef]
18. Hajipour, M.; Malek, A. High accurate modified WENO method for the solution of Black–Scholes equation. *Comput. Appl. Math.* **2014**, *34*, 125–140. [CrossRef]
19. Cen, Z.; Huang, J.; Xu, A. A posteriori grid method for a time-fractional Black-Scholes equation. *AIMS Math.* **2022**, *7*, 20962–20978. [CrossRef]
20. Sugandha, A.; Rusyaman, E.; Sukono; Carnia, E. A New Solution to the Fractional Black–Scholes Equation Using the Daftardar-Gejji Method. *Mathematics* **2023**, *11*, 4887. [CrossRef]
21. Erturk, V.S.; Momani, S.; Odibat, Z. Application of generalized differential transform method to multi-order fractional differential equations. *Commun. Nonlinear Sci. Numer. Simul.* **2008**, *13*, 1642–1654. [CrossRef]
22. Sahraee, Z.; Arabameri, M. A Semi-Discretization Method Based on Finite Difference and Differential Transform Methods to Solve the Time-Fractional Telegraph Equation. *Symmetry* **2023**, *15*, 1759. [CrossRef]

mathematics

MDPI

Article

A Study of Some New Hermite–Hadamard Inequalities via Specific Convex Functions with Applications

Moin-ud-Din Junjua [1], Ather Qayyum [2,*], Arslan Munir [3], Hüseyin Budak [4], Muhammad Mohsen Saleem [5] and Siti Suzlin Supadi [2]

[1] School of Mathematical Sciences, Zhejiang Normal University, Jinhua 321004, China; moinuddin@zjnu.edu.cn
[2] Institute of Mathematical Sciences, Universiti Malaya, Kuala Lumpur 50603, Malaysia; suzlin@um.edu.my
[3] Department of Mathematics, COMSATS University Islamabad, Sahiwal Campus, Sahiwal 57000, Pakistan; munirarslan999@gmail.com
[4] Department of Mathematics, Faculty of Science and Arts, Düzce University, Düzce 81620, Türkiye; hsyn.budak@gmail.com
[5] Department of Mathematics, Pakistan International College Jeddah, Jeddah 23342, Saudi Arabia; mohsenkamboh@gmail.com
* Correspondence: dratherqayyum@um.edu.my

Abstract: Convexity plays a crucial role in the development of fractional integral inequalities. Many fractional integral inequalities are derived based on convexity properties and techniques. These inequalities have several applications in different fields such as optimization, mathematical modeling and signal processing. The main goal of this article is to establish a novel and generalized identity for the Caputo–Fabrizio fractional operator. With the help of this specific developed identity, we derive new fractional integral inequalities via exponential convex functions. Furthermore, we give an application to some special means.

Keywords: exponential convex function; fractional integrals; Hölder's inequality; power-mean inequality

MSC: 26A33; 26D07; 26D10; 26D15

1. Introduction

Fractional calculus has gained significant recognition and application in various areas of mathematics. These contemporary developments in fractional calculus reflect the growing interest in exploring fractional derivatives and integrals to address complex problems in various fields. Fractional derivatives have become a powerful mathematical tool for researchers, enabling them to formulate more accurate models [1–3]. As a result, researchers across various scientific and engineering disciplines continue to rely on both Caputo and Riemann Liouville fractional derivatives to better understand and model complex phenomena (see [4]). The use of innovative fractional general operators of distinct, local, and nonlocal kernels has also been studied by other authors [5].

Moreover, fractional integrals have found practical applications across a diverse range engineering and science fields, such as electromagnetic studies, photoelasticity, fluid mechanics, electrochemistry, biological population modeling, optics, and signal processing. On the other side, the theory of convexity has been proven to have many potential applications in a wide range of research fields including, coding theory, machine learning, and data science. Convex mapping is arguably the most fundamental and significant mapping method in the theory of mathematical inequality since it has vast applications in mechanics [6], statistics [7], pure and applied mathematics [8], and economics [9]. The well-known definition of a convex function [10] is given below.

$$\hat{G}(\Lambda\psi + (1-\Lambda)\pi) \leq \Lambda\hat{G}(\psi) + (1-\Lambda)\hat{G}(\pi),$$

for all $\psi, \pi \in I$ and $\Lambda \in [0,1]$.

Theorem 1 ([11]). *Suppose the function $\hat{G} : I \subset \mathbb{R} \to \mathbb{R}$ is a convex mapping defined on I, where $\psi, \pi \in I$ with $\psi < \pi$, then*

$$\hat{G}\left(\frac{\psi+\pi}{2}\right) \leq \frac{1}{\pi-\psi}\int_{\psi}^{\pi} \hat{G}(x)dx \leq \frac{\hat{G}(\psi)+\hat{G}(\pi)}{2}.$$

This inequality, known as the Hermite–Hadamard inequality, was established by C. Hermite and J. Hadamard. For more information concerning the Hermite–Hadamard inequality, see [12]. Hermite–Hadamard and trapezoidal inequalities have recently been established by Sarikaya et al. [13] using Riemann–Liouville fractional integrals. Several authors have used different classes of function to generalizes the Hermite–Hadmard-type inequality. Additionally, a number of mathematicians have developed Hermite–Hadmard-type inequality inequalities for differentiable convex mappings [14], s-convex functions [15], m-convex mappings [16], and Green's functions [17]. Numerous scholars have presented applications for fractional operators, see, for example [18,19]. Kadakal and Iscan gave a new description for the exponential-type convex function [20]. Additionally, they again demonstrated the Hermite–Hadamard inequalities in [20] using the definition given below.

Definition 1 ([20]). *$\hat{G} : I \to \mathbb{R}$ is said to be an exponential convex function if the inequality*

$$\hat{G}(\Lambda\psi + (1-\Lambda)\pi) \leq \left(e^{\Lambda}-1\right)\hat{G}(\psi) + \left(e^{1-\Lambda}-1\right)\hat{G}(\pi),$$

holds for all $\psi, \pi \in I$ and $\Lambda \in [0,1]$.

Definition 2 ([21]). *The function $\hat{G} : I \subseteq R \to R_0 = [0,\infty)$ is said to be an s-convex function if the inequality*

$$\hat{G}(\Lambda\psi + (1-\Lambda)\pi) \leq \Lambda^s\hat{G}(\psi) + (1-\Lambda)^s\hat{G}(\pi),$$

holds for all $\psi, \pi \in I$, $s \in (0,1]$ and $\Lambda \in [0,1]$.

Theorem 2. *The function $\hat{G} : [\psi,\pi] \to \mathbb{R}$ is an exponential function. If $\psi < \pi$ and $\hat{G} \in L[\psi,\pi]$, then*

$$\frac{1}{(2\sqrt{e}-1)}\hat{G}\left(\frac{\psi+\pi}{2}\right) \leq \frac{1}{\pi-\psi}\int_{\psi}^{\pi} \hat{G}(x)dx \leq (e-2)\left(\hat{G}(\psi)+\hat{G}(\pi)\right).$$

Hölder's inequality is indeed a fundamental inequality in mathematics, particularly in the context of L_p spaces. İşcan introduced a new form of Hölder's inequality in [22] which is given below. Suppose $p > 1$ and $\frac{1}{p}+\frac{1}{q} = 1$. If $\hat{G}$ and g are real functions defined on $[\psi,\pi]$ and if $|\hat{G}|^p$ and $|g|^q$ are integrable on $[\psi,\pi]$, we have

$$\begin{aligned}\int_{\psi}^{\pi} |\hat{G}(x)g(x)|dx \leq\ & \frac{1}{\pi-\psi}\Bigg[\left(\int_{\psi}^{\pi}(\pi-x)|\hat{G}(x)|^p dx\right)^{\frac{1}{p}}\left(\int_{\psi}^{\pi}(\pi-x)|g(x)|^q dx\right)^{\frac{1}{q}} \\ & +\left(\int_{\psi}^{\pi}(x-\psi)|\hat{G}(x)|^p dx\right)^{\frac{1}{p}}\left(\int_{\psi}^{\pi}(x-\psi)|g(x)|^q dx\right)^{\frac{1}{q}}\Bigg].\end{aligned}$$

The development of the Hölder–İşcan inequality and its use in obtaining better upper bounds demonstrates the ongoing progress and innovation in mathematical inequalities.

Different authors have used fractional operators to generalize the Hermite–Hadamard inequality. In this context, we confine our focus to the Caputo–Fabrizio fractional integral operator. The distinguishing factors between these operators lie in their singularities and local characteristics, with the operator's kernel expression involving functions such as the power law, the exponential function, or a Mittag–Leffler function. Notably, the Caputo–Fabrizio operator stands out due to its kernel-lacking singularity. The key characteristic of this operator is best described as a real power transformed into an integer through the Laplace transformation, thereby facilitating the straightforward derivation of exact solutions for various problems. Xiaobin Wang et al. [23] presented the Hermite–Hadmard-type inequality for modified h-convex functions utilizing a Caputo–Fabrizio integral operator. Butt et al. [24] exponentially obtained different inequalities for s- and (s,m)-convex functions using Caputo fractional integrals and derivatives. Furthermore, Abbasi et al. [25] constructed new variants of the Hermite–Hadamard-type inequalities for s-convex functions via a Caputo–Fabrizio integral operator. Li et al. [26] proved analogous inequalities for strongly convex functions. In 2015, Caputo and Fabrizio introduced the Caputo–Fabrizio fractional operator as follows:

Definition 3 ([27]). *Let $H^1(\psi,\pi)$ be the Sobolev space of order one defined as*

$$H^1(\psi,\pi) = \left\{\hat{G} \in L^2(\psi,\pi) : \hat{G}' \in L^2(\psi,\pi)\right\},$$

where

$$L^2(\psi,\pi) = \left\{\hat{G}(z) : \left(\int_\psi^\pi \hat{G}^2(z)dz\right)^{\frac{1}{2}} < \infty\right\}.$$

Let $\hat{G} \in H^1(\psi,\pi)$, where $\psi < \pi$ and $\alpha \in [0,1]$; the nth notion of left derivative in the sense of Caputo–Fabrizio is defined as

$$\left({}_{\psi}^{CFD}D^\alpha \hat{G}\right)(x) = \frac{\beta(\alpha)}{1-\alpha}\int_\psi^x \hat{G}'(\Lambda)e^{\frac{-\alpha(x-\Lambda)^\alpha}{1-\alpha}}d\Lambda,$$

$x > \alpha$ and the associated integral operator is

$$\left({}_{\psi}^{CF}I^\alpha \hat{G}\right)(x) = \frac{1-\alpha}{\beta(\alpha)}\hat{G}(x) + \frac{\alpha}{\beta(\alpha)}\int_\psi^x \hat{G}(\Lambda)d\Lambda,$$

where $\beta(\alpha) > 0$ is the normalization function satisfying $\beta(0) = \beta(1) = 1$. For $\alpha = 0$ and $\alpha = 1$, the left derivative is, respectively, defined as follows

$$\begin{aligned}\left({}_{\psi}^{CFD}D^0 \hat{G}\right)(x) &= \hat{G}'(x) \\ \left({}_{\psi}^{CFD}D^1 \hat{G}\right)(x) &= \hat{G}(x) - \hat{G}(\psi).\end{aligned}$$

For the right derivative operator

$$\left({}_{\pi}^{CFD}D^\alpha \hat{G}\right)(x) = \frac{\beta(\alpha)}{1-\alpha}\int_x^\pi \hat{G}'(\Lambda)e^{\frac{-\alpha(\Lambda-x)^\alpha}{1-\alpha}}d\Lambda,$$

$x < \pi$ and the associated integral operator is

$$\left({}^{CF}I_\pi^\alpha \hat{G}\right)(x) = \frac{1-\alpha}{\beta(\alpha)}\hat{G}(x) + \frac{\alpha}{\beta(\alpha)}\int_x^\pi \hat{G}(\Lambda)d\Lambda.$$

In [10], Nasir et al. presented the following trapezoidal-type inequalities for the Caputo–Fabrizio fractional operator.

Theorem 3. *The function $\hat{G} : [\psi, \pi] \to \mathbb{R}$ is a differentiable function on I, where $\psi, \pi \in I$ with $\psi < \pi$. If $|\hat{G}'|$ is s-convex on $[\psi, \pi]$ and some $s \in (0,1]$, $\Lambda \in [0,1]$, then the following inequality holds*

$$\begin{aligned}&\Bigg|\frac{\hat{G}(\psi)+\hat{G}(\pi)}{2}+\frac{4(1-\alpha)}{\beta(\alpha)}\\&-\frac{\beta(\alpha)}{\alpha(\pi-\psi)}\left[\left(\left({}^{CF}_{\psi}I^{\alpha}\hat{G}\right)(k)+\left({}^{CF}I^{\alpha}_{\frac{\psi+\pi}{2}}\hat{G}\right)(k)\right)+\left({}^{CF}_{\frac{\psi+\pi}{2}}I^{\alpha}\hat{G}\right)(k)\left({}^{CF}I^{\alpha}_{\pi}\hat{G}\right)(k)\right]\Bigg|\\ \le\ &\frac{\pi-\psi}{4}\left(\frac{2se^{\ln(2)s}+1}{2^s(s+1)(s+2)}+\frac{\beta(s+1,s)}{2^s}\right)\left[|\hat{G}'(\pi)|+|\hat{G}'(\psi)|\right].\end{aligned}$$

In [28], Sahoo obtained new error bounds for the midpoint-type inequality via the s-convex function given below:

Theorem 4. *The function $\hat{G} : [\psi, \pi] \to \mathbb{R}$ is a differentiable function on I, where $\psi, \pi \in I$ with $\psi < \pi$. If $|\hat{G}'|$ is s-convex on $[\psi, \pi]$ and some $s \in (0,1]$, $\Lambda \in [0,1]$, then*

$$\begin{aligned}&\left|\frac{\beta(\alpha)}{\alpha(\pi-\psi)}\left[\left({}^{CF}_{\frac{\psi+\pi}{2}-}I^{\alpha}\hat{G}\right)(k)+\left({}^{CF}I^{\alpha}_{\frac{\psi+\pi}{2}+}\hat{G}\right)(k)\right]-\hat{G}\left(\frac{\psi+\pi}{2}\right)-\frac{(1-\alpha)}{\beta(\alpha)}(\hat{G}(\psi)+\hat{G}(\pi))\right|\\ \le\ &\frac{\pi-\psi}{4}\left(\frac{\hat{G}'(\psi)+\hat{G}'(\pi)}{2}\right).\end{aligned}$$

Motivated by ongoing research in recent years on the generalizations of Hermite–Hadamard-type inequalities for different convex functions and the Caputo–Fabrizio fractional integral operator. We established a new identity for the Caputo-Fabrizio fractional integral operator and the functions whose absolute value of the second derivative is convex. By using this identity, we obtained several new Hermite–Hadmard-type inequalities to derive several new fractional inequalities for exponential convex functions. This paper is structured as follows: In Section 1, we delve into the established definitions and outcomes pertaining to the Caputo–Fabrizio fractional integral. Section 2 introduces novel Hermite–Hadamard-type inequalities concerning the fractional operator. Moving on to Section 3, we explore intriguing applications linked to special means. Lastly, Section 4 encompasses the conclusion along with prospects for future research.

2. Main Results

Here, we first establish a general identity for the famous fractional operator (Caputo–Fabrizio) and then use the following identity which plays a central role to develop new inequalities. It is expected that the obtained inequality in this section will point to novel developments in the field of fractional integrals. In addition, by putting specific values of $\vartheta = 1$ in the auxiliary result, we will obtain a variety of valuable results which were previously obtained.

Lemma 1. *The function $\hat{G} : I^o \subset \mathbb{R} \to \mathbb{R}$ is a differentiable function on I^o, where $\psi, \pi \in I^o$ with $\psi < \pi$ and $\vartheta \in N$. If $\hat{G}'' \in L[\psi, \pi]$ and $\Lambda \in [0,1]$, then*

$$\begin{aligned}&\sum_{i=0}^{\vartheta-1}\frac{1}{2\vartheta}\left[\hat{G}\left(\frac{(\vartheta-i)\psi+i\pi}{\vartheta}\right)+\hat{G}\left(\frac{(\vartheta-i-1)\psi+(i+1)\pi}{\vartheta}\right)\right]\\&-\frac{\beta(\alpha)}{\alpha(\pi-\psi)}\left[\left({}^{CF}_{\psi}I^{\alpha}\hat{G}\right)(k)+\left({}^{CF}I^{\alpha}_{\pi}\hat{G}\right)(k)\right]+\frac{2(1-\alpha)}{\beta(\alpha)}\hat{G}(k)\\=\ &\sum_{i=0}^{\vartheta-1}\frac{(\pi-\psi)^2}{2\vartheta^3}\left[\int_0^1\Lambda(1-\Lambda)\hat{G}''\left(\Lambda\frac{(\vartheta-i)\psi+i\pi}{\vartheta}+(1-\Lambda)\frac{(\vartheta-i-1)\psi+(i+1)\pi}{\vartheta}\right)d\Lambda\right].\end{aligned}\tag{1}$$

Proof. Using integration by parts, we obtain

$$\begin{aligned}
\Omega_i &= \int_0^1 \Lambda(1-\Lambda)\hat{G}''\left(\Lambda\frac{(\vartheta-i)\psi+i\pi}{\vartheta}+(1-\Lambda)\frac{(\vartheta-i-1)\psi+(i+1)\pi}{\vartheta}\right)d\Lambda \\
&= \frac{\vartheta}{\psi-\pi}\left(\Lambda-\Lambda^2\right)\hat{G}'\left(\Lambda\frac{(\vartheta-i)\psi+i\pi}{\vartheta}+(1-\Lambda)\frac{(\vartheta-i-1)\psi+(i+1)\pi}{\vartheta}\right)\Bigg|_0^1 \\
&\quad -\frac{\vartheta}{\psi-\pi}\int_0^1(1-2\Lambda)\hat{G}'\left(\Lambda\frac{(\vartheta-i)\psi+i\pi}{\vartheta}+(1-\Lambda)\frac{(\vartheta-i-1)\psi+(i+1)\pi}{\vartheta}\right)d\Lambda \\
&= \frac{\vartheta}{\pi-\psi}\int_0^1(1-2\Lambda)\hat{G}'\left(\Lambda\frac{(\vartheta-i)\psi+i\pi}{\vartheta}+(1-\Lambda)\frac{(\vartheta-i-1)\psi+(i+1)\pi}{\vartheta}\right)d\Lambda \\
&= \frac{\vartheta}{\pi-\psi}\left(\frac{\vartheta(1-2\Lambda)}{\psi-\pi}\hat{G}\left(\Lambda\frac{(\vartheta-i)\psi+i\pi}{\vartheta}+(1-\Lambda)\frac{(\vartheta-i-1)\psi+(i+1)\pi}{\vartheta}\right)\Bigg|_0^1\right. \\
&\quad \left.+\frac{2\vartheta}{\psi-\pi}\int_0^1\hat{G}'\left(\Lambda\frac{(\vartheta-i)\psi+i\pi}{\vartheta}+(1-\Lambda)\frac{(\vartheta-i-1)\psi+(i+1)\pi}{\vartheta}\right)d\Lambda\right) \\
&= \frac{\vartheta^2}{(\pi-\psi)^2}\left(\hat{G}\left(\Lambda\frac{(\vartheta-i)\psi+i\pi}{\vartheta}+(1-\Lambda)\frac{(\vartheta-i-1)\psi+(i+1)\pi}{\vartheta}\right)\right) \\
&\quad -\frac{2\vartheta^2}{(\pi-\psi)^2}\int_0^1\hat{G}'\left(\Lambda\frac{(\vartheta-i)\psi+i\pi}{\vartheta}+(1-\Lambda)\frac{(\vartheta-i-1)\psi+(i+1)\pi}{\vartheta}\right)d\Lambda \\
&= \frac{\vartheta^2}{(\pi-\psi)^2}\left(\hat{G}\left(\Lambda\frac{(\vartheta-i)\psi+i\pi}{\vartheta}+(1-\Lambda)\frac{(\vartheta-i-1)\psi+(i+1)\pi}{\vartheta}\right)\right)-\frac{2\vartheta^3}{(\pi-\psi)^3}\int_{\frac{(\vartheta-i)\psi+i\pi}{\vartheta}}^{\frac{(\vartheta-i-1)\psi+(i+1)\pi}{\vartheta}}\hat{G}(u)du.
\end{aligned} \tag{2}$$

By multiplying by $\frac{(\pi-\psi)^3\alpha}{2\vartheta^3\beta(\alpha)}$ with the equality in (2) and subtracting $\frac{2(1-\alpha)}{\Lambda\beta(\alpha)}\hat{G}(k)$, we obtain

$$\begin{aligned}
&\Omega_i\frac{(\pi-\psi)^3\alpha}{2\vartheta^3\beta(\alpha)}-\frac{2(1-\alpha)}{\Lambda\beta(\alpha)}\hat{G}(k) \\
&= \frac{\vartheta^2}{(\pi-\psi)^2}\frac{(\pi-\psi)^3\alpha}{2\vartheta^3\beta(\alpha)}\left(\hat{G}\left(\Lambda\frac{(\vartheta-i)\psi+i\pi}{\vartheta}+(1-\Lambda)\frac{(\vartheta-i-1)\psi+(i+1)\pi}{\vartheta}\right)\right) \\
&\quad -\frac{\alpha}{\beta(\alpha)}\int_{\frac{(\vartheta-i)\psi+i\pi}{\vartheta}}^{\frac{(\vartheta-i-1)\psi+(i+1)\pi}{\vartheta}}\hat{G}(u)du-\frac{2(1-\alpha)}{\Lambda\beta(\alpha)}\hat{G}(k) \\
&= \frac{(\pi-\psi)\alpha}{2\vartheta\beta(\alpha)}\left(\hat{G}\left(\Lambda\frac{(\vartheta-i)\psi+i\pi}{\vartheta}+(1-\Lambda)\frac{(\vartheta-i-1)\psi+(i+1)\pi}{\vartheta}\right)\right) \\
&\quad -\frac{\alpha}{\beta(\alpha)}\int_{\frac{(\vartheta-i)\psi+i\pi}{\vartheta}}^{\frac{(\vartheta-i-1)\psi+(i+1)\pi}{\vartheta}}\hat{G}(u)du-\frac{2(1-\alpha)}{\Lambda\beta(\alpha)}\hat{G}(k).
\end{aligned}$$

Consequently, we have

$$\begin{aligned}
&\sum_{i=0}^{\vartheta-1}\Omega_i\frac{(\pi-\psi)^3\alpha}{2\vartheta^3\beta(\alpha)}-\frac{2(1-\alpha)}{\beta(\alpha)}\hat{G}(k) \\
&= \sum_{i=0}^{\vartheta-1}\frac{(\pi-\psi)\alpha}{2\vartheta\beta(\alpha)}\left(\hat{G}\left(\Lambda\frac{(\vartheta-i)\psi+i\pi}{\vartheta}+(1-\Lambda)\frac{(\vartheta-i-1)\psi+(i+1)\pi}{\vartheta}\right)\right) \\
&\quad -\frac{\alpha}{\beta(\alpha)}\int_\psi^\pi\hat{G}(u)du-\frac{2(1-\alpha)}{\beta(\alpha)}\hat{G}(k) \\
&= \sum_{i=0}^{\vartheta-1}\frac{(\pi-\psi)\alpha}{2\vartheta\beta(\alpha)}\left(\hat{G}\left(\Lambda\frac{(\vartheta-i)\psi+i\pi}{\vartheta}+(1-\Lambda)\frac{(\vartheta-i-1)\psi+(i+1)\pi}{\vartheta}\right)\right) \\
&\quad -\left(\frac{\alpha}{\beta(\alpha)}\int_\psi^k\hat{G}(u)du-\frac{(1-\alpha)}{\beta(\alpha)}\hat{G}(k)+\frac{\alpha}{\beta(\alpha)}\int_k^\pi\hat{G}(u)du-\frac{(1-\alpha)}{\beta(\alpha)}\hat{G}(k)\right) \\
&= \sum_{i=0}^{\vartheta-1}\frac{(\pi-\psi)\alpha}{2\vartheta\beta(\alpha)}\left(\hat{G}\left(\Lambda\frac{(\vartheta-i)\psi+i\pi}{\vartheta}+(1-\Lambda)\frac{(\vartheta-i-1)\psi+(i+1)\pi}{\vartheta}\right)\right) \\
&\quad -\left[\left({}^{CF}_{\psi}I^{\alpha}\hat{G}\right)(k)+\left({}^{CF}I^{\alpha}_{\pi}\hat{G}\right)(k)\right].
\end{aligned}$$

Thus, we have

$$\begin{aligned}
&\sum_{i=0}^{\vartheta-1}\frac{1}{2\vartheta}\left[\hat{G}\left(\frac{(\vartheta-i)\psi+i\pi}{\vartheta}\right)+\hat{G}\left(\frac{(\vartheta-i-1)\psi+(i+1)\pi}{\vartheta}\right)\right]\\
&-\frac{\beta(\alpha)}{\alpha(\pi-\psi)}\left[\left({}_{\psi}^{CF}I^{\alpha}\hat{G}\right)(k)+\left({}^{CF}I_{\pi}^{\alpha}\hat{G}\right)(k)\right]+\frac{2(1-\alpha)}{\beta(\alpha)}\hat{G}(k)\\
=&\sum_{i=0}^{\vartheta-1}\frac{(\pi-\psi)^2}{2\vartheta^3}\left[\int_0^1\Lambda(1-\Lambda)\hat{G}''\left(\Lambda\frac{(\vartheta-i)\psi+i\pi}{\vartheta}+(1-\Lambda)\frac{(\vartheta-i-1)\psi+(i+1)\pi}{\vartheta}\right)d\Lambda\right].
\end{aligned}$$

Thus, the proof of Lemma 1 is complete. □

Corollary 1. *If we set $\vartheta=1$ into Lemma 1, we then obtain*

$$\begin{aligned}
&\frac{\hat{G}(\psi)+\hat{G}(\pi)}{2}-\frac{\beta(\alpha)}{\alpha(\pi-\psi)}\left[\left({}_{\psi}^{CF}I^{\alpha}\hat{G}\right)(k)+\left({}^{CF}I_{\pi}^{\alpha}\hat{G}\right)(k)\right]+\frac{2(1-\alpha)}{\beta(\alpha)}\hat{G}(k) \qquad (3)\\
=&\frac{(\pi-\psi)^2}{2}\int_0^1\Lambda(1-\Lambda)\hat{G}''(\Lambda\psi+(1-\Lambda)\pi)d\Lambda.
\end{aligned}$$

Remark 1. *If we set $\alpha=1$ and $\beta(0)=\beta(1)=1$ in Corollary 1, we then obtain*

$$\frac{\hat{G}(\psi)+\hat{G}(\pi)}{2}-\frac{1}{\pi-\psi}\int_{\psi}^{\pi}\hat{G}(x)dx=\frac{(\pi-\psi)^2}{2}\int_0^1\Lambda(1-\Lambda)\hat{G}''(\Lambda\psi+(1-\Lambda)\pi)d\Lambda,$$

which was obtained by Alomari et al. [11].

Corollary 2. *If we set $\vartheta=2$ into Lemma 1, we then have*

$$\begin{aligned}
&\frac{1}{2}\left(\frac{\hat{G}(\psi)+\hat{G}(\pi)}{2}+\hat{G}\left(\frac{\psi+\pi}{2}\right)\right)\\
&-\frac{\beta(\alpha)}{\alpha(\pi-\psi)}\left[\left({}_{\psi}^{CF}I^{\alpha}\hat{G}\right)(k)+\left({}^{CF}I_{\pi}^{\alpha}\hat{G}\right)(k)\right]+\frac{2(1-\alpha)}{\beta(\alpha)}\hat{G}(k) \qquad (4)\\
=&\frac{(\pi-\psi)^2}{16}\left[\int_0^1\Lambda(1-\Lambda)\hat{G}''\left(\Lambda\psi+(1-\lambda)\frac{\psi+\pi}{2}\right)d\Lambda\right.\\
&\left.+\int_0^1\Lambda(1-\Lambda)\hat{G}''\left(\Lambda\frac{\psi+\pi}{2}+(1-\Lambda)\pi\right)d\Lambda\right].
\end{aligned}$$

Remark 2. *If we set $\alpha=1$ and $\beta(0)=\beta(1)=1$ in Corollary 2, we then have*

$$\begin{aligned}
&\frac{1}{2}\left(\frac{\hat{G}(\psi)+\hat{G}(\pi)}{2}+\hat{G}\left(\frac{\psi+\pi}{2}\right)\right)-\frac{1}{\pi-\psi}\int_{\psi}^{\pi}\hat{G}(x)dx\\
=&\frac{(\pi-\psi)^2}{16}\left[\int_0^1\Lambda(1-\Lambda)\hat{G}''\left(\Lambda\psi+(1-\Lambda)\frac{\psi+\pi}{2}\right)d\Lambda\right.\\
&\left.+\int_0^1\Lambda(1-\Lambda)\hat{G}''\left(\Lambda\frac{\psi+\pi}{2}+(1-\Lambda)\pi\right)d\Lambda\right],
\end{aligned}$$

which was obtained by B.Y. et al. [29]. The above inequalities can also be proven by other fractional integral operators and convexity, for example, quasi-convex function, strongly quasi-convex function, etc.

Theorem 5. *Under the assumption of Lemma 1, if $|\hat{G}''|$ is an exponential convex function on $[\psi,\pi]$, then the following fractional inequality holds*

$$\left|\sum_{i=0}^{\mathring{\vartheta}-1} \frac{1}{2\mathring{\vartheta}}\left[\hat{G}\left(\frac{(\mathring{\vartheta}-i)\psi+i\pi}{\mathring{\vartheta}}\right)+\hat{G}\left(\frac{(\mathring{\vartheta}-i-1)\psi+(i+1)\pi}{\mathring{\vartheta}}\right)\right]\right.$$
$$\left.-\frac{\beta(\alpha)}{\alpha(\pi-\psi)}\left[\left({}^{CF}_{\psi}I^{\alpha}\hat{G}\right)(k)+\left({}^{CF}I^{\alpha}_{\pi}\hat{G}\right)(k)\right]+\frac{2(1-\alpha)}{\beta(\alpha)}\hat{G}(k)\right| \tag{5}$$
$$\leq \sum_{i=0}^{\mathring{\vartheta}-1} \frac{(\pi-\psi)^2}{\mathring{\vartheta}^3}\left(\frac{17}{6}-e\right)A\left(\hat{G}''\left|\frac{(\mathring{\vartheta}-i)\psi+i\pi}{\mathring{\vartheta}}\right|, \hat{G}''\left|\frac{(\mathring{\vartheta}-i-1)\psi+(i+1)\pi}{\mathring{\vartheta}}\right|\right),$$

where $A(\psi,\pi)$ is the arithmetic mean.

Proof. By using the Lemma 1, since $|\hat{G}''|$ is an exponential convex function, we have

$$\left|\sum_{i=0}^{\mathring{\vartheta}-1} \frac{1}{2\mathring{\vartheta}}\left[\hat{G}\left(\frac{(\mathring{\vartheta}-i)\psi+i\pi}{\mathring{\vartheta}}\right)+\hat{G}\left(\frac{(\mathring{\vartheta}-i-1)\psi+(i+1)\pi}{\mathring{\vartheta}}\right)\right]\right.$$
$$\left.-\frac{\beta(\alpha)}{\alpha(\pi-\psi)}\left[\left({}^{CF}_{\psi}I^{\alpha}\hat{G}\right)(k)+\left({}^{CF}I^{\alpha}_{\pi}\hat{G}\right)(k)\right]+\frac{2(1-\alpha)}{\beta(\alpha)}\hat{G}(k)\right|$$
$$\leq \sum_{i=0}^{\mathring{\vartheta}-1} \frac{(\pi-\psi)^2}{2\mathring{\vartheta}^3}\left[\int_0^1|\Lambda(1-\Lambda)|\left|\hat{G}''\left(\Lambda\frac{(\mathring{\vartheta}-i)\psi+i\pi}{\mathring{\vartheta}}+(1-\Lambda)\frac{(\mathring{\vartheta}-i-1)\psi+(i+1)\pi}{\mathring{\vartheta}}\right)\right|d\Lambda\right]$$
$$= \sum_{i=0}^{\mathring{\vartheta}-1} \frac{(\pi-\psi)^2}{2\mathring{\vartheta}^3}\left[\int_0^1\left|\Lambda-\Lambda^2\right|\left\{\left(e^{\Lambda}-1\right)\left|\hat{G}''\left(\frac{(\mathring{\vartheta}-i)\psi+i\pi}{\mathring{\vartheta}}\right)\right|\right|\right.$$
$$\left.+\left|\left(e^{1-\Lambda}-1\right)\left|\hat{G}''\left(\frac{(\mathring{\vartheta}-i-1)\psi+(i+1)\pi}{\mathring{\vartheta}}\right)\right|\right\}\right]d\Lambda$$
$$= \sum_{i=0}^{\mathring{\vartheta}-1} \frac{(\pi-\psi)^2}{2\mathring{\vartheta}^3}\left[\int_0^1\left|\Lambda-\Lambda^2\right|\left(e^{\Lambda}-1\right)\left|\hat{G}''\left(\frac{(\mathring{\vartheta}-i)\psi+i\pi}{\mathring{\vartheta}}\right)\right|d\Lambda\right.$$
$$\left.+\int_0^1\left|\Lambda-\Lambda^2\right|\left(e^{1-\Lambda}-1\right)\left|\hat{G}''\left(\frac{(\mathring{\vartheta}-i-1)\psi+(i+1)\pi}{\mathring{\vartheta}}\right)\right|d\Lambda\right]$$
$$\leq \sum_{i=0}^{\mathring{\vartheta}-1} \frac{(\pi-\psi)^2}{\mathring{\vartheta}^3}\left(\frac{17}{6}-e\right)A\left(\hat{G}''\left|\frac{(\mathring{\vartheta}-i)\psi+i\pi}{\mathring{\vartheta}}\right|, \hat{G}''\left|\frac{(\mathring{\vartheta}-i-1)\psi+(i+1)\pi}{\mathring{\vartheta}}\right|\right).$$

This completes the proof. □

Corollary 3. *If we set $\mathring{\vartheta}=1$ in Theorem 5, the following trapezoidal-type inequality holds*

$$\left|\frac{\hat{G}(\psi)+\hat{G}(\pi)}{2}-\frac{\beta(\alpha)}{\alpha(\pi-\psi)}\left[\left({}^{CF}_{\psi}I^{\alpha}\hat{G}\right)(k)+\left({}^{CF}I^{\alpha}_{\pi}\hat{G}\right)(k)\right]+\frac{2(1-\alpha)}{\beta(\alpha)}\hat{G}(k)\right|$$
$$\leq \frac{(\pi-\psi)^2}{2}\left(\frac{17}{6}-e\right)\left(|\hat{G}''(\psi)|+|\hat{G}''(\pi)|\right)$$

Corollary 4. *If we set $\mathring{\vartheta}=2$ in Theorem 5, the following Bullen-type inequality holds*

$$\left|\frac{1}{4}\left(\hat{G}(\psi)+2\hat{G}\left(\frac{\psi+\pi}{2}\right)+\hat{G}(\pi)\right)\right.$$
$$\left.-\frac{\beta(\alpha)}{\alpha(\pi-\psi)}\left[\left({}^{CF}_{\psi}I^{\alpha}\hat{G}\right)(k)+\left({}^{CF}I^{\alpha}_{\pi}\hat{G}\right)(k)\right]+\frac{2(1-\alpha)}{\beta(\alpha)}\hat{G}(k)\right|$$
$$\leq \frac{(\pi-\psi)^2}{8}\left(\frac{17}{6}-e\right)\left(\frac{|\hat{G}''(\pi)|+|\hat{G}''(\psi)|}{2}+\left|\hat{G}''\left(\frac{\psi+\pi}{2}\right)\right|\right)$$

Theorem 6. *Using the assumption in Lemma 1, if $|\hat{G}''|^q$ is an exponential convex function on $[\psi,\pi]$ and $q>1$, then*

$$
\begin{aligned}
&\left|\sum_{i=0}^{\vartheta-1}\frac{1}{2\vartheta}\left[\hat{G}\left(\frac{(\vartheta-i)\psi+i\pi}{\vartheta}\right)+\hat{G}\left(\frac{(\vartheta-i-1)\psi+(i+1)\pi}{\vartheta}\right)\right]\right. \\
&\left.-\frac{\beta(\alpha)}{\alpha(\pi-\psi)}\left[\left({}^{CF}_{\psi}I^{\alpha}\hat{G}\right)(k)+\left({}^{CF}I^{\alpha}_{\pi}\hat{G}\right)(k)\right]+\frac{2(1-\alpha)}{\beta(\alpha)}\hat{G}(k)\right| \\
\leq\;&\sum_{i=0}^{\vartheta-1}\frac{(\pi-\psi)^2}{2^{1-\frac{1}{q}}\vartheta^3}\beta^{\frac{1}{p}}(p+1,p+1)(e-2)^{\frac{1}{q}} \\
&\times A^{\frac{1}{q}}\left(\left|\hat{G}''\left(\frac{(\vartheta-i)\psi+i\pi}{\vartheta}\right)\right|^q,\left|\hat{G}''\left(\frac{(\vartheta-i-1)\psi+(i+1)\pi}{\vartheta}\right)\right|^q\right).
\end{aligned}
\tag{6}
$$

Proof. By employing Lemma 1, the modulus properties, and the Hölder inequality, since $|\hat{G}''|^q$ is an exponential convex function, we obtain

$$
\begin{aligned}
&\left|\sum_{i=0}^{\vartheta-1}\frac{1}{2\vartheta}\left[\hat{G}\left(\frac{(\vartheta-i)\psi+i\pi}{\vartheta}\right)+\hat{G}\left(\frac{(\vartheta-i-1)\psi+(i+1)\pi}{\vartheta}\right)\right]\right. \\
&\left.-\frac{\beta(\alpha)}{\alpha(\pi-\psi)}\left[\left({}^{CF}_{\psi}I^{\alpha}\hat{G}\right)(k)+\left({}^{CF}I^{\alpha}_{\pi}\hat{G}\right)(k)\right]+\frac{2(1-\alpha)}{\beta(\alpha)}\hat{G}(k)\right| \\
\leq\;&\sum_{i=0}^{\vartheta-1}\frac{(\pi-\psi)^2}{2\vartheta^3}\left[\int_0^1|\Lambda(1-\Lambda)|\left|\hat{G}''\left(\Lambda\frac{(\vartheta-i)\psi+i\pi}{\vartheta}+(1-\Lambda)\frac{(\vartheta-i-1)\psi+(i+1)\pi}{\vartheta}\right)\right|d\Lambda\right] \\
\leq\;&\sum_{i=0}^{\vartheta-1}\frac{(\pi-\psi)^2}{2\vartheta^3}\left[\left(\int_0^1\left|\Lambda-\Lambda^2\right|^p d\Lambda\right)^{\frac{1}{p}}\left\{\left(e^{\Lambda}-1\right)\left|\hat{G}''\left(\frac{(\vartheta-i)\psi+i\pi}{\vartheta}\right)\right|^q\right.\right. \\
&\left.\left.+\left(e^{1-\Lambda}-1\right)\left|\hat{G}''\left(\frac{(\vartheta-i-1)\psi+(i+1)\pi}{\vartheta}\right)\right|^q\right\}^{\frac{1}{q}}d\Lambda\right] \\
\leq\;&\sum_{i=0}^{\vartheta-1}\frac{(\pi-\psi)^2}{2^{1-\frac{1}{q}}\vartheta^3}\beta^{\frac{1}{p}}(p+1,p+1)(e-2)^{\frac{1}{q}} \\
&\times A^{\frac{1}{q}}\left(\left|\hat{G}''\left(\frac{(\vartheta-i)\psi+i\pi}{\vartheta}\right)\right|^q,\left|\hat{G}''\left(\frac{(\vartheta-i-1)\psi+(i+1)\pi}{\vartheta}\right)\right|^q\right).
\end{aligned}
$$

This completes the proof. □

Corollary 5. *If we set $\vartheta = 1$ in Theorem 6, the following trapezoidal-type inequality holds*

$$
\begin{aligned}
&\left|\frac{\hat{G}(\psi)+\hat{G}(\pi)}{2}-\frac{\beta(\alpha)}{\alpha(\pi-\psi)}\left[\left({}^{CF}_{\psi}I^{\alpha}\hat{G}\right)(k)+\left({}^{CF}I^{\alpha}_{\pi}\hat{G}\right)(k)\right]+\frac{2(1-\alpha)}{\beta(\alpha)}\hat{G}(k)\right| \\
\leq\;&\frac{(\pi-\psi)^2}{2^{1-\frac{1}{q}}}\beta^{\frac{1}{p}}(p+1,p+1)(e-2)^{\frac{1}{q}}\left(\frac{|\hat{G}''(\psi)|^q+|\hat{G}''(\pi)|^q}{2}\right)^{\frac{1}{q}}.
\end{aligned}
$$

Corollary 6. *If we set $\vartheta = 2$ in Theorem 6, the following Bullen-type inequality holds*

$$
\begin{aligned}
&\left|\frac{1}{4}\left(\hat{G}(\psi)+2\hat{G}\left(\frac{\psi+\pi}{2}\right)+\hat{G}(\pi)\right)\right. \\
&\left.-\frac{\beta(\alpha)}{\alpha(\pi-\psi)}\left[\left({}^{CF}_{\psi}I^{\alpha}\hat{G}\right)(k)+\left({}^{CF}I^{\alpha}_{\pi}\hat{G}\right)(k)\right]+\frac{2(1-\alpha)}{\beta(\alpha)}\hat{G}(k)\right| \\
\leq\;&\frac{(\pi-\psi)^2}{2^{4-\frac{1}{q}}}\beta^{\frac{1}{p}}(p+1,p+1)(e-2)^{\frac{1}{q}} \\
&\times\left[\left(\frac{|\hat{G}''(\psi)|^q+\left|\hat{G}''\left(\frac{\psi+\pi}{2}\right)\right|^q}{2}\right)^{\frac{1}{q}}+\left(\frac{\left|\hat{G}''\left(\frac{\psi+\pi}{2}\right)\right|^q+|\hat{G}''(\pi)|^q}{2}\right)^{\frac{1}{q}}\right].
\end{aligned}
$$

Theorem 7. *Using the assumption in Lemma 1, if $|\hat{G}''|^q$ is an exponential convex function on $[\psi, \pi]$ and $q \geq 1$, then*

$$\begin{aligned}&\left|\sum_{i=0}^{\vartheta-1}\frac{1}{2\vartheta}\left[\hat{G}\left(\frac{(\vartheta-i)\psi+i\pi}{\vartheta}\right)+\hat{G}\left(\frac{(\vartheta-i-1)\psi+(i+1)\pi}{\vartheta}\right)\right]\right.\\&\left.-\frac{\beta(\alpha)}{\alpha(\pi-\psi)}\left[\left({}_{\psi}^{CF}I^{\alpha}\hat{G}\right)(k)+\left({}^{CF}I_{\pi}^{\alpha}\hat{G}\right)(k)\right]+\frac{2(1-\alpha)}{\beta(\alpha)}\hat{G}(k)\right|\\&\leq\sum_{i=0}^{\vartheta-1}\frac{(\pi-\psi)^2}{12^{1-\frac{1}{q}}\vartheta^3}\left(\frac{17}{6}-e\right)^{\frac{1}{q}}\times A^{\frac{1}{q}}\left(\left|\hat{G}''\left(\frac{(\vartheta-i)\psi+i\pi}{\vartheta}\right)\right|^q,\left|\left(\hat{G}''\frac{(\vartheta-i-1)\psi+(i+1)\pi}{\vartheta}\right)\right|^q\right).\end{aligned} \tag{7}$$

Proof. By utilizing Lemma 1, modulus properties, and the power-mean inequality, since $|\hat{G}''|^q$ is an exponential convex function, we obtain

$$\begin{aligned}&\left|\sum_{i=0}^{\vartheta-1}\frac{1}{2\vartheta}\left[\hat{G}\left(\frac{(\vartheta-i)\psi+i\pi}{\vartheta}\right)+\hat{G}\left(\frac{(\vartheta-i-1)\psi+(i+1)\pi}{\vartheta}\right)\right]\right.\\&\left.-\frac{\beta(\alpha)}{\alpha(\pi-\psi)}\left[\left({}_{\psi}^{CF}I^{\alpha}\hat{G}\right)(k)+\left({}^{CF}I_{\pi}^{\alpha}\hat{G}\right)(k)\right]+\frac{2(1-\alpha)}{\beta(\alpha)}\hat{G}(k)\right|\\
\leq&\sum_{i=0}^{\vartheta-1}\frac{(\pi-\psi)^2}{2\vartheta^3}\left[\int_0^1|\Lambda(1-\Lambda)|\left|\hat{G}''\left(\Lambda\frac{(\vartheta-i)\psi+i\pi}{\vartheta}+(1-\Lambda)\frac{(\vartheta-i-1)\psi+(i+1)\pi}{\vartheta}\right)\right|d\Lambda\right]\\
\leq&\sum_{i=0}^{\vartheta-1}\frac{(\pi-\psi)^2}{2\vartheta^3}\left[\left(\int_0^1\left|\Lambda-\Lambda^2\right|d\Lambda\right)^{1-\frac{1}{q}}\left\{\int_0^1\left|\Lambda-\Lambda^2\right|\left(\left(e^{\Lambda}-1\right)\left|\hat{G}''\left(\frac{(\vartheta-i)\psi+i\pi}{\vartheta}\right)\right|^q\right.\right.\right.\\&\left.\left.\left.+\left(e^{1-\Lambda}-1\right)\hat{G}''\left|\frac{(\vartheta-i-1)\psi+(i+1)\pi}{\vartheta}\right|^q\right)d\Lambda\right\}^{\frac{1}{q}}\right]\\
=&\sum_{i=0}^{\vartheta-1}\frac{(\pi-\psi)^2}{2\vartheta^3}\left(\frac{1}{6}\right)^{1-\frac{1}{q}}\left[\int_0^1\left|\Lambda-\Lambda^2\right|\left(e^{\Lambda}-1\right)\left|\hat{G}''\left(\frac{(\vartheta-i)\psi+i\pi}{\vartheta}\right)\right|^q d\Lambda\right.\\&\left.+\int_0^1\left|\Lambda-\Lambda^2\right|\left(e^{1-\Lambda}-1\right)\left|\frac{(\vartheta-i-1)\psi+(i+1)\pi}{\vartheta}\right|^q d\Lambda\right]^{\frac{1}{q}}\\
=&\sum_{i=0}^{\vartheta-1}\frac{(\pi-\psi)^2}{12^{1-\frac{1}{q}}\vartheta^3}\left(\frac{17}{6}-e\right)^{\frac{1}{q}}\times A^{\frac{1}{q}}\left(\left|\hat{G}''\left(\frac{(\vartheta-i)\psi+i\pi}{\vartheta}\right)\right|^q,\left|\left(\hat{G}''\frac{(\vartheta-i-1)\psi+(i+1)\pi}{\vartheta}\right)\right|^q\right).\end{aligned}$$

This completes the proof. □

Remark 3. *Under the assumption in Theorem 7, if we set $q = 1$, we can obtain Theorem 5.*

Corollary 7. *If we set $\vartheta = 1$ in Theorem 7, the following trapezoidal-type inequality holds*

$$\begin{aligned}&\left|\frac{\hat{G}(\psi)+\hat{G}(\pi)}{2}-\frac{\beta(\alpha)}{\alpha(\pi-\psi)}\left[\left({}_{\psi}^{CF}I^{\alpha}\hat{G}\right)(k)+\left({}^{CF}I_{\pi}^{\alpha}\hat{G}\right)(k)\right]+\frac{2(1-\alpha)}{\beta(\alpha)}\hat{G}(k)\right|\\&\leq\frac{(\pi-\psi)^2}{12^{1-\frac{1}{q}}}\left(\frac{17}{6}-e\right)^{\frac{1}{q}}\left(\frac{|\hat{G}''(\psi)|^q+|\hat{G}''(\pi)|^q}{2}\right)^{\frac{1}{q}}.\end{aligned}$$

Corollary 8. *If we set $\vartheta = 2$ in Theorem 7, the following Bullen-type inequality holds*

$$\begin{aligned}&\left|\frac{1}{4}\left(\hat{G}(\psi)+2\hat{G}\left(\frac{\psi+\pi}{2}\right)+\hat{G}(\pi)\right)\right.\\&\left.-\frac{\beta(\alpha)}{\alpha(\pi-\psi)}\left[\left({}_{\psi}^{CF}I^{\alpha}\hat{G}\right)(k)+\left({}^{CF}I_{\pi}^{\alpha}\hat{G}\right)(k)\right]+\frac{2(1-\alpha)}{\beta(\alpha)}\hat{G}(k)\right|\\&\leq\frac{(\pi-\psi)^2}{12^{1-\frac{1}{q}}\times 8}\left(\frac{17}{6}-e\right)^{\frac{1}{q}}\left[\left(\frac{|\hat{G}''(\psi)|^q+\left|\hat{G}''\left(\frac{\psi+\pi}{2}\right)\right|^q}{2}\right)^{\frac{1}{q}}+\left|\left(\frac{\left|\hat{G}''\left(\frac{\psi+\pi}{2}\right)\right|^q+|\hat{G}''(\pi)|^q}{2}\right)^{\frac{1}{q}}\right|\right].\end{aligned}$$

Theorem 8. *Using the assumption in Lemma 1, if* $|\hat{G}''|^q$ *is s-convex function on* $[\psi, \pi]$ *and some* $s \in (0,1]$, *and* $q > 1$, *then the following holds*

$$\begin{aligned}
&\left|\sum_{i=0}^{\vartheta-1} \frac{1}{2\vartheta}\left[\hat{G}\left(\frac{(\vartheta-i)\psi+i\pi}{\vartheta}\right)+\hat{G}\left(\frac{(\vartheta-i-1)\psi+(i+1)\pi}{\vartheta}\right)\right]\right.\\
&\left.-\frac{\beta(\alpha)}{\alpha(\pi-\psi)}\left[\left({}^{CF}_{\psi}I^{\alpha}\hat{G}\right)(k)+\left({}^{CF}I^{\alpha}_{\pi}\hat{G}\right)(k)\right]+\frac{2(1-\alpha)}{\beta(\alpha)}\hat{G}(k)\right| \qquad (8)\\
\leq\ &\sum_{i=0}^{\vartheta-1} \frac{\pi-\psi}{2\vartheta^3}\beta^{\frac{1}{p}}(p+1,p+1)\left(\frac{1}{s+1}\right)^{\frac{1}{q}}\\
&\times\left(\hat{G}''\left|\frac{(\vartheta-i)\psi+i\pi}{\vartheta}\right|^q, \hat{G}''\left|\frac{(\vartheta-i-1)\psi+(i+1)\pi}{\vartheta}\right|^q\right)^{\frac{1}{q}}
\end{aligned}$$

Proof. By employing Lemma 1, modulus properties, and the Hölder inequality, since $|\hat{G}''|^q$ is an s-convex function, we obtain

$$\begin{aligned}
&\left|\sum_{i=0}^{\vartheta-1} \frac{1}{2\vartheta}\left[\hat{G}\left(\frac{(\vartheta-i)\psi+i\pi}{\vartheta}\right)+\hat{G}\left(\frac{(\vartheta-i-1)\psi+(i+1)\pi}{\vartheta}\right)\right]\right.\\
&\left.-\frac{\beta(\alpha)}{\alpha(\pi-\psi)}\left[\left({}^{CF}_{\psi}I^{\alpha}\hat{G}\right)(k)+\left({}^{CF}I^{\alpha}_{\pi}\hat{G}\right)(k)\right]+\frac{2(1-\alpha)}{\beta(\alpha)}\hat{G}(k)\right|\\
\leq\ &\sum_{i=0}^{\vartheta-1} \frac{(\pi-\psi)^2}{2\vartheta^3}\left[\int_0^1 |\Lambda(1-\Lambda)|\left|\hat{G}''\left(\Lambda\frac{(\vartheta-i)\psi+i\pi}{\vartheta}+(1-\Lambda)\frac{(\vartheta-i-1)\psi+(i+1)\pi}{\vartheta}\right)\right|d\Lambda\right]\\
\leq\ &\sum_{i=0}^{\vartheta-1} \frac{(\pi-\psi)^2}{2\vartheta^3}\left[\left(\int_0^1 \left|\Lambda-\Lambda^2\right|^p d\Lambda\right)^{\frac{1}{p}}\left\{\Lambda^s\left|\hat{G}''\left(\frac{(\vartheta-i)\psi+i\pi}{\vartheta}\right)\right|^q\right.\right.\\
&\left.\left.+(1-\Lambda)^s\left|\hat{G}''\left(\frac{(\vartheta-i-1)\psi+(i+1)\pi}{\vartheta}\right)\right|^q\right\}^{\frac{1}{q}}d\Lambda\right]\\
\leq\ &\sum_{i=0}^{\vartheta-1} \frac{\pi-\psi}{2\vartheta^3}\beta^{\frac{1}{p}}(p+1,p+1)\left(\frac{1}{s+1}\right)^{\frac{1}{q}}\\
&\times\left(\hat{G}''\left|\frac{(\vartheta-i)\psi+i\pi}{\vartheta}\right|^q, \hat{G}''\left|\frac{(\vartheta-i-1)\psi+(i+1)\pi}{\vartheta}\right|^q\right)^{\frac{1}{q}}.
\end{aligned}$$

Thus, the proof of Theorem 8 is complete. □

Corollary 9. *If we set* $s = 1$ *in Theorem 8, then*

$$\begin{aligned}
&\left|\sum_{i=0}^{\vartheta-1} \frac{1}{2\vartheta}\left[\hat{G}\left(\frac{(\vartheta-i)\psi+i\pi}{\vartheta}\right)+\hat{G}\left(\frac{(\vartheta-i-1)\psi+(i+1)\pi}{\vartheta}\right)\right]\right.\\
&\left.-\frac{\beta(\alpha)}{\alpha(\pi-\psi)}\left[\left({}^{CF}_{\psi}I^{\alpha}\hat{G}\right)(k)+\left({}^{CF}I^{\alpha}_{\pi}\hat{G}\right)(k)\right]+\frac{2(1-\alpha)}{\beta(\alpha)}\hat{G}(k)\right|\\
\leq\ &\sum_{i=0}^{\vartheta-1} \frac{\pi-\psi}{2^{1+\frac{1}{q}}\vartheta^3}\beta^{\frac{1}{p}}(p+1,p+1)\left(\hat{G}''\left|\frac{(\vartheta-i)\psi+i\pi}{\vartheta}\right|^q, \hat{G}''\left|\frac{(\vartheta-i-1)\psi+(i+1)\pi}{\vartheta}\right|^q\right)^{\frac{1}{q}}
\end{aligned}$$

holds.

Corollary 10. *If we set $\mathring{\vartheta} = 2$ in Theorem 8, we then obtain the following Bullen-type inequality:*

$$\begin{aligned}
&\left|\frac{1}{4}\left(\hat{G}(\psi) + 2\hat{G}\left(\frac{\psi+\pi}{2}\right) + \hat{G}(\pi)\right)\right. \\
&\left. - \frac{\beta(\alpha)}{\alpha(\pi-\psi)}\left[\left({}^{CF}_{\psi}I^{\alpha}\hat{G}\right)(k) + \left({}^{CF}I^{\alpha}_{\pi}\hat{G}\right)(k)\right] + \frac{2(1-\alpha)}{\beta(\alpha)}\hat{G}(k)\right| \\
\leq\; & \frac{\pi-\psi}{16}\beta^{\frac{1}{p}}(p+1,p+1)\left(\frac{1}{s+1}\right)^{\frac{1}{q}} \\
&\left[\left(\frac{|\hat{G}''(\psi)|^q + \left|\hat{G}''\left(\frac{\psi+\pi}{2}\right)\right|^q}{2}\right)^{\frac{1}{q}} + \left|\left(\frac{\left|\hat{G}''\left(\frac{\psi+\pi}{2}\right)\right|^q + |\hat{G}''(\pi)|^q}{2}\right)^{\frac{1}{q}}\right|\right].
\end{aligned}$$

Theorem 9. *Using the assumption in Lemma 1, if $|\hat{G}''|^q$ is an s-convex function on $[\psi, \pi]$ and some $s \in (0,1]$, and $q \geq 1$, then*

$$\begin{aligned}
&\left|\sum_{i=0}^{\mathring{\vartheta}-1}\frac{1}{2\mathring{\vartheta}}\left[\hat{G}\left(\frac{(\mathring{\vartheta}-i)\psi+i\pi}{\mathring{\vartheta}}\right) + \hat{G}\left(\frac{(\mathring{\vartheta}-i-1)\psi+(i+1)\pi}{\mathring{\vartheta}}\right)\right]\right. \\
&\left. - \frac{\beta(\alpha)}{\alpha(\pi-\psi)}\left[\left({}^{CF}_{\psi}I^{\alpha}\hat{G}\right)(k) + \left({}^{CF}I^{\alpha}_{\pi}\hat{G}\right)(k)\right] + \frac{2(1-\alpha)}{\beta(\alpha)}\hat{G}(k)\right| \\
\leq\; & \sum_{i=0}^{\mathring{\vartheta}-1}\frac{(\pi-\psi)^2}{2\mathring{\vartheta}^3}\left(\frac{1}{6}\right)^{1-\frac{1}{q}}\left(\frac{1}{(s+2)(s+3)}\right)^{\frac{1}{q}}\left[\left|\hat{G}''\left(\frac{(\mathring{\vartheta}-i)\psi+i\pi}{\mathring{\vartheta}}\right)\right|^q + \left|\hat{G}''\left(\frac{(\mathring{\vartheta}-i-1)\psi+(i+1)\pi}{\mathring{\vartheta}}\right)\right|^q\right]^{\frac{1}{q}}
\end{aligned} \tag{9}$$

holds.

Proof. By utilizing Lemma 1, modulus properties of, and the power-mean inequality, since $|\hat{G}''|^q$ is an s-convex function, we obtain

$$\begin{aligned}
&\left|\sum_{i=0}^{\mathring{\vartheta}-1}\frac{1}{2\mathring{\vartheta}}\left[\hat{G}\left(\frac{(\mathring{\vartheta}-i)\psi+i\pi}{\mathring{\vartheta}}\right) + \hat{G}\left(\frac{(\mathring{\vartheta}-i-1)\psi+(i+1)\pi}{\mathring{\vartheta}}\right)\right]\right. \\
&\left. - \frac{\beta(\alpha)}{\alpha(\pi-\psi)}\left[\left({}^{CF}_{\psi}I^{\alpha}\hat{G}\right)(k) + \left({}^{CF}I^{\alpha}_{\pi}\hat{G}\right)(k)\right] + \frac{2(1-\alpha)}{\beta(\alpha)}\hat{G}(k)\right| \\
\leq\; & \sum_{i=0}^{\mathring{\vartheta}-1}\frac{(\pi-\psi)^2}{2\mathring{\vartheta}^3}\left[\int_0^1|\Lambda(1-\Lambda)|\left|\hat{G}''\left(\Lambda\frac{(\mathring{\vartheta}-i)\psi+i\pi}{\mathring{\vartheta}} + (1-\Lambda)\frac{(\mathring{\vartheta}-i-1)\psi+(i+1)\pi}{\mathring{\vartheta}}\right)\right|d\Lambda\right] \\
\leq\; & \sum_{i=0}^{\mathring{\vartheta}-1}\frac{(\pi-\psi)^2}{2\mathring{\vartheta}^3}\left[\left(\int_0^1\left|\Lambda-\Lambda^2\right|d\Lambda\right)^{1-\frac{1}{q}}\left\{\int_0^1\left|\Lambda-\Lambda^2\right|\left(\Lambda^s\left|\hat{G}''\left(\frac{(\mathring{\vartheta}-i)\psi+i\pi}{\mathring{\vartheta}}\right)\right|^q\right.\right.\right. \\
&\left.\left.\left. + (1-\Lambda)^s\left|\hat{G}''\left(\frac{(\mathring{\vartheta}-i-1)\psi+(i+1)\pi}{\mathring{\vartheta}}\right)\right|^q\right)d\Lambda\right\}^{\frac{1}{q}}\right] \\
\leq\; & \sum_{i=0}^{\mathring{\vartheta}-1}\frac{(\pi-\psi)^2}{2\mathring{\vartheta}^3}\left(\frac{1}{6}\right)^{1-\frac{1}{q}}\left[\int_0^1\left|\Lambda-\Lambda^2\right|\Lambda^s\left|\hat{G}''\left(\frac{(\mathring{\vartheta}-i)\psi+i\pi}{\mathring{\vartheta}}\right)\right|^q d\Lambda\right. \\
&\left. + \int_0^1\left|\Lambda-\Lambda^2\right|(1-\Lambda)^s\left|\hat{G}''\left(\frac{(\mathring{\vartheta}-i-1)\psi+(i+1)\pi}{\mathring{\vartheta}}\right)\right|^q d\Lambda\right]^{\frac{1}{q}} \\
\leq\; & \sum_{i=0}^{\mathring{\vartheta}-1}\frac{(\pi-\psi)^2}{2\mathring{\vartheta}^3}\left(\frac{1}{6}\right)^{1-\frac{1}{q}}\left(\frac{1}{(s+2)(s+3)}\right)^{\frac{1}{q}}\left[\left|\hat{G}''\left(\frac{(\mathring{\vartheta}-i)\psi+i\pi}{\mathring{\vartheta}}\right)\right|^q + \left|\hat{G}''\left(\frac{(\mathring{\vartheta}-i-1)\psi+(i+1)\pi}{\mathring{\vartheta}}\right)\right|^q\right]^{\frac{1}{q}}.
\end{aligned}$$

Thus, the proof of Theorem 9 is complete. □

Corollary 11. *If we set $s = 1$ in Theorem 9, then*

$$
\begin{aligned}
&\left|\sum_{i=0}^{\vartheta-1}\frac{1}{2\vartheta}\left[\hat{G}\left(\frac{(\vartheta-i)\psi+i\pi}{\vartheta}\right)+\hat{G}\left(\frac{(\vartheta-i-1)\psi+(i+1)\pi}{\vartheta}\right)\right]\right.\\
&\left.-\frac{\beta(\alpha)}{\alpha(\pi-\psi)}\left[\left({}_{\psi}^{CF}I^{\alpha}\hat{G}\right)(k)+\left({}^{CF}I_{\pi}^{\alpha}\hat{G}\right)(k)\right]+\frac{2(1-\alpha)}{\beta(\alpha)}\hat{G}(k)\right|\\
\leq\ &\sum_{i=0}^{\vartheta-1}\frac{(\pi-\psi)^2}{2\vartheta^3}\left(\frac{1}{6}\right)^{\frac{1}{q}}\left[\left|\hat{G}''\left(\frac{(\vartheta-i)\psi+i\pi}{\vartheta}\right)\right|^q+\left|\hat{G}''\left(\frac{(\vartheta-i-1)\psi+(i+1)\pi}{\vartheta}\right)\right|^q\right]^{\frac{1}{q}}
\end{aligned}
$$

holds.

Corollary 12. *If we set $\vartheta=2$ in Corollary 11, we then obtian the following Bullen-type inequality*

$$
\begin{aligned}
&\left|\frac{1}{4}\left(\hat{G}(\psi)+2\hat{G}\left(\frac{\psi+\pi}{2}\right)+\hat{G}(\pi)\right)\right.\\
&\left.-\frac{\beta(\alpha)}{\alpha(\pi-\psi)}\left[\left({}_{\psi}^{CF}I^{\alpha}\hat{G}\right)(k)+\left({}^{CF}I_{\pi}^{\alpha}\hat{G}\right)(k)\right]+\frac{2(1-\alpha)}{\beta(\alpha)}\hat{G}(k)\right|\\
\leq\ &\frac{(\pi-\psi)^2}{16}\left(\frac{1}{6}\right)^{\frac{1}{q}}\left[\left(\frac{\left|\hat{G}''(\psi)\right|^q+\left|\hat{G}''\left(\frac{\psi+\pi}{2}\right)\right|^q}{2}\right)^{\frac{1}{q}}+\left|\left(\frac{\left|\hat{G}''\left(\frac{\psi+\pi}{2}\right)\right|^q+\left|\hat{G}''(\pi)\right|^q}{2}\right)^{\frac{1}{q}}\right|\right].
\end{aligned}
$$

3. Applications to Special Means

(a) Arithmetic mean:

$$A=A(\psi,\pi):=\frac{\psi+\pi}{2},\ \psi,\pi\in\mathbb{R};$$

(b) Logarithmic mean:

$$L=L(\psi,\pi):=\frac{\pi-\psi}{\ln\pi-\ln\psi},\ \psi,\pi\in\mathbb{R},\ \psi\neq\pi;$$

(c) The generalized logarithmic mean:

$$L_r=L_r(\psi,\pi):=\left[\frac{\pi^{r+1}-\psi^{r+1}}{(r+1)(\pi-\psi)}\right]\ r\in\mathbb{R}\backslash\{-1,0\},\ \psi,\pi\in\mathbb{R},\ \psi\neq\pi;$$

Proposition 1. *Let $\psi,\pi\in\mathbb{R}$, $0<\psi<\pi$ and $\Lambda\in\mathbb{N}$, $\Lambda\geq 3$, then we have*

$$
\begin{aligned}
&\left|\sum_{i=0}^{\vartheta-1}\frac{1}{\vartheta}A\left(\left(\frac{(\vartheta-i)\psi+i\pi}{\vartheta}\right)^{\Lambda},\left(\frac{(\vartheta-i-1)\psi+(i+1)\pi}{\vartheta}\right)^{\Lambda}\right)-L_{\Lambda}^{\Lambda}(\psi,\pi)\right|\\
\leq\ &\sum_{i=0}^{\vartheta-1}\frac{(\pi-\psi)^2\Lambda(\Lambda-1)}{\vartheta^3}\left(\frac{17}{6}-e\right)A\left(\left|\frac{(\vartheta-i)\psi+i\pi}{\vartheta}\right|^{\Lambda-2},\left|\frac{(\vartheta-i-1)\psi+(i+1)\pi}{\vartheta}\right|^{\Lambda-2}\right).
\end{aligned}
$$

Proof. The assertion follows from Theorem 5, applying $\hat{G}(x)=x^{\Lambda}$, $x\in[\psi,\pi]$. □

Proposition 2. *Let $\psi, \pi \in \mathbb{R}$, $0 < \psi < \pi$ and $\Lambda \in \mathbb{N}$, $\Lambda \geq 3$, we have*

$$\left|\sum_{i=0}^{\mathring{\vartheta}-1} \frac{1}{\mathring{\vartheta}} A\left(\left(\frac{(\mathring{\vartheta}-i)\psi+i\pi}{\mathring{\vartheta}}\right)^{\Lambda}, \left(\frac{(\mathring{\vartheta}-i-1)\psi+(i+1)\pi}{\mathring{\vartheta}}\right)^{\Lambda}\right) - L_{\Lambda}^{\Lambda}(\psi,\pi)\right|$$
$$\leq \sum_{i=0}^{\mathring{\vartheta}-1} \frac{(\pi-\psi)^2\Lambda(\Lambda-1)}{2^{1-\frac{1}{q}}\mathring{\vartheta}^3} \beta^{\frac{1}{p}}(p+1,p+1)(e-2)^{\frac{1}{q}}$$
$$\times A^{\frac{1}{q}}\left(\left|\frac{(\mathring{\vartheta}-i)\psi+i\pi}{\mathring{\vartheta}}\right|^{(\Lambda-2)q}, \left|\frac{(\mathring{\vartheta}-i-1)\psi+(i+1)\pi}{\mathring{\vartheta}}\right|^{(\Lambda-2)q}\right)^{\frac{1}{q}}.$$

Proof. The assertion follows from Theorem 6, applying $\hat{G}(x) = x^{\Lambda}$, $x \in [\psi, \pi]$. □

Proposition 3. *Let $\psi, \pi \in \mathbb{R}$, $0 < \psi < \pi$ and $\Lambda \in \mathbb{N}$, $\Lambda \geq 3$, we have*

$$\left|\sum_{i=0}^{\mathring{\vartheta}-1} \frac{1}{\mathring{\vartheta}} A\left(\left(\frac{(\mathring{\vartheta}-i)\psi+i\pi}{\mathring{\vartheta}}\right)^{\Lambda}, \left(\frac{(\mathring{\vartheta}-i-1)\psi+(i+1)\pi}{\mathring{\vartheta}}\right)^{\Lambda}\right) - L_{\Lambda}^{\Lambda}(\psi,\pi)\right|$$
$$\sum_{i=0}^{\mathring{\vartheta}-1} \frac{(\pi-\psi)^2\Lambda(\lambda-1)}{12^{1-\frac{1}{q}}\mathring{\vartheta}^3}\left(\frac{17}{6}-e\right) \times A^{\frac{1}{q}}\left(\left|\frac{(\mathring{\vartheta}-i)\psi+i\pi}{\mathring{\vartheta}}\right|^{(\Lambda-2)q}, \left|\frac{(\mathring{\vartheta}-i-1)\psi+(i+1)\pi}{\mathring{\vartheta}}\right|^{(\Lambda-2)q}\right)^{\frac{1}{q}}.$$

Proof. The assertion follows from Theorem 7, applying $\hat{G}(x) = x^{\Lambda}$, $x \in [\psi, \pi]$. □

4. Conclusions

The investigation of fractional Hermite Hadamard-type inequalities is an informative and active area of research that reflects the growing importance of fractional calculus in modern science and engineering. Here, we established a new lemma (Lemma 1) and produced new Hermite–Hadamard-type inequalities for the exponential convex function. Additionally, several types of fractional integral inequalities were obtained based on this identity (different outcomes were found for various values of $\mathring{\vartheta}$, $\mathring{\vartheta} \in \mathbb{N}$). From the developed corollaries, Corollaries 1 and 2, one can observe that by taking specific values of $\mathring{\vartheta} = 1$ for the factors, all the existing results were reduced to the results obtained by Alomari et al. [11] and B.Y et al. [29]. In future, authors can apply these new techniques and useful ideas, e.g., coordinates, and other fractional operators, produced in this paper. Furthermore, one can obtain likewise, parameterized inequalities via the Caputo–Fabrizio fractional integral operator for convex functions using quantum calculus. Additionally, our findings could potentially have specific implementations in numerical integration, optimization, and other related areas.

Author Contributions: Conceptualization, M.-u.-D.J. and A.M.; investigation, A.Q. and H.B.; methodology, M.M.S. and S.S.S.; validation, M.-u.-D.J. and M.M.S.; visualization, H.B.; writing—original draft, A.Q. and A.M.; writing—review and editing, S.S.S. and H.B. All authors have read and agreed to the published version of the manuscript.

Funding: This research received no external funding.

Data Availability Statement: Data sharing is not applicable to this paper as no data sets were generated or analyzed during the current study.

Conflicts of Interest: The authors declare no conflict of interest.

References

1. Uchaikin, V.V. *Fractional Derivatives for Physicists and Engineers*; Springer: Berlin, Germany, 2013; Volume 2.
2. Trujillo, J.J.; Scalas, E.; Diethelm, K.; Baleanu, D. *Fractional Calculus: Models and Numerical Methods*; World Scientific: Singapore, 2016; Volume 5, p. 417.
3. Anastassiou, G.A. *Generalized Fractional Calculus*; Studies in Systems, Decision and Control; Springer: Cham, Switzerland, 2021; p. 305.

4. Magin, R.L. *Fractional Calculus in Bioengineering*; Begell House Publishers: Danbury, CT, USA, 2006.
5. Atangana, A.; Baleanu, D. New fractional derivatives with nonlocal and non-singular kernel: Theory and application to heat transfer model. *arXiv* **2016**, arXiv:1602.03408.
6. Okubo, S.; Isihara, A. Inequality for convex functions in quantum-statistical mechanics. *Physica* **1972**, *59*, 228–240. [CrossRef]
7. Pecaric, J.E.; Tong, Y.L. *Convex Functions, Partial Orderings, and Statistical Applications*; Academic Press: Cambridge, MA, USA, 1992.
8. Krishna, V.; Maenner, E. Convex potentials with an application to mechanism design. *Econometrica* **2001**, *69*, 1113–1119. [CrossRef]
9. Murota, K.; Tamura, A. New characterizations of M -convex functions and their applications to economic equilibrium models with indivisibilities. *Discret. Appl. Math.* **2003**, *131*, 495–512. [CrossRef]
10. Nasir, J.; Qaisar, S.; Qayyum, A.; Budak, H. New results on Hermite-Hadamard type inequalities via Caputo-Fabrizio fractional integral for s-convex function. *Filomat* **2023**, *37*, 4943–4957.
11. Alomari, M.; Darus, M.; Dragomir, S.S. *Inequalities of Hermite-Hadamard's Type for Functions Whose Derivatives Absolute Values Are Quasi-Convex*; Research Report Collection; Victoria University: Melbourne, Australia, 2009.
12. Budak, H.; Ali, M.A.; Alp, N.; Awais, H.M. Some new q-Hermite-Hadamard type inequalities for the product of convex functions. *J. Interdiscip. Math.* **2022**, *25*, 2141–2166. [CrossRef]
13. Sarikaya, M.Z.; Filiz, H.; Kiris, M.E. On some generalized integral inequalities for Riemann-Liouville fractional integrals. *Filomat* **2015**, *29*, 1307–1314. [CrossRef]
14. Xi, B.Y.; Qi, F. Some integral inequalities of Hermite-Hadamard type for convex functions with applications to means. *J. Funct. Spaces* **2012**, *2012*, 980438. [CrossRef]
15. Özcan, S.; İşcan, İ. Some new Hermite-Hadamard type inequalities for s-convex functions and their applications. *J. Inequal. Appl.* **2019**, *2019*, 201. [CrossRef]
16. Serap, Ö. Hermite–Hadamard type inequalities for m-convex and(α, m)-convex functions. *J. Inequal. Appl.* **2020**, *2020*, 175.
17. Adil Khan, M.; Iqbal, A.; Suleman, M.; Chu, Y.M. Hermite-Hadamard type inequalities for fractional integrals via Green's function. *J. Inequal. Appl.* **2018**, *2018*, 161. [CrossRef]
18. Sezer, S. The Hermite-Hadamard inequality for s -Convex functions in the third sense. *Aims Math* **2021**, *6*, 7719–7732. [CrossRef]
19. Samraiz, M.; Malik, M.; Naheed, S.; Rahman, G.; Nonlaopon, K. Hermite-Hadamard-type inequalities via different convexities with applications. *J. Inequal. Appl.* **2023**, *2023*, 70. [CrossRef]
20. Kadakal, M.; İşcan, İ. Exponential type convexity and some related inequalities. *J. Inequal. Appl.* **2020**, *2020*, 82. [CrossRef]
21. Hudzik, H.; Maligranda, L. Some remarks on s -convex functions. *Aequationes Math.* **1994**, *48*, 100–111. [CrossRef]
22. İşcan, İ. New refinements for integral and sum forms of Hölder inequality. *J. Inequal. Appl.* **2019**, *2019*, 304. [CrossRef]
23. Wang, X.; Saleem, M.S.; Aslam, K.N.; Wu, X.; Zhou, T. On Caputo-Fabrizio fractional integral inequalities of Hermite-Hadamard type for modified h-convex functions. *J. Math.* **2020**, *2020*, 8829140. [CrossRef]
24. Butt, S.I.; Nadeem, M.; Farid, G. On Caputo fractional derivatives via exponential (s, m)-convex functions. *Eng. Appl. Sci. Lett.* **2020**, *3*, 32–39.
25. Abbasi, A.M.K.; Anwar, M. Hermite-Hadamard inequality involving Caputo-Fabrizio fractional integrals and related inequalities via s-convex functions in the second sense. *AIMS Math.* **2022**, *7*, 18565–18575. [CrossRef]
26. Li, Q.; Saleem, M.S.; Yan, P.; Zahoor, M.S.; Imran, M. On strongly convex functions via Caputo-Fabrizio-type fractional integral and some applications. *J. Math.* **2021**, *2021*, 6625597. [CrossRef]
27. Caputo, M.; Fabrizio, M. A new definition of fractional derivative without singular kernel. *Prog. Fract. Differ. Appl.* **2015**, *1*, 73–85.
28. Sahoo, S.K.; Mohammed, P.O.; Kodamasingh, B.; Tariq, M.; Hamed, Y.S. New fractional integral inequalities for convex functions pertaining to Caputo–Fabrizio operator. *Fractal Fract.* **2022**, *6*, 171. [CrossRef]
29. Xi, B.Y.; Qi, F. Some inequalities of Hermite-Hadamard type for h-convex functions. *Adv. Inequal. Appl.* **2013**, *2*, 1–15.

mathematics

MDPI

Article

On Λ-Fractional Wave Propagation in Solids

Kostantinos A. Lazopoulos [1,*] and Anastasios K. Lazopoulos [2]

1 Independent Researcher, 19009 Rafina, Greece
2 Mathematical Sciences Department, Hellenic Army Academy, 16673 Vari, Greece; orfeakos74@gmail.com
* Correspondence: kolazop@mail.ntua.gr

Abstract: Wave propagation in solids is discussed, based upon inherently non-local Λ-fractional analysis. Following the governing equations of Λ-fractional continuum mechanics, the Λ-fractional wave equations are derived. Since the variational procedures are only global, in the present Λ-fractional analysis, various jumpings, either in the strain or the stress, may be shown. The proposed theory is applied to impact-induced transitions in two-phase elastic materials and viscoelastic materials.

Keywords: Λ-fractional derivative; Λ-fractional space; initial space; global stability; coexistence of phases; strain jumping; stress jumping

MSC: 26A33

1. Introduction

Lately, mechanics have adapted various fractional calculus models to describe viscoelastic behavior and simulating experiments, Bagley et al. [1,2]. Atanackovic [3] and Mainardi [4] have presented various viscoelastic and wave propagation models in mechanics. The fundamental characteristic of fractional calculus is its global dependence. Lazopoulos [5], based upon fractional calculus, proposed the deformation of a non-homogeneous bar with possible voids. In that case, Noll's axiom of local action, Truesdell [6], fails to be valid. According to Eringen [7], micro- and nanomaterials should be based on the axiom of non-local action. In fact, the strains in the neighborhood of that point define the stress.

Introducing non-local derivatives, fractional calculus has recently been applied to physics advances, engineering, mechanics, bioengineering, physics, biology, etc. In fact, Leibniz [8] foresaw the importance of fractional derivatives because they acquire properties quite different from common derivatives. Their strikingly different property is the non-locality they inherently possess, contrary to the common derivatives expressing locality. Many famous mathematicians like Liouville [9], Lagrange, Poincare, and Riemann [10] have worked on fractional derivatives. Information concerning fractional calculus may be found in various texts, like Miller et al. [11], Poldubny [12], Samko et al. [13], and Oldham et al. [14]. Nevertheless, fractional derivatives are not mathematical derivatives according to differential topology, which Chillingworth [15] satisfies:

1. Linearity $\mathrm{D}(\mathrm{af}(\mathrm{x}) + \mathrm{bg}(\mathrm{x})) = \mathrm{aDf}(\mathrm{x}) + bDg(x)$.
2. Leibniz rule $D(f(x) \bullet g(x)) = Df(x) \bullet g(x) + f(x)Dg(x)$.
3. Chain rule $D(g(f))(x) = Dg(f(x) \bullet Df(x)$.

Although fractional calculus is considered necessary when studying various problems in physics, engineering, biology, etc., fractional geometry does not exist. Hence the mathematical analysis of the presented problems does not possess the accuracy demanded by mathematics.

Nevertheless, the application of fractional calculus is considered quite important in various scientific areas requiring the consideration of non-local procedures. Lazopoulos [16–20] introduced the Λ-fractional derivative, because it is a unique fractional derivative satisfying all the prerequisites of differential topology for being a mathematical derivative. Hence it is a unique fractional differential procedure formulating fractional differential geometry and correct differential equations with the existence and uniqueness theorem applied in physics and mechanics. Another essential feature of fractional calculus is the necessity for the consideration of global variational procedures with the additional Weierstrass–Erdmann corner conditions, Lazopoulos [21]. Hence, the co-existence of phases phenomena, Ericksen in [22], may be revealed.

Wave propagation is studied in the context of Λ-fractional analysis. Due to global variation procedures, jumps in the strain and stress may be revealed. Jumping in strain or stress with non-linear elasticity has already been discussed in [23]. In fact, the evolution of phase transitions is present in the wave propagation of strains in non-local Λ-fractional mechanics. The Λ-fractional impact-induced transitions in two-phase elastic materials are discussed. Further, the Λ-fractional wave propagation with possible jumping is discussed in the context of viscoelastic materials.

2. The Λ-Fractional Analysis

The importance of fractional derivatives was suggested by Leibnitz in 1695. The main characteristic of fractional calculus is non-locality. Non-local properties are exhibited mainly by micro and nanomaterials [7].

For a fractional order $0 < \gamma \leq 1$, the left and right fractional integrals are expressed by

$$ {}_aI_x^{\gamma}f(x) = \frac{1}{\Gamma(\gamma)}\int_a^x \frac{f(s)}{(x-s)^{1-\gamma}}ds \tag{1} $$

$$ {}_xI_b^{\gamma}f(x) = \frac{1}{\Gamma(\gamma)}\int_x^b \frac{f(s)}{(s-x)^{1-\gamma}}ds \tag{2} $$

where $\Gamma(\gamma)$ denotes Euler's Gamma function. There exist many fractional derivatives. However, there is only one fractional integral. The Riemann–Liouville (*RL*) fractional derivative (FR) is the most common fractional derivative. In fact, the left RL fractional derivative is defined by

$$ {}_a^{RL}D_x^{\gamma}f(x) = \frac{d}{dx}\left({}_aI_x^{1-\gamma}(f(x))\right) = \frac{1}{\Gamma(1-\gamma)}\frac{d}{dx}\int_a^x \frac{f(s)}{(x-s)^{\gamma}}ds, \tag{3} $$

whereas, the right *RL* fractional derivative (*RL*) is expressed by

$$ {}_x^{RL}D_b^{\gamma}f(x) = \frac{d}{dx}\left({}_xI_b^{1-\gamma}(f(x))\right) = -\frac{1}{\Gamma(1-\gamma)}\frac{d}{dx}\int_x^b \frac{f(s)}{(s-x)^{\gamma}}ds \tag{4} $$

Fractional integrals and derivatives are connected through the relation

$$ {}_x^{RL}D_x^{\gamma}\left({}_aI_x^{\gamma}f(x)\right) = f(x) \tag{5} $$

It is well known that fractional derivatives fail to satisfy the differential topology prerequisites, Chillingworth [15], for creating the differential geometry necessary for describing physical problems. Nevertheless, well-known fractional derivatives have been used in physics, mechanics, biomechanics, etc., without being able to generate the geometry necessary for the study of the physical problems

The Λ-fractional analysis, proposed by Lazopoulos [16], is consistent with the prerequisites of differential topology, and Λ-fractional derivatives may correctly generate differential geometry. Λ-fractional analysis has already been applied to geometry, physics, mechanics, differential equations, etc., Lazopoulos [16–20].

The Λ-fractional derivative (Λ-FD) is defined as

$$ {}^{\Lambda}_{a}D^{\gamma}_{x}f(x) = \frac{{}^{RL}_{\alpha}D^{\gamma}_{x}f(x)}{{}^{RL}_{a}D^{\gamma}_{x}x}. \quad (6)$$

In addition, the Λ-FD becomes

$$ {}^{\Lambda}_{a}D^{\gamma}_{x}f(x) = \frac{\frac{d_a I_x^{1-\gamma} f(x)}{dx}}{\frac{d_a I_x^{1-\gamma} x}{dx}} = \frac{d_a I_x{}^{1-\gamma} f(x)}{d_a I_x{}^{1-\gamma} x}, \quad (7)$$

with the help of Equation (3). Moreover, the Λ-fractional space is constructed using $(X,F(X))$ with

$$ X =_a I_x{}^{1-\gamma} x, \;\; F(X) =_a I_x{}^{1-\gamma} f(x(X)). \quad (8)$$

Taking into consideration Equation (5), the results generated by analysis in the Λ-fractional space may be transferred into the original space. Hence,

$$ f(x) = {}^{RL}_{a}D^{1-\gamma}_{x} F(X(x)) = {}^{RL}_{\alpha}D^{1-\gamma}_{x}\left(I^{1-\gamma} f(x)\right). \quad (9)$$

The Λ-fractional procedure presents similarities to Laplace's transformation applied to fractional calculus. However, Λ-fractional transformation applies only to functions, not to derivatives, and the corresponding functions in the Λ-fractional space form various derivatives. Applying analysis in the Λ-fractional space, the various results may be transferred back into the initial space as simple functions only.

Another essential feature of Λ-fractional analysis is the global stable features of the various fractional problems. The defect was pointed out in [18], and the governing continuum mechanics laws were corrected in a recent work by Lazopoulos [24]. Following Ericksen [22], the various globally stable states in the introduced Λ-fractional space should satisfy the conditions of Erdmann–Weierstrass, Gelfand, and Fomin [25]. Those ideas have already been applied to biological balloons under pressure. The same procedures will employed in the present study of Λ-fractional waves.

3. Waves with Shocks in Λ-Fractional Non-Linear Elasticity

Consider a one-dimensional bar in the interval $0 \leq X \leq L$ in Λ-fractional space. That is considered the reference placement of the bar in the Λ-fractional space. During its motion, the particle at X is transferred into its current placement Y, with

$$ Y(X,T) = X + U(X,T), \quad (10)$$

where, $U(X,T)$ is the continuous displacement. The displacement might accept first and second piecewise continuous derivatives with respect to space and time. The assumed smoothness for the displacement $U(X,T)$ allows for jump discontinuities in the strain $G = U_X(X,T)$ and velocity $V = U_T(X,T)$. Considering the portion of the bar lying in the interval $[X_1, X_2]$, in the absence of body force, the balance of momentum in the sub-bar $[X_1, X_2]$ is expressed by

$$ \Sigma X_2, T - \Sigma X_1, T = \frac{D}{DT}\int_{X_1}^{X_2} \rho V(X,T)dX, \quad (11)$$

where ρ denotes the constant mass per unit referential volume.

For smooth fields, the momentum balance law yields

$$ \Sigma_X(X,T) = \rho V_T(X,T). \quad (12)$$

Moreover,

$$ V_X(X,T) = G_T(X,T) \quad (13)$$

$$\text{with } G(X,T) = \frac{\partial U(X,T)}{\partial X}. \tag{14}$$

If the motion exhibits a single strain discontinuity point between $[X_1, X_2]$ with a location in the reference configuration $X = S(T)$, then the momentum balance equation, Equation (11), and the assumed smoothness of the displacement yield the jump conditions

$$[\boldsymbol{\Sigma}] = -\rho\dot{S}\,[V], \tag{15}$$

$$[V] = -\dot{S}\,[G]. \tag{16}$$

Further, the constitutive law

$$\boldsymbol{\Sigma} = \boldsymbol{\Sigma}(G), \tag{17}$$

with the jumping conditions, Equations (15) and (16), yield the expression of the velocity of the discontinuity and the strains $G^{\pm}$ on either side.

$$\rho\dot{S}^2 = \frac{\Sigma(G^+) - \Sigma(G^-)}{G^+ - G^-}. \tag{18}$$

Transferring the velocity of the jump discontinuities, as a function, into the initial space with the help of Equation (9), considering the space fractional order γ_1 and time fractional order γ_2, yields

$$\dot{s}(x) = {}_0^{RL}D_t^{1-\gamma_2}\,{}_\alpha^{RL}D_x^{1-\gamma_1}\dot{S}(X(x), T(t)) = {}_0^{RL}D_t^{1-\gamma_2}\,{}_\alpha^{RL}D_x^{1-\gamma_1}\left(I^{1-\gamma_2}I^{1-\gamma_1}\dot{S}(x,t)\right). \tag{19}$$

Equation (19) includes both effects of the fractional space and the time distributions.

4. The Fractional Impact Problem for Two-Phase Materials

Let us consider a one-dimensional rod in the Λ-fractional space in its reference configuration with the strains $G(X,0) = 0$ and velocities $V(X,0) = 0$. Further, a constant velocity $V(0,T) = V_0$ is applied at time $T = 0$ and remains constant at all times T at the initial point $X = 0$. Therefore, the dynamical problem of the bar is defined by the equations

$$\Sigma'(G)G_X = \rho\, V_T \text{ for X } \geq 0, \text{ T } \geq 0 \tag{20}$$

$$V_X = G_T \tag{21}$$

and the initial conditions,

$$G(X,0) = V(X,0) = 0, \textit{ for } X \geq 0 \tag{22}$$

and the boundary conditions,

$$V(0,T) = V_0 \textit{ for } T \geq 0. \tag{23}$$

Let us consider $W(G)$ the strain energy density per unit reference volume concerning the uniaxial deformation of the rod. The stress is defined through

$$\boldsymbol{\Sigma} = W^{\sim\prime}(G) = \Sigma(G). \tag{24}$$

The diagram of Figure 1 is the most straightforward stress–strain diagram for developing two-phase deformation in compression.

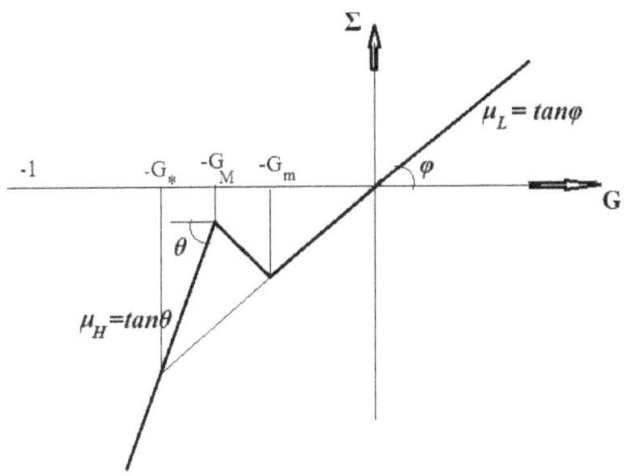

Figure 1. The trilinear non-convex stress–strain diagram.

For the material presented in Figure 1, the stress is defined by

$$\Sigma(G) = \mu_L G \, for > -G_m, \tag{25}$$

$$\Sigma(G) = \mu_H(G + G_T) \, for \ -1 < G < -G_m, \tag{26}$$

Hence, two branches exist: the low-pressure stress–strain deformation section with $G > -G_m$ and the high-pressure deformation with $-1 < G < -G_M$.
Therefore, Equation (25) yields for low-pressure shock the velocity

$$\dot{S_L} = \sqrt{\frac{\mu_L}{\rho}} \tag{27}$$

Further, the velocity of the shock wave for the high-pressure phase is defined by

$$\dot{S_H} = \sqrt{\frac{\mu_H}{\rho}} \tag{28}$$

Moreover, Figure 2 denotes the stress-strain diagram with jumping of strains. For the transition from the low-pressure phase to the high-pressure phase, Equation (18) will be recalled.

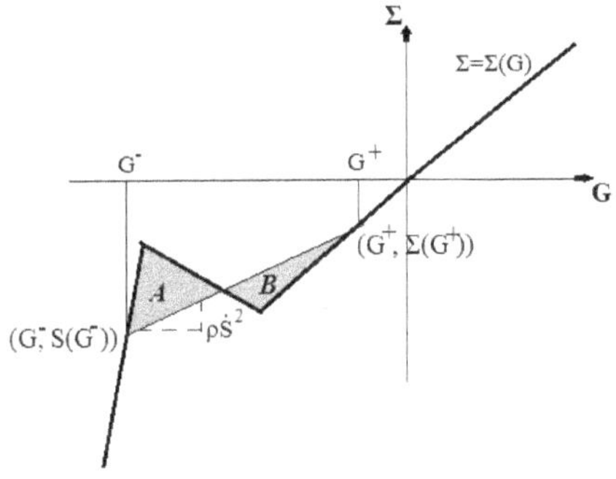

Figure 2. The stress–strain diagram with jumping of strains.

Therefore, Equation (18) yields

$$\rho\dot{S}^2 = \frac{\Sigma(G^+) - \Sigma(G^-)}{G^+ - G^-} \tag{29}$$

Therefore, three separate cases are pointed out, corresponding to the impact problem:

i. The low-pressure phase shock wave case.
ii. The low-pressure phase shock wave followed by a low-pressure phase followed by a high-pressure phase boundary.
iii. A phase boundary from the low-pressure phase to the high-pressure phase. No shock wave is involved.

For further information see Abeyaratne and Knowles [23]. The results gathered in the Λ-fractional space may be transferred into the initial space through the transformation Equation (19).

5. Waves with Shocks in Λ-Fractional Viscoelasticity

There is a result concerning the shock front in viscoelastic fractal media calculated by Demnie et al. [26], who point out that the fractality of the rod does not affect the jumping solution of the stress. Of course, there exist two comments concerning that result. The first is that fractional calculus, adhered to in that reference, fails to exhibit fractional derivatives acquiring the properties of a derivative, and secondly, the fractional time behavior has not been taken into consideration in the viscoelastic response.

Following [26], the stress Σ and the displacement $U(X)$ in the Λ-fractional space are connected through the governing equation

$$\Sigma_{,X} = \rho U_{,TT} \tag{30}$$

with ρ the constant mass density and the boundary conditions

$$U(0,T) = U_{,T}(X,0) = 0. \tag{31}$$

Furthermore, the initial conditions are expressed by

$$\Sigma(0,T) = -\Sigma_0 H(T). \tag{32}$$

where H is the Heaviside function.

Following [26], the jumping of the stress Σ in the Λ-Fractional space is connected with the jumping of the wave velocity $U_{,T}$ through the relation

$$[\Sigma] = -\rho C\,[U_{,T}], \tag{33}$$

where $[\Phi]$ denotes the jumping in Φ.

Moreover, the linear viscoelastic process in the Λ-fractional space starting at time $T = T_0^+$ is defined by

$$\Sigma(T) = E(0)U_{,X}(T) + \int_{T_0^+}^{T} E_{,T}(T-S)U_{,S}dS, \tag{34}$$

where, $E(T)$ is the relaxation function.

Recalling the conservation of the governing linear momentum equation,

$$[\Sigma_{,x}] = \rho\,[U_{,TT}], \tag{35}$$

the solution for the jumping of $[\Sigma]$ in the Λ-fractional space is defined by, see [26],

$$[\Sigma(T)] = \Sigma_0 exp\left\{\frac{1}{2}\frac{E_{,T}(0)}{E(0)}T\right\}, \tag{36}$$

As it has been pointed out, the fractality of the space does not enter into the jumping distribution of the stress Σ in the Λ-fractional space. However, transferring the jumping distribution from the Λ-space to the initial one, the fractional order of the space γ_1 and the time γ_2 should be taken into consideration. Indeed, taking into consideration Equations (8) and (9) transforms the initial space (x,t) into the Λ-fractional space (X,T) with

$$X = \frac{x^{2-\gamma_1}}{\Gamma(3-\gamma_1)} \tag{37}$$

$$T = \frac{t^{2-\gamma_2}}{\Gamma(3-\gamma_2)}. \tag{38}$$

Indeed, the transformation of Equation (36) into the initial space demands the following steps:

a. Substitution of the T variable by the equivalent of T in Equation (36). Hence,

$$[\Sigma(T)] = [\Sigma(\frac{t^{2-\gamma_2}}{\Gamma(3-\gamma_2)})] = Y(t) \tag{39}$$

b. Transferring the jumping function of the stress into the initial space just to yield the function

$$[\sigma(\mathrm{x},\mathrm{t})] = \frac{1}{\Gamma(1-\gamma_1)\Gamma(1-\gamma_2)}\frac{d}{\mathrm{dx}}\int_0^{\mathrm{x}}\frac{1}{(\mathrm{x}-\mathrm{s})^{\gamma_1}}ds\frac{d}{\mathrm{dt}}\int_0^t\frac{\mathrm{Y}(\tau)}{(\mathrm{t}-\tau)^{\gamma_2}}d\tau \tag{40}$$

Simplifying Equation (41), the jumping function of the stress into the initial space is defined by

$$[\sigma(\mathrm{x},\mathrm{t})] = \frac{x^{-\gamma_1}}{\Gamma(1-\gamma_1)\Gamma(1-\gamma_2)}\frac{d}{\mathrm{dt}}\int_0^t\frac{Y(\tau)}{(\mathrm{t}-\tau)^{\gamma_2}}d\tau \tag{41}$$

6. Conclusions—Further Results

The present analysis concerns Λ-fractional wave propagation into elastic and viscoelastic media. The main characteristic of the present analysis is the development of various jumpings, either in strain or stress, due to the globally stable conditions derived from the Erdmann–Weierstrass conditions. The wave propagation with strain jumping in a two-phase material, due to the trilinear stress–strain diagram, and the propagation of stress jumping in viscoelastic media is discussed. The present analysis will be transferred into fractional fluids, where the various shocks will be studied. Further information concerning the fractional propagation of waves in solids may be found in [27–31]. In fact, fractional derivatives are non-local, contrary to the fractal waves that access local derivatives [32]. Nevertheless, there exists the influence of fractional order calculus upon the fractal dimensions [33–36].

Author Contributions: Conceptualization, K.A.L.; methodology, K.A.L.; validation, K.A.L., A.K.L.; formal analysis, K.A.L.; investigation, K.A.L.; resources, K.A.L., A.K.L.; data curation, K.A.L., A.K.L.; writing—original draft preparation, K.A.L., A.K.L.; writing—review and editing, A.K.L.; supervision, K.A.L.; project administration K.A.L., A.K.L. All authors have read and agreed to the published version of the manuscript.

Funding: This research received no external funding.

Data Availability Statement: No data is available.

Conflicts of Interest: The authors declare no conflict of interest.

References

1. Bagley, R.L.; Torvik, P.J. On the fractional calculus model of viscoelastic behavior. *J. Rheol.* **1986**, *30*, 133–155. [CrossRef]
2. Bagley, R.L.; Torvik, P.J. A Theoretical for the application of fractional calculus to viscoelasticity. *J. Rheol.* **1983**, *27*, 201–210. [CrossRef]
3. Atanackovic, T.M.; Stankovic, B. Dynamics of a viscoelastic rod of fractional derivative type. *ZAMM* **2002**, *82*, 377–386. [CrossRef]
4. Mainardi, F. *Fractional Calculus and Waves in Linear Viscoelasticity*; Imperial College Press: London, UK, 2010.

5. Lazopoulos, K.A. Non-local continuum mechanics and fractional calculus. *Mech. Res. Commun.* **2006**, *33*, 753–757. [CrossRef]
6. Truesdell, C.; Noll, W. The non-linear field theories of mechanics. In *Handbuch der Physik*; Fluegge, S., Ed.; Springer: Berlin/Heidelberg, Germany, 1965; Volume III/3.
7. Eringen, A.C. *Non-Local Continuum Field Theories*; Springer: New York, NY, USA, 2002.
8. Leibniz, G.W. *Letter to G.A. L'Hospital, Leibnitzen Mathematishe Schriften*; A. Asher: Berlin, Germany, 1849; Volume 2, pp. 301–302.
9. Liouville, J. Sur le calcul des differentielles a indices quelconques. *Ec. Polytech.* **1832**, *13*, 71–162.
10. Riemann, B. Versuch einer allgemeinen Auffassung der Integration and Differentiation. In *Gesammelte Werke*; Cambridge University Press: Cambridge, UK, 1876; p. 62.
11. Miller, K.; Ross, B. *An Introduction to the Fractional Calculus and Fractional Differential Equations*; John Wiley & Sons: New York, NY, USA, 1993.
12. Podlubny, I. *Fractional Differential Equations An Introduction to Fractional Derivatives, Fractional Differential Equations, Some Methods of Their Solution and Some of Their Applications*; Academic Press: Cambridge, MA, USA, 1999.
13. Samko, S.G.; Kilbas, A.A.; Marichev, O.I. *Fractional Integrals and Derivatives: Theory and Applications*; Gordon and Breach: Amsterdam, The Netherlands, 1993.
14. Oldham, K.B.; Spanier, J. *The Fractional Calculus*; Academic Press: New York, NY, USA; London, UK, 1974.
15. Chillingworth, D.R.J. *Differential Topology with a View to Applications*; Pitman: London, UK; San Francisco, CA, USA, 1976.
16. Lazopoulos, K.A.; Lazopoulos, A.K. On the Mathematical Formulation of Fractional Derivatives. *Prog. Fract. Diff. Appl.* **2019**, *5*, 261–267.
17. Lazopoulos, K.A.; Lazopoulos, A.K. On fractional bending of beams with Λ-fractional derivative. *Arch. Appl. Mech.* **2020**, *90*, 573–584. [CrossRef]
18. Lazopoulos, K.A.; Lazopoulos, A.K. On plane Λ-fractional linear elasticity theory. *Theor. Appl. Mech. Lett.* **2020**, *10*, 270–275. [CrossRef]
19. Lazopoulos, K.A.; Lazopoulos, A.K. On the fractional deformation of a linearly elastic bar. *J. Mech. Behav. Mater.* **2019**, *28*, 9–18. [CrossRef]
20. Lazopoulos, K.A.; Lazopoulos, A.K. On Λ-fractional Elastic Solid Mechanics. *Meccanica* **2022**, *57*, 775–791. [CrossRef]
21. Lazopoulos, K.A. Stability criteria and Λ-fractional mechanics. *Fractal Fract.* **2023**, *7*, 248. [CrossRef]
22. Ericksen, J.L. Equilibrium of bars. *J. Elast.* **1975**, *5*, 191–201. [CrossRef]
23. Abeyaratne, R.; Knowles, J.K. *Evolution of Phase Transitions, a Continuum Theory*; Cambridge University Press: Camgridge, UK, 2006.
24. Lazopoulos, K.A.; Lazopoulos, A.K. On Λ-fractional continuum mechanics fields. *Fractal Fract.* **2020**; *submitted*.
25. Gelfand, I.H.; Fomin, S.V. *Calculus of Variations*; Prentice Hall: Englewood Cliffs, NJ, USA, 1963.
26. Demmie, P.N.; Ostoya-Starzewski, M. Waves in fractal media. *J. Elast.* **2011**, *104*, 187–2011. [CrossRef]
27. Nadeem, M.; He, J.-H. The homotopy perturbation method for fractional differential equations: Part 2, two-scale transform. *Int. J. Numer. Methods Heat Fluid Flow* **2022**, *32*, 559–567. [CrossRef]
28. Nadeem, M.; He, J.-H.; Sedighi, H.M. Numerical analysis of multi-dimensional time-fractional diffusion problems under the Atangana-Baleanu Caputo derivative. *Math. Biosci. Eng.* **2023**, *20*, 8190–8207. [CrossRef] [PubMed]
29. Carpinteri, A.; Chiaia, B.; Cornetti, P. Static-kinematic duality and the principle of virtual work in the mechanics of fractal media. *Comp. Math. Appl. Mech. Eng.* **2001**, *191*, 3–19. [CrossRef]
30. Luchko, Y. Fractional wave equation and damped waves. *J. Math. Phys.* **2013**, *54*, 031505.
31. Sander, T.; Tomovski, Z. *Fractional Wave Equations, Development in Mathematics*; DEVM Volume 61 ; Cambridge University Press: Cambridge, UK, 2019.
32. Liang, Y.; Su, W. Connection between the order of fractional calculus and the fractional dimension of a type of fractal functions. *Anal. Theory Appl.* **2007**, *23*, 354–362. [CrossRef]
33. He, J.-H. Fractal calculus and its geometrical explanation. *Results Phys.* **2018**, *10*, 272–276. [CrossRef]
34. Liang, Y.S.; Su, W.Y. The relationship between the fractal dimension of a type of fractal functions and the order of their fractional calculus. *Chaos Solitons Fractals* **2007**, *34*, 682–692. [CrossRef]
35. Liang, Y. On the fractional Calculus of Besicovitch function. *Chaos Solitons Fractals* **2009**, *42*, 2741–2747. [CrossRef]
36. Yao, K.; Su, W.Y.; Zhou, S.P. On the connection between the order of fractional calculus and the dimensions of a fractal function. *Chaos Solitons Fractals* **2005**, *23*, 621–629. [CrossRef]

mathematics

MDPI

Article

A Numerical Approach for Dealing with Fractional Boundary Value Problems

Abeer A. Al-Nana [1,*], Iqbal M. Batiha [2,3] and Shaher Momani [3,4]

1 Department of Mathematics, Prince Sattam Bin Abdulaziz University, Alkharj 11942, Saudi Arabia
2 Department of Mathematics, Al Zaytoonah University of Jordan, Amman 11733, Jordan; i.batiha@zuj.edu.jo
3 Nonlinear Dynamics Research Center (NDRC), Ajman University, Ajman 346, United Arab Emirates; s.momani@ajman.ac.ae
4 Department of Mathematics, Faculty of Science, The University of Jordan, Amman 11942, Jordan
* Correspondence: a.alnana@psau.edu.sa

Abstract: This paper proposes a novel numerical approach for handling fractional boundary value problems. Such an approach is established on the basis of two numerical formulas; the fractional central formula for approximating the Caputo differentiator of order α and the fractional central formula for approximating the Caputo differentiator of order 2α, where $0 < \alpha \leq 1$. The first formula is recalled here, whereas the second one is derived based on the generalized Taylor theorem. The stability of the proposed approach is investigated in view of some formulated results. In addition, several numerical examples are included to illustrate the efficiency and applicability of our approach.

Keywords: fractional boundary value problem; fractional central formulas; Caputo differentiator

MSC: 34B05; 26A33

1. Introduction

The significance of fractional differential equations (FDEs) has grown significantly in recent decades. This is, of course, due to their value in modeling various phenomena in many practical and industrial applications such as science, physics, dynamics, mechanics, engineering, etc. When dealing with ordinary/partial differential equations, one might be concerned about obtaining solutions to these equations so that they satisfy specific conditions [1,2]. In general, we will have initial conditions once certain conditions are provided at a single point of an independent variable, whereas we will have boundary conditions once the conditions are provided at more than a single point of that variable. Actually, obtaining a solution of a fractional-order problem in accordance with n-boundary conditions is called an FBVP. Such a problem in its linear and 2α-order cases is regarded as a very important problem due to its various applications in technology and science. In this work, two boundary conditions are typically assumed at end points of an interval, as in most physical applications. In particular, we consider the following FBVP:

$$pD^{2\alpha}y(x) + qD^{\alpha}y(x) + ry(x) = f(x), \quad (1)$$

subject to the boundary conditions

$$y(a) = y_a \quad y(b) = y_b, \quad a < x < b, \quad (2)$$

where p, q, r are constants and $0 < \alpha \leq 1$ and y_a, y_b are given real numbers.

The boundary value problems consisting of FDEs have contributed to a deep understanding of many processes in different sciences, as different types of these equations can be solved using certain mathematical methods which meet specific boundary conditions.

Given the impossibility of solving nonlinear types of the BVPs analytically, several numerical approaches are used, see [3–7]. It should be noted that the finite difference method can provide very good numerical solutions for different types of FDES, see, e.g., [8–10]. From this point of view, we here propose to use the fractional central formula for approximating the Caputo differentiator of order α established in [11], and another formula called the fractional central formula for approximating the Caputo differentiator of order 2α, to find approximate solutions to a type of FBVPs given in (1), where $0 < \alpha \leq 1$. The stability of the proposed method is then examined, and several numerical examples are provided for completeness.

This paper is coordinated as follows. In Section 2, necessary preliminaries and some properties connected with fractional calculus are presented. Section 3 displays the methodology of the proposed method coupled with its stability. Section 4 provides a number of examples with some figures and tabulated results attached to illustrate the fulfilled findings. Section 5 finishes this work by declaring a conclusion.

2. Preliminaries

In this section, we mention some basic and necessary definitions in fractional calculus, such as the Riemann–Liouville integral and derivative, the Caputo derivative, and properties of the operators, which will be applied throughout the paper.

Definition 1 ([12,13]). *The Riemann–Liouville fractional integral of the function f of order γ is outlined as*

$$\mathcal{J}^{\gamma}f(t) = \frac{1}{\Gamma(\gamma)}\int_0^t (t-\tau)^{\gamma-1}f(\tau)d\tau, \tag{3}$$

where $t > 0$ and $0 < \gamma \leq 1$.

Remark 1 ([12,13]). *It is useful to mention some characteristics of the Riemann–Liouville integral operator, which are listed below for completeness:*

- *The identity property, i.e.,*

$$\mathcal{J}^{0}f(t) = f(t). \tag{4}$$

- *The power rule property, i.e.,*

$$\mathcal{J}^{\gamma}t^{m} = \frac{\Gamma(m+1)}{\Gamma(m+\gamma+1)}t^{m+\gamma}, \quad m \in \mathbb{Z}^{+}. \tag{5}$$

- *The commutation property, i.e.,*

$$\mathcal{J}^{\gamma}\mathcal{J}^{\mathcal{B}}f(t) = \mathcal{J}^{\gamma+\mathcal{B}}f(t) = \mathcal{J}^{\mathcal{B}}\mathcal{J}^{\gamma}f(t), \quad \gamma, \mathcal{B} \geq 0. \tag{6}$$

Definition 2 ([12,13]). *Let $n-1 < \gamma \leq n$ such that n is a positive integer and $\gamma \in \mathbb{R}^{+}$. The Riemann–Liouville derivative of fractional-order γ is outlined as*

$$D^{\gamma}f(t) = \frac{1}{\Gamma(n-\gamma)}\frac{d^n}{dt^n}\int_0^t \frac{f^{(n)}(\tau)}{(t-\tau)^{\gamma+1-n}}d\tau. \tag{7}$$

Definition 3 ([12,13]). *The Caputo fractional differential operator of order γ is outlined as*

$$D^{\gamma}f(x) = \frac{1}{\Gamma(n-\gamma)}\int_0^t \frac{f^{(n)}(\tau)}{(t-\tau)^{\gamma+1-n}}d\tau, \tag{8}$$

where $t > 0$ and $n-1 < \gamma \leq n$ such that $n \in \mathbb{N}$.

Remark 2 ([12,13]). *The Caputo fractional derivative satisfies the following properties:*

- *The power rule property, i.e.,*

$$D^{\gamma}t^{\varepsilon} = \begin{cases} \frac{\Gamma(\varepsilon+1)}{\Gamma(\varepsilon-\gamma+1)}t^{\varepsilon-\gamma}, & n-1<\alpha<n, \varepsilon>n-1, \varepsilon\in\mathbb{R} \\ 0, & n-1<\alpha<n, \varepsilon\leq n-1, \varepsilon\in\mathbb{N} \end{cases}. \tag{9}$$

- *The constant property, i.e.,*

$$D^{\gamma}c = 0, \tag{10}$$

where c *is constant.*

- *Interpolation property, i.e.,*

$$\lim_{\gamma\to n} D^{\gamma}f(t) = D^{n}f(t). \tag{11}$$

- *Linearity property, i.e.,*

$$D^{\gamma}(\lambda_1 f(t) + \lambda_2 g(t)) = \lambda_1 D^{\gamma}f(t) + \lambda_2 D^{\gamma}g(t), \tag{12}$$

where λ_1 *and* λ_2 *are two constants.*

- *Non-commutation property, i.e.,*

$$D^{\gamma}D^{\mu}f(t) \neq D^{\mu}D^{\gamma}f(t), \tag{13}$$

where $n-1<\gamma,\ \mu\leq n$ *such that* $n\in\mathbb{N}$.

Theorem 1 ([14]). *Suppose that* $D^{k\alpha}f(x)\in C^{n+1}(0,b]$ *for* $k=0,1,\cdots,n+1$, *where* $0<\alpha\leq 1$. *Then, the function* f *can be expanded about* $x=x_0$ *as follows:*

$$f(x) = \sum_{i=0}^{n}\frac{(x-x_0)^{i\alpha}}{\Gamma(i\alpha+1)}D^{i\alpha}f(x_0) + \frac{(x-x_0)^{(n+1)\alpha}}{\Gamma((n+1)\alpha+1)}D^{(n+1)\alpha}f(\xi), \tag{14}$$

where $0<\xi<b$ *and* $x\in(0,b]$.

3. Methodology and Stability

In this section, we attempt to develop a novel numerical approach to deal with FBVPs. This approach is accomplished based upon a recent formula established in [11] called the fractional central formula for approximating the Caputo differentiator of order α, and another formula called the fractional central formula for approximating the Caputo differentiator of order 2α, which would be established here, where $0<\alpha\leq 1$. But before all of this, we recall below the first formula by stating the following theorem.

Theorem 2 ([11]). *Let* $f\in C^3(0,b]$ *and* x_0,x_1,x_3 *be three distinct points in the interval* $(0,b]$ *such that* $0=x_0<x_1=x_0+h<x_2=x_0+2h=b$, *where* $h>0$. *Then, for any* $x\in(0,b]$, *the fractional central formula for approximating the Caputo differentiator of order* α *is determined by*

$$\begin{aligned} D_t^{\alpha}f(x) =& \frac{x^{2-\alpha}}{h^{2\alpha}\Gamma(3-\alpha)}\Big(f(x_0)-2f(x_1)+f(x_2)\Big) \\ &- \frac{x^{1-\alpha}}{2h^{2\alpha}\Gamma(2-\alpha)}\Big(f(x_0)(x_1+x_2)-2f(x_1)(x_0+x_2)+f(x_2)(x_0+x_1)\Big) \\ &+ \frac{f^{(3)}(\xi)}{6}\Big(\frac{6}{\Gamma(4-\alpha)}x^{3-\alpha} - \frac{2(x_0+x_1+x_2)}{\Gamma(3-\alpha)}x^{2-\alpha} + \frac{(x_0x_1+x_0x_2+x_1x_2)}{\Gamma(2-\alpha)}x^{1-\alpha}\Big), \end{aligned} \tag{15}$$

where $0<\alpha\leq 1$, *for an unknown* $\xi\in(0,b)$.

3.1. Approximating Caputo Differentiator of Order 2α

Herein, on the basis of the generalized Taylor Theorem 1, we intend to derive a novel formula called the fractional central formula for approximating the Caputo differentiator of order 2α, where $0<\alpha\leq 1$.

Theorem 3. *Suppose that $f \in C^4(0,b]$ and x_0, x_1, x_2 are distinct points in the interval $(0,b]$ such that $0 = x_0 < x_1 = x_0 + h < x_2 = x_0 + 2h = b$ with $h > 0$. Let $0 < \alpha \leq 1$, then the fractional central formula for approximating the Caputo differentiator of order 2α is determined by*

$$D^{2\alpha} f(x) = \frac{\Gamma(2\alpha+1)}{2h^{2\alpha}}(f(x_0) - 2f(x_1) + f(x_2)) - \frac{\Gamma(2\alpha+1)}{\Gamma(4\alpha+1)} h^{2\alpha} D^{4\alpha} f(\xi), \tag{16}$$

where $x \in (0,b)$ for an unknown $\xi \in (0,b)$.

Proof. To prove this result, we first expand the function f about x_0 using Theorem 1 to obtain

$$f(x) = f(x_0) + \frac{(x-x_0)^\alpha}{\Gamma(\alpha+1)} D^\alpha f(x_0) + \frac{(x-x_0)^{2\alpha}}{\Gamma(2\alpha+1)} D^{2\alpha} f(x_0) + \frac{(x-x_0)^{3\alpha}}{\Gamma(3\alpha+1)} D^{3\alpha} f(x_0) + \frac{(x-x_0)^{4\alpha}}{\Gamma(4\alpha+1)} D^{4\alpha} f(\xi_1). \tag{17}$$

Consequently, we can approximate the function f at $x_1 = x_0 + h$. In other words, we can have

$$f(x_0+h) = f(x_0) + \frac{h^\alpha}{\Gamma(\alpha+1)} D^\alpha f(x_0) + \frac{h^{2\alpha}}{\Gamma(2\alpha+1)} D^{2\alpha} f(x_0) + \frac{h^{3\alpha}}{\Gamma(3\alpha+1)} D^{3\alpha} f(x_0) + \frac{h^{4\alpha}}{\Gamma(4\alpha+1)} D^{4\alpha} f(\xi_1). \tag{18}$$

From this point of view, we can use the transform variables for both x_0 and $x_1 = x_0 + h$ to be x and $x + h$, respectively. This would immediately give

$$f(x+h) = f(x) + \frac{h^\alpha}{\Gamma(\alpha+1)} D^\alpha f(x) + \frac{h^{2\alpha}}{\Gamma(2\alpha+1)} D^{2\alpha} f(x) + \frac{h^{3\alpha}}{\Gamma(3\alpha+1)} D^{3\alpha} f(x) + \frac{h^{4\alpha}}{\Gamma(4\alpha+1)} D^{4\alpha} f(\xi_1). \tag{19}$$

In a similar manner, we can get

$$f(x-h) = f(x) - \frac{h^\alpha}{\Gamma(\alpha+1)} D^\alpha f(x) + \frac{h^{2\alpha}}{\Gamma(2\alpha+1)} D^{2\alpha} f(x) - \frac{h^{3\alpha}}{\Gamma(3\alpha+1)} D^{3\alpha} f(x) + \frac{h^{4\alpha}}{\Gamma(4\alpha+1)} D^{4\alpha} f(\xi_{-1}), \tag{20}$$

where $x - h < \xi_{-1} < x < \xi_1 < x + h$. Adding (19) to (20) yields

$$f(x+h) + f(x-h) = 2f(x) + \frac{2h^{2\alpha}}{\Gamma(2\alpha+1)} D^{2\alpha} f(x) + \frac{h^{4\alpha}}{\Gamma(4\alpha+1)} \left(D^{4\alpha} f(\xi_1) + D^{4\alpha} f(\xi_{-1})\right). \tag{21}$$

Now, due to $\frac{1}{2}(D^{4\alpha} f(\xi_1) + D^{4\alpha} f(\xi_{-1}))$ lying between $D^{4\alpha} f(\xi_1)$ and $D^{4\alpha} f(\xi_{-1})$, by the Intermediate Value Theorem we can infer that ξ exists between ξ_1 and ξ_1, and so in $(x-h, x+h)$. Thus, we have

$$D^{4\alpha} f(\xi) = \frac{1}{2}\left(D^{4\alpha} f(\xi_1) + D^{4\alpha} f(\xi_{-1})\right).$$

This consequently implies

$$\frac{\Gamma(2\alpha+1)}{2h^{2\alpha}}(f(x-h) - 2f(x) + f(x+h)) = D^{2\alpha} f(x) + \frac{\Gamma(2\alpha+1)}{\Gamma(4\alpha+1)} h^{2\alpha} D^{4\alpha} f(\xi), \tag{22}$$

which immediately gives the desired result. □

Remark 3. *It is obvious that, if we take $\alpha = 1$ in formula (16), then the conventional second derivative midpoint formula will be immediately yielded.*

3.2. Analysis of the Method

At the beginning of this section, we intend to depict the procedure of solving the FBVP given in (1) and (2). For this purpose, we apply Theorems 2 and 3 to approximate $D^\alpha y(x)$ and $D^{2\alpha} y(x)$, respectively. In other words, we have

$$D^\alpha y(x) \approx \frac{x_1^{2-\alpha}}{h^{2\alpha}\Gamma(3-\alpha)}(y(x_0) - 2y(x_1) + y(x_2)) \tag{23}$$

and

$$D^{2\alpha}y(x) \approx \frac{\Gamma(2\alpha+1)}{2h^{2\alpha}}(y(x_0) - 2y(x_1) + y(x_2)), \tag{24}$$

where h, x_0, x_1, x_2 are defined previously in Theorem 3, and $0 < \alpha \leq 1$. For the purpose of developing a novel approach to find the solution of the problem (1) and (2), we divide the interval $[a, b]$ into n subintervals through $x_i = a + ih$, for $i = 0, 1, 2, \ldots, N$, such that $a = x_0$ and $b = x_n$, where $h = \frac{b-a}{N}$. Now, at the point $x = x_i$, we have

$$D^{\alpha}y(x_i) \approx \frac{{x_i}^{2-\alpha}}{h^{2\alpha}\Gamma(3-\alpha)}(y(x_{i-1}) - 2y(x_i) + y(x_{i+1})), \tag{25}$$

and

$$D^{2\alpha}y(x_i) \approx \frac{\Gamma(2\alpha+1)}{2h^{2\alpha}}(y(x_{i-1}) - 2y(x_i) + y(x_{i+1})), \tag{26}$$

for $i = 1, 2, \ldots, N$. By substituting (25) and (26) in (1), we get

$$\frac{\Gamma(2\alpha+1)}{2h^{2\alpha}}(y(x_{i-1}) - 2y(x_i) + y(x_{i+1})) + \frac{q{x_i}^{2-\alpha}}{h^{2\alpha}\Gamma(3-\alpha)}(y(x_{i-1}) - 2y(x_i) + y(x_{i+1})) + ry(x_i) = f(x_i), \tag{27}$$

for $i = 1, 2, \ldots, N$. Actually, formula (27) can be rewritten in the form

$$\begin{aligned} \left(\frac{\Gamma(2\alpha+1)}{2} + \frac{q{x_i}^{2-\alpha}}{\Gamma(3-\alpha)}\right)y(x_{i-1}) - \left(\Gamma(2\alpha+1) + \frac{2q{x_i}^{2-\alpha}}{\Gamma(3-\alpha)} + r\right)y(x_i) \\ + \left(\frac{\Gamma(2\alpha+1)}{2} + \frac{q{x_i}^{2-\alpha}}{\Gamma(3-\alpha)}\right)y(x_{i+1}) = h^{2\alpha}f(x_i), \end{aligned} \tag{28}$$

for $i = 1, 2, \ldots, N$. For simplicity, we set the following assumptions:

$$a_i = \frac{\Gamma(2\alpha+1)}{2} + \frac{qx_i^{2-\alpha}}{\Gamma(3-\alpha)} \tag{29}$$

and

$$b_i = -\left(\Gamma(2\alpha+1) + \frac{2qx_i^{2-\alpha}}{\Gamma(3-\alpha)} + r\right), \tag{30}$$

for $i = 1, 2, \ldots, N$. This immediately converts (28) to

$$a_i(y(x_{i-1}) + y(x_{i+1})) + b_i y(x_i) = h^2 f(x_i), \tag{31}$$

for $i = 1, 2, \ldots, N$. In fact, the above formulas can be expressed in the matrix form as follows:

$$\begin{pmatrix} b_1 & a_1 & 0 & 0 & \ldots & 0 & 0 & 0 \\ a_2 & b_2 & a_2 & 0 & \ldots & 0 & 0 & 0 \\ 0 & a_3 & b_3 & a_3 & \ldots & 0 & 0 & 0 \\ \vdots & \vdots & \vdots & \vdots & \ddots & \vdots & \vdots & \vdots \\ 0 & 0 & 0 & 0 & \ldots & a_{N-1} & b_{N-1} & a_{N-1} \\ 0 & 0 & 0 & 0 & \ldots & 0 & a_N & b_N \end{pmatrix} \begin{pmatrix} y_1 \\ y_2 \\ y_3 \\ \vdots \\ y_{N-1} \\ y_N \end{pmatrix} = h^{2\alpha} \begin{pmatrix} f(x_1) \\ f(x_2) \\ f(x_3) \\ \vdots \\ f(x_{N-1}) \\ f(x_N) \end{pmatrix} - \begin{pmatrix} a_1 y_a \\ 0 \\ 0 \\ \vdots \\ 0 \\ a_N y_b \end{pmatrix}. \tag{32}$$

The above linear system can be denoted by $A\mathbf{X} = \mathbf{M}$, where

$$A = \begin{pmatrix} b_1 & a_1 & 0 & 0 & \ldots & 0 & 0 & 0 \\ a_2 & b_2 & a_2 & 0 & \ldots & 0 & 0 & 0 \\ 0 & a_3 & b_3 & a_3 & \ldots & 0 & 0 & 0 \\ \vdots & \vdots & \vdots & \vdots & \ddots & \vdots & \vdots & \vdots \\ 0 & 0 & 0 & 0 & \ldots & a_{N-1} & b_{N-1} & a_{N-1} \\ 0 & 0 & 0 & 0 & \ldots & 0 & a_N & b_N \end{pmatrix} \tag{33}$$

$$\mathbf{X} = [y_1, y_2, y_3, \cdots, y_{N-1}, y_N]^T$$

and

$$\mathbf{M} = \left[h^{2\alpha} f(x_1) - a_1 y_a, h^{2\alpha} f(x_2), h^{2\alpha} f(x_3), \cdots, h^{2\alpha} f(x_{N-1}), h^{2\alpha} f(x_N) - a_N y_N\right]^T.$$

As a matter of fact, system (32) is called tridiagonal and could be solved algebraically using the Thomas algorithm [15]. In particular, if we take formula (31) again as follows:

$$a_i(y_{i-1} + y_{i+1}) + b_i y_i = d_i, \tag{34}$$

where $d_i = h^{2\alpha} f(x_i)$ for $i = 1, 2, \ldots, N$. Now, formula (34) can be written in the form:

$$\begin{aligned}
&b_1 y_1 + a_1 y_2 = d_1^* \\
&b_2 y_2 + a_2(y_1 + y_3) = d_2 \\
&b_3 y_3 + a_3(y_2 + y_4) = d_3 \\
&\vdots \\
&b_{N-1} y_{N-1} + a_{N-1}(y_{N-2} + y_N) = d_{N-1} \\
&a_N y_{N-1} + b_N y_N = d_N^*,
\end{aligned} \tag{35}$$

where $d_1^* = h^{2\alpha} f(x_1) - a_1 y_a$ and $d_N^* = h^{2\alpha} f(x_N) - a_N y_b$. By considering the Thomas algorithm, we assume $b_1 \neq 0$ and eliminate y_1 from the second equation of system (35). This gives

$$b_2' y_2 + a_2 y_3 = d_2',$$

where $b_2' = b_2 - a_1 \frac{a_2}{b_1}$ and $d_2' = d_2 - d_1 \frac{a_2}{b_1}$. Next, assuming $b_2' \neq 0$ and eliminating y_2 from the third equation of system (35) yields

$$b_3' y_3 + a_3 y_4 = d_3',$$

where $b_3' = b_3 - a_2 \frac{a_3}{b_2'}$ and $d_3' = d_3 - d_2' \frac{a_3}{b_2'}$. Similarly, if we assume that $b_k' \neq 0$ and eliminating y_k from the $(k+1)$th-equation of the system (35), we obtain

$$b_{k+1}' y_{k+1} + a_{k+1} y_{k+2} = d_{k+1}',$$

where $b_{k+1}' = b_{k+1} - a_k \frac{a_{k+1}}{b_k'}$ and $d_{k+1}' = d_{k+1} - d_k' \frac{a_{k+1}}{b_k'}$, for $k = 1, 2, \ldots, N-1$. Consequently, by back substituting N and assuming $b_N' \neq 0$ in which $y_N = \frac{d_N'}{b_N'}$, we have

$$y_k = \frac{d_k' - a_k y_{k+1}}{b_k'},$$

for $k = N-1, N-2, \ldots, 1$. This finishes the Thomas algorithm and, hence, by proper MATLAB code, we can obtain the desired numerical solution of the aimed system (1) and (2).

3.3. Stability of the Method

In order to insure of the stability of the fractional central formula for approximating the Caputo differentiator of order 2α, where $0 < \alpha \leq 1$, we consider the following FBVP:

$$D^{2\alpha} y(x) = f(x), \tag{36}$$

with the boundary conditions

$$y(a) = y_a, \; y(b) = y_b, \tag{37}$$

where $a < x < b$. The important question to be asked here is how would $\hat{\mathbf{Y}} = [y_1, y_2, y_3, \cdots, y_{N-1}]^T$ be regarded a good approximation of solution of problem (36) and (37). To answer this question, we need to estimate the error in the discrete values $y_1, y_2, \ldots, y_N$ related to the true solution $y(x)$. In this regard, we assume the pointwise error is of the form $y_i - y(x_i)$, for $i = 0, 1, \ldots, N$, and the true vector is of the form $\mathbf{Y} = [y_1, y_2, y_3, \ldots, y_{N-1}, y_N]^T$. This gives the error of the form

$$\mathbf{E} = \hat{\mathbf{Y}} - \mathbf{Y},$$

which contains all error at each grid point. To obtain a bound on the magnitude of the above vector error, we need to estimate $O(h^{2\alpha})$ as $h \to 0$. To do this, we consider

$$||\mathbf{E}||_\infty = \max_{1 \leq i \leq 0} |E_i| = \max_{1 \leq i \leq 0} |y_i - y(x_i)|,$$

which represents the largest error order in the interval $[a, b]$. Therefore, if $||\mathbf{E}||_\infty = O(h^{2\alpha})$, then

$$|y_i - y(x_i)| = O(h^{2\alpha}),$$

for $i = 0, 1, \ldots, N$.

Next, our aim is to estimate the error in our proposed difference approach. To do so, we should be concerned with the local truncation error, and then with the stability of this approach for the purpose of justifying the boundedness of the global error. So, let us start with the local truncation error, which would be as follows:

$$T_i = \frac{\Gamma(2\alpha+1)}{2h^{2\alpha}} \Big(y(x_{i-1}) - 2y(x_i) + y(x_{i+1}) \Big) - f(x_i), \tag{38}$$

or

$$T_i = D^{2\alpha} y(x_i) - \frac{h^{2\alpha}\Gamma(2\alpha+1)}{\Gamma(4\alpha+1)} D^{4\alpha} y(\xi_i) + O(h^{4\alpha}) - f(x_i), \tag{39}$$

for $i = 1, 2, \ldots, N$. Now, by using $D^{2\alpha} y(x) = f(x)$, we have

$$T_i = -\frac{h^{2\alpha}\Gamma(2\alpha+1)}{\Gamma(4\alpha+1)} D^{4\alpha} y(\xi_i) + O(h^{4\alpha}). \tag{40}$$

Now, though $D^{4\alpha} y(\xi_i)$ is unknown fixed and is independent of h, we have $T_i \sim O(h^{4\alpha})$ as $h \to 0$. If we define $\mathbf{T}$ as a vector containing T_i, then

$$\mathbf{T} = A\mathbf{Y} - \mathbf{M},$$

which implies

$$A\mathbf{Y} = \mathbf{M} + \mathbf{T}. \tag{41}$$

Now, to address the global error, we can have from (41) the following approximation:

$$A\hat{\mathbf{Y}} = \mathbf{M}. \tag{42}$$

So, the global error is defined as

$$\mathbf{E} = \hat{\mathbf{Y}} - \mathbf{Y}.$$

Now, subtracting (41) and (42) yields

$$A(\hat{\mathbf{Y}} - \mathbf{Y}) = -\mathbf{T},$$

or

$$A\mathbf{E} = -\mathbf{T}. \tag{43}$$

This implies

$$\frac{\Gamma(2\alpha+1)}{2h^{2\alpha}} (E_{i-1} - 2E_i + E_{i+1}) = -T(x_i), \tag{44}$$

with boundary conditions

$$E_0 = 0, \;\; E_{N+1} = 0, \tag{45}$$

for $i = 1, 2, \ldots, N$. Note that problems (44) and (45) are the same as the difference equation reported previously for y_i, except $f(x_i) = -T(x_i)$, for $i = 1, 2, \ldots, N$. Actually, problems (44) and (45) can be expressed as

$$D^{2\alpha} e(x) = -\tau(x), \tag{46}$$

with boundary conditions

$$e(a) = 0, \;\; e(b) = 0, \tag{47}$$

where $a \leq x \leq b$ and

$$\tau(x) = \frac{\Gamma(2\alpha+1)}{\Gamma(4\alpha+1)} D^{4\alpha} y(x).$$

Now, if we operate $\mathcal{J}^{\alpha}$ in Equation (46), we get

$$D^{\alpha} e(x) = -h^{2\alpha} \frac{\Gamma(2\alpha+1)}{\Gamma(4\alpha+1)} (D^{3\alpha} y(x) - \{D^{2\alpha}\} y(0)),$$

or

$$D^{\alpha} e(x) = h^{2\alpha} \frac{\Gamma(2\alpha+1)}{\Gamma(4\alpha+1)} D^{2\alpha} y(0) - h^{2\alpha} \frac{\Gamma(2\alpha+1)}{\Gamma(4\alpha+1)} D^{3\alpha} y(x). \tag{48}$$

By operating $\mathcal{J}^{\alpha}$ twice again in Equation (48), we obtain

$$e(x) = h^{2\alpha} \frac{\Gamma(2\alpha+1)}{\Gamma(4\alpha+1)} \frac{x^{\alpha}}{\Gamma(\alpha+1)} D^{2\alpha} y(0) - h^{2\alpha} \frac{\Gamma(2\alpha+1)}{\Gamma(4\alpha+1)} \Big(D^{2\alpha} y(x) - D^{\alpha} y(0) \Big),$$

or

$$e(x) = -h^{2\alpha} \frac{\Gamma(2\alpha+1)}{\Gamma(4\alpha+1)} D^{2\alpha} y(x) + h^{2\alpha} \frac{\Gamma(2\alpha+1)}{\Gamma(4\alpha+1)} \left(\frac{x^{\alpha}}{\Gamma(\alpha+1)} D^{2\alpha} y(0) - D^{\alpha} y(0) \right).$$

This implies $\|\mathbf{E}\|_{\infty} \approx O(h^{2\alpha})$, which represents the desired estimation for the global error.

Now, with aim of dealing with the stability of the proposed difference scheme, we consider again system (43) in which A is the corresponding tridiagonal matrix, $\mathbf{E}$ is the global error matrix, and $\mathbf{T}$ is the local truncation error matrix. In fact, system (43) can be rewritten as

$$A^h \mathbf{E}^h = -\mathbf{T}^h, \tag{49}$$

for a given $h = \frac{1}{n+1}$. It is important to mention that $A^h_{m \times m}$, and as a result the dimension of A^h will grow as $h \to 0$. Now, let $(A^h)^{-1}$ exist. Then, we have

$$\mathbf{E}^h = -(A^h)^{-1} \mathbf{T}^h. \tag{50}$$

Consequently, we obtain

$$\left\| \mathbf{E}^h \right\| = \left\| (A^h)^{-1} \mathbf{T}^h \right\| \leq \left\| (A^h)^{-1} \right\| \left\| \mathbf{T}^h \right\|.$$

But we have $\left\| \mathbf{T}^h \right\| \sim O(h^{2\alpha})$. So, we expect the same for $\left\| \mathbf{E}^h \right\|$. Thus, for $\left\| \mathbf{E}^h \right\| \sim O(h^{2\alpha})$, then $\left\| (A^h)^{-1} \right\|$ is independent of h as $h \to 0$, say $\left\| (A^h)^{-1} \right\| \leq c$, for sufficiently small h, where c is constant. Therefore, we have

$$\left\| \mathbf{E}^h \right\| \leq c \left\| \mathbf{T}^h \right\|,$$

and hence the stability is ensured.

4. Numerical Experiments

In this section, we validate our proposed numerical approach discussed in the previous section by illustrating three numerical examples including FBVPs of the forms (1) and (2). We use MATLAB-2020 software to simulate the results in a few fractional-order values.

Example 1. *Consider the following FBVP:*

$$D^{2\alpha}y + 2y = 0, \tag{51}$$

with boundary conditions

$$y(0) = 1, \;\; y(\pi) = 0. \tag{52}$$

The exact solution for problems (51) and (52) is of the form

$$y(x) = \cos(\sqrt{2}x) - \cot(\sqrt{2}\pi)\sin(\sqrt{2}x). \tag{53}$$

In order to validate such an approach in handling the FBVPs, we track the proposed numerical approach discussed in Section 3. This would provide us with several approximate solutions for problem (51) and (52) with different fractional-order values, i.e., $\alpha = 1, 0.8, 0.6, 0.4$. Some of these approximate solutions are plot and compared with the exact solution (53) as can be seen in Figure 1 and Table 1.

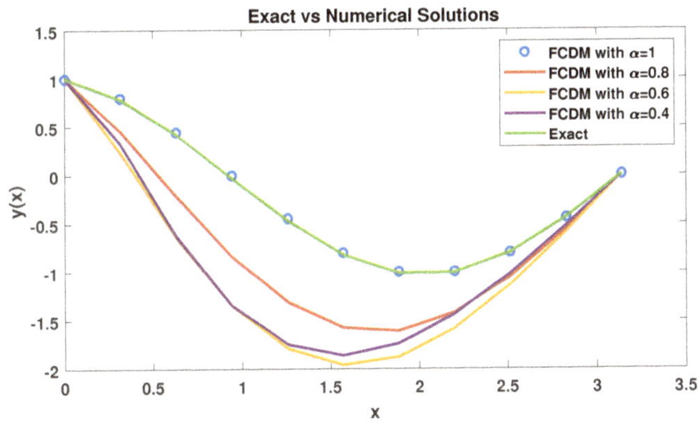

Figure 1. Exact solution vs. numerical solutions of problems (51) and (52) for $\alpha = 1, 0.8, 0.6, 0.4$.

In light of the previous numerical results, one can clearly observe that the approximate solutions generated by our approach converge to the exact solution as α gets closer to 1, confirming the validity of the proposed method.

Table 1. Exact solution vs. numerical solutions of problems (51) and (52) for $\alpha = 1, 0.8, 0.6, 0.4$.

x	$\alpha = 0.4$	$\alpha = 0.6$	$\alpha = 0.8$	$\alpha = 1$	Exact Solution
0	1.0000	1.0000	1.0000	1.0000	1.0000
0.1	0.3280	0.2289	0.4551	0.7989	0.7842
0.2	−0.6303	−0.6484	−0.2165	0.4401	0.4161
0.3	−1.3491	−1.3529	−0.8424	−0.0056	−0.0328
0.4	−1.7529	−1.7965	−1.3172	−0.4501	−0.4753
0.5	−1.8669	−1.9651	−1.5815	−0.8058	−0.8255
0.6	−1.7447	−1.8819	−1.6146	−1.0025	−1.0154
0.7	−1.4452	−1.5903	−1.4282	−1.0013	−1.0082
0.8	−1.0235	−1.1431	−1.0593	−0.8024	−0.8052
0.9	−0.5283	−0.5954	−0.5622	−0.4451	−0.4459
1.0	0.0000	0.0000	0.0000	0.0000	0.0000

Example 2. *Consider the following FBVP:*

$$D^{2\alpha}y = y + x, \tag{54}$$

with boundary conditions

$$y(0) = 0, \;\; y(1) = 0. \tag{55}$$

The exact solution for problems (54) and (55) is of the form

$$y(x) = \frac{\sinh x}{\sinh 1} - x. \tag{56}$$

With the aim of verifying the correctness of our proposed technique in handling the FBVPs, we follow the same manner used in Example 1 coupled with using the numerical approach discussed in the previous section. This would provide us with several approximate solutions for problems (54) and (55) with different fractional-order values, i.e., $\alpha = 1, 0.8, 0.6, 0.4$. *Some of these approximate solutions are plotted and compared with the exact solution (56) as can be seen in Figure 2 and Table 2.*

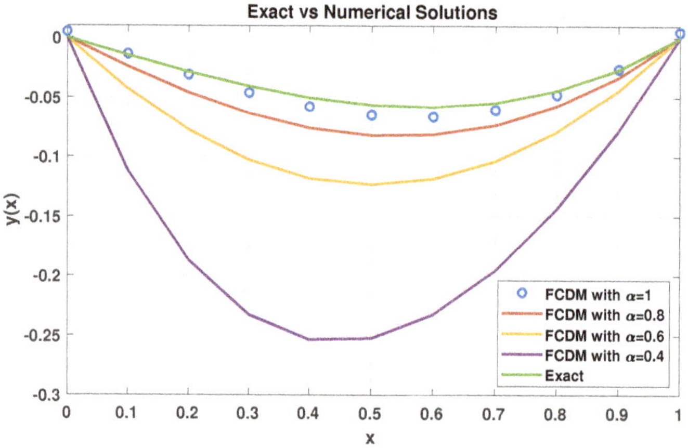

Figure 2. Exact solution vs. numerical solutions of problems (54) and (55) for $\alpha = 1, 0.8, 0.6, 0.4$.

Table 2. Exact solution vs. numerical solutions of problems (54) and (55) for $\alpha = 1, 0.8, 0.6, 0.4$.

x	$\alpha = 0.4$	$\alpha = 0.6$	$\alpha = 0.8$	$\alpha = 1$	Exact Solution
0	0.0000	0.0000	0.0000	0.0000	0.0000
0.1	−0.1120	−0.0429	−0.0244	−0.0150	−0.0148
0.2	−0.1870	−0.0775	−0.0460	−0.0299	−0.0287
0.3	−0.2326	−0.1026	−0.0635	−0.0412	−0.0409
0.4	−0.2533	−0.1180	−0.0758	−0.0508	−0.0505
0.5	−0.2524	−0.1233	−0.0819	−0.0568	−0.0566
0.6	−0.2324	−0.1185	−0.0813	−0.0589	−0.0583
0.7	−0.1955	−0.1036	−0.0732	−0.566	−0.0545
0.8	−0.1435	−0.0788	−0.0572	−0.0476	−0.0443
0.9	−0.0778	−0.0442	−0.0329	−0.0269	−0.0265
1.0	0.0000	0.0000	0.0000	0.0000	0.0000

Herein, we can also notice that the approximate solutions generated by our numerical scheme converge to the exact solution as α *gets closer to 1.*

Example 3. *Consider the following FBVP:*

$$D^{2\alpha}y + 5D^{\alpha}y + 4y = 1, \tag{57}$$

with boundary conditions

$$y(0) = 0, \ \ y(1) = 0. \tag{58}$$

The exact solution for problems (57) and (58) is of the form

$$y(x) = \left(\frac{e^{-3} - e}{4(1 - e^{-3})}\right)e^{-x} + \left(-\frac{1}{4} - \left(\frac{e^{-3} - e}{4(1 - e^{-3})}\right)\right)e^{-4x} + \frac{1}{4}. \tag{59}$$

In a similar manner to the previous two examples, we generate here several approximate solutions for problems (57) and (58) with different fractional-order values, i.e., $\alpha = 1, 0.8, 0.6, 0.4$. *Some of these approximate solutions are plotted and compared with the exact solution (59) as can be seen in Figure 3 and Table 3.*

Note that the approximate solutions obtained by the proposed scheme also converge to the exact solution as α *gets closer to 1.*

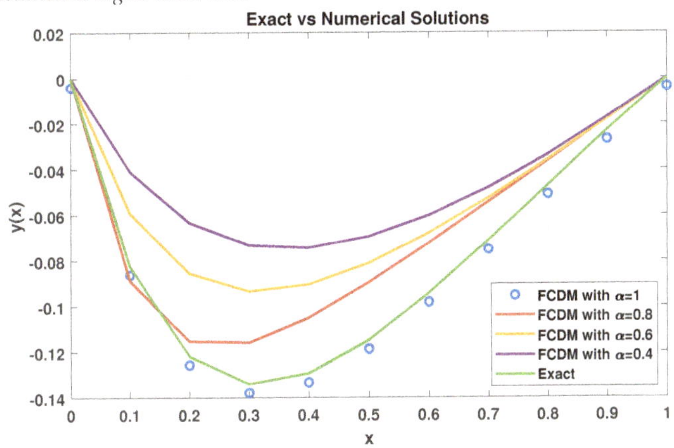

Figure 3. Exact solution vs. numerical solutions of problems (57) and (58) for $\alpha = 1, 0.8, 0.6, 0.4$.

Table 3. Exact solution vs. numerical solutions of problems (57) and (58) for $\alpha = 1, 0.8, 0.6, 0.4$.

x	$\alpha = 0.4$	$\alpha = 0.6$	$\alpha = 0.8$	$\alpha = 1$	Exact Solution
0	0.0000	0.0000	0.0000	0.0000	0.0000
0.1	−0.1365	−0.0409	−0.0591	−0.0862	−0.0822
0.2	−0.1479	−0.0633	−0.0855	−0.1257	−0.1217
0.3	−0.1323	−0.0732	−0.0934	−0.1379	−0.1339
0.4	−0.1120	−0.0743	−0.0905	−0.1333	−0.1293
0.5	−0.0919	−0.0695	−0.0811	−0.1188	−0.1146
0.6	−0.0727	−0.0603	−0.0680	−0.0981	−0.0943
0.7	−0.0542	−0.0481	−0.0527	−0.0752	−0.0712
0.8	−0.0360	−0.0336	−0.0359	−0.0510	−0.0470
0.9	−0.0180	−0.0175	−0.0183	−0.0271	−0.0231
1.0	0.0000	0.0000	0.0000	0.0000	0.0000

5. Conclusions

In this paper, a novel numerical approach has been successfully proposed to deal with fractional boundary value problems. This has been carried out by utilizing two numerical formulas—the fractional central formula for approximating the Caputo differentiator of order α and the fractional central formula for approximating the Caputo differentiator of order 2α, where $0 < \alpha \leq 1$. The stability analysis of the proposed approach has been discussed, and several numerical examples have been illustrated to show the applicability of the proposed method. Thus, in light of this study, we believe that we can address many other kinds of fractional-order problems in a similar manner, such as the fractional-order system of differential equations, fractional partial differential equations, and fractional integrodifferential equations. This is left to the future for further consideration.

Author Contributions: Conceptualization, A.A.A.-N.; Methodology, I.M.B.; Validation, A.A.A.-N.; Formal analysis, I.M.B.; Resources, S.M.; Writing—original draft, A.A.A.-N.; Writing—review & editing, I.M.B.; Visualization, S.M.; Supervision, S.M. All authors have read and agreed to the published version of the manuscript.

Funding: This research was funded by Deputyship for research & Innovation, Ministry of Education in Saudi Arabia for funding this research through the project number (IF2/PSAU/2022/01/22174).

Data Availability Statement: Not applicable.

Acknowledgments: The authors extend their appreciation to the Deputyship for research & Innovation, Ministry of Education in Saudi Arabia for funding this research through the project number (IF2/PSAU/2022/01/22174).

Conflicts of Interest: The authors declare no conflict of interest.

References

1. Aydemir, K.; Olğar, H.; Mukhtarov, O.S.; Muhtarov, F.S. Differential Operator Equations with Interface Conditions in Modified Direct Sum Spaces. *Filomat* **2018**, *32*, 921–931. [CrossRef]
2. Bezziou, M.; Dahmani, Z.; Jebril, I.; Belhamiti, M.M. Solvability for a Differential System of Duffing Type Via Caputo-Hadamard Approach. *Appl. Math. Inf. Sci.* **2022**, *16*, 341–352.
3. Abu-Zaid, I.T.; El-Gebeily, M.A. A finite-difference method for the spectral approximation of a class of singular two-point boundary value problems. *IMA J. Numer. Anal.* **1994**, *14*, 545–562. [CrossRef]
4. Fulton, C.T. Two-point boundary value problems with eigenvalue parameter contained in the boundary conditions. *Proc. Roy. Soc. Edinb.* **1977**, *77A*, 293–308. [CrossRef]
5. Mukhtarov, O.; Olğar, H.; Aydemir, K. Resolvent Operator and Spectrum of New Type Boundary Value Problems. *Filomat* **2015**, *29*, 1671–1680. [CrossRef]
6. Keller, H.B. *Numerical Methods for Two-Point Boundary-Value Problems*; Courier Dover Publications: Mineola, NY, USA, 2018.
7. Endeshaw B. Finite Difference Method for Boundary Value Problems in Ordinary Differential Equations. *Math. Theory Model.* **2019**, *9*, 17–27.
8. Zhang, T.; Li, Y. Exponential Euler scheme of multi-delay Caputo–Fabrizio fractional-order differential equations. *Appl. Math. Lett.* **2022**, *124*, 107709. [CrossRef]
9. Albadarneh, R.B.; Batiha, I.M.; Zurigat, M. Numerical solutions for linear fractional differential equations of order $1 < \alpha < 2$ using finite difference method (FFDM). *Int. J. Math. Comput. Sci.* **2016**, *16*, 103–111.
10. Albadarneh, R.B.; Zerqat, M.; Batiha, I.M. Numerical solutions for linear and non-linear fractional differential equations. *Int. J. Pure Appl. Math.* **2016**, *106*, 859–871. [CrossRef]
11. Batiha, I.M.; Alshorm, S.; Ouannas, A.; Momani, S.; Ababneh, O.Y.; Albdareen, M. Modified Three-Point Fractional Formulas with Richardson Extrapolation. *Mathematics* **2022**, *10*, 3489. [CrossRef]
12. Kilbas, A.A. *Theory and Application of Fractional Differential Equations*; Elsevier: Amsterdam, The Netherlands, 2006.
13. Mainardi, F. Fractional Calculus. In *Fractals and Fractional Calculus in Continuum Mechanics*; Springer: Berlin, Germany, 1997; pp. 291–348.
14. Odibat, Z.M.; Momani, S. An algorithm for the numerical solution of differential equations of fractional order. *J. Appl. Math. Inform.* **2008**, *26*, 15–27.
15. Bittelli; Marco; Campbell, G.S.; Tomei, F. *Soil Physics with Python: Transport in the Soil–Plant–Atmosphere System*; Oxford Academic: Oxford, UK, 2015.:oso/9780199683093.001.0001. [CrossRef]

mathematics

MDPI

Article

Integro-Differential Boundary Conditions to the Sequential ψ_1-Hilfer and ψ_2-Caputo Fractional Differential Equations

Surang Sitho [1], Sotiris K. Ntouyas [2], Chayapat Sudprasert [3] and Jessada Tariboon [3,*]

[1] Department of Social and Applied Science, College of Industrial Technology, King Mongkut's University of Technology North Bangkok, Bangkok 10800, Thailand
[2] Department of Mathematics, University of Ioannina, 451 10 Ioannina, Greece
[3] Intelligent and Nonlinear Dynamic Innovations Research Center, Department of Mathematics, Faculty of Applied Science, King Mongkut's University of Technology North Bangkok, Bangkok 10800, Thailand
* Correspondence: jessada.t@sci.kmutnb.ac.th

Abstract: In this paper, we introduce and study a new class of boundary value problems, consisting of a mixed-type ψ_1-Hilfer and ψ_2-Caputo fractional order differential equation supplemented with integro-differential nonlocal boundary conditions. The uniqueness of solutions is achieved via the Banach contraction principle, while the existence of results is established by using the Leray–Schauder nonlinear alternative. Numerical examples are constructed illustrating the obtained results.

Keywords: ψ-Hilfer fractional derivative; Caputo fractional derivative; boundary value problems; nonlocal boundary conditions; existence; uniqueness; fixed point

MSC: 26A33; 34A08; 34B10

1. Introduction

Fractional order differential equations have recently proved to be valuable tools in the modeling of many phenomena in various fields of mathematics, physics, viscoelasticity, electrochemistry, engineering, control, porous media, electromagnetic, etc., see [1–5] and references cited therein. For a theoretical approach of fractional calculus, see the monographs [6–11]. Many processes in physics and engineering can be described accurately by using differential equations containing different types of fractional derivatives such as Riemann–Liouville, Caputo, Hadamard, Erdeyl–Kober, Hilfer, Caputo–Hadamard, etc. Hilfer proposed in [12] a fractional derivative operator generalizing both Riemann–Liouville and Caputo fractional derivative operators. For the advantages of the Hilfer derivative, see [13]. In [14], the ψ-Hilfer fractional derivative operator was introduced. Initial and boundary value problems including the ψ-Hilfer fractional derivative operator have been studied by many researchers, see [15–20] and references therein.

In the present paper, we investigate a new class of boundary value problems, consisting of mixed-type fractional differential equations including ψ_1-Hilfer and ψ_2-Caputo fractional derivative operators supplemented with nonlocal integro-differential boundary conditions. More precisely, we consider the following sequential ψ_1-Hilfer and ψ_2-Caputo fractional differential equation with nonlocal integro-differential boundary conditions

$$\begin{cases} {}^{H}\mathbb{D}^{\alpha,\beta;\psi_1}({}^{C}\mathbb{D}^{\gamma;\psi_2}\pi)(t) = \Pi(t,\pi(t)), \quad 0<\alpha,\beta,\gamma<1,\ t\in[0,x_1], \\ {}^{C}\mathbb{D}^{\gamma;\psi_2}\pi(0)=0, \quad \pi(T)=\sum_{i=1}^{m}\lambda_i\,{}^{C}\mathbb{D}^{\gamma;\psi_2}\pi(\eta_i)+\sum_{j=1}^{n}\delta_j\,\mathbb{I}^{\mu_j;\psi_2}\pi(\xi_j), \end{cases} \tag{1}$$

where ${}^{H}\mathbb{D}^{\alpha,\beta;\psi_1}$ and ${}^{C}\mathbb{D}^{\gamma;\psi_2}$ are the ψ_1-Hilfer and ψ_2-Caputo fractional derivatives with respect to functions ψ_1 and ψ_2, respectively, when $\psi_1'(t),\psi_2'(t)>0$ for all $t\in[0,x_1]$.

In addition, the given constants $\lambda_i, \delta_j \in \mathbb{R}$ and some points $\eta_i, \xi_j \in (0, x_1)$, $\mathbb{I}^{\mu_j;\psi_2}$ is the Riemann–Liouville fractional integral of order $\mu_j > 0$, with respect to a function ψ_2, for $i = 1, \cdots, m$, $j = 1, \cdots, n$ and $\Pi : [0, x_1] \times \mathbb{R} \to \mathbb{R}$ is a nonlinear continuous function. Existence and uniqueness are established via Banach's fixed point theorem and the Leray–Schauder nonlinear alternative.

The novelty of this study lies in the fact that we introduce a new class of nonlocal boundary value problems in which we combine ψ_1-Hilfer and ψ_2-Caputo fractional derivative operators and as far as we know, this is the only paper dealing with this combination. By fixing the parameters in the nonlocal integro-differential fractional boundary value problem (1), we obtain some new results as special cases. For example, we get to:

(i) Hilfer and Caputo fractional nonlocal integro-differential boundary value problem if $\psi_1(t) = \psi_2(t) = t$;

(ii) ψ_2-Hilfer and Caputo-type fractional nonlocal integro-differential boundary value problem if $\psi_1(t) = t$;

(iii) ψ_1-Hilfer and Caputo-type nonlocal integro-differential boundary value problem if $\psi_2(t) = t$.

The remaining part of this article is organized as follows: in Section 2, some preliminary definitions and results that will be applied in the next sections are recalled. In addition, an auxiliary result is proved to convert the problem (1) into a fixed point problem. In Section 3, the main results for the nonlocal integro-differential boundary value problem (1) are established, while in Section 4, these results are discussed for some special cases. Section 5 includes some numerical examples illustrating the main results.

2. Preliminaries

Now, some notations and definitions of fractional calculus are recalled. In the following, we assume that $\psi \in C^1([0, x_1], \mathbb{R})$ is an increasing function with $\psi'(t) > 0$ for all $t \in [0, x_1]$.

Definition 1 ([7]). *Given $\alpha > 0$ and $\hat{h} \in L^1([0, x_1], \mathbb{R})$, the ψ-Riemann–Liouville fractional integral of order α of a function $\hat{h}$ with respect to ψ is defined by*

$$\mathbb{I}_0^{\alpha;\psi}\hat{h}(t) = \frac{1}{\Gamma(\alpha)} \int_a^t \psi'(s)(\psi(t) - \psi(s))^{\alpha-1}\hat{h}(s)ds.$$

To abbreviate, we use $\mathbb{I}_0^{\alpha;\psi}\hat{h}(t)$ as $\mathbb{I}^{\alpha;\psi}\hat{h}(t)$ throughout this paper.

Definition 2 ([14]). *Suppose that $n - 1 < \alpha < n$, $n \in \mathbb{N}$ and $\hat{h}, \psi \in C^n([0, x_1], \mathbb{R})$. The ψ-Hilfer fractional derivative ${}^H\mathbb{D}^{\alpha,\beta;\psi}(\cdot)$ of order α of a function $\hat{h}$ with a parameter $\beta \in [0, 1]$ is defined by*

$${}^H\mathbb{D}^{\alpha,\beta;\psi}\hat{h}(t) = \mathbb{I}^{\beta(n-\alpha);\psi}\left(\frac{1}{\psi'(t)}\frac{d}{dt}\right)^n \mathbb{I}^{(1-\beta)(n-\alpha);\psi}\hat{h}(t),$$

provided that the right-hand side exists.

Definition 3 ([21]). *The ψ-Caputo fractional derivative ${}^C\mathbb{D}^{\alpha;\psi}(\cdot)$ of order α of a function $\hat{h}$ is expressed as*

$${}^C\mathbb{D}^{\alpha;\psi}\hat{h}(t) = \mathbb{I}^{n-\alpha;\psi}\left(\frac{1}{\psi'(t)}\frac{d}{dt}\right)^n \hat{h}(t),$$

where $n - 1 < \alpha < n$, $n \in \mathbb{N}$ and $\hat{h}, \psi \in C^n([0, x_1], \mathbb{R})$.

Remark 1 ([22]). *The following relations hold:*

$$\rho = \alpha + \beta(n - \alpha), \quad n - 1 < \alpha, \quad \rho < n, \quad 0 \leq \beta \leq 1,$$

and

$$\rho \geq \alpha, \quad \rho > \beta, \quad n - \rho < n - \beta(n - \alpha).$$

Lemma 1 ([14]). *Let $\alpha, \mu > 0$ and $\delta > 1$ be constants. Then, we have:*
(i) $\mathbb{I}^{\alpha;\psi}\mathbb{I}^{\mu;\psi}\hat{h}(t) = \mathbb{I}^{\alpha+\mu;\psi}\hat{h}(t)$;
(ii) $\mathbb{I}^{\alpha;\psi}(\psi(t) - \psi(0))^{\delta-1} = \dfrac{\Gamma(\delta)}{\Gamma(\alpha+\delta)}(\psi(t) - \psi(0))^{\alpha+\delta-1}$.

Lemma 2. *Let $\hat{h} \in L(0, x_1)$, $n - 1 < \alpha \leq n$, $n \in \mathbb{N}$, $0 \leq \beta \leq 1$, $\rho = \alpha + n\beta - \alpha\beta$, $\left(\mathbb{I}^{(n-\alpha)(1-\beta);\psi}\hat{h}\right) \in AC^k[0, x_1]$. (Here, by $AC^k[0, x_1]$, we denote the space of k times absolutely continuous functions on $[0, x_1]$.) Then, we have*

$$\left(\mathbb{I}^{\alpha;\psi}\, {}^H\mathbb{D}^{\alpha,\beta;\psi}\hat{h}\right)(t) = \hat{h}(t) - \sum_{k=1}^{n} \frac{(\psi(t) - \psi(a))^{\rho-k}}{\Gamma(\rho - k + 1)} \hat{h}_{\psi}^{[n-k]}\left(\mathbb{I}^{(1-\beta)(n-\alpha);\psi}\hat{h}\right)(a),$$

where $\hat{h}_{\psi}^{[n-k]} = \left(\dfrac{1}{\psi'(t)}\dfrac{d}{dt}\right)^{n-k}$ *and*

$$\left(\mathbb{I}^{\alpha;\psi}\, {}^C\mathbb{D}^{\alpha;\psi}\hat{h}\right)(t) = \hat{h}(t) - \sum_{k=0}^{n-1} \frac{\hat{h}_{\psi}^{[k]}\hat{h}(a)}{k!}(\psi(t) - \psi(a))^k.$$

A linear variant of the sequential Hilfer–Caputo fractional integro-differential boundary value problem (1) is investigated in the next lemma.

Lemma 3. *Let $h \in C([0, x_1], \mathbb{R})$ be a given function and all constants are as in boundary value problem (1). Then, the sequential Hilfer–Caputo fractional integro-differential linear boundary value problem*

$$\begin{cases} {}^H\mathbb{D}^{\alpha,\beta;\psi_1}({}^C\mathbb{D}^{\gamma;\psi_2}\pi)(t) = h(t), \quad t \in [0, x_1], \\ {}^C\mathbb{D}^{\gamma;\psi_2}\pi(0) = 0, \quad \pi(x_1) = \sum\limits_{i=1}^{m} \lambda_i\, {}^C\mathbb{D}^{\gamma;\psi_2}\pi(\eta_i) + \sum\limits_{j=1}^{n} \delta_j\, \mathbb{I}^{\mu_j;\psi_2}\pi(\xi_j) \end{cases} \tag{2}$$

is equivalent to the integral equation

$$\begin{aligned} \pi(t) \;=\; & \frac{1}{A}\left(\sum_{i=1}^{m} \lambda_i \mathbb{I}^{\alpha;\psi_1}h(\eta_i) + \sum_{j=1}^{n} \delta_j \mathbb{I}^{\mu_j+\gamma;\psi_2}\mathbb{I}^{\alpha;\psi_1}h(\xi_j) - \mathbb{I}^{\gamma;\psi_2}\mathbb{I}^{\alpha;\psi_1}h(x_1)\right) \\ & + \mathbb{I}^{\gamma;\psi_2}\mathbb{I}^{\alpha;\psi_1}h(t), \end{aligned} \tag{3}$$

where it is assumed that

$$A := 1 - \sum_{j=1}^{n} \delta_j \frac{[\psi_2(\xi_j) - \psi_2(0)]^{\mu_j}}{\Gamma(\mu_j + 1)} \neq 0. \tag{4}$$

Proof. Operating the fractional integral $\mathbb{I}^{\alpha;\psi_1}$ to both sides of the first equation in (2) and applying Lemma 2, we obtain for $t \in [0, x_1]$, that

$${}^C\mathbb{D}^{\gamma;\psi_2}\pi(t) = \frac{c_0}{\Gamma(\rho_1)}(\psi_1(t) - \psi_1(0))^{\rho_1-1} + \mathbb{I}^{\alpha;\psi_1}h(t),$$

where $\rho_1 = \alpha + (1-\alpha)\beta$ and $c_0 \in \mathbb{R}$. Since $\rho_1 \in (\alpha, 1)$, by Remark 1, from ${}^C\mathbb{D}^{\gamma;\psi_2}\pi(0) = 0$, we have $c_0 = 0$. Therefore, we get

$${}^C\mathbb{D}^{\gamma;\psi_2}\pi(t) = \mathbb{I}^{\alpha;\psi_1}h(t), \tag{5}$$

which leads to

$$\sum_{i=1}^{m} \lambda_i\, {}^{C}\mathbb{D}^{\gamma;\psi_2}\pi(\eta_i) = \sum_{i=1}^{m} \lambda_i \mathbb{I}^{\alpha;\psi_1} h(\eta_i). \tag{6}$$

Acting $\mathbb{I}^{\gamma;\psi_2}$ in (5) yields

$$\pi(t) = c_1 + \mathbb{I}^{\gamma;\psi_2}\mathbb{I}^{\alpha;\psi_1} h(t). \tag{7}$$

In addition, we have

$$\sum_{j=1}^{n} \delta_j \mathbb{I}^{\mu_j;\psi_2}\pi(\xi_j) = c_1 \sum_{j=1}^{n} \delta_j \frac{[\psi_2(\xi_j) - \psi_2(0)]^{\mu_j}}{\Gamma(\mu_j+1)} + \sum_{j=1}^{n} \delta_j \mathbb{I}^{\mu_j+\gamma;\psi_2}\mathbb{I}^{\alpha;\psi_1} h(\xi_j). \tag{8}$$

From the second boundary condition (2) with (6) and (8), we get

$$c_1 = \frac{1}{A}\left[\sum_{i=1}^{m} \lambda_i \mathbb{I}^{\alpha;\psi_1} h(\eta_i) + \sum_{j=1}^{n} \delta_j \mathbb{I}^{\mu_j+\gamma;\psi_2}\mathbb{I}^{\alpha;\psi_1} h(\xi_j) - \mathbb{I}^{\gamma;\psi_2}\mathbb{I}^{\alpha;\psi_1} h(x_1)\right], \tag{9}$$

where A is defined in (4). Substituting the value of c_1 in (7), we get the solution (3). On the other hand, by taking the fractional differential operator of ψ_2-Caputo and ψ_1-Hilfer of orders γ and α, respectively, we get the first equation in problem (2). By direct computation, it is easy to see that (3) satisfies the two boundary conditions in (2). Therefore, the proof is completed. □

3. Main Results

In this section, we establish existence and uniqueness of solutions to the sequential Hilfer–Caputo fractional integro-differential boundary value problem (1) on an interval $J = [0, x_1]$. At first, we denote the Banach space of all continuous functions from J to $\mathbb{R}$ equipped with the norm $\|\pi\| = \sup\{|\pi(t)| : t \in J\}$ by $\mathcal{C} = C(J, \mathbb{R})$. Having in mind Lemma 3, we define an operator $\mathbb{W} : \mathcal{C} \to \mathcal{C}$ by

$$\begin{aligned}(\mathbb{W}\pi)(t) &= \frac{1}{A}\Big[\sum_{i=1}^{m} \lambda_i \mathbb{I}^{\alpha;\psi_1}\Pi(\eta_i, \pi(\eta_i)) + \sum_{j=1}^{n} \delta_j \mathbb{I}^{\mu_j+\gamma;\psi_2}\mathbb{I}^{\alpha;\psi_1}\Pi(\xi_j, \pi(\xi_j)) \\ &\quad - \mathbb{I}^{\gamma;\psi_2}\mathbb{I}^{\alpha;\psi_1}\Pi(x_1, \pi(x_1))\Big] + \mathbb{I}^{\gamma;\psi_2}\mathbb{I}^{\alpha;\psi_1}\Pi(t, \pi(t)),\end{aligned} \tag{10}$$

where

$$\mathbb{I}^{\alpha;\psi_1}\Pi(\eta_i, \pi(\eta_i)) = \frac{1}{\Gamma(\alpha)}\int_0^{\eta_i} \psi_1'(s)(\psi_1(\eta_i) - \psi_1(s))^{\alpha-1}\Pi(s, \pi(s))ds$$

and

$$\begin{aligned}&\mathbb{I}^{\phi;\psi_2}\mathbb{I}^{\alpha;\psi_1}\Pi(l, \pi(l)) \\ =\ &\frac{1}{\Gamma(\alpha)\Gamma(\phi)}\int_0^{l}\int_0^{u} \psi_1'(s)\psi_2'(u)(\psi_1(u) - \psi_1(s))^{\alpha-1}(\psi_2(l) - \psi_2(u))^{\phi-1}\Pi(s, \pi(s))dsdu,\end{aligned}$$

with $\phi \in \{\gamma, \mu_j + \gamma\}$ and $l \in \{t, x_1, \xi_j\}$. Note that if $\Pi(t, \pi) \equiv 1$, we have

$$\begin{aligned}\mathbb{I}^{\phi;\psi_2}\mathbb{I}^{\alpha;\psi_1}(1)(l) &= \frac{1}{\Gamma(\alpha+1)\Gamma(\phi)}\int_0^{l} \psi_2'(u)(\psi_1(u) - \psi_1(0))^{\alpha}(\psi_2(l) - \psi_2(u))^{\phi-1}du \\ &:= A^{\alpha,\phi}_{\psi_1,\psi_2}(l).\end{aligned}$$

For convenience, we put

$$A_1 = \frac{1}{|A|}\left(\sum_{i=1}^{m} |\lambda_i| \frac{[\psi_1(\eta_i) - \psi_1(0)]^{\alpha}}{\Gamma(\alpha+1)} + \sum_{j=1}^{n} |\delta_j| A^{\alpha,\mu_j+\gamma}_{\psi_1,\psi_2}(\xi_j)\right)$$

$$+\left(\frac{|A|+1}{|A|}\right)A^{\alpha,\gamma}_{\psi_1,\psi_2}(x_1). \tag{11}$$

In the following theorem, we prove the existence and uniqueness of solutions of the fractional integro-differential boundary value problem of sequential Hilfer and Caputo fractional derivatives (1) by applying the Banach contraction mapping principle.

Theorem 1. *Let $\Pi : J \times \mathbb{R} \to \mathbb{R}$ such that:*
$(\mathbb{H}_1)$ There exists $\mathbb{L} > 0$ such that

$$|\Pi(t,\pi_1) - \Pi(t,\pi_2)| \le \mathbb{L}|\pi_1 - \pi_2|, \tag{12}$$

$\forall t \in J$ and $\pi_1, \pi_2 \in \mathbb{R}$.
If

$$A_1\mathbb{L} < 1, \tag{13}$$

where A_1 is given by (11). Then, the fractional integro-differential boundary value problem of sequential Hilfer and Caputo fractional derivatives (1) *has a unique solution on J.*

Proof. Let $M = \sup\{|\Pi(t,0)| : t \in J\}$ and $B_r = \{\pi \in \mathcal{C} : \|\pi\| \le r^*\}$ with

$$r^* \ge \frac{MA_1}{1 - A_1\mathbb{L}}. \tag{14}$$

Now, we will show that $\mathbb{W}B_{r^*} \subseteq B_{r^*}$. For any $\pi \in B_{r^*}$, we obtain

$$\begin{aligned}
|\mathbb{W}\pi(t)| &\le \sup_{t\in J}|\mathbb{W}\pi(t)| \\
&\le \frac{1}{|A|}\Bigg[\sum_{i=1}^{m}|\lambda_i|\mathbb{I}^{\alpha;\psi_1}(|\Pi(\eta_i,\pi(\eta_i)) - \Pi(\eta_i,0)| + |\Pi(\eta_i,0)|) \\
&\quad + \sum_{j=1}^{n}|\delta_j|\mathbb{I}^{\mu_j+\gamma;\psi_2}\mathbb{I}^{\alpha;\psi_1}(|\Pi(\xi_j,\pi(\xi_j)) - \Pi(\xi_j,0)| + |\Pi(\xi_j,0)|) \\
&\quad + \mathbb{I}^{\gamma;\psi_2}\mathbb{I}^{\alpha;\psi_1}(|\Pi(x_1,\pi(x_1)) - \Pi(x_1,0)| + |\Pi(x_1,0)|)\Bigg] \\
&\quad + \mathbb{I}^{\gamma;\psi_2}\mathbb{I}^{\alpha;\psi_1}(|\Pi(x_1,\pi(x_1)) - \Pi(x_1,0)| + |\Pi(x_1,0)|) \\
&\le \frac{1}{|A|}\Bigg[\sum_{i=1}^{m}|\lambda_i|(\mathbb{L}r^* + M)I^{\alpha;\psi_1}(1)(\eta_i) \\
&\quad + \sum_{j=1}^{n}|\delta_j|(\mathbb{L}r^* + M)I^{\mu_j+\gamma;\psi_2}I^{\alpha;\psi_1}(1)(\xi_j) \\
&\quad + (\mathbb{L}r^* + M)I^{\gamma;\psi_2}I^{\alpha;\psi_1}(1)(x_1)\Bigg] + (\mathbb{L}r^* + M)I^{\gamma;\psi_2}I^{\alpha;\psi_1}(1)(x_1) \\
&= \frac{1}{|A|}\Bigg[(\mathbb{L}r^* + M)\sum_{i=1}^{m}|\lambda_i|\frac{[\psi_1(\eta_i) - \psi_1(0)]^{\alpha}}{\Gamma(\alpha+1)} \\
&\quad + (\mathbb{L}r^* + M)\sum_{j=1}^{n}|\delta_j|A^{\alpha,\mu_j+\gamma}_{\psi_1,\psi_2}(\xi_j) + (\mathbb{L}r^* + M)A^{\alpha,\gamma}_{\psi_1,\psi_2}(x_1)\Bigg] \\
&\quad + (\mathbb{L}r^* + M)A^{\alpha,\gamma}_{\psi_1,\psi_2}(x_1) \\
&= (\mathbb{L}r^* + M)A_1 \le r^*,
\end{aligned}$$

which holds from (14). This shows that $\mathbb{W}B_{r^*} \subseteq B_{r^*}$. Next, we let $\pi_1, \pi_2 \in B_{r^*}$, then we have

$$\begin{aligned}
|\mathbb{W}\pi_1(t) - \mathbb{W}\pi_2(t)| &\leq \sup_{t\in J} |\mathbb{W}\pi_1(t) - \mathbb{W}\pi_2(t)| \\
&\leq \frac{1}{|A|}\left[\sum_{i=1}^{m} |\lambda_i|\mathbb{I}^{\alpha;\psi_1}|\Pi(\eta_i, \pi_1(\eta_i)) - \Pi(\eta_i, \pi_2(\eta_i))|\right. \\
&\quad + \sum_{j=1}^{n} |\delta_j|\mathbb{I}^{\mu_j+\gamma;\psi_2}\mathbb{I}^{\alpha;\psi_1}|\Pi(\xi_j, \pi_1(\xi_j)) - \Pi(\xi_j, \pi_2(\xi_j))| \\
&\quad \left. + \mathbb{I}^{\gamma;\psi_2}\mathbb{I}^{\alpha;\psi_1}|\Pi(x_1, \pi_1(x_1)) - \Pi(x_1, \pi_2(x_1))|\right] \\
&\quad + \mathbb{I}^{\gamma;\psi_2}\mathbb{I}^{\alpha;\psi_1}|\Pi(x_1, \pi_1(x_1)) - \Pi(x_1, \pi_2(x_1))|, \\
&\leq \frac{\mathbb{L}}{|A|}\left[\|\pi_1 - \pi_2\| \sum_{i=1}^{m} |\lambda_i|\mathbb{I}^{\alpha;\psi_1}(1)(\eta_i)\right. \\
&\quad + \|\pi_1 - \pi_2\| \sum_{j=1}^{n} |\delta_j|\mathbb{I}^{\mu_j+\gamma;\psi_2}\mathbb{I}^{\alpha;\psi_1}(1)(\xi_j) \\
&\quad \left. + \|\pi_1 - \pi_2\|\mathbb{I}^{\gamma;\psi_2}\mathbb{I}^{\alpha;\psi_1}(1)(x_1)\right] + L\|\pi_1 - \pi_2\|\mathbb{I}^{\gamma;\psi_2}\mathbb{I}^{\alpha;\psi_1}(1)(x_1) \\
&= A_1\mathbb{L}\|\pi_1 - \pi_2\|.
\end{aligned}$$

Therefore, the operator $\mathbb{W}$ satisfies the inequality $\|\mathbb{W}\pi_1 - \mathbb{W}\pi_2\| \leq A_1\mathbb{L}\|\pi_1 - \pi_2\|$. Since, $A_1\mathbb{L} < 1$, $\mathbb{W}$ is a contraction. Therefore, the operator $\mathbb{W}$ has a unique fixed point in the ball B_r, by Banach's contraction mapping. Consequently, the sequential Hilfer–Caputo fractional integro-differential boundary value problem (1) has a unique solution on J. □

Next, the nonlinear alternative of the Leray–Schauder-type [23] is used to prove the existence of at least one solution to the sequential Hilfer–Caputo fractional integro-differential boundary value problem (1).

Theorem 2. *Assume that $\Pi : J \times \mathbb{R} \to \mathbb{R}$ is a continuous function satisfying the conditions:*

$(\mathbb{H}_2)$ *There exists a continuous function $\Omega : [0, \infty) \to (0, \infty)$ which is nondecreasing and $u_1, u_2 : J \to \mathbb{R}^+$ two continuous functions such that*

$$|\Pi(t, \pi)| \leq u_1(t)\Omega(|\pi|) + u_2(t), \tag{15}$$

for all $t \in J$ and $\pi \in \mathbb{R}$;

$(\mathbb{H}_3)$ *There exists a positive constant K such that*

$$\frac{K}{(\|u_1\|\Omega(K) + \|u_2\|)A_1} > 1. \tag{16}$$

Then, the sequential Hilfer–Caputo fractional integro-differential boundary value problem (1) *has at least one solution on J.*

Proof. We show that the operator $\mathbb{W}$ defined by (10) is compact on a bounded ball B_ρ, when $B_\rho = \{\pi \in C : \|\pi\| \leq \rho\}$. For any $\pi \in B_\rho$, we have

$$\begin{aligned}
|\mathbb{W}\pi(t)| &\leq \sup_{t\in J} |\mathbb{W}\pi(t)| \\
&\leq \frac{1}{|A|}\left[\sum_{i=1}^{m} |\lambda_i|\mathbb{I}^{\alpha;\psi_1}|\Pi(\eta_i, \pi(\eta_i))| + \sum_{j=1}^{n} |\delta_j|\mathbb{I}^{\mu_j+\gamma;\psi_2}\mathbb{I}^{\alpha;\psi_1}|\Pi(\xi_j, \pi(\xi_j))|\right.
\end{aligned}$$

$$
\begin{aligned}
& +\mathbb{I}^{\gamma;\psi_2}\mathbb{I}^{\alpha;\psi_1}|\Pi(x_1,\pi(x_1))|\Bigg] + \mathbb{I}^{\gamma;\psi_2}\mathbb{I}^{\alpha;\psi_1}|\Pi(x_1,\pi(x_1))|, \\
\leq\ & \frac{1}{|A|}\Bigg[(\|u_1\|\Omega(\rho)+\|u_2\|)\sum_{i=1}^{m}|\lambda_i|\mathbb{I}^{\alpha;\psi_1}(\eta_i) \\
& +(\|u_1\|\Omega(\rho)+\|u_2\|)\sum_{j=1}^{n}|\delta_j|\mathbb{I}^{\mu_j+\gamma;\psi_2}\mathbb{I}^{\alpha;\psi_1}(\xi_j) \\
& +(\|u_1\|\Omega(\rho)+\|u_2\|)\mathbb{I}^{\gamma;\psi_2}\mathbb{I}^{\alpha;\psi_1}(x_1)\Bigg] + (\|u_1\|\Omega(\rho)+\|u_2\|)\mathbb{I}^{\gamma;\psi_2}\mathbb{I}^{\alpha;\psi_1}(x_1) \\
=\ & (\|u_1\|\Omega(\rho)+\|u_2\|)A_1 := \Phi, \quad \text{a constant,}
\end{aligned}
$$

which yields $\|\mathbb{W}\pi\| \leq \Phi$. Therefore, the set $\mathbb{W}(B_\rho)$ is uniformly bounded. To show that $\mathbb{W}(B_\rho)$ is an equicontinuous set, we let t_1 and t_2 be the two points in J such that $t_1 < t_2$. Thus, for any $\pi \in B_\rho$, we have

$$
\begin{aligned}
& |\mathbb{W}\pi(t_2) - \mathbb{W}\pi(t_1)| \\
=\ & \Bigg|\frac{1}{\Gamma(\alpha)\Gamma(\gamma)}\int_0^{t_2}\int_0^{u}\psi_1'(s)\psi_2'(u)(\psi_1(u)-\psi_1(s))^{\alpha-1} \\
& \times(\psi_2(t_2)-\psi_2(u))^{\alpha-1}\Pi(s,\pi(s))dsdu \\
& -\frac{1}{\Gamma(\alpha)\Gamma(\gamma)}\int_0^{t_1}\int_0^{u}\psi_1'(s)\psi_2'(u)(\psi_1(u)-\psi_1(s))^{\alpha-1} \\
& \times(\psi_2(t_1)-\psi_2(u))^{\alpha-1}\Pi(s,\pi(s))dsdu\Bigg| \\
=\ & \Bigg|\frac{1}{\Gamma(\alpha)\Gamma(\gamma)}\int_0^{t_1}\int_0^{u}\psi_1'(s)\psi_2'(u)(\psi_1(u)-\psi_1(s))^{\alpha-1} \\
& \times(\psi_2(t_2)-\psi_2(u))^{\alpha-1}\Pi(s,\pi(s))dsdu \\
& +\frac{1}{\Gamma(\alpha)\Gamma(\gamma)}\int_{t_1}^{t_2}\int_0^{u}\psi_1'(s)\psi_2'(u)(\psi_1(u)-\psi_1(s))^{\alpha-1} \\
& \times(\psi_2(t_2)-\psi_2(u))^{\alpha-1}\Pi(s,\pi(s))dsdu \\
& -\frac{1}{\Gamma(\alpha)\Gamma(\gamma)}\int_0^{t_1}\int_0^{u}\psi_1'(s)\psi_2'(u)(\psi_1(u)-\psi_1(s))^{\alpha-1} \\
& \times(\psi_2(t_1)-\psi_2(u))^{\alpha-1}\Pi(s,\pi(s))dsdu\Bigg| \\
=\ & \Bigg|\frac{1}{\Gamma(\alpha)\Gamma(\gamma)}\int_0^{t_1}\int_0^{u}\psi_1'(s)\psi_2'(u)(\psi_1(u)-\psi_1(s))^{\alpha-1}\Big\{(\psi_2(t_2)-\psi_2(u))^{\alpha-1} \\
& -(\psi_2(t_1)-\psi_2(u))^{\alpha-1}\Big\}\Pi(s,\pi(s))dsdu \\
& +\frac{1}{\Gamma(\alpha)\Gamma(\gamma)}\int_{t_1}^{t_2}\int_0^{u}\psi_1'(s)\psi_2'(u)(\psi_1(u)-\psi_1(s))^{\alpha-1} \\
& \times(\psi_2(t_2)-\psi_2(u))^{\alpha-1}\Pi(s,\pi(s))dsdu\Bigg| \\
\leq\ & \frac{1}{\Gamma(\alpha)\Gamma(\gamma)}\int_0^{t_1}\int_0^{u}\psi_1'(s)\psi_2'(u)(\psi_1(u)-\psi_1(s))^{\alpha-1} \\
& \times\Big|(\psi_2(t_2)-\psi_2(u))^{\alpha-1}-(\psi_2(t_1)-\psi_2(u))^{\alpha-1}\Big||\Pi(s,\pi(s))|dsdu \\
& +\frac{1}{\Gamma(\alpha)\Gamma(\gamma)}\int_{t_1}^{t_2}\int_0^{u}\psi_1'(s)\psi_2'(u)(\psi_1(u)-\psi_1(s))^{\alpha-1} \\
& \times(\psi_2(t_2)-\psi_2(u))^{\alpha-1}|\Pi(s,\pi(s))|dsdu \\
\leq\ & \frac{(\|u_1\|\Omega(\rho)+\|u_2\|)}{\Gamma(\alpha)\Gamma(\gamma)}\int_0^{t_1}\int_0^{u}\psi_1'(s)\psi_2'(u)(\psi_1(u)-\psi_1(s))^{\alpha-1}
\end{aligned}
$$

$$\times\left|(\psi_2(t_2)-\psi_2(u))^{\alpha-1}-(\psi_2(t_1)-\psi_2(u))^{\alpha-1}\right|dsdu$$
$$+\frac{(\|u_1\|\Omega(\rho)+\|u_2\|)}{\Gamma(\alpha)\Gamma(\gamma)}\int_{t_1}^{t_2}\int_0^u\psi_1'(s)\psi_2'(u)(\psi_1(u)-\psi_1(s))^{\alpha-1}$$
$$\times(\psi_2(t_2)-\psi_2(u))^{\alpha-1}dsdu.$$

Observe that if $t_1 \to t_2$, then we have $|\mathbb{W}\pi(t_2)-\mathbb{W}\pi(t_1)| \to 0$ independently of π. Therefore, the set $\mathbb{W}(B_\rho)$ is an equicontinuous set. Hence, the set $\mathbb{W}(B_\rho)$ is relatively compact. By applying the Arzelá–Ascoli theorem, the operator $\mathbb{W}$ is completely continuous.

Finally, we show that the set of all solutions to equations $\pi=\lambda\mathbb{W}\pi$ is bounded for $\lambda\in(0,1)$. Let $\pi\in C$ and $\pi=\lambda\mathbb{W}\pi$ for some $\lambda\in(0,1)$. Then, for any $t\in J$, as in the first step, we obtain

$$\begin{aligned}|\pi(t)| &= \lambda|\mathbb{W}\pi(t)|\le\sup_{t\in J}|\mathbb{W}\pi(t)|\\ &\le (\|u_1\|\Omega(\|\pi\|)+\|u_2\|)A_1,\end{aligned}$$

and, consequently,

$$\frac{\|\pi\|}{(\|u_1\|\Omega(\|\pi\|)+\|u_2\|)A_1}\le 1.$$

From $(\mathbb{H}_3)$, $\|\pi\|\neq K$. After that, we define $U=\{\pi\in B_\rho:\|\pi\|<K\}$. Now, we can see that $\mathbb{W}:\overline{U}\to C$ is continuous and completely continuous. Thus, there is no $\pi\in\partial U$ such that $\pi=\lambda\mathbb{W}\pi$ with $0<\lambda<1$. By the nonlinear alternative of the Leray–Schauder-type, we get that the operator $\mathbb{W}$ has a fixed point $\pi\in\overline{U}$, which is a solution of the nonlocal fractional integro-differential sequential Hilfer and Caputo boundary value problem (17) on J. The proof is completed. □

4. Some Special Cases

In this section, we present some special cases and some interesting behavior of solutions to the investigated problem (1).

Corollary 1. *Assume that $\Pi: J\times\mathbb{R}\to\mathbb{R}$ is a continuous function.*

(a) *If $|\Pi(t,\pi)|\le M$, where M is a positive constant, then the nonlocal fractional integro-differential sequential Hilfer and Caputo boundary value problem* (17) *has at least one solution J.*

(b) *If $u_1(t)=1$, $\Omega(u)=Bu+C$, $u_2(t)=D$, where $B\ge 0$, $C,D>0$, then the nonlocal fractional integro-differential sequential Hilfer and Caputo boundary value problem* (17) *has at least one solution J if $A_1B<1$.*

(c) *If $u_1(t)=1$, $\Omega(u)=Bu^2+C$, $u_2(t)=D$, where $B\ge 0$, $C,D>0$, then the nonlocal fractional integro-differential sequential Hilfer and Caputo boundary value problem* (17) *has at least one solution J, if $4A_1^2B(C+D)<1$.*

If we put $\psi_1(t)=\psi_2(t)=\psi(t)$, then the nonlocal fractional integro-differential sequential Hilfer and Caputo boundary value problem (17) is reduced to

$$\begin{cases}{}^{H}\mathbb{D}^{\alpha,\beta;\psi}({}^{C}\mathbb{D}^{\gamma;\psi}\pi)(t)=\Pi(t,\pi(t)), \quad 0<\alpha,\beta,\gamma<1,\ t\in[0,x_1],\\ {}^{C}\mathbb{D}^{\gamma;\psi}\pi(0)=0, \quad \pi(x_1)=\sum_{i=1}^{m}\lambda_i\,{}^{C}\mathbb{D}^{\gamma;\psi}\pi(\eta_i)+\sum_{j=1}^{n}\delta_j\,\mathbb{I}^{\mu_j;\psi}\pi(\xi_j).\end{cases} \tag{17}$$

The following constants are used in the next corollaries.

$$A^* = 1-\sum_{j=1}^{n}\delta_j\frac{[\psi(\xi_j)-\psi(0)]^{\mu_j}}{\Gamma(\mu_j+1)},$$

$$
\begin{aligned}
A_1^* &= \frac{1}{|A^*|}\left(\sum_{i=1}^{m}|\lambda_i|\frac{[\psi(\eta_i)-\psi(0)]^{\alpha}}{\Gamma(\alpha+1)}+\sum_{j=1}^{n}|\delta_j|\frac{(\psi(\xi_j)-\psi(0))^{\alpha+\mu_j+\gamma}}{\Gamma(\alpha+\mu_j+\gamma+1)}\right)\\
&\quad+\left(\frac{|A^*|+1}{|A^*|}\right)\frac{(\psi(x_1)-\psi(0))^{\alpha+\gamma}}{\Gamma(\alpha+\gamma+1)}.
\end{aligned}
$$

Corollary 2. *If f satisfies the Lipschitz condition in $(\mathbb{H}_1)$ and if $A_1^*L<1$, then the nonlocal fractional integro-differential sequential Hilfer and Caputo boundary value problem* (17) *has a unique solution on J.*

Corollary 3. *If the continuous function f satisfies $(\mathbb{H}_2)$ in Theorem 2 and if there exists a positive constant M such that*

$$
\frac{M}{(\|u_1\|\Omega(M)+\|u_2\|)A_1^*}>1,
$$

then the nonlocal fractional integro-differential sequential Hilfer and Caputo boundary value problem (17) *has at least one solutions on J.*

If $n=p+q$, and $\mu_w=0$ for $w=1,\ldots,q$, then the problem (17) can be reduced to the following problem with integro-differential multi-point boundary conditions as

$$
\begin{cases}
{}^{H}\mathbb{D}^{\alpha,\beta;\psi}({}^{C}\mathbb{D}^{\gamma;\psi}\pi)(t)=\Pi(t,\pi(t)), \quad 0<\alpha,\beta,\gamma<1,\ t\in[0,x_1],\\
{}^{C}\mathbb{D}^{\gamma;\psi}\pi(0)=0, \quad \pi(x_1)=\sum_{i=1}^{m}\lambda_i{}^{C}\mathbb{D}^{\gamma;\psi}\pi(\eta_i)+\sum_{j=1}^{p}\delta_j\mathbb{I}^{\mu_j;\psi}\pi(\xi_j)+\sum_{w=p+1}^{q}\zeta_w\,\pi(\theta_w).
\end{cases} \tag{18}
$$

In addition, we put

$$
\begin{aligned}
\hat{A} &= 1-\sum_{j=1}^{p}\delta_j\frac{[\psi(\xi_j)-\psi(0)]^{\mu_j}}{\Gamma(\mu_j+1)}-\sum_{w=p+1}^{q}\zeta_w,\\
\hat{A}_1 &= \frac{1}{|\hat{A}|}\left\{\sum_{i=1}^{m}|\lambda_i|\frac{[\psi(\eta_i)-\psi(0)]^{\alpha}}{\Gamma(\alpha+1)}+\sum_{j=1}^{p}|\delta_j|\frac{(\psi(\xi_j)-\psi(0))^{\alpha+\mu_j+\gamma}}{\Gamma(\alpha+\mu_j+\gamma+1)}\right.\\
&\quad\left.+\sum_{w=p+1}^{q}|\zeta_w|\frac{(\psi(\theta_w)-\psi(0))^{\alpha+\gamma}}{\Gamma(\alpha+\gamma+1)}\right\}+\left(\frac{|\hat{A}|+1}{|\hat{A}|}\right)\frac{(\psi(x_1)-\psi(0))^{\alpha+\gamma}}{\Gamma(\alpha+\gamma+1)}.
\end{aligned}
$$

The existence and uniqueness results for the integro-differential multi-point boundary value problem (18) are similar to the Corollaries 2 and 3 by replacing $\hat{A}_1$ with A_1^*.

5. Illustrative Examples

Example 1. *Let us consider the following integro-differential boundary conditions to the sequential ψ_1-Hilfer and ψ_2-Caputo fractional differential equation of the form*

$$
{}^{H}\mathbb{D}^{\frac{1}{4},\frac{3}{4};e^{\frac{1}{10}t}}\left({}^{C}\mathbb{D}^{\frac{1}{2};t^2+t}\pi\right)(t)=\Pi(t,\pi(t)), \quad 0<t<\frac{9}{8}, \tag{19}
$$

$$
\begin{aligned}
&{}^{C}\mathbb{D}^{\frac{1}{2};t^2+t}\pi(0)=0, \quad \pi\left(\frac{9}{8}\right)=\frac{3}{67}{}^{C}\mathbb{D}^{\frac{1}{2};t^2+t}\pi\left(\frac{3}{8}\right)+\frac{5}{77}{}^{C}\mathbb{D}^{\frac{1}{2};t^2+t}\pi\left(\frac{5}{8}\right)\\
&+\frac{7}{87}{}^{C}\mathbb{D}^{\frac{1}{2};t^2+t}\pi\left(\frac{7}{8}\right)+\frac{2}{39}\mathbb{I}^{\frac{4}{5};t^2+t}\pi\left(\frac{1}{2}\right)+\frac{4}{59}\mathbb{I}^{\frac{7}{5};t^2+t}\pi\left(\frac{3}{4}\right).
\end{aligned} \tag{20}
$$

From the boundary value problem (19), we set constants as $\alpha=1/4$, $\beta=3/4$, $\gamma=1/2$, $x_1=9/8$, $\lambda_1=3/67$, $\lambda_2=5/77$, $\lambda_3=7/87$, $\eta_1=3/8$, $\eta_2=5/8$, $\eta_3=7/8$, $\delta_1=2/39$, $\delta_2=4/59$, $\mu_1=4/5$, $\mu_2=7/5$, $\xi_1=1/2$, $\xi_2=3/4$ and functions $\psi_1(t)=e^{(1/10)t}$ and $\psi_2(t)=t^2+t$. From above information, we can compute that $A\approx 0.8763925133$ and $A_1\approx 2.374946616$. Observe that the two functions satisfy $\psi_1',\psi_2'>0$.

(i) If the function Π is defined by

$$\Pi(t,\pi(t)) = \frac{1}{2t+5}\left(\frac{2|\pi|+\pi^2}{1+|\pi|}\right) + \frac{1}{7}t^2 + 8t + \frac{1}{9}. \tag{21}$$

From the given nonlinear unbounded Lipschitzian function in (21), we get $|\Pi(t,\pi) - \Pi(t,z)| \leq (2/5)|\pi - z|$ for $t \in [0,9/8]$, $\pi, z \in \mathbb{R}$. Setting $L = 2/5$, we have $A_1 L \approx 0.9499786464 < 1$ which fulfills the condition in (13). The result in Theorem 1 can be used to conclude that the boundary value problem (19) and (20) with the given function in (21) has a unique solution on $[0,9/8]$

(ii) Let the function Π be defined as

$$\Pi(t,\pi(t)) = \frac{1}{t+4}\left(\frac{\pi^{2024}}{5(1+\pi^{2022})} + \frac{1}{3t+6}\right) + \frac{1}{2t+7}. \tag{22}$$

We have

$$|\Pi(t,\pi)| \leq \frac{1}{t+4}\left(\frac{1}{5}\pi^2 + \frac{1}{6}\right) + \frac{1}{2t+7}.$$

Choosing $u_1(t) = 1/(t+4)$, $u_2(t) = 1/(2t+7)$ and $\Omega(\pi) = (1/5)\pi^2 + (1/6)$, we get $\|u_1\| = 1/4$, $\|u_2\| = 1/7$ and then, there exists a $K \in (0.463775263, 7.957466657)$ satisfying the inequality in (16). Therefore, all assumptions in Theorem 2 agree with function Π in (22). Then, using integro-differential boundary conditions to the sequential ψ_1-Hilfer and ψ_2-Caputo fractional differential Equations (19), (20) and (22) have at least one solution on $[0,9/8]$.

(iii) If $\psi_1(t) = \psi_2(t) = t^2 + t$, then (19) is expressed as

$$^{H}\mathbb{D}^{\frac{1}{4},\frac{3}{4};t^2+t}\left({}^{C}\mathbb{D}^{\frac{1}{2};t^2+t}\pi\right)(t) = \Pi(t,\pi(t)), \quad 0 < t < \frac{9}{8}, \tag{23}$$

and we can find that $A^* \approx 0.8763925133$, $A_1^* \approx 4.810643110$. If

$$\Pi(t,pi) = \frac{1}{2t+10}\left(\frac{2|\pi|+\pi^2}{1+|x|}\right) + \frac{1}{7}t^2 + 8t + \frac{1}{9}. \tag{24}$$

Then, $L = 1/5$ and we have $A_1^* L \approx 0.9621286220$. This means that boundary value problem (23), (20) and (24) has a unique solution on $[0,9/8]$.

In addition, if function Π in (23) is given in (22), then there exists a constant $K \in (0.235228817, 3.922219479)$ which satisfies the Corollary 3. So, the boundary value problem (23), (20) and (22) has at least one solution on $[0,9/8]$.

(iv) If the boundary conditions in (20) is replaced by

$$\begin{aligned} {}^{C}\mathbb{D}^{\frac{1}{2};t^2+t}\pi(0) = 0, \quad & \pi\left(\frac{9}{8}\right) = \frac{3}{67}{}^{C}\mathbb{D}^{\frac{1}{2};t^2+t}\pi\left(\frac{3}{8}\right) + \frac{5}{77}{}^{C}\mathbb{D}^{\frac{1}{2};t^2+t}\pi\left(\frac{5}{8}\right) \\ & + \frac{7}{87}{}^{C}\mathbb{D}^{\frac{1}{2};t^2+t}\pi\left(\frac{7}{8}\right) + \frac{2}{39}\mathbb{I}^{\frac{4}{5};t^2+t}\pi\left(\frac{1}{2}\right) + \frac{4}{59}\pi\left(\frac{3}{4}\right). \end{aligned} \tag{25}$$

Then, we get $\hat{A} \approx 0.8884626894$, $\hat{A}_1 \approx 4.816166032$. If

$$\Pi(t,\pi) = W\pi^2 + Z, \tag{26}$$

where constants $W, Z > 0$ and $WZ < 1/(4\hat{A}_1^2) \approx 0.01077797341$. Then, there exists a positive constant M satisfying the Corollary 3 when replacing A_1^* by $\hat{A}_1$. Hence, the boundary value problem (23), (25) and (26) has at least one solution on $[0,9/8]$.

6. Conclusions

In this paper, we have studied a new kind of boundary value problem consisting of a combination of two fractional derivative operators, one ψ_1-Hilfer and one ψ_2-Caputo, supplemented with nonlocal integro-differential boundary conditions. This combination, as far as we know, is new in the literature. Our uniqueness result is derived via Banach's contraction principle, while the Leray–Schauder nonlinear alternative is used to derive the existence result. The main results are well illustrated by constructing numerical examples.

Author Contributions: Conceptualization, S.K.N. and J.T.; methodology, S.S., S.K.N., C.S. and J.T.; formal analysis, S.S., S.K.N., C.S. and J.T.; writing—original draft preparation, S.S. and C.S.; writing—review and editing, S.K.N. and J.T.; supervision, S.K.N.; funding acquisition, J.T. All authors have read and agreed to the published version of the manuscript.

Funding: This research was funded by King Mongkut's University of Technology North Bangkok. Contract no. KMUTNB-62-KNOW-41.

Conflicts of Interest: The authors declare no conflict of interest.

References

1. Gaul, L.; Klein, P.; Kempfle, S. Damping description involving fractional operators. *Mech. Syst. Signal Process.* **1991**, *5*, 81–88. [CrossRef]
2. Glockle, W.G.; Nonnenmacher, T.F. A fractional calculus approach of self-similar protein dynamics. *Biophys. J.* **1995**, *68*, 46–53. [CrossRef] [PubMed]
3. Hilfer, R. Experimental evidence for fractional time evolution in glass forming materials. *J. Chem. Phys.* **2002**, *284*, 399–408. [CrossRef]
4. Mainardi, F. Fractional calculus: Some basic problems in continuum and statistical mechanics. In *Fractals and Fractional Calculus in Continuum Mechanics*; Carpinteri, A., Mainardi, F., Eds.; Springer: Vienna, Austria, 1997; pp. 291–348.
5. Metzler, F.; Schick, W.; Kilian, H.G.; Nonnenmacher, T.F. Relaxation in filled polymers: A fractional calculus approach. *J. Chem. Phys.* **1995**, *103*, 7180–7186. [CrossRef]
6. Diethelm, K. *The Analysis of Fractional Differential Equations*; Lecture Notes in Mathematics; Springer: New York, NY, USA, 2010.
7. Kilbas, A.A.; Srivastava, H.M.; Trujillo, J.J. *Theory and Applications of the Fractional Differential Equations*; North-Holland Mathematics Studies; Elsevier: Amsterdam, The Netherlands, 2006; Volume 204.
8. Miller, K.S.; Ross, B. *An Introduction to the Fractional Calculus and Differential Equations*; John Wiley: NewYork, NY, USA, 1993.
9. Podlubny, I. *Fractional Differential Equations*; Academic Press: New York, NY, USA, 1999.
10. Zhou, Y. *Basic Theory of Fractional Differential Equations*; World Scientific: Singapore, 2014.
11. Ahmad, B.; Ntouyas, S.K. *Nonlocal Nonlinear Fractional-Order Boundary Value Problems*; World Scientific: Singapore, 2021.
12. Hilfer, R. (Ed.) *Applications of Fractional Calculus in Physics*; World Scientific: Singapore, 2000.
13. Kamocki, R. A new representation formula for the Hilfer fractional derivative and its application. *J. Comput. Appl. Math.* **2016**, *308*, 39–45. [CrossRef]
14. Vanterler da Sousa, J.; de Oliveira, E.C. On the ψ-Hilfer fractional derivative. *Commun. Nonlinear Sci. Numer. Simul.* **2018**, *60*, 72–91. [CrossRef]
15. Vanterler da Sousa, J.; Kucche, K.D.; de Oliveira, E.C. On the Ulam-Hyers stabilities of the solutions of ψ-Hilfer fractional differential equation with abstract Volterra operator. *Math. Methods Appl. Sci.* **2019**, *42*, 3021–3032. [CrossRef]
16. Vanterler da Sousa, J.; de Oliveira, E.C. On the Ulam–Hyers–Rassias stability for nonlinear fractional differential equations using the ψ–Hilfer operator. *J. Fixed Point Theory Appl.* **2018**, *20*, 96. [CrossRef]
17. Ahmad, B.; Ntouyas, S.K.; Alsaedi, A.; Alotaibi, F.M. Existence results for a ψ-Hilfer type nonlocal fractional boundary value problem via topological degree theory. *Dyn. Syst. Appl.* **2021**, *30*, 1091–1103. [CrossRef]
18. Sitho, S.; Ntouyas, S.K.; Samadi, A.; Tariboon, J. Boundary value problems for ψ-Hilfer type sequential fractional differential equations and inclusions with integral multi-point boundary conditions. *Mathematics* **2021**, *9*, 1001. [CrossRef]
19. Kiataramkul, C.; Ntouyas, S.K.; Tariboon, J. Existence results for ψ-Hilfer fractional integro-differential hybrid boundary value problems for differential equations and inclusions. *Adv. Math. Phys.* **2021**, *2021*, 9044313. [CrossRef]
20. Kiataramkul, C.; Ntouyas, S.K.; Tariboon, J. An existence result for ψ-Hilfer fractional integro-differential hybrid three-point boundary value problems. *Fractal. Fract.* **2021**, *5*, 136. [CrossRef]
21. Almeida, R. A Caputo fractional derivative of a function with respect to another function. *Commun. Nonlinear Sci. Numer. Simul.* **2017**, *44*, 460–481. [CrossRef]

22. Mallah, I.; Ahmed, I.; Akgul, A.; Jarad, F.; Alha, S. On ψ-Hilfer generalized proportional fractional operators. *AIMS Math.* **2021**, *7*, 82–103. [CrossRef]
23. Granas, A.; Dugundji, J. *Fixed Point Theory*; Springer: New York, NY, USA, 2003.

mathematics

MDPI

Article

An Investigation on Existence, Uniqueness, and Approximate Solutions for Two-Dimensional Nonlinear Fractional Integro-Differential Equations

Tahereh Eftekhari * and Jalil Rashidinia

School of Mathematics, Iran University of Science & Technology (IUST), Narmak, Tehran 16846 13114, Iran
* Correspondence: t.eftekhari2009@gmail.com

Abstract: In this research, we provide sufficient conditions to prove the existence of local and global solutions for the general two-dimensional nonlinear fractional integro-differential equations. Furthermore, we prove that these solutions are unique. In addition, we use operational matrices of two-variable shifted Jacobi polynomials via the collocation method to reduce the equations into a system of equations. Error bounds of the presented method are obtained. Five test problems are solved. The obtained numerical results show the accuracy, efficiency, and applicability of the proposed approach.

Keywords: the mixed Riemann–Liouville integral; fixed-point theorems; shifted Jacobi polynomials; operational matrices; collocation method; error bound

MSC: 26A33, 33C45, 65N35

1. Introduction

In the last decades, many problems, such as acoustic wave problems [1], groundwater pollution and groundwater flow problems [2–6], among others [7–10], have been shown by using fractional calculus. In addition, many engineering and physical problems, such as problems from control, electrochemistry, rheology, coupling and particle mechanics, viscoelasticity, electromagnetism fluid structure, and porous media (see e.g., [11–14]), have been mathematically formulated by fractional integro-differential equations (FIDEs). Recently, numerical methods for solving FIDEs have attracted the attention of many researchers. Taheri et al. [15] solved stochastic FIDEs by using the shifted Legendre spectral collocation method. Rahimkhani et al. [16] proposed the Bernoulli pseudo-spectral method for solving nonlinear Volterra FIDEs. Wang et al. [17] developed an approximate scheme based on fractional-order Euler functions to solve weakly singular FIDEs. Babaei et al. [18] considered a sixth-kind Chebyshev collocation method to solve a nonlinear quadratic FIDEs of variable order.

In the presented research, we focus on the following general two-dimensional nonlinear fractional integro-differential Equations (2D-NFIDEs):

$$\begin{aligned} &af_{yy}(x,y) + bf_{xx}(x,y) + cf_{yx}(x,y) + f(x,y) + \lambda I^{\varrho} f(x,y) = g(x,y) + \Theta(x,y) \\ &+ \Lambda(x,y) + \rho(x,y) + \varphi(x,y), \end{aligned} \tag{1}$$

with the initial conditions of:

$$f(x,0) = d_1(x), \quad f(0,y) = d_2(y), \quad f_y(x,0) = d_3(x), \quad f_x(0,y) = d_4(y), \quad f_x(x,0) = d_5(x), \tag{2}$$

where $(x,y) \in \mathfrak{D} = [0,\ell_1) \times [0,\ell_2)$; $\varrho = (\varrho_1, \varrho_2) \in (0,\infty) \times (0,\infty)$; and a, b, c, λ are constants, and

$$\Theta(x,y) = \int_0^x \int_0^y k_1(x,t,y,s) f^{p_1}(t,s)\, \mathrm{d}s\, \mathrm{d}t,$$
$$\Lambda(x,y) = \frac{1}{\Gamma(\varrho_1)\Gamma(\varrho_2)} \int_0^x \int_0^y (x-t)^{\varrho_1 - 1}(y-s)^{\varrho_2 - 1} k_2(x,t,y,s) f^{p_2}(t,s)\, \mathrm{d}s\, \mathrm{d}t,$$
$$\rho(x,y) = \frac{1}{\Gamma(\varrho_1)\Gamma(\varrho_2)} \int_0^{\ell_1} \int_0^{\ell_2} (\ell_1-t)^{\varrho_1 - 1}(\ell_2-s)^{\varrho_2 - 1} k_3(x,t,y,s) f^{p_3}(t,s)\, \mathrm{d}s\, \mathrm{d}t,$$
$$\varphi(x,y) = \int_0^{\ell_1} \int_0^{\ell_2} k_4(x,t,y,s) f^{p_4}(t,s)\, \mathrm{d}s\, \mathrm{d}t.$$

Here, functions $d_i(.)$, $i = 1,2,3,4,5$, $k_j(x,t,y,s)$, $j = 1,2,3,4$, $g(x,y)$ are known, and $f(x,y)$ is unknown; $I^{\varrho} f(x,y)$ is the left-sided mixed Riemann–Liouville integral of order $\varrho = (\varrho_1, \varrho_2) \in (0,\infty) \times (0,\infty)$ of f denoted by [19]

$$I^{\varrho} f(x,y) = \frac{1}{\Gamma(\varrho_1)\Gamma(\varrho_2)} \int_0^x \int_0^y (x-t)^{\varrho_1 - 1}(y-s)^{\varrho_2 - 1} f(t,s)\, \mathrm{d}s\, \mathrm{d}t;$$

and $p_j \geq 1$, $j = 1,2,3,4$ are constants.

While several numerical techniques have been proposed for solving many different problems (see, for instance, [20–35] and references therein), there were few research studies that developed numerical methods for solving Equations (1) and (2). For example, Najafalizadeh and Ezzati [36] obtained approximate solutions of these equations by using operational matrices of two-dimensional block pulse functions (2D-BPFs) with the order of convergence $O(\frac{1}{N})$, $N \in \mathbb{N}$. Maleknejad et al. [37] applied operational matrices based on a hybrid of two-dimensional block-pulse functions and shifted Legendre polynomials (2D-HBPSLs) to solve the general 2D-NFIDEs. The order of convergence of this method was $O(\frac{1}{2^{2M-1} N^M M!})$.

According to the best of our knowledge, the existence and uniqueness of solutions for Equations (1) and (2) have not been discussed so far. In this research, we provide sufficient conditions to prove that there exist local and global solutions for the general 2D-NFIDEs. Then, we prove that the solutions of these equations are unique. Additionally, we prepare an efficient numerical approach to approximate solutions of the general 2D-NFIDEs with high accuracy.

The rest of this paper is organized as follows: in Section 2, some theorems for the existence and uniqueness of solutions of general 2D-NFIDEs are proved. In Section 3, an introduction of one- and two-variable shifted Jacobi polynomials (1D-SJPs and 2D-SJPs) is provided. Additionally, some operational matrices are introduced. In Section 4, by using the collocation method via these operational matrices, approximate solutions for Equations (1) and (2) are obtained. In Section 5, error bounds of approximations are obtained. In Section 6, five test problems are solved to show the accuracy of the proposed method. In Section 7, a conclusion is presented.

2. Existence and Uniqueness of Solutions

Now, by using Schauder's fixed-point theorem [38], a local existence of solutions of general 2D-NIDEFs is proved in a Banach space.

Theorem 1. *Suppose that*

(C1) $0 \leq t \leq x \leq \ell_1$, $0 \leq s \leq y \leq \ell_2$, $g, g_1, f, v \in C(\mathfrak{D}, \mathbb{R}^n)$, $k_1, k_2, k_3, k_4 \in C(\mathfrak{D} \times \mathfrak{D} \times \mathbb{R}^n, \mathbb{R}^n)$;

(C2) $\|f_{yy}(x,y) - v_{yy}(x,y)\| < \frac{\varepsilon}{24a}$, $\|f_{\lambda\lambda}(x,y) - v_{\lambda\lambda}(x,y)\| < \frac{\varepsilon}{24b}$, $\|f_{y\lambda}(x,y) - v_{y\lambda}(x,y)\| < \frac{\varepsilon}{24c}$, $\|I^{\varrho} f(x,y) - I^{\varrho} v(x,y)\| < \frac{\varepsilon}{24\lambda}$;

(C3) $\|g(x,y) - g_1(x,y)\| < \frac{\varepsilon}{6}$;

(C4) $\|k_i(x,t,y,s,f(t,s)) - k_i(x,t,y,s,v(t,s))\| < \frac{\varepsilon}{6\alpha\beta}$, $i = 1,4$, $0 < \alpha < \ell_1$, $0 < \beta < \ell_2$;

(C5) $\|k_j(x,t,y,s,f(t,s)) - k_j(x,t,y,s,v(t,s))\| < \frac{\varepsilon\Gamma(\varrho_1+1)\Gamma(\varrho_2+1)}{6\alpha^{\varrho_1}\beta^{\varrho_2}}$, $j = 2,3$, $0 < \alpha < \ell_1$, $0 < \beta < \ell_2$.

Then, there exists at least one solution for the 2D-NIDEF on $0 \le t \le \alpha$, $0 \le s \le \beta$.

Proof. Suppose that $\mathcal{D} = \{(x,t,y,s,f) : (x,t,y,s) \in \mathfrak{D} \times \mathfrak{D}, |f| \le b'\}$. Let $|f_{yy}(x,y)| \le \frac{b'}{16a}$, $|f_{xx}(x,y)| \le \frac{b'}{16b}$, $|f_{yx}(x,y)| \le \frac{b'}{16c}$, $|I^{\varrho}f(x,y)| \le \frac{b'}{16\lambda}$, $|g(x,y)| \le \frac{b'}{4}$,

$$\max\{|k_i(x_1,t,y_1,s,f(t,s))|, |k_i(x_2,t,y_2,s,f(t,s))|\} = \xi_i, \quad i = 1,2,3,4,$$

on $\mathcal{D}$. Choose $(\xi_1 + \xi_4)\alpha\beta \le \frac{b'}{4}$, $\frac{(\xi_2+\xi_3)\alpha^{\varrho_1}\beta^{\varrho_2}}{\Gamma(\varrho_1+1)\Gamma(\varrho_2+1)} \le \frac{b'}{4}$. Consider $\Pi_0 = \{f : f \in C(\mathfrak{D}_0, \mathbb{R}^n)$, $|f| \le b'\}$ such that $\|f\| = \max_{(x,y)\in\mathfrak{D}_0} |f(x,y)|$, $\mathfrak{D}_0 = [0,\alpha] \times [0,\beta]$. Clearly, Π_0 is bounded, closed, and convex. Now, for any $f \in \Pi_0$, define the operator

$$\begin{aligned} \mathcal{T}f(x,y) =& -af_{yy}(x,y) - bf_{xx}(x,y) - cf_{yx}(x,y) - \lambda I^{\varrho}f(x,y) + g(x,y) + \Theta(x,y) \\ &+ \Lambda(x,y) + \rho(x,y) + \varphi(x,y), \quad (x,y) \in \mathfrak{D}_0. \end{aligned} \tag{3}$$

It is clear that

$$\begin{aligned} &|\Theta(x,y)| \le \xi_1\alpha\beta, \\ &|\Lambda(x,y)| \le \frac{\xi_2\alpha^{\varrho_1}\beta^{\varrho_2}}{\Gamma(\varrho_1+1)\Gamma(\varrho_2+1)}, \\ &|\rho(x,y)| \le \frac{\xi_3\alpha^{\varrho_1}\beta^{\varrho_2}}{\Gamma(\varrho_1+1)\Gamma(\varrho_2+1)}, \\ &|\varphi(x,y)| \le \xi_4\alpha\beta. \end{aligned}$$

Therefore, we obtain

$$\begin{aligned} |\mathcal{T}f(x,y)| \le& |af_{yy}(x,y)| + |bf_{xx}(x,y)| + |cf_{yx}(x,y)| + |\lambda I^{\varrho}f(x,y)| + |g(x,y)| + |\Theta(x,y)| \\ &+ |\Lambda(x,y)| + |\rho(x,y)| + |\varphi(x,y)| \\ \le& \frac{b'}{2} + (\xi_1 + \xi_4)\alpha\beta + \frac{(\xi_2+\xi_3)\alpha^{\varrho_1}\beta^{\varrho_2}}{\Gamma(\varrho_1+1)\Gamma(\varrho_2+1)} \le b', \end{aligned}$$

which implies that $\mathcal{T}(\Pi_0) \subset \Pi_0$. Furthermore, for any $(x_1,y_1), (x_2,y_2) \in \mathfrak{D}_0$, such that $x_2 > x_1$ and $y_2 > y_1$, we obtain

$$\begin{aligned} |\mathcal{T}f(x_2,y_2) - \mathcal{T}f(x_1,y_1)| \le& a|f_{yy}(x_2,y_2) - f_{yy}(x_1,y_1)| + b|f_{xx}(x_2,y_2) - f_{xx}(x_1,y_1)| \\ &+ c|f_{yx}(x_2,y_2) - f_{yx}(x_1,y_1)| + \lambda|I^{\varrho}f(x_2,y_2) - I^{\varrho}f(x_1,y_1)| \\ &+ |g(x_2,y_2) - g(x_1,y_1)| + |\Theta(x_2,y_2) - \Theta(x_1,y_1)| \\ &+ |\Lambda(x_2,y_2) - \Lambda(x_1,y_1)| + |\rho(x_2,y_2) - \rho(x_1,y_1)| \\ &+ |\varphi(x_2,y_2) - \varphi(x_1,y_1)|. \end{aligned} \tag{4}$$

Additionally, we have

$$
\begin{aligned}
&|I^{\varrho}f(x_2,y_2) - I^{\varrho}f(x_1,y_1)| \\
&\leq \frac{1}{\Gamma(\varrho_1)\Gamma(\varrho_2)}\left|\int_0^{x_2}\int_0^{y_2}(x_2-t)^{\varrho_1-1}(y_2-s)^{\varrho_2-1}f(t,s)\mathrm{d}s\mathrm{d}t\right. \\
&\left.-\int_0^{x_1}\int_0^{y_1}(x_1-t)^{\varrho_1-1}(y_1-s)^{\varrho_2-1}f(t,s)\mathrm{d}s\mathrm{d}t\right| \\
&\leq \frac{1}{\Gamma(\varrho_1)\Gamma(\varrho_2)}\left|\int_0^{x_1}\int_0^{y_1}(x_2-t)^{\varrho_1-1}(y_2-s)^{\varrho_2-1}f(t,s)\mathrm{d}s\mathrm{d}t\right. \\
&+\int_{x_1}^{x_2}\int_{y_1}^{y_2}(x_2-t)^{\varrho_1-1}(y_2-s)^{\varrho_2-1}f(t,s)\mathrm{d}s\mathrm{d}t \\
&\left.-\int_0^{x_1}\int_0^{y_1}(x_1-t)^{\varrho_1-1}(y_1-s)^{\varrho_2-1}f(t,s)\,\mathrm{d}s\,\mathrm{d}t\right| \\
&\leq \frac{1}{\Gamma(\varrho_1)\Gamma(\varrho_2)}\left|\int_0^{x_1}\int_0^{y_1}\left((x_2-t)^{\varrho_1-1}(y_2-s)^{\varrho_2-1}-(x_1-t)^{\varrho_1-1}(y_1-s)^{\varrho_2-1}\right)f(t,s)\,\mathrm{d}s\,\mathrm{d}t\right. \\
&\left.+\int_{x_1}^{x_2}\int_{y_1}^{y_2}(x_2-t)^{\varrho_1-1}(y_2-s)^{\varrho_2-1}f(t,s)\mathrm{d}s\mathrm{d}t\right| \\
&\leq \frac{b'}{\Gamma(\varrho_1+1)\Gamma(\varrho_2+1)}\left(\int_0^{x_1}\int_0^{y_1}\left((x_2-t)^{\varrho_1-1}(y_2-s)^{\varrho_2-1}-(x_1-t)^{\varrho_1-1}(y_1-s)^{\varrho_2-1}\right)\mathrm{d}s\,\mathrm{d}t\right. \\
&\left.+\int_{x_1}^{x_2}\int_{y_1}^{y_2}(x_2-t)^{\varrho_1-1}(y_2-s)^{\varrho_2-1}\mathrm{d}s\mathrm{d}t\right) \\
&\leq \frac{b'}{\Gamma(\varrho_1+1)\Gamma(\varrho_2+1)}((x_2-x_1)^{\varrho_1}(y_2-y_1)^{\varrho_2}-x_2^{\varrho_1}y_2^{\varrho_2}+x_1^{\varrho_1}y_1^{\varrho_2}-(x_2-x_1)^{\varrho_1}(y_2-y_1)^{\varrho_2}) \\
&=0.
\end{aligned}
$$

Therefore,

$$
|\mathcal{T}f(x_2,y_2) - \mathcal{T}f(x_1,y_1)| = 0. \tag{5}
$$

Moreover, we can obtain

$$
\begin{aligned}
&|\Lambda(x_2,y_2)-\Lambda(x_1,y_1)| \leq \frac{1}{\Gamma(\varrho_1)\Gamma(\varrho_2)}\left|\int_0^{x_2}\int_0^{y_2}(x_2-t)^{\varrho_1-1}(y_2-s)^{\varrho_2-1}k_2(x_2,t,y_2,s,f(t,s))\mathrm{d}s\mathrm{d}t\right. \\
&\left.-\int_0^{x_1}\int_0^{y_1}(x_1-t)^{\varrho_1-1}(y_1-s)^{\varrho_2-1}k_2(x_1,t,y_1,s,f(t,s))\mathrm{d}s\mathrm{d}t\right| \\
&=\frac{1}{\Gamma(\varrho_1)\Gamma(\varrho_2)}\left|\int_0^{x_1}\int_0^{y_1}(x_2-t)^{\varrho_1-1}(y_2-s)^{\varrho_2-1}k_2(x_2,t,y_2,s,f(t,s))\mathrm{d}s\mathrm{d}t\right. \\
&+\int_{x_1}^{x_2}\int_{y_1}^{y_2}(x_2-t)^{\varrho_1-1}(y_2-s)^{\varrho_2-1}k_2(x_2,t,y_2,s,f(t,s))\mathrm{d}s\mathrm{d}t \\
&\left.-\int_0^{x_1}\int_0^{y_1}(x_1-t)^{\varrho_1-1}(y_1-s)^{\varrho_2-1}k_2(x_1,t,y_1,s,f(t,s))\mathrm{d}s\mathrm{d}t\right| \\
&=\frac{1}{\Gamma(\varrho_1)\Gamma(\varrho_2)}\left|\int_0^{x_1}\int_0^{y_1}\left((x_2-t)^{\varrho_1-1}(y_2-s)^{\varrho_2-1}k_2(x_2,t,y_2,s,f(t,s))\right.\right. \\
&\left.-(x_1-t)^{\varrho_1-1}(y_1-s)^{\varrho_2-1}k_2(x_1,t,y_1,s,f(t,s))\right)\mathrm{d}s\mathrm{d}t \\
&\left.+\int_{x_1}^{x_2}\int_{y_1}^{y_2}(x_2-t)^{\varrho_1-1}(y_2-s)^{\varrho_2-1}k_2(x_2,t,y_2,s,f(t,s))\mathrm{d}s\mathrm{d}t\right| \\
&\leq \frac{1}{\Gamma(\varrho_1)\Gamma(\varrho_2)}\int_0^{x_1}\int_0^{y_1}\left((x_2-t)^{\varrho_1-1}(y_2-s)^{\varrho_2-1}|k_2(x_2,t,y_2,s,f(t,s))|\right. \\
&\left.+(x_1-t)^{\varrho_1-1}(y_1-s)^{\varrho_2-1}|k_2(x_1,t,y_1,s,f(t,s))|\right)\mathrm{d}s\mathrm{d}t \\
&+\frac{1}{\Gamma(\varrho_1)\Gamma(\varrho_2)}\int_{x_1}^{x_2}\int_{y_1}^{y_2}(x_2-t)^{\varrho_1-1}(y_2-s)^{\varrho_2-1}|k_2(x_2,t,y_2,s,f(t,s))|\mathrm{d}s\mathrm{d}t \\
&\leq \frac{\xi_2}{\Gamma(\varrho_1)\Gamma(\varrho_2)}\left(\int_0^{x_1}\int_0^{y_1}\left((x_2-t)^{\varrho_1-1}(y_2-s)^{\varrho_2-1}+(x_1-t)^{\varrho_1-1}(y_1-s)^{\varrho_2-1}\right)\mathrm{d}s\mathrm{d}t\right. \\
&\left.+\int_{x_1}^{x_2}\int_{y_1}^{y_2}(x_2-t)^{\varrho_1-1}(y_2-s)^{\varrho_2-1}\mathrm{d}s\mathrm{d}t\right) \\
&\leq \frac{\xi_2}{\Gamma(\varrho_1+1)\Gamma(\varrho_2+1)}((x_2-x_1)^{\varrho_1}(y_2-y_1)^{\varrho_2}-x_2^{\varrho_1}y_2^{\varrho_2}+x_1^{\varrho_1}y_1^{\varrho_2}+(x_2-x_1)^{\varrho_1}(y_2-y_1)^{\varrho_2}) \\
&\leq \frac{2\xi_2}{\Gamma(\varrho_1+1)\Gamma(\varrho_2+1)}(x_2-x_1)^{\varrho_1}(y_2-y_1)^{\varrho_2}.
\end{aligned} \tag{6}
$$

Similarly,

$$|\Theta(x_2,y_2)-\Theta(x_1,y_1)|\leq \xi_1(x_2y_2-x_1y_1), \tag{7}$$

$$|\rho(x_2,y_2)-\rho(x_1,y_1)|\leq \xi_3\left(\frac{\alpha^{\varrho_1}\beta^{\varrho_2}}{\Gamma(\varrho_1+1)\Gamma(\varrho_2+1)}-\frac{\alpha^{\varrho_1}\beta^{\varrho_2}}{\Gamma(\varrho_1+1)\Gamma(\varrho_2+1)}\right)=0, \tag{8}$$

$$|\varphi(x_2,y_2)-\varphi(x_1,y_1)|\leq \xi_4(\alpha\beta-\alpha\beta)=0. \tag{9}$$

Applying inequalities (5)–(9) in (4) gives

$$\begin{aligned}|\mathcal{T}f(x_2,y_2)-\mathcal{T}f(x_1,y_1)|\leq&|(\mathscr{F}f)(x_2,y_2)-(\mathscr{F}f)(x_1,y_1)|+\lambda|I^{\varrho}f(x_2,y_2)-I^{\varrho}f(x_1,y_1)|\\&+|g(x_2,y_2)-g(x_1,y_1)|+\xi_1(x_2y_2-x_1y_1)\\&+\frac{2\xi_2}{\Gamma(\varrho_1+1)\Gamma(\varrho_2+1)}(x_2-x_1)^{\varrho_1}(y_2-y_1)^{\varrho_2},\end{aligned} \tag{10}$$

where

$$(\mathscr{F}f)(x,y)=-af_{yy}(x,y)-bf_{xx}(x,y)-cf_{yx}(x,y).$$

It is clear that the right-hand side of (10) tends to zero as $x_2\to x_1$, $y_2\to y_1$. Thus, $\mathcal{T}:\Pi_0\to\Pi_0$ is equicontinuous. Therefore, by using the Arzela–Ascoli theorem [39], the compactness of the closure of $\mathcal{T}(\Pi_0)$ can be concluded.

Now, we need to show that $\mathcal{T}$ is continuous. For this propose, define

$$\mathcal{T}v(x,y)=(\mathscr{F}v)(x,y)-\lambda I^{\varrho}v(x,y)+g_1(x,y)+\Theta_v(x,y)+\Lambda_v(x,y)+\rho_v(x,y)+\varphi_v(x,y),$$

$$v(x,0)=d_1(x),\ v(0,y)=d_2(y),\ v_y(x,0)=d_3(x),\ v_x(0,y)=d_4(y),\ v_x(x,0)=d_5(x),$$

where $(x,y)\in\mathfrak{D}_0$, $v\in\Pi_0$, and

$$\begin{aligned}(\mathscr{F}v)(x,y)&=-av_{yy}(x,y)-bv_{xx}(x,y)-cv_{yx}(x,y),\\ \Theta_v(x,y)&=\int_0^x\int_0^y k_1(x,t,y,s,v(t,s))\mathrm{d}s\mathrm{d}t,\\ \Lambda_v(x,y)&=\frac{1}{\Gamma(\varrho_1)\Gamma(\varrho_2)}\int_0^x\int_0^y(x-t)^{\varrho_1-1}(y-s)^{\varrho_2-1}k_2(x,t,y,s,v(t,s))\mathrm{d}s\mathrm{d}t,\\ \rho_v(x,y)&=\frac{1}{\Gamma(\varrho_1)\Gamma(\varrho_2)}\int_0^\alpha\int_0^\beta(\alpha-t)^{\varrho_1-1}(\beta-s)^{\varrho_2-1}k_3(x,t,y,s,v(t,s))\mathrm{d}s\mathrm{d}t,\\ \varphi_v(x,y)&=\int_0^\alpha\int_0^\beta k_4(x,t,y,s,v(t,s))\mathrm{d}s\mathrm{d}t.\end{aligned}$$

Since k_i, $i=1,2,3,4$, are uniformly continuous, we can write

$$\forall\varepsilon>0,\ \exists\delta>0:\quad |f(x,y)-v(x,y)|<\delta.$$

Suppose that the assumptions (**C1**)–(**C5**) hold; therefore,

$$\begin{aligned}|\mathcal{T}f(x,y)-\mathcal{T}v(x,y)|\leq&|(\mathscr{F}f)(x,y)-(\mathscr{F}v)(x,y)|+\lambda|I^{\varrho}f(x,y)-I^{\varrho}v(x,y)|\\&+|g(x,y)-g_1(x,y)|+|\Theta(x,y)-\Theta_v(x,y)|\\&+|\Lambda(x,y)-\Lambda_v(x,y)|+|\rho(x,y)-\rho_v(x,y)|\\&+|\varphi(x,y)-\varphi_v(x,y)|.\end{aligned}$$

Furthermore, we can easily obtain the following inequalities:

$$|\Theta(x,y)-\Theta_v(x,y)| \le \frac{\varepsilon}{6\alpha\beta}\int_0^x\int_0^y \mathrm{d}s\mathrm{d}t \le \frac{\varepsilon}{6},$$
$$|\Lambda(x,y)-\Lambda_v(x,y)| \le \frac{1}{\Gamma(\varrho_1)\Gamma(\varrho_2)}\frac{\varepsilon\Gamma(\varrho_1+1)\Gamma(\varrho_2+1)}{6\alpha^{\varrho_1}\beta^{\varrho_2}}\int_0^x\int_0^y (x-t)^{\varrho_1-1}(y-s)^{\varrho_2-1}\mathrm{d}s\mathrm{d}t \le \frac{\varepsilon}{6},$$
$$|\rho(x,y)-\rho_v(x,y)| \le \frac{1}{\Gamma(\varrho_1)\Gamma(\varrho_2)}\frac{\varepsilon\Gamma(\varrho_1+1)\Gamma(\varrho_2+1)}{6\alpha^{\varrho_1}\beta^{\varrho_2}}\int_0^\alpha\int_0^\beta (\alpha-t)^{\varrho_1-1}(\beta-s)^{\varrho_2-1}\mathrm{d}s\mathrm{d}t = \frac{\varepsilon}{6},$$
$$|\varphi(x,y)-\varphi_v(x,y)| \le \frac{\varepsilon}{6\alpha\beta}\int_0^\alpha\int_0^\beta \mathrm{d}s\mathrm{d}t = \frac{\varepsilon}{6}.$$

Thus, we have

$$|\mathcal{T}f(x,y)-\mathcal{T}v(x,y)| \le \varepsilon,$$

and the proof is completed. □

In the following theorem, by using Tychonoff's fixed-point theorem [38], the global existence of solutions of the general 2D-NFIDEs will be discussed.

Theorem 2. *Suppose that*

(D1) $G_i \in C(\mathbb{R}_+^5, \mathbb{R}^n)$, $k_i \in C(\mathbb{R}_+^4 \times \mathbb{R}^n, \mathbb{R}^n)$, $i = 1,2,3,4$;

(D2) *For each* $(x,t,y,s) \in \mathbb{R}_+^4$, $G_i(x,t,y,s,u(t,s))$, $i = 1,2,3,4$, *are monotonically non-decreasing in* u;

(D3) $|k_i(x,t,y,s,f(t,s))| \le G_i(x,t,y,s,|f(t,s)|)$, $(x,t,y,s,f(t,s)) \in \mathbb{R}_+^4 \times \mathbb{R}^n$, $i = 1,2,3,4$;

(D4) $|(\mathscr{F}f)(x,y)| \le (\mathscr{F}u)(x,y)$.

Then, for every $x,y \ge 0$, *the generalized two-dimensional nonlinear fractional integro-differential equation*

$$u(x,y) = (\mathscr{F}u)(x,y) + \lambda' I^{\varrho}u(x,y) + q(x,y) + \Theta_u(x,y) + \Lambda_u(x,y) + \rho_u(x,y) + \varphi_u(x,y), \tag{11}$$

has a solution $u(x,y)$ *with initial conditions*

$$u(x,0) = d_1(x),\ u(0,y) = d_2(y),\ u_y(x,0) = d_3(x),\ u_x(0,y) = d_4(y),\ u_x(x,0) = d_5(x), \tag{12}$$

and

$$(\mathscr{F}u)(x,y) = -a\,u_{yy}(x,y) - b\,u_{xx}(x,y) - c\,u_{yx}(x,y),$$
$$I^{\varrho}u(x,y) = \frac{1}{\Gamma(\varrho_1)\Gamma(\varrho_2)}\int_0^x\int_0^y (x-t)^{\varrho_1-1}(y-s)^{\varrho_2-1}u(t,s)\mathrm{d}s\mathrm{d}t,$$
$$\Theta_u(x,y) = \int_0^x\int_0^y G_1(x,t,y,s,u(t,s))\mathrm{d}s\mathrm{d}t,$$
$$\Lambda_u(x,y) = \frac{1}{\Gamma(\varrho_1)\Gamma(\varrho_2)}\int_0^x\int_0^y (x-t)^{\varrho_1-1}(y-s)^{\varrho_2-1}G_2(x,t,y,s,u(t,s))\mathrm{d}s\mathrm{d}t,$$
$$\rho_u(x,y) = \frac{1}{\Gamma(\varrho_1)\Gamma(\varrho_2)}\int_0^{\ell_1}\int_0^{\ell_2} (\ell_1-t)^{\varrho_1-1}(\ell_2-s)^{\varrho_2-1}G_3(x,t,y,s,u(t,s))\mathrm{d}s\mathrm{d}t,$$
$$\varphi_u(x,y) = \int_0^{\ell_1}\int_0^{\ell_2} G_4(x,t,y,s,u(t,s))\mathrm{d}s\mathrm{d}t.$$

Additionally, for every $x,y \ge 0$ *and* $q(x,y) \in \mathbb{R}_+^2$, *such that* $|g(x,y)| \le q(x,y)$, *there exists a solution* $f(x,y)$ *for Equations* (1) *and* (2) *satisfying* $|f(x,y)| \le u(x,y)$ *and* $|\lambda| \le \lambda'$.

Proof. Let $\mathcal{Q}$ be a real space of all continuous functions from $(0,\infty)\times(0,\infty)$ into $\mathbb{R}^n$. The topology on $\mathcal{Q}$ is that induced by the family of pseudo-norms $\{\mathcal{Q}_{m',m}(f)\}_{m',m=1}^{\infty}$, where $\mathcal{Q}_{m',m}(f) = \sup_{0\leq x\leq m', 0\leq y\leq m} |f(x,y)|$ for $f \in \mathcal{Q}$. Consider $\{\mathcal{S}_{m',m}\}_{m',m=1}^{\infty}$ as a set of neighborhoods with $\mathcal{S}_{m',m} = \{f \in \mathcal{Q} : \ \mathcal{Q}_{m',m}(f) \leq 1\}$. Under this topology, $\mathcal{Q}$ is complete, locally convex, and a linear space.

Let

$$\mathcal{Q}_0 = \{f \in \mathcal{Q} : \ |f(x,y)| \leq u(x,y), \ x,y \geq 0\} \subseteq \mathcal{Q},$$

where $u(x,y)$ is a solution of Equations (11) and (12). Obviously, in the topology of $\mathcal{Q}$, $\mathcal{Q}_0$ is closed, convex, and bounded.

Note that a fixed point of Equations (11) and (12) corresponds to a solution of Equations (1) and (2). Since, in the topology of $\mathcal{Q}$, $\mathcal{T}$ is compact and $\mathcal{Q}_0$ is bounded, therefore, the closure of $T(\mathcal{Q}_0)$ is compact.

Considering assumptions (**D1**)–(**D4**) yields

$$\begin{aligned}
|\Theta(x,y)| &\leq \int_0^x \int_0^y |k_1(x,t,y,s,f(t,s))| \mathrm{d}s\mathrm{d}t \leq \int_0^x \int_0^y G_1(x,t,y,s,|f(t,s)|)\mathrm{d}s\mathrm{d}t \\
&\leq \int_0^x \int_0^y G_1(x,t,y,s,u(t,s))\mathrm{d}s\mathrm{d}t = \Theta_u(x,y).
\end{aligned}$$

Similarly,

$$|\Lambda(x,y)| \leq \Lambda_u(x,y), \quad |\rho(x,y)| \leq \rho_u(x,y), \quad |\varphi(x,y)| \leq \varphi_u(x,y), \quad |I^{\varrho} f(x,y)| \leq u(x,y).$$

Since $u(x,y)$ is a solution of Equations (11) and (12), the definition of $\mathcal{Q}_0$ yields $|\mathcal{T}f(x,y)| \leq u(x,y)$. Therefore, $\mathcal{T}(\mathcal{Q}_0) \subset \mathcal{Q}_0$. Now, by using Tychonoff's fixed-point theorem [38], we can deduce that $\mathcal{T}$ has a fixed point in $\mathcal{Q}_0$, and this completes the proof. □

In the following theorem, we prove that the general 2D-NFIDE has a unique solution.

Theorem 3. *Consider $k_i \in C(\mathfrak{D} \times \mathfrak{D} \times \mathbb{R}^n, \mathbb{R}^n)$ $(i = 1,2,3,4)$, $f \in C(\mathfrak{D}, \mathbb{R}^n)$. Assume that there exist $0 < L_j < 1$ $(j = 1,2,3)$ such that:*

$$\left|f_{yy}(x,y) - \bar{f}_{yy}(x,y)\right| \leq L_1 \left|f(x,y) - \bar{f}(x,y)\right|, \tag{13}$$

$$\left|f_{xx}(x,y) - \bar{f}_{xx}(x,y)\right| \leq L_2 \left|f(x,y) - \bar{f}(x,y)\right|, \tag{14}$$

$$\left|f_{yx}(x,y) - \bar{f}_{yx}(x,y)\right| \leq L_3 \left|f(x,y) - \bar{f}(x,y)\right|, \tag{15}$$

$$\left|k_i(x,t,y,s,f(t,s)) - k_i(x,t,y,s,\bar{f}(t,s))\right| \leq \eta_i \left|f(t,s) - \bar{f}(t,s)\right|, \quad i = 1,2,3,4. \tag{16}$$

If

$$\left((aL_1 + bL_2 + cL_3) + \frac{\ell_1^{\varrho_1} \ell_2^{\varrho_2}}{\Gamma(\varrho_1+1)\Gamma(\varrho_2+1)} (\lambda + \eta_1 + \eta_2 + \eta_3 + \eta_4) \right) < 1, \tag{17}$$

then the general 2D-NIDEF has a unique solution.

Proof. Let

$$\mathcal{T}\bar{f}(x,y) = (\mathscr{F}\bar{f})(x,y) - \lambda I^{\varrho} \bar{f}(x,y) + g(x,y) + \bar{\Theta}(x,y) + \bar{\Lambda}(x,y) + \bar{\rho}(x,y) + \bar{\varphi}(x,y),$$

with

$$\bar{f}(x,0) = d_1(x), \quad \bar{f}(0,y) = d_2(y), \quad \bar{f}_y(x,0) = d_3(x), \quad \bar{f}_x(0,y) = d_4(y), \quad \bar{f}_x(x,0) = d_5(x),$$

and

$$
\begin{aligned}
(\mathscr{F}\overline{f})(x,y) &= -a\overline{f}_{yy}(x,y) - b\overline{f}_{xx}(x,y) - c\overline{f}_{yx}(x,y),\\
\overline{\Theta}(x,y) &= \int_0^x \int_0^y k_1(x,t,y,s)\overline{f}^{p_1}(t,s)\mathrm{d}s\mathrm{d}t,\\
\overline{\Lambda}(x,y) &= \frac{1}{\Gamma(\varrho_1)\Gamma(\varrho_2)} \int_0^x \int_0^y (x-t)^{\varrho_1-1}(y-s)^{\varrho_2-1}k_2(x,t,y,s)\overline{f}^{p_2}(t,s)\mathrm{d}s\mathrm{d}t,\\
\overline{\rho}(x,y) &= \frac{1}{\Gamma(\varrho_1)\Gamma(\varrho_2)} \int_0^{\ell_1} \int_0^{\ell_2} (\ell_1-t)^{\varrho_1-1}(\ell_2-s)^{\varrho_2-1}k_3(x,t,y,s)\overline{f}^{p_3}(t,s)\mathrm{d}s\mathrm{d}t,\\
\overline{\varphi}(x,y) &= \int_0^{\ell_1} \int_0^{\ell_2} k_4(x,t,y,s)\overline{f}^{p_4}(t,s)\mathrm{d}s\mathrm{d}t.
\end{aligned}
$$

for $(x,y) \in \mathfrak{D}$.

Using (13)–(16) yields

$$
\begin{aligned}
\left|(\mathscr{F}f)(x,y) - (\mathscr{F}\overline{f})(x,y)\right| &\leq (aL_1 + bL_2 + cL_3)\left\|f - \overline{f}\right\|,\\
\left|I^{\varrho}f(x,y) - \lambda I^{\varrho}\overline{f}(x,y)\right| &\leq \frac{\ell_1^{\varrho_1}\ell_2^{\varrho_2}}{\Gamma(\varrho_1+1)\Gamma(\varrho_2+1)}\left\|f - \overline{f}\right\|,\\
|\Theta(x,y) - \bar{\Theta}(x,y)| &\leq \frac{\eta_1\ell_1^{\varrho_1}\ell_2^{\varrho_2}}{\Gamma(\varrho_1+1)\Gamma(\varrho_2+1)}\left\|f - \overline{f}\right\|,\\
|\Lambda(x,y) - \bar{\Lambda}(x,y)| &\leq \frac{\eta_2\ell_1^{\varrho_1}\ell_2^{\varrho_2}}{\Gamma(\varrho_1+1)\Gamma(\varrho_2+1)}\left\|f - \overline{f}\right\|,\\
|\rho(x,y) - \bar{\rho}(x,y)| &\leq \frac{\eta_3\ell_1^{\varrho_1}\ell_2^{\varrho_2}}{\Gamma(\varrho_1+1)\Gamma(\varrho_2+1)}\left\|f - \overline{f}\right\|,\\
|\varphi(x,y) - \bar{\varphi}(x,y)| &\leq \frac{\eta_4\ell_1^{\varrho_1}\ell_2^{\varrho_2}}{\Gamma(\varrho_1+1)\Gamma(\varrho_2+1)}\left\|f - \overline{f}\right\|.
\end{aligned}
$$

Now, we can write

$$
\begin{aligned}
\left|\mathcal{T}f(x,y) - \mathcal{T}\overline{f}(x,y)\right| \leq& \left|(\mathscr{F}f)(x,y) - (\mathscr{F}\overline{f})(x,y)\right| + \lambda\left|I^{\varrho}f(x,y) - \lambda I^{\varrho}\overline{f}(x,y)\right|\\
&+ |\Theta(x,y) - \bar{\Theta}(x,y)| + |\Lambda(x,y) - \bar{\Lambda}(x,y)|\\
&+ |\rho(x,y) - \bar{\rho}(x,y)| + |\varphi(x,y) - \bar{\varphi}(x,y)|\\
\leq& \left(aL_1 + bL_2 + cL_3 + \frac{\ell_1^{\varrho_1}\ell_2^{\varrho_2}}{\Gamma(\varrho_1+1)\Gamma(\varrho_2+1)}(\lambda + \eta_1 + \eta_2 + \eta_3 + \eta_4)\right)\left\|f - \overline{f}\right\|,
\end{aligned}
$$

for any $(x,y) \in \mathfrak{D}$ and $f, \overline{f} \in C(\mathfrak{D}, \mathbb{R}^n)$. Therefore,

$$
\left\|\mathcal{T}f - \mathcal{T}\overline{f}\right\| \leq \left(aL_1 + bL_2 + cL_3 + \frac{\ell_1^{\varrho_1}\ell_2^{\varrho_2}}{\Gamma(\varrho_1+1)\Gamma(\varrho_2+1)}(\lambda + \eta_1 + \eta_2 + \eta_3 + \eta_4)\right)\left\|f - \overline{f}\right\|.
$$

From (17), $\mathcal{T}$ is a contraction map in $C(\mathfrak{D}, \mathbb{R}^n)$, and thus, it has a unique fixed point. Therefore, $f \in C(\mathfrak{D}, \mathbb{R}^n)$ is a unique solution for the general 2D-NIDEF. □

3. The 1D-SJPs and 2D-SJPs and Their Operational Matrices

3.1. The 1D-SJPs

The 1D-SJPs are defined on the interval $[0, \ell)$ by

$$
\mathcal{J}_{\ell,l}^{(\tau,\varsigma)}(x) = \sum_{j=0}^{l} (-1)^{l-j} \frac{\Gamma(l+\varsigma+1)\Gamma(l+j+\tau+\varsigma+1)}{\Gamma(j+\varsigma+1)\Gamma(l+\tau+\varsigma+1)(l-j)!j!\ell^j} x^j.
$$

These polynomials are orthogonal on the interval $[0, \ell)$; therefore,

$$\int_0^{\ell_1} \mathcal{J}_{\ell,i}^{(\tau,\varsigma)}(x)\mathcal{J}_{\ell,i'}^{(\tau,\varsigma)}(x)w_\ell^{(\tau,\varsigma)}(x)\,\mathrm{d}x = \delta_{ii'}h_{\ell,i}^{(\tau,\varsigma)},$$

where $w_\ell^{(\tau,\varsigma)}(x) = x^\varsigma(\ell - x)^\tau$ is a weight function, $\delta_{ii'}$ is Kronecker delta, and

$$h_{\ell,l}^{(\tau,\varsigma)} = \frac{\ell^{\tau+\varsigma+1}\Gamma(l+\tau+1)\Gamma(l+\varsigma+1)}{(2l+\tau+\varsigma+1)l!\Gamma(l+\tau+\varsigma+1)}.$$

Additionally, these polynomials have the following property:

$$\frac{d^i}{dx^i}\mathcal{J}_{\ell,l}^{(\tau,\varsigma)}(x) = \frac{\Gamma(l+\tau+\varsigma+i+1)}{\Gamma(l+\tau+\varsigma+1)}\mathcal{J}_{\ell,l-i}^{(\tau+i,\varsigma+i)}(x). \tag{18}$$

The vector of 1D-SJPs is as follows:

$$\Psi(x) = \begin{pmatrix} \mathcal{J}_{\ell,0}^{(\tau,\varsigma)}(x) & \mathcal{J}_{\ell,1}^{(\tau,\varsigma)}(x) & \dots & \mathcal{J}_{\ell,N}^{(\tau,\varsigma)}(x) \end{pmatrix}^T. \tag{19}$$

3.2. 2D-SJPs and Function Approximation

The 2D-SJPs are defined on the domain $\mathfrak{D} = [0, \ell_1) \times [0, \ell_2)$ by

$$\mathcal{J}_{i,j}^{(\tau,\varsigma)}(x,y) = \mathcal{J}_{\ell_1,i}^{(\tau,\varsigma)}(x)\mathcal{J}_{\ell_2,j}^{(\tau,\varsigma)}(y), \quad i,j = 0,1,\dots,N.$$

These polynomials are orthogonal on $\mathfrak{D}$; therefore,

$$\int_0^{\ell_1}\int_0^{\ell_2} \mathcal{J}_{i,j}^{(\tau,\varsigma)}(x,y)\mathcal{J}_{i',j'}^{(\tau,\varsigma)}(x,y)\omega^{(\tau,\varsigma)}(x,y)\,\mathrm{d}y\,\mathrm{d}x = \delta_{ii'}\delta_{jj'}h_{\ell_1,i}^{(\tau,\varsigma)}h_{\ell_2,j}^{(\tau,\varsigma)},$$

where $\omega^{(\tau,\varsigma)}(x,y) = w_{\ell_1}^{(\tau,\varsigma)}(x)w_{\ell_2}^{(\tau,\varsigma)}(y)$ is a weight function.

By using 2D-SJPs, we can approximate a continuous function $f(x,y)$ on the domain $\mathfrak{D} = [0, \ell_1) \times [0, \ell_2)$ as follows:

$$f(x,y) \simeq f_N(x,y) = \sum_{i=0}^{N}\sum_{j=0}^{N} \hat{f}_{ij}\mathcal{J}_{i,j}^{(\tau,\varsigma)}(x,y) = \Psi^T(x,y)\hat{F} = \hat{F}^T\Psi(x,y), \tag{20}$$

where

$$\hat{F} = \begin{pmatrix} \hat{f}_{00} & \hat{f}_{01} & \dots \hat{f}_{0N} & \hat{f}_{10} & \hat{f}_{11} & \dots & \hat{f}_{1N} & \dots & \hat{f}_{N0} & \hat{f}_{N1} & \dots & \hat{f}_{NN} \end{pmatrix}^T,$$

with entries

$$\hat{f}_{ij} = \frac{1}{h_{\ell_1,i}^{(\tau,\varsigma)}h_{\ell_2,j}^{(\tau,\varsigma)}}\int_0^{\ell_1}\int_0^{\ell_2} f(x,y)\mathcal{J}_{i,j}^{(\tau,\varsigma)}(x,y)\omega^{(\tau,\varsigma)}(x,y)\,\mathrm{d}y\,\mathrm{d}x, \quad i,j = 0,1,\dots,N,$$

and

$$\begin{aligned}\Psi(x,y) = &\Big(\mathcal{J}_{0,0}^{(\tau,\varsigma)}(x,y),\dots\mathcal{J}_{0,N}^{(\tau,\varsigma)}(x,y), \mathcal{J}_{1,0}^{(\tau,\varsigma)}(x,y),\dots\mathcal{J}_{1,N}^{(\tau,\varsigma)}(x,y)\\ &\dots, \mathcal{J}_{N,0}^{(\tau,\varsigma)}(x,y),\dots\mathcal{J}_{N,N}^{(\tau,\varsigma)}(x,y)\Big)^T,\end{aligned} \tag{21}$$

are $(N+1)^2 \times 1$ vectors.

Additionally, we can expand a function $k(x,t,y,s)$ on the domain $\mathfrak{D} \times \mathfrak{D}$ with respect to 2D-SJPs as follows:

$$k(x,t,y,s) \simeq \Psi^T(x,y)K\Psi(t,s). \tag{22}$$

Here, K is a matrix with entries

$$K_{i,j} = \frac{\int_0^{\ell_1}\int_0^{\ell_2}\int_0^{\ell_1}\int_0^{\ell_2} \mathcal{J}^{(\tau,\varsigma)}_{q'[i],q''[i]}(x,y)k(x,t,y,s)\mathcal{J}^{(\tau,\varsigma)}_{q'[j],q''[j]}(t,s)\omega^{(\tau,\varsigma)}(x,y)\omega^{(\tau,\varsigma)}(t,s)\mathrm{d}s\mathrm{d}t\mathrm{d}y\mathrm{d}x}{h^{(\tau,\varsigma)}_{\ell_1,q'[i]}h^{(\tau,\varsigma)}_{\ell_2,q''[i]}h^{(\tau,\varsigma)}_{\ell_1,q'[j]}h^{(\tau,\varsigma)}_{\ell_2,q''[j]}},$$

where

$$q' = [0,\dots,0,1,\dots,1,\dots,N,\dots,N],$$
$$q'' = [0,\dots,N,0,\dots,N,\dots,0,\dots,N],$$

and $i,j = 1,\dots,(N+1)^2$.

3.3. Operational Matrices of Two-Dimensional Integration

In [40], the authors computed the one-dimensional integration of $\Psi(t)$ for $t \in [0,1)$. Similarly, we compute the one-dimensional integration of this vector for $t \in [0,\ell)$, as follows:

$$\int_0^x \Psi(t)\,\mathrm{d}t \simeq \mathbf{P}_x\,\Psi(x),$$

where $\mathbf{P}_x$ is a one-dimensional operational matrix of integration, defined in the following form:

$$\mathbf{P}_x = \begin{pmatrix} p_{00} & p_{01} & \cdots & p_{0N} \\ p_{10} & p_{11} & \cdots & p_{1N} \\ \vdots & \vdots & \ddots & \vdots \\ p_{N0} & p_{N1} & \cdots & p_{NN} \end{pmatrix}, \tag{23}$$

with the following entries:

$$p_{kl} = \sum_{j=0}^{k}\left(\frac{(-1)^{k-j}\Gamma(l+\varsigma+1)\Gamma(k+\varsigma+1)\Gamma(k+j+\tau+\varsigma+1)\Gamma(\tau+1)}{h_l\Gamma(l+\tau+\varsigma+1)\Gamma(j+\varsigma+1)\Gamma(k+\tau+\varsigma+1)(j+1)!(k-j)!\ell^j}\right.$$
$$\left.\times\sum_{i=0}^{l}\frac{(-1)^{l-i}\Gamma(l+i+\tau+\varsigma+1)\Gamma(i+j+\varsigma+2)\ell}{\Gamma(i+\varsigma+1)\Gamma(i+j+\tau+\varsigma+3)i!(l-i)!}\right), \quad k,l = 0,1,\dots,N.$$

Since $\Psi(x,y) = \Psi(x)\otimes\Psi(y)$, the two-dimensional integration of $\Psi(t,s)$ can be obtained as follows:

$$\int_0^x\int_0^y \Psi(t,s)\,\mathrm{d}s\,\mathrm{d}t \simeq (\mathbf{P}_x\otimes\mathbf{P}_y)\,\Psi(x,y), \qquad x\in[0,\ell_1),\ y\in[0,\ell_2), \tag{24}$$

where $\otimes$ denotes the Kronecker product; $\mathbf{P}_x\otimes\mathbf{P}_y$ is the $(N+1)^2\times(N+1)^2$ operational matrix of the two-dimensional integration; and $\mathbf{P}_x$, $\mathbf{P}_y$ are $(N+1)\times(N+1)$ one-dimensional operational matrices of integration, defined in Equation (23).

Additionally, it is easy to conclude the following result:

$$\int_0^{\ell_1}\int_0^{\ell_2}\Psi(t,s)\,\mathrm{d}s\,\mathrm{d}t = A_1\otimes A_2, \tag{25}$$

where

$$A_1 = \begin{pmatrix} a_0 & a_1 & \dots & a_N \end{pmatrix}^T, \qquad A_2 = \begin{pmatrix} a'_0 & a'_1 & \dots & a'_N \end{pmatrix}^T,$$

with the entries:

$$a_r = \sum_{j=0}^{r} (-1)^{r-j} \frac{\Gamma(r+\varsigma+1)\Gamma(r+j+\tau+\varsigma+1)\ell_1}{\Gamma(j+\varsigma+1)\Gamma(r+\tau+\varsigma+1)(r-j)!(j+1)!},$$

$$a'_r = \sum_{j=0}^{r} (-1)^{r-j} \frac{\Gamma(r+\varsigma+1)\Gamma(r+j+\tau+\varsigma+1)\ell_2}{\Gamma(j+\varsigma+1)\Gamma(r+\tau+\varsigma+1)(r-j)!(j+1)!},$$

for $r = 0, 1, \dots, N$.

3.4. Operational Matrices of Fractional-Order Integration

In [27], the authors defined an operational matrix of the Riemann–Liouville integral operator of order κ by

$$\mathbf{I}^{\ell,\kappa} = \begin{pmatrix} S_{00} & S_{01} & \dots & S_{0N} \\ S_{10} & S_{11} & \dots & S_{1N} \\ \vdots & \vdots & \ddots & \vdots \\ S_{N0} & S_{N1} & \dots & S_{NN} \end{pmatrix},$$

with the entries

$$S_{lr} = \sum_{m=0}^{l} \Bigg(\frac{(-1)^{l-m}\Gamma(l+\varsigma+1)\Gamma(l+m+\tau+\varsigma+1)\Gamma(m+1)}{\Gamma(m+\varsigma+1)\Gamma(l+\tau+\varsigma+1)(l-m)!m!\Gamma(m+\kappa+1)\ell^m}$$
$$\times \sum_{m'=0}^{r} \frac{(-1)^{r-m'}(2r+\tau+\varsigma+1)\Gamma(r+1)\Gamma(r+m'+\tau+\varsigma+1)\Gamma(m+\kappa+m'+\varsigma+1)\Gamma(\kappa+1)\ell^\kappa}{\Gamma(r+\tau+1)\Gamma(m'+\varsigma+1)(r-m')!m'!\Gamma(m+\kappa+m'+\varsigma+\tau+2)} \Bigg),$$

for $l, r = 0, 1, \dots, N$.

Theorem 4 (see [34]). *Let $\varrho = (\varrho_1, \varrho_2) \in (0,\infty) \times (0,\infty)$ and $\Psi(x,y)$ be the vector of 2D-SJPs. Then*

$$I^{\varrho}\Psi(x,y) \simeq (\mathbf{I}^{\ell_1,\varrho_1} \otimes \mathbf{I}^{\ell_2,\varrho_2})\Psi(x,y), \qquad (x,y) \in [0,\ell_1) \times [0,\ell_2). \tag{26}$$

Here, $\mathbf{I}^{\ell_1,\varrho_1}$ and $\mathbf{I}^{\ell_2,\varrho_2}$ are operational matrices of a fractional Riemann–Liouville integration of orders ϱ_1 and ϱ_2, respectively.

Theorem 5 (see [34]). *Let $\kappa > 0$. Assume that $\Psi(s)$, defined in (19), is the vector of 1D-SJPs. Then,*

$$\frac{1}{\Gamma(\kappa)} \int_0^{\ell} (\ell - s)^{\kappa-1}\Psi(s)\,\mathrm{d}s = \Upsilon, \tag{27}$$

where $\Upsilon = \begin{pmatrix} \gamma_0 & \gamma_1 & \dots & \gamma_N \end{pmatrix}^T$ *and*

$$\gamma_r = \sum_{j=0}^{r} (-1)^{r-j} \frac{\Gamma(r+\varsigma+1)\Gamma(r+j+\tau+\varsigma+1)\ell^{\kappa-1}}{\Gamma(j+\varsigma+1)\Gamma(r+\tau+\varsigma+1)(r-j)!\Gamma(j+\kappa+1)}, \qquad r = 0, 1, \dots, N. \tag{28}$$

Theorem 6 (see [34]). *Let $\varrho_1, \varrho_2 > 0$. Assume that $\Psi(t,s)$, defined in* (21), *is the vector of 2D-SJPs. Then*

$$\frac{1}{\Gamma(\varrho_1)\Gamma(\varrho_2)}\int_0^{\ell_1}\int_0^{\ell_2}(\ell_1-t)^{\varrho_1-1}(\ell_2-s)^{\varrho_2-1}\Psi(t,s)\,\mathrm{d}s\,\mathrm{d}t = \Upsilon_1\otimes\Upsilon_2, \tag{29}$$

where

$$\Upsilon_1 = \begin{pmatrix}\gamma1_0 & \gamma1_1 & \dots & \gamma1_N\end{pmatrix}^T, \qquad \Upsilon_2 = \begin{pmatrix}\gamma2_0 & \gamma2_1 & \dots & \gamma2_N\end{pmatrix}^T,$$

and

$$\gamma1_r = \sum_{j=0}^{r}(-1)^{r-j}\frac{\Gamma(r+\varsigma+1)\Gamma(r+j+\tau+\varsigma+1)\ell_1^{\varrho_1}}{\Gamma(j+\varsigma+1)\Gamma(r+\tau+\varsigma+1)(r-j)!\Gamma(j+\varrho_1+1)},$$
$$\gamma2_r = \sum_{j=0}^{r}(-1)^{r-j}\frac{\Gamma(r+\varsigma+1)\Gamma(r+j+\tau+\varsigma+1)\ell_2^{\varrho_2}}{\Gamma(j+\varsigma+1)\Gamma(r+\tau+\varsigma+1)(r-j)!\Gamma(j+\varrho_2+1)},$$

for $r = 0,1,\dots,N$.

3.5. Operational Matrix of Product

Assume that $\Psi(x,y)$, defined in (21), is the vector of 2D-SJPs. In [34], Rashidinia et al. introduced the operational matrix of the product as follows:

$$\Psi(x,y)\Psi^T(x,y)\hat{F} \simeq \tilde{\hat{F}}\Psi(x,y), \tag{30}$$

for $(x,y)\in[0,\ell_1)\times[0,\ell_2)$. Here, $\tilde{\hat{F}}$ is the operational matrix of the product with the entries

$$\tilde{\hat{F}}_{m_1(N+1)+n_1+1,m_2(N+1)+n_2+1} = \frac{1}{h^{(\tau,\varsigma)}_{\ell_1,m_2}h^{(\tau,\varsigma)}_{\ell_2,n_2}}\sum_{j=0}^{N}\sum_{k=0}^{N}\hat{f}_{jk}v_{m_1jm_2}v_{n_1kn_2},$$

where

$$v_{m_1jm_2} = \int_0^{\ell_1}\mathcal{J}^{(\tau,\varsigma)}_{\ell_1,m_1}(x)\mathcal{J}^{(\tau,\varsigma)}_{\ell_1,j}(x)\mathcal{J}^{(\tau,\varsigma)}_{\ell_1,m_2}(x)w^{(\tau,\varsigma)}_{\ell_1}(x)\,\mathrm{d}x,$$
$$v_{n_1kn_2} = \int_0^{\ell_2}\mathcal{J}^{(\tau,\varsigma)}_{\ell_2,n_1}(y)\mathcal{J}^{(\tau,\varsigma)}_{\ell_2,k}(y)\mathcal{J}^{(\tau,\varsigma)}_{\ell_2,n_2}(y)w^{(\tau,\varsigma)}_{\ell_2}(y)\,\mathrm{d}y,$$

for $m_1, n_1, m_2, n_2 = 0,1,\dots,N$.

4. Method of Solution

Here, by using the method proposed in Section 3, we solve the general 2D-NFIDEs. First of all, we define

$$f_{yy}(x,y) \simeq f_{yy}^T\Psi(x,y), \tag{31}$$
$$f_{xx}(x,y) \simeq f_{xx}^T\Psi(x,y), \tag{32}$$
$$f_{yx}(x,y) \simeq f_{yx}^T\Psi(x,y), \tag{33}$$
$$g(x,y) \simeq \Psi^T(x,y)G, \tag{34}$$
$$k_i(x,t,y,s) \simeq \Psi^T(x,y)k_i\Psi(t,s), \quad i = 1,2,3,4, \tag{35}$$

$$d_1(x) = f(x,0) \simeq F_{x0}^T \Psi(x,y), \tag{36}$$
$$d_2(y) = f(0,y) \simeq F_{0y}^T \Psi(x,y), \tag{37}$$
$$d_3(x) = f_y(x,0) \simeq F_{yx0}^T \Psi(x,y), \tag{38}$$
$$d_4(y) = f_x(0,y) \simeq F_{x0y}^T \Psi(x,y), \tag{39}$$
$$d_5(x) = f_x(x,0) \simeq F_{xx0}^T \Psi(x,y). \tag{40}$$

Now, from the Appendix in [36], we can obtain:

$$f_{yy}^T = ((f^T - F_{x0}^T)(I \otimes \mathbf{P}_y)^{-1} - F_{yx0}^T)(I \otimes \mathbf{P}_y)^{-1}, \tag{41}$$
$$f_{xx}^T = ((f^T - F_{0y}^T)(\mathbf{P}_x \otimes I)^{-1} - F_{x0y}^T)(\mathbf{P}_x \otimes I)^{-1}, \tag{42}$$
$$f_{yx}^T = ((f^T - F_{0y}^T)(\mathbf{P}_x \otimes I)^{-1} - F_{xx0}^T)(I \otimes \mathbf{P}_y)^{-1}. \tag{43}$$

Using (26) for $I^{\varrho} f(x,y)$ yields

$$I^{\varrho} f(x,y) \simeq I^{\varrho} \hat{F}^T \Psi(x,y) = \hat{F}^T I^{\varrho} \Psi(x,y) = \hat{F}^T \left(\mathbf{I}^{\ell_1,\varrho_1} \otimes \mathbf{I}^{\ell_2,\varrho_2}\right) \Psi(x,y). \tag{44}$$

Additionally, by using (20) and (30), we have

$$f^2(x,y) \simeq \hat{F}^T \Psi(x,y) \Psi^T(x,y) \hat{F} = \underbrace{\hat{F}^T \tilde{\hat{F}}}_{\hat{F}_2} \Psi(x,y) = \hat{F}_2 \Psi(x,y),$$

$$f^3(x,y) \simeq \hat{F}^T \Psi(x,y) \hat{F}_2 \Psi(x,y) = \hat{F}^T \Psi(x,y) \Psi^T(x,y) \hat{F}_2^T = \underbrace{\hat{F}^T \widetilde{\hat{F}_2^T}}_{\hat{F}_3} \Psi(x,y) = \hat{F}_3 \Psi(x,y).$$

Similarly, we obtain

$$f^p(x,y) \simeq \hat{F}_p \Psi(x,y). \tag{45}$$

Now, using (24), (35), and (45) gives

$$\begin{aligned}
\Theta(x,y) &= \int_0^x \int_0^y k_1(x,t,y,s) f^{p_1}(t,s)\, \mathrm{d}s\, \mathrm{d}t \\
&\simeq \int_0^x \int_0^y \Psi^T(x,y) k_1 \Psi(t,s) \hat{F}_{p_1} \Psi(t,s)\, \mathrm{d}s\, \mathrm{d}t \\
&= \int_0^x \int_0^y \Psi^T(x,y) k_1 \widetilde{\hat{F}_{p_1}^T} \Psi(t,s)\, \mathrm{d}s\, \mathrm{d}t \\
&= \Psi^T(x,y) k_1 \widetilde{\hat{F}_{p_1}^T} \int_0^x \int_0^y \Psi(t,s)\, \mathrm{d}s\, \mathrm{d}t \\
&= \Psi^T(x,y) k_1 \widetilde{\hat{F}_{p_1}^T} (\mathbf{P}_x \otimes \mathbf{P}_y) \Psi(x,y).
\end{aligned} \tag{46}$$

Similarly, using (25), (35), and (45) for $\varphi(x,y)$, we can write

$$\begin{aligned}
\varphi(x,y) &= \int_0^{\ell_1} \int_0^{\ell_2} k_4(x,t,y,s) f^{p_4}(t,s)\, \mathrm{d}s\, \mathrm{d}t \\
&\simeq \int_0^{\ell_1} \int_0^{\ell_2} \Psi^T(x,y) k_4 \Psi(t,s) \hat{F}_{p_4} \Psi(t,s)\, \mathrm{d}s\, \mathrm{d}t \\
&= \int_0^{\ell_1} \int_0^{\ell_2} \Psi^T(x,y) k_4 \widetilde{\hat{F}_{p_4}^T} \Psi(t,s)\, \mathrm{d}s\, \mathrm{d}t \\
&= \Psi^T(x,y) k_4 \widetilde{\hat{F}_{p_4}^T} \int_0^{\ell_1} \int_0^{\ell_2} \Psi(t,s)\, \mathrm{d}s\, \mathrm{d}t \\
&= \Psi^T(x,y) k_4 \widetilde{\hat{F}_{p_4}^T} (A_1 \otimes A_2).
\end{aligned} \tag{47}$$

Additionally, using (26), (35), and (45), $\Lambda(x,y)$ can be determined as:

$$\begin{aligned}\Lambda(x,y) &= \frac{1}{\Gamma(\varrho_1)\Gamma(\varrho_2)}\int_0^x\int_0^y (x-t)^{\varrho_1-1}(y-s)^{\varrho_2-1}k_2(x,t,y,s)f^{p_2}(t,s)\,\mathrm{d}s\,\mathrm{d}t \\ &\simeq \frac{1}{\Gamma(\varrho_1)\Gamma(\varrho_2)}\int_0^x\int_0^y (x-t)^{\varrho_1-1}(y-s)^{\varrho_2-1}\Psi^T(x,y)k_2\Psi(t,s)\hat{F}_{p_2}\Psi(t,s)\,\mathrm{d}s\,\mathrm{d}t \\ &= \frac{1}{\Gamma(\varrho_1)\Gamma(\varrho_2)}\int_0^x\int_0^y (x-t)^{\varrho_1-1}(y-s)^{\varrho_2-1}\Psi^T(x,y)k_2\widetilde{\hat{F}^T_{p_2}}\Psi(t,s)\,\mathrm{d}s\,\mathrm{d}t \\ &= \Psi^T(x,y)k_2\widetilde{\hat{F}^T_{p_2}}\left(\frac{1}{\Gamma(\varrho_1)\Gamma(\varrho_2)}\int_0^x\int_0^y (x-t)^{\varrho_1-1}(y-s)^{\varrho_2-1}\Psi(t,s)\,\mathrm{d}s\,\mathrm{d}t\right) \\ &= \Psi^T(x,y)k_2\widetilde{\hat{F}^T_{p_2}}\left(\mathbf{I}^{\ell_1,\varrho_1}\otimes\mathbf{I}^{\ell_2,\varrho_2}\right)\Psi(x,y). \end{aligned} \tag{48}$$

Using (29), (35), and (45) for $\rho(x,y)$, we obtain

$$\begin{aligned}\rho(x,y) &= \frac{1}{\Gamma(\varrho_1)\Gamma(\varrho_2)}\int_0^{\ell_1}\int_0^{\ell_2} (\ell_1-t)^{\varrho_1-1}(\ell_2-s)^{\varrho_2-1}k_3(x,t,y,s)f^{p_3}(t,s)\,\mathrm{d}s\,\mathrm{d}t \\ &\simeq \frac{1}{\Gamma(\varrho_1)\Gamma(\varrho_2)}\int_0^{\ell_1}\int_0^{\ell_2} (\ell_1-t)^{\varrho_1-1}(\ell_2-s)^{\varrho_2-1}\Psi^T(x,y)k_3\Psi(t,s)\hat{F}_{p_3}\Psi(t,s)\,\mathrm{d}s\,\mathrm{d}t \\ &= \frac{1}{\Gamma(\varrho_1)\Gamma(\varrho_2)}\int_0^{\ell_1}\int_0^{\ell_2} (\ell_1-t)^{\varrho_1-1}(\ell_2-s)^{\varrho_2-1}\Psi^T(x,y)k_3\widetilde{\hat{F}^T_{p_3}}\Psi(t,s)\,\mathrm{d}s\,\mathrm{d}t \\ &= \Psi^T(x,y)k_3\widetilde{\hat{F}^T_{p_3}}\left(\frac{1}{\Gamma(\varrho_1)\Gamma(\varrho_2)}\int_0^{\ell_1}\int_0^{\ell_2} (\ell_1-t)^{\varrho_1-1}(\ell_2-s)^{\varrho_2-1}\Psi(t,s)\,\mathrm{d}s\,\mathrm{d}t\right) \\ &= \Psi^T(x,y)k_3\widetilde{\hat{F}^T_{p_3}}(\Upsilon_1\otimes\Upsilon_2). \end{aligned} \tag{49}$$

Now, by substituting (31)–(34), (36)–(44), and (46)–(49) into (1), a system of equations can be obtained as follows:

$$\begin{aligned}&af^T_{yy}\Psi(x,y)+bf^T_{xx}\Psi(x,y)+cf^T_{yx}\Psi(x,y)+\hat{F}^T\Psi(x,y)+\lambda\hat{F}^T\left(\mathbf{I}^{\ell_1,\varrho_1}\otimes\mathbf{I}^{\ell_2,\varrho_2}\right)\Psi(x,y) \\ &\simeq \Psi^T(x,y)G+\Psi^T(x,y)k_1\widetilde{\hat{F}^T_{p_1}}(\mathbf{P}_x\otimes\mathbf{P}_y)\Psi(x,y)+\Psi^T(x,y)k_2\widetilde{\hat{F}^T_{p_2}}\left(\mathbf{I}^{\ell_1,\varrho_1}\otimes\mathbf{I}^{\ell_2,\varrho_2}\right)\Psi(x,y) \\ &+\Psi^T(x,y)k_3\widetilde{\hat{F}^T_{p_3}}(\Upsilon_1\otimes\Upsilon_2)+\Psi^T(x,y)k_4\widetilde{\hat{F}^T_{p_4}}(A_1\otimes A_2). \end{aligned} \tag{50}$$

In the above system, the coefficients $\hat{f}_{mm'}$, $m,m'=0,1,\dots,N$ are unknown. Using the roots of $\mathcal{J}^{(\tau,\varsigma)}_{\ell_1,N+1}(x)$ and $\mathcal{J}^{(\tau,\varsigma)}_{\ell_2,N+1}(y)$ for an appropriate N determines these unknown coefficients. By collocating Equation (50) at points $\{(x_m,y'_m)\}^N_{m,m'=0}$, we obtain $(N+1)^2$ equations and solve this system using the Newton method. Therefore, we obtain the unknown coefficients and determine an approximate solution from (20).

5. Error Bounds

Let $\mathfrak{D}=[0,\ell_1)\times[0,\ell_2)$ and $L^2_{\omega^{(\tau,\varsigma)}}(\mathfrak{D})$ be a weighted space of square integrable functions on $\mathfrak{D}$. We recall the following inner product and norm on $L^2_{\omega^{(\tau,\varsigma)}}(\mathfrak{D})$ to discuss the convergence of the new method:

$$\begin{aligned}\langle f,g\rangle_{\omega^{(\tau,\varsigma)}} &= \int_0^{\ell_1}\int_0^{\ell_2} f(x,y)g(x,y)\omega^{(\tau,\varsigma)}(x,y)\,\mathrm{d}y\,\mathrm{d}x, \qquad \forall f,g\in L^2_{\omega^{(\tau,\varsigma)}}(\mathfrak{D}), \\ \|f\|_{\omega^{(\tau,\varsigma)}} &= \left(\int_0^{\ell_1}\int_0^{\ell_2}(f(x,y))^2\omega^{(\tau,\varsigma)}(x,y)\,\mathrm{d}y\,\mathrm{d}x\right)^{\frac{1}{2}}, \qquad \forall f\in L^2_{\omega^{(\tau,\varsigma)}}(\mathfrak{D}).\end{aligned}$$

Theorem 7. *Consider the following finite-dimensional polynomial space:*

$$\mathscr{P}_N = span\{\mathcal{J}^{(\tau,\varsigma)}_{m,m'}(x,y),\quad 0\le m,m'\le N\}.$$

Suppose that

$$\frac{\partial^i}{\partial x^{i_1}\partial y^{i_2}} f(x,y) \in C(\mathfrak{D}), \quad i_1 + i_2 = i,\ i = 0,1,\ldots,N.$$

If $f_N(x,y)$ is the best approximation from $\mathscr{P}_N$ to $f(x,y)$ and $\widetilde{f}_N(x,y)$ is the Taylor expansion of $f(x,y)$ of order N with respect to each variables x and y, then

$$\|f - f_N\|_{\omega^{(\tau,\varsigma)}} \leq \frac{\mu 2^{N+1}}{(N+1)!}\sqrt{(\ell_1\ell_2)^{\tau+\varsigma+1}B(\tau+1,\varsigma+1)}, \tag{51}$$

where

$$\mu = \max_{i=0,1,\ldots,N}\left\{\ell_1^{N+1-i}\ell_2^i \max_{(x,y)\in\mathfrak{D}}\left|\frac{\partial^{N+1}}{\partial x^{N+1-i}\partial y^i} f(x,y)\right|\right\}, \tag{52}$$

and $B(.,.)$ is a beta function.

Proof. Since $f_N(x,y)$ is the best approximation to $f(x,y)$, it is obvious that from the definition of best approximation, we have

$$\|f - f_N\|_{\omega^{(\tau,\varsigma)}} \leq \left\|f - \widetilde{f}_N\right\|_{\omega^{(\tau,\varsigma)}}. \tag{53}$$

The Taylor expansion of $f(x,y)$ about $(0^+,0^+)$ yields

$$\begin{aligned}
\left|f(x,y) - \widetilde{f}_N(x,y)\right| &= \left|f(x,y) - \sum_{r=0}^{N}\sum_{m=0}^{r}\frac{x^{r-m}y^m}{(r-m)!m!}\frac{\partial^r}{\partial x^{r-m}\partial y^m}f(0^+,0^+)\right| \\
&= \left|\sum_{r=0}^{N+1}\frac{x^{N+1-r}y^r}{(N+1-r)!r!}\frac{\partial^{N+1}}{\partial x^{N+1-r}\partial y^i}f(\eta_x,\eta_y)\right| \\
&\leq \sum_{r=0}^{N+1}\frac{\ell_1^{N+1-r}\ell_2^r}{(N+1-r)!r!}\left|\frac{\partial^{N+1}}{\partial x^{N+1-r}\partial y^r}f(\eta_x,\eta_y)\right| \\
&\leq \sum_{r=0}^{N+1}\frac{\ell_1^{N+1-r}\ell_2^r}{(N+1-r)!r!}\max_{(x,y)\in\mathfrak{D}}\left|\frac{\partial^{N+1}}{\partial x^{N+1-r}\partial y^r}f(x,y)\right| \\
&\leq \mu\sum_{r=0}^{N+1}\frac{1}{(N+1-r)!r!} \\
&= \frac{\mu}{(N+1)!}\sum_{r=0}^{N+1}\binom{N+1}{r} \\
&= \frac{\mu 2^{N+1}}{(N+1)!},
\end{aligned}$$

where $(\eta_x,\eta_y) \in [0,x]\times[0,y]$ and $(x,y)\in\mathfrak{D}$. Since $\widetilde{f}_N \in \mathscr{P}_N$, we can write

$$\begin{aligned}
\|f - f_N\|^2_{\omega^{(\tau,\varsigma)}} &\leq \int_0^{\ell_1}\int_0^{\ell_2}\left(\frac{\mu 2^{N+1}}{(N+1)!}\right)^2\omega^{(\tau,\varsigma)}(x,y)\,\mathrm{d}y\,\mathrm{d}x \\
&= \left(\frac{\mu 2^{N+1}}{(N+1)!}\right)^2(\ell_1\ell_2)^{\tau+\varsigma+1}(B(\tau+1,\varsigma+1))^2.
\end{aligned}$$

Taking the square roots of the above inequality gives the inequality (51). □

Definition 1. *A Jacobi-weighted Sobolev space of measurable functions is denoted by* $\mathscr{P}^{\varepsilon}_{\omega^{(\tau,\varsigma)}}(\mathfrak{D})$ *and is defined with the following norm and semi-norm:*

$$\|f\|_{\varepsilon,\omega^{(\tau,\varsigma)}} = \left(\sum_{l=0}^{\varepsilon} \left\| \partial_{\Delta}^{l} f \right\|^2_{\omega^{(\tau+l,\varsigma+l)}} \right)^{\frac{1}{2}} < \infty, \quad \Delta = (x,y), \quad \varepsilon \in \mathbb{N},$$
$$|f|_{\varepsilon,\omega^{(\tau,\varsigma)}} = \|\partial_{\Delta}^{\varepsilon} f\|_{\omega^{(\tau+\varepsilon,\varsigma+\varepsilon)}},$$

where

$$\partial_{\Delta}^{l} f = \frac{\partial^{l}}{\partial x^{l_1} \partial y^{l_2}} f, \quad l_1 + l_2 = l,$$

$$\omega^{(\tau+l,\varsigma+l)}(x,y) = \omega^{(\tau+l_1,\varsigma+l_1)}(x)\omega^{(\tau+l_2,\varsigma+l_2)}(y).$$

Theorem 8. *For any* $f \in \mathscr{P}^{\varepsilon}_{\omega^{(\tau,\varsigma)}}(\mathfrak{D})$, $\varepsilon \in \mathbb{N}$, *and* $0 \le \epsilon \le \varepsilon$, *we have*

$$\|f - f_N\|_{\epsilon,\omega^{(\tau,\varsigma)}} \le \eta (N(N+\tau+\varsigma)(1+\tau+\varsigma))^{\frac{\epsilon-\varepsilon}{2}} |f|_{\varepsilon,\omega^{(\tau,\varsigma)}}, \tag{54}$$

where η *is a positive constant.*

Proof. From (18), we can write

$$\begin{aligned}
\partial_{\Delta}^{l}(f(x,y) - f_N(x,y)) = & \sum_{j=0}^{\infty} \sum_{k=N+1}^{\infty} \hat{f}_{jk} \partial_{\Delta}^{l} \mathcal{J}^{(\tau,\varsigma)}_{\ell_1,j}(x) \mathcal{J}^{(\tau,\varsigma)}_{\ell_2,k}(y) \\
& + \sum_{j=N+1}^{\infty} \sum_{k=0}^{\infty} \hat{f}_{jk} \partial_{\Delta}^{l} \mathcal{J}^{(\tau,\varsigma)}_{\ell_1,j}(x) \mathcal{J}^{(\tau,\varsigma)}_{\ell_2,k}(y) \\
= & \sum_{j=0}^{\infty} \sum_{k=N+1}^{\infty} \hat{f}_{jk} \nu_{j,l_1} \nu_{k,l_2} \mathcal{J}^{(\tau+l_1,\varsigma+l_1)}_{\ell_1,j-l_1}(x) \mathcal{J}^{(\tau+l_2,\varsigma+l_2)}_{\ell_2,k-l_2}(y) \\
& + \sum_{j=N+1}^{\infty} \sum_{k=0}^{\infty} \hat{f}_{jk} \nu_{j,l_1} \nu_{k,l_2} \mathcal{J}^{(\tau+l_1,\varsigma+l_1)}_{\ell_1,j-l_1}(x) \mathcal{J}^{(\tau+l_2,\varsigma+l_2)}_{\ell_2,k-l_2}(y),
\end{aligned} \tag{55}$$

where

$$\nu_{j,l_1} = \frac{\Gamma(j+\tau+\varsigma+l_1+1)}{\Gamma(j+\tau+\varsigma+1)}, \qquad \nu_{k,l_2} = \frac{\Gamma(k+\tau+\varsigma+l_2+1)}{\Gamma(k+\tau+\varsigma+1)}. \tag{56}$$

Taking the $L^2_{\omega^{(\tau,\varsigma)}}$−norm of Equation (55) yields

$$\left\| \partial_{\Delta}^{l}(f - f_N) \right\|^2_{\omega^{(\tau+l,\varsigma+l)}} = \sum_{j=0}^{\infty} \sum_{k=N+1}^{\infty} \hat{f}^2_{jk} a_{j,k} + \sum_{j=N+1}^{\infty} \sum_{k=0}^{\infty} \hat{f}^2_{jk} a_{j,k} + 2 \sum_{j=N+1}^{\infty} \sum_{k=N+1}^{\infty} \hat{f}^2_{jk} a_{j,k}, \tag{57}$$

where

$$a_{j,k} = \nu^2_{j,l_1} \nu^2_{k,l_2} h^{(\tau+l_1,\varsigma+l_1)}_{\ell_1,j-l_1}(x) h^{(\tau+l_2,\varsigma+l_2)}_{\ell_2,k-l_2}(y).$$

Similarly,

$$\left\| \partial_{\Delta}^{l} f \right\|^2_{\omega^{(\tau+\varepsilon,\varsigma+\varepsilon)}} = \sum_{j=0}^{\infty} \sum_{k=N+1}^{\infty} \hat{f}^2_{jk} b_{j,k} + \sum_{j=N+1}^{\infty} \sum_{k=0}^{\infty} \hat{f}^2_{jk} b_{j,k} + 2 \sum_{j=N+1}^{\infty} \sum_{k=N+1}^{\infty} \hat{f}^2_{jk} b_{j,k}, \tag{58}$$

where

$$b_{j,k}=v_{j,\varepsilon_1}^2 v_{k,\varepsilon_2}^2 h_{\ell_1,j-\varepsilon_1}^{(\tau+\varepsilon_1,\varsigma+\varepsilon_1)}(x) h_{\ell_2,k-\varepsilon_2}^{(\tau+\varepsilon_2,\varsigma+\varepsilon_2)}(y).$$

Using (18) and the Stirling formula

$$\Gamma(z+1)=\sqrt{2\pi z}z^z \mathrm{e}^{-z}\left(1+O\left(z^{-\frac{1}{5}}\right)\right), \tag{59}$$

and from

$$(m+\kappa)^{m+\kappa}=m^{m+\kappa}\mathrm{e}^{(m+\kappa)\sum\limits_{i=1}^{\infty}\frac{(-1)^i}{i}\left(\frac{\kappa}{m}\right)^i}, \tag{60}$$

we have

$$\frac{a_{j,k}}{b_{j,k}} \leq \eta j^{l_1-\varepsilon_1} k^{l_2-\varepsilon_2} (j+\tau+\varsigma)^{l_1-\varepsilon_1} (k+\tau+\varsigma)^{l_2-\varepsilon_2}. \tag{61}$$

From the relations (63)–(65), we obtain

$$\begin{aligned}
&|f(x,y)-f_N(x,y)|^2_{l,\omega^{(\tau,\varsigma)}} = \left\|\partial_\Delta^l (f-f_N)\right\|^2_{\omega^{(\tau+l,\varsigma+l)}} \\
&= \sum_{j=0}^{\infty}\sum_{k=N+1}^{\infty} \frac{a_{j,k}}{b_{j,k}} b_{j,k}\hat{f}_{jk}^2 + \sum_{j=N+1}^{\infty}\sum_{k=0}^{\infty} \frac{a_{j,k}}{b_{j,k}} b_{j,k}\hat{f}_{jk}^2 + 2\sum_{j=N+1}^{\infty}\sum_{k=N+1}^{\infty} \frac{a_{j,k}}{b_{j,k}} b_{j,k}\hat{f}_{jk}^2 \\
&\leq \sum_{j=0}^{\infty}\sum_{k=N+1}^{\infty} \eta j^{l_1-\varepsilon_1} k^{l_2-\varepsilon_2} (j+\tau+\varsigma)^{l_1-\varepsilon_1} (k+\tau+\varsigma)^{l_2-\varepsilon_2} b_{j,k}\hat{f}_{jk}^2 \\
&+ \sum_{j=N+1}^{\infty}\sum_{k=0}^{\infty} \eta j^{l_1-\varepsilon_1} k^{l_2-\varepsilon_2} (j+\tau+\varsigma)^{l_1-\varepsilon_1} (k+\tau+\varsigma)^{l_2-\varepsilon_2} b_{j,k}\hat{f}_{jk}^2 \\
&+ 2\sum_{j=N+1}^{\infty}\sum_{k=N+1}^{\infty} \eta j^{l_1-\varepsilon_1} k^{l_2-\varepsilon_2} (j+\tau+\varsigma)^{l_1-\varepsilon_1} (k+\tau+\varsigma)^{l_2-\varepsilon_2} b_{j,k}\hat{f}_{jk}^2 \\
&\leq \eta N^{l_2-\varepsilon_2}(1+\tau+\varsigma)^{l_1-\varepsilon_1}(N+\tau+\varsigma)^{l_2-\varepsilon_2} \sum_{j=0}^{\infty}\sum_{k=N+1}^{\infty} b_{j,k}\hat{f}_{jk}^2 \\
&+ \eta N^{l_1-\varepsilon_1}(N+\tau+\varsigma)^{l_1-\varepsilon_1}(1+\tau+\varsigma)^{l_2-\varepsilon_2} \sum_{j=N+1}^{\infty}\sum_{k=0}^{\infty} b_{j,k}\hat{f}_{jk}^2 \\
&+ 2\eta N^{l_1-\varepsilon_1} N^{l_2-\varepsilon_2}(N+\tau+\varsigma)^{l_1-\varepsilon_1}(N+\tau+\varsigma)^{l_2-\varepsilon_2} \sum_{j=N+1}^{\infty}\sum_{k=N+1}^{\infty} b_{j,k}\hat{f}_{jk}^2 \\
&\leq \eta N^{l_n-\varepsilon}(N+\tau+\varsigma)^{l_n-\varepsilon}(1+\tau+\varsigma)^{l_n-\varepsilon}\left(\sum_{j=0}^{\infty}\sum_{k=N+1}^{\infty} b_{j,k}\hat{f}_{jk}^2 + \sum_{j=N+1}^{\infty}\sum_{k=0}^{\infty} b_{j,k}\hat{f}_{jk}^2 + 2\sum_{j=N+1}^{\infty}\sum_{k=N+1}^{\infty} b_{j,k}\hat{f}_{jk}^2\right) \\
&= \eta N^{l_n-\varepsilon}(N+\tau+\varsigma)^{l_n-\varepsilon}(1+\tau+\varsigma)^{l_n-\varepsilon}\left\|\partial_\Delta^l f\right\|^2_{\omega^{(\tau+\varepsilon,\varsigma+\varepsilon)}} \\
&= \eta N^{l_n-\varepsilon}(N+\tau+\varsigma)^{l_n-\varepsilon}(1+\tau+\varsigma)^{l_n-\varepsilon}|f|^2_{\varepsilon,\omega^{(\tau,\varsigma)}},
\end{aligned}$$

for any $l_n \leq \varepsilon_n$, where

$$l_n-\varepsilon_n=\min_{i=1,2}\{l_i-\varepsilon_i\}, \quad 0 \leq l_i \leq \varepsilon_i \leq \varepsilon,\ i=1,2.$$

Therefore, we obtain

$$\|f-f_N\|_{\epsilon,\omega^{(\tau,\varsigma)}} \leq \eta(N(N+\tau+\varsigma)(1+\tau+\varsigma))^{\frac{\epsilon-\varepsilon}{2}}|f|_{\varepsilon,\omega^{(\tau,\varsigma)}}, \quad 0 \leq \epsilon \leq \varepsilon.$$

□

Theorem 9. *For any* $f \in \mathscr{P}^{\varepsilon}_{\omega^{(\tau,\varsigma)}}(\mathfrak{D})$, $\varepsilon \in \mathbb{N}$, *and* $0 \le \epsilon \le \varepsilon$, *we have*

$$\left\| \frac{\partial^2 f}{\partial y^2} - \left(\frac{\partial^2 f}{\partial y^2}\right)_N \right\|_{\epsilon,\omega^{(\tau,\varsigma)}} \le \eta_1 (N(N+\tau+\varsigma)(1+\tau+\varsigma))^{\frac{\epsilon-\varepsilon}{2}} |f|_{\varepsilon,\omega^{(\tau,\varsigma)}}, \tag{62}$$

where η_1 *is a positive constant.*

Proof. From (18) and (56), we have

$$\begin{aligned}
\partial^l_\Delta\left(\frac{\partial^2 f(x,y)}{\partial y^2} - \left(\frac{\partial^2 f(x,y)}{\partial y^2}\right)_N\right) &= \sum_{j=0}^{\infty}\sum_{k=N+1}^{\infty} \hat{f}_{jk}\partial_\Delta^{l_1+l_2+2}\mathcal{J}^{(\tau,\varsigma)}_{\ell_1,j}(x)\mathcal{J}^{(\tau,\varsigma)}_{\ell_2,k}(y)\\
&+ \sum_{j=N+1}^{\infty}\sum_{k=0}^{\infty} \hat{f}_{jk}\partial_\Delta^{l_1+l_2+2}\mathcal{J}^{(\tau,\varsigma)}_{\ell_1,j}(x)\mathcal{J}^{(\tau,\varsigma)}_{\ell_2,k}(y)\\
&= \sum_{j=0}^{\infty}\sum_{k=N+1}^{\infty} \hat{f}_{jk}\nu_{j,l_1}\nu_{k,l_2+2}\mathcal{J}^{(\tau+l_1,\varsigma+l_1)}_{\ell_1,j-l_1}(x)\mathcal{J}^{(\tau+l_2+2,\varsigma+l_2+2)}_{\ell_2,k-l_2-2}(y)\\
&+ \sum_{j=N+1}^{\infty}\sum_{k=0}^{\infty} \hat{f}_{jk}\nu_{j,l_1}\nu_{k,l_2+2}\mathcal{J}^{(\tau+l_1,\varsigma+l_1)}_{\ell_1,j-l_1}(x)\mathcal{J}^{(\tau+l_2+2,\varsigma+l_2+2)}_{\ell_2,k-l_2-2}(y).
\end{aligned}$$

By taking the $L^2_{\omega^{(\tau,\varsigma)}}-$norm of the above equation, we obtain

$$\left\|\partial^l_\Delta\left(\frac{\partial^2 f}{\partial y^2} - \left(\frac{\partial^2 f}{\partial y^2}\right)_N\right)\right\|^2_{\omega^{(\tau+l,\varsigma+l)}} = \sum_{j=0}^{\infty}\sum_{k=N+1}^{\infty} \hat{f}^2_{jk}c_{j,k} + \sum_{j=N+1}^{\infty}\sum_{k=0}^{\infty} \hat{f}^2_{jk}c_{j,k} + 2\sum_{j=N+1}^{\infty}\sum_{k=N+1}^{\infty} \hat{f}^2_{jk}c_{j,k}, \tag{63}$$

where

$$c_{j,k} = \nu^2_{j,l_1}\nu^2_{k,l_2+2}h^{(\tau+l_1,\varsigma+l_1)}_{\ell_1,j-l_1}(x)h^{(\tau+l_2+2,\varsigma+l_2+2)}_{\ell_2,k-l_2-2}(y).$$

Similarly,

$$\left\|\partial^l_\Delta\left(\frac{\partial^2 f}{\partial y^2}\right)\right\|^2_{\omega^{(\tau+\varepsilon,\varsigma+\varepsilon)}} = \sum_{j=0}^{\infty}\sum_{k=N+1}^{\infty} \hat{f}^2_{jk}d_{j,k} + \sum_{j=N+1}^{\infty}\sum_{k=0}^{\infty} \hat{f}^2_{jk}d_{j,k} + 2\sum_{j=N+1}^{\infty}\sum_{k=N+1}^{\infty} \hat{f}^2_{jk}d_{j,k}, \tag{64}$$

where

$$d_{j,k} = \nu^2_{j,\varepsilon_1}\nu^2_{k,\varepsilon_2+2}h^{(\tau+\varepsilon_1,\varsigma+\varepsilon_1)}_{\ell_1,j-\varepsilon_1}(x)h^{(\tau+\varepsilon_2+2,\varsigma+\varepsilon_2+2)}_{\ell_2,k-\varepsilon_2-2}(y).$$

Using (18), (59), and (60), we obtain

$$\frac{c_{j,k}}{d_{j,k}} \le \eta_1 j^{l_1-\varepsilon_1}k^{l_2-\varepsilon_2-2}(j+\tau+\varsigma)^{l_1-\varepsilon_1}(k+\tau+\varsigma)^{l_2-\varepsilon_2-2}. \tag{65}$$

From the relations (63)–(65), we can write

$$\left|\frac{\partial^2 f(x,y)}{\partial y^2}-\left(\frac{\partial^2 f(x,y)}{\partial y^2}\right)_N\right|^2_{l,\omega^{(\tau,\varsigma)}}=\left\|\partial^l_\Delta\left(\frac{\partial^2 f}{\partial y^2}-\left(\frac{\partial^2 f}{\partial y^2}\right)_N\right)\right\|^2_{\omega^{(\tau+l,\varsigma+l)}}$$
$$=\sum_{j=0}^{\infty}\sum_{k=N+1}^{\infty}\frac{c_{j,k}}{d_{j,k}}d_{j,k}\hat{f}^2_{jk}+\sum_{j=N+1}^{\infty}\sum_{k=0}^{\infty}\frac{c_{j,k}}{d_{j,k}}d_{j,k}\hat{f}^2_{jk}+2\sum_{j=N+1}^{\infty}\sum_{k=N+1}^{\infty}\frac{c_{j,k}}{d_{j,k}}d_{j,k}\hat{f}^2_{jk}$$
$$\leq\sum_{j=0}^{\infty}\sum_{k=N+1}^{\infty}\eta_1 j^{l_1-\varepsilon_1}k^{l_2-\varepsilon_2-2}(j+\tau+\varsigma)^{l_1-\varepsilon_1}(k+\tau+\varsigma)^{l_2-\varepsilon_2-2}d_{j,k}\hat{f}^2_{jk}$$
$$+\sum_{j=N+1}^{\infty}\sum_{k=0}^{\infty}\eta_1 j^{l_1-\varepsilon_1}k^{l_2-\varepsilon_2-2}(j+\tau+\varsigma)^{l_1-\varepsilon_1}(k+\tau+\varsigma)^{l_2-\varepsilon_2-2}d_{j,k}\hat{f}^2_{jk}$$
$$+2\sum_{j=N+1}^{\infty}\sum_{k=N+1}^{\infty}\eta_1 j^{l_1-\varepsilon_1}k^{l_2-\varepsilon_2-2}(j+\tau+\varsigma)^{l_1-\varepsilon_1}(k+\tau+\varsigma)^{l_2-\varepsilon_2-2}d_{j,k}\hat{f}^2_{jk}$$
$$\leq\eta_1 N^{l_2-\varepsilon_2-2}(1+\tau+\varsigma)^{l_1-\varepsilon_1}(N+\tau+\varsigma)^{l_2-\varepsilon_2-2}\sum_{j=0}^{\infty}\sum_{k=N+1}^{\infty}d_{j,k}\hat{f}^2_{jk}$$
$$+\eta_1 N^{l_1-\varepsilon_1}(N+\tau+\varsigma)^{l_1-\varepsilon_1}(1+\tau+\varsigma)^{l_2-\varepsilon_2-2}\sum_{j=N+1}^{\infty}\sum_{k=0}^{\infty}d_{j,k}\hat{f}^2_{jk}$$
$$+2\eta_1 N^{l_1-\varepsilon_1}N^{l_2-\varepsilon_2-2}(N+\tau+\varsigma)^{l_1-\varepsilon_1}(N+\tau+\varsigma)^{l_2-\varepsilon_2-2}\sum_{j=N+1}^{\infty}\sum_{k=N+1}^{\infty}d_{j,k}\hat{f}^2_{jk}$$
$$\leq\eta_1 N^{l_n-\varepsilon}(N+\tau+\varsigma)^{l_n-\varepsilon}(1+\tau+\varsigma)^{l_n-\varepsilon}\left(\sum_{j=0}^{\infty}\sum_{k=N+1}^{\infty}d_{j,k}\hat{f}^2_{jk}+\sum_{j=N+1}^{\infty}\sum_{k=0}^{\infty}d_{j,k}\hat{f}^2_{jk}+2\sum_{j=N+1}^{\infty}\sum_{k=N+1}^{\infty}d_{j,k}\hat{f}^2_{jk}\right)$$
$$=\eta_1 N^{l_n-\varepsilon}(N+\tau+\varsigma)^{l_n-\varepsilon}(1+\tau+\varsigma)^{l_n-\varepsilon}\left\|\partial^l_\Delta f\right\|^2_{\omega^{(\tau+\varepsilon,\varsigma+\varepsilon)}}$$
$$=\eta_1 N^{l_n-\varepsilon}(N+\tau+\varsigma)^{l_n-\varepsilon}(1+\tau+\varsigma)^{l_n-\varepsilon}|f|^2_{\varepsilon,\omega^{(\tau,\varsigma)}},$$

where

$$l_n-\varepsilon_n=\min_{i=1,2}\{l_i-\varepsilon_i\},\quad 0\leq l_i\leq\varepsilon_i\leq\varepsilon,\ i=1,2,$$

for any $l_n\leq\varepsilon_n$. Therefore,

$$\left\|\frac{\partial^2 f}{\partial y^2}-\left(\frac{\partial^2 f}{\partial y^2}\right)_N\right\|_{\epsilon,\omega^{(\tau,\varsigma)}}\leq\eta(N(N+\tau+\varsigma)(1+\tau+\varsigma))^{\frac{\epsilon-\varepsilon}{2}}|f|_{\varepsilon,\omega^{(\tau,\varsigma)}},\quad 0\leq\epsilon\leq\varepsilon.$$

□

Theorem 10. *For any $f\in\mathscr{P}^{\varepsilon}_{\omega^{(\tau,\varsigma)}}(\mathfrak{D})$, $\varepsilon\in\mathbb{N}$, and $0\leq\epsilon\leq\varepsilon$, we can conclude that*

$$\left\|\frac{\partial^2 f}{\partial x^2}-\left(\frac{\partial^2 f}{\partial x^2}\right)_N\right\|_{\epsilon,\omega^{(\tau,\varsigma)}}\leq\eta_2(N(N+\tau+\varsigma)(1+\tau+\varsigma))^{\frac{\epsilon-\varepsilon}{2}}|f|_{\varepsilon,\omega^{(\tau,\varsigma)}},\tag{66}$$

where η_2 is a positive constant.

Proof. The proof of this theorem is similar to the proof of Theorem 9. □

Theorem 11. *For any $f\in\mathscr{P}^{\varepsilon}_{\omega^{(\tau,\varsigma)}}(\mathfrak{D})$, $\varepsilon\in\mathbb{N}$, and $0\leq\epsilon\leq\varepsilon$, we have*

$$\left\|\frac{\partial^2 f}{\partial y\partial x}-\left(\frac{\partial^2 f}{\partial y\partial x}\right)_N\right\|_{\epsilon,\omega^{(\tau,\varsigma)}}\leq\eta_3(N(N+\tau+\varsigma)(1+\tau+\varsigma))^{\frac{\epsilon-\varepsilon}{2}}|f|_{\varepsilon,\omega^{(\tau,\varsigma)}},\tag{67}$$

where η_3 is a positive constant.

Proof. The proof of this theorem is similar to the proof of Theorem 9. □

Remark 1. *Inequality (54) implies that if N tends to infinity, then $f - f_N \to 0$.*

6. Numerical Results

Here, we solve five examples tested by Maple 2018. The number of bases are denoted by $\mathfrak{B}$. The absolute errors and maximum absolute errors are obtained by

$$\begin{aligned}&|f(x,y) - f_N(x,y)|, \qquad (x,y) \in [0,\ell_1) \times [0,\ell_2),\ N \in \mathbb{N},\\ &MAE := \max_{i,j=0,1,\ldots,N} \{|f(x_i,y_j) - f_N(x_i,y_j)|\},\end{aligned}$$

respectively, where (x_i, y_j) are roots of 2D-SJPs in $\mathfrak{D} = [0,\ell_1) \times [0,\ell_2)$ for different values of τ and ς.

Moreover, using

$$\max_{j=0,1,\ldots,N} \{|f(x,y_j) - f_N(x,y_j)|\}, \qquad x \in [0,\ell_1),$$

we plot maximum absolute errors where y_j are roots of 1D-SJPs in $[0,\ell_2)$ for $j = 0,1,\ldots,N$.

Example 1. *Consider the following 2D-NFIDE studied by [36]:*

$$f_{yx}(x,y) + f(x,y) + I^{(\frac{7}{2},\frac{11}{2})} f(x,y) = g(x,y) + \Theta(x,y) + \Lambda(x,y) + \rho(x,y) + \varphi(x,y),$$

with the initial conditions

$$f(x,0) = f(0,y) = f_y(y,0) = 0,\ f_x(0,y) = y,\ f_y(x,0) = x,$$

where $(x,y) \in [0,1) \times [0,1)$ and

$$\begin{aligned}\Theta(x,y) &= \int_0^x \int_0^y (yt - xs) f^2(t,s)\, \mathrm{d}s\, \mathrm{d}t,\\ \Lambda(x,y) &= \frac{1}{\Gamma(\frac{7}{2})\Gamma(\frac{11}{2})} \int_0^x \int_0^y (x-t)^{\frac{5}{2}} (y-s)^{\frac{9}{2}} \log(s-t) f(t,s)\, \mathrm{d}s\, \mathrm{d}t,\\ \rho(x,y) &= \frac{1}{\Gamma(\frac{7}{2})\Gamma(\frac{11}{2})} \int_0^1 \int_0^1 (1-t)^{\frac{5}{2}} (1-s)^{\frac{9}{2}} y(t-s) f^2(t,s)\, \mathrm{d}s\, \mathrm{d}t,\\ \varphi(x,y) &= \int_0^1 \int_0^1 (1+y)(t^2 - s^2) f^2(t,s)\, \mathrm{d}s\, \mathrm{d}t,\\ g(x,y) &= \frac{4096}{127702575\pi} x^{\frac{9}{2}} y^{\frac{13}{2}} + xy - \frac{524288}{1552224799125\pi} y + 1.\end{aligned}$$

The exact solution is $f(x,y) = yx$.

Tables 1 and 2 report the obtained numerical results and absolute errors, respectively, using the new approach and choosing $\tau = \varsigma = 0$ and $N = 2,3$. Additionally, Table 3 reports maximum absolute errors by selecting various values of τ, ς and $N = 2$. These tables show that by choosing $\mathfrak{B} = (N+1)^2 = 16$ numbers of 2D-SJPs, our obtained results are more accurate than the results reported in [36,37] and use $\mathfrak{B} = N^2M^2 = 16$ and $\mathfrak{B} = m^2 = 4096$ numbers of 2D-HBPSLs and 2D-BPFs, respectively, for solving this problem. From Figure 1, the accuracy and efficiency of proposed method is illustrated.

Table 1. Numerical results with $\tau = \varsigma = 0$ for Example 1.

$x = y$	Exact Solution	2D-SJPs $N = 2$, $\mathfrak{B} = 9$	2D-SJPs $N = 3$, $\mathfrak{B} = 16$	2D-HBPSLs [37] $M = N = 2$, $\mathfrak{B} = 16$	2D-BPFs [36] $N = 64$, $\mathfrak{B} = 4096$
0	0	-1.45834×10^{-8}	-1.93165×10^{-9}	-5.39368×10^{-10}	6.06689×10^{-5}
0.2	0.04	0.04	0.04	0.04	0.0379181
0.4	0.16	0.16	0.16	0.16	0.1578
0.6	0.36	0.36	0.36	0.36	0.359706
0.8	0.64	0.64	0.64	0.640001	0.643637
0.99	0.9801	0.980099	0.9801	0.980101	0.978529
Max error	0	1.908184×10^{-5}	2.081128×10^{-7}	1.185071×10^{-5}	2.09569×10^{-3}

Table 2. Absolute errors with $\tau = \varsigma = 0$ for Example 1.

$x = y$	2D-SJPs $N = 2$, $\mathfrak{B} = 9$	2D-SJPs $N = 3$, $\mathfrak{B} = 16$	2D-HBPSLs [37] $M = N = 2$, $\mathfrak{B} = 16$
0	1.458338×10^{-8}	1.931649×10^{-9}	5.393684×10^{-10}
0.1	4.839152×10^{-9}	2.920296×10^{-11}	1.049377×10^{-8}
0.2	1.620866×10^{-8}	3.409101×10^{-10}	4.526134×10^{-8}
0.3	3.955156×10^{-8}	5.296828×10^{-11}	1.037633×10^{-7}
0.4	7.048566×10^{-8}	1.150183×10^{-10}	1.859998×10^{-7}
0.5	1.093869×10^{-7}	2.445786×10^{-10}	2.674698×10^{-7}
0.6	1.613894×10^{-7}	5.844627×10^{-10}	4.343939×10^{-7}
0.7	2.363855×10^{-7}	4.051722×10^{-9}	5.646382×10^{-7}
0.8	3.490255×10^{-7}	3.485633×10^{-8}	6.582027×10^{-7}
0.9	5.187180×10^{-7}	1.445669×10^{-7}	7.150874×10^{-7}

Table 3. Maximum absolute errors with $N = 2$ for Example 1.

(τ, ς)	MAE	(τ, ς)	MAE
$(0,0)$	1.908184×10^{-5}	$(1,1)$	5.525558×10^{-5}
$(1,2)$	1.657651×10^{-4}	$(2,1)$	1.682304×10^{-5}
$(2,2)$	6.110782×10^{-5}	$(3,2)$	2.426797×10^{-5}

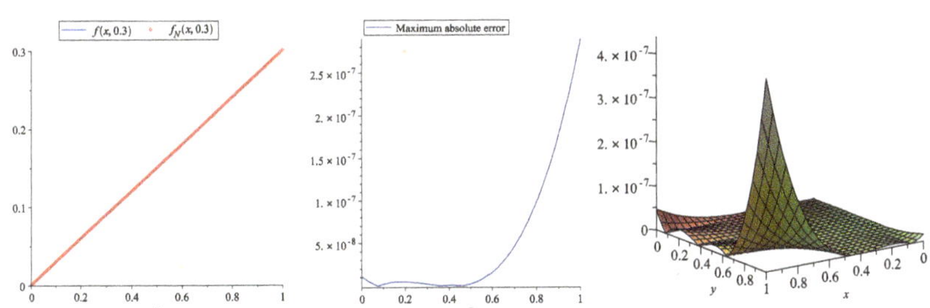

Figure 1. Plots of the exact and approximate solutions (**left**), maximum absolute error (**middle**) at $y = 0.3$, and absolute error (**right**) obtained by the 2D-SJPs with $N = 3$ and $\tau = \varsigma = 0$ for Example 1.

Example 2. *Consider the following 2D-NFIDE studied by [36]:*

$$f_{yy}(x,y) + f_{yx}(x,y) + f(x,y) + I^{(\frac{5}{2},1)} f(x,y) = g(x,y) + \rho(x,y) + \varphi(x,y),$$

with initial conditions

$$f(x,0) = f_x(x,0) = f_y(x,0) = f_x(0,y) = 0,\ f(0,y) = \frac{y^2}{4},$$

where $(x,y) \in [0,1) \times [0,1)$ *and*

$$\rho(x,y) = \frac{1}{\Gamma(\frac{5}{2})\Gamma(1)} \int_0^1 \int_0^1 (1-t)^{\frac{3}{2}} y^{\frac{8}{3}} x^{\frac{7}{2}} t^3 f(t,s)\, \mathrm{d}s\, \mathrm{d}t,$$

$$\varphi(x,y) = \int_0^1 \int_0^1 \frac{3360}{46} xy(x+y) f^2(t,s)\, \mathrm{d}s\, \mathrm{d}t,$$

$$g(x,y) = -\frac{608}{153153\sqrt{\pi}} x^{\frac{7}{2}} y^{\frac{8}{3}} + \frac{1}{4}(x^3+1)y^2 + \frac{1}{2}(x^3+1) - \frac{3}{2}xy^2 + \frac{2(16x^3+231)x^{\frac{5}{2}}y^3}{10395\sqrt{\pi}}.$$

The exact solution is $f(x,y) = \frac{y^2}{4}(x^3+1)$.

Tables 4 and 5 report the obtained numerical results and absolute errors, respectively, using the new approach and choosing $\tau = \varsigma = 0$ *and* $N = 2,3$. *Additionally, Table 6 reports maximum absolute errors by selecting various values of* τ, ς *and* $N = 2$. *These tables show that by choosing* $\mathfrak{B} = (N+1)^2 = 16$ *numbers of 2D-SJPs, our obtained results are more accurate than the results reported in [36,37] and use* $\mathfrak{B} = N^2M^2 = 36$ *and* $\mathfrak{B} = m^2 = 1024$ *numbers of 2D-HBPSLs and 2D-BPFs, respectively, for solving this problem. In Figure 2, the accuracy and efficiency of proposed method is illustrated.*

Table 4. Numerical results with $\tau = \varsigma = 0$ for Example 2.

$x = y$	Exact Solution	2D-SJPs		2D-HBPSLs [37]	2D-BPFs [36]
		$N = 2$, $\mathfrak{B} = 9$	$N = 3$, $\mathfrak{B} = 16$	$N = 2, M = 3$, $\mathfrak{B} = 36$	$m = 32$, $\mathfrak{B} = 1024$
0	0	3.50087×10^{-8}	-1.75105×10^{-11}	-1.70722×10^{-8}	5.31008×10^{-5}
0.2	0.01008	0.00990005	0.01008	0.0100625	9.04921×10^{-3}
0.4	0.04256	0.0419991	0.04256	0.0426493	0.035166
0.6	0.10944	0.110691	0.10944	0.109233	0.099042
0.8	0.24192	0.244764	0.24192	0.242178	0.208004
0.99	0.482773	0.471861	0.482772	0.481524	0.411787
Max error	0	5.746197×10^{-5}	4.748580×10^{-8}	3.570347×10^{-4}	7.0986×10^{-2}

Table 5. Absolute errors with $\tau = \varsigma = 0$ for Example 2.

$x = y$	2D-SJPs		2D-HBPSLs [37]
	$N = 2$, $\mathfrak{B} = 9$	$N = 3$, $\mathfrak{B} = 16$	$N = 2, M = 3$, $\mathfrak{B} = 36$
0	3.500869×10^{-8}	1.751047×10^{-11}	1.707223×10^{-8}
0.1	9.992949×10^{-6}	1.282426×10^{-12}	5.623240×10^{-6}
0.2	1.799480×10^{-4}	1.250557×10^{-11}	1.752097×10^{-5}
0.3	4.950320×10^{-4}	7.129280×10^{-11}	3.919885×10^{-5}
0.4	5.608532×10^{-4}	3.100506×10^{-10}	8.934775×10^{-5}
0.5	3.355656×10^{-6}	1.029452×10^{-9}	3.884051×10^{-4}
0.6	1.251167×10^{-3}	2.924318×10^{-9}	2.071935×10^{-4}
0.7	2.676069×10^{-3}	7.479405×10^{-9}	2.249140×10^{-4}
0.8	2.844359×10^{-3}	1.753510×10^{-8}	2.583723×10^{-4}
0.9	8.713086×10^{-4}	7.185571×10^{-8}	4.152332×10^{-4}

Table 6. Maximum absolute errors with $N = 2$ for Example 2.

(τ, ς)	MAE	(τ, ς)	MAE
$(0, 0)$	5.746197×10^{-5}	$(1, 1)$	2.502457×10^{-3}
$(1, 2)$	2.374060×10^{-2}	$(2, 1)$	1.116405×10^{-2}
$(2, 2)$	3.419813×10^{-3}	$(3, 2)$	9.826693×10^{-3}

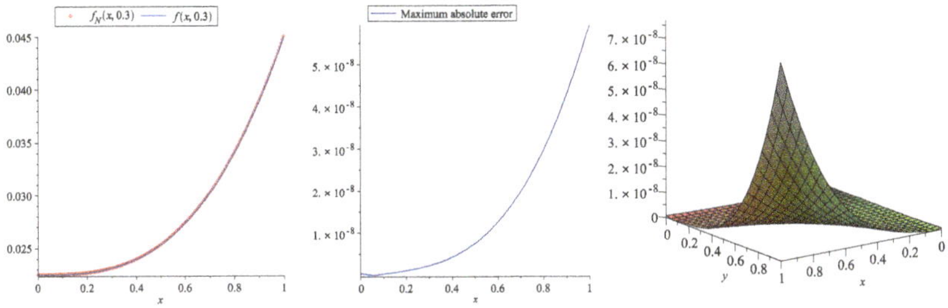

Figure 2. Plots of the exact and approximate solutions (**left**), maximum absolute error (**middle**) at $y = 0.3$, and absolute error (**right**) obtained by the 2D-SJPs with $N = 3$ and $\tau = \varsigma = 0$ for Example 2.

Example 3. *Consider the following 2D-NFIDE:*

$$f_{yy}(x, y) + f_{yx}(x, y) + f(x, y) = g(x, y) + \rho(x, y),$$

with initial conditions

$$f(x, 0) = f_x(x, 0) = f_y(x, 0) = \mathrm{e}^x, \; f(0, y) = \mathrm{e}^y,$$

where $(x, y) \in [0, 2) \times [0, 2)$

$$\rho(x, y) = \frac{1}{\Gamma(\frac{3}{2})\Gamma(\frac{3}{2})} \int_0^2 \int_0^2 (2-t)^{\frac{1}{2}}(2-s)^{\frac{1}{2}}(x+y)(t^2+s^2) f(t, s)\, \mathrm{d}s\, \mathrm{d}t,$$

$$g(x, y) = 3\mathrm{e}^{x+y} - 4(x+y)\left(\frac{11}{\pi} - \frac{9\mathrm{e}^2\sqrt{2}\mathrm{erf}(\sqrt{2})}{\sqrt{\pi}} + \frac{7\mathrm{e}^4(\mathrm{erf}(\sqrt{2}))^2}{8}\right).$$

The exact solution is $f(x, y) = \mathrm{e}^{x+y}$. *Note that* $\mathrm{erf}(x) = \frac{2\int_0^x \mathrm{e}^{-x^2}\,\mathrm{d}x}{\sqrt{\pi}}$.

Tables 7 and 8 report the obtained numerical results and absolute errors, respectively, using the new approach and choosing $\tau = \varsigma = 0$ *and* $N = 4, 5$. *These tables show that by choosing* $\mathfrak{B} = (N+1)^2 = 36$ *numbers of 2D-SJPs, our obtained results are more accurate than the results reported in [37] and use* $\mathfrak{B} = N^2M^2 = 64$ *numbers of 2D-HBPSLs for solving this problem. From Figure 3, the accuracy and efficiency of the proposed method is illustrated.*

Table 7. Numerical results with $\tau = \varsigma = 0$ for Example 3.

$x = y$	Exact Solution	2D-SJPs		2D-HBPSLs [37]
		$N = 4$ $\mathfrak{B} = 25$	$N = 5$ $\mathfrak{B} = 36$	$N = 2, M = 4$ $\mathfrak{B} = 64$
0	1	0.999498	1.00004	0.99811
0.2	1.49182	1.49209	1.49181	1.49284
0.4	2.22554	2.22543	2.22556	2.22493
0.6	3.32012	3.31979	3.32012	3.31909
0.8	4.95303	4.95305	4.953	4.95461
1	7.38906	7.38946	7.38905	7.37414
1.2	11.0232	11.0233	11.0232	11.0301
1.4	16.4446	16.4439	16.4446	16.4394
1.6	24.5325	24.5318	24.5325	24.5242
1.8	36.5982	36.5992	36.5983	36.6095
Max error	0	3.352898×10^{-4}	2.293543×10^{-5}	1.118645×10^{-2}

Table 8. Absolute errors with $\tau = \varsigma = 0$ for Example 3.

$x = y$	2D-SJPs		2D-HBPSLs [37]
	$N = 4$ $\mathfrak{B} = 25$	$N = 5$ $\mathfrak{B} = 36$	$N = 2, M = 4$ $\mathfrak{B} = 64$
0	5.018269×10^{-4}	3.878596×10^{-5}	1.890271×10^{-3}
0.2	2.646095×10^{-4}	1.323019×10^{-5}	1.016898×10^{-3}
0.4	1.156163×10^{-4}	1.971321×10^{-5}	6.116798×10^{-4}
0.6	3.222169×10^{-4}	1.006197×10^{-6}	1.030940×10^{-3}
0.8	1.401881×10^{-5}	2.886721×10^{-5}	1.578274×10^{-3}
1	4.053898×10^{-4}	7.535908×10^{-6}	1.491810×10^{-2}
1.2	1.410474×10^{-4}	3.456475×10^{-5}	6.949542×10^{-3}
1.4	7.246987×10^{-4}	6.085008×10^{-7}	5.233810×10^{-3}
1.6	7.533610×10^{-4}	7.863965×10^{-5}	8.312774×10^{-3}
1.8	9.833575×10^{-4}	3.723796×10^{-5}	1.126113×10^{-2}

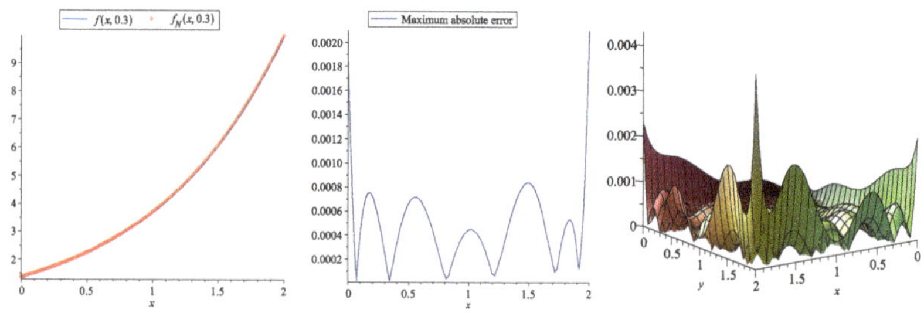

Figure 3. Plots of the exact and approximate solutions (**left**), maximum absolute error (**middle**) at $y = 0.3$, and absolute error (**right**) obtained by the 2D-SJPs with $N = 5$ and $\tau = \varsigma = 0$ for Example 3.

Example 4. *Consider the following 2D-NFIDE:*

$$f_{xx}(x,y) + f(x,y) + I^{(\frac{3}{2},1)}f(x,y) = g(x,y) + \Theta(x,y),$$

with initial conditions

$$f(x,0) = f(0,y) = f_y(x,0) = f_x(0,y) = f_x(x,0) = 0,$$

where $(x,y) \in [0,1) \times [0,1)$ and

$$\Theta(x,y) = \int_0^x \int_0^y (yt - xs) f^2(t,s)\, ds\, dt,$$

$$g(x,y) = -\frac{1}{360\pi^{\frac{9}{2}}}\Bigg(y((-360x^2 - 720)\sin(\pi y) + x^6y^3)\pi^{\frac{9}{2}} + 24y^2\left(\cos(\pi y)^2 - \frac{1}{2}\right)x^6\pi^{\frac{5}{2}} + \frac{768\pi^2(\pi y\cos(\pi y) - \sin(\pi y))x^{\frac{7}{2}}}{7} - 27x^6\left(\frac{1}{9}\pi^{\frac{3}{2}}y\sin(\pi y)\cos(\pi y)\left(-2\pi^2y^2 + 13\right) + \cos(\pi y)^2\sqrt{\pi} - \sqrt{\pi}\right)\Bigg).$$

The exact solution is $f(x,y) = x^2 y\sin(\pi y)$.

Tables 9 and 10 report the obtained numerical results and absolute errors, respectively, using the new approach and choosing $\tau = \varsigma = 0$ and $N = 3,4$. Additionally, Table 11 reports maximum absolute errors by selecting various values of τ, ς and $N = 2$. These tables show that by choosing $\mathfrak{B} = (N+1)^2 = 25$ numbers of 2D-SJPs, our obtained results are more accurate than the results obtained by the 2D-HBPSL method [37] and use $\mathfrak{B} = N^2M^2 = 36$ bases for solving this problem. In Figure 4, the accuracy and efficiency of the proposed method is illustrated.

Table 9. Numerical results with $\tau = \varsigma = 0$ for Example 4.

$x = y$	Exact Solution	2D-SJPs		2D-HBPSLs [37]	
		$N = 3$ $\mathfrak{B} = 16$	$N = 4$ $\mathfrak{B} = 25$	$M = N = 2$ $\mathfrak{B} = 16$	$N = 2$, $M = 3$ $\mathfrak{B} = 36$
0	0	1.42563×10^{-6}	-1.53250×10^{-7}	0.00304418	-5.40176×10^{-8}
0.2	0.00470228	0.00503905	0.00461625	0.00860387	0.00502286
0.4	0.0608676	0.0606074	0.0615685	0.0582732	0.0592075
0.6	0.205428	0.201651	0.203813	0.2084	0.206665
0.8	0.300946	0.309229	0.302467	0.253177	0.299392
Max error	0	4.183049×10^{-3}	2.691559×10^{-4}	1.686288×10^{-2}	6.519558×10^{-3}

Table 10. Absolute errors with $\tau = \varsigma = 0$ for Example 4.

$x = y$	2D-SJPs		2D-HBPSLs [37]	
	$N = 3$ $\mathfrak{B} = 16$	$N = 4$ $\mathfrak{B} = 25$	$M = N = 2$ $\mathfrak{B} = 16$	$N = 2$, $M = 3$ $\mathfrak{B} = 36$
0	1.425634×10^{-6}	1.532497×10^{-7}	3.044182×10^{-3}	5.401763×10^{-8}
0.1	2.359796×10^{-6}	5.799964×10^{-5}	1.304790×10^{-6}	8.310324×10^{-5}
0.2	3.367631×10^{-4}	8.603064×10^{-5}	3.901591×10^{-3}	3.205808×10^{-4}
0.3	6.244970×10^{-4}	3.609740×10^{-4}	6.081376×10^{-3}	6.170073×10^{-4}
0.4	2.601698×10^{-4}	7.008446×10^{-4}	2.594409×10^{-3}	1.660119×10^{-3}
0.5	2.479625×10^{-3}	5.263376×10^{-5}	1.670057×10^{-2}	2.207590×10^{-3}
0.6	3.776819×10^{-3}	1.615412×10^{-3}	2.972021×10^{-3}	1.236545×10^{-3}
0.7	3.370614×10^{-4}	1.772158×10^{-3}	3.193363×10^{-2}	1.625204×10^{-5}
0.8	8.282794×10^{-3}	1.521422×10^{-3}	4.776857×10^{-2}	1.553977×10^{-3}
0.9	9.162584×10^{-3}	4.275932×10^{-3}	5.981687×10^{-3}	4.222491×10^{-4}

Table 11. Maximum absolute errors with $N = 2$ for Example 4.

(τ,ς)	MAE	(τ,ς)	MAE
$(0,0)$	4.183049×10^{-3}	$(1,1)$	7.254076×10^{-3}
$(1,2)$	6.743181×10^{-3}	$(2,1)$	4.492349×10^{-3}
$(2,2)$	4.903053×10^{-3}	$(3,2)$	3.081034×10^{-3}

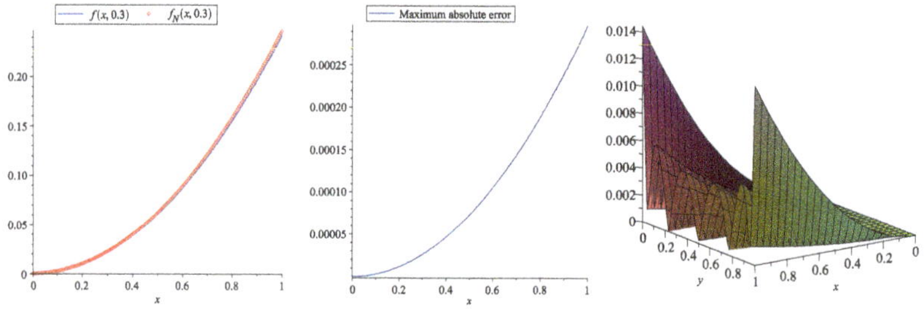

Figure 4. Plots of the exact and approximate solutions (**left**), maximum absolute error (**middle**) at $y = 0.3$, and absolute error (**right**) obtained by the 2D-SJPs with $N = 4$ and $\tau = \varsigma = 0$ for Example 4.

Example 5. *Consider the following 2D-NFIDE:*

$$f_{yy}(x,y) + f_{yx}(x,y) + f(x,y) + I^{(\frac{3}{2},1)}f(x,y) = g(x,y) + \Theta(x,y) + \varphi(x,y),$$

with initial conditions

$$f(x,0) = 0,\ f(0,y) = \sin(\pi y),\ f_y(x,0) = \pi e^x,\ f_x(0,y) = \sin(\pi y),\ f_x(x,0) = 0,$$

where $(x,y) \in [0,1) \times [0,1)$ *and*

$$\Theta(x,y) = \int_0^x \int_0^y xys f^2(t,s)\,ds\,dt,$$
$$\varphi(x,y) = \int_0^1 \int_0^1 x^2y^3t^2 f^2(t,s)\,ds\,dt,$$
$$g(x,y) = -\frac{1}{8\pi^{\frac{5}{2}}}\left(\left(xy^2\left(x-\frac{1}{2}\right)e^{2x} + e^2x^2y^3 - x^2y^3 + \frac{1}{2}xy^2 - 8e^x\sin(\pi y)\right)\pi^{\frac{5}{2}}\right.$$
$$+ \left(\left(-2\sin(\pi y)yx\left(x-\frac{1}{2}\right)e^{2x} - \sin(\pi y)yx + 8e^x\operatorname{erf}(\sqrt{x})\right)\cos(\pi y) - 8e^x\operatorname{erf}(\sqrt{x})\right)\pi^{\frac{3}{2}}$$
$$- 8\pi^{\frac{7}{2}}e^x\cos(\pi y) + 8\pi^{\frac{9}{2}}e^x\sin(\pi y) - (-1+\cos(\pi y))\left(x\left(\frac{1}{2} + \left(x-\frac{1}{2}\right)e^{2x}\right)\sqrt{\pi}\cos(\pi y)\right.$$
$$\left.\left. + x\sqrt{\pi}\left(x-\frac{1}{2}\right)e^{2x} + \frac{1}{2}x\sqrt{\pi} + 16\pi\sqrt{x}\right)\right).$$

The exact solution is $f(x,y) = e^x\sin(\pi y)$.

Tables 12 and 13 report the obtained numerical results and absolute errors, respectively, using the new approach and choosing $\tau = \varsigma = 0$ *and* $N = 3, 4$. *Additionally, Table 14 reports maximum absolute errors by selecting various values of* τ, ς *and* $N = 3$. *These tables show that by choosing* $\mathfrak{B} = (N+1)^2 = 25$ *numbers of 2D-SJPs, our obtained results are more accurate than the results obtained by the 2D-HBPSL method [37] and use* $\mathfrak{B} = N^2M^2 = 36$ *bases for solving this problem. In Figure 5, the accuracy and efficiency of proposed method is illustrated.*

Table 12. Numerical results with $\tau = \varsigma = 0$ for Example 5.

$x = y$	Exact Solution	2D-SJPs		2D-HBPSLs [37]	
		$N = 3$ $\mathfrak{B} = 16$	$N = 4$ $\mathfrak{B} = 25$	$M = N = 2$ $\mathfrak{B} = 16$	$N = 2, M = 3$ $\mathfrak{B} = 36$
0	0	−0.0498894	0.00126408	0.106466	−0.0269479
0.2	0.717923	0.743648	0.718851	0.644168	0.713975
0.4	1.41881	1.39875	1.41815	1.33223	1.3479
0.6	1.73294	1.70905	1.73227	1.43579	1.40505
0.8	1.30814	1.35737	1.31117	0.694829	0.506292
Max error	0	4.900771×10^{-3}	2.890626×10^{-3}	7.161353×10^{-1}	1.625743

Table 13. Absolute errors with $\tau = \varsigma = 0$ for Example 5.

$x = y$	2D-SJPs		2D-HBPSLs [37]	
	$N = 3$ $\mathfrak{B} = 16$	$N = 4$ $\mathfrak{B} = 25$	$M = N = 2$ $\mathfrak{B} = 16$	$N = 2, M = 3$ $\mathfrak{B} = 36$
0	4.988938×10^{-2}	1.264079×10^{-3}	1.064657×10^{-1}	2.694793×10^{-2}
0.1	1.314614×10^{-2}	2.544488×10^{-4}	1.500519×10^{-2}	7.810507×10^{-3}
0.2	2.572567×10^{-2}	9.282027×10^{-4}	7.375466×10^{-2}	3.947639×10^{-3}
0.3	7.178138×10^{-3}	6.978147×10^{-4}	1.226548×10^{-1}	3.448407×10^{-2}
0.4	2.005857×10^{-2}	6.560525×10^{-4}	8.657965×10^{-2}	7.090727×10^{-2}
0.5	3.495032×10^{-2}	1.518547×10^{-3}	1.553134×10^{-1}	3.482695×10^{-1}
0.6	2.389001×10^{-2}	6.632893×10^{-4}	2.971477×10^{-1}	3.278872×10^{-1}
0.7	1.206528×10^{-2}	1.561235×10^{-3}	4.595629×10^{-1}	5.951170×10^{-1}
0.8	4.922751×10^{-2}	3.025826×10^{-3}	6.133115×10^{-1}	8.018483×10^{-1}
0.9	3.323691×10^{-2}	2.322792×10^{-3}	7.485747×10^{-1}	1.408296

Table 14. Maximum absolute errors with $N = 3$ for Example 5.

(τ, ς)	MAE	(τ, ς)	MAE
$(0,0)$	4.90077×10^{-3}	$(1,1)$	3.494379×10^{-2}
$(1,2)$	1.159618×10^{-1}	$(2,1)$	1.718043×10^{-2}
$(2,2)$	6.089228×10^{-2}	$(3,2)$	3.330454×10^{-2}

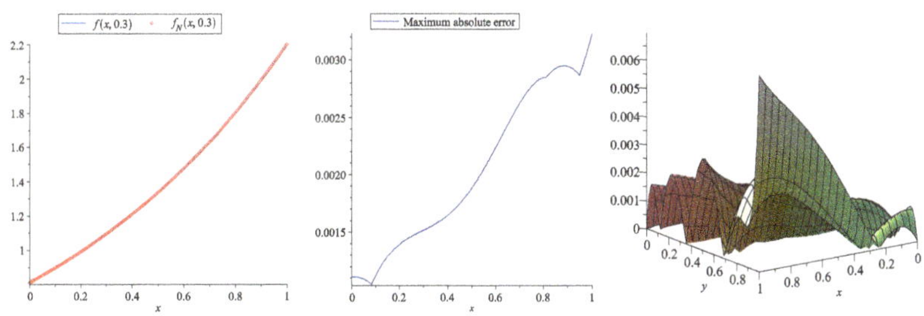

Figure 5. Plots of the exact and approximate solutions (**left**), maximum absolute error (**middle**) at $y = 0.3$, and absolute error (**right**) obtained by the 2D-SJPs with $N = 4$ and $\tau = \varsigma = 0$ for Example 5.

7. Conclusions

In this research, sufficient conditions for the existence and uniqueness of local and global solutions of general 2D-NFIDEs were provided. Additionally, the collocation method and operational matrices based on 2D-SJPs were used for solving these equations. Moreover, error bounds of the proposed method were obtained. We showed that the order of convergence of the method is $O\left(\frac{1}{(N(N+\tau+\varsigma))^{\frac{\varepsilon-\epsilon}{2}}}\right)$ in the Jacobi-weighted Sobolev space. Finally, we evaluated the presented method by solving five test problems. The obtained numerical results showed that a favorable approximate solution can be obtained by using lower numbers of basis functions.

Author Contributions: Conceptualization, T.E.; methodology, T.E.; software, T.E.; validation, T.E. and J.R.; investigation, T.E.; resources, T.E.; writing—original draft preparation, T.E.; writing—review and editing, T.E. and J.R.; supervision, J.R. All authors have read and agreed to the published version of the manuscript.

Funding: This research received no external funding.

Data Availability Statement: Not applicable.

Acknowledgments: The authors express their sincere thanks to anonymous reviewers for their valuable comments and suggestions that improved the quality of this paper.

Conflicts of Interest: The authors declare no conflict of interest.

References

1. Atangana, A.; Kılıçman, A. A possible generalization of acoustic wave equation using the concept of perturbed derivative order. *Math. Probl. Eng.* **2013**, *2013*, 696597. [CrossRef]
2. Atangana, A.; Kılıçman, A. Analytical solutions of the spacetime fractional derivative of advection dispersion equation. *Math. Probl. Eng.* **2013**, *2013*, 853127. [CrossRef]
3. Benson, D.A.; Wheatcraft, S.W.; Meerschaert, M.M. Application of a fractional advection-dispersion equation. *Water Resour. Res.* **2000**, *36*, 1403–1412. [CrossRef]
4. Caputo, M. Linear models of dissipation whose Q is almost frequency independent-part II. *Geophys. J. Int.* **1967**, *13*, 529–539. [CrossRef]
5. Cloot, A.; Botha, J.F. A generalised groundwater flow equation using the concept of non-integer order derivatives. *Water SA* **2006**, *32*, 55–78. [CrossRef]
6. Meerschaert, M.M.; Tadjeran, C. Finite difference approximations for fractional advection-dispersion flow equations. *J. Comput. Appl. Math.* **2004**, *172*, 65–77. [CrossRef]
7. Chen, C.M.; Liu, F.; Turner, I.; Anh, V. A Fourier method for the fractional diffusion equation describing sub-diffusion. *J. Comput. Phys.* **2007**, *227*, 886–897. [CrossRef]
8. Mainardi, F. Fractional calculus: Some basic problems in continuum and statistical mechanics. In *Fractals and Fractional Calculus in Continuum Mechanics*; Carpinteri, A., Mainardi, F., Eds.; Springer: New York, NY, USA, 1997; pp. 291–348.
9. Yuste, S.B.; Acedo, L. An explicit finite difference method and a new von Neumann-type stability analysis for fractional diffusion equations. *SIAM J. Numer. Anal.* **2005**, *42*, 1862–1874. [CrossRef]
10. Zhuang, P.; Liu, F.; Anh, V.; Turner, I. Numerical methods for the variable-order fractional advection-diffusion equation with a nonlinear source term. *SIAM J. Numer. Anal.* **2009**, *47*, 1760–1781. [CrossRef]
11. Carpinteri, A.; Mainardi, F. *Fractals and Fractional Calculus in Continuum Mechanics*; Springer: New York, NY, USA, 1997; pp. 223–276.
12. Metzler, F.; Schick, W.; Kilian, H.G.; Nonnenmacher, T.F. Relaxation in filled polymers: A fractional calculus approach. *J. Chem. Phys.* **1995**, *103*, 7180–7186. [CrossRef]
13. Oldham, K.B.; Spanier, J. *The Fractional Calculus*; Academic Press: New York, NY, USA; London, UK, 1974.
14. Thomas, R.; Fehmi, C. An immersed finite element method with integral equation correction. *Int. J. Numer. Methods Eng.* **2010**, *86*, 93–114.
15. Taheri, Z.; Javadi, S.; Babolian, E. Numerical solution of stochastic fractional integro-differential equation by the spectral collocation method. *J. Comput. Appl. Math.* **2017**, *321*, 336–347. [CrossRef]
16. Rahimkhania, P.; Ordokhani, Y.; Babolian, E. A numerical scheme for solving nonlinear fractional Volterra integro-differential equations. *Iran. J. Math. Sci. Inform.* **2018**, *13*, 111–132.
17. Wang, Y.; Zhu, L.; Wang, Z. Fractional-order Euler functions for solving fractional integro-differential equations with weakly singular kernel. *Adv. Differ. Equ.* **2018**, *2018*, 254. [CrossRef]
18. Babaei, A.; Jafari, H.; Banihashemi, S. Numerical solution of variable order fractional nonlinear quadratic integro-differential equations based on the sixth-kind Chebyshev collocation method. *J. Comput. Appl. Math.* **2020**, *377*, 112908. [CrossRef]
19. Abbas, S.; Benchohra, M. Fractional order integral equations of two independent variables. *Appl. Math. Comput.* **2014**, *227*, 755–761. [CrossRef]
20. Asgari, M.; Ezzati, R.; Jafari, H. Solution of 2D Fractional Order Integral Equations by Bernstein Polynomials Operational Matrices. *Nonlinear Dyn. Syst. Theory* **2019**, *19*, 10–20.

21. Babolian, E.; Maleknejad, K.; Roodaki, M.; Almasieh, H. Two-dimensional triangular functions and their applications to nonlinear 2d Volterra-Fredholm integral equations. *Comput. Math. Appl.* **2010**, *60*, 1711–1722. [CrossRef]
22. Eftekhari, T.; Hosseini, S.M. A new and efficient approach for solving linear and nonlinear time-fractional diffusion equations of distributed-order. *Comput. Appl. Math.* **2022**, *41*, 281. [CrossRef]
23. Eftekhari, T.; Rashidinia, J. A novel and efficient operational matrix for solving nonlinear stochastic differential equations driven by multi-fractional Gaussian noise. *Appl. Math. Comput.* **2022**, *429*, 127218. [CrossRef]
24. Eftekhari, T.; Rashidinia, J. A new operational vector approach for time-fractional subdiffusion equations of distributed order based on hybrid functions. *Math. Methods Appl. Sci.* **2022**. [CrossRef]
25. Eftekhari, T.; Rashidinia, J.; Maleknejad, K. Existence, uniqueness, and approximate solutions for the general nonlinear distributed-order fractional differential equations in a Banach space. *Adv. Differ. Equ.* **2021**, *2021*, 461. [CrossRef]
26. Hesameddini, E.; Shahbazi, M. Two-dimensional shifted Legendre polynomials operational matrix method for solving the two-dimensional integral equations of fractional order. *Appl. Math. Comput.* **2018**, *322*, 40–54. [CrossRef]
27. Khalil, H.; Khan, R.A. The use of Jacobi polynomials in the numerical solution of coupled system of fractional differential equations. *Int. J. Comput. Math.* **2015**, *92*, 1452–1472. [CrossRef]
28. Maleknejad, K.; Rashidinia, J.; Eftekhari, T. A new and efficient numerical method based on shifted fractional-order Jacobi operational matrices for solving some classes of two-dimensional nonlinear fractional integral equations. *Numer. Methods Partial Differ. Equ.* **2021**, *37*, 2687–2713. [CrossRef]
29. Maleknejad, K.; Rashidinia, J.; Eftekhari, T. Numerical solutions of distributed order fractional differential equations in the time domain using the Müntz-Legendre wavelets approach. *Numer. Methods Partial Differ. Equ.* **2021**, *37*, 707–731. [CrossRef]
30. Maleknejad, K.; Rashidinia, J.; Eftekhari, T. Existence, uniqueness, and numerical analysis of solutions for some classes of two-dimensional nonlinear fractional integral equations in a Banach space. *Comput. Appl. Math.* **2020**, *39*, 271. [CrossRef]
31. Maleknejad, K.; Rashidinia, J.; Eftekhari, T. Numerical solution of three-dimensional Volterra-Fredholm integral equations of the first and second kinds based on Bernstein's approximation. *Appl. Math. Comput.* **2018**, *339*, 272–285. [CrossRef]
32. Mirzaee, F.; Samadyar, N. Numerical solution based on two-dimensional orthonormal Bernstein polynomials for solving some classes of two-dimensional nonlinear integral equations of fractional order. *Appl. Math. Comput.* **2019**, *344*, 191–203. [CrossRef]
33. Najafalizadeh, S.; Ezzati, R. Numerical methods for solving two-dimensional nonlinear integral equations of fractional order by using two-dimensional block pulse operational matrix. *Appl. Math. Comput.* **2016**, *280*, 46–56. [CrossRef]
34. Rashidinia, J.; Eftekhari, T.; Maleknejad, K. Numerical solutions of two-dimensional nonlinear fractional Volterra and Fredholm integral equations using shifted Jacobi operational matrices via collocation method. *J. King Saud Univ.-Sci.* **2021**, *33*, 101244. [CrossRef]
35. Rashidinia, J.; Eftekhari, T.; Maleknejad, K. A novel operational vector for solving the general form of distributed order fractional differential equations in the time domain based on the second kind Chebyshev wavelets. *Numer. Algorithms* **2021**, *88*, 1617–1639. [CrossRef]
36. Najafalizadeh, S.; Ezzati, R. A block pulse operational matrix method for solving two-dimensional nonlinear integro-differential equations of fractional order. *J. Comput. Appl. Math.* **2017**, *326*, 159–170. [CrossRef]
37. Maleknejad, K.; Rashidinia, J.; Eftekhari, T. Operational matrices based on hybrid functions for solving general nonlinear two-dimensional fractional integro-differential equations. *Comp. Appl. Math.* **2020**, *39*, 103. [CrossRef]
38. Zeidler, E. Applied Functional Analysis: Applications to Mathematical Physics. *Appl. Math. Sci.* **1995**, *108*.
39. Conway, J.B. *A Course in Functional Analysis*; Springer: Berlin/Heidelberg, Germany, 2007.
40. Borhanifar, A.; Sadri, K. A Generalized Operational Method for Solving Integro-Partial Differential Equations Based on Jacobi Polynomials. *Hacet. J. Math. Stat.* **2016**, *45*, 311–335.

mathematics

MDPI

Article

Topological Structure and Existence of Solutions Set for q-Fractional Differential Inclusion in Banach Space

Ali Rezaiguia [1,2,*] and Taher S. Hassan [1,3]

[1] Department of Mathematics, College of Science, University of Hail, Hail 2440, Saudi Arabia; tshassan@mans.edu.eg
[2] Department of Computer Science and Mathematics, Mouhamed Cherif Messadia University, Souk Ahras BP 1553, Algeria
[3] Department of Mathematics, Faculty of Science, Mansoura University, Mansoura 35516, Egypt
* Correspondence: ali_rezaig@yahoo.fr

Abstract: In this work, we concentrate on the existence of the solutions set of the following problem ${}^cD_q^\alpha\sigma(t) \in F(t,\sigma(t),{}^c D_q^\alpha\sigma(t)), t \in I = [0,T]$ $\sigma(0) = \sigma_0 \in E$, as well as its topological structure in Banach space E. By transforming the problem posed into a fixed point problem, we provide the necessary conditions for the existence and compactness of solutions set. Finally, we present an example as an illustration of main results.

Keywords: Caputo fractional q-difference inclusion; measure of non-compactness; Darbo point theorem; selection theory

MSC: 34A60; 34K30; 34A08

1. Introduction

One of the most important branches of modern mathematics is the study of the fractional differential equations and inclusion, which are considered as powerful and effective tools for studying many problems in science and engineering, thermodynamics, finance, astrophysics, bioengineering, hydrology, mathematical physics, biophysics, statistical mechanics, control theory, and cosmology, see [1–5] and its references mentioned.

Recently, many authors have been attracted by the study of fractional q-difference boundary value problems in Banach Spaces, for recent contributions are included in [6–13].

During the year 2020, the authors in [8], through the use of multi-valued analysis, Kuratowski measure of non-compactness and fixed-point theory on Banach space, they discussed the existence of solutions for the fractional q-differential inclusion of the form

$$^{c}D_q^\alpha\sigma(t) \in F(t,\sigma(t)), t \in I = [0,T]$$

with

$$\sigma(0) = \sigma_0 \in E,$$

where α, q are constants with $\alpha \in (0,1], q \in (0,1), T > 0, F : I \times E \to \mathcal{P}(E)$ is a is a multi-valued map, and ${}^cD_q^\alpha$ is the Caputo fractional q-difference derivative of order α. By employing some fixed point theorems in Banach spaces, the authors proved the existence of solution set defined on I.

During the following year, in [14], the author was given some conditions for the existence solution set and Filippov-type results for the fractional q-differential equation

$$^{c}D_q^\alpha\sigma(t) \in F(t,\sigma(t),{}^c D_q^\alpha\sigma(t)), t \in [0,T]$$

with

$$\upsilon(0) = \upsilon_0,$$

where $q \in (0,1)$ and $\alpha \in (0,1], T > 0, F : [0,T] \times \mathbb{R} \to \mathcal{P}(\mathbb{R})$ is a multi-valued map, and $\mathcal{P}(\mathbb{R})$ is the family of all subsets of $\mathbb{R}$, and ${}^cD_q^\alpha$ is the Caputo fractional q-difference derivative of order α.

The purpose of this article is to study the q-fractional differential inclusion of the form:

$$ {}^cD_q^\alpha \sigma(t) \in F(t, \sigma(t), {}^cD_q^\alpha \sigma(t)), t \in I = [0,T] \tag{1} $$

$$ \sigma(0) = \sigma_0 \in E, \tag{2} $$

where $(E, \|.\|)$ is a real or complex Banach space, $\alpha \in (0,1], q \in (0,1), T > 0, F : I \times E \times E \to \mathcal{P}(E)$ is a multi-valued map, and ${}^cD_q^\alpha$ is the Caputo fractional q-difference derivative of order α. By using the set-valued analysis, *Kuratowski* measure of non-compactness and *Darbo* fixed point theorem, we concentrate on the existence and the topological structure of the solutions set for the problem (1) and (2).

This work is structured as follows: in Section 2, we mention some theorems and lemmas which play an important role in our proofs. In Section 3, we present two results, the first obtained by combining the selection theory with *Kuratowski* measure of non-compactness, and the Darbo fixed-point theorem. For the second result, we study the compactness of the solution set for the problem (1) and (2). The last section is for an example as an illustration of our results.

2. Preliminaries

Firstly, we introduce some useful spaces. The classical Banach spaces $C(I,E) = \{\sigma : I \to E,\ \sigma \text{ is continuous functions}\}$, with the norm $\|\sigma\|_\infty = \sup_{t \in I}\{\|\sigma(t)\|, t \in I\}$, where $(E, \|.\|)$ is a separable Banach spaces. The space $L^1(I,E)$ of measurable functions $\varphi : I \to E$ which are Bochner integrable, normed by $\|\varphi\|_{L^1} = \int_I \|\varphi(t)\| dt$. We also use the Banach space $C_q^\alpha(I,E)$ defined by

$$ C_q^\alpha(I,E) = \left\{\sigma : \sigma \in C(I,E), {}^cD_q^\alpha \sigma \in C(I,E)\right\}, $$

equipped with the norm $\|\sigma\|_q = \max\left\{\|\sigma\|_\infty, \left\|{}^cD_q^\alpha \sigma\right\|_\infty\right\}$.

Now we mention some basic definitions, lemmas, and theorems related to multi-valued analysis that we need. Let (E,e) be a metric space generated by the normed space $(E, \|.\|)$. We denote by $\mathcal{P}_0(E) = \{S \in \mathcal{P}(E), S \neq \emptyset\}$, $\mathcal{P}_{cl}(E) = \{S \in \mathcal{P}_0(E) : S \text{ is closed}\}$, $\mathcal{P}_b(E) = \{S \in \mathcal{P}_0(E) : S \text{ is bounded}\}$, $\mathcal{P}_c(E) = \{S \in \mathcal{P}_0(E) : S \text{ is compact}\}$, $\mathcal{P}_v(E) = \{S \in \mathcal{P}_0(E) : S \text{ is convex}\}$, $\mathcal{P}_{cl,b}(E) = \mathcal{P}_{cl}(E) \cap \mathcal{P}_b(E)$.

Let the distance $H_e : \mathcal{P}(E) \times \mathcal{P}(E) \to \mathbb{R} \cup \{\infty\}$ given by

$$ H_e(C,D) = \max\left\{\sup_{c \in C} e(c,D), \sup_{d \in D} e(d,C)\right\}, $$

where $e(c,D) = \inf_{d \in D} e(c,d)$ and $e(d,C) = \inf_{c \in C} e(d,c)$, then $(\mathcal{P}_{b,cl}(E), H_e)$ is a metric space see [15].

Let E be a separable Banach space, $C \in \mathcal{P}_{cl}(E)$ and $F : C \to \mathcal{P}_{cl}(E)$ a multi-valued operator. F has convex (closed) values if $F(x)$ is convex (closed) for all $x \in E$. F is said to be upper semi-continuous $(u.s.c)$ at a point $c_0 \in C$ if for every open $O \subseteq C$, such that $F(c_0) \subset O$ there exists a neighborhood N of c_0, such that $F(N) \subset O$. F has a closed graph, that is, $x_n \to x, y_n \to y, y_n \in F(x_n)$ imply that $y \in F(x)$. We say that F is bounded on bounded sets if $F(\Omega)$ is bounded in E for each bounded set Ω of E (i.e., $\sup_{x \in \Omega}\{\sup\{\|\overline{x}\| : \overline{x} \in F(x)\}\} < +\infty$). F is completely continuous if $F(\Omega)$ is relatively compact for every $\Omega \in \mathcal{P}_b(X)$. Suppose that $F : C \to \mathcal{P}_c(E)$ is completely continuous, then F is upper semi-continuous (u,s,c), is equivalent to F has a closed graph. If $x \in F(x)$, we say that F has a fixed point in E. F is said to be measurable if the function $f : I \to \mathbb{R}$ defined by $f(t) = e(x, F(t)) = \inf\{\|x - y\| : y \in F(t)\}$ is measurable.

Lemma 1 ([16], *Thm*19,7). *Let E be a separable metric space and F a multi-valued map with non-empty closed values. Then F has a measurable selection.*

Definition 1. *$F : I \times E \times E \to \mathcal{P}(E)$ is Caratheodory multi-valued map, if:*
(1) *$t \to F(t, x_1, x_2)$ is measurable for each $x_1, x_2 \in E$,*
(2) *$(x_1, x_2) \to F(t, x_1, x_2)$ is upper semi-continuous for almost all $t \in I$,*
F is called L^1−Caratheodory if F is Caratheodory and,
(3) *for each $r > 0$, there exists $\varphi_r \in L^1(I, \mathbb{R}^+)$, such that*

$$\|F(t, x_1, x_2)\| = \sup\{\|x\|_\infty : x \in F(t, x_1, x_2)\} \leq \varphi_r(t).$$

For more details of the multi-valued analysis, we refer the reader to the following books [15,17–20].

Definition 2. *A function $\kappa : \mathcal{P}_b(E) \to \mathbb{R}^+$ is called a measure of non-compactness on E, if for each subsets $C, C_1, C_2 \in \mathcal{P}_b(E)$, the following conditions are hold :*
(1) $\kappa(C) = 0$ if and only if C is precompact,
(2) $\kappa(C) = \kappa(\overline{C})$,
(3) $\kappa(C_1 \cup C_2) = max\{\kappa(C_1), \kappa(C_2)\}$.

Let $\mathcal{B}_E$ the family of bounded subsets of a Banach space E.

Definition 3 ([21,22]). *The Kuratowski measure of non-compactness is defined as $\kappa : \mathcal{B}_E \to \mathbb{R}^+$, such that, $\kappa(C) = \inf\{\varepsilon > 0 | C \subset \cup_{i=1}^{n} C_i, diam(C_i) \leq \varepsilon\}, C \in \mathcal{B}_E$.*

Definition 4. *A multi-valued mapping $\Phi : E \to \mathcal{P}_{cl,b}(E)$ is said to be γ-Lipschitz, if there exists a constant $\gamma > 0$, such that $\kappa(\Phi(\Omega)) \leq \gamma\kappa(\Omega)$ for all closed bounded set Ω in E with $\Phi(\Omega)$ is a closed bounded set in E.*
If $\gamma < 1$, then Φ is called a γ-contraction on E.

Let us recall some definitions and properties of fractional q-calculus [23–27]. For $x \in \mathbb{R}$, let $q \in (0,1)$

$$[x]_q = \frac{q^x - 1}{q - 1} = 1 + q + q^2 + \ldots + q^{x-1}, x \in \mathbb{R}.$$

The q-analogue of the power function $(x - y)^n$, $n \in \mathbb{N}$ is

$$(x - y)^0 = 1, (x - y)^n = \prod_{k=0}^{n-1}\left(x - yq^k\right), x, y \in \mathbb{R}, n \in \mathbb{N}.$$

If $\alpha \in \mathbb{R}$, then

$$(x - y)^{(\alpha)} = x^\alpha \prod_{k=0}^{+\infty} \frac{x - yq^i}{x - yq^{\alpha+i}}.$$

When $y = 0$, then

$$x^{(\alpha)} = x^\alpha.$$

The q-gamma function is given by:

$$\Gamma_q(\alpha) = \frac{(1 - q)^{(\alpha-1)}}{(1 - q)^{\alpha-1}}, \alpha \in \mathbb{R}\backslash\{\ldots, -2, -1, 0, 1, 2, \ldots\}, 0 < q < 1$$

and verifies that

$$\Gamma_q(\alpha + 1) = [\alpha]_q \Gamma_q(\alpha).$$

The q-derivative of a function $h(x)$ is defined by

$$D_q h(x) = \frac{d_q h(x)}{d_q x} = \frac{h(qx) - h(x)}{(q-1)x}, x \neq 0.$$

The higher order q-derivative of $h(x)$ is given as the following formula

$$D_q^n h(x) = \begin{cases} h(x), & \text{if } n = 0, \\ D_q D_q^{n-1} h(x), & \text{if } n \in \mathbb{N}. \end{cases}$$

Let h a function defined on $[0,b]$,the q-integral of is given by

$$\int_0^t h(x) d_q x = t(1-q) \sum_{n \geq 0} h(tq^n) q^n, 0 \leq |q| < 1,\ t \in [0,b].$$

If $a \in [0,b]$, then

$$\int_a^b h(x) d_q x = \int_0^b h(x) d_q x - \int_0^a h(x) d_q x.$$

Similarly as performed for derivatives, it can be defined an operator I_q^n, namely,

$$\left(I_q^0 h\right)(x) = h(x) \text{ and } \left(I_q^n h\right)(x) = I_q\left(I_q^{n-1} h\right)(x),\ n \in \mathbb{N}.$$

The fundamental theorem of calculus applies to these operators I_q and D_q, i.e

$$D_q (I_q h)(x) = h(x),$$

if h is continuous at $x = 0$, then

$$I_q (D_q h)(x) = h(x) - h(0).$$

For more information and basic properties of these operators, we recommend [28] to the reader.

Definition 5. *Let $\alpha \geq 0$ and h be a function defined on I. The fractional q-integral of the Riemann–Liouville type is*

$$\left(I_q^\alpha h\right)(x) = \begin{cases} h(x), & \text{if } \alpha = 0 \\ \frac{1}{\Gamma_q(\alpha)} \int_0^x (x - qs)^{(\alpha-1)} h(s) d_q s, & \text{if } \alpha > 0 \end{cases},\ x \in I.$$

Definition 6. *The fractional q-derivative of the Riemann–Liouville with order $\alpha \geq 0$ is defined by*

$$\left(D_q^\alpha h\right)(x) = \begin{cases} h(x), & \text{if } \alpha = 0 \\ \left(D_q^{[\alpha]}\left(I_q^{[\alpha]-\alpha} h\right)\right)(x), & \text{if } \alpha > 0 \end{cases},\ x \in I,$$

where $[.]$ is the smallest integer greater than or equal to α.

Definition 7. *The fractional q-derivative of Caputo with order $\alpha \geq 0$ is defined by*

$$\left({}^c D_q^\alpha h\right)(x) = \begin{cases} h(x), & \text{if } \alpha = 0 \\ \left(I_q^{[\alpha]-\alpha}\left(D_q^{[\alpha]} h\right)\right)(x), & \text{if } \alpha > 0 \end{cases},\ x \in I.$$

Lemma 2. *Let $\alpha \geq 0$. Then we have*

$$I_q^\alpha \left({}^c D_q^\alpha h\right)(x) = h(x) - \sum_{n=0}^{[\alpha]-\alpha} h(tq^n) \frac{t^n}{\Gamma_q(n+1)} \left(D_q^\alpha h\right)(0),$$

and if $\alpha \in (0,1)$, *then*

$$I_q^\alpha \left({}^c D_q^\alpha h \right)(x) = h(x) - h(0).$$

Now we give the Darbo fixed point theorems, which our results will be based on:

Theorem 1 ([29])**.** *Let E be a Banach space, a set* $\mathcal{C} \in \mathcal{P}_{cl,b}(E) \cap \mathcal{P}_v(E)$ *and let* $\psi : \mathcal{C} \to \mathcal{P}_{cl,b}(\mathcal{C})$ *be a closed and* γ*-contraction. Then* ψ *has a fixed point.*

3. Existence Results

In this section, by applying Darbo fixed point theorem [29] for multi-valued map, we prove the existence of solutions for the problem (1) and (2).

First, we introduce the definition of the solution of the problem (1) and (2).

Definition 8. *A function* $\sigma \in C_q^\alpha(I,E)$ *is called a solution of problem (1) and (2) if there exists a function* $h \in L^1(I,\mathbb{R})$ *with* $h \in F(t,\sigma(t), {}^c D_q^\alpha \sigma(t))$, *a.e.*$t \in I$, *such that* ${}^c D_q^\alpha \sigma(t) = h(t)$, *a.e.*$t \in I$ *and condition* (2) *is satisfied.*

Now, we assume the following assumptions:

(H_1) $F : I \times E \times E \to \mathcal{P}_c(E)$ be a L^1-Caratheodory multi-valued mapping.

(H_2) There exists a function $\phi \in L^1(I,\mathbb{R}^+)$, such that, for each set, $B_1, B_2 \in \mathcal{P}_{cl,b}(C(I,E))$ and $t \in I$, we have

$$\kappa(F(t,B_1(t),B_2(t))) \le \phi(t)\max(\kappa(B_1(t)),\kappa(B_2(t))).$$

Theorem 2. *Assume that* (H_1), (H_2), $\max\left\{ \|\sigma_0\|_\infty + \varphi_r^* \frac{T^{(\alpha)}}{\Gamma_q(\alpha+1)}, \varphi_r^* \right\} \le r$, *and* $\phi(t) \le 1$, *for each* $t \in I$, *hold, then the problem (1) and (2) has at least one solution in* $C_q^\alpha(I,E)$, *for all* $t \in I$.

Proof. For each $x \in C(I,E)$, define the set of selections of F by

$$S_{F,\sigma} = \left\{ \varsigma \in L^1(I,E) : \varsigma(t) \in F(t,\sigma(t), {}^c D_q^\alpha \sigma(t)), \text{ for all } t \in I \right\}.$$

Let for $r \in \mathbb{R}^+$, the set $\mathcal{C}_r \in \mathcal{P}_{cl,b}(C_q^\alpha(I,E)) \cap \mathcal{P}_v(C_q^\alpha(I,E))$, defined by

$$\mathcal{C}_r = \left\{ \sigma \in C_q^\alpha(I,E),\ \|\sigma\|_q \le r \right\}.$$

Now, we consider the multi-valued operator $\psi : C_q^\alpha(I,E) \to \mathcal{P}_{cl,b}\left(C_q^\alpha(I,E)\right)$ defined by

$$\psi(\sigma) = \left\{ \rho \in C_q^\alpha(I,E) : \rho(t) = \sigma_0 + \left(I_q^\alpha \varsigma\right)(t),\ \text{for } \varsigma \in S_{F,\sigma} \right\}.$$

Observe that, for each $\sigma \in C_q^\alpha(I,E)$ then the set $S_{F,\sigma} \neq \emptyset$, by the hypothesis H_1, the multi-valued function F has a measurable selection. We shall prove that the operator ψ fulfills the conditions of Darbo fixed point theorem.

Step 1. We prove that $\psi(\sigma) \in \mathcal{P}_b(\mathcal{C}_r)$.

Let $\sigma \in \mathcal{C}_r$ and $\rho \in \psi(\sigma)$, then there exists $\varsigma \in S_{F,\sigma}$, such that for each $t \in I$, we have

$$\rho(t) = \sigma_0 + \left(I_q^\alpha \varsigma\right)(t).$$

then

$$\begin{aligned}\|\rho(t)\| &\leq \|\sigma\| + \int_0^t \frac{(t-qs)^{(\alpha-1)}}{\Gamma_q(\alpha)}\|\varsigma(s)\|d_qs \\ &\leq \|\sigma_0\| + \int_0^t \frac{(t-qs)^{(\alpha-1)}}{\Gamma_q(\alpha)}\varphi_r(s)d_qs \\ &\leq \|\sigma_0\| + \int_0^T \frac{(T-qs)^{(\alpha-1)}}{\Gamma_q(\alpha)}\varphi_r(s)d_qs.\end{aligned}$$

Let *ess* sup $\varphi_r = \varphi_r^*$, then

$$\|\rho\|_\infty \leq \|\sigma_0\|_\infty + \varphi_r^* \frac{T^{(\alpha)}}{\Gamma_q(\alpha+1)},$$

and

$$\begin{aligned}\left\|{}^cD_q^\alpha \rho(t)\right\| &= \|\varsigma(t)\|, \\ &\leq \varphi_r(t), \\ &\leq \varphi_r^*.\end{aligned}$$

Then

$$\left\|{}^cD_q^\alpha \rho\right\|_\infty \leq \varphi_r^*,$$

So,

$$\|\rho\|_q \leq \max\left\{\|\sigma_0\|_\infty + \varphi_r^* \frac{T^{(\alpha)}}{\Gamma_q(\alpha+1)}, \varphi_r^*\right\} \leq r.$$

Step 2. We show that $\psi(\sigma) \in \mathcal{P}_{cl}(\mathcal{C}_r)$.

Let $\{\rho_n\}_{n\in\mathbb{N}}$ a sequence in $\psi(\sigma)$, such that $\rho_n \to \rho$ $(n \to \infty)$ in $C_q^\alpha(I, E)$. Then for each $t \in I$ there exists $\varsigma_n \in S_{F,\sigma}$ such that

$$\rho_n(t) = \sigma_0 + I_q^\alpha \varsigma_n(t),$$

As F has compact values, we pass on to a subsequence to get that ς_n converge to ς in $L^1(I \times E)$. Thus $\varsigma \in S_{F,\sigma}$ and for each $t \in I$,

$$\rho_n(t) \to \rho(t)$$

with $\rho(t) = \sigma_0 + I_q^\alpha \varsigma(s)$. Hence $\rho \in \psi(\sigma)$, then $\psi(\sigma)$ is closed in $\mathcal{C}_r$ for each $\sigma \in \mathcal{C}_r$.

Step 3. We prove that ψ a is γ-contraction.

Let $B \in \mathcal{P}_{cl,b}(\mathcal{C}_r)$, then for each $t \in I$, we have

$$\kappa(\psi(B)) = \kappa\{\psi(\sigma) : \sigma \in B\}.$$

Let $\rho \in \psi(\sigma)$ Then there exists $\varsigma \in S_{F,\sigma}$ such that, for each $t \in I$,

$$\rho(t) = \sigma_0 + I_q^\alpha \varsigma(t).$$

For each x and ${}^cD_q^\alpha x \in B$, we have

$$\begin{aligned}\kappa(\psi(B)(t)) &= \kappa\left(\rho \in C_q^\alpha(I, E) : \rho(t) \in F(t, \sigma(t), {}^cD_q^\alpha \sigma(t))\right) \\ &\leq \kappa\left(F(t, \sigma(t), {}^cD_q^\alpha \sigma(t))\right) \\ &\leq \phi(t)\kappa(B),\end{aligned}$$

so the operator ψ is a γ-contraction. By the Theorem 1, we deduce that ψ has a fixed point that is a solution of the problem (1) and (2). □

Now, we give some conditions that guarantee the compactness of solutions set for our problem.

Theorem 3. *Let* (H_1) *holds. Then the set* $\mathcal{S} = \{\sigma \in C_q^{\alpha}(I,E) : \sigma$ *is solution of the problem* (1) *and* (2)$\}$ *is an element of* $\mathcal{P}_c(C_q^{\alpha}(I,E))$.

Proof. From Theorem 2, the set $\mathcal{S}$ is not empty. Now, we prove that $\mathcal{S} \in \mathcal{P}_c(C_q^{\alpha}(I,E))$. Let $(\sigma_n)_{n\in\mathbb{N}} \in \mathcal{S}$, then there exist $\varsigma_n \in S_{F,\sigma_n}$ such that

$$\sigma_n(t) = \sigma_0 + I_q^{\alpha}\varsigma_n(t).$$

Step 1. We show that the set $\{\sigma_n, n \in \mathbb{N}\}$ is equicontinuous in $C_q^{\alpha}(I,E)$.
Let $t_1, t_2 \in I$, with $t_1 < t_2$, we obtain

$$\begin{aligned}
\|\sigma_n(t_2) - \sigma_n(t_1)\| &= \left\| I_q^{\alpha}\varsigma_n(t_2) - I_q^{\alpha}\varsigma_n(t_1) \right\| \\
&\leq \frac{1}{\Gamma_q(\alpha)}\left(\int_0^{t_1} \left|(t_2 - qs)^{(\alpha-1)} - (t_2 - qs)^{(\alpha-1)}\right| \|\varsigma_n(s)\| d_q s + \right. \\
&\left. \int_{t_1}^{t_2} \left|(t_2 - qs)^{(\alpha-1)}\right| \|\varsigma_n(s)\| d_q s \right) \\
&\leq \frac{1}{\Gamma_q(\alpha)}\left(\int_0^{t_1} \left|(t_2 - qs)^{(\alpha-1)} - (t_2 - qs)^{(\alpha-1)}\right| \varphi_r(s) d_q s + \right. \\
&\left. \int_{t_1}^{t_2} \left|(t_2 - qs)^{(\alpha-1)}\right| \varphi_r(s) d_q s \right)
\end{aligned}$$

and

$$\left\| {}^c D_q^{\alpha}\sigma_n(t_2) - {}^c D_q^{\alpha}\sigma_n(t_1) \right\| = \|\varsigma_n(t_2) - \varsigma_n(t_1)\|.$$

Then, when $t_2 \to t_1$, we get

$$\|\sigma_n(t_2) - \sigma_n(t_1)\|_q \to 0.$$

With the theorem of Arzela–Ascoli, we conclude that, there exists a subsequence $\{\sigma_{n_k}\}$, such that σ_{n_k} converges to some σ in $C_q^{\alpha}(I,E)$. Now we prove that there exists $\varsigma(.) \in F(.,\sigma(.),{}^c D_q^{\alpha}\sigma(.))$, such that

$$\sigma(t) = \sigma_0 + I_q^{\alpha}\varsigma(t).$$

Since $F(t,.,.)$ is upper semi-continuous, then for every $\varepsilon > 0$, there exists $n_0(\varepsilon)$, such that for every $n \geq n_0$, we have

$$\varsigma_n(t) \in F(t,\sigma_n(t),{}^c D_q^{\alpha}\sigma_n(t)) \subset F(t,\sigma(t),{}^c D_q^{\alpha}\sigma(t)) + B(0,\varepsilon),\ a.e.t \in I.$$

As $F(.,.,.) \in \mathcal{P}_c(C_q^{\alpha}(I,E))$ then there exists a subsequence ς_{n_m}, such that

$$\varsigma_{n_m}(.) \to \varsigma(.) \text{ as } m \to +\infty$$

and

$$\varsigma(t) \in F(t,\sigma(t),{}^c D_q^{\alpha}\sigma(t)),\ a.e.t \in I \text{ for all } m \in \mathbb{N}.$$

Since, $\varsigma_{n_m}(t) \leq \varphi_r(t)$, *a.e.t* $\in I$, Lebesgue's Dominated Convergence Theorem give us that $\varsigma(t) \in L^1(I \times E)$ implies $\varsigma \in S_{F,\sigma}$. Therefore, $\sigma(t) = \sigma_0 + I_q^{\alpha}\varsigma(t)$. So $\mathcal{S} \in \mathcal{P}_c\left(C_q^{\alpha}(I,E)\right)$. □

4. An Example

Now, we give an example as an illustration of the results obtained in Theorem 2 and Theorem 3.

Example 1. *Let* $E = C([0,1])$ *be the Banach space of all real continuous function on* $[0,1]$ *equipped with the norm*

$$\|f\| = \sup_{t\in[0,1]} \{|f(t)|\}.$$

Now we consider the q-fractional differential inclusion, given by:

$$^{c}D_{0.5}^{0.2}\sigma(t) \in F(t,\sigma(t),^{c} D_{0.5}^{0.2}\sigma(t)), t \in I = [0,1] \quad (3)$$

$$\sigma(0) = t\cosh(t). \quad (4)$$

where $\alpha = 0.2$, $q = 0.5$, $T = 1$, *and*

$$F(t,\sigma(t),^{c} D_{0.5}^{0.2}\sigma(t)) = \frac{1}{\|\sigma\|_q}\left(\frac{1}{1+t+e^t}\right).\left\{f \in C([0,1]) : \|f\| \leq \|\sigma\|_q\right\}.$$

Let

$$\mathcal{C}_3 = \left\{\sigma \in C_{0.5}^{0.2}(I,E) : \|\sigma\|_q \leq 3\right\}.$$

For each $\sigma \in E$ *and* $t \in I$, *we have*

$$\|F(t,\sigma,\sigma_1)\| \leq \frac{1}{1+t+e^t} = \varphi_3(t) \textit{ implies } \varphi_3^* = 0.5$$

and for each $B \in \mathcal{P}_{cl,b}(\mathcal{C}_3)$, *we get*

$$\kappa(\psi(B)(t)) \leq e^{t-2}\kappa(B) = \phi(t)\kappa(B),$$

$$\max\left\{\|\sigma_0\|_\infty + \varphi_3^*\frac{T^{(0.2)}}{\Gamma_{0.5}(0.2+1)}, \varphi_3^*\right\} \approx 2.07 < 3,$$

and

$$\phi(t) \leq 1, \textit{for all } t \in I.$$

Then Theorem 2 and Theorem 3 guarantee that the set of solutions of the problem (3) and (4) is not empty and also is compact.

Author Contributions: Conceptualization, A.R.; Methodology, A.R.; Formal analysis, A.R.; Writing—review and editing A.R.; Funding acquisition, A.R.; Supervision, review and reading, T.S.H.; Investigation, T.S.H.; Methodology, T.S.H.; Validation, T.S.H. All authors have read and agreed to the published version of the manuscript.

Funding: This research received no external funding.

Data Availability Statement: Not applicable.

Conflicts of Interest: The authors declare no conflicts of interest.

References

1. Ahmad, B.; Otero-Espinar, V. Existence of Solutions for Fractional Differential Inclusions with Antiperiodic Boundary Conditions. *Bound. Value Probl.* **2009**, *2009*, 625347. [CrossRef]
2. Chang, Y.-K.; Nieto, J.J. Some new existence results for fractional differential inclusions with boundary conditions. *Math. Comput. Model.* **2009**, *49*, 605–609. [CrossRef]
3. Rezaiguia, A.; Kelaiaia, S. Existence of Solution, Filippov's Theorem and Compactness of the Set of Solutions for a Third-Order Differential Inclusion with Three- Point Boundary Conditions. *Mathematics* **2018**, *6*, 40. [CrossRef]
4. Tarasov, V.E. *Fractional Dynamics: Application of Fractional Calculus to Dynamics of Particles, Fields and Media*; Springer: Heidelberg, Germany; Higher Education Press: Beijing, China, 2010.
5. Stojiljkovic, V. A new conformable fractional derivative and applications (Una nueva derivada fraccionaria conforme y aplicaciones). *Sel. Mat.* **2022**, *9*, 370–380 [CrossRef]

6. Abbas, A.; Ahmad, B.; Benchohra, M.; Ntouyas, S.K. Weak solutions for caputo-pettis fractional q-difference inclusion. *Fract. Differ. Calc.* **2020**, *10*, 141–152. [CrossRef]
7. Allouch, N.; Graef, J.R.; Hamani, S. Boundary Value Problem for Fractional q-Difference Equations with Integral Conditions in Banach Spaces. *Fractal Fract.* **2022**, *6*, 237. [CrossRef]
8. Alqahtani, B.; Abbas, S.; Benchohra, M.; Salem Alzaid, S. Fractional q-Difference Inclusions in Banach Spaces. *Mathematics* **2020**, *8*, 91. [CrossRef]
9. Ahmad, B.; Etemad, S.; Ettefagh, M.; Rezapour, S. On the existence of solutions for fractional q-difference inclusions with q-antiperiodic boundary conditions. *Bull. Math. Soc. Sci. Math. Roum.* **2016**, *59*, 119–134.
10. Bragdi, M.; Debbouche, A.; Baleanu, D. Existence of Solutions for Fractional Differential Inclusions with Separated Boundary Conditions in Banach Space. *Adv. Math. Phys.* **2013**, *2013*, 426061. [CrossRef]
11. El-Shahed, M.; Hassan, H.A. Positive solutions of q-difference equation. *Proc. Amer. Math. Soc.* **2010**, *138*, 1733–1738. [CrossRef]
12. Gefter, S.L.; Piven, A.L. Implicit Linear q-Difference Equations in Banach Spaces. *J. Math. Sci.* **2020**, *251*, 787–796. [CrossRef]
13. Liang, S.; Samei, M.E. New approach to solutions of a class of singular fractional q-differential problem via quantum calculus. *Adv. Differ. Equ.* **2020**, *2020*, 14. [CrossRef]
14. Rezaiguia, A. Existence Results For q-Fractional Differential Inclusion With Non-Convex Right Hand Side. *Acta Math. Univ.* **2021**, *90*, 277–288.
15. Aubin, J.P.; Cellina, A. *Differential Inclusions*; Springer: Berlin/Heidelberg, Germany, 1984.
16. Castaing, C.; Valadier, M. Convex Analysis and Measurable Multifunctions. In *Lecture Notes in Mathematics*; Springer: Berlin/Heidelberg, Germany, 1977.
17. Aubin, J.P.; Frankowska, H. *Set-Valued Analysis*; Birkhauser: Boston, MA, USA, 1990.
18. Deimling, K. *Multivalued Differential Equations*; Walter De Gruyter: Berlin, Germany, 1992.
19. Gorniewicz, L. Topological Fixed Point Theory of Multivalued Map pings. In *Mathematics and Its Applications*; Kluwer Academic Publishers: Dordrecht, The Netherlands, 1999.
20. Papageorgiou, N.; Hu, S. *Handbook of Multivalued Analysis, Volume I: Theory*; Kluwer Academic Publishers: Dordrecht, The Netherlands; Boston, MA, USA; London, UK, 1997.
21. Banas, J.; Goebel, K. *Measures of Noncompactness in Banach Spaces*; Marcel Dekker: New York, NY, USA, 1980.
22. Toledano, J.M.A.; Benavides, T.D.; Acedo, G.L. *Measures of Noncompactness in Metric Fixed Point Theory, Operator Theory, Advances and Applications*; Birkhauser: Basel, Switzerland; Boston, MA, USA; Berlin, Germany, 1997; Volume 99.
23. Al-Salam, W.A. Some fractional q-integrals and q-derivatives. *Proc. Edinb. Math. Soc.* **1966**, *15*, 135–140. [CrossRef]
24. Agarwal, R.P. Certain fractional q-integrals and q-derivatives. *Proc. Cambridge Philos. Soc.* **1969**, *66*, 365–370. [CrossRef]
25. Ahmad, B.; Ntouyas, S.K.; Tariboon, J. *Quantum Calculus. New Concepts, Impulsive IVPs and BVPs, Inequalities. Trends in Abstract and Applied Analysis*; World Scientific Publishing Co., Pte. Ltd.: Hackensack, NJ, USA, 2016.
26. Etemad, S.; Sotiris, K. Ntouyas and Bashir Ahmad Existence Theory for a Fractional q-Integro-Difference Equation with q-Integral Boundary Conditions of Different Orders. *Mathematics* **2019**, *7*, 659. [CrossRef]
27. Kac, V.; Cheung, P. Quantum Calculus; Springer: New York, NY, USA, 2002.
28. Rajkovic, P.M.; Marinkovic, S.D.; Stankovic, M.S. On q-analogues of Caputo derivative and Mittag-Leffler function. *Fract. Calc. Appl. Anal.* **2007**, *10*, 359–373
29. Dhage, B.C. Some generalization of multi-valued version of Schauderís fixed point theorem with applications. *Cubo* **2010**, *12*, 139–151. [CrossRef]

mathematics

Article

New Hermite–Hadamard and Ostrowski-Type Inequalities for Newly Introduced Co-Ordinated Convexity with Respect to a Pair of Functions

Muhammad Aamir Ali [1], Fongchan Wannalookkhee [2], Hüseyin Budak [3], Sina Etemad [4,*] and Shahram Rezapour [5,6,7,*]

1 Jiangsu Key Laboratory for NSLSCS, School of Mathematical Sciences, Nanjing Normal University, Nanjing 210023, China
2 Department of Mathematics, Faculty of Science, Khon Kaen University, Khon Kaen 40002, Thailand
3 Department of Mathematics, Faculty of Science and Arts, Düzce University, Düzce 81620, Turkey
4 Department of Mathematics, Azarbaijan Shahid Madani University, Tabriz 3751-71379, Iran
5 Institute of Research and Development, Duy Tan University, Da Nang 550000, Vietnam
6 Faculty of Natural Sciences, Duy Tan University, Da Nang 550000, Vietnam
7 Department of Medical Research, China Medical University Hospital, China Medical University, Taichung 40402, Taiwan
* Correspondence: sina.etemad@azaruniv.ac.ir (S.E.); rezapourshahram@yahoo.ca or shahramrezapour@duytan.edu.vn or sh.rezapour@mail.cmuh.org.tw (S.R.)

Abstract: In both pure and applied mathematics, convex functions are used in many different problems. They are crucial to investigate both linear and non-linear programming issues. Since a convex function is one whose epigraph is a convex set, the theory of convex functions falls under the umbrella of convexity. However, it is a significant theory that affects practically all areas of mathematics. In this paper, we introduce the notions of (g,h)-convexity or convexity with respect to a pair of functions on co-ordinates and discuss its fundamental properties. Moreover, we establish some novel Hermite–Hadamard- and Ostrowski-type inequalities for newly introduced co-ordinated convexity. Additionally, it is presented that the newly introduced notion of the convexity and given inequalities are generalizations of existing studies in the literature. Lastly, we look at various mathematical examples and graphs to confirm the validity of the newly found inequalities.

Keywords: Hermite–Hadamard inequality; Ostrowski inequalities; convex functions; co-ordinated convex function

MSC: 26D10; 26D15; 26A51; 26B25

1. Introduction

In different branches of mathematical analysis, inequalities play a fundamental role in proving many famous theorems. Additionally, in recent years, such inequalities have been used in most papers discussing fractional mathematical models, fractional boundary value problems, etc. The application of some of them can be found in numerous articles, including [1–11]. These applications show the importance of study on different generalizations of inequalities.

Throughout this paper, we let $I=[\sigma,\rho]\subset\mathbb{R}$ and $\triangle:=[\sigma,\rho]\times[\varsigma,d]\subseteq\mathbb{R}^2$. The Hermite–Hadamard inequality is a fudamental inequality which is presented as: if $F:I\to\mathbb{R}$ is a convex function, then

$$F\left(\frac{\sigma+\rho}{2}\right)\leq\frac{1}{\rho-\sigma}\int_{\sigma}^{\rho}F(\varkappa)\,d\varkappa\leq\frac{F(\sigma)+F(\rho)}{2}. \tag{1}$$

The double inequality (1) was discussed by Hermite [12] in 1883, and ten years later in 1893, it was proved by Hadamard [13].

Another famous inequality is the Ostrowski inequality, which was established by Ostrowski [14] in 1938.

Theorem 1. *Let $\digamma : I \to \mathbb{R}$ be differentiable on I° (interior of I) with a bounded derivative, that is, $\|\digamma'\|_\infty := \sup_{\varkappa\in(\sigma,\rho)} |\digamma'(\varkappa)| < \infty$. Then, we have*

$$\left|\digamma(\varkappa) - \frac{1}{\rho-\sigma}\int_\sigma^\rho \digamma(\varkappa)\,d\varkappa\right| \le \left[\frac{1}{4} + \frac{(\varkappa - \frac{\sigma+\rho}{2})}{(\rho-\sigma)^2}\right](\rho-\sigma)\|\digamma'\|_\infty, \tag{2}$$

for all $\varkappa \in I$. The constant $\frac{1}{4}$ is the best possible.

The inequality (2) can be rewritten in the equivalent form

$$\left|\digamma(\varkappa) - \frac{1}{\rho-\sigma}\int_\sigma^\rho \digamma(\varkappa)\,d\varkappa\right| \le \left[\frac{(\varkappa-\sigma)^2 + (\rho-\varkappa)^2}{2(\rho-\sigma)}\right]\|\digamma'\|_\infty.$$

The Hermite–Hadamard inequality and Ostrowski inequality have been extensively studied by a number of researchers; see [15–20] and the references therein.

In 2001, S. S. Dragomir defined a new concept of a co-ordinated convex function.

Definition 1 ([21]). *$\digamma : \triangle \to \mathbb{R}$ is a co-ordinated convex map, if*

$$\digamma_\varkappa : [\varsigma, d] \ni v \mapsto \digamma(\varkappa, v) \in \mathbb{R} \quad \& \quad \digamma_\gamma : [\sigma, \rho] \ni u \mapsto \digamma(u, \gamma) \in \mathbb{R}, \tag{3}$$

are convex ($\forall\, \varkappa \in (\sigma,\rho), \forall\, \gamma \in (\varsigma, d)$).

A formal equivalent definition of such functions can be stated as the following:

Definition 2 ([21]). *$\digamma : \triangle \to \mathbb{R}$ is co-ordinated convex if*

$$\begin{aligned}\digamma(\xi\varkappa + (1-\xi)z, \lambda\gamma + (1-\lambda)w) \; &\le \xi\lambda\digamma(\varkappa,\gamma) + \xi(1-\lambda)\digamma(\varkappa, w) \\ &\quad + (1-\xi)\lambda\digamma(z,\gamma) + (1-\xi)(1-\lambda)\digamma(z,w),\end{aligned} \tag{4}$$

$\forall\, \xi, \lambda \in [0,1]$ and $\forall\, (\varkappa,\gamma), (z,w) \in \triangle$.

He also presented the following version of Hermite–Hadamard-type inequalities for the aforesaid functions:

Theorem 2 ([21]). *If $\digamma : \triangle \to \mathbb{R}$ is a co-ordinated convex function, then*

$$\begin{aligned}\digamma\left(\frac{\sigma+\rho}{2}, \frac{\varsigma+d}{2}\right) &\le \frac{1}{2}\left[\frac{1}{\rho-\sigma}\int_\sigma^\rho \digamma\left(\varkappa, \frac{\varsigma+d}{2}\right)d\varkappa + \frac{1}{d-\varsigma}\int_\varsigma^d \digamma\left(\frac{\sigma+\rho}{2}, \gamma\right)d\gamma\right] \\ &\le \frac{1}{(\rho-\sigma)(d-\varsigma)}\int_\sigma^\rho\int_\varsigma^d \digamma(\varkappa,\gamma)\,d\gamma\,d\varkappa \\ &\le \frac{1}{4}\left[\frac{1}{\rho-\sigma}\left(\int_\sigma^\rho \digamma(\varkappa,\varsigma)\,d\varkappa + \int_\sigma^\rho \digamma(\varkappa,d)\,d\varkappa\right)\right. \\ &\quad \left. + \frac{1}{d-\varsigma}\left(\int_\varsigma^d \digamma(\sigma,\gamma)\,d\gamma + \int_\varsigma^d \digamma(\rho,\gamma)\,d\gamma\right)\right] \\ &\le \frac{1}{4}[\digamma(\sigma,\varsigma) + \digamma(\rho,\varsigma) + \digamma(\sigma,d) + \digamma(\rho,d)].\end{aligned} \tag{5}$$

In relation to the convex functions on co-ordinates, Latif et al. [22] presented the following Ostrowski-type inequality in 2010:

Theorem 3 ([22]). *Let $F : \Delta \to \mathbb{R}$ be a function with the twice-partial differentiability property on Δ° and $\frac{\partial^2 F}{\partial\eta\,\partial\xi}$ be continuous and integrable on Δ. When $\left|\frac{\partial^2 F}{\partial\eta\,\partial\xi}\right|$ is co-ordinated convex on Δ and $\left|\frac{\partial^2 F}{\partial\eta\,\partial\xi}(\varkappa,\gamma)\right| \le M$, $(\varkappa,\gamma)\in\Delta$, then*

$$\left|F(\varkappa,\gamma) + \frac{1}{(\rho-\sigma)(d-\varsigma)}\int_\sigma^\rho\int_\varsigma^d F(u,v)\,d\eta\,d\xi - A\right|$$
$$\le M\left[\frac{(\varkappa-\sigma)^2+(\rho-\varkappa)^2}{2(\rho-\sigma)}\right]\left[\frac{(\gamma-\varsigma)^2+(d-\gamma)^2}{2(d-\varsigma)}\right], \quad (6)$$

where

$$A(\varkappa,\gamma) = \frac{1}{d-\varsigma}\int_\varsigma^d F(\varkappa,v)\,dv + \frac{1}{\rho-\sigma}\int_\sigma^\varsigma F(u,\gamma)\,du. \quad (7)$$

Theorem 4 ([22]). *Let $F : \Delta \to \mathbb{R}$ be a function with the twice-partial differentiability property on Δ°, and let $\frac{\partial^2 F}{\partial\eta\,\partial\xi}$ be continuous and integrable on Δ. When $\left|\frac{\partial^2 F}{\partial\eta\,\partial\xi}\right|^q$ is co-ordinated convex on Δ, where $q > 1$ with $\frac{1}{p}+\frac{1}{q}=1$, and $\left|\frac{\partial^2 F}{\partial\eta\,\partial\xi}(\varkappa,\gamma)\right| \le M$, $(\varkappa,\gamma)\in\Delta$, then*

$$\left|F(\varkappa,\gamma) + \frac{1}{(\rho-\sigma)(d-\varsigma)}\int_\sigma^\rho\int_\varsigma^d F(u,v)\,dv\,du - A\right|$$
$$\le \frac{M}{(1+p)^{2/p}}\left[\frac{(\varkappa-\sigma)^2+(\rho-\varkappa)^2}{\rho-\sigma}\right]\quad\left[\frac{(\gamma-\varsigma)^2+(d-\gamma)^2}{d-\varsigma}\right], \quad (8)$$

where A is defined as in (7).

Theorem 5 ([22]). *Let $F : \Delta \to \mathbb{R}$ be a function with the twice-partial differentiability property on Δ°, and let $\frac{\partial^2 F}{\partial\eta\,\partial\xi}$ be continuous and integrable on Δ. When $\left|\frac{\partial^2 F}{\partial\eta\,\partial\xi}\right|^q$ is co-ordinated convex on Δ, where $q \ge 1$, and $\left|\frac{\partial^2 F}{\partial\eta\,\partial\xi}(\varkappa,\gamma)\right| \le M$, $(\varkappa,\gamma)\in\Delta$, then*

$$\left|F(\varkappa,\gamma) + \frac{1}{(\rho-\sigma)(d-\varsigma)}\int_\sigma^\rho\int_\varsigma^d F(u,v)\,dv\,du - A\right|$$
$$\le \frac{M}{4}\left[\frac{(\varkappa-\sigma)^2+(\rho-\varkappa)^2}{\rho-\sigma}\right]\left[\frac{(\gamma-\varsigma)^2+(d-\gamma)^2}{d-\varsigma}\right], \quad (9)$$

where A is defined as in (7).

In [23], B. Samet introduced a new class of convex functions with respect to a pair of functions, which is defined as:

Definition 3. *Let $g,h : I \to \mathbb{R}$ be two mappings. A mapping $F : I \to \mathbb{R}$ is called (g,h) convex if the following inequality holds for $M(\varkappa,\gamma) = g(\varkappa)h(\gamma) + g(\gamma)h(\varkappa)$*

$$F(\xi\varkappa + (1-\xi)\gamma) \le \xi^2 F(\varkappa) + (1-\xi)^2 F(\gamma) + \xi(1-\xi)M(\varkappa,\gamma), \quad (10)$$

for all $\xi\in[0,1]$ and $\varkappa,\gamma\in I$.

Remark 1. *If $g,h : I \subset \mathbb{R} \to [0,\infty)$ are two convex mappings, then $F = gh$ is (g,h)-convex mapping.*

B. Samet also established a Hermite–Hadamard inequality (double inequality) for newly class of convex functions with respect to a pair of functions, presented as:

Theorem 6 ([23]). *Let $F : I \to \mathbb{R}$ be a (g,h)-convex function over I with $g,h : I \to \mathbb{R}$. If $F \in L^1(I)$ and $g,h \in L^2(I)$, then*

$$\begin{aligned} & 2F\left(\tfrac{\sigma+\rho}{2}\right) - \tfrac{1}{\rho-\sigma}\int_\sigma^\rho g(\sigma+\rho-\varkappa)h(\varkappa)d\varkappa \\ = \; & 2F\left(\tfrac{\sigma+\rho}{2}\right) - \tfrac{1}{\rho-\sigma}\int_\sigma^\rho g(\varkappa)h(\sigma+\rho-\varkappa)d\varkappa \\ \le \; & \tfrac{1}{\rho-\sigma}\int_\sigma^\rho F(\varkappa)d\varkappa \\ \le \; & \tfrac{F(\sigma)+F(\rho)}{3} + \tfrac{M(\sigma,\rho)}{6}. \end{aligned} \tag{11}$$

Remark 2. *In Theorem 6, if we set $g = F$ and $h = 1$ or $h = F$ and $g = 1$, then inequality (11) becomes the inequality (1).*

After that, Ali et al. [24] and Xie et al. [25] used the (g,h)-convexity and established the following fractional Hermite–Hadamard-type inequality.

Theorem 7 ([24,25]). *Consider $F : I \to \mathbb{R}$ as a (g,h)-convex function on I with $g,h : I \to \mathbb{R}$. If $F \in L^1(I)$ and $g,h \in L^2(I)$, then*

$$\begin{aligned} & 2F\left(\frac{\sigma+\rho}{2}\right) - \frac{\Gamma(\alpha+1)}{2(\rho-\sigma)^\alpha}\left[J^\alpha_{\sigma+}\Omega(\rho) + J^\alpha_{\rho-}\Omega(\sigma)\right] \\ \le \; & \frac{\Gamma(\alpha+1)}{2(\rho-\sigma)^\alpha}\left[J^\alpha_{\sigma+}F(\rho) + J^\alpha_{\rho-}F(\sigma)\right] \\ \le \; & \frac{F(\sigma)+F(\rho)}{2}\left[\frac{\alpha}{\alpha+2} + \frac{2}{\alpha^2+3\alpha+2}\right] + \frac{\alpha}{\alpha^2+3\alpha+2}M(\sigma,\rho), \end{aligned} \tag{12}$$

$$\begin{aligned} & 2F\left(\frac{\sigma+\rho}{2}\right) - \frac{2^{\alpha-1}\Gamma(\alpha+1)}{(\rho-\sigma)^\alpha}\left[J^\alpha_{\sigma+}\Omega\left(\frac{\sigma+\rho}{2}\right) + J^\alpha_{\rho-}\Omega\left(\frac{\sigma+\rho}{2}\right)\right] \\ \le \; & \frac{2^{\alpha-1}\Gamma(\alpha+1)}{(\rho-\sigma)^\alpha}\left[J^\alpha_{\sigma+}F\left(\frac{\sigma+\rho}{2}\right) + J^\alpha_{\rho-}F\left(\frac{\sigma+\rho}{2}\right)\right] \\ \le \; & \frac{[F(\sigma)+F(\rho)](\alpha+1)}{2(\alpha+2)} + \frac{M(\sigma,\rho)}{2(\alpha+2)}, \end{aligned}$$

and

$$\begin{aligned} & 2F\left(\tfrac{\sigma+\rho}{2}\right) - \tfrac{2^{\alpha-1}\Gamma(\alpha+1)}{(\rho-\sigma)^\alpha}\left[J^\alpha_{\frac{\sigma+\rho}{2}+}\Omega(\rho) + J^\alpha_{\frac{\sigma+\rho}{2}-}\Omega(\sigma)\right] \\ \le \; & \tfrac{2^{\alpha-1}\Gamma(\alpha+1)}{(\rho-\sigma)^\alpha}\left[J^\alpha_{\frac{\sigma+\rho}{2}+}F(\rho) + J^\alpha_{\frac{\sigma+\rho}{2}-}F(\sigma)\right] \\ \le \; & \tfrac{[F(\sigma)+F(\rho)]}{4}\left[2 - \tfrac{\alpha(\alpha+3)}{(\alpha+1)(\alpha+2)}\right] + \tfrac{M(\sigma,\rho)\alpha(\alpha+3)}{4(\alpha+1)(\alpha+2)}, \end{aligned} \tag{13}$$

where $\Omega(\varkappa) = g(\varkappa)h(\sigma+\rho-\varkappa)$.

For more results on Simpson- and Ostrowski-type inequalities via (g,h)-convexity, one can consult [23–25].

Motivated by the above literature, we conduct an anlaysis on some new generalizations of Hermite–Hadamard and Ostrowski type inequalities via the co-ordinated convex functions by defining a new notion of co-ordinated (g,h)-convexity or convexity with respect to a pair of functions. It is also shown that the newly established inequalities and class of convex functions are generalizations of the existing results in the literature.

A description of the paper is as follows: in Section 2, the notion of co-ordinated (g,h)-convexity is introduced. We also prove some of its important properties and give an example of a co-ordinated (g,h)-convex function. In Section 3, we establish some

Hermite–Hadamard-type inequalities for co-ordinated (g,h)-convex functions. In Section 4, we derive some new Ostrowski-type inequalities under the differentiable (g,h)-convexity. The examples showing the consistency of newly discussed inequalities are in Section 5. Section 6 concludes our work briefly.

2. Co-Ordinated (g,h)-Convex Functions

In this section, we introduce a new concept of the co-ordinated (g,h)-convex function, and then some of its properties are proved. We also give an example of a co-ordinated (g,h)-convex function at the end of the section.

Definition 4. *Let $g,h:\triangle\to\mathbb{R}$ be two given functions. A function $F:\triangle\to\mathbb{R}$ is called co-ordinated (g,h)-convex, if*

$$\begin{aligned}F(\xi\varkappa+(1-\xi)z,\eta\gamma+(1-\eta)w) &\le \xi^2\eta^2F(\varkappa,\gamma)+\xi^2(1-\eta)^2F(\varkappa,w)\\&+(1-\xi)^2\eta^2F(z,\gamma)+(1-\xi)^2(1-\eta)^2F(z,w)+\xi^2\eta(1-\eta)M_1(\varkappa,\gamma,w)\\&+\xi\eta(1-\xi)(1-\eta)M_2(\varkappa,z,\gamma,w)+\xi\eta^2(1-\xi)M_3(\varkappa,z,\gamma)+\xi\eta(1-\xi)(1-\eta)M_4(\varkappa,z,\gamma,w)\\&+\xi(1-\xi)(1-\eta)^2M_5(\varkappa,z,w)+\eta(1-\xi)^2(1-\eta)M_6(z,\gamma,w),\end{aligned}$$

where

$$\begin{aligned}M_1(\varkappa,\gamma,w)&=h(\varkappa,w)g(\varkappa,\gamma)+h(\varkappa,\gamma)g(\varkappa,w),\\M_2(\varkappa,z,\gamma,w)&=h(\varkappa,w)g(z,\gamma)+h(z,\gamma)g(\varkappa,w),\\M_3(\varkappa,z,\gamma)&=h(\varkappa,\gamma)g(z,\gamma)+h(z,\gamma)g(\varkappa,\gamma),\\M_4(\varkappa,z,\gamma,w)&=h(\varkappa,\gamma)g(z,w)+h(z,w)g(\varkappa,\gamma),\\M_5(\varkappa,z,w)&=h(\varkappa,w)g(z,w)+h(z,w)g(\varkappa,w),\end{aligned}$$

and

$$M_6(z,\gamma,w)=h(z,\gamma)g(z,w)+h(z,w)g(z,\gamma),$$

for all $\xi,\eta\in[0,1]$, $\varkappa,z\in[\sigma,\rho]$ and $\gamma,w\in[\varsigma,d]$.

Some properties of co-ordinated (g,h)-convexity are proved as follows:

Proposition 1. *Let $g,h:\triangle\to\mathbb{R}$ be two given functions. Then, we have that*

(i) F is co-ordinated (g,h)-convex if F is co-ordinated (h,g)-convex.

(ii) If F is co-ordinated (g,h)-convex, then F is co-ordinated $(\sigma^{-1}g,\sigma h)$-convex for all $\sigma\in\mathbb{R}$, $\sigma\neq 0$.

(iii) If $F,\overline{F}$ are co-ordinated (g,h)-convex, in this case, $F+\overline{F}$ is co-ordinated $(2g,h)$-convex and co-ordinated $(g,2h)$-convex.

(iv) If F is co-ordinated (g,h)-convex, then σF is co-ordinated $(\sigma g,h)$-convex and co-ordinated $(g,\sigma h)$-convex for all $\sigma>0$.

(v) Let F be co-ordinated (g,h)-convex, $F\ge 0$ and $(g\ge 0,h\le 0)$ or $(g\le 0,h\ge 0)$. Then F is co-ordinated convex.

(vi) If F is co-ordinated (g,h)-convex and $\overline{F}$ are co-ordinated $(g,\overline{h})$-convex, then $F+\overline{F}$ is co-ordinated $(g,h+\overline{h})$-convex.

(vii) If F is co-ordinated (g,h)-convex and $\overline{F}$ are co-ordinated $(\overline{g},h)$-convex, then $F+\overline{F}$ is co-ordinated $(g+\overline{g},h)$-convex.

(viii) If F is co-ordinated (g,h)-convex, then

$$F\left(\frac{\varkappa+z}{2},\frac{\gamma+w}{2}\right)\leq\frac{F(\varkappa,\gamma)+F(\varkappa,w)+F(z,\gamma)+F(z,w)}{16}$$
$$+\frac{M_1(\varkappa,\gamma,w)+M_2(\varkappa,z,\gamma,w)+M_3(\varkappa,z,\gamma)+M_4(\varkappa,z,\gamma,w)+M_5(\varkappa,z,w)+M_6(z,\gamma,w)}{16},$$

for all $\varkappa, z \in [\sigma,\rho]$ *and* $\gamma, w \in [\varsigma, d]$.

Proof. (i) It is immediately true by Definition 4.
(ii) We simply consider that

$$h(\varkappa,w)g(\varkappa,\gamma)+h(\varkappa,\gamma)g(\varkappa,w)=(\sigma h(\varkappa,w))\left(\sigma^{-1}g(\varkappa,\gamma)\right)+(\sigma h(\varkappa,\gamma))\left(\sigma^{-1}g(\varkappa,w)\right),$$
$$h(\varkappa,w)g(z,\gamma)+h(z,\gamma)g(\varkappa,w)=(\sigma h(\varkappa,w))\left(\sigma^{-1}g(z,\gamma)\right)+(\sigma h(z,\gamma))\left(\sigma^{-1}g(\varkappa,w)\right),$$
$$h(\varkappa,\gamma)g(z,\gamma)+h(z,\gamma)g(\varkappa,\gamma)=(\sigma h(\varkappa,\gamma))\left(\sigma^{-1}g(z,\gamma)\right)+(\sigma h(z,\gamma))\left(\sigma^{-1}g(\varkappa,\gamma)\right),$$
$$h(\varkappa,\gamma)g(z,w)+h(z,w)g(\varkappa,\gamma)=(\sigma h(\varkappa,\gamma))\left(\sigma^{-1}g(z,w)\right)+(\sigma h(z,w))\left(\sigma^{-1}g(\varkappa,\gamma)\right),$$
$$h(\varkappa,w)g(z,w)+h(z,w)g(\varkappa,w)=(\sigma h(\varkappa,w))\left(\sigma^{-1}g(z,w)\right)+(\sigma h(z,w))\left(\sigma^{-1}g(\varkappa,w)\right),$$

and

$$h(z,\gamma)g(z,w)+h(z,w)g(z,\gamma)=(\sigma h(z,\gamma))\left(\sigma^{-1}g(z,w)\right)+(\sigma h(z,w))\left(\sigma^{-1}g(z,\gamma)\right).$$

(iii) Since $F, \overline{F}$ are co-ordinated (g,h)-convex, we have

$$\begin{aligned}F(\xi\varkappa &+(1-\xi)z,\eta\gamma+(1-\eta)w)\leq\xi^2\eta^2F(\varkappa,\gamma)+\xi^2(1-\eta)^2F(\varkappa,w)\\ &+(1-\xi)^2\eta^2F(z,\gamma)+(1-\xi)^2(1-\eta)^2F(z,w)\\ &+\xi^2\eta(1-\eta)M_1(\varkappa,\gamma,w)+\xi\eta(1-\xi)(1-\eta)M_2(\varkappa,z,\gamma,w)\\ &+\xi\eta^2(1-\xi)M_3(\varkappa,z,\gamma)+\xi\eta(1-\xi)(1-\eta)M_4(\varkappa,z,\gamma,w)\\ &+\xi(1-\xi)(1-\eta)^2M_5(\varkappa,z,w)+\eta(1-\xi)^2(1-\eta)M_6(z,\gamma,w),\end{aligned}\tag{14}$$

and

$$\begin{aligned}\overline{F}(\xi\varkappa &+(1-\xi)z,\eta\gamma+(1-\eta)w)\leq\xi^2\eta^2\overline{F}(\varkappa,\gamma)+\xi^2(1-\eta)^2\overline{F}(\varkappa,w)\\ &+(1-\xi)^2\eta^2\overline{F}(z,\gamma)+(1-\xi)^2(1-\eta)^2\overline{F}(z,w)\\ &+\xi^2\eta(1-\eta)M_1(\varkappa,\gamma,w)+\xi\eta(1-\xi)(1-\eta)M_2(\varkappa,z,\gamma,w)\\ &+\xi\eta^2(1-\xi)M_3(\varkappa,z,\gamma)+\xi\eta(1-\xi)(1-\eta)M_4(\varkappa,z,\gamma,w)\\ &+\xi(1-\xi)(1-\eta)^2M_5(\varkappa,z,w)+\eta(1-\xi)^2(1-\eta)M_6(z,\gamma,w),\end{aligned}\tag{15}$$

for all $\xi,\eta\in[0,1]$, $\varkappa,z\in[\sigma,\rho]$ and $\gamma,w\in[\varsigma,d]$. Adding (14) and (15), we obtain

$$\begin{aligned}(F+\overline{F})(\xi\varkappa+(1-\xi)z,\eta\gamma+(1-\eta)w)&\leq\xi^2\eta^2(F+\overline{F})(\varkappa,\gamma)+\xi^2(1-\eta)^2(F+\overline{F})(\varkappa,w)\\ &+(1-\xi)^2\eta^2(F+\overline{F})(z,\gamma)+(1-\xi)^2(1-\eta)^2(F+\overline{F})(z,w)\\ &+2\xi^2\eta(1-\eta)M_1(\varkappa,\gamma,w)+2\xi\eta(1-\xi)(1-\eta)M_2(\varkappa,z,\gamma,w)\\ &+2\xi\eta^2(1-\xi)M_3(\varkappa,z,\gamma)+2\xi\eta(1-\xi)(1-\eta)M_4(\varkappa,z,\gamma,w)\\ &+2\xi(1-\xi)(1-\eta)^2M_5(\varkappa,z,w)+2\eta(1-\xi)^2(1-\eta)M_6(z,\gamma,w),\end{aligned}$$

which means that $F + \overline{F}$ is co-ordinated $(2g, h)$-convex and co-ordinated $(g, 2h)$-convex.

(iv) Let F be co-ordinated (g, h)-convex. In this case, multiplying (14) by $\sigma \geq 0$ yields

$$\begin{aligned}(\sigma F)(\xi\varkappa + (1-\xi)z, \eta\gamma + (1-\eta)w) &\leq \xi^2\eta^2(\sigma F)(\varkappa,\gamma) + \xi^2(1-\eta)^2(\sigma F)(\varkappa, w)\\ &+ (1-\xi)^2\eta^2(\sigma F)(z,\gamma) + (1-\xi)^2(1-\eta)^2(\sigma F)(z,w)\\ &+ \xi^2\eta(1-\eta)\sigma M_1(\varkappa,\gamma,w) + \xi\eta(1-\xi)(1-\eta)\sigma M_2(\varkappa,z,\gamma,w)\\ &+ \xi\eta^2(1-\xi)\sigma M_3(\varkappa,z,\gamma) + \xi\eta(1-\xi)(1-\eta)\sigma M_4(\varkappa,z,\gamma,w)\\ &+ \xi(1-\xi)(1-\eta)^2\sigma M_5(\varkappa,z,w) + \eta(1-\xi)^2(1-\eta)\sigma M_6(z,\gamma,w),\end{aligned}$$

which shows that σF is co-ordinated $(\sigma g, h)$-convex and co-ordinated $(g, \sigma h)$-convex.

(v) Let $F \geq 0$ be co-ordinated (g, h)-convex, where $g \geq 0$ and $h \leq 0$. Then, for all $\xi, \eta \in [0,1]$, $\varkappa, z \in [\sigma, \rho]$ and $\gamma, w \in [\varsigma, d]$, we have

$$\begin{aligned}F(\xi\varkappa + (1-\xi)z, \eta\gamma + (1-\eta)w) &\leq \xi^2\eta^2F(\varkappa,\gamma) + \xi^2(1-\eta)^2F(\varkappa,w) + (1-\xi)^2\eta^2F(z,\gamma)\\ &+ (1-\xi)^2(1-\eta)^2F(z,w) + \xi^2\eta(1-\eta)M_1(\varkappa,\gamma,w)\\ &+ \xi\eta(1-\xi)(1-\eta)M_2(\varkappa,z,\gamma,w) + \xi\eta^2(1-\xi)M_3(\varkappa,z,\gamma)\\ &+ \xi\eta(1-\xi)(1-\eta)M_4(\varkappa,z,\gamma,w) + \xi(1-\xi)(1-\eta)^2M_5(\varkappa,z,w)\\ &+ \eta(1-\xi)^2(1-\eta)M_6(z,\gamma,w)\\ &\leq \xi\eta F(\varkappa,\gamma) + \xi(1-\eta)F(\varkappa,w) + (1-\xi)\eta F(z,\gamma) + (1-\xi)(1-\eta)F(z,w),\end{aligned}$$

which shows that F is co-ordinated convex. This holds similarly in the case of $g \leq 0$ and $h \geq 0$.

(vi) If F is co-ordinated (g, h)-convex and $\overline{F}$ are co-ordinated $(g, \overline{h})$-convex, we may write

$$\begin{aligned}F(\xi\varkappa &+ (1-\xi)z, \eta\gamma + (1-\eta)w) \leq \xi^2\eta^2F(\varkappa,\gamma) + \xi^2(1-\eta)^2F(\varkappa,w)\\ &+ (1-\xi)^2\eta^2F(z,\gamma) + (1-\xi)^2(1-\eta)^2F(z,w) + \xi^2\eta(1-\eta)M_1(\varkappa,\gamma,w)\\ &+ \xi\eta(1-\xi)(1-\eta)M_2(\varkappa,z,\gamma,w) + \xi\eta^2(1-\xi)M_3(\varkappa,z,\gamma)\\ &+ \xi\eta(1-\xi)(1-\eta)M_4(\varkappa,z,\gamma,w) + \xi(1-\xi)(1-\eta)^2M_5(\varkappa,z,w)\\ &+ \eta(1-\xi)^2(1-\eta)M_6(z,\gamma,w),\end{aligned} \tag{16}$$

and

$$\begin{aligned}\overline{F}(\xi\varkappa &+ (1-\xi)z, \eta\gamma + (1-\eta)w) \leq \xi^2\eta^2\overline{F}(\varkappa,\gamma) + \xi^2(1-\eta)^2\overline{F}(\varkappa,w)\\ &+ (1-\xi)^2\eta^2\overline{F}(z,\gamma) + (1-\xi)^2(1-\eta)^2\overline{F}(z,w) + \xi^2\eta(1-\eta)M_7(\varkappa,\gamma,w)\\ &+ \xi\eta(1-\xi)(1-\eta)M_8(\varkappa,z,\gamma,w) + \xi\eta^2(1-\xi)M_9(\varkappa,z,\gamma)\\ &+ \xi\eta(1-\xi)(1-\eta)M_{10}(\varkappa,z,\gamma,w) + \xi(1-\xi)(1-\eta)^2M_{11}(\varkappa,z,w)\\ &+ \eta(1-\xi)^2(1-\eta)M_{12}(z,\gamma,w),\end{aligned} \tag{17}$$

where

$$M_7(\varkappa,\gamma,w) = \overline{h}(\varkappa,w)g(\varkappa,\gamma) + \overline{h}(\varkappa,\gamma)g(\varkappa,w),$$

$$M_8(\varkappa,z,\gamma,w) = \overline{h}(\varkappa,w)g(z,\gamma) + \overline{h}(z,\gamma)g(\varkappa,w),$$

$$M_9(\varkappa,z,\gamma) = \overline{h}(\varkappa,\gamma)g(z,\gamma) + \overline{h}(z,\gamma)g(\varkappa,\gamma),$$

$$M_{10}(\varkappa,z,\gamma,w)=\overline{h}(\varkappa,\gamma)g(z,w)+\overline{h}(z,w)g(\varkappa,\gamma),$$

$$M_{11}(\varkappa,z,w)=\overline{h}(\varkappa,w)g(z,w)+\overline{h}(z,w)g(\varkappa,w),$$

and

$$M_{12}(z,\gamma,w)=\overline{h}(z,\gamma)g(z,w)+\overline{h}(z,w)g(z,\gamma),$$

for all $\xi,\eta\in[0,1]$, $\varkappa,z\in[\sigma,\rho]$ and $\gamma,w\in[\varsigma,d]$. Adding (16) and (17), we obtain that $F+\overline{F}$ is co-ordinated $(g,h+\overline{h})$-convex.

(vii) The proof is similar to that of (vi).

(viii) Taking $\xi=\eta=\frac{1}{2}$ in (14), the desired inequality is obtained.

□

Proposition 2. *Let $F:\triangle\to\mathbb{R}$ be a co-ordinated convex function. Then, F is co-ordinated $(F,1_{\mathbb{R}\times\mathbb{R}})$-convex.*

Proof. Let $\xi,\eta\in[0,1]$, $\varkappa,z\in[\sigma,\rho]$ and $\gamma,w\in[\varsigma,d]$. By the co-ordinated convexity of F, we write

$$\begin{aligned}
&F(\xi\varkappa+(1-\xi)z,\eta\gamma+(1-\eta)w)\\
&\leq \xi\eta F(\varkappa,\gamma)+\xi(1-\eta)F(\varkappa,v)+(1-\xi)\eta F(z,\gamma)+(1-\xi)(1-\eta)F(z,w)\\
&=\xi^2\eta^2F(\varkappa,\gamma)+\xi^2(1-\eta)^2F(\varkappa,w)+(1-\xi)^2\eta^2F(z,\gamma)+(1-\xi)^2(1-\eta)^2F(z,w)\\
&\quad+\xi^2\eta(1-\eta)(F(\varkappa,\gamma)+F(\varkappa,w))+\xi\eta(1-\xi)(1-\eta)(F(z,\gamma)+F(\varkappa,w))\\
&\quad+\xi\eta^2(1-\xi)(F(z,\gamma)+F(\varkappa,\gamma))+\xi\eta(1-\xi)(1-\eta)(F(z,w)+F(\varkappa,\gamma))\\
&\quad+\xi(1-\xi)(1-\eta)^2(F(z,w)+F(\varkappa,w))+\eta(1-\xi)^2(1-\eta)(F(z,w)+F(z,\gamma))\\
&=\xi^2\eta^2F(\varkappa,\gamma)+\xi^2(1-\eta)^2F(\varkappa,w)+(1-\xi)^2\eta^2F(z,\gamma)+(1-\xi)^2(1-\eta)^2F(z,w)\\
&\quad+\xi^2\eta(1-\eta)(1_{\mathbb{R}\times\mathbb{R}}(\varkappa,w)F(\varkappa,\gamma)+1_{\mathbb{R}\times\mathbb{R}}(\varkappa,\gamma)F(\varkappa,w))\\
&\quad+\xi\eta(1-\xi)(1-\eta)(1_{\mathbb{R}\times\mathbb{R}}(\varkappa,w)F(z,\gamma)+1_{\mathbb{R}\times\mathbb{R}}(z,\gamma)F(\varkappa,w))\\
&\quad+\xi\eta^2(1-\xi)(1_{\mathbb{R}\times\mathbb{R}}(\varkappa,\gamma)F(z,\gamma)+1_{\mathbb{R}\times\mathbb{R}}(z,\gamma)F(\varkappa,\gamma))\\
&\quad+\xi\eta(1-\xi)(1-\eta)(1_{\mathbb{R}\times\mathbb{R}}(\varkappa,\gamma)F(z,w)+1_{\mathbb{R}\times\mathbb{R}}(z,w)F(\varkappa,\gamma))\\
&\quad+\xi(1-\xi)(1-\eta)^2(1_{\mathbb{R}\times\mathbb{R}}(\varkappa,w)F(z,w)+1_{\mathbb{R}\times\mathbb{R}}(z,w)F(\varkappa,w))\\
&\quad+\eta(1-\xi)^2(1-\eta)(1_{\mathbb{R}\times\mathbb{R}}(z,\gamma)F(z,w)+1_{\mathbb{R}\times\mathbb{R}}(z,w)F(z,\gamma)),
\end{aligned}$$

which proves that F is co-ordinated $(F,1_{\mathbb{R}\times\mathbb{R}})$-convex. □

Proposition 3. *Let $g,h:\triangle\to\mathbb{R}$ be two co-ordinated convex functions. Then, $F=gh$ is co-ordinated (g,h)-convex.*

Proof. Let $\xi,\eta\in[0,1]$, $\varkappa,z\in[\sigma,\rho]$ and $\gamma,w\in[\varsigma,d]$. Since $g,h:\triangle\to\mathbb{R}$ are two functions with the co-ordinated convexity property, we have

$$\begin{aligned}
&F(\xi\varkappa+(1-\xi)z,\eta\gamma+(1-\eta)w)\\
&\quad=g(\xi\varkappa+(1-\xi)z,\eta\gamma+(1-\eta)w)h(\xi\varkappa+(1-\xi)z,\eta\gamma+(1-\eta)w)\\
&\quad\leq[\xi\eta g(\varkappa,\gamma)+\xi(1-\eta)g(\varkappa,w)+(1-\xi)\eta g(z,\gamma)+(1-\xi)(1-\eta)g(z,w)]
\end{aligned}$$

$$\times [\xi\eta h(\varkappa,\gamma) + \xi(1-\eta)h(\varkappa,w) + (1-\xi)\eta h(z,\gamma) + (1-\xi)(1-\eta)h(z,w)]$$
$$= \xi^2\eta^2 F(\varkappa,\gamma) + \xi^2(1-\eta)^2 F(\varkappa,w) + (1-\xi)^2\eta^2 F(z,\gamma) + (1-\xi)^2(1-\eta)^2 F(z,w)$$
$$+ \xi^2\eta(1-\eta)M_1(\varkappa,\gamma,w) + \xi\eta(1-\xi)(1-\eta)M_2(\varkappa,z,\gamma,w) + \xi\eta^2(1-\xi)M_3(\varkappa,z,\gamma)$$
$$+ \xi\eta(1-\xi)(1-\eta)M_4(\varkappa,z,\gamma,w) + \xi(1-\xi)(1-\eta)^2 M_5(\varkappa,z,w)$$
$$+ \eta(1-\xi)^2(1-\eta)M_6(z,\gamma,w).$$

This gurantees that F is co-ordinated (g,h)-convex. □

Example 1. *Let $F : [0,1]^2 \to \mathbb{R}$ be a function as*

$$F(\varkappa,\gamma) = \varkappa\gamma\, e^{-\varkappa-\gamma}.$$

Consider the functions $g,h : [0,1]\times[0,1] \to \mathbb{R}$ defined by

$$g(\varkappa,\gamma) = \varkappa\gamma,$$

and

$$h(\varkappa,\gamma) = e^{-\varkappa-\gamma}.$$

Since g,h are non-negative co-ordinated convex functions, by Proposition 3, $F = gh$ is a co-ordinated (g,h)-convex function.

3. Hermite–Hadamard-Type Inequalities

Now, we here derive some new Hermite–Hadamard-type inequalities for co-ordinated (g,h)-convex functions. We also show that our results can be reduced to previous work.

Theorem 8. *Let $F : \triangle \to \mathbb{R}$ be a function with the co-ordinated (g,h)-convexity on $\triangle$. If $F \in L^1(\triangle)$ and $g,h \in L^2(\triangle)$, then the following Hermite–Hadamard-type inequalities are formulated as*

$$\begin{aligned}
&4F\left(\tfrac{\sigma+\rho}{2},\tfrac{\varsigma+d}{2}\right) - \tfrac{1}{(\rho-\sigma)(d-\varsigma)}\int_\sigma^\rho\int_\varsigma^d h(\varkappa,\gamma)[g(\varkappa,\varsigma+d-\gamma) + g(\sigma+\rho-\varkappa,\gamma)\\
&\quad + g(\sigma+\rho-\varkappa,\varsigma+d-\gamma)]\,d\gamma\,d\varkappa\\
&\le \tfrac{1}{(\rho-\sigma)(d-\varsigma)}\int_\sigma^\rho\int_\varsigma^d F(\varkappa,\gamma)\,d\gamma\,d\varkappa\\
&\le \tfrac{1}{9}\Big[F(\sigma,\varsigma) + F(\sigma,d) + F(\rho,\varsigma) + F(\rho,d) + \tfrac{K(\sigma,\varsigma,d)+P(\rho,\varsigma,d)+M(\sigma,\rho,\varsigma)+O(\sigma,\rho,d)}{2}\\
&\quad + \tfrac{L(\sigma,\rho,\varsigma,d)+N(\sigma,\rho,\varsigma,d)}{4}\Big],
\end{aligned} \tag{18}$$

where

$$K(\sigma,\varsigma,d) = h(\sigma,d)g(\sigma,\varsigma) + h(\sigma,\varsigma)g(\sigma,d),$$
$$L(\sigma,\rho,\varsigma,d) = h(\sigma,d)g(\rho,\varsigma) + h(\rho,\varsigma)g(\sigma,d),$$
$$M(\sigma,\rho,\varsigma) = h(\sigma,\varsigma)g(\rho,\varsigma) + h(\rho,\varsigma)g(\sigma,\varsigma),$$
$$N(\sigma,\rho,\varsigma,d) = h(\sigma,\varsigma)g(\rho,d) + h(\rho,d)g(\sigma,\varsigma),$$
$$O(\sigma,\rho,d) = h(\sigma,d)g(\rho,d) + h(\rho,d)g(\sigma,d),$$

and

$$P(\rho,\varsigma,d) = h(\rho,\varsigma)g(\rho,d) + h(\rho,d)g(\rho,\varsigma).$$

Proof. Let

$$u_1(\xi) = \xi\sigma + (1-\xi)\rho, \quad u_2(\xi) = (1-\xi)\sigma + \xi\rho,$$
$$v_1(\eta) = \eta\varsigma + (1-\eta)d, \quad v_2(\eta) = (1-\eta)\varsigma + \eta d,$$

for $\xi, \eta \in [0,1]$.

By the co-ordinated (g,h)-convexity of F on $[\sigma,\rho] \times [\varsigma, d]$, we have

$$\begin{aligned} 16F\left(\tfrac{\sigma+\rho}{2}, \tfrac{\varsigma+d}{2}\right) &= 16F\left(\tfrac{u_1(\xi)+u_2(\xi)}{2}, \tfrac{v_1(\eta)+v_2(\eta)}{2}\right) \\ &\le F(u_1(\xi),v_1(\eta)) + F(u_1(\xi),v_2(\eta)) + F(u_2(\xi),v_1(\eta)) + F(u_2(\xi),v_2(\eta)) \\ &\quad + M_1(u_1(\xi),v_1(\eta),v_2(\eta)) + M_2(u_1(\xi),u_2(\xi),v_1(\eta),v_2(\eta)) + M_3(u_1(\xi),u_2(\xi),v_1(\eta)) \\ &\quad + M_4(u_1(\xi),u_2(\xi),v_1(\eta),v_2(\eta)) + M_5(u_1(\xi),u_2(\xi),v_2(\eta)) + M_6(u_2(\xi),v_1(\eta),v_2(\eta)). \end{aligned} \tag{19}$$

Integrating both sides of (19) over $[0,1] \times [0,1]$ with respect to ξ and η, we obtain

$$\begin{aligned} 16F\left(\tfrac{\sigma+\rho}{2}, \tfrac{\varsigma+d}{2}\right) &\le \int_0^1\int_0^1 F(u_1(\xi),v_1(\eta)) + F(u_1(\xi),v_2(\eta)) + F(u_2(\xi),v_1(\eta)) \\ &\quad + F(u_2(\xi),v_2(\eta)) + M_1(u_1(\xi),v_1(\eta),v_2(\eta)) + M_2(u_1(\xi),u_2(\xi),v_1(\eta),v_2(\eta)) \\ &\quad + M_3(u_1(\xi),u_2(\xi),v_1(\eta)) + M_4(u_1(\xi),u_2(\xi),v_1(\eta),v_2(\eta)) \\ &\quad + M_5(u_1(\xi),u_2(\xi),v_2(\eta)) + M_6(u_2(\xi),v_1(\eta),v_2(\eta))\, d\eta\, d\xi. \end{aligned} \tag{20}$$

We consider

$$\begin{aligned} \int_0^1\int_0^1 F(u_1(\xi),v_1(\eta))\, d\eta\, d\xi &= \int_0^1\int_0^1 F(\xi\sigma+(1-\xi)\rho, \eta\varsigma+(1-\eta)d)\, d\eta\, d\xi \\ &= \frac{1}{(\rho-\sigma)(d-\varsigma)}\int_\sigma^\rho\int_\varsigma^d F(\varkappa,\gamma)\, d\gamma\, d\varkappa \\ &= \int_0^1\int_0^1 F(u_1(\xi),v_2(\eta))\, d\eta\, d\xi \\ &= \int_0^1\int_0^1 F(u_2(\xi),v_1(\eta))\, d\eta\, d\xi \\ &= \int_0^1\int_0^1 F(u_2(\xi),v_2(\eta))\, d\eta\, d\xi. \end{aligned}$$

Moreover, we have

$$\begin{aligned} \int_0^1\int_0^1 M_1(u_1(\xi),v_1(\eta),v_2(\eta))\, d\eta\, d\xi &= \int_0^1\int_0^1 h(u_1(\xi),v_2(\eta))g(u_1(\xi),v_1(\eta))\, d\eta\, d\xi \\ &\quad + \int_0^1\int_0^1 h(u_1(\xi),v_1(\eta))g(u_1(\xi),v_2(\eta))\, d\eta\, d\xi \\ &= \int_0^1\int_0^1 h(\xi\sigma+(1-\xi)\rho,(1-\eta)\varsigma+\eta d)g(\xi\sigma+(1-\xi)\rho,\eta\varsigma+(1-\eta)d)\, d\eta\, d\xi \\ &\quad + \int_0^1\int_0^1 h(\xi\sigma+(1-\xi)\rho,\eta\varsigma+(1-\eta)d)g(\xi\sigma+(1-\xi)\rho,(1-\eta)\varsigma+\eta d)\, d\eta\, d\xi \\ &= \frac{2}{(\rho-\sigma)(d-\varsigma)}\int_\sigma^\rho\int_\varsigma^d h(\varkappa,\gamma)g(\varkappa,\varsigma+d-\gamma)\, d\gamma\, d\varkappa. \end{aligned}$$

Similarly, we get

$$\int_0^1\int_0^1 M_2(u_1(\xi),u_2(\xi),v_1(\eta),v_2(\eta))\,d\eta\,d\xi = \frac{2}{(\rho-\sigma)(d-\varsigma)}\int_\sigma^\rho\int_\varsigma^d h(\varkappa,\gamma)g(\sigma+\rho-\varkappa,\varsigma+d-\gamma)\,d\gamma\,d\varkappa,$$

$$\int_0^1\int_0^1 M_3(u_1(\xi),u_2(\xi),v_1(\eta))\,d\eta\,d\xi = \frac{2}{(\rho-\sigma)(d-\varsigma)}\int_\sigma^\rho\int_\varsigma^d h(\varkappa,\gamma)g(\sigma+\rho-\varkappa,\varsigma+d-\gamma)\,d\gamma\,d\varkappa,$$

$$\int_0^1\int_0^1 M_4(u_1(\xi),u_2(\xi),v_1(\eta),v_2(\eta))\,d\eta\,d\xi = \frac{2}{(\rho-\sigma)(d-\varsigma)}\int_\sigma^\rho\int_\varsigma^d h(\varkappa,\gamma)g(\sigma+\rho-\varkappa,\varsigma+d-\gamma)\,d\gamma\,d\varkappa,$$

$$\int_0^1\int_0^1 M_5(u_1(\xi),u_2(\xi),v_2(\eta))\,d\eta\,d\xi = \frac{2}{(\rho-\sigma)(d-\varsigma)}\int_\sigma^\rho\int_\varsigma^d h(\varkappa,\gamma)g(\sigma+\rho-\varkappa,\gamma)\,d\gamma\,d\varkappa,$$

and

$$\int_0^1\int_0^1 M_5(u_2(\xi),v_1(\eta),v_2(\eta))\,d\eta\,d\xi = \frac{2}{(\rho-\sigma)(d-\varsigma)}\int_\sigma^\rho\int_\varsigma^d h(\varkappa,\gamma)g(\varkappa,\varsigma+d-\gamma)\,d\gamma\,d\varkappa.$$

Thus, (20) becomes

$$\begin{aligned}4F\left(\frac{\sigma+\rho}{2},\frac{\varsigma+d}{2}\right) &\le \frac{1}{(\rho-\sigma)(d-\varsigma)}\int_\sigma^\rho\int_\varsigma^d F(\varkappa,\gamma)\,d\gamma\,d\varkappa\\ &+\frac{1}{(\rho-\sigma)(d-\varsigma)}\int_\sigma^\rho\int_\varsigma^d h(\varkappa,\gamma)[g(\varkappa,\varsigma+d-\gamma)\\ &+g(\sigma+\rho-\varkappa,\gamma)+g(\sigma+\rho-\varkappa,\varsigma+d-\gamma)]\,d\gamma\,d\varkappa.\end{aligned}$$

Therefore, the first inequality of (18) is proven.

Since F is co-ordinated (g,h)-convex on $[\sigma,\rho]\times[\varsigma,d]$, we have

$$\begin{aligned}&F(\xi\sigma+(1-\xi)\rho,\eta\varsigma+(1-\eta)d)\\ &\le \xi^2\eta^2F(\sigma,\varsigma)+\xi^2(1-\eta)^2F(\sigma,d)+(1-\xi)^2\eta^2F(\rho,\varsigma)+(1-\xi)^2(1-\eta)^2F(\rho,d)\\ &\quad+\xi^2\eta(1-\eta)M_1(\sigma,\varsigma,d)+\xi\eta(1-\xi)(1-\eta)M_2(\sigma,\rho,\varsigma,d)+\xi\eta^2(1-\xi)M_3(\sigma,\rho,\varsigma)\\ &\quad+\xi\eta(1-\xi)(1-\eta)M_4(\sigma,\rho,\varsigma,d)+\xi(1-\xi)(1-\eta)^2M_5(\sigma,\rho,d)+\eta(1-\xi)^2(1-\eta)M_6(\rho,\varsigma,d)\\ &= \xi^2\eta^2F(\sigma,\varsigma)+\xi^2(1-\eta)^2F(\sigma,d)+(1-\xi)^2\eta^2F(\rho,\varsigma)+(1-\xi)^2(1-\eta)^2F(\rho,d)\\ &\quad+\xi^2\eta(1-\eta)K(\sigma,\varsigma,d)+\xi\eta(1-\xi)(1-\eta)L(\sigma,\rho,\varsigma,d)+\xi\eta^2(1-\xi)M(\sigma,\rho,\varsigma)\\ &\quad+\xi\eta(1-\xi)(1-\eta)N(\sigma,\rho,\varsigma,d)+\xi(1-\xi)(1-\eta)^2O(\sigma,\rho,d)+\eta(1-\xi)^2(1-\eta)P(\rho,\varsigma,d),\end{aligned} \tag{21}$$

$$\begin{aligned}&F(\xi\sigma+(1-\xi)\rho,(1-\eta)\varsigma+\eta d)\\ &\le \xi^2\eta^2F(\sigma,d)+\xi^2(1-\eta)^2F(\sigma,\varsigma)+(1-\xi)^2\eta^2F(\rho,d)+(1-\xi)^2(1-\eta)^2F(\rho,\varsigma)\\ &\quad+\xi^2\eta(1-\eta)M_1(\sigma,d,\varsigma)+\xi\eta(1-\xi)(1-\eta)M_2(\sigma,\rho,d,\varsigma)+\xi\eta^2(1-\xi)M_3(\sigma,\rho,d)\\ &\quad+\xi\eta(1-\xi)(1-\eta)M_4(\sigma,\rho,d,\varsigma)+\xi(1-\xi)(1-\eta)^2M_5(\sigma,\rho,\varsigma)+\eta(1-\xi)^2(1-\eta)M_6(\rho,d,\varsigma)\\ &= \xi^2\eta^2F(\sigma,d)+\xi^2(1-\eta)^2F(\sigma,\varsigma)+(1-\xi)^2\eta^2F(\rho,d)+(1-\xi)^2(1-\eta)^2F(\rho,\varsigma)\\ &\quad+\xi^2\eta(1-\eta)K(\sigma,\varsigma,d)+\xi\eta(1-\xi)(1-\eta)N(\sigma,\rho,\varsigma,d)+\xi\eta^2(1-\xi)O(\sigma,\rho,d)\\ &\quad+\xi\eta(1-\xi)(1-\eta)L(\sigma,\rho,\varsigma,d)+\xi(1-\xi)(1-\eta)^2M(\sigma,\rho,\varsigma)+\eta(1-\xi)^2(1-\eta)P(\rho,\varsigma,d),\end{aligned} \tag{22}$$

$$
\begin{aligned}
&F((1-\xi)\sigma+\xi\rho,\eta\varsigma+(1-\eta)d)\\
&\leq \xi^2\eta^2F(\rho,\varsigma)+\xi^2(1-\eta)^2F(\rho,d)+(1-\xi)^2\eta^2F(\sigma,\varsigma)+(1-\xi)^2(1-\eta)^2F(\sigma,d)\\
&\quad+\xi^2\eta(1-\eta)M_1(\rho,\varsigma,d)+\xi\eta(1-\xi)(1-\eta)M_2(\rho,\sigma,\varsigma,d)+\xi\eta^2(1-\xi)M_3(\rho,\sigma,\varsigma)\\
&\quad+\xi\eta(1-\xi)(1-\eta)M_4(\rho,\sigma,\varsigma,d)+\xi(1-\xi)(1-\eta)^2M_5(\rho,\sigma,d)+\eta(1-\xi)^2(1-\eta)M_6(\sigma,\varsigma,d)\\
&=\xi^2\eta^2F(\rho,\varsigma)+\xi^2(1-\eta)^2F(\rho,d)+(1-\xi)^2\eta^2F(\sigma,\varsigma)+(1-\xi)^2(1-\eta)^2F(\sigma,d)\\
&\quad+\xi^2\eta(1-\eta)P(\rho,\varsigma,d)+\xi\eta(1-\xi)(1-\eta)N(\sigma,\rho,\varsigma,d)+\xi\eta^2(1-\xi)M(\sigma,\rho,\varsigma)\\
&\quad+\xi\eta(1-\xi)(1-\eta)L(\sigma,\rho,\varsigma,d)+\xi(1-\xi)(1-\eta)^2O(\sigma,\rho,d)+\eta(1-\xi)^2(1-\eta)K(\sigma,\varsigma,d),
\end{aligned}
\tag{23}
$$

and

$$
\begin{aligned}
&F((1-\xi)\sigma+\xi\rho,(1-\eta)\varsigma+\eta d)\\
&\leq \xi^2\eta^2F(\rho,d)+\xi^2(1-\eta)^2F(\rho,\varsigma)+(1-\xi)^2\eta^2F(\sigma,d)+(1-\xi)^2(1-\eta)^2F(\sigma,\varsigma)\\
&\quad+\xi^2\eta(1-\eta)M_1(\rho,d,\varsigma)+\xi\eta(1-\xi)(1-\eta)M_2(\rho,\sigma,d,\varsigma)+\xi\eta^2(1-\xi)M_3(\rho,\sigma,d)\\
&\quad+\xi\eta(1-\xi)(1-\eta)M_4(\rho,\sigma,d,\varsigma)+\xi(1-\xi)(1-\eta)^2M_5(\rho,\sigma,\varsigma)+\eta(1-\xi)^2(1-\eta)M_6(\sigma,d,\varsigma)\\
&=\xi^2\eta^2F(\rho,d)+\xi^2(1-\eta)^2F(\rho,\varsigma)+(1-\xi)^2\eta^2F(\sigma,d)+(1-\xi)^2(1-\eta)^2F(\sigma,\varsigma)\\
&\quad+\xi^2\eta(1-\eta)P(\rho,\varsigma,d)+\xi\eta(1-\xi)(1-\eta)L(\sigma,\rho,\varsigma,d)+\xi\eta^2(1-\xi)O(\sigma,\rho,d)\\
&\quad+\xi\eta(1-\xi)(1-\eta)N(\sigma,\rho,\varsigma,d)+\xi(1-\xi)(1-\eta)^2M(\sigma,\rho,\varsigma)+\eta(1-\xi)^2(1-\eta)K(\sigma,\varsigma,d).
\end{aligned}
\tag{24}
$$

Combining (21)–(24), we get

$$
\begin{aligned}
&F(\xi\sigma+(1-\xi)\rho,\eta\varsigma+(1-\eta)d)+F(\xi\sigma+(1-\xi)\rho,(1-\eta)\varsigma+\eta d)\\
&\quad+F((1-\xi)\sigma+\xi\rho,\eta\varsigma+(1-\eta)d)+F((1-\xi)\sigma+\xi\rho,(1-\eta)\varsigma+\eta d)\\
&\leq(1-2\xi+2\xi^2)(1-2\eta+2\eta^2)[F(\sigma,\varsigma)+F(\sigma,d)+F(\rho,\varsigma)+F(\rho,d)]\\
&\quad+2\eta(1-\eta)(1-2\xi+2\xi^2)[K(\sigma,\varsigma,d)+P(\rho,\varsigma,d)]\\
&\quad+2\xi(1-\xi)(1-2\eta+2\eta^2)[M(\sigma,\rho,\varsigma)+O(\sigma,\rho,d)]\\
&\quad+4\xi\eta(1-\xi)(1-\eta)[K(\sigma,\varsigma,d)+P(\rho,\varsigma,d)].
\end{aligned}
\tag{25}
$$

Integrating both sides of (25) over $[0,1]\times[0,1]$ with respect to ξ and η, we obtain

$$
\begin{aligned}
\frac{4}{(\rho-\sigma)(d-\varsigma)}\int_\sigma^\rho\int_\varsigma^d F(\varkappa,\gamma)\,d\gamma\,d\varkappa &= \int_0^1\int_0^1 F(\xi\sigma+(1-\xi)\rho,\eta\varsigma+(1-\eta)d)\,d\eta\,d\xi\\
&\quad+\int_0^1\int_0^1 F(\xi\sigma+(1-\xi)\rho,(1-\eta)\varsigma+\eta d)\,d\eta\,d\xi\\
&\quad+\int_0^1\int_0^1 F((1-\xi)\sigma+\xi\rho,\eta\varsigma+(1-\eta)d)\,d\eta\,d\xi\\
&\quad+\int_0^1\int_0^1 F((1-\xi)\sigma+\xi\rho,(1-\eta)\varsigma+\eta d)\,d\eta\,d\xi\\
&\leq[F(\sigma,\varsigma)+F(\sigma,d)+F(\rho,\varsigma)+F(\rho,d)]\\
&\quad\times\int_0^1\int_0^1(1-2\xi+2\xi^2)(1-2\eta+2\eta^2)\,d\eta\,d\xi\\
&\quad+[K(\sigma,\varsigma,d)+P(\rho,\varsigma,d)]\int_0^1\int_0^1 2\eta(1-\eta)(1-2\xi+2\xi^2)\,d\eta\,d\xi
\end{aligned}
$$

$$+ [M(\sigma,\rho,\varsigma) + O(\sigma,\rho,d)] \int_0^1 \int_0^1 2\xi(1-\xi)(1-2\eta+2\eta^2)\, d\eta\, d\xi$$

$$+ [K(\sigma,\varsigma,d) + P(\rho,\varsigma,d)] \int_0^1 \int_0^1 4\xi\eta(1-\xi)(1-\eta)\, d\eta\, d\xi$$

$$= \frac{4}{9}\big[F(\sigma,\varsigma) + F(\sigma,d) + F(\rho,\varsigma) + F(\rho,d)\big] + \frac{2}{9}\big[K(\sigma,\varsigma,d) + P(\rho,\varsigma,d)$$

$$+ M(\sigma,\rho,\varsigma) + O(\sigma,\rho,d)\big] + \frac{1}{9}\big[K(\sigma,\varsigma,d) + P(\rho,\varsigma,d)\big].$$

Multiplying the above inequality by $\frac{1}{4}$, the second inequality of (18) is derived. □

Remark 3. *If we consider $h(\varkappa,\gamma) = F(\varkappa,\gamma)$ and $g(\varkappa,\gamma) = 1$, then the inequalities* (18) *reduces to the inequalities*

$$F\left(\frac{\sigma+\rho}{2}, \frac{\varsigma+d}{2}\right) \le \frac{1}{(\rho-\sigma)(d-\varsigma)} \int_\sigma^\rho \int_\varsigma^d F(\varkappa,\gamma)\, d\gamma\, d\varkappa \le \frac{F(\sigma,\varsigma) + F(\sigma,d) + F(\rho,\varsigma) + F(\rho,d)}{4}.$$

This inequality is presented in Theorem 2.

4. Ostrowski-Type Inequalities

In this position, we derive some new Ostrowski-type inequalities for (g,h)-convex functions. To establish the inequalities of the current section, we receive help from a lemma.

Lemma 1 ([22]). *Let $F : \triangle \to \mathbb{R}$ be a twice-partial differentiable function on $\triangle^\circ$. If $\frac{\partial^2}{\partial\xi\,\partial\eta} \in L(\triangle)$, then*

$$\begin{aligned} F(\varkappa,\gamma) &+ \tfrac{1}{(\rho-\sigma)(d-\varsigma)} \int_\sigma^\rho \int_\varsigma^d F(u,v)\, dv\, du - A \\ &= \tfrac{(\varkappa-\sigma)^2(\gamma-\varsigma)^2}{(\rho-\sigma)(d-\varsigma)} \int_0^1 \int_0^1 \xi\eta\, \frac{\partial^2}{\partial\xi\,\partial\eta} F(\xi\varkappa + (1-\xi)\sigma, \eta\gamma + (1-\eta)\varsigma)\, d\eta\, d\xi \\ &- \tfrac{(\varkappa-\sigma)^2(d-\gamma)^2}{(\rho-\sigma)(d-\varsigma)} \int_0^1 \int_0^1 \xi\eta\, \frac{\partial^2}{\partial\xi\,\partial\eta} F(\xi\varkappa + (1-\xi)\sigma, \eta\gamma + (1-\eta)d)\, d\eta\, d\xi \\ &- \tfrac{(\rho-\varkappa)^2(\gamma-\varsigma)^2}{(\rho-\sigma)(d-\varsigma)} \int_0^1 \int_0^1 \xi\eta\, \frac{\partial^2}{\partial\xi\,\partial\eta} F(\xi\varkappa + (1-\xi)\rho, \eta\gamma + (1-\eta)\varsigma)\, d\eta\, d\xi \\ &+ \tfrac{(\rho-\varkappa)^2(d-\gamma)^2}{(\rho-\sigma)(d-\varsigma)} \int_0^1 \int_0^1 \xi\eta\, \frac{\partial^2}{\partial\xi\,\partial\eta} F(\xi\varkappa + (1-\xi)\rho, \eta\gamma + (1-\eta)d)\, d\eta\, d\xi, \end{aligned} \tag{26}$$

for all $(\varkappa,\gamma) \in \triangle$, where A is defined in (7).

Theorem 9. *Under the assumptions of Lemma 1, if $\left|\frac{\partial^2 F}{\partial\xi\,\partial\eta}\right|$ is co-ordinated (g,h)-convex on $\triangle$, then*

$$\begin{aligned} &\left|F(\varkappa,\gamma) + \tfrac{1}{(\rho-\sigma)(d-\varsigma)} \int_\sigma^\rho \int_\varsigma^d F(u,v)\, dv\, du - A\right| \le \tfrac{1}{144(\rho-\sigma)(d-\varsigma)} \\ &\times\Big\{(\varkappa-\sigma)^2(\gamma-\varsigma)^2\Big[9\left|\frac{\partial^2}{\partial\xi\,\partial\eta}F(\varkappa,\gamma)\right| + 3\left|\frac{\partial^2}{\partial\xi\,\partial\eta}F(\varkappa,\varsigma)\right| + 3\left|\frac{\partial^2}{\partial\xi\,\partial\eta}F(\sigma,\gamma)\right| + \left|\frac{\partial^2}{\partial\xi\,\partial\eta}F(\sigma,\varsigma)\right| \\ &+ 3K(\varkappa,\gamma,\varsigma) + L(\varkappa,\sigma,\gamma,\varsigma) + 3M(\varkappa,\sigma,\gamma) + N(\varkappa,\sigma,\gamma,\varsigma) + O(\varkappa,\sigma,\varsigma) + P(\sigma,\gamma,\varsigma)\Big] \\ &+ (\varkappa-\sigma)^2(d-\gamma)^2\Big[9\left|\frac{\partial^2}{\partial\xi\,\partial\eta}F(\varkappa,\gamma)\right| + 3\left|\frac{\partial^2}{\partial\xi\,\partial\eta}F(\varkappa,d)\right| + 3\left|\frac{\partial^2}{\partial\xi\,\partial\eta}F(\sigma,\gamma)\right| + \left|\frac{\partial^2}{\partial\xi\,\partial\eta}F(\sigma,d)\right| \end{aligned} \tag{27}$$

$$+3K(\varkappa,\gamma,d)+L(\varkappa,\sigma,\gamma,d)+3M(\varkappa,\sigma,\gamma)+N(\varkappa,\sigma,\gamma,d)+O(\varkappa,\sigma,d)+P(\sigma,\gamma,d)]$$

$$+(\rho-\varkappa)^2(\gamma-\varsigma)^2\Big[9\left|\frac{\partial^2}{\partial\xi\,\partial\eta}F(\varkappa,\gamma)\right|+3\left|\frac{\partial^2}{\partial\xi\,\partial\eta}F(\varkappa,\varsigma)\right|+3\left|\frac{\partial^2}{\partial\xi\,\partial\eta}F(\rho,\gamma)\right|+\left|\frac{\partial^2}{\partial\xi\,\partial\eta}F(\rho,\varsigma)\right|$$
$$+3K(\varkappa,\gamma,\varsigma)+L(\varkappa,\rho,\gamma,\varsigma)+3M(\varkappa,\rho,\gamma)+N(\varkappa,\rho,\gamma,\varsigma)+O(\varkappa,\rho,\varsigma)+P(\rho,\gamma,\varsigma)]$$

$$+(\rho-\varkappa)^2(d-\gamma)^2\Big[9\left|\frac{\partial^2}{\partial\xi\,\partial\eta}F(\varkappa,\gamma)\right|+3\left|\frac{\partial^2}{\partial\xi\,\partial\eta}F(\varkappa,d)\right|+3\left|\frac{\partial^2}{\partial\xi\,\partial\eta}F(\rho,\gamma)\right|+\left|\frac{\partial^2}{\partial\xi\,\partial\eta}F(\rho,d)\right|$$
$$+3K(\varkappa,\gamma,d)+L(\varkappa,\rho,\gamma,\varsigma)+3M(\varkappa,\rho,\gamma)+N(\varkappa,\rho,\gamma,d)+O(\varkappa,\rho,d)+P(\rho,\gamma,d)]\},$$

where A is defined as in (7), and K, L, M, N, O, P are defined as in Theorem 8.

Proof. The conclusion of Lemma 1 yields

$$\begin{aligned}
&\left|F(\varkappa,\gamma)+\tfrac{1}{(\rho-\sigma)(d-\varsigma)}\int_\sigma^\rho\int_\varsigma^d F(u,v)\,dv\,du-A\right|\\
&\le \tfrac{(\varkappa-\sigma)^2(\gamma-\varsigma)^2}{(\rho-\sigma)(d-\varsigma)}\int_0^1\int_0^1\xi\eta\left|\frac{\partial^2}{\partial\xi\,\partial\eta}F(\xi\varkappa+(1-\xi)\sigma,\eta\gamma+(1-\eta)\varsigma)\right|d\eta\,d\xi\\
&+\tfrac{(\varkappa-\sigma)^2(d-\gamma)^2}{(\rho-\sigma)(d-\varsigma)}\int_0^1\int_0^1\xi\eta\left|\frac{\partial^2}{\partial\xi\,\partial\eta}F(\xi\varkappa+(1-\xi)\sigma,\eta\gamma+(1-\eta)d)\right|d\eta\,d\xi\\
&+\tfrac{(\rho-\varkappa)^2(\gamma-\varsigma)^2}{(\rho-\sigma)(d-\varsigma)}\int_0^1\int_0^1\xi\eta\left|\frac{\partial^2}{\partial\xi\,\partial\eta}F(\xi\varkappa+(1-\xi)\rho,\eta\gamma+(1-\eta)\varsigma)\right|d\eta\,d\xi\\
&+\tfrac{(\rho-\varkappa)^2(d-\gamma)^2}{(\rho-\sigma)(d-\varsigma)}\int_0^1\int_0^1\xi\eta\left|\frac{\partial^2}{\partial\xi\,\partial\eta}F(\xi\varkappa+(1-\xi)\rho,\eta\gamma+(1-\eta)d)\right|d\eta\,d\xi.
\end{aligned}\tag{28}$$

By the co-ordinated (g,h)-convexity of $\left|\frac{\partial^2 F}{\partial\xi\,\partial\eta}\right|$, we obtain

$$\begin{aligned}
&\int_0^1\int_0^1\xi\eta\left|\frac{\partial^2}{\partial\xi\,\partial\eta}F(\xi\varkappa+(1-\xi)\sigma,\eta\gamma+(1-\eta)\varsigma)\right|d\eta\,d\xi\\
&\le\int_0^1\int_0^1\xi\eta\Big[\xi^2\eta^2\left|\frac{\partial^2}{\partial\xi\,\partial\eta}F(\varkappa,\gamma)\right|+\xi^2(1-\eta)^2\left|\frac{\partial^2}{\partial\xi\,\partial\eta}F(\varkappa,\varsigma)\right|\\
&+(1-\xi)^2\eta^2\left|\frac{\partial^2}{\partial\xi\,\partial\eta}F(\sigma,\gamma)\right|+(1-\xi)^2(1-\eta)^2\left|\frac{\partial^2}{\partial\xi\,\partial\eta}F(\sigma,\varsigma)\right|\\
&+\xi^2\eta(1-\eta)M_1(\varkappa,\gamma,\varsigma)+\xi\eta(1-\xi)(1-\eta)M_2(\varkappa,\sigma,\gamma,\varsigma)\\
&+\xi\eta^2(1-\xi)M_3(\varkappa,\sigma,\gamma)+\xi\eta(1-\xi)(1-\eta)M_4(\varkappa,\sigma,\gamma,\varsigma)\\
&+\xi(1-\xi)(1-\eta)^2M_5(\varkappa,\sigma,\varsigma)+\eta(1-\xi)^2(1-\eta)M_6(\sigma,\gamma,\varsigma)\Big]\,d\eta\,d\xi\\
&=\tfrac{1}{16}\left|\frac{\partial^2}{\partial\xi\,\partial\eta}F(\varkappa,\gamma)\right|+\tfrac{1}{48}\left|\frac{\partial^2}{\partial\xi\,\partial\eta}F(\varkappa,\varsigma)\right|+\tfrac{1}{48}\left|\frac{\partial^2}{\partial\xi\,\partial\eta}F(\sigma,\gamma)\right|+\tfrac{1}{144}\left|\frac{\partial^2}{\partial\xi\,\partial\eta}F(\sigma,\varsigma)\right|\\
&+\tfrac{1}{48}K(\varkappa,\gamma,\varsigma)+\tfrac{1}{144}L(\varkappa,\sigma,\gamma,\varsigma)+\tfrac{1}{48}M(\varkappa,\sigma,\gamma)\\
&+\tfrac{1}{144}N(\varkappa,\sigma,\gamma,\varsigma)+\tfrac{1}{144}O(\varkappa,\sigma,\varsigma)+\tfrac{1}{144}P(\sigma,\gamma,\varsigma).
\end{aligned}\tag{29}$$

Similarly, we have

$$\begin{aligned}
&\int_0^1\int_0^1\xi\eta\left|\frac{\partial^2}{\partial\xi\,\partial\eta}F(\xi\varkappa+(1-\xi)\sigma,\eta\gamma+(1-\eta)d)\right|d\eta\,d\xi\\
&\le\tfrac{1}{16}\left|\frac{\partial^2}{\partial\xi\,\partial\eta}F(\varkappa,\gamma)\right|+\tfrac{1}{48}\left|\frac{\partial^2}{\partial\xi\,\partial\eta}F(\varkappa,d)\right|+\tfrac{1}{48}\left|\frac{\partial^2}{\partial\xi\,\partial\eta}F(\sigma,\gamma)\right|+\tfrac{1}{144}\left|\frac{\partial^2}{\partial\xi\,\partial\eta}F(\sigma,d)\right|
\end{aligned}\tag{30}$$

$$+\tfrac{1}{48}K(\varkappa,\gamma,d)+\tfrac{1}{144}L(\varkappa,\sigma,\gamma,d)+\tfrac{1}{48}M(\varkappa,\sigma,\gamma)$$
$$+\tfrac{1}{144}N(\varkappa,\sigma,\gamma,d)+\tfrac{1}{144}O(\varkappa,\sigma,d)+\tfrac{1}{144}P(\sigma,\gamma,d),$$

$$\begin{aligned}\int_0^1\int_0^1 \; & \xi\eta\left|\frac{\partial^2}{\partial\xi\,\partial\eta}F(\xi\varkappa+(1-\xi)\rho,\eta\gamma+(1-\eta)\varsigma)\right|d\eta\,d\xi\\ &\leq \tfrac{1}{16}\left|\frac{\partial^2}{\partial\xi\,\partial\eta}F(\varkappa,\gamma)\right|+\tfrac{1}{48}\left|\frac{\partial^2}{\partial\xi\,\partial\eta}F(\varkappa,\varsigma)\right|+\tfrac{1}{48}\left|\frac{\partial^2}{\partial\xi\,\partial\eta}F(\rho,\gamma)\right|+\tfrac{1}{144}\left|\frac{\partial^2}{\partial\xi\,\partial\eta}F(\rho,\varsigma)\right|\\ &\quad+\tfrac{1}{48}K(\varkappa,\gamma,\varsigma)+\tfrac{1}{144}L(\varkappa,\rho,\gamma,\varsigma)+\tfrac{1}{48}M(\varkappa,\rho,\gamma)\\ &\quad+\tfrac{1}{144}N(\varkappa,\rho,\gamma,\varsigma)+\tfrac{1}{144}O(\varkappa,\rho,\varsigma)+\tfrac{1}{144}P(\rho,\gamma,\varsigma),\end{aligned} \tag{31}$$

and

$$\begin{aligned}\int_0^1\int_0^1 \; & \xi\eta\left|\frac{\partial^2}{\partial\xi\,\partial\eta}F(\xi\varkappa+(1-\xi)\rho,\eta\gamma+(1-\eta)d)\right|d\eta\,d\xi\\ &\leq \tfrac{1}{16}\left|\frac{\partial^2}{\partial\xi\,\partial\eta}F(\varkappa,\gamma)\right|+\tfrac{1}{48}\left|\frac{\partial^2}{\partial\xi\,\partial\eta}F(\varkappa,d)\right|+\tfrac{1}{48}\left|\frac{\partial^2}{\partial\xi\,\partial\eta}F(\rho,\gamma)\right|+\tfrac{1}{144}\left|\frac{\partial^2}{\partial\xi\,\partial\eta}F(\rho,d)\right|\\ &\quad+\tfrac{1}{48}K(\varkappa,\gamma,d)+\tfrac{1}{144}L(\varkappa,\rho,\gamma,\varsigma)+\tfrac{1}{48}M(\varkappa,\rho,\gamma)\\ &\quad+\tfrac{1}{144}N(\varkappa,\rho,\gamma,d)+\tfrac{1}{144}O(\varkappa,\rho,d)+\tfrac{1}{144}P(\rho,\gamma,d).\end{aligned} \tag{32}$$

Substituting the inequalities (29)–(32) in the inequality (28), we obtain

$$\begin{aligned}&\left|F(\varkappa,\gamma)+\frac{1}{(\rho-\sigma)(d-\varsigma)}\int_\sigma^\rho\int_\varsigma^d F(u,v)\,dv\,du-A\right|\leq\frac{1}{144(\rho-\sigma)(d-\varsigma)}\\ &\times\Bigg\{(\varkappa-\sigma)^2(\gamma-\varsigma)^2\Bigg[9\left|\frac{\partial^2}{\partial\xi\,\partial\eta}F(\varkappa,\gamma)\right|+3\left|\frac{\partial^2}{\partial\xi\,\partial\eta}F(\varkappa,\varsigma)\right|+3\left|\frac{\partial^2}{\partial\xi\,\partial\eta}F(\sigma,\gamma)\right|+\left|\frac{\partial^2}{\partial\xi\,\partial\eta}F(\sigma,\varsigma)\right|\\ &+3K(\varkappa,\gamma,\varsigma)+L(\varkappa,\sigma,\gamma,\varsigma)+3M(\varkappa,\sigma,\gamma)+N(\varkappa,\sigma,\gamma,\varsigma)+O(\varkappa,\sigma,\varsigma)+P(\sigma,\gamma,\varsigma)\Bigg]\\ &+(\varkappa-\sigma)^2(d-\gamma)^2\Bigg[9\left|\frac{\partial^2}{\partial\xi\,\partial\eta}F(\varkappa,\gamma)\right|+3\left|\frac{\partial^2}{\partial\xi\,\partial\eta}F(\varkappa,d)\right|+3\left|\frac{\partial^2}{\partial\xi\,\partial\eta}F(\sigma,\gamma)\right|+\left|\frac{\partial^2}{\partial\xi\,\partial\eta}F(\sigma,d)\right|\\ &+3K(\varkappa,\gamma,d)+L(\varkappa,\sigma,\gamma,d)+3M(\varkappa,\sigma,\gamma)+N(\varkappa,\sigma,\gamma,d)+O(\varkappa,\sigma,d)+P(\sigma,\gamma,d)\Bigg]\\ &+(\rho-\varkappa)^2(\gamma-\varsigma)^2\Bigg[9\left|\frac{\partial^2}{\partial\xi\,\partial\eta}F(\varkappa,\gamma)\right|+3\left|\frac{\partial^2}{\partial\xi\,\partial\eta}F(\varkappa,\varsigma)\right|+3\left|\frac{\partial^2}{\partial\xi\,\partial\eta}F(\rho,\gamma)\right|+\left|\frac{\partial^2}{\partial\xi\,\partial\eta}F(\rho,\varsigma)\right|\\ &+3K(\varkappa,\gamma,\varsigma)+L(\varkappa,\rho,\gamma,\varsigma)+3M(\varkappa,\rho,\gamma)+N(\varkappa,\rho,\gamma,\varsigma)+O(\varkappa,\rho,\varsigma)+P(\rho,\gamma,\varsigma)\Bigg]\\ &+(\rho-\varkappa)^2(d-\gamma)^2\Bigg[9\left|\frac{\partial^2}{\partial\xi\,\partial\eta}F(\varkappa,\gamma)\right|+3\left|\frac{\partial^2}{\partial\xi\,\partial\eta}F(\varkappa,d)\right|+3\left|\frac{\partial^2}{\partial\xi\,\partial\eta}F(\rho,\gamma)\right|+\left|\frac{\partial^2}{\partial\xi\,\partial\eta}F(\rho,d)\right|\\ &+3K(\varkappa,\gamma,d)+L(\varkappa,\rho,\gamma,\varsigma)+3M(\varkappa,\rho,\gamma)+N(\varkappa,\rho,\gamma,d)+O(\varkappa,\rho,d)+P(\rho,\gamma,d)\Bigg]\Bigg\}.\end{aligned}$$

The proof is completed. □

Remark 4. *Set* $h(\varkappa,\gamma)=\left|\frac{\partial^2}{\partial\xi\,\partial\eta}F(\varkappa,\gamma)\right|$, $g(\varkappa,\gamma)=1$ *and* $\left|\frac{\partial^2}{\partial\xi\,\partial\eta}F(\varkappa,\gamma)\right|\leq M$ *for all* $(\varkappa,\gamma)\in\triangle$. *In that case, the inequality* (28) *reduces to the inequality* (6).

Theorem 10. *Under the assumptions of Lemma 1, if* $\left|\frac{\partial^2 F}{\partial\xi\,\partial\eta}\right|^q$ *is co-ordinated* (g,h)*-convex on* $\triangle$ *for* $\frac{1}{p}+\frac{1}{q}=1$ *and* $p,q>1$, *then*

$$\left|F(\varkappa,\gamma)+\frac{1}{(\rho-\sigma)(d-\varsigma)}\int_\sigma^\rho\int_\varsigma^d F(u,v)\,dv\,du-A\right|\le\frac{1}{(\rho-\sigma)(d-\varsigma)(p+1)^{2/p}}\left(\frac{1}{36}\right)^{1/q}$$
$$\times\left\{(\varkappa-\sigma)^2(\gamma-\varsigma)^2\left[4\left|\frac{\partial^2}{\partial\xi\,\partial\eta}F(\varkappa,\gamma)\right|^q+4\left|\frac{\partial^2}{\partial\xi\,\partial\eta}F(\varkappa,\varsigma)\right|^q+4\left|\frac{\partial^2}{\partial\xi\,\partial\eta}F(\sigma,\gamma)\right|^q+4\left|\frac{\partial^2}{\partial\xi\,\partial\eta}F(\sigma,\varsigma)\right|^q\right.\right.$$
$$\left.+2K(\varkappa,\gamma,\varsigma)+L(\varkappa,\sigma,\gamma,\varsigma)+2M(\varkappa,\sigma,\gamma)+N(\varkappa,\sigma,\gamma,\varsigma)+2O(\varkappa,\sigma,\varsigma)+2P(\sigma,\gamma,\varsigma)\right]^{1/q}$$
$$+(\varkappa-\sigma)^2(d-\gamma)^2\left[4\left|\frac{\partial^2}{\partial\xi\,\partial\eta}F(\varkappa,\gamma)\right|^q+4\left|\frac{\partial^2}{\partial\xi\,\partial\eta}F(\varkappa,d)\right|^q+4\left|\frac{\partial^2}{\partial\xi\,\partial\eta}F(\sigma,\gamma)\right|^q+4\left|\frac{\partial^2}{\partial\xi\,\partial\eta}F(\sigma,d)\right|^q\right.$$
$$\left.+2K(\varkappa,\gamma,d)+L(\varkappa,\sigma,\gamma,d)+2M(\varkappa,\sigma,\gamma)+N(\varkappa,\sigma,\gamma,d)+2O(\varkappa,\sigma,d)+2P(\sigma,\gamma,d)\right]^{1/q}\tag{33}$$
$$+(\rho-\varkappa)^2(\gamma-\varsigma)^2\left[4\left|\frac{\partial^2}{\partial\xi\,\partial\eta}F(\varkappa,\gamma)\right|^q+4\left|\frac{\partial^2}{\partial\xi\,\partial\eta}F(\varkappa,\varsigma)\right|^q+4\left|\frac{\partial^2}{\partial\xi\,\partial\eta}F(\rho,\gamma)\right|^q+4\left|\frac{\partial^2}{\partial\xi\,\partial\eta}F(\rho,\varsigma)\right|^q\right.$$
$$\left.+2K(\varkappa,\gamma,\varsigma)+L(\varkappa,\rho,\gamma,\varsigma)+2M(\varkappa,\rho,\gamma)+N(\varkappa,\rho,\gamma,\varsigma)+2O(\varkappa,\rho,\varsigma)+2P(\rho,\gamma,\varsigma)\right]^{1/q}$$
$$+(\rho-\varkappa)^2(d-\gamma)^2\left[4\left|\frac{\partial^2}{\partial\xi\,\partial\eta}F(\varkappa,\gamma)\right|^q+4\left|\frac{\partial^2}{\partial\xi\,\partial\eta}F(\varkappa,d)\right|^q+4\left|\frac{\partial^2}{\partial\xi\,\partial\eta}F(\rho,\gamma)\right|^q+4\left|\frac{\partial^2}{\partial\xi\,\partial\eta}F(\rho,d)\right|^q\right.$$
$$\left.\left.+2K(\varkappa,\gamma,d)+L(\varkappa,\rho,\gamma,\varsigma)+2M(\varkappa,\rho,\gamma)+N(\varkappa,\rho,\gamma,d)+2O(\varkappa,\rho,d)+2P(\rho,\gamma,d)\right]^{1/q}\right\},$$

where A is defined as in (7) and K, L, M, N, O, P are defined as in Theorem 8.

Proof. By the Hölder inequality for double integrals and co-ordinated (g,h)-convexity of $\left|\frac{\partial^2 F}{\partial\xi\,\partial\eta}\right|^q$, with the help of Lemma 1, we have

$$\begin{aligned}
&\int_0^1\int_0^1 \xi\eta\left|\frac{\partial^2}{\partial\xi\,\partial\eta}F(\xi\varkappa+(1-\xi)\sigma,\eta\gamma+(1-\eta)\varsigma)\right|d\eta\,d\xi\\
&\le\left(\int_0^1\int_0^1\xi^p\eta^p\,d\eta\,d\xi\right)^{1/p}\left(\int_0^1\int_0^1\left|\frac{\partial^2}{\partial\xi\,\partial\eta}F(\xi\varkappa+(1-\xi)\sigma,\eta\gamma+(1-\eta)\varsigma)\right|^q d\eta\,d\xi\right)^{1/q}\\
&\le\frac{1}{(p+1)^{2/p}}\left(\int_0^1\int_0^1\xi^2\eta^2\left|\frac{\partial^2}{\partial\xi\,\partial\eta}F(\varkappa,\gamma)\right|^q+\xi^2(1-\eta)^2\left|\frac{\partial^2}{\partial\xi\,\partial\eta}F(\varkappa,\varsigma)\right|^q\right.\\
&\quad+(1-\xi)^2\eta^2\left|\frac{\partial^2}{\partial\xi\,\partial\eta}F(\sigma,\gamma)\right|^q+(1-\xi)^2(1-\eta)^2\left|\frac{\partial^2}{\partial\xi\,\partial\eta}F(\sigma,\varsigma)\right|^q
\end{aligned}\tag{34}$$
$$+\xi^2\eta(1-\eta)M_1(\varkappa,\gamma,\varsigma)+\xi\eta(1-\xi)(1-\eta)M_2(\varkappa,\sigma,\gamma,\varsigma)+\xi\eta^2(1-\xi)M_3(\varkappa,\sigma,\gamma)$$
$$\left.+\xi\eta(1-\xi)(1-\eta)M_4(\varkappa,\sigma,\gamma,\varsigma)+\xi(1-\xi)(1-\eta)^2M_5(\varkappa,\sigma,\varsigma)+\eta(1-\xi)^2(1-\eta)M_6(\sigma,\gamma,\varsigma)\,d\eta\,d\xi\right)^{1/q}$$
$$=\frac{1}{(p+1)^{2/p}}\left(\frac{1}{9}\left|\frac{\partial^2}{\partial\xi\,\partial\eta}F(\varkappa,\gamma)\right|^q+\frac{1}{9}\left|\frac{\partial^2}{\partial\xi\,\partial\eta}F(\varkappa,\varsigma)\right|^q+\frac{1}{9}\left|\frac{\partial^2}{\partial\xi\,\partial\eta}F(\sigma,\gamma)\right|^q+\frac{1}{9}\left|\frac{\partial^2}{\partial\xi\,\partial\eta}F(\sigma,\varsigma)\right|^q\right.$$
$$+\frac{1}{18}K(\varkappa,\gamma,\varsigma)+\frac{1}{36}L(\varkappa,\sigma,\gamma,\varsigma)+\frac{1}{18}M(\varkappa,\sigma,\gamma)$$
$$\left.+\frac{1}{36}N(\varkappa,\sigma,\gamma,\varsigma)+\frac{1}{18}O(\varkappa,\sigma,\varsigma)+\frac{1}{18}P(\sigma,\gamma,\varsigma)\right)^{1/q}.$$

Similarly, we obtain

$$\int_0^1\int_0^1 \xi\eta\left|\frac{\partial^2}{\partial\xi\,\partial\eta}F(\xi\varkappa+(1-\xi)\sigma,\eta\gamma+(1-\eta)d)\right|d\eta\,d\xi$$
$$\leq \tfrac{1}{(p+1)^{2/p}}\Big(\tfrac{1}{9}\left|\frac{\partial^2}{\partial\xi\,\partial\eta}F(\varkappa,\gamma)\right|^q+\tfrac{1}{9}\left|\frac{\partial^2}{\partial\xi\,\partial\eta}F(\varkappa,d)\right|^q+\tfrac{1}{9}\left|\frac{\partial^2}{\partial\xi\,\partial\eta}F(\sigma,\gamma)\right|^q$$
$$+\tfrac{1}{9}\left|\frac{\partial^2}{\partial\xi\,\partial\eta}F(\sigma,d)\right|^q+\tfrac{1}{18}K(\varkappa,\gamma,d)+\tfrac{1}{36}L(\varkappa,\sigma,\gamma,d)+\tfrac{1}{18}M(\varkappa,\sigma,\gamma)$$
$$+\tfrac{1}{36}N(\varkappa,\sigma,\gamma,d)+\tfrac{1}{18}O(\varkappa,\sigma,d)+\tfrac{1}{18}P(\sigma,\gamma,d)\Big)^{1/q}, \tag{35}$$

$$\int_0^1\int_0^1 \xi\eta\left|\frac{\partial^2}{\partial\xi\,\partial\eta}F(\xi\varkappa+(1-\xi)\rho,\eta\gamma+(1-\eta)\varsigma)\right|d\eta\,d\xi$$
$$\leq \tfrac{1}{(p+1)^{2/p}}\Big(\tfrac{1}{9}\left|\frac{\partial^2}{\partial\xi\,\partial\eta}F(\varkappa,\gamma)\right|^q+\tfrac{1}{9}\left|\frac{\partial^2}{\partial\xi\,\partial\eta}F(\varkappa,\varsigma)\right|^q+\tfrac{1}{9}\left|\frac{\partial^2}{\partial\xi\,\partial\eta}F(\rho,\gamma)\right|^q$$
$$+\tfrac{1}{9}\left|\frac{\partial^2}{\partial\xi\,\partial\eta}F(\rho,\varsigma)\right|^q+\tfrac{1}{18}K(\varkappa,\gamma,\varsigma)+\tfrac{1}{36}L(\varkappa,\rho,\gamma,\varsigma)+\tfrac{1}{18}M(\varkappa,\rho,\gamma)$$
$$+\tfrac{1}{36}N(\varkappa,\rho,\gamma,\varsigma)+\tfrac{1}{18}O(\varkappa,\rho,\varsigma)+\tfrac{1}{18}P(\rho,\gamma,\varsigma)\Big)^{1/q}, \tag{36}$$

and

$$\int_0^1\int_0^1 \xi\eta\left|\frac{\partial^2}{\partial\xi\,\partial\eta}F(\xi\varkappa+(1-\xi)\rho,\eta\gamma+(1-\eta)d)\right|d\eta\,d\xi$$
$$\leq \tfrac{1}{(p+1)^{2/p}}\Big(\tfrac{1}{9}\left|\frac{\partial^2}{\partial\xi\,\partial\eta}F(\varkappa,\gamma)\right|^q+\tfrac{1}{9}\left|\frac{\partial^2}{\partial\xi\,\partial\eta}F(\varkappa,d)\right|^q+\tfrac{1}{9}\left|\frac{\partial^2}{\partial\xi\,\partial\eta}F(\rho,\gamma)\right|^q$$
$$+\tfrac{1}{9}\left|\frac{\partial^2}{\partial\xi\,\partial\eta}F(\rho,d)\right|^q+\tfrac{1}{18}K(\varkappa,\gamma,d)+\tfrac{1}{36}L(\varkappa,\rho,\gamma,\varsigma)+\tfrac{1}{18}M(\varkappa,\rho,\gamma)$$
$$+\tfrac{1}{36}N(\varkappa,\rho,\gamma,d)+\tfrac{1}{18}O(\varkappa,\rho,d)+\tfrac{1}{18}P(\rho,\gamma,d)\Big)^{1/q}. \tag{37}$$

If we substitute the inequalities (35)–(37) in the inequality (28), we obtain

$$\left|F(\varkappa,\gamma)+\frac{1}{(\rho-\sigma)(d-\varsigma)}\int_\sigma^\rho\int_\varsigma^d F(u,v)\,dv\,du-A\right|\leq\frac{1}{(\rho-\sigma)(d-\varsigma)(p+1)^{2/p}}\left(\frac{1}{36}\right)^{1/q}$$
$$\times\Bigg\{(\varkappa-\sigma)^2(\gamma-\varsigma)^2\Bigg[4\left|\frac{\partial^2}{\partial\xi\,\partial\eta}F(\varkappa,\gamma)\right|^q+4\left|\frac{\partial^2}{\partial\xi\,\partial\eta}F(\varkappa,\varsigma)\right|^q+4\left|\frac{\partial^2}{\partial\xi\,\partial\eta}F(\sigma,\gamma)\right|^q+4\left|\frac{\partial^2}{\partial\xi\,\partial\eta}F(\sigma,\varsigma)\right|^q$$
$$+2K(\varkappa,\gamma,\varsigma)+L(\varkappa,\sigma,\gamma,\varsigma)+2M(\varkappa,\sigma,\gamma)+N(\varkappa,\sigma,\gamma,\varsigma)+2O(\varkappa,\sigma,\varsigma)+2P(\sigma,\gamma,\varsigma)]^{1/q}$$
$$+(\varkappa-\sigma)^2(d-\gamma)^2\Bigg[4\left|\frac{\partial^2}{\partial\xi\,\partial\eta}F(\varkappa,\gamma)\right|^q+4\left|\frac{\partial^2}{\partial\xi\,\partial\eta}F(\varkappa,d)\right|^q+4\left|\frac{\partial^2}{\partial\xi\,\partial\eta}F(\sigma,\gamma)\right|^q+4\left|\frac{\partial^2}{\partial\xi\,\partial\eta}F(\sigma,d)\right|^q$$
$$+2K(\varkappa,\gamma,d)+L(\varkappa,\sigma,\gamma,d)+2M(\varkappa,\sigma,\gamma)+N(\varkappa,\sigma,\gamma,d)+2O(\varkappa,\sigma,d)+2P(\sigma,\gamma,d)]^{1/q}$$
$$+(\rho-\varkappa)^2(\gamma-\varsigma)^2\Bigg[4\left|\frac{\partial^2}{\partial\xi\,\partial\eta}F(\varkappa,\gamma)\right|^q+4\left|\frac{\partial^2}{\partial\xi\,\partial\eta}F(\varkappa,\varsigma)\right|^q+4\left|\frac{\partial^2}{\partial\xi\,\partial\eta}F(\rho,\gamma)\right|^q+4\left|\frac{\partial^2}{\partial\xi\,\partial\eta}F(\rho,\varsigma)\right|^q$$
$$+2K(\varkappa,\gamma,\varsigma)+L(\varkappa,\rho,\gamma,\varsigma)+2M(\varkappa,\rho,\gamma)+N(\varkappa,\rho,\gamma,\varsigma)+2O(\varkappa,\rho,\varsigma)+2P(\rho,\gamma,\varsigma)]^{1/q}$$
$$+(\rho-\varkappa)^2(d-\gamma)^2\Bigg[4\left|\frac{\partial^2}{\partial\xi\,\partial\eta}F(\varkappa,\gamma)\right|^q+4\left|\frac{\partial^2}{\partial\xi\,\partial\eta}F(\varkappa,d)\right|^q+4\left|\frac{\partial^2}{\partial\xi\,\partial\eta}F(\rho,\gamma)\right|^q+4\left|\frac{\partial^2}{\partial\xi\,\partial\eta}F(\rho,d)\right|^q$$
$$+2K(\varkappa,\gamma,d)+L(\varkappa,\rho,\gamma,\varsigma)+2M(\varkappa,\rho,\gamma)+N(\varkappa,\rho,\gamma,d)+2O(\varkappa,\rho,d)+2P(\rho,\gamma,d)]^{1/q}\Bigg\}.$$

The proof is ended. □

Remark 5. *Set* $h(\varkappa,\gamma) = \left|\frac{\partial^2}{\partial\xi\,\partial\eta}F(\varkappa,\gamma)\right|^q$, $g(\varkappa,\gamma) = 1$ *and* $\left|\frac{\partial^2}{\partial\xi\,\partial\eta}F(\varkappa,\gamma)\right| \leq M$ *for all* $(\varkappa,\gamma) \in \triangle$. *Then, the inequality (33) reduces to the inequality (8).*

Theorem 11. *Under the assumptions of Lemma 1, if* $\left|\frac{\partial^2 F}{\partial\xi\,\partial\eta}\right|^q$ *is co-ordinated* (g,h)*-convex on* $\triangle$ *for* $q \geq 1$*, then*

$$\begin{aligned}
&\left|F\quad(\varkappa,\gamma) + \tfrac{1}{(\rho-\sigma)(d-\varsigma)}\int_\sigma^\rho\int_\varsigma^d F(u,v)\,dv\,du - A\right| \leq \tfrac{1}{4(\rho-\sigma)(d-\varsigma)}\left(\tfrac{1}{36}\right)^{1/q} \\
&\times\Bigg\{(\varkappa-\sigma)^2(\gamma-\varsigma)^2\Bigg[9\left|\frac{\partial^2}{\partial\xi\,\partial\eta}F(\varkappa,\gamma)\right|^q + 3\left|\frac{\partial^2}{\partial\xi\,\partial\eta}F(\varkappa,\varsigma)\right|^q + 3\left|\frac{\partial^2}{\partial\xi\,\partial\eta}F(\sigma,\gamma)\right|^q + \left|\frac{\partial^2}{\partial\xi\,\partial\eta}F(\sigma,\varsigma)\right|^q \\
&+3K(\varkappa,\gamma,\varsigma) + L(\varkappa,\sigma,\gamma,\varsigma) + 3M(\varkappa,\sigma,\gamma) + N(\varkappa,\sigma,\gamma,\varsigma) + O(\varkappa,\sigma,\varsigma) + P(\sigma,\gamma,\varsigma)\Bigg]^{1/q} \\
&+(\varkappa-\sigma)^2(d-\gamma)^2\Bigg[9\left|\frac{\partial^2}{\partial\xi\,\partial\eta}F(\varkappa,\gamma)\right|^q + 3\left|\frac{\partial^2}{\partial\xi\,\partial\eta}F(\varkappa,d)\right|^q + 3\left|\frac{\partial^2}{\partial\xi\,\partial\eta}F(\sigma,\gamma)\right|^q + \left|\frac{\partial^2}{\partial\xi\,\partial\eta}F(\sigma,d)\right|^q \\
&+3K(\varkappa,\gamma,d) + L(\varkappa,\sigma,\gamma,d) + 3M(\varkappa,\sigma,\gamma) + N(\varkappa,\sigma,\gamma,d) + O(\varkappa,\sigma,d) + P(\sigma,\gamma,d)\Bigg]^{1/q} \\
&+(\rho-\varkappa)^2(\gamma-\varsigma)^2\Bigg[9\left|\frac{\partial^2}{\partial\xi\,\partial\eta}F(\varkappa,\gamma)\right|^q + 3\left|\frac{\partial^2}{\partial\xi\,\partial\eta}F(\varkappa,\varsigma)\right|^q + 3\left|\frac{\partial^2}{\partial\xi\,\partial\eta}F(\rho,\gamma)\right|^q + \left|\frac{\partial^2}{\partial\xi\,\partial\eta}F(\rho,\varsigma)\right|^q \\
&+3K(\varkappa,\gamma,\varsigma) + L(\varkappa,\rho,\gamma,\varsigma) + 3M(\varkappa,\rho,\gamma) + N(\varkappa,\rho,\gamma,\varsigma) + O(\varkappa,\rho,\varsigma) + P(\rho,\gamma,\varsigma)\Bigg]^{1/q} \\
&+(\rho-\varkappa)^2(d-\gamma)^2\Bigg[9\left|\frac{\partial^2}{\partial\xi\,\partial\eta}F(\varkappa,\gamma)\right|^q + 3\left|\frac{\partial^2}{\partial\xi\,\partial\eta}F(\varkappa,d)\right|^q + 3\left|\frac{\partial^2}{\partial\xi\,\partial\eta}F(\rho,\gamma)\right|^q + \left|\frac{\partial^2}{\partial\xi\,\partial\eta}F(\rho,d)\right|^q \\
&+ 3K(\varkappa,\gamma,d) + L(\varkappa,\rho,\gamma,\varsigma) + 3M(\varkappa,\rho,\gamma) + N(\varkappa,\rho,\gamma,d) + O(\varkappa,\rho,d) + P(\rho,\gamma,d)\Bigg]^{1/q}\Bigg\},
\end{aligned} \tag{38}$$

where A is defined as in (7) and K, L, M, N, O, P are defined as in Theorem 8.

Proof. By vitue of the power mean inequality in relation to double integrals and by the co-ordinated (g,h)-convexity of $\left|\frac{\partial^2 F}{\partial\xi\,\partial\eta}\right|^q$, with the help of Lemma 1, we have

$$\begin{aligned}
&\int_0^1\int_0^1 \quad \xi\eta\left|\frac{\partial^2}{\partial\xi\,\partial\eta}F(\xi\varkappa + (1-\xi)\sigma, \eta\gamma + (1-\eta)\varsigma)\right| d\eta\,d\xi \\
&\leq \left(\int_0^1\int_0^1 \xi\eta\,d\eta\,d\xi\right)^{1-1/q}\left(\int_0^1\int_0^1 \xi\eta\left|\frac{\partial^2}{\partial\xi\,\partial\eta}F(\xi\varkappa + (1-\xi)\sigma, \eta\gamma + (1-\eta)\varsigma)\right|^q d\eta\,d\xi\right)^{1/q} \\
&\leq \left(\tfrac{1}{4}\right)^{1-1/q}\Bigg(\int_0^1\int_0^1 \xi\eta\Bigg[\xi^2\eta^2\left|\frac{\partial^2}{\partial\xi\,\partial\eta}F(\varkappa,\gamma)\right|^q + \xi^2(1-\eta)^2\left|\frac{\partial^2}{\partial\xi\,\partial\eta}F(\varkappa,\varsigma)\right|^q \\
&+(1-\xi)^2\eta^2\left|\frac{\partial^2}{\partial\xi\,\partial\eta}F(\sigma,\gamma)\right|^q + (1-\xi)^2(1-\eta)^2\left|\frac{\partial^2}{\partial\xi\,\partial\eta}F(\sigma,\varsigma)\right|^q \\
&+\xi^2\eta(1-\eta)M_1(\varkappa,\gamma,\varsigma) + \xi\eta(1-\xi)(1-\eta)M_2(\varkappa,\sigma,\gamma,\varsigma) + \xi\eta^2(1-\xi)M_3(\varkappa,\sigma,\gamma) \\
&+ \xi\eta(1-\xi)(1-\eta)M_4(\varkappa,\sigma,\gamma,\varsigma) + \xi(1-\xi)(1-\eta)^2M_5(\varkappa,\sigma,\varsigma) + \eta(1-\xi)^2(1-\eta)M_6(\sigma,\gamma,\varsigma)\Bigg]\,d\eta\,d\xi\Bigg)^{1/q} \\
&= \left(\tfrac{1}{4}\right)^{1-1/q}\Bigg(\tfrac{1}{16}\left|\frac{\partial^2}{\partial\xi\,\partial\eta}F(\varkappa,\gamma)\right|^q + \tfrac{1}{48}\left|\frac{\partial^2}{\partial\xi\,\partial\eta}F(\varkappa,\varsigma)\right|^q + \tfrac{1}{48}\left|\frac{\partial^2}{\partial\xi\,\partial\eta}F(\sigma,\gamma)\right|^q + \tfrac{1}{144}\left|\frac{\partial^2}{\partial\xi\,\partial\eta}F(\sigma,\varsigma)\right|^q \\
&+\tfrac{1}{48}K(\varkappa,\gamma,\varsigma) + \tfrac{1}{144}L(\varkappa,\sigma,\gamma,\varsigma) + \tfrac{1}{48}M(\varkappa,\sigma,\gamma) \\
&+ \tfrac{1}{111}N(\varkappa,\sigma,\gamma,\varsigma) + \tfrac{1}{144}O(\varkappa,\sigma,\varsigma) + \tfrac{1}{144}P(\sigma,\gamma,\varsigma)\Bigg)^{1/q}
\end{aligned} \tag{39}$$

In a similar way, one can obtain

$$
\begin{aligned}
&\int_0^1\int_0^1 \xi\eta\left|\frac{\partial^2}{\partial\xi\,\partial\eta}F(\xi\varkappa+(1-\xi)\sigma,\eta\gamma+(1-\eta)d)\right|d\eta\,d\xi \\
&\leq\left(\tfrac{1}{4}\right)^{1-1/q}\left(\tfrac{1}{16}\left|\frac{\partial^2}{\partial\xi\,\partial\eta}F(\varkappa,\gamma)\right|^q+\tfrac{1}{48}\left|\frac{\partial^2}{\partial\xi\,\partial\eta}F(\varkappa,d)\right|^q+\tfrac{1}{48}\left|\frac{\partial^2}{\partial\xi\,\partial\eta}F(\sigma,\gamma)\right|^q+\tfrac{1}{144}\left|\frac{\partial^2}{\partial\xi\,\partial\eta}F(\sigma,d)\right|^q\right. \\
&\quad+\tfrac{1}{48}K(\varkappa,\gamma,d)+\tfrac{1}{144}L(\varkappa,\sigma,\gamma,d)+\tfrac{1}{48}M(\varkappa,\sigma,\gamma) \\
&\quad\left.+\tfrac{1}{144}N(\varkappa,\sigma,\gamma,d)+\tfrac{1}{144}O(\varkappa,\sigma,d)+\tfrac{1}{144}P(\sigma,\gamma,d)\right)^{1/q},
\end{aligned}
\tag{40}
$$

$$
\begin{aligned}
&\int_0^1\int_0^1 \xi\eta\left|\frac{\partial^2}{\partial\xi\,\partial\eta}F(\xi\varkappa+(1-\xi)\rho,\eta\gamma+(1-\eta)\varsigma)\right|d\eta\,d\xi \\
&\leq\left(\tfrac{1}{4}\right)^{1-1/q}\left(\tfrac{1}{16}\left|\frac{\partial^2}{\partial\xi\,\partial\eta}F(\varkappa,\gamma)\right|^q+\tfrac{1}{48}\left|\frac{\partial^2}{\partial\xi\,\partial\eta}F(\varkappa,\varsigma)\right|^q+\tfrac{1}{48}\left|\frac{\partial^2}{\partial\xi\,\partial\eta}F(\rho,\gamma)\right|^q+\tfrac{1}{144}\left|\frac{\partial^2}{\partial\xi\,\partial\eta}F(\rho,\varsigma)\right|^q\right. \\
&\quad+\tfrac{1}{48}K(\varkappa,\gamma,\varsigma)+\tfrac{1}{144}L(\varkappa,\rho,\gamma,\varsigma)+\tfrac{1}{48}M(\varkappa,\rho,\gamma) \\
&\quad\left.+\tfrac{1}{144}N(\varkappa,\rho,\gamma,\varsigma)+\tfrac{1}{144}O(\varkappa,\rho,\varsigma)+\tfrac{1}{144}P(\rho,\gamma,\varsigma)\right)^{1/q},
\end{aligned}
\tag{41}
$$

and

$$
\begin{aligned}
&\int_0^1\int_0^1 \xi\eta\left|\frac{\partial^2}{\partial\xi\,\partial\eta}F(\xi\varkappa+(1-\xi)\rho,\eta\gamma+(1-\eta)d)\right|d\eta\,d\xi \\
&\leq\left(\tfrac{1}{4}\right)^{1-1/q}\left(\tfrac{1}{16}\left|\frac{\partial^2}{\partial\xi\,\partial\eta}F(\varkappa,\gamma)\right|^q+\tfrac{1}{48}\left|\frac{\partial^2}{\partial\xi\,\partial\eta}F(\varkappa,d)\right|^q+\tfrac{1}{48}\left|\frac{\partial^2}{\partial\xi\,\partial\eta}F(\rho,\gamma)\right|^q+\tfrac{1}{144}\left|\frac{\partial^2}{\partial\xi\,\partial\eta}F(\rho,d)\right|^q\right. \\
&\quad+\tfrac{1}{48}K(\varkappa,\gamma,d)+\tfrac{1}{144}L(\varkappa,\rho,\gamma,\varsigma)+\tfrac{1}{48}M(\varkappa,\rho,\gamma) \\
&\quad\left.+\tfrac{1}{144}N(\varkappa,\rho,\gamma,d)+\tfrac{1}{144}O(\varkappa,\rho,d)+\tfrac{1}{144}P(\rho,\gamma,d)\right)^{1/q}.
\end{aligned}
\tag{42}
$$

By substituting the inequalities (39)–(42) in the inequality (28), we obtain

$$
\begin{aligned}
&\left|F(\varkappa,\gamma)+\frac{1}{(\rho-\sigma)(d-\varsigma)}\int_\sigma^\rho\int_\varsigma^d F(u,v)\,dv\,du-A\right|\leq\frac{1}{4(\rho-\sigma)(d-\varsigma)}\left(\frac{1}{36}\right)^{1/q} \\
&\times\left\{(\varkappa-\sigma)^2(\gamma-\varsigma)^2\left[9\left|\frac{\partial^2}{\partial\xi\,\partial\eta}F(\varkappa,\gamma)\right|^q+3\left|\frac{\partial^2}{\partial\xi\,\partial\eta}F(\varkappa,\varsigma)\right|^q+3\left|\frac{\partial^2}{\partial\xi\,\partial\eta}F(\sigma,\gamma)\right|^q+\left|\frac{\partial^2}{\partial\xi\,\partial\eta}F(\sigma,\varsigma)\right|^q\right.\right. \\
&+3K(\varkappa,\gamma,\varsigma)+L(\varkappa,\sigma,\gamma,\varsigma)+3M(\varkappa,\sigma,\gamma)+N(\varkappa,\sigma,\gamma,\varsigma)+O(\varkappa,\sigma,\varsigma)+P(\sigma,\gamma,\varsigma)\Big]^{1/q} \\
&+(\varkappa-\sigma)^2(d-\gamma)^2\left[9\left|\frac{\partial^2}{\partial\xi\,\partial\eta}F(\varkappa,\gamma)\right|^q+3\left|\frac{\partial^2}{\partial\xi\,\partial\eta}F(\varkappa,d)\right|^q+3\left|\frac{\partial^2}{\partial\xi\,\partial\eta}F(\sigma,\gamma)\right|^q+\left|\frac{\partial^2}{\partial\xi\,\partial\eta}F(\sigma,d)\right|^q\right. \\
&+3K(\varkappa,\gamma,d)+L(\varkappa,\sigma,\gamma,d)+3M(\varkappa,\sigma,\gamma)+N(\varkappa,\sigma,\gamma,d)+O(\varkappa,\sigma,d)+P(\sigma,\gamma,d)\Big]^{1/q} \\
&+(\rho-\varkappa)^2(\gamma-\varsigma)^2\left[9\left|\frac{\partial^2}{\partial\xi\,\partial\eta}F(\varkappa,\gamma)\right|^q+3\left|\frac{\partial^2}{\partial\xi\,\partial\eta}F(\varkappa,\varsigma)\right|^q+3\left|\frac{\partial^2}{\partial\xi\,\partial\eta}F(\rho,\gamma)\right|^q+\left|\frac{\partial^2}{\partial\xi\,\partial\eta}F(\rho,\varsigma)\right|^q\right. \\
&+3K(\varkappa,\gamma,\varsigma)+L(\varkappa,\rho,\gamma,\varsigma)+3M(\varkappa,\rho,\gamma)+N(\varkappa,\rho,\gamma,\varsigma)+O(\varkappa,\rho,\varsigma)+P(\rho,\gamma,\varsigma)\Big]^{1/q} \\
&+(\rho-\varkappa)^2(d-\gamma)^2\left[9\left|\frac{\partial^2}{\partial\xi\,\partial\eta}F(\varkappa,\gamma)\right|^q+3\left|\frac{\partial^2}{\partial\xi\,\partial\eta}F(\varkappa,d)\right|^q+3\left|\frac{\partial^2}{\partial\xi\,\partial\eta}F(\rho,\gamma)\right|^q+\left|\frac{\partial^2}{\partial\xi\,\partial\eta}F(\rho,d)\right|^q\right.
\end{aligned}
$$

$$+\ 3K(\varkappa,\gamma,d)+L(\varkappa,\rho,\gamma,\varsigma)+3M(\varkappa,\rho,\gamma)+N(\varkappa,\rho,\gamma,d)+O(\varkappa,\rho,d)+P(\rho,\gamma,d)]^{1/q}\Big\}.$$

The proof is completed. □

Remark 6. *Set* $h(\varkappa,\gamma)=\left|\frac{\partial^2}{\partial\xi\,\partial\eta}F(\varkappa,\gamma)\right|^q$, $g(\varkappa,\gamma)=1$ *and* $\left|\frac{\partial^2}{\partial\xi\,\partial\eta}F(\varkappa,\gamma)\right|\leq M$ *for all* $(\varkappa,\gamma)\in\Delta$. *In that case, the inequality* (38) *reduces to* (9).

5. Examples

In the section of examples, we give some examples to demonstrate and confirm the consistency of our main findings.

Example 2. *Let* $g,h,F:[0,1]\times[0,1]\to\mathbb{R}$ *be given by* $g(\varkappa,\gamma)=\varkappa\gamma$, $h(\varkappa,\gamma)=\mathrm{e}^{-\varkappa-\gamma}$ *and* $F(\varkappa,\gamma)=\varkappa\gamma\,\mathrm{e}^{-\varkappa-\gamma}$. *By Example 1, F is co-ordinated* (g,h)*-convex. Applying Theorem 8, the first inequality of* (18) *is*

$$\begin{aligned}0.038126\ldots&=\frac{1}{\mathrm{e}}-2\left(\frac{-2}{\mathrm{e}}+1\right)\left(\frac{1}{\mathrm{e}}\right)-\left(\frac{1}{\mathrm{e}^2}\right)\\&=4F\left(\frac{1}{2},\frac{1}{2}\right)-\int_0^1\int_0^1\mathrm{e}^{-\varkappa-\gamma}[\varkappa(1-\gamma)+(1-\varkappa)\gamma+(1-\varkappa)(1-\gamma)]\,d\gamma\,d\varkappa\\&\leq\int_0^1\int_0^1\varkappa\gamma\,\mathrm{e}^{-\varkappa-\gamma}\,d\gamma\,d\varkappa=\frac{4}{\mathrm{e}^2}-\frac{4}{\mathrm{e}}+1=0.069823\ldots.\end{aligned}$$

Additionally, the second inequality of (18) *is*

$$\begin{aligned}0.069823\ldots&=\int_0^1\int_0^1\varkappa\gamma\,\mathrm{e}^{-\varkappa-\gamma}\,d\gamma\,d\varkappa\leq\frac{1}{9}\Big[F(0,0)+F(0,1)+F(1,0)+F(1,1)\\&+\frac{K(0,0,1)+P(1,0,1)+M(0,1,0)+O(0,1,1)}{2}+\frac{L(0,1,0,1)+N(0,1,0,1)}{4}\Big]\\&=\frac{1}{9}\left[\frac{1}{\mathrm{e}^2}+\frac{1}{\mathrm{e}}+\frac{1}{4}\right]=0.083690\ldots.\end{aligned}$$

It is clear that

$$0.038126\ldots\leq 0.069823\ldots\leq 0.083690\ldots.$$

This confirms the correctness of the result established in Theorem 8.

Example 3. *Let* $g,h,F:[0,1]\times[0,1]\to\mathbb{R}$ *be formulated by* $g(\varkappa,\gamma)=(1-\varkappa)(1-\gamma)$, $h(\varkappa,\gamma)=\mathrm{e}^{-\varkappa-\gamma}$ *and* $F(\varkappa,\gamma)=\varkappa\gamma\,\mathrm{e}^{-\varkappa-\gamma}$ *(see Figure 1). Then, F is partially differentiable on* $(0,1)\times(0,1)$*, and its partial derivative is integrable and co-ordinated* (g,h)*-convex on* $[0,1]\times[0,1]$*. By utilizing Theorem 9, we have*

$$\begin{aligned}&\left|\varkappa\gamma\,\mathrm{e}^{-\varkappa-\gamma}+\left(\frac{4}{\mathrm{e}^2}-\frac{4}{\mathrm{e}}+1\right)+\left(\varkappa\,\mathrm{e}^{-\varkappa}\right)\left(\frac{2}{\mathrm{e}}-1\right)+\left(\gamma\,\mathrm{e}^{-\gamma}\right)\left(\frac{2}{\mathrm{e}}-1\right)\right|\\&=\left|\varkappa\gamma\,\mathrm{e}^{-\varkappa-\gamma}+\int_0^1\int_0^1 uv\,\mathrm{e}^{-u-v}\,dv\,du-\int_0^1 u\gamma\,\mathrm{e}^{-u-\gamma}\,du-\int_0^1\varkappa v\,\mathrm{e}^{-\varkappa-v}\,dv\right|\\&\leq\frac{1}{144}\Big\{\varkappa^2\gamma^2[9(1-\varkappa)(1-\gamma)\,\mathrm{e}^{-\varkappa-\gamma}+3(1-\varkappa)\,\mathrm{e}^{-\varkappa}+3(1-\gamma)\,\mathrm{e}^{-\gamma}+1\\&+3(1-\varkappa)(1-\gamma)\,\mathrm{e}^{-\varkappa}+3(1-\varkappa)\,\mathrm{e}^{-\varkappa-\gamma}+(1-\gamma)\,\mathrm{e}^{-\varkappa}+(1-\varkappa)\,\mathrm{e}^{-\gamma}\\&+3(1-\gamma)\,\mathrm{e}^{-\varkappa-\gamma}+3(1-\varkappa)(1-\gamma)\,\mathrm{e}^{-\gamma}+\mathrm{e}^{-\varkappa-\gamma}+(1-\varkappa)(1-\gamma)\end{aligned}$$

$$+ e^{-\varkappa} + (1-\varkappa) + e^{-\gamma} + (1-\gamma)\big] + \varkappa^2(1-\gamma)^2\big[9(1-\varkappa)(1-\gamma)\,e^{-\varkappa-\gamma} + 3(1-\gamma)\,e^{-\gamma}$$
$$+ 3(1-\varkappa)(1-\gamma)\,e^{-\varkappa-1} + (1-\gamma)\,e^{-\varkappa-1} + 3(1-\gamma)\,e^{-\varkappa-\gamma} + 3(1-\varkappa)(1-\gamma)\,e^{-\gamma}$$
$$+(1-\varkappa)(1-\gamma)\,e^{-1} + (1-\gamma)\,e^{-1}\Big] + (1-\varkappa)^2\gamma^2\big[9(1-\varkappa)(1-\gamma)\,e^{-\varkappa-\gamma} + 3(1-\varkappa)\,e^{-\varkappa}$$
$$+ 3(1-\varkappa)(1-\gamma)\,e^{-\varkappa} + 3(1-\varkappa)\,e^{-\varkappa-\gamma} + (1-\varkappa)\,e^{-\gamma-1} + 3(1-\varkappa)(1-\gamma)\,e^{-\gamma-1}$$
$$+ (1-\varkappa)(1-\gamma)\,e^{-\gamma-1} + (1-\varkappa)(1-\gamma)\,e^{-1} + (1-\varkappa)\,e^{-1}\Big]$$
$$+ (1-\varkappa)^2(1-\gamma)^2\Big[9(1-\varkappa)(1-\gamma)\,e^{-\varkappa-\gamma} + 3(1-\varkappa)(1-\gamma)\,e^{-\varkappa-1} + (1-\gamma)\,e^{-\varkappa-1}$$
$$+3(1-\varkappa)(1-\gamma)\,e^{-\gamma-1}\Big]\Big\}.$$

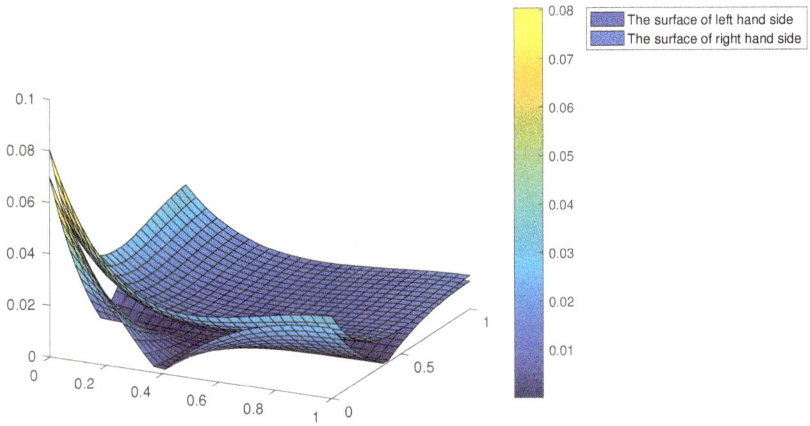

Figure 1. The image description for Theorem 9.

Example 4. *Let $g, h, F : [0,1] \times [0,1] \to \mathbb{R}$ be defined by $g(\varkappa,\gamma) = (1-\varkappa)^2(1-\gamma)^2$, $h(\varkappa,\gamma) = e^{-2\varkappa-2\gamma}$ and $F(\varkappa,\gamma) = \varkappa\gamma\,e^{-\varkappa-\gamma}$ (see Figure 2). Then, F is partially differentiable on $(0,1)\times(0,1)$, its partial derivative is integrable and $\left|\frac{\partial^2 F}{\partial\xi\,\partial\eta}\right|^2$ is co-ordinated (g,h)-convex on $[0,1]^2$. Via Theorem 10 with $p = q = 2$, we have*

$$\left|\varkappa\gamma\,e^{-\varkappa-\gamma} + \left(\frac{4}{e^2} - \frac{4}{e} + 1\right) + (\varkappa\,e^{-\varkappa})\left(\frac{2}{e} - 1\right) + (\gamma\,e^{-\gamma})\left(\frac{2}{e} - 1\right)\right|$$
$$= \left|\varkappa\gamma\,e^{-\varkappa-\gamma} + \int_0^1\int_0^1 uv\,e^{-u-v}\,dv\,du - \int_0^1 u\gamma\,e^{-u-\gamma}\,du - \int_0^1 \varkappa v\,e^{-\varkappa-v}\,dv\right|$$
$$\le \frac{1}{18}\Big\{\varkappa^2\gamma^2\Big[4(1-\varkappa)^2(1-\gamma)^2\,e^{-2\varkappa-2\gamma} + 4(1-\varkappa)^2\,e^{-2\varkappa} + 4(1-\gamma)^2\,e^{-2\gamma} + 4$$
$$+ 2(1-\varkappa)^2(1-\gamma)^2\,e^{-2\varkappa} + 2(1-\varkappa)^2\,e^{-2\varkappa-2\gamma} + (1-\gamma)^2\,e^{-2\varkappa} + (1-\varkappa)^2\,e^{-2\gamma}$$
$$+ 2(1-\gamma)^2\,e^{-2\varkappa-2\gamma} + 2(1-\varkappa)^2(1-\gamma)^2\,e^{-2\gamma} + e^{-2\varkappa-2\gamma} + (1-\varkappa)^2(1-\gamma)^2$$
$$+ 2e^{-2\varkappa} + 2(1-\varkappa)^2 + 2e^{-2\gamma} + 2(1-\gamma)^2\Big]^{1/2} + \varkappa^2(1-\gamma)^2\Big[4(1-\varkappa)^2(1-\gamma)^2\,e^{-2\varkappa-2\gamma} + 4(1-\gamma)^2\,e^{-2\gamma}$$
$$+ 2(1-\varkappa)^2(1-\gamma)^2\,e^{-2\varkappa-2} + (1-\gamma)^2\,e^{-2\varkappa-2} + 2(1-\gamma)^2\,e^{-2\varkappa-2\gamma} + (1-\varkappa)^2(1-\gamma)^2\,e^{-2\gamma}$$

$$+2(1-\varkappa)^2(1-\gamma)^2 e^{-2} + 2(1-\gamma)^2 e^{-2}\Big]^{1/2} + (1-\varkappa)^2\gamma^2\Big[4(1-\varkappa)^2(1-\gamma)^2 e^{-2\varkappa-2\gamma} + 4(1-\varkappa)^2 e^{-2\varkappa}$$
$$+ 2(1-\varkappa)^2(1-\gamma)^2 e^{-2\varkappa} + 2(1-\varkappa)^2 e^{-2\varkappa-2\gamma} + (1-\varkappa)^2 e^{-2\gamma-2} + 2(1-\varkappa)^2(1-\gamma)^2 e^{-2\gamma-2}$$
$$+ (1-\varkappa)^2(1-\gamma)^2 e^{-2\gamma-2} + 2(1-\varkappa)^2(1-\gamma)^2 e^{-2} + 2(1-\varkappa)^2 e^{-2}\Big]^{1/2}$$
$$+ (1-\varkappa)^2(1-\gamma)^2\Big[4(1-\varkappa)^2(1-\gamma)^2 e^{-2\varkappa-2\gamma} + 2(1-\varkappa)^2(1-\gamma)^2 e^{-2\varkappa-2} + (1-\gamma)^2 e^{-2\varkappa-2}$$
$$+2(1-\varkappa)^2(1-\gamma)^2 e^{-2\gamma-2}\Big]^{1/2}\Big\}.$$

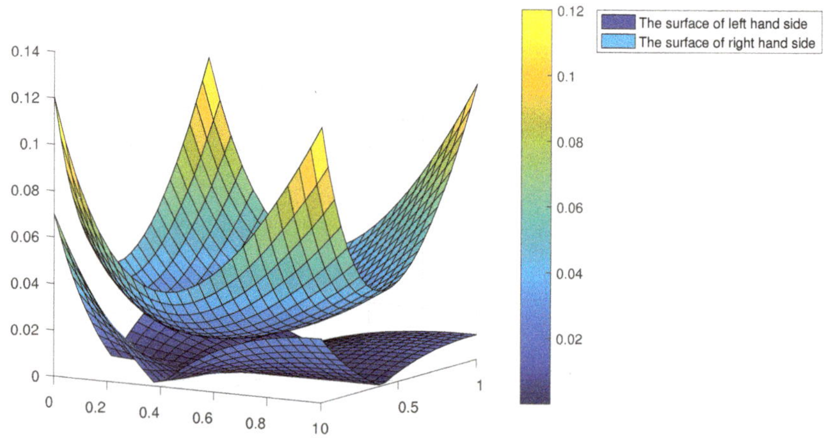

Figure 2. The image description for Theorem 10.

Example 5. *Consider the functions $g, h, F : [0,1]^2 \to \mathbb{R}$ formulated as $g(\varkappa,\gamma) = (1-\varkappa)(1-\gamma)$, $h(\varkappa,\gamma) = e^{-\varkappa-\gamma}$ and $F(\varkappa,\gamma) = \varkappa\gamma e^{-\varkappa-\gamma}$ (see Figure 3). Then, F is partially differentiable on $(0,1)\times(0,1)$, its partial derivative is integrable and $\left|\frac{\partial^2 F}{\partial\xi\,\partial\eta}\right|^2$ is co-ordinated (g,h)-convex on $[0,1]^2$. The utilization of Theorem 11 with $q = 2$ gives*

$$\left|\varkappa\gamma e^{-\varkappa-\gamma} + \left(\frac{4}{e^2} - \frac{4}{e} + 1\right) + \left(\varkappa e^{-\varkappa}\right)\left(\frac{2}{e} - 1\right) + \left(\gamma e^{-\gamma}\right)\left(\frac{2}{e} - 1\right)\right|$$
$$= \left|\varkappa\gamma e^{-\varkappa-\gamma} + \int_0^1\int_0^1 uv\, e^{-u-v}\, dv\, du - \int_0^1 u\gamma\, e^{-u-\gamma}\, du - \int_0^1 \varkappa v\, e^{-\varkappa-v}\, dv\right|$$
$$\leq \frac{1}{24}\Big\{\varkappa^2\gamma^2\Big[9(1-\varkappa)^2(1-\gamma)^2 e^{-2\varkappa-2\gamma} + 3(1-\varkappa)^2 e^{-2\varkappa} + 3(1-\gamma)^2 e^{-2\gamma} + 1$$
$$+ 3(1-\varkappa)^2(1-\gamma)^2 e^{-2\varkappa} + 3(1-\varkappa)^2 e^{-2\varkappa-2\gamma} + (1-\gamma)^2 e^{-2\varkappa} + (1-\varkappa)^2 e^{-2\gamma}$$
$$+ 3(1-\gamma)^2 e^{-2\varkappa-2\gamma} + 3(1-\varkappa)^2(1-\gamma)^2 e^{-2\gamma} + e^{-2\varkappa-2\gamma} + (1-\varkappa)^2(1-\gamma)^2$$
$$+ e^{-2\varkappa} + (1-\varkappa)^2 + e^{-2\gamma} + (1-\gamma)^2\Big]^{1/2} + \varkappa^2(1-\gamma)^2\Big[9(1-\varkappa)^2(1-\gamma)^2 e^{-2\varkappa-2\gamma} + 3(1-\gamma)^2 e^{-2\gamma}$$
$$+ 3(1-\varkappa)^2(1-\gamma)^2 e^{-2\varkappa-2} + (1-\gamma)^2 e^{-2\varkappa-2} + 3(1-\gamma)^2 e^{-2\varkappa-2\gamma} + 3(1-\varkappa)^2(1-\gamma)^2 e^{-2\gamma}$$
$$+(1-\varkappa)^2(1-\gamma)^2 e^{-2} + (1-\gamma)^2 e^{-2}\Big]^{1/2} + (1-\varkappa)^2\gamma^2\Big[9(1-\varkappa)^2(1-\gamma)^2 e^{-2\varkappa-2\gamma} + 3(1-\varkappa)^2 e^{-2\varkappa}$$

$$+ 3(1-\varkappa)^2(1-\gamma)^2\,e^{-2\varkappa} + 3(1-\varkappa)^2\,e^{-2\varkappa-2\gamma} + (1-\varkappa)^2\,e^{-2\gamma-2} + 3(1-\varkappa)^2(1-\gamma)^2\,e^{-2\gamma-2}$$

$$+ (1-\varkappa)^2(1-\gamma)^2\,e^{-2\gamma-2} + (1-\varkappa)^2(1-\gamma)^2\,e^{-2} + (1-\varkappa)^2\,e^{-2}\Big]^{1/2}$$

$$+ (1-\varkappa)^2(1-\gamma)^2\Big[9(1-\varkappa)^2(1-\gamma)^2\,e^{-2\varkappa-2\gamma} + 3(1-\varkappa)^2(1-\gamma)^2\,e^{-2\varkappa-2} + (1-\gamma)^2\,e^{-2\varkappa-2}$$

$$+3(1-\varkappa)^2(1-\gamma)^2\,e^{-2\gamma-2}\Big]^{1/2}\Bigg\}.$$

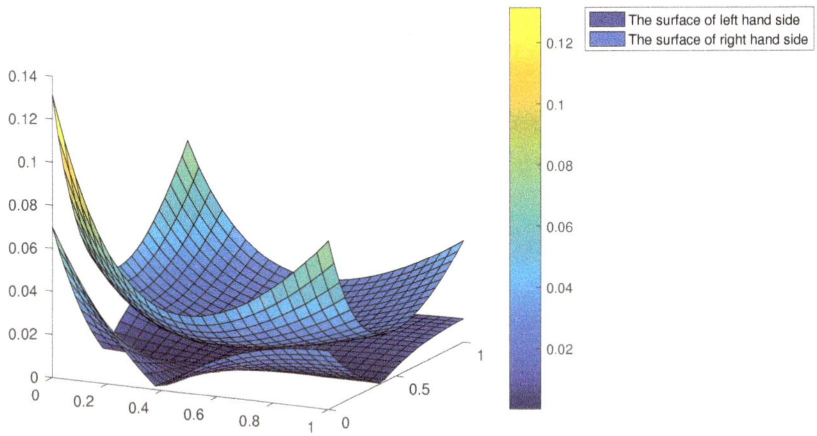

Figure 3. The image description for Theorem 11.

6. Conclusions

We gave a definition of newly defined co-ordinated (g,h)-convexity, which is a generalization of co-ordinated convexity. We also proved some of its significant properties. We established some new Hermite–Hadamard- and Ostrowski-type inequalities in relation to such co-ordinated (g,h)-convex functions. We established that the inequalities derived in this paper generalize the results given in earlier works. Lastly, we gave some examples to demonstrate and show the correctness of the main results. In the next works, one can extend similar theorems to other types of generalized convexity.

Author Contributions: Conceptualization, M.A.A., F.W., H.B.; formal analysis, M.A.A., F.W., H.B., S.E. and S.R.; funding acquisition, S.R.; methodology, M.A.A., F.W., H.B., S.E. and S.R.; software, M.A.A., F.W., H.B. and S.E. All authors have read and agreed to the published version of the manuscript.

Funding: This research received no external funding.

Institutional Review Board Statement: Not applicable.

Informed Consent Statement: Not applicable.

Data Availability Statement: Data sharing is not applicable to this article as no datasets were generated nor analyzed during the current study.

Acknowledgments: S.E. and S.R. would like to thank Azarbaijan Shahid Madani University. Additionally, the authors would like to thank dear reviewers for their constructive comments to improve the quality of the paper.

Conflicts of Interest: The authors declare no conflict of interest.

References

1. Ye, H.; Gao, J.; Ding, Y. A generalized Gronwall inequality and its application to a fractional differential equation. *J. Math. Anal. Appl.* **2007**, *328*, 1075–1081. [CrossRef]
2. Rezapour, S.; Ntouyas, S.K.; Amara, A.; Etemad, S.; Tariboon, J. Some existence and dependence criteria of solutions to a fractional integro-differential boundary value problem via the generalized Gronwall inequality. *Mathematics* **2021**, *9*, 1165. [CrossRef]
3. Rahman, G.; Ullah, Z.; Khan, A.; Set, E.; Nisar, K.S. Certain Chebyshev-type inequalities involving fractional conformable integral operators. *Mathematics* **2019**, *7*, 364. [CrossRef]
4. Alzabut, J.; Abdeljawad, T. A generalized discrete fractional Gronwall inequality and its application on the uniqueness of solutions for nonlinear delay fractional difference system. *Appl. Anal. Discr. Math.* **2018**, *12*, 36–48. [CrossRef]
5. Mohammadi, H.; Baleanu, D.; Etemad, S.; Rezapour, S. Criteria for existence of solutions for a Liouville–Caputo boundary value problem via generalized Gronwall's inequality. *J. Inequal. Appl.* **2021**, *2021*, 36. [CrossRef]
6. Wang, Y.; Liang, S.; Xia, C. A Lyapunov-type inequality for a fractional differential equation under Sturm-Liouville boundary conditions. *Math. Inequal. Appl.* **2017**, *20*, 139–148. [CrossRef]
7. Matar, M.M.; Abu Jarad, M.; Ahmad, M.; Zada, A.; Etemad, S.; Rezapour, S. On the existence and stability of two positive solutions of a hybrid differential system of arbitrary fractional order via Avery–Anderson–Henderson criterion on cones. *Adv. Differ. Equ.* **2021**, *2021*, 423. [CrossRef]
8. Mohammad, H.; Kumar, S.; Rezapour, S.; Etemad, S. A theoretical study of the Caputo–Fabrizio fractional modeling for hearing loss due to Mumps virus with optimal control. *Chaos Solitons Fractals* **2021**, *144*, 110668. [CrossRef]
9. Etemad, S.; Avcı, İ.; Kumar, P.; Baleanu, D.; Rezapour, S. Some novel mathematical analysis on the fractal–fractional model of the AH1N1/09 virus and its generalized Caputo-type version. *Chaos Solitons Fractals* **2022**, *162*, 112511. [CrossRef]
10. Najafi, H.; Etemad, S.; Patanarapeelert, N.; Asamoah, J.K.K.; Rezapour, S.; Sitthiwirattham, T. A study on dynamics of $CD4^+$ T-cells under the effect of HIV-1 infection based on a mathematical fractal-fractional model via the Adams-Bashforth scheme and Newton polynomials. *Mathematics* **2022**, *10*, 1366. [CrossRef]
11. Baleanu, D.; Etemad, S.; Rezapour, S. A hybrid Caputo fractional modeling for thermostat with hybrid boundary value conditions. *Bound. Value Probl.* **2020**, *2020*, 64. [CrossRef]
12. Hermite, C. Sur deux limites d'une integrale de finie. *Mathesis* **1883**, *3*, 82.
13. Hadamard, J. Etude sur les fonctions entiees et en particulier d'une fonction consideree par Riemann. *J. Math. Pures Appl.* **1893**, *58*, 171–215.
14. Ostrowski, A. Uber die absolutabweichung einer differentiebaren funcktion von iherem integralmittelwert. *Comment. Math. Helv.* **1938**, *10*, 226–227. [CrossRef]
15. Ozdemir, M.E.; Avci, M.; Set, E. On some inequalities of Hermite-Hadamard type via m-convexity. *Math. Lett.* **2010**, *23*, 1065–1070. [CrossRef]
16. Ozdemir, M.E.; Avci, M.; Kavurmaci, H. Hermite-Hadamard-type inequalities via (σ, m)-convexity. *Comput. Math. Appl.* **2011**, *61*, 2614–2620. [CrossRef]
17. Lü, Z. On sharp inequalities of Simpson type and Ostrowski type in two independent variables. *Comput. Math. Appl.* **2008**, *56*, 2043–2047. [CrossRef]
18. Sarikaya, M.Z.; Set, E.; Yaldiz, H.; Başak, N. Hermite-Hadamard's inequalities for fractional integrals and related fractional inequalities. *Math. Comput. Model.* **2013**, *57*, 2403–2407. [CrossRef]
19. Set, E. New inequalities of Ostrowski type for mappings whose derivatives are η-convex in the second sense via fractional integrals. *Comput. Math. Appl.* **2012**, *63*, 1147–1154. [CrossRef]
20. İşcan, İ.; Wu, S. Hermite-Hadamard type inequalities for harmonically convex functions via fractional integrals. *Appl. Math. Comput.* **2014**, *238*, 237–244. [CrossRef]
21. Dragomir, S.S. On the Hadamard's inequality for convex functions on the co-ordinates in a rectangle from the plane. *Taiwan. J. Math.* **2001**, *5*, 775–788. [CrossRef]
22. Latif, M.A.; Hussain, S.; Dragomir, S.S. New Ostrowski type inequalities for co-ordinated convex functions. *TJMM* **2012**, *4*, 125–136.
23. Samet, B. A convexity concept with respect to a pair of functions. *Numer. Funct. Anal. Optim.* **2022**, *43*, 522–540. [CrossRef]
24. Ali, M.A.; Soontharanon, J.; Budak, H.; Sitthiwirattham, T.; Fečkon, M. Fractional Hermite-Hadamard inequality and error estimates for Simpson's formula through convexity with respect to pair of functions. *Miskolc Math. Notes* 2022, *in press*.
25. Xie, J.; Ali, M.A.; Budak, H.; Fečkon, M.; Sitthiwirattham, T. Fractional Hermite-Hadamard inequality, Simpson's and Ostrowski's type inequalities for convex functions with respect to a pair of functions. *Rocky Mt. J. Math.* 2022, *in press*.

mathematics

MDPI

Article

Sequential Fractional Hybrid Inclusions: A Theoretical Study via Dhage's Technique and Special Contractions

Sina Etemad [1], Sotiris K. Ntouyas [2,3], Bashir Ahmad [3], Shahram Rezapour [1,4,*] and Jessada Tariboon [5,*]

1 Department of Mathematics, Azarbaijan Shahid Madani University, Tabriz 53751-71379, Iran; sina.etemad@azaruniv.ac.ir
2 Department of Mathematics, University of Ioannina, 451 10 Ioannina, Greece; sntouyas@uoi.gr
3 Nonlinear Analysis and Applied Mathematics (NAAM)-Research Group, Department of Mathematics, Faculty of Science, King Abdulaziz University, P.O. Box 80203, Jeddah 21589, Saudi Arabia; bashir_qau@yahoo.com
4 Department of Medical Research, China Medical University Hospital, China Medical University, Taichung 404332, Taiwan
5 Intelligent and Nonlinear Dynamic Innovations Research Center, Department of Mathematics, Faculty of Applied Science, King Mongkut's University of Technology North Bangkok, Bangkok 10800, Thailand
* Correspondence: rezapourshahram@yahoo.ca (S.R.); jessada.t@sci.kmutnb.ac.th (J.T.)

Abstract: The most important objective of the present research is to establish some theoretical existence results on a novel combined configuration of a Caputo sequential inclusion problem and the hybrid integro-differential one in which the boundary conditions are also formulated as the hybrid multi-order integro-differential conditions. In this respect, firstly, some inequalities are proven in relation to the corresponding integral equation. Then, we employ some newly defined theoretical techniques with the help of the product operators on a Banach algebra and also with the aid of some special functions including α-ψ-contractions and α-admissible mappings to extract the existence criteria corresponding to the given mixed sequential hybrid BVPs. Some important useful properties such as the approximate endpoint property, (C_α)-property, and the compactness play a key role in this regard. The final part of the manuscript is devoted to formulating and computing two applicable examples to guarantee the correctness of the obtained results.

Keywords: α-ψ-contractive maps; endpoint; Dhage's fixed point result; sequential derivative; sequential hybrid inclusion problem

MSC: 26A33; 34B10; 47H10

1. Introduction

Human beings need to recognize different interesting phenomena more than ever before. An appropriate approach to meet this demand is to employ the methods and techniques that are available in fractional calculus and, specifically, the fractional operators in modeling of events and processes. Many operators of this fractional type have appeared in recent years, and their consistency and flexibility are becoming known to mathematicians everyday. In such a way, it is convenient that we design complicated and general abstract mathematical models of processes in the format of applicable fractional BVPs. Several examples of the usability of such operators can be seen in branches of science including biomathematics, medical science, engineering, and so on; see [1–4]. All of these points imply that a wide range of scientists are attracted to work on various angles of applicability of such fractional BVPs along with some dynamical behaviors of solutions of these fractional systems. In the mentioned context, most mathematicians have turned toward studying advanced fractional modelings and relevant theoretical findings and graphical behaviors of solutions for these kinds of BVPs; see [5–11].

Miller with the help of Ross [12] introduced sequential structures of derivatives, which are illustrated by a product of the given derivatives. Later, new findings about different forms of these operators resulted in the publishing of several articles on sequential BVPs in fractional settings. Recently, Alsaedi et al. [13] addressed the primary version of the sequential fractional boundary problem of the Caputo type given by

$$\begin{cases} ({}^{C}\mathcal{D}_{0^+}^{\eta^*} + \mu^{*C}\mathcal{D}_{0^+}^{\eta^*-1})\hbar(z) = \breve{g}_*(z,\hbar(z)), \\ \hbar(0) = 0, \quad \hbar'(0) = 0, \quad \hbar(\sigma) = \gamma^{RL}\mathcal{I}_{0^+}^{\theta^*}\hbar(\delta) \end{cases}$$

so that $\eta^* \in (2,3]$, $\delta \in (0,1)$, $\sigma \in (\delta,1)$ with $\theta^* > 0$, $z \in [0,1]$, $\gamma, \mu^* \in \mathbb{R}^+$, and $\breve{g}_* \in \mathcal{C}([0,1] \times \mathbb{R}, \mathbb{R})$. The authors in relation to the existence results used some usual notions of the nonlinear analysis theory [13]. For more details, check [14].

During the past few years, a new framework of problems called hybrid differential ones supplemented with abstract types of boundary conditions have been in the spotlight of most mathematicians; see, for example, [15–20]. In 2010, the study of this category of equations began with a brilliant paper by Lakshmikantham with the aid of Dhage [21]. Both of them regarded a newly designed hybrid differential equation and obtained its extremal possible solutions by proving several inequalities [21]. After this work, Zhao et al. [22] presented a fractional general extension of the aforementioned BVP in [21] and considered an FBVP consisting of fractional hybrid differential equations. Gradually, researchers have been attracted to this category of modern differential equations. For example, Ahmad et al. [23] carried out a pure mathematical analysis to find the necessary conditions for the existence results of the following Caputo nonlocal hybrid inclusion problem illustrated by

$${}^{C}\mathcal{D}_{0^+}^{\eta^*}\left[\frac{\varpi(z) - \sum_{j=1}^{k}{}^{RL}\mathcal{I}_{0^+}^{\theta_j^*}h_j^*(z,\varpi(z))}{g^*(z,\varpi(z))}\right] \in \mathfrak{O}(z,\varpi(z)),$$

equipped with conditions $\varpi(0) = \beta(z)$ and $\varpi(1) = \alpha \in \mathbb{R}$, where $\eta^* \in (1,2]$ and ${}^{RL}\mathcal{I}_{0^+}^{\theta^*}$ stands for the RL integral of order $\theta^* > 0$ with $\theta^* \in \{\theta_1^*, \theta_2^*, \ldots, \theta_k^*\}$.

In 2020, Baleanu, Etemad, and Rezapour [24] developed a novel hybrid version of the thermostat fractional model, which describes its performance. Indeed, this model checks an amount of ambient heat and controls it according to the temperature assessed by active sensors. We can review the mentioned thermostat hybrid model as

$${}^{C}\mathcal{D}_{0^+}^{\eta^*}\left[\frac{\mu(s)}{w^*(s,\mu(s))}\right] + \tilde{\Phi}(s,\mu(s)) = 0, \quad (\eta^* \in (1,2], s \in [0,1])$$

subject to the fractional hybrid boundary conditions

$$\begin{cases} {}^{C}\mathcal{D}_{0^+}^{1}\left[\frac{\mu(s)}{w^*(s,\mu(s))}\right]\Big|_{s=0} = 0, \\ \lambda_*{}^{C}\mathcal{D}_{0^+}^{\eta^*-1}\left[\frac{\mu(s)}{w^*(s,\mu(s))}\right]\Big|_{s=1} + \left[\frac{\mu(s)}{w^*(s,\mu(s))}\right]\Big|_{s=\delta} = 0, \end{cases}$$

where λ_* is a positive parameter, $\delta \in [0,1]$, and $\eta^* - 1 \in (0,1]$. Furthermore, ${}^{C}\mathcal{D}_{0^+}^{1} = \frac{\mathrm{d}}{\mathrm{d}z}$, ${}^{C}\mathcal{D}_{0^+}^{\gamma^*}$ illustrates the Caputo derivative of order $\gamma^* \in \{\eta^*, \eta^* - 1\}$ and $\tilde{\Phi}, w^* \in \mathcal{C}([0,1] \times \mathbb{R}, \mathbb{R})$ with $w^* \neq 0$. The analytical techniques utilized by the authors rely on some fixed point concepts on self-maps and multifunctions.

In 2021, Abbas and Ragusa [25] dealt with a novel category of hybrid FDEs via proportional derivatives depending to a certain function as

$$\begin{cases} {}^{\varrho}\mathcal{D}^{\delta,\vartheta}_{a^+}\left[\dfrac{\mu(s)}{w^*(s,\mu(s))}\right] = \tilde{\Phi}(s,\mu(s)), \\ {}^{\varrho}\mathcal{I}^{1-\delta,\vartheta}_{a^+}\left[\dfrac{\mu(s)}{w^*(s,\mu(s))}\right]\Big|_{s=a} = b \in \mathbb{R}, \end{cases}$$

where $\varrho, \delta \in (0,1]$ and ${}^{\varrho}\mathcal{D}^{\delta,\vartheta}_{a^+}$ displays the δth-proportional derivative depending on the increasing mapping ϑ with $\vartheta'(s) > 0$. They discussed the continuity of solutions of this BVP in terms of some inputs.

By considering and mixing the ideas of the above problems, we formulate a new combined structure of a Caputo sequential hybrid integro-differential inclusion as follows

$$\mu_1^*({}^{C}\mathcal{D}^{\eta^*}_{0^+} + \mu_2^* {}^{C}\mathcal{D}^{\eta^*-1}_{0^+})\left[\frac{\varpi(z)}{\tilde{S}^*(z,\varpi(z), {}^{RL}\mathcal{I}^{\delta_1^*}_{0^+}\varpi(z),\ldots, {}^{RL}\mathcal{I}^{\delta_k^*}_{0^+}\varpi(z))}\right] \in \tilde{\mathfrak{D}}(z,\varpi(z)) \quad (1)$$

furnished with three-point hybrid multi-order integro-differential conditions:

$$\begin{cases} \left[\dfrac{\varpi(z)}{\tilde{S}^*(z,\varpi(z), {}^{RL}\mathcal{I}^{\delta_1^*}_{0^+}\varpi(z),\ldots, {}^{RL}\mathcal{I}^{\delta_k^*}_{0^+}\varpi(z))}\right]\Big|_{z=0} = 0, \\ {}^{C}\mathcal{D}^{1}_{0^+}\left[\dfrac{\varpi(z)}{\tilde{S}^*(z,\varpi(z), {}^{RL}\mathcal{I}^{\delta_1^*}_{0^+}\varpi(z),\ldots, {}^{RL}\mathcal{I}^{\delta_k^*}_{0^+}\varpi(z))}\right]\Big|_{z=0} = 0, \\ {}^{RL}\mathcal{I}^{\theta_1^*}_{0^+}\left[\dfrac{\varpi(z)}{\tilde{S}^*(z,\varpi(z), {}^{RL}\mathcal{I}^{\delta_1^*}_{0^+}\varpi(z),\ldots, {}^{RL}\mathcal{I}^{\delta_k^*}_{0^+}\varpi(z))}\right]\Big|_{z=1} \\ \qquad + {}^{RL}\mathcal{I}^{\theta_2^*}_{0^+}\left[\dfrac{\varpi(z)}{\tilde{S}^*(z,\varpi(z), {}^{RL}\mathcal{I}^{\delta_1^*}_{0^+}\varpi(z),\ldots, {}^{RL}\mathcal{I}^{\delta_k^*}_{0^+}\varpi(z))}\right]\Big|_{z=\sigma} = 0, \end{cases} \quad (2)$$

where $z \in \mathfrak{T} := [0,1]$, $\eta^* \in [2,3)$, $\eta^* - 1 \in [1,2)$, $\sigma \in (0,1)$, $\mu_1^*, \mu_2^*, \theta_1^*, \theta_2^* > 0$ with $\theta_1^* - 1 > 0$ and $\theta_2^* - 1 > 0$. Furthermore, for $k \in \mathbb{N}$, $\delta_1^*, \delta_2^*, \ldots, \delta_k^* > 0$. Here, ${}^{C}\mathcal{D}^{(\cdot)}_{0^+}$ and ${}^{RL}\mathcal{I}^{(\cdot)}_{0^+}$ display the Caputo derivative and the RL integral. Further, notice that ${}^{C}\mathcal{D}^{1}_{0^+} = \frac{\mathrm{d}}{\mathrm{d}z}$. The continuous real-valued function $\tilde{S}^* \neq 0$ is defined on $\mathfrak{T} \times \mathbb{R}^{k+1}$, and the set-valued map $\tilde{\mathfrak{D}}$ is assumed to be considered on $\mathfrak{T} \times \mathbb{R}$ having some properties that are pointed out in the sequel. In the next stage, we turn to a special nonhybrid form of the above FBVP as follows:

$$\begin{cases} \mu_1^*({}^{C}\mathcal{D}^{\eta^*}_{0^+} + \mu_2^* {}^{C}\mathcal{D}^{\eta^*-1}_{0^+})\varpi(z) \in \tilde{\mathfrak{D}}(z,\varpi(z)), \\ \varpi(0) = 0, \qquad \varpi'(0) = 0, \qquad {}^{RL}\mathcal{I}^{\theta_1^*}_{0^+}\varpi(1) + {}^{RL}\mathcal{I}^{\theta_2^*}_{0^+}\varpi(\sigma) = 0, \end{cases} \quad (3)$$

where $\eta^* \in [2,3)$, $\eta^* - 1 \in [1,2)$, $z \in \mathfrak{T} := [0,1]$, $0 < \sigma < 1$, $\mu_1^*, \mu_2^* \in \mathbb{R}_+$, and ${}^{RL}\mathcal{I}^{(\cdot)}_{0^+}$ illustrates the RL integral of both orders $\theta_1^*, \theta_2^* > 0$ with $\theta_1^* - 1 > 0$ and $\theta_2^* - 1 > 0$. As you see, it is notable that we derive the Caputo sequential inclusion problem (3) if we take $\tilde{S}^*(z,\varpi(z), {}^{RL}\mathcal{I}^{\delta_1^*}_{0^+}\varpi(z),\ldots, {}^{RL}\mathcal{I}^{\delta_k^*}_{0^+}\varpi(z)) = 1$ in the given problem (1) and (2). The readers should pay attention to this point that the combined construction of a sequential problem and a hybrid one is a novel and unique fractional modeling, and this kind of mixed sequential hybrid integro-differential inclusion problem has not been discussed in any literature so far. We organize the rest of the research as follows. In Section 2, we review some primitive notions briefly. In Section 3, we develop some newly defined theoretical methods to derive the required existence criteria corresponding to the given mixed BVPs by (1)–(3). Some existing important properties on operators and the existing space including the approximate endpoint property, the (C_α)-property and the compactness play a key role in this regard. The last section of this manuscript is devoted to formulating and computing two simulation examples to validate the correctness of the results.

2. Preliminaries

This part of the paper is devoted to recalling some basic notions and auxiliary concepts briefly. First of all, we assume that $\eta^* > 0$. Then, one can recall the definition of the Riemann–Liouville integral for $\varpi : [0, +\infty) \to \mathbb{R}$ in the format of ${}^{RL}\mathcal{I}_{0^+}^{\eta^*}\varpi(z) = \int_0^z \frac{(z-q)^{\eta^*-1}}{\Gamma(\eta^*)}\varpi(q)\,\mathrm{d}q$ such that there exists the R.H.S. value finitely [26,27]. Hereafter, we regard $\eta^* \in (n-1, n)$. For $\varpi \in \mathcal{AC}_{\mathbb{R}}^{(n)}([0, +\infty))$, the derivative in the Caputo sense can be defined by the following framework:

$$ {}^{C}\mathcal{D}_{0^+}^{\eta^*}\varpi(z) = \int_0^z \frac{(z-q)^{n-\eta^*-1}}{\Gamma(n-\eta^*)}\varpi^{(n)}(q)\,\mathrm{d}q $$

such that the R.H.S integral exists [26,27]. In addition, for an arbitrary sufficiently smooth map $\varpi : [0, +\infty) \to \mathbb{R}$, one can define the sequential fractional derivative as follows:

$$ \mathcal{D}_{0^+}^{\eta^*}\varpi(z) = (\mathcal{D}_{0^+}^{\eta_1^*}\mathcal{D}_{0^+}^{\eta_2^*}\ldots\mathcal{D}_{0^+}^{\eta_n^*})\varpi(z), $$

where $\eta^* = (\eta_1^*, \eta_2^*, \ldots, \eta_n^*)$ is a multi-index [12]. It is notable that the sequential derivative operator $\mathcal{D}_{0^+}^{\eta^*}$ can be considered one of the Caputo, RL, Hadamard, Caputo–Hadamard, etc. In the present research, we shall utilize the sequential derivative in the Caputo setting, which is illustrated by the following. For $n = 1 + [\eta^*]$, the Caputo sequential derivative of the given map $\varpi : [0, +\infty) \to \mathbb{R}$ is arranged as

$$ {}^{C}\mathcal{D}_{0^+}^{\eta^*}\varpi(z) = \mathcal{D}_{0^+}^{-(n-\eta^*)}\left(\frac{\mathrm{d}}{\mathrm{d}z}\right)^n\varpi(z), $$

where $\mathcal{D}_{0^+}^{-(n-\eta^*)}\varpi(z) = {}^{RL}\mathcal{I}_{0^+}^{(n-\eta^*)}\varpi(z)$ stands for the RL integral of order $n - \eta^*$ [26]. In a monograph presented by Miller and Ross [12], it was demonstrated that the general solution of ${}^{C}\mathcal{D}_{0^+}^{\eta^*}\varpi(z) = 0$ is illustrated by $\varpi(z) = c_0 + c_1 z + c_2 z^2 + \ldots + c_{n-1}z^{n-1}$, and we obtain

$$ {}^{RL}\mathcal{I}_{0^+}^{\eta^*}({}^{C}\mathcal{D}_{0^+}^{\eta^*}\varpi(z)) = \varpi(z) + \sum_{k=0}^{n-1} c_k z^k = \varpi(z) + c_0 + c_1 z + c_2 z^2 + \ldots + c_{n-1}z^{n-1}, $$

in which c_i are real numbers with $n = [\eta^*] + 1$. Assuming the normed space $(\mathfrak{W}, \|\cdot\|_{\mathfrak{W}})$, we introduce the notations $\mathcal{P}(\mathfrak{W})$, $\mathcal{P}_{cls}(\mathfrak{W})$, $\mathcal{P}_{bnd}(\mathfrak{W})$, $\mathcal{P}_{cmp}(\mathfrak{W})$, and $\mathcal{P}_{cvx}(\mathfrak{W})$ to illustrate the set of all nonempty, closed, bounded, compact, and convex subsets of $\mathfrak{W}$, respectively. A metric $\mathbb{PH}_{d_{\mathfrak{W}}} : \mathcal{P}(\mathfrak{W}) \times \mathcal{P}(\mathfrak{W}) \to \mathbb{R}^*$ is named as the Pompeiu–Hausdorff metric if

$$ \mathbb{PH}_{d_{\mathfrak{W}}}(\mathcal{E}_1, \mathcal{E}_2) = \max\{\sup_{e_1\in\mathcal{E}_1} d_{\mathfrak{W}}(e_1, \mathcal{E}_2), \sup_{e_2\in\mathcal{E}_2} d_{\mathfrak{W}}(\mathcal{E}_1, e_2)\} $$

so that $d_{\mathfrak{W}}(\mathcal{E}_1, e_2) = \inf_{e_1\in\mathcal{E}_1} d_{\mathfrak{W}}(e_1, e_2)$ and $d_{\mathfrak{W}}(e_1, \mathcal{E}_2) = \inf_{e_2\in\mathcal{E}_2} d_{\mathfrak{W}}(e_1, e_2)$ [28]. We represent all selections of $\tilde{\mathfrak{H}}$ at point $\varpi \in \mathcal{C}_{\mathbb{R}}(\mathfrak{T})$ by

$$ (\mathbb{SEL})_{\tilde{\mathfrak{H}},\varpi} := \{\hat{\kappa} \in \mathcal{L}_{\mathbb{R}}^1(\mathfrak{T}) : \hat{\kappa}(z) \in \tilde{\mathfrak{H}}(z, \varpi(z))\} $$

for a.e. $z \in \mathfrak{T} := [0,1]$ [28,29]. Further, $(\mathbb{SEL})_{\tilde{\mathfrak{H}},\varpi} \neq \emptyset$ if $\dim(\mathfrak{W}) < \infty$ [28].

A novel category of nonnegative nondecreasing mappings as $\psi : [0, \infty) \to [0, \infty)$ was constructed by Samet et al. [30] in which $\sum_{n=1}^{\infty}\psi^n(z) < \infty$. This category of functions is illustrated by the notation Ψ. The most important property of these functions is that $\psi(z) < z$ for each $z > 0$ [30]. After this work, Mohammadi et al. introduced a generalized framework for set-valued maps as follows [31]. A multifunction $\tilde{\mathfrak{H}} : \mathfrak{W} \to \mathcal{P}_{bnd,cls}(\mathfrak{W})$ is named an α-ψ-contraction whenever for each $\varpi, \varpi' \in \mathfrak{W}$, we have

$$\alpha(\varpi,\varpi')\mathbb{PH}_{d_{\mathfrak{W}}}(\tilde{\mathfrak{H}}\varpi,\tilde{\mathfrak{H}}\varpi') \leq \psi(d_{\mathfrak{W}}(\varpi,\varpi')).$$

We also say that the normed space $\mathfrak{W}$ possesses the (C_α)-property if for each convergent sequence $\{\varpi_n\} \subseteq \mathfrak{W}$ with $\varpi_n \to \varpi$ and $\alpha(\varpi_n,\varpi_{n+1}) \geq 1$ for any $n \in \mathbb{N}$, there exists a subsequence $\{\varpi_{n_j}\}$ of $\{\varpi_n\}$ provided that $\alpha(\varpi_{n_j},\varpi) \geq 1$ for each $j \in \mathbb{N}$. In the same direction, we say that $\tilde{\mathfrak{H}}$ is α-admissible if for every $\varpi \in \mathfrak{W}$ and $\varpi' \in \tilde{\mathfrak{H}}(\varpi)$ with $\alpha(\varpi,\varpi') \geq 1$, we have $\alpha(\varpi',\varpi'') \geq 1$ for all $\varpi'' \in \tilde{\mathfrak{H}}(\varpi')$ [31]. Eventually, an element $\varpi \in \mathfrak{W}$ is said to be the endpoint of $\tilde{\mathfrak{H}} : \mathfrak{W} \to \mathcal{P}(\mathfrak{W})$ if the equality $\tilde{\mathfrak{H}}(\varpi) = \{\varpi\}$ holds [32]. In addition, $\tilde{\mathfrak{H}}$ is a set-valued map having an approximate endpoint property (APPX-endpoint property) if $\inf_{\varpi\in\mathfrak{W}} \sup_{\varrho\in\tilde{\mathfrak{H}}\varpi} d_{\mathfrak{W}}(\varpi,\varrho) = 0$ [32]. We need the following lemmas to establish theoretical results about the existence criteria of solutions in this research.

Lemma 1 ([33]). *The Banach space $\mathfrak{W}$ is assumed to be separable. Suppose that the multi-function $\tilde{\mathfrak{H}} : [0,1] \times \mathfrak{W} \to \mathcal{P}_{cmp,cvx}(\mathfrak{W})$ is $\mathcal{L}^1$-Carathéodory and the linear mapping $\tilde{\mathbb{P}}^* : \mathcal{L}^1_{\mathfrak{W}}([0,1]) \to \mathcal{C}_{\mathfrak{W}}([0,1])$ is continuous. Then, $\tilde{\mathbb{P}}^* \circ (\mathbb{SEL})_{\tilde{\mathfrak{H}}} : \mathcal{C}_{\mathfrak{W}}([0,1]) \to \mathcal{P}_{cmp,cvx}(\mathcal{C}_{\mathfrak{W}}([0,1]))$ defines an operator in $\mathcal{C}_{\mathfrak{W}}([0,1]) \times \mathcal{C}_{\mathfrak{W}}([0,1])$ via action*

$$\varpi \mapsto (\tilde{\mathbb{P}}^* \circ (\mathbb{SEL})_{\tilde{\mathfrak{H}}})(\varpi) = \tilde{\mathbb{P}}^*((\mathbb{SEL})_{\tilde{\mathfrak{H}},\varpi})$$

which has a closed graph.

Lemma 2 ([34]). *Let $\mathfrak{W}$ be a Banach algebra and some items be valid for $\mathbb{A}_1^* : \mathfrak{W} \to \mathfrak{W}$ and $\mathbb{A}_2^* : \mathfrak{W} \to \mathcal{P}_{cmp,cvx}(\mathfrak{W})$ including:*

(1S) $\mathbb{A}_1^*$ is Lipschitz with $l^* > 0$;
(2S) $\mathbb{A}_2^*$ has the upper semi-continuity and the compactness properties;
(3S) $2l^*\hat{\mathbb{O}} < 1$, provided that $\hat{\mathbb{O}} = \|\mathbb{A}_2^*(\mathfrak{W})\|$.

In that case, either (a) $\Sigma^* = \{v^* \in \mathfrak{W} \mid \alpha_0 v^* \in (\mathbb{A}_1^* v^*)(\mathbb{A}_2^* v^*),\ \ \alpha_0 > 1\}$ is unbounded or (b) a member exists in $\mathfrak{W}$ with $\varpi \in (\mathbb{A}_1^*\varpi)(\mathbb{A}_2^*\varpi)$.

Lemma 3 ([31]). *Let the metric space $(\mathfrak{W}, d_{\mathfrak{W}})$ be complete and α be a nonnegative mapping defined on $\mathfrak{W}^2$, $\psi \in \Psi$ be a map that increases strictly, and $\tilde{\mathfrak{H}} : \mathfrak{W} \to \mathcal{P}_{cls,bnd}(\mathfrak{W})$ be α-admissible and an α-ψ-contraction via $\alpha(\varpi,\varpi') \geq 1$ for some $\varpi \in \mathfrak{W}$ and $\varpi' \in \tilde{\mathfrak{H}}(\varpi)$. In this case, $\tilde{\mathfrak{H}}$ includes a fixed point if $\mathfrak{W}$ contains the (C_α)-property.*

Lemma 4 ([32]). *Let the metric space $(\mathfrak{W}, d_{\mathfrak{W}})$ be complete and $\psi : [0,\infty) \to [0,\infty)$ involve the upper semi-continuity specification via $\psi(z) < z$ and $\liminf_{z\to\infty}(z - \psi(z)) > 0$ for all $z > 0$. Besides, we assume that $\tilde{\mathfrak{H}} : \mathfrak{W} \to \mathcal{P}_{cls,bnd}(\mathfrak{W})$ is such that $\mathbb{PH}_{d_{\mathfrak{W}}}(\tilde{\mathfrak{H}}\varpi,\tilde{\mathfrak{H}}\varpi') \leq \psi(d_{\mathfrak{W}}(\varpi,\varpi'))$ for each $\varpi,\varpi' \in \mathfrak{W}$. Then, $\tilde{\mathfrak{H}}$ involves an endpoint uniquely iff $\tilde{\mathfrak{H}}$ possesses the APPX-endpoint property.*

3. Main Results

In two previous sections, we assembled some auxiliary and useful notions to achieve our main goals. Now, in the following, we establish other required lemmas to derive the main existence items. To do this, we first regard the sup norm given by $\|\varpi\|_{\mathfrak{W}} = \sup_{z\in\mathfrak{T}} |\varpi(z)|$ on the space $\mathfrak{W} = \{\varpi(z) : \varpi(z) \in \mathcal{C}_{\mathbb{R}}(\mathfrak{T})\}$. In this case, the Banach space $(\mathfrak{W}, \|\cdot\|_{\mathfrak{W}})$ along with the multiplication action defined as $(\varpi \cdot \varpi')(z) = \varpi(z)\varpi'(z)$ is a

Banach algebra for all $\varpi, \varpi' \in \mathfrak{W}$. In addition, we specify the following constant for the sake of simplicity in computation:

$$\hat{\Omega}_* := \frac{\mu_2^*}{\Gamma(\theta_1^*+2)} - \frac{1}{\Gamma(\theta_1^*+1)} + \frac{\mu_2^*\sigma^{\theta_2^*+1}}{\Gamma(\theta_2^*+2)} - \frac{\sigma^{\theta_2^*}}{\Gamma(\theta_2^*+1)}$$

$$+ \int_0^1 \frac{(1-q)^{\theta_1^*-1}}{\Gamma(\theta_1^*)} e^{-\mu_2^* q} \mathrm{d}q + \int_0^\sigma \frac{(\sigma-q)^{\theta_2^*-1}}{\Gamma(\theta_2^*)} e^{-\mu_2^* q} \mathrm{d}q \neq 0. \tag{4}$$

On this basis, we explore an integral framework for the possible solution of the proposed Caputo sequential hybrid boundary problem of the inclusion version (1) and (2).

Lemma 5. *Let $\tilde{h}_* \in \mathfrak{W}$, $\eta^* \in [2,3)$, $\eta^*-1 \in [1,2)$, $\sigma \in (0,1)$, $\mu_1^*, \mu_2^*, \theta_1^*, \theta_2^* > 0$ with $\theta_1^*-1>0$ and $\theta_2^*-1>0$. Furthermore, for $k \in \mathbb{N}$, $\delta_1^*, \delta_2^*, \ldots, \delta_k^* > 0$. Then, a solution for the sequential hybrid FDE:*

$$\mu_1^*\left({}^{C}\mathcal{D}_{0^+}^{\eta^*} + \mu_2^* {}^{C}\mathcal{D}_{0^+}^{\eta^*-1}\right)\left[\frac{\varpi(z)}{\tilde{S}^*\left(z,\varpi(z), {}^{RL}\mathcal{I}_{0^+}^{\delta_1^*}\varpi(z), \ldots, {}^{RL}\mathcal{I}_{0^+}^{\delta_k^*}\varpi(z)\right)}\right] = \tilde{h}_*(z) \tag{5}$$

furnished with hybrid multi-order integro-differential conditions:

$$\begin{cases} \left[\dfrac{\varpi(z)}{\tilde{S}^*\left(z,\varpi(z), {}^{RL}\mathcal{I}_{0^+}^{\delta_1^*}\varpi(z), \ldots, {}^{RL}\mathcal{I}_{0^+}^{\delta_k^*}\varpi(z)\right)}\right]\Big|_{z=0} = 0, \\ {}^{C}\mathcal{D}_{0^+}^{1}\left[\dfrac{\varpi(z)}{\tilde{S}^*\left(z,\varpi(z), {}^{RL}\mathcal{I}_{0^+}^{\delta_1^*}\varpi(z), \ldots, {}^{RL}\mathcal{I}_{0^+}^{\delta_k^*}\varpi(z)\right)}\right]\Big|_{z=0} = 0, \\ {}^{RL}\mathcal{I}_{0^+}^{\theta_1^*}\left[\dfrac{\varpi(z)}{\tilde{S}^*\left(z,\varpi(z), {}^{RL}\mathcal{I}_{0^+}^{\delta_1^*}\varpi(z), \ldots, {}^{RL}\mathcal{I}_{0^+}^{\delta_k^*}\varpi(z)\right)}\right]\Big|_{z=1} \\ \qquad + {}^{RL}\mathcal{I}_{0^+}^{\theta_2^*}\left[\dfrac{\varpi(z)}{\tilde{S}^*\left(z,\varpi(z), {}^{RL}\mathcal{I}_{0^+}^{\delta_1^*}\varpi(z), \ldots, {}^{RL}\mathcal{I}_{0^+}^{\delta_k^*}\varpi(z)\right)}\right]\Big|_{z=\sigma} = 0, \end{cases} \tag{6}$$

is displayed as $\varpi(z)$ iff

$$\varpi(z) = \tilde{S}^*\left(z,\varpi(z), {}^{RL}\mathcal{I}_{0^+}^{\delta_1^*}\varpi(z), \ldots, {}^{RL}\mathcal{I}_{0^+}^{\delta_k^*}\varpi(z)\right)\left(\frac{1}{\mu_1^*}\int_0^z e^{-\mu_2^*(z-q)}\int_0^q \frac{(q-r)^{\eta^*-2}}{\Gamma(\eta^*-1)}\tilde{h}_*(r)\,\mathrm{d}r\mathrm{d}q\right.$$

$$+ \frac{1-e^{-\mu_2^* z}-\mu_2^* z}{\mu_1^*\hat{\Omega}_*}\left[\int_0^1 \frac{(1-q)^{\theta_1^*-1}}{\Gamma(\theta_1^*)}\int_0^q e^{-\mu_2^*(q-m)}\int_0^m \frac{(m-r)^{\eta^*-2}}{\Gamma(\eta^*-1)}\tilde{h}_*(r)\,\mathrm{d}r\mathrm{d}m\mathrm{d}q\right.$$

$$\left.\left.+ \int_0^\sigma \frac{(\sigma-q)^{\theta_2^*-1}}{\Gamma(\theta_2^*)}\int_0^q e^{-\mu_2^*(q-m)}\int_0^m \frac{(m-r)^{\eta^*-2}}{\Gamma(\eta^*-1)}\tilde{h}_*(r)\,\mathrm{d}r\mathrm{d}m\mathrm{d}q\right]\right), \tag{7}$$

where $\hat{\Omega}_*$ is given in (4).

Proof. We suppose that the function $\tilde{\varpi}_0^*$ satisfies the given Caputo sequential hybrid Equation (5). Then,

$$\mu_1^* {}^{C}\mathcal{D}_{0^+}^{\eta^*}\left(1+\mu_2^* {}^{C}\mathcal{D}_{0^+}^{-1}\right)\left[\frac{\tilde{\varpi}_0^*(z)}{\tilde{S}^*\left(z,\tilde{\varpi}_0^*(z), {}^{RL}\mathcal{I}_{0^+}^{\delta_1^*}\tilde{\varpi}_0^*(z), \ldots, {}^{RL}\mathcal{I}_{0^+}^{\delta_k^*}\tilde{\varpi}_0^*(z)\right)}\right] = \tilde{h}_*(z).$$

In the next step, by taking the η^*-th order integral of the Riemann–Liouville type on the above equality, the following non-homogeneous integro-differential equation results:

$$\mu_1^*(1+\mu_2^{*C}\mathcal{D}_{0^+}^{-1})\left[\frac{\tilde{\omega}_0^*(z)}{\tilde{S}^*(z,\tilde{\omega}_0^*(z),{}^{RL}\mathcal{I}_{0^+}^{\delta_1^*}\tilde{\omega}_0^*(z),\dots,{}^{RL}\mathcal{I}_{0^+}^{\delta_k^*}\tilde{\omega}_0^*(z))}\right]={}^{RL}\mathcal{I}_{0^+}^{\eta^*}\tilde{h}_*(z)+c_0+c_1z+c_2z^2.$$

We try to find these unknowns $c_0, c_1, c_2 \in \mathbb{R}$ provided

$$\mu_1^*\left[\frac{\tilde{\omega}_0^*(z)}{\tilde{S}^*(z,\tilde{\omega}_0^*(z),{}^{RL}\mathcal{I}_{0^+}^{\delta_1^*}\tilde{\omega}_0^*(z),\dots,{}^{RL}\mathcal{I}_{0^+}^{\delta_k^*}\tilde{\omega}_0^*(z))}\right]={}^{RL}\mathcal{I}_{0^+}^{\eta^*}\tilde{h}_*(z)+c_0+c_1z+c_2z^2$$
$$-\mu_1^*\mu_2^*\int_0^z\left[\frac{\tilde{\omega}_0^*(q)}{\tilde{S}^*(q,\tilde{\omega}_0^*(q),{}^{RL}\mathcal{I}_{0^+}^{\delta_1^*}\tilde{\omega}_0^*(q),\dots,{}^{RL}\mathcal{I}_{0^+}^{\delta_k^*}\tilde{\omega}_0^*(q))}\right]\mathrm{d}q. \tag{8}$$

The latter equality implies that $\mu_1^*\left[\frac{\tilde{\omega}_0^*(0)}{\tilde{S}^*\left(0,\tilde{\omega}_0^*(0),{}^{RL}\mathcal{I}_{0^+}^{\delta_1^*}\tilde{\omega}_0^*(0),\dots,{}^{RL}\mathcal{I}_{0^+}^{\delta_k^*}\tilde{\omega}_0^*(0)\right)}\right]=c_0$. In addition, by taking the Caputo derivative of Equation (8) of the first order with respect to z, we obtain

$$\mu_1^{*C}\mathcal{D}_{0^+}^{1}\left[\frac{\tilde{\omega}_0^*(z)}{\tilde{S}^*(z,\tilde{\omega}_0^*(z),{}^{RL}\mathcal{I}_{0^+}^{\delta_1^*}\tilde{\omega}_0^*(z),\dots,{}^{RL}\mathcal{I}_{0^+}^{\delta_k^*}\tilde{\omega}_0^*(z))}\right]={}^{RL}\mathcal{I}_{0^+}^{\eta^*-1}\tilde{h}_*(z)+c_1+2c_2z$$
$$-\mu_1^*\mu_2^*\left[\frac{\tilde{\omega}_0^*(z)}{\tilde{S}^*(z,\tilde{\omega}_0^*(z),{}^{RL}\mathcal{I}_{0^+}^{\delta_1^*}\tilde{\omega}_0^*(z),\dots,{}^{RL}\mathcal{I}_{0^+}^{\delta_k^*}\tilde{\omega}_0^*(z))}\right].$$

By multiplying both sides of the above equality by $e^{\mu_2^*z}$, one can write

$$\mu_1^{*C}\mathcal{D}_{0^+}^{1}\left[\frac{\tilde{\omega}_0^*(z)}{\tilde{S}^*(z,\tilde{\omega}_0^*(z),{}^{RL}\mathcal{I}_{0^+}^{\delta_1^*}\tilde{\omega}_0^*(z),\dots,{}^{RL}\mathcal{I}_{0^+}^{\delta_k^*}\tilde{\omega}_0^*(z))}\right]e^{\mu_2^*z}=e^{\mu_2^*z}{}^{RL}\mathcal{I}_{0^+}^{\eta^*-1}\tilde{h}_*(z)+c_1e^{\mu_2^*z}$$
$$+2c_2ze^{\mu_2^*z}-\mu_1^*\mu_2^*\left[\frac{\tilde{\omega}_0^*(z)}{\tilde{S}^*(z,\tilde{\omega}_0^*(z),{}^{RL}\mathcal{I}_{0^+}^{\delta_1^*}\tilde{\omega}_0^*(z),\dots,{}^{RL}\mathcal{I}_{0^+}^{\delta_k^*}\tilde{\omega}_0^*(z))}\right]e^{\mu_2^*z}.$$

After performing some direct computations and necessary simplifications, we obtain

$$\frac{\tilde{\omega}_0^*(z)}{\tilde{S}^*(z,\tilde{\omega}_0^*(z),{}^{RL}\mathcal{I}_{0^+}^{\delta_1^*}\tilde{\omega}_0^*(z),\dots,{}^{RL}\mathcal{I}_{0^+}^{\delta_k^*}\tilde{\omega}_0^*(z))}=\frac{1}{\mu_1^*}\int_0^z e^{-\mu_2^*(z-q)}\int_0^q\frac{(q-r)^{\eta^*-2}}{\Gamma(\eta^*-1)}\tilde{h}_*(r)\,\mathrm{d}r\mathrm{d}q$$
$$+\frac{c_0}{\mu_1^*}e^{-\mu_2^*z}+\frac{c_1}{\mu_1^*\mu_2^*}(1-e^{-\mu_2^*z})+\frac{2c_2}{\mu_1^*\mu_2^{*2}}(\mu_2^*z-1+e^{-\mu_2^*z}). \tag{9}$$

Here, in light of the hybrid multi-order integro-differential conditions (6), we obtain $c_0=c_1=0$ and

$$c_2=-\frac{\mu_2^{*2}}{2\hat{\Omega}_*}\int_0^1\frac{(1-q)^{\theta_1^*-1}}{\Gamma(\theta_1^*)}\int_0^q e^{-\mu_2^*(q-m)}\int_0^m\frac{(m-r)^{\eta^*-2}}{\Gamma(\eta^*-1)}\tilde{h}_*(r)\,\mathrm{d}r\mathrm{d}m\mathrm{d}q$$
$$-\frac{\mu_2^{*2}}{2\hat{\Omega}_*}\int_0^\sigma\frac{(\sigma-q)^{\theta_2^*-1}}{\Gamma(\theta_2^*)}\int_0^q e^{-\mu_2^*(q-m)}\int_0^m\frac{(m-r)^{\eta^*-2}}{\Gamma(\eta^*-1)}\tilde{h}_*(r)\,\mathrm{d}r\mathrm{d}m\mathrm{d}q,$$

where we have mentioned before the nonzero constant $\hat{\Omega}_*$ in (4). Eventually, we insert all three values c_0, c_1, and c_2 into (9) and (9) becomes

$$\tilde{\varpi}_0^*(z) = \tilde{S}^*\left(z, \tilde{\varpi}_0^*(z), {}^{RL}\mathcal{I}_{0^+}^{\delta_1^*}\tilde{\varpi}_0^*(z), \ldots, {}^{RL}\mathcal{I}_{0^+}^{\delta_k^*}\tilde{\varpi}_0^*(z)\right)\left(\frac{1}{\mu_1^*}\int_0^z e^{-\mu_2^*(z-q)}\int_0^q \frac{(q-r)^{\eta^*-2}}{\Gamma(\eta^*-1)}\tilde{h}_*(r)\,\mathrm{d}r\mathrm{d}q\right.$$

$$+\frac{1-e^{-\mu_2^* z}-\mu_2^* z}{\mu_1^*\hat{\Omega}_*}\left[\int_0^1 \frac{(1-q)^{\theta_1^*-1}}{\Gamma(\theta_1^*)}\int_0^q e^{-\mu_2^*(q-m)}\int_0^m \frac{(m-r)^{\eta^*-2}}{\Gamma(\eta^*-1)}\tilde{h}_*(r)\,\mathrm{d}r\mathrm{d}m\mathrm{d}q\right.$$

$$\left.\left.+\int_0^\sigma \frac{(\sigma-q)^{\theta_2^*-1}}{\Gamma(\theta_2^*)}\int_0^q e^{-\mu_2^*(q-m)}\int_0^m \frac{(m-r)^{\eta^*-2}}{\Gamma(\eta^*-1)}\tilde{h}_*(r)\,\mathrm{d}r\mathrm{d}m\mathrm{d}q\right]\right). \tag{10}$$

This indicates that the function $\tilde{\varpi}_0^*$ can be regarded as a solution for (7), and the argument is finished. The converse is evident. □

Next, we present the following inequalities, which are useful in the sequel.

Lemma 6. *Let $\tilde{h}_* : \mathfrak{T} \to \mathbb{R}$ be continuous via $\|\tilde{h}_*\| = \sup_{z\in\mathfrak{T}}|\tilde{h}_*(z)|$. Then, the following inequalities are valid:*

(E1) $\left|\int_0^z e^{-\mu_2^*(z-q)}\int_0^q \frac{(q-r)^{\eta^*-2}}{\Gamma(\eta^*-1)}\tilde{h}_*(r)\,\mathrm{d}r\mathrm{d}q\right| \le \frac{1-e^{-\mu_2^*}}{\mu_2^*\Gamma(\eta^*)}\|\tilde{h}_*\|;$

(E2) $\left|\int_0^1 \frac{(1-q)^{\theta_1^*-1}}{\Gamma(\theta_1^*)}\int_0^q e^{-\mu_2^*(q-m)}\int_0^m \frac{(m-r)^{\eta^*-2}}{\Gamma(\eta^*-1)}\tilde{h}_*(r)\,\mathrm{d}r\mathrm{d}m\mathrm{d}q\right| \le \frac{\mu_2^*+e^{-\mu_2^*}-1}{\mu_2^{*2}\Gamma(\theta_1^*)\Gamma(\eta^*)}\|\tilde{h}_*\|;$

(E3) $\left|\int_0^\sigma \frac{(\sigma-q)^{\theta_2^*-1}}{\Gamma(\theta_2^*)}\int_0^q e^{-\mu_2^*(q-m)}\int_0^m \frac{(m-r)^{\eta^*-2}}{\Gamma(\eta^*-1)}\tilde{h}_*(r)\,\mathrm{d}r\mathrm{d}m\mathrm{d}q\right| \le$
$\frac{\sigma^{\theta_2^*+\eta^*-1}(\mu_2^*\sigma+e^{-\mu_2^*\sigma}-1)}{\mu_2^{*2}\Gamma(\theta_2^*)\Gamma(\eta^*)}\|\tilde{h}_*\|.$

Proof. (E1) In the first stage, a simple computation yields

$$\int_0^q \frac{(q-r)^{\eta^*-2}}{\Gamma(\eta^*-1)}\mathrm{d}r = -\frac{(q-r)^{\eta^*-1}}{\Gamma(\eta^*)}\bigg|_0^q = \frac{q^{\eta^*-1}}{\Gamma(\eta^*)}.$$

In the next step, one can write

$$\int_0^z e^{-\mu_2^*(z-q)}\int_0^q \frac{(q-r)^{\eta^*-2}}{\Gamma(\eta^*-1)}\mathrm{d}r\mathrm{d}q = \int_0^z e^{-\mu_2^*(z-q)}\frac{q^{\eta^*-1}}{\Gamma(\eta^*)}\mathrm{d}q \le \frac{z^{\eta^*-1}}{\Gamma(\eta^*)}\int_0^z e^{-\mu_2^*(z-q)}\mathrm{d}q$$

$$\le \frac{1}{\Gamma(\eta^*)}\left(-\frac{1}{\mu_2^*}e^{-\mu_2^*(z-q)}\right)\bigg|_0^z = -\frac{1}{\mu_2^*\Gamma(\eta^*)}(1-e^{-\mu_2^* z}).$$

Thus, we obtain

$$\left|\int_0^z e^{-\mu_2^*(z-q)}\int_0^q \frac{(q-r)^{\eta^*-2}}{\Gamma(\eta^*-1)}\tilde{h}_*(r)\,\mathrm{d}r\mathrm{d}q\right| \le \frac{1-e^{-\mu_2^*}}{\mu_2^*\Gamma(\eta^*)}\|\tilde{h}_*\|.$$

(E2) By some easy calculations, we have

$$\int_0^m \frac{(m-r)^{\eta^*-2}}{\Gamma(\eta^*-1)}\mathrm{d}r = -\frac{(m-r)^{\eta^*-1}}{\Gamma(\eta^*)}\bigg|_0^m = \frac{m^{\eta^*-1}}{\Gamma(\eta^*)}. \tag{11}$$

In addition, one may write

$$\int_0^q e^{-\mu_2^*(q-m)} \int_0^m \frac{(m-r)^{\eta^*-2}}{\Gamma(\eta^*-1)}\, \mathrm{d}r\mathrm{d}m = \int_0^q e^{-\mu_2^*(q-m)} \frac{m^{\eta^*-1}}{\Gamma(\eta^*)}\, \mathrm{d}m \le \frac{q^{\eta^*-1}}{\Gamma(\eta^*)} \int_0^q e^{-\mu_2^*(q-m)} \mathrm{d}m$$

$$= \frac{q^{\eta^*-1}}{\Gamma(\eta^*)}\Big(-\frac{1}{\mu_2^*} e^{-\mu_2^*(q-m)}\Big)\Big|_0^q = -\frac{q^{\eta^*-1}}{\mu_2^*\Gamma(\eta^*)}(1-e^{-\mu_2^* q}). \tag{12}$$

Then, by mixing the above results, we obtain

$$\Big|\int_0^1 \frac{(1-q)^{\theta_1^*-1}}{\Gamma(\theta_1^*)} \int_0^q e^{-\mu_2^*(q-m)} \int_0^m \frac{(m-r)^{\eta^*-2}}{\Gamma(\eta^*-1)} \tilde{h}_*(r)\, \mathrm{d}r\mathrm{d}m\mathrm{d}q\Big|$$

$$\le \|\tilde{h}_*\| \int_0^1 \frac{(1-q)^{\theta_1^*-1}}{\Gamma(\theta_1^*)} \frac{q^{\eta^*-1}(1-e^{-\mu_2^* q})}{\mu_2^*\Gamma(\eta^*)}\, \mathrm{d}q$$

$$\le \|\tilde{h}_*\| \frac{1}{\mu_2^*\Gamma(\theta_1^*)\Gamma(\eta^*)} \int_0^1 (1-e^{-\mu_2^* q})\, \mathrm{d}q = \|\tilde{h}_*\| \frac{1}{\mu_2^*\Gamma(\theta_1^*)\Gamma(\eta^*)}(1+\frac{1}{\mu_2^*}e^{-\mu_2^*} - \frac{1}{\mu_2^*})$$

$$= \|\tilde{h}_*\| \frac{1}{\mu_2^{*2}\Gamma(\theta_1^*)\Gamma(\eta^*)}(\mu_2^* + e^{-\mu_2^*} - 1).$$

(E3) By similar computations and according to (11) and (12), we have

$$\int_0^q e^{-\mu_2^*(q-m)} \int_0^m \frac{(m-r)^{\eta^*-2}}{\Gamma(\eta^*-1)}\, \mathrm{d}r\mathrm{d}m \le -\frac{q^{\eta^*-1}}{\mu_2^*\Gamma(\eta^*)}(1-e^{-\mu_2^* q}).$$

Thus,

$$\Big|\int_0^\sigma \frac{(\sigma-q)^{\theta_2^*-1}}{\Gamma(\theta_2^*)} \int_0^q e^{-\mu_2^*(q-m)} \int_0^m \frac{(m-r)^{\eta^*-2}}{\Gamma(\eta^*-1)} \tilde{h}_*(r)\, \mathrm{d}r\mathrm{d}m\mathrm{d}q\Big|$$

$$\le \|\tilde{h}_*\| \int_0^\sigma \frac{(\sigma-q)^{\theta_2^*-1}}{\Gamma(\theta_2^*)} \frac{q^{\eta^*-1}(1-e^{-\mu_2^* q})}{\mu_2^*\Gamma(\eta^*)}\, \mathrm{d}q$$

$$\le \|\tilde{h}_*\| \frac{1}{\mu_2^*\Gamma(\theta_2^*)\Gamma(\eta^*)} \int_0^\sigma \sigma^{\theta_2^*-1}\sigma^{\eta^*-1}(1-e^{-\mu_2^* q})\, \mathrm{d}q$$

$$\le \|\tilde{h}_*\| \frac{\sigma^{\theta_2^*+\eta^*-1}}{\mu_2^*\Gamma(\theta_2^*)\Gamma(\eta^*)} \int_0^\sigma (1-e^{-\mu_2^* q})\, \mathrm{d}q = \|\tilde{h}_*\| \frac{\sigma^{\theta_2^*+\eta^*-1}}{\mu_2^*\Gamma(\theta_2^*)\Gamma(\eta^*)}(\sigma + \frac{1}{\mu_2^*}e^{-\mu_2^*\sigma} - \frac{1}{\mu_2^*})$$

$$= \|\tilde{h}_*\| \frac{\sigma^{\theta_2^*+\eta^*-1}}{\mu_2^{*2}\Gamma(\theta_2^*)\Gamma(\eta^*)}(\mu_2^*\sigma + e^{-\mu_2^*\sigma} - 1).$$

□

Definition 1. *A function $\varpi \in \mathcal{AC}_{\mathbb{R}}(\mathfrak{T})$ is a solution of the suggested sequential multi-order hybrid inclusion boundary problem* (1) *and* (2) *if some function $\mathfrak{k} \in \mathcal{L}^1_{\mathbb{R}}(\mathfrak{T})$ exists with $\mathfrak{k}(z) \in \tilde{\mathfrak{H}}(z, \varpi(z))$ for almost all $z \in \mathfrak{T}$ that satisfies the following hybrid multi-order integro-differential boundary conditions:*

$$\begin{cases} \left[\dfrac{\varpi(z)}{\tilde{S}^*(z,\varpi(z),{}^{RL}\mathcal{I}_{0^+}^{\delta_1^*}\varpi(z),\ldots,{}^{RL}\mathcal{I}_{0^+}^{\delta_k^*}\varpi(z))}\right]\Big|_{z=0}=0, \\ {}^{C}\mathcal{D}_{0^+}^{1}\left[\dfrac{\varpi(z)}{\tilde{S}^*(z,\varpi(z),{}^{RL}\mathcal{I}_{0^+}^{\delta_1^*}\varpi(z),\ldots,{}^{RL}\mathcal{I}_{0^+}^{\delta_k^*}\varpi(z))}\right]\Big|_{z=0}=0, \\ {}^{RL}\mathcal{I}_{0^+}^{\theta_1^*}\left[\dfrac{\varpi(z)}{\tilde{S}^*(z,\varpi(z),{}^{RL}\mathcal{I}_{0^+}^{\delta_1^*}\varpi(z),\ldots,{}^{RL}\mathcal{I}_{0^+}^{\delta_k^*}\varpi(z))}\right]\Big|_{z=1} \\ \qquad +{}^{RL}\mathcal{I}_{0^+}^{\theta_2^*}\left[\dfrac{\varpi(z)}{\tilde{S}^*(z,\varpi(z),{}^{RL}\mathcal{I}_{0^+}^{\delta_1^*}\varpi(z),\ldots,{}^{RL}\mathcal{I}_{0^+}^{\delta_k^*}\varpi(z))}\right]\Big|_{z=\sigma}=0, \end{cases}$$

and

$$\varpi(z)=\tilde{S}^*(z,\varpi(z),{}^{RL}\mathcal{I}_{0^+}^{\delta_1^*}\varpi(z),\ldots,{}^{RL}\mathcal{I}_{0^+}^{\delta_k^*}\varpi(z))\left(\frac{1}{\mu_1^*}\int_0^z e^{-\mu_2^*(z-q)}\int_0^q\frac{(q-r)^{\eta^*-2}}{\Gamma(\eta^*-1)}\hat{\kappa}(r)\,\mathrm{d}r\mathrm{d}q\right.$$

$$+\frac{1-e^{-\mu_2^*z}-\mu_2^*z}{\mu_1^*\hat{\Omega}_*}\left[\int_0^1\frac{(1-q)^{\theta_1^*-1}}{\Gamma(\theta_1^*)}\int_0^q e^{-\mu_2^*(q-m)}\int_0^m\frac{(m-r)^{\eta^*-2}}{\Gamma(\eta^*-1)}\hat{\kappa}(r)\,\mathrm{d}r\mathrm{d}m\mathrm{d}q\right.$$

$$\left.\left.+\int_0^\sigma\frac{(\sigma-q)^{\theta_2^*-1}}{\Gamma(\theta_2^*)}\int_0^q e^{-\mu_2^*(q-m)}\int_0^m\frac{(m-r)^{\eta^*-2}}{\Gamma(\eta^*-1)}\hat{\kappa}(r)\,\mathrm{d}r\mathrm{d}m\mathrm{d}q\right]\right)$$

for any $z\in\mathfrak{T}$.

For now, by taking into account Lemmas 5 and 6, we provide some existence theorems for two Caputo sequential multi-order BVPs (1)–(3).

Theorem 1. *Assume that a continuous real mapping* $\tilde{S}^*\neq 0$ *is defined on product space* $\mathfrak{T}\times\mathfrak{W}^{k+1}$ *and* $\tilde{\mathfrak{H}}:\mathfrak{T}\times\mathfrak{W}\to\mathcal{P}_{cvx,cmp}(\mathfrak{W})$. *Along with these, the following statements are valid:*

(HPS1) *There exists a bounded positive-valued mapping* $\tilde{v}:\mathfrak{T}\to\mathbb{R}^+$ *so that for each member* $\varpi_1,\ldots,\varpi_{k+1},\varpi_1',\ldots,\varpi_{k+1}'\in\mathfrak{W}$ *and* $z\in\mathfrak{T}$, *we have*

$$|\tilde{S}^*(z,\varpi_1(z),\ldots,\varpi_{k+1}(z))-\tilde{S}^*(z,\varpi_1'(z),\ldots,\varpi_{k+1}'(z))|\leq\tilde{v}(z)\sum_{i=1}^{k+1}|\varpi_i(z)-\varpi_i'(z)|;$$

(HPS2) $\tilde{\mathfrak{H}}:\mathfrak{T}\times\mathfrak{W}\to\mathcal{P}_{cvx,cmp}(\mathfrak{W})$ *is supposed to be* $\mathcal{L}^1$*-Caratheodory;*

(HPS3) *There is a positive function* $x^*\in\mathcal{L}^1_{\mathbb{R}^+}(\mathfrak{T})$ *such that for any* $\varpi\in\mathfrak{W}$ *and for almost all* $z\in\mathfrak{T}$, *we have*

$$\|\tilde{\mathfrak{H}}(z,\varpi)\|=\sup\{|\hat{\kappa}|:\ \hat{\kappa}\in\tilde{\mathfrak{H}}(z,\varpi(z))\}\leq x^*(z);$$

(HPS4) *There is a number* $r_*\in\mathbb{R}^+$ *provided that*

$$r_*>\frac{\mathbb{S}^*\mathbb{M}_*\|x^*\|}{1-\tilde{v}^*\left(1+\dfrac{1}{\Gamma(\delta_1^*+1)}+\ldots+\dfrac{1}{\Gamma(\delta_k^*+1)}\right)\mathbb{M}_*\|x^*\|},\tag{13}$$

where $\|x^*\|=\sup_{z\in\mathfrak{T}}\{|x(z)|\}$, $\mathbb{S}^*=\sup_{z\in\mathfrak{T}}|\tilde{S}^*(z,0,\ldots,0)|$, $\tilde{v}^*=\sup_{z\in\mathfrak{T}}|\tilde{v}(z)|$ *and*

$$\mathbb{M}_*=\frac{|1-e^{-\mu_2^*}|}{\mu_1^*\mu_2^*\Gamma(\eta^*)}+\frac{|1-e^{-\mu_2^*}|+\mu_2^*}{\mu_1^*|\hat{\Omega}_*|}\left(\frac{|\mu_2^*+e^{-\mu_2^*}-1|}{\mu_2^{*2}\Gamma(\theta_1^*)\Gamma(\eta^*)}+\frac{\sigma^{\theta_2^*+\eta^*-1}|\mu_2^*\sigma+e^{-\mu_2^*\sigma}-1|}{\mu_2^{*2}\Gamma(\theta_2^*)\Gamma(\eta^*)}\right).\tag{14}$$

Then, the Caputo sequential hybrid multi-order integro-differential inclusion BVP (1) *and* (2) *has a solution if an inequality* $\tilde{\upsilon}^*\left(1+\frac{1}{\Gamma(\delta_1^*+1)}+\ldots+\frac{1}{\Gamma(\delta_k^*+1)}\right)\mathbb{M}_*\|x^*\|<\frac{1}{2}$ *holds strictly.*

Proof. First of all, for every $\varpi \in \mathfrak{W}$, we construct the following collection of selections for $\tilde{\mathfrak{H}}$ as follows:

$$(\mathbb{SEL})_{\tilde{\mathfrak{H}},\varpi}=\left\{\hat{\kappa}\in\mathcal{L}^1(\mathfrak{T}):\hat{\kappa}(z)\in\tilde{\mathfrak{H}}(z,\varpi(z))\right\}$$

for almost all $z \in \mathfrak{T}$. In addition, we consider a set-valued map $\mathcal{G}^*:\mathfrak{W}\to\mathcal{P}(\mathfrak{W})$ by $\mathcal{G}^*(\varpi)=\{g^*\in\mathfrak{W}:g^*(z)=\rho^*(z)\text{ for }z\in\mathfrak{T}\}$, where

$$\rho^*(z)=\tilde{S}^*\left(z,\varpi(z),{}^{RL}\mathcal{I}_{0^+}^{\delta_1^*}\varpi(z),\ldots,{}^{RL}\mathcal{I}_{0^+}^{\delta_k^*}\varpi(z)\right)\left(\frac{1}{\mu_1^*}\int_0^z e^{-\mu_2^*(z-q)}\int_0^q\frac{(q-r)^{\eta^*-2}}{\Gamma(\eta^*-1)}\hat{\kappa}(r)\,\mathrm{d}r\mathrm{d}q\right.$$

$$+\frac{1-e^{-\mu_2^*z}-\mu_2^*z}{\mu_1^*\hat{\Omega}_*}\left[\int_0^1\frac{(1-q)^{\theta_1^*-1}}{\Gamma(\theta_1^*)}\int_0^q e^{-\mu_2^*(q-m)}\int_0^m\frac{(m-r)^{\eta^*-2}}{\Gamma(\eta^*-1)}\hat{\kappa}(r)\,\mathrm{d}r\mathrm{d}m\mathrm{d}q\right.$$

$$\left.\left.+\int_0^\sigma\frac{(\sigma-q)^{\theta_2^*-1}}{\Gamma(\theta_2^*)}\int_0^q e^{-\mu_2^*(q-m)}\int_0^m\frac{(m-r)^{\eta^*-2}}{\Gamma(\eta^*-1)}\hat{\kappa}(r)\,\mathrm{d}r\mathrm{d}m\mathrm{d}q\right]\right)$$

for some $\hat{\kappa}\in(\mathbb{SEL})_{\tilde{\mathfrak{H}},\varpi}$. It is evident that $g_0^*\in\mathfrak{W}$ is considered as a solution for the Caputo sequential hybrid multi-order inclusion BVP (1) and (2) iff g_0^* is a fixed point of $\mathcal{G}^*$. To begin the main proof, with due attention to Lemma 5, we formulate two different structural mappings $\mathbb{A}_1^*:\mathfrak{W}\to\mathfrak{W}$ by $(\mathbb{A}_1^*\varpi)(z)=\tilde{S}^*\left(z,\varpi(z),{}^{RL}\mathcal{I}_{0^+}^{\delta_1^*}\varpi(z),\ldots,{}^{RL}\mathcal{I}_{0^+}^{\delta_k^*}\varpi(z)\right)$ and $\mathbb{A}_2^*:\mathfrak{W}\to\mathcal{P}(\mathfrak{W})$ by

$$(\mathbb{A}_2^*\varpi)(z)=\{v\in\mathfrak{W}:v(z)=\varphi(z)\text{ for }z\in\mathfrak{T}\},$$

where

$$\varphi(z)=\frac{1}{\mu_1^*}\int_0^z e^{-\mu_2^*(z-q)}\int_0^q\frac{(q-r)^{\eta^*-2}}{\Gamma(\eta^*-1)}\hat{\kappa}(r)\,\mathrm{d}r\mathrm{d}q$$

$$+\frac{1-e^{-\mu_2^*z}-\mu_2^*z}{\mu_1^*\hat{\Omega}_*}\left[\int_0^1\frac{(1-q)^{\theta_1^*-1}}{\Gamma(\theta_1^*)}\int_0^q e^{-\mu_2^*(q-m)}\int_0^m\frac{(m-r)^{\eta^*-2}}{\Gamma(\eta^*-1)}\hat{\kappa}(r)\,\mathrm{d}r\mathrm{d}m\mathrm{d}q\right.$$

$$\left.+\int_0^\sigma\frac{(\sigma-q)^{\theta_2^*-1}}{\Gamma(\theta_2^*)}\int_0^q e^{-\mu_2^*(q-m)}\int_0^m\frac{(m-r)^{\eta^*-2}}{\Gamma(\eta^*-1)}\hat{\kappa}(r)\,\mathrm{d}r\mathrm{d}m\mathrm{d}q\right]$$

for some $\hat{\kappa}\in(\mathbb{SEL})_{\tilde{\mathfrak{H}},\varpi}$. Then, one can represent the product operator equation:

$$\mathcal{G}^*(\varpi)=\mathbb{A}_1^*\varpi\mathbb{A}_2^*\varpi.$$

The basic aim at present is to verify that $\mathbb{A}_1^*$ and $\mathbb{A}_2^*$ settle all hypotheses of Lemma 2. We in the first place intend to confirm that $\mathbb{A}_1^*$ is Lipschitz on space $\mathfrak{W}$. Let $\varpi_1,\varpi_2\in\mathfrak{W}$ be arbitrary. By proceeding under the hypothesis (HPS1), it is deduced that

$$\left|(\mathbb{A}_1^*\varpi_1)(z)-(\mathbb{A}_1^*\varpi_2)(z)\right|=\left|\tilde{S}^*\left(z,\varpi_1(z),{}^{RL}\mathcal{I}_{0^+}^{\delta_1^*}\varpi_1(z),\ldots,{}^{RL}\mathcal{I}_{0^+}^{\delta_k^*}\varpi_1(z)\right)\right.$$

$$\left.-\tilde{S}^*\left(z,\varpi_2(z),{}^{RL}\mathcal{I}_{0^+}^{\delta_1^*}\varpi_2(z),\ldots,{}^{RL}\mathcal{I}_{0^+}^{\delta_k^*}\varpi_2(z)\right)\right|$$

$$\leq\tilde{\upsilon}(z)\left(|\varpi_1(z)-\varpi_2(z)|+\frac{1}{\Gamma(\delta_1^*+1)}|\varpi_1(z)-\varpi_2(z)|+\ldots+\frac{1}{\Gamma(\delta_k^*+1)}|\varpi_1(z)-\varpi_2(z)|\right)$$

$$= \tilde{v}(z)(1+\frac{1}{\Gamma(\delta_1^*+1)}+\ldots+\frac{1}{\Gamma(\delta_k^*+1)})|\varpi_1(z)-\varpi_2(z)|$$

for all $z \in \mathfrak{T} := [0,1]$. Hence, we obtain

$$\|\mathbb{A}_1^*\varpi_1 - \mathbb{A}_1^*\varpi_2\|_{\mathfrak{W}} \leq \tilde{v}^*\Big(1+\frac{1}{\Gamma(\delta_1^*+1)}+\ldots+\frac{1}{\Gamma(\delta_k^*+1)}\Big)\|\varpi_1-\varpi_2\|_{\mathfrak{W}}$$

for all $\varpi_1, \varpi_2 \in \mathfrak{W}$. It follows that the single-valued mapping $\mathbb{A}_1^*$ is Lipschitz via constant $\tilde{v}^*\Big(1+\frac{1}{\Gamma(\delta_1^*+1)}+\ldots+\frac{1}{\Gamma(\delta_k^*+1)}\Big)$. In the subsequent stage, we proceed to determine that $\mathbb{A}_2^*$ involves convex values. To emphasize the correctness of such a claim, let $\varpi_1, \varpi_2 \in \mathbb{A}_2^*\varpi$ be arbitrary. Choose functions $\hat{\kappa}_1, \hat{\kappa}_2 \in (\mathbb{SEL})_{\tilde{\mathfrak{H}},\varpi}$ such that

$$\varpi_l(z) = \frac{1}{\mu_1^*}\int_0^z e^{-\mu_2^*(z-q)}\int_0^q \frac{(q-r)^{\eta^*-2}}{\Gamma(\eta^*-1)}\hat{\kappa}_l(r)\,drdq$$

$$+\frac{1-e^{-\mu_2^* z}-\mu_2^* z}{\mu_1^*\hat{\Omega}_*}\Bigg[\int_0^1 \frac{(1-q)^{\theta_1^*-1}}{\Gamma(\theta_1^*)}\int_0^q e^{-\mu_2^*(q-m)}\int_0^m \frac{(m-r)^{\eta^*-2}}{\Gamma(\eta^*-1)}\hat{\kappa}_l(r)\,drdmdq$$

$$+\int_0^\sigma \frac{(\sigma-q)^{\theta_2^*-1}}{\Gamma(\theta_2^*)}\int_0^q e^{-\mu_2^*(q-m)}\int_0^m \frac{(m-r)^{\eta^*-2}}{\Gamma(\eta^*-1)}\hat{\kappa}_l(r)\,drdmdq\Bigg]$$

for all $z \in \mathfrak{T}$ (a.e.) and for $l = 1,2$. Further, let $\lambda \in (0,1)$. In this case, one may write

$$\lambda\varpi_1(z)+(1-\lambda)\varpi_2(z) = \frac{1}{\mu_1^*}\int_0^z e^{-\mu_2^*(z-q)}\int_0^q \frac{(q-r)^{\eta^*-2}}{\Gamma(\eta^*-1)}[\lambda\hat{\kappa}_1(r)+(1-\lambda)\hat{\kappa}_2(r)]\,drdq$$

$$+\frac{1-e^{-\mu_2^* z}-\mu_2^* z}{\mu_1^*\hat{\Omega}_*}\Bigg[\int_0^1 \frac{(1-q)^{\theta_1^*-1}}{\Gamma(\theta_1^*)}\int_0^q e^{-\mu_2^*(q-m)}\int_0^m \frac{(m-r)^{\eta^*-2}}{\Gamma(\eta^*-1)}[\lambda\hat{\kappa}_1(r)+(1-\lambda)\hat{\kappa}_2(r)]\,drdmdq$$

$$+\int_0^\sigma \frac{(\sigma-q)^{\theta_2^*-1}}{\Gamma(\theta_2^*)}\int_0^q e^{-\mu_2^*(q-m)}\int_0^m \frac{(m-r)^{\eta^*-2}}{\Gamma(\eta^*-1)}[\lambda\hat{\kappa}_1(r)+(1-\lambda)\hat{\kappa}_2(r)]\,drdmdq\Bigg]$$

for all $z \in \mathfrak{T}$ (a.e.). By assumption, we know that $\tilde{\mathfrak{H}}$ is convex-valued; thus, we immediately realize that $(\mathbb{SEL})_{\tilde{\mathfrak{H}},\varpi}$ is a convex set. Therefore, we obtain that $\lambda\hat{\kappa}_1(z)+(1-\lambda)\hat{\kappa}_2(z) \in (\mathbb{SEL})_{\tilde{\mathfrak{H}},\varpi}$ for each $z \in \mathfrak{T}$, and so, $\mathbb{A}_2^* w$ belongs to collection $\mathcal{P}_{cvx}(\mathfrak{W})$ for each $\varpi \in \mathfrak{W}$.

By continuing the proof process, we are going to investigate the complete continuity of $\mathbb{A}_2^*$ on $\mathfrak{W}$. To reach this aim, we have to prove two notions for the set $\mathbb{A}_2^*(\mathfrak{W})$ including equi-continuity and uniform boundedness. We first check that $\mathbb{A}_2^*$ relatesevery bounded set to a bounded one in $\mathfrak{W}$. For an arbitrary number $\tilde{r}_* \in \mathbb{R}^+$, we build a bounded ball $\mathbb{V}_{\tilde{r}_*} = \{\varpi \in \mathfrak{W} : \|\varpi\|_{\mathfrak{W}} \leq \tilde{r}_*\}$. In that phase, for every $\varpi \in \mathbb{V}_{\tilde{r}_*}$ and $v \in \mathbb{A}_2^*\varpi$, there is a function $\hat{\kappa} \in (\mathbb{SEL})_{\tilde{\mathfrak{H}},\varpi}$ provided that

$$v(z) = \frac{1}{\mu_1^*}\int_0^z e^{-\mu_2^*(z-q)}\int_0^q \frac{(q-r)^{\eta^*-2}}{\Gamma(\eta^*-1)}\hat{\kappa}(r)\,drdq$$

$$+\frac{1-e^{-\mu_2^* z}-\mu_2^* z}{\mu_1^*\hat{\Omega}_*}\Bigg[\int_0^1 \frac{(1-q)^{\theta_1^*-1}}{\Gamma(\theta_1^*)}\int_0^q e^{-\mu_2^*(q-m)}\int_0^m \frac{(m-r)^{\eta^*-2}}{\Gamma(\eta^*-1)}\hat{\kappa}(r)\,drdmdq$$

$$+\int_0^\sigma \frac{(\sigma-q)^{\theta_2^*-1}}{\Gamma(\theta_2^*)}\int_0^q e^{-\mu_2^*(q-m)}\int_0^m \frac{(m-r)^{\eta^*-2}}{\Gamma(\eta^*-1)}\kappa(r)\,drdmdq\Bigg]$$

for each $z \in \mathfrak{T}$. Then, the estimate of v is implemented as follows:

$$|v(z)| \leq \frac{1}{\mu_1^*}\int_0^z e^{-\mu_2^*(z-q)}\int_0^q \frac{(q-r)^{\eta^*-2}}{\Gamma(\eta^*-1)}|\hat{\kappa}(r)|\,\mathrm{d}r\mathrm{d}q$$

$$+\frac{|1-e^{-\mu_2^* z}|+\mu_2^* z}{\mu_1^*|\hat{\Omega}_*|}\left[\int_0^1 \frac{(1-q)^{\theta_1^*-1}}{\Gamma(\theta_1^*)}\int_0^q e^{-\mu_2^*(q-m)}\int_0^m \frac{(m-r)^{\eta^*-2}}{\Gamma(\eta^*-1)}|\hat{\kappa}(r)|\,\mathrm{d}r\mathrm{d}m\mathrm{d}q\right.$$

$$\left.+\int_0^\sigma \frac{(\sigma-q)^{\theta_2^*-1}}{\Gamma(\theta_2^*)}\int_0^q e^{-\mu_2^*(q-m)}\int_0^m \frac{(m-r)^{\eta^*-2}}{\Gamma(\eta^*-1)}|\hat{\kappa}(r)|\,\mathrm{d}r\mathrm{d}m\mathrm{d}q\right]$$

$$\leq \frac{1}{\mu_1^*}\int_0^z e^{-\mu_2^*(z-q)}\int_0^q \frac{(q-r)^{\eta^*-2}}{\Gamma(\eta^*-1)}x^*(r)\,\mathrm{d}r\mathrm{d}q$$

$$+\frac{|1-e^{-\mu_2^* z}|+\mu_2^* z}{\mu_1^*|\hat{\Omega}_*|}\left[\int_0^1 \frac{(1-q)^{\theta_1^*-1}}{\Gamma(\theta_1^*)}\int_0^q e^{-\mu_2^*(q-m)}\int_0^m \frac{(m-r)^{\eta^*-2}}{\Gamma(\eta^*-1)}x^*(r)\,\mathrm{d}r\mathrm{d}m\mathrm{d}q\right.$$

$$\left.+\int_0^\sigma \frac{(\sigma-q)^{\theta_2^*-1}}{\Gamma(\theta_2^*)}\int_0^q e^{-\mu_2^*(q-m)}\int_0^m \frac{(m-r)^{\eta^*-2}}{\Gamma(\eta^*-1)}x^*(r)\,\mathrm{d}r\mathrm{d}m\mathrm{d}q\right]$$

$$\leq \left[\frac{1-e^{-\mu_2^*}}{\mu_1^*\mu_2^*\Gamma(\eta^*)}+\frac{|1-e^{-\mu_2^*}|+\mu_2^*}{\mu_1^*|\hat{\Omega}_*|}\left(\frac{\mu_2^*+e^{-\mu_2^*}-1}{\mu_2^{*2}\Gamma(\theta_1^*)\Gamma(\eta^*)}+\frac{\sigma^{\theta_2^*+\eta^*-1}(\mu_2^*\sigma+e^{-\mu_2^*\sigma}-1)}{\mu_2^{*2}\Gamma(\theta_2^*)\Gamma(\eta^*)}\right)\right]\|x^*\|$$

$$=\mathbb{M}_*\|x^*\|,$$

so that $\mathbb{M}_*$ is illustrated by (14). Therefore, $\|v\| \leq \mathbb{M}_*\|x^*\|$, which confirms the uniform boundedness of $\mathbb{A}_2^*(\mathfrak{W})$. In the subsequent step, we verify that $\mathbb{A}_2^*$ maps every bounded set to an equi-continuous subset. Let $\varpi \in \mathbb{V}_{\tilde{r}_*}$ and $v \in \mathbb{A}_2^*\varpi$. We select a function $\hat{\kappa} \in (\mathbb{SEL})_{\mathfrak{H},\varpi}$ so that

$$v(z) = \frac{1}{\mu_1^*}\int_0^z e^{-\mu_2^*(z-q)}\int_0^q \frac{(q-r)^{\eta^*-2}}{\Gamma(\eta^*-1)}\hat{\kappa}(r)\,\mathrm{d}r\mathrm{d}q$$

$$+\frac{1-e^{-\mu_2^* z}-\mu_2^* z}{\mu_1^*\hat{\Omega}_*}\left[\int_0^1 \frac{(1-q)^{\theta_1^*-1}}{\Gamma(\theta_1^*)}\int_0^q e^{-\mu_2^*(q-m)}\int_0^m \frac{(m-r)^{\eta^*-2}}{\Gamma(\eta^*-1)}\hat{\kappa}(r)\,\mathrm{d}r\mathrm{d}m\mathrm{d}q\right.$$

$$\left.+\int_0^\sigma \frac{(\sigma-q)^{\theta_2^*-1}}{\Gamma(\theta_2^*)}\int_0^q e^{-\mu_2^*(q-m)}\int_0^m \frac{(m-r)^{\eta^*-2}}{\Gamma(\eta^*-1)}\hat{\kappa}(r)\,\mathrm{d}r\mathrm{d}m\mathrm{d}q\right]$$

for all $z \in \mathfrak{T}$. Let us suppose that $z_1, z_2 \in \mathfrak{T}$ along with $z_1 < z_2$. Then, we can write

$$|v(z_2)-v(z_1)| \leq \left|\frac{1}{\mu_1^*}\int_0^{z_2} e^{-\mu_2^*(z_2-q)}\int_0^q \frac{(q-r)^{\eta^*-2}}{\Gamma(\eta^*-1)}\tilde{r}_*\,\mathrm{d}r\mathrm{d}q\right.$$

$$\left.-\frac{1}{\mu_1^*}\int_0^{z_1} e^{-\mu_2^*(z_1-q)}\int_0^q \frac{(q-r)^{\eta^*-2}}{\Gamma(\eta^*-1)}\tilde{r}_*\,\mathrm{d}r\mathrm{d}q\right|$$

$$+\frac{(e^{-\mu_2^* z_1}-e^{-\mu_2^* z_2})+\mu_2^*(z_2-z_1)}{\mu_1^*|\hat{\Omega}_*|}\left[\int_0^1 \frac{(1-q)^{\theta_1^*-1}}{\Gamma(\theta_1^*)}\int_0^q e^{-\mu_2^*(q-m)}\int_0^m \frac{(m-r)^{\eta^*-2}}{\Gamma(\eta^*-1)}\tilde{r}_*\,\mathrm{d}r\mathrm{d}m\mathrm{d}q\right.$$

$$+\int_0^\sigma \frac{(\sigma-q)^{\theta_2^*-1}}{\Gamma(\theta_2^*)}\int_0^q e^{-\mu_2^*(q-m)}\int_0^m \frac{(m-r)^{\eta^*-2}}{\Gamma(\eta^*-1)}\tilde{r}_*\,\mathrm{d}r\mathrm{d}m\mathrm{d}q\Bigg].$$

In light of the above arguments, we realize that the limit value of the right-hand expressions equals zero without depending on $\varpi \in \mathbb{V}_{\tilde{r}_*}$ whenever $z_1 \to z_2$. Consequently, we are in a position that one can refer to as the Arzela–Ascoli theorem to deduce that the operator $\mathbb{A}_2^* : \mathcal{C}_{\mathbb{R}}(\mathfrak{T}) \to \mathcal{P}(\mathcal{C}_{\mathbb{R}}(\mathfrak{T})$ is completely continuous. In the sequel, we intend to prove that $\mathbb{A}_2^*$ is an operator having a closed graph, which implies its upper semi-continuity property. Let $\varpi_n \in \mathbb{V}_{\tilde{r}_*}$ and $v_n \in \mathbb{A}_2^*\varpi_n$ so that $\varpi_n \to \varpi^*$ and $v_n \to v^*$. We claim that the inclusion $v^* \in \mathbb{A}_2^*\varpi^*$ is valid. For each $n \geq 1$ and $v_n \in \mathbb{A}_2^*\varpi_n$, choose $\hat{\kappa}_n \in (\mathbb{SEL})_{\mathfrak{H},\varpi_n}$ so that

$$\begin{aligned}
v_n(z) = {} & \frac{1}{\mu_1^*}\int_0^z e^{-\mu_2^*(z-q)}\int_0^q \frac{(q-r)^{\eta^*-2}}{\Gamma(\eta^*-1)}\hat{\kappa}_n(r)\,\mathrm{d}r\mathrm{d}q \\
& + \frac{1-e^{-\mu_2^* z}-\mu_2^* z}{\mu_1^*\hat{\Omega}_*}\Bigg[\int_0^1 \frac{(1-q)^{\theta_1^*-1}}{\Gamma(\theta_1^*)}\int_0^q e^{-\mu_2^*(q-m)}\int_0^m \frac{(m-r)^{\eta^*-2}}{\Gamma(\eta^*-1)}\hat{\kappa}_n(r)\,\mathrm{d}r\mathrm{d}m\mathrm{d}q \\
& + \int_0^\sigma \frac{(\sigma-q)^{\theta_2^*-1}}{\Gamma(\theta_2^*)}\int_0^q e^{-\mu_2^*(q-m)}\int_0^m \frac{(m-r)^{\eta^*-2}}{\Gamma(\eta^*-1)}\hat{\kappa}_n(r)\,\mathrm{d}r\mathrm{d}m\mathrm{d}q\Bigg]
\end{aligned}$$

for any $z \in \mathfrak{T}$. We have to check the existence of a function $\hat{\kappa}^* \in (\mathbb{SEL})_{\mathfrak{H},\varpi^*}$ provided that

$$\begin{aligned}
v^*(z) = {} & \frac{1}{\mu_1^*}\int_0^z e^{-\mu_2^*(z-q)}\int_0^q \frac{(q-r)^{\eta^*-2}}{\Gamma(\eta^*-1)}\hat{\kappa}^*(r)\,\mathrm{d}r\mathrm{d}q \\
& + \frac{1-e^{-\mu_2^* z}-\mu_2^* z}{\mu_1^*\hat{\Omega}_*}\Bigg[\int_0^1 \frac{(1-q)^{\theta_1^*-1}}{\Gamma(\theta_1^*)}\int_0^q e^{-\mu_2^*(q-m)}\int_0^m \frac{(m-r)^{\eta^*-2}}{\Gamma(\eta^*-1)}\hat{\kappa}^*(r)\,\mathrm{d}r\mathrm{d}m\mathrm{d}q \\
& + \int_0^\sigma \frac{(\sigma-q)^{\theta_2^*-1}}{\Gamma(\theta_2^*)}\int_0^q e^{-\mu_2^*(q-m)}\int_0^m \frac{(m-r)^{\eta^*-2}}{\Gamma(\eta^*-1)}\hat{\kappa}^*(r)\,\mathrm{d}r\mathrm{d}m\mathrm{d}q\Bigg]
\end{aligned}$$

for each $z \in \mathfrak{T}$. To achieve this aim, we construct the continuous linear map $\tilde{\mathbb{P}}^* : \mathcal{L}^1_{\mathbb{R}}(\mathfrak{T}) \to \mathfrak{W} = \mathcal{C}_{\mathbb{R}}(\mathfrak{T})$ as follows:

$$\begin{aligned}
\tilde{\mathbb{P}}^*(\hat{\kappa})(z) = \varpi(z) = {} & \frac{1}{\mu_1^*}\int_0^z e^{-\mu_2^*(z-q)}\int_0^q \frac{(q-r)^{\eta^*-2}}{\Gamma(\eta^*-1)}\hat{\kappa}(r)\,\mathrm{d}r\mathrm{d}q \\
& + \frac{1-e^{-\mu_2^* z}-\mu_2^* z}{\mu_1^*\hat{\Omega}_*}\Bigg[\int_0^1 \frac{(1-q)^{\theta_1^*-1}}{\Gamma(\theta_1^*)}\int_0^q e^{-\mu_2^*(q-m)}\int_0^m \frac{(m-r)^{\eta^*-2}}{\Gamma(\eta^*-1)}\hat{\kappa}(r)\,\mathrm{d}r\mathrm{d}m\mathrm{d}q \\
& + \int_0^\sigma \frac{(\sigma-q)^{\theta_2^*-1}}{\Gamma(\theta_2^*)}\int_0^q e^{-\mu_2^*(q-m)}\int_0^m \frac{(m-r)^{\eta^*-2}}{\Gamma(\eta^*-1)}\hat{\kappa}(r)\,\mathrm{d}r\mathrm{d}m\mathrm{d}q\Bigg]
\end{aligned}$$

for any $z \in \mathfrak{T}$. One can directly confirm

$$\begin{aligned}
\|v_n(z)-v^*(z)\| = {} & \Bigg\|\frac{1}{\mu_1^*}\int_0^z e^{-\mu_2^*(z-q)}\int_0^q \frac{(q-r)^{\eta^*-2}}{\Gamma(\eta^*-1)}(\hat{\kappa}_n(r)-\hat{\kappa}^*(r))\,\mathrm{d}r\mathrm{d}q \\
& + \frac{1-e^{-\mu_2^* z}-\mu_2^* z}{\mu_1^*\hat{\Omega}_*}\Bigg[\int_0^1 \frac{(1-q)^{\theta_1^*-1}}{\Gamma(\theta_1^*)}\int_0^q e^{-\mu_2^*(q-m)}\int_0^m \frac{(m-r)^{\eta^*-2}}{\Gamma(\eta^*-1)}(\hat{\kappa}_n(r)-\hat{\kappa}^*(r))\,\mathrm{d}r\mathrm{d}m\mathrm{d}q
\end{aligned}$$

$$+\int_0^{\sigma}\frac{(\sigma-q)^{\theta_2^*-1}}{\Gamma(\theta_2^*)}\int_0^q e^{-\mu_2^*(q-m)}\int_0^m\frac{(m-r)^{\eta^*-2}}{\Gamma(\eta^*-1)}\left(\hat{\kappa}_n(r)-\hat{\kappa}^*(r)\right)drdmdq\Bigg]\Bigg\|\to 0.$$

Hence, by the assumptions of Lemma 2, it is realized that $\tilde{\mathbb{P}}^*\circ(\mathbb{SEL})_{\mathfrak{H}}$ has a closed graph. For the sake of holding the inclusion $v_n\in\tilde{\mathbb{P}}^*((\mathbb{SEL})_{\mathfrak{H},\varpi_n})$ and also $\varpi_n\to\varpi^*$, there exists a function $\hat{\kappa}^*\in(\mathbb{SEL})_{\mathfrak{H},\varpi^*}$ provided that

$$v^*(z)=\frac{1}{\mu_1^*}\int_0^z e^{-\mu_2^*(z-q)}\int_0^q\frac{(q-r)^{\eta^*-2}}{\Gamma(\eta^*-1)}\hat{\kappa}^*(r)\,drdq$$

$$+\frac{1-e^{-\mu_2^*z}-\mu_2^*z}{\mu_1^*\hat{\Omega}_*}\left[\int_0^1\frac{(1-q)^{\theta_1^*-1}}{\Gamma(\theta_1^*)}\int_0^q e^{-\mu_2^*(q-m)}\int_0^m\frac{(m-r)^{\eta^*-2}}{\Gamma(\eta^*-1)}\hat{\kappa}^*(r)\,drdmdq\right.$$

$$\left.+\int_0^{\sigma}\frac{(\sigma-q)^{\theta_2^*-1}}{\Gamma(\theta_2^*)}\int_0^q e^{-\mu_2^*(q-m)}\int_0^m\frac{(m-r)^{\eta^*-2}}{\Gamma(\eta^*-1)}\hat{\kappa}^*(r)\,drdmdq\right]$$

for all $z\in\mathfrak{T}$. Hence, $v^*\in\mathbb{A}_2^*\varpi^*$ and so $\mathbb{A}_2^*$ is an operator having a closed graph. From this point, we find that $\mathbb{A}_2^*$ is upper semi-continuous. Meanwhile, notice that by assumption, we know that $\mathbb{A}_2^*$ is compact-valued. In the following, by taking into account the hypothesis (HPS3) and continuing a similar argument, we have

$$\hat{\mathbb{O}}=\|\mathbb{A}_2^*(\mathfrak{W})\|=\sup_{z\in\mathfrak{T}}\{|\mathbb{A}_2^*\varpi|:\varpi\in\mathfrak{W}\}$$

$$\leq\left[\frac{1-e^{-\mu_2^*}}{\mu_1^*\mu_2^*\Gamma(\eta^*)}+\frac{|1-e^{-\mu_2^*}|+\mu_2^*}{\mu_1^*|\hat{\Omega}_*|}\left(\frac{\mu_2^*+e^{-\mu_2^*}-1}{\mu_2^{*2}\Gamma(\theta_1^*)\Gamma(\eta^*)}+\frac{\sigma^{\theta_2^*+\eta^*-1}(\mu_2^*\sigma+e^{-\mu_2^*\sigma}-1)}{\mu_2^{*2}\Gamma(\theta_2^*)\Gamma(\eta^*)}\right)\right]\|x^*\|$$

$$=\mathbb{M}_*\|x^*\|.$$

As we can observe, an inequality $\hat{\mathbb{O}}\leq\mathbb{M}_*\|x^*\|$ holds. Therefore, one can write

$$\tilde{v}^*\left(1+\frac{1}{\Gamma(\delta_1^*+1)}+\ldots+\frac{1}{\Gamma(\delta_k^*+1)}\right)\hat{\mathbb{O}}\leq\tilde{v}^*\left(1+\frac{1}{\Gamma(\delta_1^*+1)}+\ldots+\frac{1}{\Gamma(\delta_k^*+1)}\right)\mathbb{M}_*\|x^*\|<\frac{1}{2}.$$

By setting $l^*=\tilde{v}^*\left(1+\frac{1}{\Gamma(\delta_1^*+1)}+\ldots+\frac{1}{\Gamma(\delta_k^*+1)}\right)$, clearly $l^*\hat{\mathbb{O}}<\frac{1}{2}$. Until now, it is seen that Lemma 2 is settled on $\mathbb{A}_1^*$ and $\mathbb{A}_2^*$. In this position, it is sufficient to check that one of (a) or (b) holds. Our claim is that (b) is not valid. To confirm this claim, with due attention to Lemma 2 and hypothesis (HPS4), one can suppose that ϖ is an arbitrary member belonging to Σ^* with $\|\varpi\|=r_*$. Obviously, $\alpha_0\varpi(z)\in\mathbb{A}_1^*\varpi(z)\mathbb{A}_2^*\varpi(z)$ for any $\alpha_0>1$. By selecting a suitable function $\hat{\kappa}\in(\mathbb{SEL})_{\mathfrak{H},\varpi}$, one can write

$$\varpi(z)=\frac{1}{\alpha_0}\tilde{S}^*(z,\varpi(z),{}^{RL}\mathcal{I}_{0^+}^{\delta_1^*}\varpi(z),\ldots,{}^{RL}\mathcal{I}_{0^+}^{\delta_k^*}\varpi(z))\left(\frac{1}{\mu_1^*}\int_0^z e^{-\mu_2^*(z-q)}\int_0^q\frac{(q-r)^{\eta^*-2}}{\Gamma(\eta^*-1)}\hat{\kappa}(r)\,drdq\right.$$

$$+\frac{1-e^{-\mu_2^*z}-\mu_2^*z}{\mu_1^*\hat{\Omega}_*}\left[\int_0^1\frac{(1-q)^{\theta_1^*-1}}{\Gamma(\theta_1^*)}\int_0^q e^{-\mu_2^*(q-m)}\int_0^m\frac{(m-r)^{\eta^*-2}}{\Gamma(\eta^*-1)}\hat{\kappa}(r)\,drdmdq\right.$$

$$\left.\left.+\int_0^{\sigma}\frac{(\sigma-q)^{\theta_2^*-1}}{\Gamma(\theta_2^*)}\int_0^q e^{-\mu_2^*(q-m)}\int_0^m\frac{(m-r)^{\eta^*-2}}{\Gamma(\eta^*-1)}\hat{\kappa}(r)\,drdmdq\right]\right)$$

for each $\alpha_0>1$ and for any $z\in\mathfrak{T}$. Therefore, we obtain:

$$|\varpi(z)| = \frac{1}{\alpha_0}|\tilde{S}^*(z,\varpi(z),{}^{RL}\mathcal{I}_{0^+}^{\delta_1^*}\varpi(z),\dots,{}^{RL}\mathcal{I}_{0^+}^{\delta_k^*}\varpi(z))|\Bigg(\frac{1}{\mu_1^*}\int_0^z e^{-\mu_2^*(z-q)}\int_0^q \frac{(q-r)^{\eta^*-2}}{\Gamma(\eta^*-1)}|\hat{\kappa}(r)|\,\mathrm{d}r\mathrm{d}q$$

$$+\frac{|1-e^{-\mu_2^* z}|+\mu_2^* z}{\mu_1^*|\hat{\Omega}_*|}\Bigg[\int_0^1 \frac{(1-q)^{\theta_1^*-1}}{\Gamma(\theta_1^*)}\int_0^q e^{-\mu_2^*(q-m)}\int_0^m \frac{(m-r)^{\eta^*-2}}{\Gamma(\eta^*-1)}|\hat{\kappa}(r)|\,\mathrm{d}r\mathrm{d}m\mathrm{d}q$$

$$+\int_0^\sigma \frac{(\sigma-q)^{\theta_2^*-1}}{\Gamma(\theta_2^*)}\int_0^q e^{-\mu_2^*(q-m)}\int_0^m \frac{(m-r)^{\eta^*-2}}{\Gamma(\eta^*-1)}|\hat{\kappa}(r)|\,\mathrm{d}r\mathrm{d}m\mathrm{d}q\Bigg]\Bigg)$$

$$=[|\tilde{S}^*(z,\varpi(z),{}^{RL}\mathcal{I}_{0^+}^{\delta_1^*}\varpi(z),\dots,{}^{RL}\mathcal{I}_{0^+}^{\delta_k^*}\varpi(z))-\tilde{S}^*(z,0,0,\dots,0)|+|\tilde{S}^*(z,0,0,\dots,0)|]$$

$$\times\Bigg(\frac{1}{\mu_1^*}\int_0^z e^{-\mu_2^*(z-q)}\int_0^q \frac{(q-r)^{\eta^*-2}}{\Gamma(\eta^*-1)}|\hat{\kappa}(r)|\,\mathrm{d}r\mathrm{d}q$$

$$+\frac{|1-e^{-\mu_2^* z}|+\mu_2^* z}{\mu_1^*|\hat{\Omega}_*|}\Bigg[\int_0^1 \frac{(1-q)^{\theta_1^*-1}}{\Gamma(\theta_1^*)}\int_0^q e^{-\mu_2^*(q-m)}\int_0^m \frac{(m-r)^{\eta^*-2}}{\Gamma(\eta^*-1)}|\hat{\kappa}(r)|\,\mathrm{d}r\mathrm{d}m\mathrm{d}q$$

$$+\int_0^\sigma \frac{(\sigma-q)^{\theta_2^*-1}}{\Gamma(\theta_2^*)}\int_0^q e^{-\mu_2^*(q-m)}\int_0^m \frac{(m-r)^{\eta^*-2}}{\Gamma(\eta^*-1)}|\hat{\kappa}(r)|\,\mathrm{d}r\mathrm{d}m\mathrm{d}q\Bigg]\Bigg)$$

$$\leq [\tilde{v}^*(1+\frac{1}{\Gamma(\delta_1^*+1)}+\dots+\frac{1}{\Gamma(\delta_k^*+1)})\|\varpi\|+\tilde{\mathbb{S}}^*]\Bigg(\frac{1}{\mu_1^*}\int_0^z e^{-\mu_2^*(z-q)}\int_0^q \frac{(q-r)^{\eta^*-2}}{\Gamma(\eta^*-1)}x^*(r)\,\mathrm{d}r\mathrm{d}q$$

$$+\frac{|1-e^{-\mu_2^* z}|+\mu_2^* z}{\mu_1^*|\hat{\Omega}_*|}\Bigg[\int_0^1 \frac{(1-q)^{\theta_1^*-1}}{\Gamma(\theta_1^*)}\int_0^q e^{-\mu_2^*(q-m)}\int_0^m \frac{(m-r)^{\eta^*-2}}{\Gamma(\eta^*-1)}x^*(r)\,\mathrm{d}r\mathrm{d}m\mathrm{d}q$$

$$+\int_0^\sigma \frac{(\sigma-q)^{\theta_2^*-1}}{\Gamma(\theta_2^*)}\int_0^q e^{-\mu_2^*(q-m)}\int_0^m \frac{(m-r)^{\eta^*-2}}{\Gamma(\eta^*-1)}x^*(r)\,\mathrm{d}r\mathrm{d}m\mathrm{d}q\Bigg]\Bigg)$$

$$\leq \left[\tilde{v}^*\left(1+\frac{1}{\Gamma(\delta_1^*+1)}+\dots+\frac{1}{\Gamma(\delta_k^*+1)}\right)\|\varpi\|+\tilde{\mathbb{S}}^*\right]\mathbb{M}_*\|x^*\|$$

for all $z \in \mathfrak{T}$. After some simplifications, we reach the following inequality

$$r_* \leq \frac{\tilde{\mathbb{S}}^*\mathbb{M}_*\|x^*\|}{1-\tilde{v}^*\left(1+\frac{1}{\Gamma(\delta_1^*+1)}+\dots+\frac{1}{\Gamma(\delta_k^*+1)}\right)\mathbb{M}_*\|x^*\|}.$$

In view of Inequality (13), the impossibility of Condition (b) of Lemma 2 is deduced. Hence, we have $\varpi \in \mathbb{A}_1^*\varpi\mathbb{A}_2^*\varpi$. Eventually, we manage to verify that there exists a fixed point for $\mathcal{G}^*$ and the sequential hybrid multi-order integro-differential inclusion BVP (1) and (2) involves a solution. □

In what follows, we carry out our procedure to derive other existence criteria for the Caputo sequential nonhybrid multi-order inclusion BVP (3) by applying two novel pure analytical theorems.

Definition 2. *The function $\varpi \in \mathcal{AC}_{\mathbb{R}}(\mathfrak{T})$ is defined to be a solution of the given Caputo sequential nonhybrid multi-order inclusion BVP* (3) *if $\hat{\kappa} \in \mathcal{L}^1_{\mathbb{R}}(\mathfrak{T})$ exists via $\hat{\kappa} \in \tilde{\mathfrak{H}}(z, \varpi(z))$ for all $z \in \mathfrak{T}$ (a.e.), which satisfies the multi-order integro-derivative boundary conditions:*

$$\varpi(0) = 0, \qquad \varpi'(0) = 0, \qquad {}^{RL}\mathcal{I}^{\theta_1^*}_{0^+}\varpi(1) + {}^{RL}\mathcal{I}^{\theta_2^*}_{0^+}\varpi(\sigma) = 0,$$

and

$$\varpi(z) = \frac{1}{\mu_1^*}\int_0^z e^{-\mu_2^*(z-q)} \int_0^q \frac{(q-r)^{\eta^*-2}}{\Gamma(\eta^*-1)}\hat{\kappa}(r)\,\mathrm{d}r\mathrm{d}q$$
$$+ \frac{1 - e^{-\mu_2^* z} - \mu_2^* z}{\mu_1^* \hat{\Omega}_*}\left[\int_0^1 \frac{(1-q)^{\theta_1^*-1}}{\Gamma(\theta_1^*)}\int_0^q e^{-\mu_2^*(q-m)}\int_0^m \frac{(m-r)^{\eta^*-2}}{\Gamma(\eta^*-1)}\hat{\kappa}(r)\,\mathrm{d}r\mathrm{d}m\mathrm{d}q\right.$$
$$\left.+ \int_0^\sigma \frac{(\sigma-q)^{\theta_2^*-1}}{\Gamma(\theta_2^*)}\int_0^q e^{-\mu_2^*(q-m)}\int_0^m \frac{(m-r)^{\eta^*-2}}{\Gamma(\eta^*-1)}\hat{\kappa}(r)\,\mathrm{d}r\mathrm{d}m\mathrm{d}q\right]$$

for any $z \in \mathfrak{T}$.

In addition, for each $\varpi \in \mathfrak{W}$, we build the following collection of selections for $\tilde{\mathfrak{H}}$:

$$(\mathbb{SEL})_{\tilde{\mathfrak{H}},\varpi} = \left\{\hat{\kappa} \in L^1(\mathfrak{T}) : \hat{\kappa}(z) \in \tilde{\mathfrak{H}}(z, \varpi(z))\right\}$$

for almost all $z \in \mathfrak{T}$. From here onwards, we consider $\mathfrak{P} : \mathfrak{W} \to \mathcal{P}(\mathfrak{W})$ by

$$\mathfrak{P}(\varpi) = \left\{\Phi \in \mathfrak{W} : \text{ there is } \hat{\kappa} \in (\mathbb{SEL})_{\tilde{\mathfrak{H}},\varpi} \text{ so that } \Phi(z) = b(z) \text{ for any } z \in \mathfrak{T}\right\}, \tag{15}$$

where

$$b(z) = \frac{1}{\mu_1^*}\int_0^z e^{-\mu_2^*(z-q)} \int_0^q \frac{(q-r)^{\eta^*-2}}{\Gamma(\eta^*-1)}\hat{\kappa}(r)\,\mathrm{d}r\mathrm{d}q$$
$$+ \frac{1 - e^{-\mu_2^* z} - \mu_2^* z}{\mu_1^* \hat{\Omega}_*}\left[\int_0^1 \frac{(1-q)^{\theta_1^*-1}}{\Gamma(\theta_1^*)}\int_0^q e^{-\mu_2^*(q-m)}\int_0^m \frac{(m-r)^{\eta^*-2}}{\Gamma(\eta^*-1)}\hat{\kappa}(r)\,\mathrm{d}r\mathrm{d}m\mathrm{d}q\right.$$
$$\left.+ \int_0^\sigma \frac{(\sigma-q)^{\theta_2^*-1}}{\Gamma(\theta_2^*)}\int_0^q e^{-\mu_2^*(q-m)}\int_0^m \frac{(m-r)^{\eta^*-2}}{\Gamma(\eta^*-1)}\hat{\kappa}(r)\,\mathrm{d}r\mathrm{d}m\mathrm{d}q\right].$$

Theorem 2. *Let $\tilde{\mathfrak{H}} : \mathfrak{T} \times \mathfrak{W} \to \mathcal{P}_{cmp}(\mathfrak{W})$ be compact. Suppose that all six hypotheses hold:*

(HPS5) *An integrable operator $\tilde{\mathfrak{H}}$ is bounded, and also, $\tilde{\mathfrak{H}}(\cdot, \varpi) : \mathfrak{T} \to \mathcal{P}_{cmp}(\mathfrak{W})$ is a measurable set for every $\varpi \in \mathfrak{W}$;*

(HPS6) *There are $\psi \in \Psi$ and $\beta \in C_{\mathbb{R}^{\geq 0}}(\mathfrak{T})$ provided that for any $z \in \mathfrak{T}$ and $\varpi, \varpi' \in \mathfrak{W}$, we have*

$$\mathbb{PH}_{d_{\mathfrak{W}}}\left(\tilde{\mathfrak{H}}(z, \varpi), \tilde{\mathfrak{H}}(z, \varpi')\right) \leq \psi(|\varpi - \varpi'|)\frac{\beta(z)}{\mathbb{M}_*\|\beta\|}, \tag{16}$$

where $\sup_{z\in\mathfrak{T}}|\beta(z)| = \|\beta\|$ and $\mathbb{M}_*$ is displayed in (14);

(HPS7) *$\tilde{\varepsilon} : \mathfrak{W} \times \mathfrak{W} \to \mathbb{R}$ exists so that $\tilde{\varepsilon}(\varpi, \varpi') \geq 0$ for each $\varpi, \varpi' \in \mathfrak{W}$;*

(HPS8) *Let $\{\varpi_n\}_{n\geq 1} \subset \mathfrak{W}$ go to ϖ and $\tilde{\varepsilon}(\varpi_n(z), \varpi_{n+1}(z)) \geq 0$ for any $z \in \mathfrak{T}$. Then, a subsequence $\{\varpi_{n_l}\}_{l\geq 1}$ of $\{\varpi_n\}$ exists such that $\tilde{\varepsilon}(\varpi_{n_l}(z), \varpi(z)) \geq 0$ for any $z \in \mathfrak{T}$ and $l \geq 1$;*

(HPS9) *There exist two elements* $\varpi_0 \in \mathfrak{W}$ *and* $\Phi \in \mathfrak{P}(\varpi_0)$ *such that* $\tilde{\mathfrak{e}}(\varpi_0(z), \Phi(z)) \geq 0$ *for all* $z \in \mathfrak{T}$, *in which* $\mathfrak{P} : \mathfrak{W} \to \mathcal{P}(\mathfrak{W})$ *is the same operator illustrated by* (15);

(HPS10) *For every* $\varpi \in \mathfrak{W}$ *and* $\Phi \in \mathfrak{P}(\varpi)$ *along with* $\tilde{\mathfrak{e}}(\varpi(z), \Phi(z)) \geq 0$, *there exists* $b \in \mathfrak{P}(\varpi)$ *provided that* $\tilde{\mathfrak{e}}(\Phi(z), b(z)) \geq 0$ *for each* $z \in \mathfrak{T}$.

Then, the Caputo sequential nonhybrid multi-order inclusion BVP (3) *has a solution.*

Proof. For the same reason as before, it is explicit that a solution of the given Caputo sequential nonhybrid multi-order FBVP (3) is a fixed point of $\mathfrak{P} : \mathfrak{W} \to \mathcal{P}(\mathfrak{W})$ defined by (15). By (HPS5), the measurability of $z \mapsto \tilde{\mathfrak{H}}(z, \varpi(z))$ is an obvious fact, and so, it is closed-valued for any $\varpi \in \mathfrak{W}$. Therefore, we realize that $\tilde{\mathfrak{H}}$ involves a measurable selection and $(\mathbb{SEL})_{\tilde{\mathfrak{H}},\varpi}$ is nonempty. Subsequently, we attempt to verify that $\mathfrak{P}(\varpi)$ is closed in $\mathfrak{W}$ for each $\varpi \in \mathfrak{W}$. To implement the process, we regard a sequence $\{\varpi_n\}_{n\geq 1}$ of $\mathfrak{P}(\varpi)$ having the property $\varpi_n \to \varpi$. For each n, we choose $\hat{\kappa}_n \in (\mathbb{SEL})_{\tilde{\mathfrak{H}},\varpi}$ so that

$$\begin{aligned}
\varpi_n(z) = & \frac{1}{\mu_1^*}\int_0^z e^{-\mu_2^*(z-q)} \int_0^q \frac{(q-r)^{\eta^*-2}}{\Gamma(\eta^*-1)} \hat{\kappa}_n(r)\, \mathrm{d}r\mathrm{d}q \\
& + \frac{1-e^{-\mu_2^* z}-\mu_2^* z}{\mu_1^*\hat{\Omega}_*}\left[\int_0^1 \frac{(1-q)^{\theta_1^*-1}}{\Gamma(\theta_1^*)} \int_0^q e^{-\mu_2^*(q-m)} \int_0^m \frac{(m-r)^{\eta^*-2}}{\Gamma(\eta^*-1)} \hat{\kappa}_n(r)\, \mathrm{d}r\mathrm{d}m\mathrm{d}q \right. \\
& \left. + \int_0^\sigma \frac{(\sigma-q)^{\theta_2^*-1}}{\Gamma(\theta_2^*)} \int_0^q e^{-\mu_2^*(q-m)} \int_0^m \frac{(m-r)^{\eta^*-2}}{\Gamma(\eta^*-1)} \hat{\kappa}_n(r)\, \mathrm{d}r\mathrm{d}m\mathrm{d}q \right]
\end{aligned}$$

for all $z \in \mathfrak{T}$ (a.e.). In light of the compactness of $\tilde{\mathfrak{H}}$, we can pass it into a subsequence to reach $\{\hat{\kappa}_n\}_{n\geq 1}$, which approaches some $\hat{\kappa} \in \mathcal{L}^1(\mathfrak{T})$. Hence, there exists $\hat{\kappa} \in (\mathbb{SEL})_{\tilde{\mathfrak{H}},\varpi}$, and so,

$$\begin{aligned}
\lim_{n\to\infty} \varpi_n(z) = & \frac{1}{\mu_1^*}\int_0^z e^{-\mu_2^*(z-q)} \int_0^q \frac{(q-r)^{\eta^*-2}}{\Gamma(\eta^*-1)} \hat{\kappa}(r)\, \mathrm{d}r\mathrm{d}q \\
& + \frac{1-e^{-\mu_2^* z}-\mu_2^* z}{\mu_1^*\hat{\Omega}_*}\left[\int_0^1 \frac{(1-q)^{\theta_1^*-1}}{\Gamma(\theta_1^*)} \int_0^q e^{-\mu_2^*(q-m)} \int_0^m \frac{(m-r)^{\eta^*-2}}{\Gamma(\eta^*-1)} \hat{\kappa}(r)\, \mathrm{d}r\mathrm{d}m\mathrm{d}q \right. \\
& \left. + \int_0^\sigma \frac{(\sigma-q)^{\theta_2^*-1}}{\Gamma(\theta_2^*)} \int_0^q e^{-\mu_2^*(q-m)} \int_0^m \frac{(m-r)^{\eta^*-2}}{\Gamma(\eta^*-1)} \hat{\kappa}(r)\, \mathrm{d}r\mathrm{d}m\mathrm{d}q \right] \\
= & \varpi(z)
\end{aligned}$$

for any $z \in \mathfrak{T}$. Based on this argument, it follows that $\varpi \in \mathfrak{P}(\varpi)$, and so, $\mathfrak{P}$ is closed-valued. According to the hypothesis of the theorem, $\tilde{\mathfrak{H}}$ is compact, so one can easily verify that $\mathfrak{P}(\varpi)$ is bounded for each $\varpi \in \mathfrak{W}$. Here, we want to show that $\mathfrak{P}$ is α-ψ-contractive. To prove this claim, we introduce $\alpha : \mathfrak{W}^2 \to [0,\infty)$ by $\alpha(\varpi, \varpi') = 1$ if $\tilde{\mathfrak{e}}(\varpi(z), \varpi'(z)) \geq 0$, and $\alpha(\varpi, \varpi') = 0$ otherwise. Assume that $\varpi, \varpi' \in \mathfrak{W}$ and $\Phi_1 \in \mathfrak{P}(\varpi')$ are arbitrary. Furthermore, we select $\hat{\kappa}_1 \in (\mathbb{SEL})_{\tilde{\mathfrak{H}},\varpi'}$ so that

$$\begin{aligned}
\Phi_1(z) = & \frac{1}{\mu_1^*}\int_0^z e^{-\mu_2^*(z-q)} \int_0^q \frac{(q-r)^{\eta^*-2}}{\Gamma(\eta^*-1)} \hat{\kappa}_1(r)\, \mathrm{d}r\mathrm{d}q \\
& + \frac{1-e^{-\mu_2^* z}-\mu_2^* z}{\mu_1^*\hat{\Omega}_*}\left[\int_0^1 \frac{(1-q)^{\theta_1^*-1}}{\Gamma(\theta_1^*)} \int_0^q e^{-\mu_2^*(q-m)} \int_0^m \frac{(m-r)^{\eta^*-2}}{\Gamma(\eta^*-1)} \hat{\kappa}_1(r)\, \mathrm{d}r\mathrm{d}m\mathrm{d}q \right. \\
& \left. + \int_0^\sigma \frac{(\sigma-q)^{\theta_2^*-1}}{\Gamma(\theta_2^*)} \int_0^q e^{-\mu_2^*(q-m)} \int_0^m \frac{(m-r)^{\eta^*-2}}{\Gamma(\eta^*-1)} \hat{\kappa}_1(r)\, \mathrm{d}r\mathrm{d}m\mathrm{d}q \right]
\end{aligned}$$

for any $z \in \mathfrak{T}$. Based on the hypothesis (16), we obtain

$$\mathbb{PH}_{d_{\mathfrak{W}}}\Big(\tilde{\mathfrak{S}}(z,\varpi(z)),\tilde{\mathfrak{S}}(z,\varpi'(z))\Big) \leq \beta(z)\psi(|\varpi(z)-\varpi'(z)|)\frac{1}{\mathbb{M}_*\|\beta\|},$$

for each $\varpi, \varpi' \in \mathfrak{W}$ having the property $\tilde{\varepsilon}(\varpi(z),\varpi'(z)) \geq 0$ for any $z \in \mathfrak{T}$. Hence, $b \in \tilde{\mathfrak{S}}(z,\varpi(z))$ exists with $|\hat{k}_1(z) - b| \leq \psi(|\varpi(z)-\varpi'(z)|)\frac{\beta(z)}{\mathbb{M}_*\|\beta\|}$. Next, we introduce $\mathcal{Q}^* : \mathfrak{T} \to \mathcal{P}(\mathfrak{W})$ given by

$$\mathcal{Q}^*(z) = \left\{b \in \mathfrak{W} : |\hat{k}_1(z) - b| \leq \psi(|\varpi(z)-\varpi'(z)|)\frac{\beta(z)}{\mathbb{M}_*\|\beta\|}\right\}$$

for each $z \in \mathfrak{T}$. Because of the measurability of both $\hat{k}_1$ and $\varrho = \beta\psi(|\varpi - \varpi'|)\frac{1}{\mathbb{M}_*\|\beta\|}$, it follows that the intersection $\mathcal{Q}^*(\cdot) \cap \tilde{\mathfrak{S}}(\cdot,\varpi(\cdot))$ is measurable. In this direction, we select $\hat{k}_2$, which belongs to $\tilde{\mathfrak{S}}(z,\varpi(z))$ so that

$$|\hat{k}_1(z) - \hat{k}_2(z)| \leq \psi(|\varpi(z)-\varpi'(z)|)\frac{\beta(z)}{\mathbb{M}_*\|\beta\|}$$

for all $z \in \mathfrak{T}$. Now, we regard the member $\Phi_2 \in \mathfrak{P}(\varpi)$ by

$$\Phi_2(z) = \frac{1}{\mu_1^*}\int_0^z e^{-\mu_2^*(z-q)}\int_0^q \frac{(q-r)^{\eta^*-2}}{\Gamma(\eta^*-1)}\hat{k}_2(r)\,\mathrm{d}r\mathrm{d}q$$

$$+\frac{1-e^{-\mu_2^* z}-\mu_2^* z}{\mu_1^*\hat{\Omega}_*}\left[\int_0^1 \frac{(1-q)^{\theta_1^*-1}}{\Gamma(\theta_1^*)}\int_0^q e^{-\mu_2^*(q-m)}\int_0^m \frac{(m-r)^{\eta^*-2}}{\Gamma(\eta^*-1)}\hat{k}_2(r)\,\mathrm{d}r\mathrm{d}m\mathrm{d}q\right.$$

$$\left.+\int_0^\sigma \frac{(\sigma-q)^{\theta_2^*-1}}{\Gamma(\theta_2^*)}\int_0^q e^{-\mu_2^*(q-m)}\int_0^m \frac{(m-r)^{\eta^*-2}}{\Gamma(\eta^*-1)}\hat{k}_2(r)\,\mathrm{d}r\mathrm{d}m\mathrm{d}q\right]$$

for any $z \in \mathfrak{T}$. Then, by computing the following estimates, we have

$$|\Phi_1(z) - \Phi_2(z)| \leq \frac{1}{\mu_1^*}\int_0^z e^{-\mu_2^*(z-q)}\int_0^q \frac{(q-r)^{\eta^*-2}}{\Gamma(\eta^*-1)}|\hat{k}_1(r)-\hat{k}_2(r)|\,\mathrm{d}r\mathrm{d}q$$

$$+\frac{|1-e^{-\mu_2^* z}|+\mu_2^* z}{\mu_1^*|\hat{\Omega}_*|}\left[\int_0^1 \frac{(1-q)^{\theta_1^*-1}}{\Gamma(\theta_1^*)}\int_0^q e^{-\mu_2^*(q-m)}\int_0^m \frac{(m-r)^{\eta^*-2}}{\Gamma(\eta^*-1)}|\hat{k}_1(r)-\hat{k}_2(r)|\,\mathrm{d}r\mathrm{d}m\mathrm{d}q\right.$$

$$\left.+\int_0^\sigma \frac{(\sigma-q)^{\theta_2^*-1}}{\Gamma(\theta_2^*)}\int_0^q e^{-\mu_2^*(q-m)}\int_0^m \frac{(m-r)^{\eta^*-2}}{\Gamma(\eta^*-1)}|\hat{k}_1(r)-\hat{k}_2(r)|\,\mathrm{d}r\mathrm{d}m\mathrm{d}q\right]$$

$$\leq \left[\frac{1-e^{-\mu_2^*}}{\mu_1^*\mu_2^*\Gamma(\eta^*)} + \frac{|1-e^{-\mu_2^*}|+\mu_2^*}{\mu_1^*|\hat{\Omega}_*|}\left(\frac{\mu_2^*+e^{-\mu_2^*}-1}{\mu_2^{*2}\Gamma(\theta_1^*)\Gamma(\eta^*)} + \frac{\sigma^{\theta_2^*+\eta^*-1}(\mu_2^*\sigma+e^{-\mu_2^*\sigma}-1)}{\mu_2^{*2}\Gamma(\theta_2^*)\Gamma(\eta^*)}\right)\right]$$

$$\times\|\beta\|\psi(\|\varpi-\varpi'\|)\frac{1}{\mathbb{M}_*\|\beta\|} = \mathbb{M}_*\|\beta\|\psi(\|\varpi-\varpi'\|)\frac{1}{\mathbb{M}_*\|\beta\|} = \psi(\|\varpi-\varpi'\|)$$

for all $z \in \mathfrak{T}$. Therefore, we obtain

$$\|\Phi_1 - \Phi_2\| = \sup_{z\in\mathfrak{T}}|\Phi_1(z)-\Phi_2(z)| \leq \psi(\|\varpi-\varpi'\|)$$

and so, we obtain

$$\alpha(\varpi,\varpi')\mathbb{PH}_{d_{\mathfrak{W}}}(\mathfrak{P}(\varpi),\mathfrak{P}(\varpi')) \leq \psi(\|\varpi-\varpi'\|)$$

for every $\varpi,\varpi' \in \mathfrak{W}$. This indicates that $\mathfrak{P}$ is α-ψ-contractive. Now, by following the proof, we consider $\varpi \in \mathfrak{W}$ and $\varpi' \in \mathfrak{P}(\varpi)$ coupled with $\alpha(\varpi,\varpi') \geq 1$. Then, by taking into account the definition of $\tilde{\varepsilon}$, we obtain $\tilde{\varepsilon}(\varpi(z),\varpi'(z)) \geq 0$, and so, there exists $b \in \mathfrak{P}(\varpi')$ so that $\tilde{\varepsilon}(\varpi'(z),b(z)) \geq 0$. Hence, $\alpha(\varpi',b) \geq 1$, and the latter inequality demonstrates that $\mathfrak{P}$ is α-admissible. To complete the proof process, we consider $\varpi_0 \in \mathfrak{W}$ and $\varpi' \in \mathfrak{P}(\varpi_0)$ so that $\tilde{\varepsilon}(\varpi_0(z),\varpi'(z)) \geq 0$ for all z. Thus, we obtain $\alpha(\varpi_0,\varpi') \geq 1$.

Moreover, consider $\{\varpi_n\}_{n\geq 1}$ in $\mathfrak{W}$ via $\varpi_n \to \varpi$ and $\alpha(\varpi_n,\varpi_{n+1}) \geq 1$ for all n. In this phase, we reach $\tilde{\varepsilon}(\varpi_n(z),\varpi_{n+1}(z)) \geq 0$. Now, by using the assumption (HPS8), we figure out that there exists a subsequence $\{\varpi_{n_l}\}_{l\geq 1}$ of $\{\varpi_n\}$ so that $\tilde{\varepsilon}(\varpi_{n_l}(z),\varpi(z)) \geq 0$ for each $z \in \mathfrak{T}$. As a consequence, $\alpha(\varpi_{n_l},\varpi) \geq 1$ for $l \geq 1$, and it is deduced that the space $\mathfrak{W}$ has the $(\mathcal{C}_\alpha)$-property. In the final step, by considering Lemma 3, we can easily realize that $\mathfrak{P}$ includes a fixed point and the sequential nonhybrid multi-order inclusion BVP (3) has at least one solution. □

As a final criterion for the existence of the solution, we review the following theorem based on a new interesting condition attributed to Amini Harandi [32]. On this basis, we shall employ the APPX-endpoint property for $\mathfrak{P}$ illustrated in (15).

Theorem 3. *Let $\tilde{\mathfrak{H}} : \mathfrak{T} \times \mathfrak{W} \to \mathcal{P}_{cmp}(\mathfrak{W})$ be compact. Further:*

(HPS11) $\psi : [0,\infty) \to [0,\infty)$ *is a nondecreasing map having the upper semi-continuity property via* $\liminf_{z\to\infty}(z-\psi(z)) > 0$ *and* $\psi(z) < z$ *for all* $z > 0$;

(HPS12) $\tilde{\mathfrak{H}} : \mathfrak{T} \times \mathfrak{W} \to \mathcal{P}_{cmp}(\mathfrak{W})$ *is bounded integrable so that* $\tilde{\mathfrak{H}}(\cdot,\varpi) : \mathfrak{T} \to \mathcal{P}_{cp}(\mathfrak{W})$ *is measurable for every* $\varpi \in \mathfrak{W}$;

(HPS13) $\Upsilon \in \mathcal{C}_{\mathbb{R}_{\geq 0}}(\mathfrak{T})$ *exists such that for all* $z \in \mathfrak{T}$ *and* $\varpi,\varpi' \in \mathfrak{W}$, *we have*

$$\mathbb{PH}_{d_{\mathfrak{W}}}(\tilde{\mathfrak{H}}(z,\varpi) - \tilde{\mathfrak{H}}(z,\varpi')) \leq \Upsilon(z)\psi(|\varpi-\varpi'|)\frac{1}{\mathbb{M}_*\|\Upsilon\|}, \tag{17}$$

where $\sup_{z\in\mathfrak{T}}|\Upsilon(z)| = \|\Upsilon\|$ *and* $\mathbb{M}_*$ *is defined by* (14);

(HPS14) $\mathfrak{P}$ *is an operator having the APPX-endpoint property, where* $\mathfrak{P}$ *is formulated by* (15).

Then, the Caputo sequential nonhybrid multi-order inclusion BVP (3) *has at least one solution.*

Proof. To begin the proof, we want to check the existence of at least one endpoint for given multifunction $\mathfrak{P} : \mathfrak{W} \to \mathcal{P}(\mathfrak{W})$. To reach this objective, we have to verify that $\mathfrak{P}(\varpi)$ is a closed set for each $\varpi \in \mathfrak{W}$. By (HPS12), due to the measurability of $z \mapsto \tilde{\mathfrak{H}}(z,\varpi(z))$ and also since it is closed-valued for all $\varpi \in \mathfrak{W}$, it follows that $\tilde{\mathfrak{H}}$ has a measurable selection and, thus, $(\mathbb{SEL})_{\tilde{\mathfrak{H}},\varpi}$ is nonempty for every $\varpi \in \mathfrak{W}$. In this case, similar to the argument of Theorem 2, one can simply see that the subset $\mathfrak{P}(\varpi)$ of $\mathfrak{W}$ is closed, and so, we omit it. From another angle, we know that $\mathfrak{P}(\varpi)$ is a set having the boundedness property for each $\varpi \in \mathfrak{W}$ due to the compactness of $\tilde{\mathfrak{H}}$. Eventually, to end our proof, we must control whether the inequality $\mathbb{PH}_{d_{\mathfrak{W}}}(\mathfrak{P}(\varpi),\mathfrak{P}(\varpi')) \leq \psi(\|\varpi-\varpi'\|)$ holds or not. To check this, let $\varpi,\varpi' \in \mathfrak{W}$ and $\Phi_1 \in \mathfrak{P}(\varpi')$. Let us select $\hbar_1 \in (\mathbb{SEL})_{\tilde{\mathfrak{H}},\varpi'}$ such that

$$\Phi_1(z) = \frac{1}{\mu_1^*}\int_0^z e^{-\mu_2^*(z-q)}\int_0^q \frac{(q-r)^{\eta^*-2}}{\Gamma(\eta^*-1)}\hbar_1(r)\,drdq$$

$$+\frac{1-e^{-\mu_2^*z}-\mu_2^*z}{\mu_1^*\hat{\Omega}_*}\left[\int_0^1 \frac{(1-q)^{\theta_1^*-1}}{\Gamma(\theta_1^*)}\int_0^q e^{-\mu_2^*(q-m)}\int_0^m \frac{(m-r)^{\eta^*-2}}{\Gamma(\eta^*-1)}\hbar_1(r)\,drdmdq\right.$$

$$+\int_0^{\sigma}\frac{(\sigma-q)^{\theta_2^*-1}}{\Gamma(\theta_2^*)}\int_0^q e^{-\mu_2^*(q-m)}\int_0^m\frac{(m-r)^{\eta^*-2}}{\Gamma(\eta^*-1)}\hat{\kappa}_1(r)\,drdmdq\Bigg]$$

for all $z\in\mathfrak{T}$ (a.e.). In light of the inequality (17) demonstrated in the assumption (HPS13), we know that

$$\mathbb{PH}_{d_{\mathfrak{W}}}(\tilde{\mathfrak{H}}(z,\varpi)-\tilde{\mathfrak{H}}(z,\varpi'))\leq \Upsilon(z)\psi(|\varpi-\varpi'|)\frac{1}{\mathbb{M}_*\|\Upsilon\|}$$

for any $z\in\mathfrak{T}$; thus; there exists $b^*\in\tilde{\mathfrak{H}}(z,\varpi(z))$ for which one can write

$$|\hat{\kappa}_1(z)-b^*|\leq \Upsilon(z)\psi(|\varpi(z)-\varpi'(z)|)\frac{1}{\mathbb{M}_*\|\Upsilon\|}$$

for each $z\in\mathfrak{T}$. Now, we introduce $\mathfrak{R}^*:\mathfrak{T}\to\mathcal{P}(\mathfrak{W})$, which is illustrated by

$$\mathfrak{R}^*(z)=\left\{b^*\in\mathfrak{W}:\ |\hat{\kappa}_1(z)-b^*|\leq \Upsilon(z)\psi(|\varpi(z)-\varpi'(z)|)\frac{1}{\mathbb{M}_*\|\Upsilon\|}\right\}.$$

For the sake of the measurability of $\hat{\kappa}_1$ and $\varrho=\Upsilon\psi(|\varpi-\varpi'|)\frac{1}{\mathbb{M}_*\|\Upsilon\|}$, we can easily realize that $\mathfrak{R}^*(\cdot)\cap\tilde{\mathfrak{H}}(\cdot,\varpi(\cdot))$ is measurable. At this moment, choose the member $\hat{\kappa}_2(z)\in\tilde{\mathfrak{H}}(z,\varpi(z))$ such that

$$|\hat{\kappa}_1(z)-\hat{\kappa}_2(z)|\leq \Upsilon(z)\psi(|\varpi(z)-\varpi'(z)|)\frac{1}{\mathbb{M}_*\|\Upsilon\|}$$

for each $z\in\mathfrak{T}$. Now, we can choose $\Phi_2\in\mathfrak{P}(\varpi)$, provided that

$$\Phi_2(z)=\frac{1}{\mu_1^*}\int_0^z e^{-\mu_2^*(z-q)}\int_0^q\frac{(q-r)^{\eta^*-2}}{\Gamma(\eta^*-1)}\hat{\kappa}_2(r)\,drdq$$

$$+\frac{1-e^{-\mu_2^*z}-\mu_2^*z}{\mu_1^*\hat{\Omega}_*}\Bigg[\int_0^1\frac{(1-q)^{\theta_1^*-1}}{\Gamma(\theta_1^*)}\int_0^q e^{-\mu_2^*(q-m)}\int_0^m\frac{(m-r)^{\eta^*-2}}{\Gamma(\eta^*-1)}\hat{\kappa}_2(r)\,drdmdq$$

$$+\int_0^{\sigma}\frac{(\sigma-q)^{\theta_2^*-1}}{\Gamma(\theta_2^*)}\int_0^q e^{-\mu_2^*(q-m)}\int_0^m\frac{(m-r)^{\eta^*-2}}{\Gamma(\eta^*-1)}\hat{\kappa}_2(r)\,drdmdq\Bigg]$$

for all $z\in\mathfrak{T}$. Hence, if we repeat the same process implemented in Theorem 2, then we arrive at inequality

$$\|\Phi_1-\Phi_2\|=\sup_{z\in\mathfrak{T}}|\Phi_1(z)-\Phi_2(z)|\leq\mathbb{M}_*\|\Upsilon\|\psi(\|\varpi-\varpi'\|)\frac{1}{\mathbb{M}_*\|\Upsilon\|}=\psi(\|\varpi-\varpi'\|).$$

These findings verify that $\mathbb{PH}_{d_{\mathfrak{W}}}(\mathfrak{P}(\varpi),\mathfrak{P}(\varpi'))\leq\psi(\|\varpi-\varpi'\|)$ holds for any $\varpi,\varpi'\in\mathfrak{W}$. In addition, from the hypothesis (HPS14), we are sure that $\mathfrak{P}$ is an operator having the APPX-endpoint property, so by referring to Lemma 4, we derive the conclusion, which shows the existence of $\varpi^*\in\mathfrak{W}$ uniquely such that $\mathfrak{P}(\varpi^*)=\{\varpi^*\}$. Therefore, it is concluded that ϖ^* is a solution of the sequential multi-order inclusion FBVP (3). □

4. Examples

This part of the current paper is devoted to supporting the obtained theoretical results by proposing two simulative examples to demonstrate the correctness and the applicability of these outcomes.

Example 1. *In view of the given boundary problem (1) and (2), we here formulate a Caputo sequential hybrid integro-differential inclusion as the following form*

$$\frac{3}{1000}\left({}^{C}\mathcal{D}^{2.34}_{0^+} + \frac{5}{1000}{}^{C}\mathcal{D}^{1.34}_{0^+}\right)\left(\frac{\varpi(z)}{z\left(\frac{\sin\varpi(z)+\arcsin({}^{RL}\mathcal{I}^{0.71}_{0^+}\varpi(z))+\arctan({}^{RL}\mathcal{I}^{0.21}_{0^+}\varpi(z))}{100000}\right)+\frac{37}{10000}}\right)$$
$$\in\left[0,\left(0.0002z^{4999}+\frac{1}{5000}\right)\cos\varpi(z)\right] \tag{18}$$

subject to hybrid multi-order integro-derivative boundary conditions

$$\begin{cases}\left(\frac{\varpi(z)}{z\left(\frac{\sin\varpi(z)+\arcsin({}^{RL}\mathcal{I}^{0.71}_{0^+}\varpi(z))+\arctan({}^{RL}\mathcal{I}^{0.21}_{0^+}\varpi(z))}{100000}\right)+\frac{37}{10000}}\right)\Bigg|_{z=0}=0,\\ {}^{C}\mathcal{D}^{1}_{0^+}\left(\frac{\varpi(z)}{z\left(\frac{\sin\varpi(z)+\arcsin({}^{RL}\mathcal{I}^{0.71}_{0^+}\varpi(z))+\arctan({}^{RL}\mathcal{I}^{0.21}_{0^+}\varpi(z))}{100000}\right)+\frac{37}{10000}}\right)\Bigg|_{z=0}=0,\\ {}^{RL}\mathcal{I}^{1.02}_{0^+}\left(\frac{\varpi(z)}{z\left(\frac{\sin\varpi(z)+\arcsin({}^{RL}\mathcal{I}^{0.71}_{0^+}\varpi(z))+\arctan({}^{RL}\mathcal{I}^{0.21}_{0^+}\varpi(z))}{100000}\right)+\frac{37}{10000}}\right)\Bigg|_{z=1}\\ \quad+{}^{RL}\mathcal{I}^{1.08}_{0^+}\left(\frac{\varpi(z)}{z\left(\frac{\sin\varpi(z)+\arcsin({}^{RL}\mathcal{I}^{0.71}_{0^+}\varpi(z))+\arctan({}^{RL}\mathcal{I}^{0.21}_{0^+}\varpi(z))}{100000}\right)+\frac{37}{10000}}\right)\Bigg|_{z=0.65}=0,\end{cases} \tag{19}$$

where $z\in\mathfrak{T}:=[0,1]$, $\eta^*=2.34$, $\eta^*-1=1.34$, $\mu_1^*=0.003$, $\mu_2^*=0.005$, $\sigma=0.65$, $\theta_1^*=1.02$. $\theta_2^*=1.08$, *and for* $k=2$, *we have* $\delta_1^*=0.71$ *and* $\delta_2^*=0.21$. *In this case, we obtain* $\hat{\Omega}_*\simeq 0.000006$. *Here, one can specify the map* $\tilde{S}^*:\mathfrak{T}\times\mathbb{R}^3\to\mathbb{R}\setminus\{0\}$ *defined continuously as follows:*

$$\tilde{S}^*(z,\varpi_1(z),\varpi_2(z),\varpi_3(z))=z\left(\frac{\sin\varpi_1(z)+\arcsin({}^{RL}\mathcal{I}^{0.71}_{0^+}\varpi_2(z))+\arctan({}^{RL}\mathcal{I}^{0.21}_{0^+}\varpi_3(z))}{100000}\right)+\frac{37}{10000}$$

in which $\tilde{\mathbb{S}}^*=\sup_{z\in\mathfrak{T}}|\tilde{S}^*(z,0,0,0)|=0.0037$. *We claim that* $\tilde{S}^*$ *is Lipschitzian. To confirm this claim, for each* $\varpi,\varpi'\in\mathbb{R}$, *we may write*

$$\begin{aligned}&\left|\tilde{S}^*(z,\varpi(z),{}^{RL}\mathcal{I}^{\delta_1^*}_{0^+}\varpi(z),{}^{RL}\mathcal{I}^{\delta_2^*}_{0^+}\varpi(z))-\tilde{S}^*(z,\varpi'(z),{}^{RL}\mathcal{I}^{\delta_1^*}_{0^+}\varpi'(z),{}^{RL}\mathcal{I}^{\delta_2^*}_{0^+}\varpi'(z))\right|\\ &\qquad\le\tilde{v}(z)\left[1+\frac{z^{\delta_1^*}}{\Gamma(\delta_1^*+1)}+\frac{z^{\delta_2^*}}{\Gamma(\delta_2^*+1)}\right]|\varpi(z)-\varpi'(z)|\\ &\qquad=\frac{z}{100000}\left[1+\frac{z^{0.71}}{\Gamma(1.71)}+\frac{z^{0.21}}{\Gamma(1.21)}\right]|\varpi(z)-\varpi'(z)|,\end{aligned}$$

where $\tilde{v}(z)=\dfrac{z}{100000}$ *and* $\tilde{v}^*=\sup_{z\in\mathfrak{T}}|\tilde{v}(z)|=0.00001$. *Hence, one can observe that the Lipschitz constant of* $\tilde{S}^*$ *equals*

$$\tilde{v}^*\left[1+\frac{1}{\Gamma(\delta_1^*+1)}+\frac{1}{\Gamma(\delta_2^*+1)}\right]=\frac{1}{100000}\left[1+\frac{1}{\Gamma(1.71)}+\frac{1}{\Gamma(1.21)}\right]\simeq 0.0000319>0.$$

In the next stage, we formulate the multifunction $\tilde{\mathfrak{H}}:\mathfrak{T}\times\mathbb{R}\to\mathcal{P}(\mathbb{R})$ *in the following framework:*

$$\tilde{\mathfrak{H}}(z,\varpi(z))=\left[0,(0.0002z^{4999}+\frac{1}{5000})\cos\varpi(z)\right].$$

As for every $v \in \tilde{\mathfrak{H}}(z, \varpi(z))$, we have

$$|v| \le \max\left[0, (0.0002z^{4999} + \frac{1}{5000})\cos\varpi(z)\right] \le 0.0002z^{4999} + 0.0002,$$

so we obtain

$$\|\tilde{\mathfrak{H}}(z, \varpi(z))\| = \sup\{|\hat{\kappa}| : \hat{\kappa} \in \tilde{\mathfrak{H}}(z, \varpi(z))\} \le 0.0002z^{4999} + 0.0002.$$

By setting $x^*(z) = 0.0002z^{4999} + 0.0002$ for any $z \in \mathfrak{T}$, we obtain $\|x^*\| = 0.0004$. Furthermore, by the above obtained values, $\mathbb{M}_* \simeq 721419.86984$. In view of the above results and by some direct calculations, we select the positive number r_* so that $r_* > 1.0776$. Then, the following inequality holds:

$$\tilde{v}^*\left[1 + \frac{1}{\Gamma(\delta_1^* + 1)} + \frac{1}{\Gamma(\delta_2^* + 1)}\right]\mathbb{M}_*\|x^*\| \simeq (0.0000319)(721419.86984)(0.0004) \simeq 0.0092053 < \frac{1}{2}.$$

The latter inequality and all the above numerical findings show that Theorem 1 is settled on the present BVP, and so, it is verified that the Caputo sequential hybrid multi-order integro-differential inclusion (18) *and* (19) *has a solution.*

Remark 1. *Note that in the above example, we can review other numerical results to check the correctness of the existence criteria of solutions for different values of order η^*. Indeed, for every $\eta^* \in [2, 3)$, we compute the corresponding values of the constant $\mathbb{M}_*$ and the minimum value of r_*. Then, by assuming $\Delta := \tilde{v}^*\left[1 + \frac{1}{\Gamma(\delta_1^* + 1)} + \frac{1}{\Gamma(\delta_2^* + 1)}\right]\mathbb{M}_*\|x^*\|$, we shall see that an inequality $\Delta < 0.5$ holds in all cases. These numerical values can be observed in Table 1 and Figure 1.*

Table 1. Numerical values for $\mathbb{M}_*$, min r_* and Δ corresponding to different values of order η^*.

η^*	$\mathbb{M}_*$	$r_* >$	$\Delta < 0.5$
2	889,292.91961	1.3313	0.011347
2.05	865,898.41669	1.2958	0.011049
2.10	841,868.56165	1.2595	0.010742
2.15	817,328.27460	1.2224	0.010429
2.20	792,395.79444	1.1847	0.010111
2.25	767,182.51010	1.1467	0.0097892
2.30	741,792.85850	1.1083	0.0094653
2.34	721,419.86984	1.0776	0.0092053
2.35	716,324.28332	1.0699	0.0091403
2.40	690,867.24816	1.0316	0.0088155
2.45	665,505.29858	0.99338	0.0084918
2.50	640,315.16705	0.95547	0.0081704
2.55	615,366.91563	0.91795	0.0078521
2.60	590,724.11123	0.88091	0.0075376
2.65	566,444.02851	0.84444	0.0072278
2.70	542,577.87603	0.80861	0.0069233
2.75	519,171.04139	0.77350	0.0066246
2.80	496,263.35146	0.73915	0.0063323
2.85	473,889.34410	0.70562	0.0060468
2.90	452,078.54815	0.67296	0.0057685
2.95	430,855.76866	0.64119	0.0054977
2.99	414,314.74663	0.61644	0.0052867

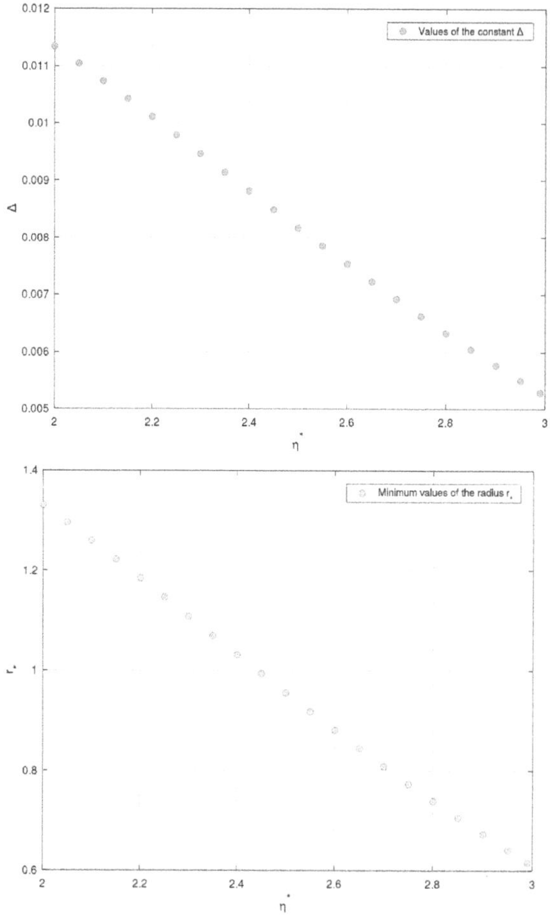

Figure 1. Values of Δ and $\min r_*$ with respect to different values of η^*.

In the last part, the analytical results obtained in Theorem 3 are investigated by the following numerical example.

Example 2. *In this example, we utilize the same given values* $\eta^* = 2.34$, $\eta^* - 1 = 1.34$, $\mu_1^* = 0.003$, $\mu_2^* = 0.005$, $\sigma = 0.65$, $\theta_1^* = 1.02$. $\theta_2^* = 1.08$. *According to the given problem* (3), *we formulate the following Caputo sequential nonhybrid multi-order differential inclusion:*

$$\frac{3}{1000}\left({}^{C}\mathcal{D}_{0^+}^{2.34} + \frac{5}{1000}{}^{C}\mathcal{D}_{0^+}^{1.34}\right)\varpi(z) \in \left[0, (z^{4999} + \frac{1}{5000})\cos\varpi(z)\right] \tag{20}$$

furnished with multi-order integro-derivative boundary conditions

$$\varpi(0) = 0, \quad {}^{C}\mathcal{D}_{0^+}^{1}\varpi(0) = 0, \quad {}^{RL}\mathcal{I}_{0^+}^{1.02}\varpi(1) + {}^{RL}\mathcal{I}_{0^+}^{1.08}\varpi(0.65) = 0 \tag{21}$$

for all $z \in \mathfrak{T}$, *where* ${}^{C}\mathcal{D}_{0^+}^{\gamma}$ *stands for the derivative of order* $\gamma \in \{2.34, 1.34\}$ *of the Caputo type and* ${}^{RL}\mathcal{I}_{0^+}^{\lambda}$ *indicates the RL integral of order* $\lambda \in \{1.02, 1.08\}$. *In a similar manner, we have* $\hat{\Omega}_* \simeq 0.000006$ *and* $\mathbb{M}_* \simeq 2354320.0929$. *To investigate the proposed problem* *precisely, we construct the Banach space as follows* $\mathfrak{W} = \{\varpi(z) : \varpi(z) \in \mathcal{C}_{\mathbb{R}}([0,1])\}$ *with* $\|\varpi\|_{\mathfrak{W}} = \sup_{z\in\mathfrak{T}} |\varpi(z)|$. *Now, we can introduce* $\tilde{\mathfrak{H}} : \mathfrak{T} \times \mathfrak{W} \to \mathcal{P}(\mathfrak{W})$ *by*

$$\tilde{\mathfrak{H}}(z, \varpi(z)) = \left[0, \frac{0.008(z+6)}{1628} \frac{|\sin\varpi(z)|}{1+|\sin\varpi(z)|}\right]$$

for each $z \in \mathfrak{T}$. *In view of the above set-valued map* $\tilde{\mathfrak{H}}$, *we reach the function* $\Upsilon \in \mathcal{C}_{\mathbb{R}^{\geq 0}}(\mathfrak{T})$, *which is demonstrated by* $\Upsilon(z) = \dfrac{0.008(z+6)}{814}$ *for any z along with* $\|\Upsilon\| = \dfrac{0.056}{814} = 0.0000687$. *In addition, the nondecreasing mapping* $\psi : [0,\infty) \to [0,\infty)$ *with the upper semi-continuity specification is regarded as* $\psi(z) = \dfrac{z}{2}$ *for* $z > 0$. *Furthermore, it is evident that* $\liminf_{z\to\infty}(z - \psi(z)) > 0$ *and* $\psi(z) < z$ *for each* $z > 0$. *For both arbitrary elements* $\varpi, \varpi' \in \mathfrak{W}$, *we estimate the following inequality:*

$$\begin{aligned}\mathbb{PH}_{d_{\mathfrak{W}}}\left(\tilde{\mathfrak{H}}(z,\varpi(z)), \tilde{\mathfrak{H}}(z,\varpi'(z))\right) &\leq \frac{0.008(z+6)}{814}\frac{1}{2}(|\varpi - \varpi'|) \\ &= \frac{0.008(z+6)}{814}\psi(|\varpi - \varpi'|) \leq \Upsilon(z)\psi(|\varpi - \varpi'|)\frac{1}{\mathbb{M}_*\|\Upsilon\|},\end{aligned}$$

where $\dfrac{1}{\mathbb{M}_*\|\Upsilon\|} \simeq 0.006182$. *Finally, with due attention to the method implemented in Theorem 3, we regard* $\mathfrak{P} : \mathfrak{W} \to \mathcal{P}(\mathfrak{W})$ *illustrated by*

$$\mathfrak{P}(\varpi) = \left\{\Phi \in \mathfrak{W} : \text{ there is } \mathfrak{k} \in (\mathbb{SEL})_{\tilde{\mathfrak{H}},\varpi} \text{ such that } \Phi(z) = b(z) \text{ for any } z \in \mathfrak{T}\right\},$$

where

$$\begin{aligned}b(z) &= \frac{1}{0.003}\int_0^z e^{-0.005(z-q)}\int_0^q \frac{(q-r)^{2.34-2}}{\Gamma(2.34-1)}\mathfrak{k}(r)\,\mathrm{d}r\mathrm{d}q \\ &+ \frac{1-e^{-0.005z} - 0.005z}{(0.003)(0.000006)}\left[\int_0^1 \frac{(1-q)^{1.02-1}}{\Gamma(1.02)}\int_0^q e^{-0.005(q-m)}\int_0^m \frac{(m-r)^{2.34-2}}{\Gamma(2.34-1)}\mathfrak{k}(r)\,\mathrm{d}r\mathrm{d}m\mathrm{d}q\right. \\ &+ \left.\int_0^{0.65}\frac{(0.65-q)^{1.08-1}}{\Gamma(1.08)}\int_0^q e^{-0.005(q-m)}\int_0^m \frac{(m-r)^{2.34-2}}{\Gamma(2.34-1)}\mathfrak{k}(r)\,\mathrm{d}r\mathrm{d}m\mathrm{d}q\right].\end{aligned}$$

Therefore, by referring to Theorem 3 based on a numerical method, it is realized that the Caputo sequential nonhybrid inclusion (20) *along with multi-order integro-differential conditions* (21) *involves a solution. This means that the numerical outcomes of the current example are compatible with all theoretical arguments given in Theorem 3.*

5. Conclusions

In this manuscript, we introduced and combined a new configuration of a Caputo sequential inclusion BVP with the hybrid integro-differential inclusion problem in which the boundary conditions are also formulated as the hybrid multi-order integro-derivative conditions. To reach the desired goal of this abstract general fractional model, we derived some theoretical existence results with the help of analytical techniques due to Dhage on the product operators for the given mixed sequential hybrid BVP (1) and (2). Next, based on some conditions on a defined space including the APPX-endpoint property, the (C_α)-property, and the compactness, we investigated the nonhybrid structure of the suggested BVP (3). Lastly, two examples were designed in this regard. For the next works, one can study the qualitative behaviors and the stability of coupled systems of such sequential hybrid inclusion BVPs by using newly defined fractional operators. Specifically, we can conduct research on the fractal–fractional hybrid models of thermostat or pantograph systems by considering different cases for fractional orders and fractal dimensions.

Author Contributions: Conceptualization, S.E. and S.R.; formal analysis, S.E., S.K.N., B.A., S.R. and J.T.; funding acquisition, J.T.; methodology, S.E., S.K.N., B.A., S.R. and J.T.; software, S.E. All authors have read and agreed to the published version of the manuscript.

Funding: This research was funded by the National Science, Research and Innovation Fund (NSRF) and King Mongkut's University of Technology North Bangkok with Contract No. KMUTNB-FF-65-36.

Institutional Review Board Statement: Not applicable.

Informed Consent Statement: Not applicable.

Data Availability Statement: Data sharing is not applicable to this article as no datasets were generated nor analyzed during the current study.

Acknowledgments: The first and fourth authors would like to thank Azarbaijan Shahid Madani University.

Conflicts of Interest: The authors declare no conflict of interest.

Abbreviations

The following abbreviations are used in this manuscript:

FBVP Fractional Boundary Value Problem

References

1. Adjabi, Y.; Samei, M.E.; Matar, M.M.; Alzabut, J. Langevin differential equation in frame of ordinary and Hadamard fractional derivatives under three point boundary conditions. *AIMS Math.* **2021**, *6*, 2796–2843. [CrossRef]
2. Mohammadi, H.; Kumar, S.; Rezapour, S.; Etemad, S. A theoretical study of the Caputo-Fabrizio fractional modeling for hearing loss due to Mumps virus with optimal control. *Chaos Solitons Fractals* **2021**, *144*, 110668. [CrossRef]
3. Thabet, S.T.M.; Abdo, M.S.; Shah, K.; Abdeljawad, T. Abdeljawad, Study of transmission dynamics of COVID-19 mathematical model under ABC fractional order derivative. *Res. Phys.* **2020**, *19*, 103507.
4. Thabet, S.T.M.; Etemad, S.; Rezapour, S. On a new structure of the pantograph inclusion problem in the Caputo conformable setting. *Bound. Value Probl.* **2020**, *2020*, 171. [CrossRef]
5. Abbas, M.I.; Ragusa, M.A. Solvability of Langevin equations with two Hadamard fractional derivatives via Mittag-Leffler functions. *Appl. Anal.* **2022**, *101*, 3231–3245. [CrossRef]
6. Abdo, M.S.; Shah, K.; Wahash, H.A.; Panchal, S.K. On a comprehensive model of the novel coronavirus (COVID-19) under Mittag-Leffler derivative. *Chaos Solitons Fractal* **2020**, *135*, 109867. [CrossRef]
7. Amara, A.; Etemad, S.; Rezapour, S. Topological degree theory and Caputo–Hadamard fractional boundary value problems. *Adv. Differ. Equ.* **2020**, *2020*, 369. [CrossRef]
8. Boucenna, D.; Boulfoul, A.; Chidouh, A.; Makhlouf, A.B.; Tellab, B. Some results for initial value problem of nonlinear fractional equation in Sobolev space. *J. Appl. Math. Comput.* **2021**, *67*, 605–621. [CrossRef]
9. Derbazi, C.; Baitiche, Z.; Abdo, M.S.; Abdeljawad, T. Qualitative analysis of fractional relaxation equation and coupled system with Ψ-Caputo fractional derivative in Banach spaces. *AIMS Math.* **2020**, *6*, 2486–2509. [CrossRef]
10. Ntouyas, S.K.; Etemad, S. On the existence of solutions for fractional differential inclusions with sum and integral boundary conditions. *Appl. Math. Comput.* **2015**, *266*, 235–243. [CrossRef]
11. Kamenskii, M.; Petrosyan, G.; Wen, C.F. An existence result for a periodic boundary value problem of fractional semilinear differential equations in a Banach space. *J. Nonlinear Var. Anal.* **2021**, *5*, 155–177.
12. Miller, K.S.; Ross, B. *An Introduction to the Fractional Calculus and Fractional Differential Equations*; Wiley-Interscience, John-Wiley and Sons: New York, NY, USA, 1993.
13. Alsaedi, A.; Ntouyas, S.K.; Agarwal, R.P.; Ahmad, B. On Caputo type sequential fractional differential equations with nonlocal integral boundary conditions. *Adv. Differ. Equations* **2015**, *2015*, 33. [CrossRef]
14. Klimek, M. Sequential fractional differential equations with Hadamard derivative. *Commun. Nonlinear Sci. Numer. Simul.* **2011**, *16*, 4689–4697. [CrossRef]
15. Baleanu, D.; Etemad, S.; Pourrazi, S.; Rezapour, S. On the new fractional hybrid boundary value problems with three-point integral hybrid conditions. *Adv. Differ. Equations* **2019**, *2019*, 473. [CrossRef]
16. Hilal, K.; Kajouni, A. Boundary value problems for hybrid differential equations with fractional order. *Adv. Differ. Equations* **2015**, *2015*, 183. [CrossRef]
17. Mohammadi, H.; Rezapour, S.; Etemad, S.; Baleanu, D. Two sequential fractional hybrid differential inclusions. *Adv. Differ. Equations* **2020**, *2020*, 385. [CrossRef]
18. Sun, S.; Zhao, Y.; Han, Z.; Li, Y. The existence of solutions for boundary value problem of fractional hybrid differential equations. *Commun. Nonlinear Sci. Numer. Simul.* **2012**, *17*, 4961–4967. [CrossRef]

19. Sutar, S.T.; Kucche, K.D. On nonlinear hybrid fractional differential equations with Atangana-Baleanu-Caputo derivative. *Chaos Solitons Fractals* **2021**, *143*, 110557. [CrossRef]
20. Dhage, B.C. Existence and attractivity theorems for nonlinear hybrid fractional integrodifferential equations with anticipation and retardation. *J. Nonlinear Funct. Anal.* **2020**, *2020*, 47. [CrossRef]
21. Dhage, B.C.; Lakshmikantham, V. Basic results on hybrid differential equation. *Nonlinear Anal. Hybrid Syst.* **2010**, *4*, 414–424. [CrossRef]
22. Zhao, Y.; Sun, S.; Han, Z.; Li, Q. Theory of fractional hybrid differential equations. *Comput. Math. Appl.* **2011**, *62*, 1312–1324. [CrossRef]
23. Ahmad, B.; Ntouyas, S.K.; Tariboon, J. On hybrid Caputo fractional integro-differential inclusions with nonlocal conditions. *J. Nonlinear Sci. Appl.* **2016**, *9*, 4235–4246. [CrossRef]
24. Baleanu, D.; Etemad, S.; Rezapour, S. A hybrid Caputo fractional modeling for thermostat with hybrid boundary value conditions. *Bound. Value Probl.* **2020**, *2020*, 64. [CrossRef]
25. Abbas, M.I.; Ragusa, M.A. On the hybrid fractional differential equations with fractional proportional derivatives of a function with respect to a certain function. *Symmetry* **2021**, *13*, 264. [CrossRef]
26. Podlubny, I. *Fractional Differential Equations*; Academic Press: San Diego, CA, USA, 1999.
27. Samko, G.; Kilbas, A.; Marichev, O. *Fractional Integrals and Derivatives: Theory and Applications*; Gordon and Breach Science Publishers: Longhorne, PA, USA, 1993.
28. Deimling, K. *Multi-Valued Differential Equations*; Walter de Gruyter: Berlin, Germany, 1992.
29. Aubin, J.; Cellna, A. *Differential Inclusions: Set-Valued Maps and Viability Theory*; Springer: Berlin/Heidelberg, Germany, 1984.
30. Samet, B.; Vetro, C.; Vetro, P. Fixed point theorems for α-ψ-contractive type mappings. *Nonlinear Anal.* **2012**, *75*, 2154–2165. [CrossRef]
31. Mohammadi, B.; Rezapour, S.; Shahzad, N. Some results on fixed points of α-ψ-Ciric generalized multifunctions. *Fixed Point Theory Appl.* **2013**, *2013*, 24. [CrossRef]
32. Amini-Harandi, A. Endpoints of set-valued contractions in metric spaces. *Nonlinear Anal.* **2010**, *72*, 132–134. [CrossRef]
33. Lasota, A.; Opial, Z. An application of the Kakutani-Ky Fan theorem in the theory of ordinary differential equations. *Bull. Acad. Pol. Sci. Set. Sci. Math. Astronom. Phy.* **1965**, *13*, 781–786.
34. Dhage, B.C. Existence results for neutral functional differential inclusions in Banach algebras. *Nonlinear Anal.* **2006**, *64*, 1290–1306. [CrossRef]

mathematics

MDPI

Review

A Survey on the Oscillation of Solutions for Fractional Difference Equations

Jehad Alzabut [1,2,*,†], Ravi P. Agarwal [3,†], Said R. Grace [4,†], Jagan M. Jonnalagadda [5,†], A. George Maria Selvam [6,†] and Chao Wang [7,†]

1 Department of Mathematics and Sciences, Prince Sultan University, Riyadh 12435, Saudi Arabia
2 Department of Industrial Engineering, OSTİM Technical University, Ankara 06374, Turkey
3 Department of Mathematics, Texas A&M University-Kingvsille, Kingsville, TX 7836, USA; ravi.agarwal@tamuk.edu
4 Department of Engineering Mathematics, Faculty of Engineering, Cairo University, Giza 12221, Egypt; saidgrace@yahoo.com
5 Department of Mathematics, Birla Institute of Technology and Science Pilani, Hyderabad 500078, Telangana, India; j.jaganmohan@hotmail.com
6 Department of Mathematics, Sacred Heart College (Autonomous), Tirupattur 635 601, Tamil Nadu, India; agmshc@gmail.com
7 Department of Mathematics, Yunnan University, Kunming 650091, China; chaowang@ynu.edu.cn
* Correspondence: jalzabut@psu.edu.sa or jehad.alzabut@ostimteknik.edu.tr
† These authors contributed equally to this work.

Abstract: In this paper, we present a systematic study concerning the developments of the oscillation results for the fractional difference equations. Essential preliminaries on discrete fractional calculus are stated prior to giving the main results. Oscillation results are presented in a subsequent order and for different types of equations. The investigation was carried out within the delta and nabla operators.

Keywords: fractional order; forward (delta) difference equation; backward (nabla) difference equation; oscillation of solutions

MSC: 26A33; 34A08; 34K11; 39A10; 39A11; 39A12; 39A13; 39A20; 39A21

1. Introduction

Over many years, the process of describing natural or real-life phenomena has been carried out using the integer-order differential equations. However, the factors involved in the phenomena are very complicated and of different natures, all of which cannot be incorporated by the ordinary differential equations. This gap in the construction of the models is covered up by arbitrary-order calculus. Fractional calculus has its origin during the same period of time as that of the classical calculus in the 17th Century. The insufficient geometrical and unsatisfactory physical interpretation of the arbitrary-order derivatives has slowed down the progress of the field. It was in the 20th Century with the development of high-speed computers and computational techniques that researchers began to understand the importance and the meaningful representation to construct and apply a certain type of nonlocal operator to real-life problems. Now, fractional calculus has turned out to be a hot topic in the fields of science and engineering. The rapid growth and inspiration of fractional calculus have been greatly due to anticipation of the memory and hereditary features that are incorporated in many phenomena by the so-called fractional differential operators [1–3]. As a result of this, the subject of fractional calculus and its widespread applications have become of great interest for the relevant audience [4]. For the same justifications that led to the investigation of the discrete analogue of integer-order differential operators, the discrete analogue of fractional differential operators, which is called fractional difference operators, has gained considerable attention, and thus, they have been significantly adopted due to their extensive applications in computations and simulations. The study of fractional difference equations was led by the pioneering works of Agarwal, Atici, Eloe, Anastassiou, Holm, Goodrich, and Peterson, who introduced a complete counterpart theory that adopts all the essential preliminaries needed to set forth similar results relevant to the qualitative theory of solutions for several types of fractional difference equations [5–11].

Every phenomenon in the world in one way or other is nonlinear in nature. Thus, the better understanding of these phenomena can be obtained from models constructed via nonlinear equations. The analytical solution of nonlinear equations is not always possible to obtain as in the case of linear equations. However, approximate solutions can be obtained for the nonlinear equations, which provide a better understanding of the behavior of the equations. In the case of nonlinear equations, without actually solving the equations, one can very well answer questions such as the existence of solutions, whether the system is stable, whether it can be controlled, whether the system is chaotic, or whether it exhibits periodicity. Thus, this direct method of analyzing the system behavior can be useful and help engineers in their research. Scientists and researchers are very much interested in the qualitative properties such as the oscillation, stability, controllability, bifurcation, chaos, and so on.

Oscillation is one of the important branches in applied mathematics and can be induced or destroyed by the introduction of nonlinearity, delay, or a stochastic term. The oscillation of differential and difference equations contributes to many realistic applications, such as torsional oscillations, the oscillation of heart beats, sinusoidal oscillation, voltage-controlled neuron models, and harmonic oscillation with damping. Not only in physical applications, oscillation theory is vital biologically in describing the synchrony in animal and plant populations due to predation and competition. Such applications have attracted the interest of many researchers who have developed systematic studies concerning the oscillation and non-oscillation of solutions of integer-order differential and difference equations; we refer the reader to the remarkable monographs [12,13]. With the explosion in the theory of fractional calculus, the oscillation of fractional-order differential equations has been under investigation in the last two decades. Grace et al. initiated this subject by studying the oscillation of fractional differential equations in [14]. Progress in this regard has continued, and several important results have been established; see for instance [15–18] and the references cited therein. In alignment with this, fractional difference equations have been the object of interested researchers in terms of the oscillation of their solutions. Several results have been reported by many researchers about the oscillation of solutions for different types of fractional difference equations.

The main aim of this work was to consolidate the recent developments in the field of the oscillation theory of discrete fractional equations and provide an insight for researchers about the future requisites in the field of the oscillations of discrete fractional calculus. The investigation in this work focused on the results for both delta- and nabla-type fractional difference equations.

2. Preliminaries

In this section, we review some notations, definitions, and well-known results of discrete fractional calculus that are widely treated throughout the remaining part of this paper. The terms and notations were adopted from different resources.

The empty sums and products were taken to be zero and one, respectively. Denote by $\mathbb{N}$ the set of all natural numbers, $\mathbb{R}$ the set of all real numbers, and $\mathbb{R}^+$ the set of all positive real numbers. Define by $\mathbb{N}_a = \{a, a+1, a+2, \dots\}$ and $\mathbb{N}_a^b = \{a, a+1, a+2, \dots, b\}$ for any $a, b \in \mathbb{R}$ such that $b - a \in \mathbb{N}_1$.

Definition 1 ([19,20])**.** *The Euler gamma function is defined by:*

$$\Gamma(z) = \int_0^\infty t^{z-1}e^{-t}dt, \quad \Re(z) > 0.$$

Using its reduction formula, the Euler gamma function can also be extended to the half-plane $\Re(z) \leq 0$ except for $z \in \{\ldots, -2, -1, 0\}$.

Definition 2 ([21]). *The generalized falling function is defined by:*

$$t^{\underline{r}} = \frac{\Gamma(t+1)}{\Gamma(t-r+1)},$$

for those values of t and r such that the right-hand side of this equation makes sense. If $t-r+1$ is a nonpositive integer and $t+1$ is not a nonpositive integer, then we use the convention that $t^{\underline{r}} = 0$. The generalized rising function is defined by:

$$t^{\overline{r}} = \frac{\Gamma(t+r)}{\Gamma(t)},$$

for those values of t and r so that the right-hand side of this equation is sensible. If t is a nonpositive integer, but $t+r$ is not a nonpositive integer, then we use the convention that $t^{\overline{r}} = 0$.

Definition 3 ([22]). *Let $u : \mathbb{N}_a^b \to \mathbb{R}$ and $N \in \mathbb{N}_1$. The first-order forward (delta) and backward (nabla) differences of u are defined by:*

$$(\Delta u)(t) = u(t+1) - u(t), \quad t \in \mathbb{N}_a^{b-1},$$

$$(\nabla u)(t) = u(t) - u(t-1), \quad t \in \mathbb{N}_{a+1}^b,$$

respectively. The Nth-order delta and nabla differences of u are defined recursively by

$$(\Delta^N u)(t) = \Big(\Delta(\Delta^{N-1}u)\Big)(t), \quad t \in \mathbb{N}_a^{b-N},$$

and:

$$(\nabla^N u)(t) = \Big(\nabla(\nabla^{N-1}u)\Big)(t), \quad t \in \mathbb{N}_{a+N}^b,$$

respectively.

Definition 4 ([21]). *Let $u : \mathbb{N}_a \to \mathbb{R}$ and $v > 0$. Then, the vth-order delta fractional sum of u based at a is defined by:*

$$(\Delta_a^{-v}u)(t) = \frac{1}{\Gamma(v)} \sum_{s=a}^{t-v} (t-s-1)^{\underline{v-1}} u(s), \quad t \in \mathbb{N}_{a+v}.$$

Definition 5 ([21]). *Let $u : \mathbb{N}_{a+1} \to \mathbb{R}$ and $v > 0$. Then, the vth-order nabla fractional sum of u based at a is defined by:*

$$(\nabla_a^{-v}u)(t) = \frac{1}{\Gamma(v)} \sum_{s=a+1}^{t} (t-s+1)^{\overline{v-1}} u(s), \quad t \in \mathbb{N}_a.$$

Definition 6 ([21]). *Let $u : \mathbb{N}_a \to \mathbb{R}$, $v > 0$, and choose $N \in \mathbb{N}_1$ such that $N-1 < v \leq N$. The vth-order Riemann–Liouville delta fractional difference of u is defined by:*

$$(\Delta_a^v u)(t) = \Big(\Delta^N(\Delta_a^{-(N-v)}u)\Big)(t), \quad t \in \mathbb{N}_{a+N-v}.$$

Definition 7 ([21]). *Let $u : \mathbb{N}_{a+1} \to \mathbb{R}$, $v > 0$, and choose $N \in \mathbb{N}_1$ such that $N-1 < v \leq N$. Then, the vth-order Riemann–Liouville nabla fractional difference of u is defined by:*

$$(\nabla_a^v u)(t) = \Big(\nabla^N(\nabla_a^{-(N-v)}u)\Big)(t), \quad t \in \mathbb{N}_{a+N}$$

Definition 8 ([23]). *Let $u : \mathbb{N}_a \to \mathbb{R}$, $\nu > 0$, and $\nu \notin \mathbb{N}$. Then, the νth-order Caputo delta fractional difference of u is defined by:*

$$(\Delta^{\nu}_{a*}u)(t) = \left(\Delta_a^{-(N-\nu)}(\Delta^N u)\right)(t), \quad t \in \mathbb{N}_{a+N-\nu},$$

where $N = [\nu] + 1$. If $\nu = N \in \mathbb{N}$, then:

$$(\Delta^{\nu}_{a*}u)(t) = (\Delta^N u)(t), \quad t \in \mathbb{N}_a.$$

Definition 9 ([24]). *Let $u : \mathbb{N}_{a-N+1} \to \mathbb{R}$ and $\nu > 0$. Then, the νth-order Caputo nabla fractional difference of u is defined by:*

$$(\nabla^{\nu}_{a*}u)(t) = \left(\nabla_a^{-(N-\nu)}(\nabla^N u)\right)(t), \quad t \in \mathbb{N}_{a+1},$$

where $N = \lceil \nu \rceil$.

3. Oscillation Results

The main results are given in this section. We carried out the presentation within delta and nabla notations.

3.1. Oscillatory Behavior of Delta Fractional Difference Equations

Consider the following higher-order nonlinear delta fractional difference equations involving the Riemann–Liouville and the Caputo operators of arbitrary order:

$$\begin{cases} (\Delta^{\nu}u)(t) + f_1(t, u(t+\nu)) = r_1(t) + f_2(t, u(t+\nu)), & t \in \mathbb{N}_a, \\ (\Delta^{-(k-\nu)}u)(t)\Big|_{t=a} = u_k \in \mathbb{R}, \quad k = 1, 2, \cdots, N, \end{cases} \tag{1}$$

and:

$$\begin{cases} (\Delta^{\nu}_{*}u)(t) + f_1(t, u(t+\nu)) = r_1(t) + f_2(t, u(t+\nu)), & t > a \geq 0, \\ (\Delta^{k}u)(t)\Big|_{t=a} = \bar{u}_k \in \mathbb{R}, \quad k = 0, 1, 2, \cdots, N-1. \end{cases} \tag{2}$$

Here, $\nu > 0$, and choose $N \in \mathbb{N}_1$ such that $N - 1 < \nu \leq N$; $f_1, f_2 : [a, \infty) \times \mathbb{R} \to \mathbb{R}$ and $r_1 : [a, \infty) \to \mathbb{R}$ are continuous. A solution u of (1) (or (2)) is said to be oscillatory if for every natural number M, there exists $t \geq M$ such that $u(t)u(t+1) \leq 0$; otherwise, it is called non-oscillatory. An equation is said to be oscillatory if all of its solutions are oscillatory.

Let $p_1, p_2 : [a, \infty) \to \mathbb{R}^+$ be continuous and β, γ be positive real numbers. We make the following assumptions:

(A1) The functions f_i satisfy the sign condition $uf_i(t, u) > 0, i = 1, 2, u \neq 0, t \geq a$;
(A2) $|f_1(t, u)| \geq p_1(t)|u|^{\beta}$ and $|f_2(t, u)| \leq p_2(t)|u|^{\gamma}$, $u \neq 0$, $t \geq a$;
(A3) $|f_1(t, u)| \leq p_1(t)|u|^{\beta}$ and $|f_2(t, u)| \geq p_2(t)|u|^{\gamma}$, $u \neq 0$, $t \geq a$.

In [25], Senem et al. established some oscillation theorems given in the sequel.

Theorem 1 ([25]). *Let (A1)–(A2) be satisfied with $\beta > \gamma$. If:*

$$\liminf_{t\to\infty} t^{(1-\nu)} \sum_{s=T}^{t-\nu} (t-s-1)^{(\nu-1)}[r_1(s) + G(s)] = -\infty,$$

and:

$$\limsup_{t\to\infty} t^{(1-\nu)} \sum_{s=T}^{t-\nu} (t-s-1)^{(\nu-1)}[r_1(s) - G(s)] = \infty,$$

for every sufficiently large T, where:

$$G(s) = \left(\frac{\beta}{\gamma} - 1\right)\left[\frac{\gamma p_2(s)}{\beta}\right]^{\frac{\beta}{\beta-\gamma}} p_1^{\frac{\gamma}{\gamma-\beta}}(s),$$

then Equation (1) is oscillatory.

Theorem 2 ([25]). *Let $\nu \geq 1$ and (A1)–(A3) be satisfied with $\beta < \gamma$. If*

$$\liminf_{t\to\infty} t^{(1-\nu)} \sum_{s=T}^{t-\nu} (t-s-1)^{(\nu-1)}[r_1(s) - G(s)] = -\infty,$$

and:

$$\limsup_{t\to\infty} t^{(1-\nu)} \sum_{s=T}^{t-\nu} (t-s-1)^{(\nu-1)}[r_1(s) + G(s)] = \infty,$$

for every sufficiently large T, where G is defined as in Theorem 1, then every bounded solution of Equation (1) is oscillatory.

Theorem 3 ([25]). *Let (A1) and (A2) be satisfied with $\beta > \gamma$. If:*

$$\liminf_{t\to\infty} t^{(1-N)} \sum_{s=T}^{t-\nu} (t-s-1)^{(\nu-1)}[r_1(s) + G(s)] = -\infty,$$

and:

$$\limsup_{t\to\infty} t^{(1-N)} \sum_{s=T}^{t-\nu} (t-s-1)^{(\nu-1)}[r_1(s) - G(s)] = \infty,$$

for every sufficiently large T, where G is defined as in Theorem 1, then Equation (2) is oscillatory.

Theorem 4 ([25]). *Let $\nu \geq 1$ and (A1)–(A3) be satisfied with $\beta < \gamma$. If:*

$$\liminf_{t\to\infty} t^{(1-N)} \sum_{s=T}^{t-\nu} (t-s-1)^{(\nu-1)}[r_1(s) - G(s)] = -\infty,$$

and:

$$\limsup_{t\to\infty} t^{(1-N)} \sum_{s=T}^{t-\nu} (t-s-1)^{(\nu-1)}[r_1(s) + G(s)] = \infty,$$

for every sufficiently large T, where G is defined as in Theorem 1, then every bounded solution of Equation (2) is oscillatory.

Following the work in [25], Li et al. [26] investigated the oscillation of forced delta fractional difference equations with the damping term of the form:

$$\begin{cases} (1+p_3(t))(\Delta\Delta^\nu u)(t) + p_3(t)(\Delta^\nu u)(t) + f_3(t,u(t)) = g_1(t), & t \in \mathbb{N}_0, \\ (\Delta^{-(1-\nu)}u)(t)\Big|_{t=0} = u_0 \in \mathbb{R}, \end{cases} \tag{3}$$

where $0 < \nu < 1$; $p_3, g_1 : \mathbb{N}_0 \to \mathbb{R}$ and $f_3 : \mathbb{N}_0 \times \mathbb{R} \to \mathbb{R}$ such that:

$$uf_3(t,u) > 0, \quad u \neq 0, \quad t \in \mathbb{N}_0,$$

and $p_3(t) > -1$ for $t \in \mathbb{N}_0$.

Theorem 5 ([26]). *For $t_0 \in \mathbb{N}_0$, suppose that:*

$$\liminf_{t\to\infty} \sum_{s=0}^{t-\nu} \frac{(t-s-1)^{(\nu-1)}}{V(s)} \left[M + \sum_{\xi=t_0}^{s-1} g_1(\xi)V(\xi) \right] < 0,$$

and:

$$\limsup_{t\to\infty} \sum_{s=0}^{t-\nu} \frac{(t-s-1)^{(\nu-1)}}{V(s)} \left[M + \sum_{\xi=t_0}^{s-1} g_1(\xi)V(\xi) \right] > 0,$$

where M is a constant and:

$$V(t) = \prod_{s=t_0}^{t-1} (1 + p_3(s)).$$

Then, Equation (3) *is oscillatory.*

Theorem 6 ([26]). *For $t_0 \in \mathbb{N}_0$, suppose that:*

$$\liminf_{t\to\infty} \sum_{s=0}^{t-1} \frac{1}{V(s)} \left[M + \sum_{\xi=t_0}^{s-1} g_1(\xi)V(\xi) \right] = -\infty,$$

and:

$$\limsup_{t\to\infty} \sum_{s=0}^{t-1} \frac{1}{V(s)} \left[M + \sum_{\xi=t_0}^{s-1} g_1(\xi)V(\xi) \right] = \infty,$$

where M is a constant and V is defined as in Theorem 5. Then, Equation (3) *is oscillatory.*

In this line, Seçer et al. [27] investigated the oscillation of the following nonlinear delta fractional difference equations:

$$\Delta\Big(p_4(t)\left[\Delta(q_1(t)((\Delta^\nu u)(t))^{\gamma_1})\right]^{\gamma_2}\Big) + q_2(t) f_4\left(\sum_{s=t_0}^{t-1+\nu} (t-s-1)^{(-\nu)} u(s) \right) = 0, \quad (4)$$

for $t \in \mathbb{N}_{t_0+1-\nu}$. Here, $0 < \nu \le 1$, γ_1 and γ_2 are the quotients of two odd positive numbers such that $\gamma_1\gamma_2 = 1$, p_4, q_1 and q_2 are positive sequences,

$$\sum_{s=t_0}^{\infty} \left(\frac{1}{p_4^{1/\gamma_2}(s)} \right) = \infty,$$

$f_4 : \mathbb{R} \to \mathbb{R}$ is continuous, and:

$$\frac{f_4(u)}{u} \ge k, \quad k \in \mathbb{R}^+, \quad u \ne 0.$$

Theorem 7 ([27]). *If there exists a positive sequence ϕ such that:*

$$\limsup_{t\to\infty} \sum_{s=t_2}^{t-1} \left[k\phi(s)q_2(s) - \frac{q_1^{1/\gamma_1}(s)[(\Delta\phi_+)(s)]^2}{4\phi(s)\Gamma(1-\nu)\delta_1^{1/\gamma_1}(s,t_1)} \right] = \infty,$$

then Equation (4) *is oscillatory. Here:*

$$\delta_1(t,t_i) = \sum_{s=t_i}^{t-1} \left(\frac{1}{p_4^{1/\gamma_2}(s)} \right), \quad i = 0,1,2,3,$$

and,

$$(\Delta\phi_+)(s) = \max\{(\Delta\phi)(s), 0\}.$$

Theorem 8 ([27]). *Let ϕ be a positive sequence. Furthermore, we assume that there exists a double sequence such that:*

$$H(t,t) = 0 \text{ for } t \geq 0, \quad H(t,s) > 0 \text{ for } t > s \geq 0,$$
$$\Delta_2 H(t,s) = H(t,s+1) - H(t,s) \leq 0 \text{ for } t > s \geq 0.$$

If:

$$\limsup_{t\to\infty} \frac{1}{H(t,t_0)} \sum_{s=t_0}^{t-1} H(t,s) \left[k\phi(s)q_2(s) - \frac{q_1^{1/\gamma_1}(s)[(\Delta\phi_+)(s)]^2}{4\phi(s)\Gamma(1-\nu)\delta_1^{1/\gamma_1}(s,t_2)} \right] = \infty.$$

Then, Equation (4) is oscillatory.

If we choose the double sequence:

$$H(t,s) = (t-s)^\lambda, \quad \lambda \geq 1, \quad t \geq s \geq 0,$$

we have the following corollary.

Corollary 1 ([27]). *Under the conditions of Theorem 8 and:*

$$\limsup_{t\to\infty} \frac{1}{(t-t_0)^\lambda} \sum_{s=t_0}^{t-1} (t-s)^\lambda \left[k\phi(s)q_2(s) - \frac{q_1^{1/\gamma_1}(s)[(\Delta\phi_+)(s)]^2}{4\phi(s)\Gamma(1-\nu)\delta_1^{1/\gamma_1}(s,t_2)} \right] = \infty,$$

then Equation (4) is oscillatory.

In [28], Chatzarakis et al. studied the oscillatory behavior of the delta fractional difference equation of the form:

$$\Delta\big((\Delta^\nu u)(t)\big)^{\gamma_3} + q_3(t) f_5(u(t)) = 0, \quad t \in \mathbb{N}_{t_0+1-\nu}, \tag{5}$$

where $0 < \nu \leq 1$; $\gamma_3 > 0$ is a quotient of odd positive integers; q_3 is a positive sequence, and $f_5 : \mathbb{R} \to \mathbb{R}$ is a continuous function such that:

$$\frac{f_5(u)}{u^n} \geq l, \quad u \neq 0, \quad l > 0, \quad n \in \mathbb{N},$$

$$\left[\frac{b}{q_3(t)}\right]^{\frac{1}{\gamma_3}} \leq -m, \quad t \geq t_0, \quad b < 0, \quad m > 0.$$

We also assume:

$$\frac{(\Delta u)(t)}{(\Delta^\nu u)(t+1)} \geq M_1, \quad \frac{(\Delta u)(t)}{(\Delta^\nu u)(t)} \geq M_2, \quad t \geq t_0,$$

for some positive constants M_1, M_2 and for all $(\Delta^\nu u)(t) \neq 0$ and $(\Delta^\nu u)(t+1) \neq 0$, and:

$$\frac{[(\Delta u)(t)]^2}{u(t)u(t+1)} \geq J_1, \quad (\Delta^2 u)(t) \geq J_2,$$

for some positive constants J_1 and J_2.

Theorem 9 ([28]). *Assume:*

$$\sum_{s=t_0}^{\infty} q_3^{\frac{1}{\gamma_3}}(s) = \infty.$$

Furthermore, assume that there exists a positive sequence $\tilde{r}$ such that:

$$\limsup_{t\to\infty}\sum_{s=t_1}^{t-1} H(t,s)\left[l\tilde{r}(s)q_3(s) - \frac{[(\Delta\tilde{r}_+)(s)]^2}{4\tilde{r}(s+1)M_1^{\gamma_3}}\right] = \infty,$$

where:

$$(\Delta\tilde{r}_+)(s) = \max\{(\Delta\tilde{r})(s), 0\}.$$

Then, Equation (5) *is oscillatory.*

Theorem 10 ([28]). *Assume:*

$$\sum_{s=t_0}^{\infty} q_3^{\frac{1}{\gamma_3}}(s) = \infty.$$

Furthermore, assume that there exists a positive sequence $\tilde{r}$ and a double positive sequence $\tilde{H}(t,s)$ such that:

$$\tilde{H}(t,t) = 0 \text{ for } t \geq t_0, \quad \tilde{H}(t,s) > 0 \text{ for } t > s \geq t_0,$$
$$\Delta_2\tilde{H}(t,s) = \tilde{H}(t,s+1) - \tilde{H}(t,s) \leq 0 \text{ for } t > s \geq t_0.$$

If:

$$\limsup_{t\to\infty}\frac{1}{\tilde{H}(t,t_0)}\sum_{s=t_0}^{t-1}\left[\tilde{r}(s)q_3(s)\tilde{H}(t,s) - \frac{\tilde{h}^2(t,s)\tilde{r}(s+1)}{4l\tilde{H}(t,s)M_1^{\gamma_3}}\right] = \infty,$$

where:

$$\tilde{h}(t,s) = \Delta_2\tilde{H}(t,s) + \frac{\tilde{H}(t,s)(\Delta\tilde{r}_+)(s)}{\tilde{r}(s+1)},$$

then Equation (5) *is oscillatory.*

Theorem 11 ([28]). *Assume that there exists a positive sequence $\tilde{r}$ such that:*

$$\limsup_{t\to\infty}\sum_{s=t_1}^{t-1} H(t,s)\left[lq_3(s) + \left(\frac{J_1}{M_2}\right)^{\gamma_3} - \frac{J_2}{M_2} - (\Delta\tilde{r}_+)(s)\right] = \infty.$$

Then, Equation (5) *is oscillatory.*

Motivated by the above works, Adiguzel [29,30] considered the oscillation behavior of the solutions of the following delta fractional difference equations:

$$\Delta\big(r_2(t)(\Delta^\nu u)(t)\big) + q_4(t)f_6\left(\sum_{s=t_0}^{t-1+\nu}(t-s-1)^{(-\nu)}u(s)\right) = 0, \quad t \in \mathbb{N}_{t_0+1-\nu}, \tag{6}$$

and:

$$\Delta\Big(c_1(t)\Delta\big(c_2(t)\big(r_2(t)(\Delta^\nu u)(t)\big)\big)\Big) + q_4(t)\left(\sum_{s=t_0}^{t-1+\nu}(t-s-1)^{(-\nu)}u(s)\right) = 0, \quad t \in \mathbb{N}_{t_0+1-\nu}, \tag{7}$$

where $0 < \nu \leq 1$, r_2, q_4, c_1, and c_2 are positive sequences and $f_6 : \mathbb{R} \to \mathbb{R}$ is a continuous function satisfying $uf_6(u) > 0$ for $u \neq 0$.

Theorem 12 ([29]). *Suppose that:*

$$\sum_{s=t_0}^{\infty} q_4(s) = \infty,$$

and:

$$\liminf_{t\to\infty} f_6(t) > 0.$$

Then, Equation (6) *is oscillatory.*

Theorem 13 ([29]). *Assume that:*

$$\sum_{s=t_0}^{\infty} R(s)q_4(s) = \infty,$$

where:

$$R(t) = \sum_{s=t_0}^{t-1} \frac{1}{r_2(s)} \text{ such that } \lim_{t\to\infty} R(t) = \infty.$$

Then, every bounded solution of Equation (6) *is oscillatory.*

Theorem 14 ([30]). *Assume that:*

$$\sum_{s=t_0}^{\infty} \frac{1}{c_1(s)} = \sum_{s=t_0}^{\infty} \frac{1}{c_2(s)} = \sum_{s=t_0}^{\infty} \frac{1}{r_2(s)} = \infty, \tag{8}$$

and there exists a positive sequence γ such that, for all sufficiently large t,

$$\limsup_{t\to\infty} \sum_{s=t_3}^{t-1} \left[\frac{\Gamma(1-\nu)\gamma(s)q_4(s)}{\theta(s)\phi(s+1)} \sum_{\tau=t_2}^{s-1} \frac{\theta(\tau)}{r_2(\tau)} \sum_{\tau=t_2}^{s-1} \frac{\phi(\tau)}{c_2(\tau)} - \frac{c_1(s)\left[(\Delta\gamma_+)(s)\right]^2}{4\gamma(s)} \right] = \infty.$$

If there exist positive sequences β, λ such that, for all sufficiently large t,

$$\frac{\lambda(t)}{r_2(t)\sum_{s=t_1}^{t-1}\frac{1}{r_2(s)}} - (\Delta\lambda)(t) \le 0, \tag{9}$$

and:

$$\limsup_{t\to\infty} \sum_{\xi=t_2}^{t-1} \left[\frac{\beta(\xi)\lambda(\xi)}{\lambda(\xi+1)c_2(\xi)} \sum_{s=\xi}^{\infty} \left(\frac{1}{c_1(s)} \sum_{\tau=s}^{\infty} q_4(\tau) \right) - \frac{r_2(\xi)\left[(\Delta\beta_+)(\xi)\right]^2}{4\Gamma(1-\nu)\beta(\xi)} \right] = \infty, \tag{10}$$

then, Equation (7) *is oscillatory. Here:*

$$\phi(t) = \sum_{s=t_1}^{t-1} \frac{1}{c_1(s)}, \quad \theta(t) = \sum_{s=t_2}^{t-1} \frac{\phi(s)}{c_2(s)}, \quad \delta(t) = \sum_{s=t_3}^{t-1} \frac{\theta(s)}{r_2(s)}.$$

Further, we have:

$$(\Delta\gamma_+)(s) = \max\{0, (\Delta\gamma)(s)\}, \quad (\Delta\beta_+)(s) = \max\{0, (\Delta\beta)(s)\}.$$

Theorem 15 ([30]). *Let* (8) *hold. Assume that there exists a positive sequence γ such that, for all sufficiently large t,*

$$\limsup_{t\to\infty} \sum_{s=t_3}^{t-1} \left[\frac{\Gamma(1-\nu)\gamma(s)q_4(s)}{\theta(s+1)} \sum_{\tau=t_2}^{s-1} \frac{\theta(\tau)}{r_2(\tau)} - \frac{c_2(s)\theta(s+1)\left[(\Delta\gamma_+)(s)\right]^2}{4\gamma(s)\theta(s)\sum_{\tau=t_0}^{s-1}\frac{1}{c_1(\tau)}} \right] = \infty. \tag{11}$$

If there exist positive sequences β, λ such that (9) *and* (10) *hold, then Equation* (7) *is oscillatory.*

Theorem 16. [30] *Let (8) hold. Assume that there exists a positive sequence γ such that, for all sufficiently large t,*

$$\limsup_{t\to\infty}\sum_{s=t_2}^{t-1}\left[\frac{\delta(s)\gamma(s)q_4(s)}{\delta(s+1)}-\frac{r_2(s)\phi(s)\left[(\Delta\gamma_+)(s)\right]^2}{4\gamma(s)\sum_{\tau=t_1}^{s-1}\frac{\phi(\tau)}{c_2(\tau)}\sum_{\tau=t_0}^{s-1}\frac{1}{c_1(\tau)}}\right]=\infty. \quad (12)$$

If there exist positive sequences β, λ such that (9) and (10) hold, then Equation (7) is oscillatory.

Motivated by the idea in [27], Bai et al. [31] was concerned with the oscillation of a class of nonlinear fractional difference equations with the damping term of the form:

$$\Delta\left(c_3(t)[\Delta(r_3(t)(\Delta^\nu u)(t))]^{\gamma_4}\right)+q_5(t)[\Delta(r_3(t)(\Delta^\nu u)(t))]^{\gamma_4}$$
$$+q_6(t)f_7\left(\sum_{s=t_0}^{t-1+\nu}(t-s-1)^{(-\nu)}u(s)\right)=0, \quad (13)$$

for $t\in\mathbb{N}_{t_0}$, $0<\nu\le 1$, $\gamma_4\ge 1$ is a quotient of two odd positive numbers, r_3, q_5, q_6, and c_3 are positive sequences such that $c_3(t)>q_5(t)$, and $f_7:\mathbb{R}\to\mathbb{R}$ is a monotone decreasing function satisfying:

$$uf_7(u)>0,\quad \frac{f_7(u)}{u^{\gamma_4}}\ge L>0,\quad u\neq 0.$$

Theorem 17 ([31]). *Define:*

$$x(t)=\prod_{s=t_0}^{t-1}\frac{c_3(s)}{c_3(s)-q_5(s)}.$$

Assume:

$$\sum_{s=t_0}^{\infty}\frac{1}{(x(s)c_3(s))^{\frac{1}{\gamma_4}}}=\infty, \quad (14)$$

$$\sum_{s=t_0}^{\infty}\frac{1}{r_3(s)}=\infty, \quad (15)$$

and:

$$\sum_{\xi=t_0}^{\infty}\frac{1}{r_3(\xi)}\sum_{\tau=\xi}^{\infty}\left[\frac{1}{c_3(\tau)x(\tau)}\sum_{s=\tau}^{\infty}x(s+1)q_6(s)\right]^{\frac{1}{\gamma_4}}=\infty. \quad (16)$$

If:

$$\limsup_{t\to\infty}\sum_{s=T}^{t-1}\left[Lx(s)q_6(s)-\frac{[(\Delta x)(s)]^2}{4x(s)x(s+1)W(s)}\right]=\infty,$$

where T is sufficiently large,

$$W(t)=\left[\frac{\Gamma(1-\nu)\delta_2(t,t_1)}{r_3(t)}\right]^{\gamma_4},$$

then Equation (13) is oscillatory or satisfies:

$$\lim_{t\to\infty}\left[\sum_{s=t_0}^{t-1+\nu}(t-s-1)^{(-\nu)}u(s)\right]=0.$$

Here:

$$\delta_2(t,t_1)=\sum_{s=t_1}^{\infty}\frac{1}{(x(s)c_3(s))^{\frac{1}{\gamma_4}}}.$$

Theorem 18 ([31]). *Define* x, W, *and* δ *as in Theorem 17. Assume that* (14)–(16) *hold and there exists a positive sequence* $\tilde{H}(t,s)$ *such that:*

$$\tilde{H}(t,t) = 0 \text{ for } t \geq t_0, \quad \tilde{H}(t,s) > 0 \text{ for } t > s \geq t_0,$$
$$\Delta_2\tilde{H}(t,s) = \tilde{H}(t,s+1) - \tilde{H}(t,s) \leq 0 \text{ for } t > s \geq t_0.$$

If:

$$\limsup_{t\to\infty} \frac{1}{\tilde{H}(t,t_0)} \sum_{s=t_0}^{t-1} \left[Lx(s)q_6(s)\tilde{H}(t,s) - \frac{h^2(t,s)x(s+1)}{4\tilde{H}(t,s)x(s)W(s)} \right] = \infty,$$

where:

$$h(t,s) = \Delta_2\tilde{H}(t,s) + \frac{\tilde{H}(t,s)(\Delta x)(s)}{x(s+1)},$$

then Equation (13) *is oscillatory or satisfies:*

$$\lim_{t\to\infty} \left[\sum_{s=t_0}^{t-1+\nu} (t-s-1)^{(-\nu)} u(s) \right] = 0.$$

In [32], Chatzarakis et al. studied the oscillatory behavior of the solutions of the delta fractional difference equation of the form:

$$\Delta\big(r_4(t)g_2((\Delta^\nu u)(t))\big) + p_4(t)f_8\left(\sum_{s=t_0}^{t-1+\nu} (t-s-1)^{(-\nu)} u(s) \right) = 0, \quad t \in \mathbb{N}_{t_0+1-\nu}, \tag{17}$$

where $0 < \nu \leq 1$, r_4, p_4, are positive sequences; g_2, $f_8 : \mathbb{R} \to \mathbb{R}$ are continuous functions with:

$$\frac{f_8(u)}{u} \geq k_1, \quad \frac{u}{g_2(u)} \geq k_2,$$

for some constants k_1, k_2 and for all $u \neq 0$. Further, we also assume that $ug_2(u) > 0$ for $u \neq 0$ and there exists a positive constant μ such that $g_2(u_1u_2) \leq \mu u_1 g_2(u_2)$ for $u_1u_2 \neq 0$.

Theorem 19 ([32]). *Assume:*

$$\sum_{s=t_1}^{\infty} g_2\left(\frac{1}{r_4(s)}\right) = \infty.$$

Furthermore, assume that there exists a positive sequence ψ *such that:*

$$\limsup_{t\to\infty} \sum_{s=t_1}^{t-1} \left[k_1\psi(s)p_4(s) - \frac{1}{k_2}R_1(s) \right] = \infty,$$

where:

$$R_1(s) = \frac{\left[(\Delta\psi_+)(s)\right]^2 r_4(s+1)}{4\psi(s+1)\Gamma(1-\nu)}, \quad (\Delta\psi_+)(s) = \max\{(\Delta\psi)(s), 0\}.$$

Then, Equation (17) *is oscillatory.*

Theorem 20 ([32]). *Assume:*

$$\sum_{s=t_1}^{\infty} g_2\left(\frac{1}{r_4(s)}\right) = \infty.$$

Furthermore, assume that there exists a positive sequence ψ *and a double positive sequence* $\tilde{H}(t,s)$ *such that:*

$$\tilde{H}(t,t) = 0 \text{ for } t \geq t_0, \quad \tilde{H}(t,s) > 0 \text{ for } t > s \geq t_0,$$
$$\Delta_2\tilde{H}(t,s) = \tilde{H}(t,s+1) - \tilde{H}(t,s) \leq 0 \text{ for } t > s \geq t_0.$$

If:

$$\limsup_{t\to\infty}\sum_{s=t_1}^{t-1}\left[\psi(s)p_4(s)\tilde{H}(t,s)-\frac{\bar{h}^2(t,s)\psi(s+1)r_4(s+1)}{4k_1k_2\tilde{H}(t,s)\Gamma(1-\nu)}\right]=\infty,$$

where:

$$\bar{h}(t,s)=\Delta_2\tilde{H}(t,s)+\frac{\tilde{H}(t,s)(\Delta\psi_+)(s)}{\psi(s+1)},$$

then Equation (17) is oscillatory.

Motivated by the above-mentioned works, Alzabut at al. [33] investigated the oscillatory behavior of the nonlinear fractional difference equation with the damping term of the form:

$$\Delta(r_5(t)(\Delta^\nu u)(t))+p_5(t)(\Delta^\nu u)(t)+q_7(t)f_9\left(\sum_{s=t_0}^{t-1+\nu}(t-s-1)^{(-\nu)}u(s)\right)=0, \tag{18}$$

for $t\in\mathbb{N}_{t_0+1-\nu}$. Here, $0<\nu\le 1$, p_5, q_7 are nonnegative sequences such that $1-p_5(t)>0$ for large t; $f_9:\mathbb{R}\to\mathbb{R}$ is a continuous function, and there exists a constant $k_3>0$ such that,

$$\frac{f_9(u)}{u}\ge k_3,$$

for all $u\neq 0$. Further, we also assume that $f_9(u_1)-f_9(u_2)=S(u_1,u_2)(u_1-u_2)$ for all u_1, $u_2\neq 0$, where S is a nonnegative function.

Theorem 21 ([33]). *Let $r_5(t)\equiv 1$ and:*

$$\sum_{t=t_0}^{\infty}\prod_{s=t_0}^{t-1}[1-p_5(s)]=\infty.$$

If there exists a positive sequence ϕ_1 such that:

$$\limsup_{t\to\infty}\sum_{s=t_1}^{t-1}\left[k_3q_7(s)\phi_1(s)-\frac{[(\Delta\phi_1)(s)-p_5(s)\phi_1(s)]^2}{4\Gamma(1-\nu)\phi_1(s)}\right]=\infty,$$

then Equation (18) is oscillatory.

Theorem 22 ([33]). *Assume that $S(u_1,u_2)\ge\xi>0$ for all u_1, $u_2\neq 0$. If there exists a positive sequence ϕ_2 such that:*

$$\sum_{s=t_0}^{\infty}\frac{1}{r_5(s)\phi_2(s)}=\infty,\quad \sum_{s=t_0}^{\infty}q_7(s)\phi_2(s+1)=\infty,\quad r_5(t)(\Delta\phi_2)(t)\ge p_5(t)\phi_2(t+1),\quad t\ge t_0,$$

$$\sum_{s=t_0}^{\infty}\frac{\phi_2(s+1)p_5^2(s)}{r_5(s)}<\infty,\quad \sum_{s=t_0}^{\infty}\frac{r_5(s)[(\Delta\phi_2)(s)]^2}{\phi_2(s+1)}<\infty,$$

then Equation (18) is oscillatory.

Theorem 23 ([33]). *Let $r_5(t)\equiv 1$ and:*

$$\sum_{t=t_0}^{\infty}\prod_{s=t_0}^{t-1}[1-p_5(s)]=\infty.$$

Furthermore, assume that there exists a positive sequence ϕ_1 *and a double positive sequence* $\tilde{H}(t,s)$ *such that:*

$$\tilde{H}(t,t) = 0 \text{ for } t \geq t_0, \quad \tilde{H}(t,s) > 0 \text{ for } t > s \geq t_0,$$
$$\Delta_2\tilde{H}(t,s) = \tilde{H}(t,s+1) - \tilde{H}(t,s) \leq 0 \text{ for } t > s \geq t_0.$$

If:

$$\limsup_{t\to\infty} \sum_{s=t_1}^{t-1} \frac{1}{\tilde{H}(t,t_0)} \left[k_3\phi_1(s)q_7(s)\tilde{H}(t,s) - \frac{\hat{h}^2(t,s)\phi_1^2(s+1)}{4\phi_1(s)\tilde{H}(t,s)\Gamma(1-\nu)} \right] = \infty, \tag{19}$$

where,

$$\hat{h}(t,s) = \Delta_2\tilde{H}(t,s) + \tilde{H}(t,s)\frac{[(\Delta\phi_1)(s) - p_5(s)\phi_1(s)]}{\phi_1(s+1)},$$

then Equation (18) is oscillatory.

If we set $\phi_1(t) = 1$ for all $t \geq t_0$ and,

$$H(t,s) = (t-s)^\lambda, \quad \lambda \geq 1, \quad t \geq s \geq t_0,$$

we have the following corollary.

Corollary 2 ([33]). *If the condition* (19) *in Theorem 23 is replaced by:*

$$\limsup_{t\to\infty} \sum_{s=t_1}^{t-1} \frac{1}{(t-t_0)^\lambda} \left[k_3q_7(s)(t-s)^\lambda - \frac{\left[\lambda(t-s-1)^{\lambda-1} + p_5(s)(t-s)^\lambda\right]^2}{4(t-s)^\lambda\Gamma(1-\nu)} \right] = \infty,$$

then Equation (18) *is oscillatory.*

Selvam et al. [34,35] examined the new oscillation criteria for forced delta fractional nonlinear difference equations of the form:

$$\Delta(r_6(t)\phi_3(u(t))(\Delta^\nu u)(t)) + q_8(t)f_{10}\left(\sum_{s=t_0}^{t-1+\nu}(t-s-1)^{(-\nu)}u(s)\right) = g_2(t), \tag{20}$$

and:

$$\Delta(r_6(t)(\Delta^\nu u)(t)) + p_6(t)(\Delta^\nu u)(t) + q_8(t)f_{11}\left(\sum_{s=t_0}^{t-1+\nu}(t-s-1)^{(-\nu)}u(s)\right) = 0, \tag{21}$$

for $t \geq t_0 > 0$. Here, $0 < \nu \leq 1$; $p_6, q_8, g_2 : [t_0,\infty) \to \mathbb{R}$ are continuous functions such that $p_6(t) < 0$, and $q_8(t) \geq 0$; $r_6 : [t_0,\infty) \to \mathbb{R}^+$ is a continuously differentiable function such that $r_6(t) \leq \lambda_1$ for some $\lambda_1 > 0$; $0 < \phi_3(u(t)) < m_1$ for some positive constant m_1 and for all $u \neq 0$:

$$f_{10}\left(\sum_{s=t_0}^{t-1+\nu}(t-s-1)^{(-\nu)}u(s)\right) \geq 0 \text{ such that } \frac{f_{10}\left(\sum_{s=t_0}^{t-1+\nu}(t-s-1)^{(-\nu)}u(s)\right)}{\sum_{s=t_0}^{t-1+\nu}(t-s-1)^{(-\nu)}u(s)} \geq k_4,$$

for some positive constant k_4 and,

$$\sum_{s=t_0}^{t-1+\nu}(t-s-1)^{(-\nu)}u(s) \neq 0, \quad t \geq t_0;$$

$f_{11}: \mathbb{R} \to \mathbb{R}$ is a continuous function with $uf_{11}(u) > 0$ for $u \neq 0$, and there exists a constant μ_1 such that,

$$\frac{f_{11}(u)}{u} \geq \mu_1, \quad u \neq 0.$$

Theorem 24 ([34]). *Assume that for any $L_1 \geq t_0$, there exists $\alpha_1, \beta_1, \alpha_2, \beta_2$ such that $L_1 \leq \alpha_1 < \beta_1 \leq \alpha_2 < \beta_2$ satisfying:*

$$g_2(t)\begin{cases} \leq 0, & t \in [\alpha_1, \beta_1], \\ \geq 0, & t \in [\alpha_2, \beta_2]. \end{cases}$$

If there exists a positive function $\rho \in C^{\nu}[[t_0, \infty), \mathbb{R}^+]$ such that:

$$\lim_{t\to\infty} \frac{\Gamma(1-\nu)}{m_1\lambda_1} \sum_{s=t_0}^{t-1} \frac{1}{\rho(s)} = \infty,$$

and:

$$\lim_{t\to\infty} \sum_{s=t_0}^{t-1} \left[k_4\rho(s)q_8(s) - \frac{(\Delta^2\rho)(s)m_1\lambda_1}{4\rho(s)\Gamma(1-\nu)} \right] = \infty,$$

then Equation (20) is oscillatory.

Theorem 25 ([34]). *Assume that for any $L_1 \geq t_0$, there exists $\alpha_1, \beta_1, \alpha_2, \beta_2$ such that $L_1 \leq \alpha_1 < \beta_1 \leq \alpha_2 < \beta_2$ satisfying:*

$$g_2(t)\begin{cases} \leq 0, & t \in [\alpha_1, \beta_1], \\ \geq 0, & t \in [\alpha_2, \beta_2]. \end{cases}$$

If there exists a positive function $\rho \in C^{\nu}[[t_0, \infty), \mathbb{R}^+]$ and a double positive sequence $\tilde{H}(t,s)$ such that:

$$\tilde{H}(t,t) = 0 \text{ for } t \geq t_0, \quad \tilde{H}(t,s) > 0 \text{ for } t > s \geq t_0,$$
$$\Delta_2\tilde{H}(t,s) = \tilde{H}(t,s+1) - \tilde{H}(t,s) \leq 0 \text{ for } t > s \geq t_0.$$

If:

$$\limsup_{t\to\infty} \sum_{s=t_0}^{t-1} \frac{1}{\tilde{H}(t,t_0)} \left[k_4\rho(s)q_8(s)\tilde{H}(t,s) - \frac{h_2^2(t,s)\rho(s)m_1\lambda_1}{4\tilde{H}(t,s)\Gamma(1-\nu)} \right] = \infty,$$

where,

$$h_2(t,s) = \Delta_2\tilde{H}(t,s) + \tilde{H}(t,s)\frac{(\Delta\rho)(s)}{\rho(s)},$$

then Equation (20) is oscillatory.

Theorem 26 ([35]). *Assume there exists a positive function $\rho_1(t)$, $t \geq t_0$, such that:*

$$\lim_{t\to\infty} \left(\frac{\Gamma(1-\nu)}{\lambda_1} \right)^{\frac{1}{2}} \sum_{s=t_0}^{t-1} \frac{1}{\rho_1(s)} = \infty,$$

and:

$$\lim_{t\to\infty} \Bigg\{ \left(\frac{1}{16\Gamma(1-\nu)\lambda_1} \right)^{\frac{1}{2}} \sum_{s=t_0}^{t-1} \Bigg[\frac{p_6^2(s)\rho_1(s)}{\lambda_1} + \frac{\lambda_1(\Delta^2\rho_1)(s)}{\rho_1(s)}$$
$$- 2p_6(s)(\Delta\rho_1)(s) - 4\mu_1\Gamma(1-\nu)\rho_1(s)q_8(s) \Bigg] + \left(\frac{1}{4\Gamma(1-\nu)} \right)^{\frac{1}{2}} (\Delta\rho_1)(s) \Bigg\} = \infty.$$

Then, Equation (21) is oscillatory.

Theorem 27 ([35]). *Assume there exists a positive function $\rho_1(t)$, $t \geq t_0$, and a double positive sequence $\tilde{H}(t,s)$ such that:*

$$\tilde{H}(t,t) = 0 \text{ for } t \geq t_0, \quad \tilde{H}(t,s) > 0 \text{ for } t > s \geq t_0,$$
$$\Delta_2 \tilde{H}(t,s) = \tilde{H}(t,s+1) - \tilde{H}(t,s) \leq 0 \text{ for } t > s \geq t_0.$$

If:

$$\limsup_{t\to\infty} \sum_{s=t_0}^{t-1} \frac{1}{\tilde{H}(t,t_0)} \left[\mu_1 \rho_1(s) q_8(s) \tilde{H}(t,s) - \frac{h_3^2(t,s)\rho_1(s)\lambda_1}{4\tilde{H}(t,s)\Gamma(1-\nu)} \right] = \infty,$$

where,

$$h_3(t,s) = \Delta_2 \tilde{H}(t,s) + \tilde{H}(t,s) \left[\frac{(\Delta\rho_1)(s)}{\rho(s)} - \frac{p_6(s)}{\lambda_1} \right],$$

then Equation (21) *is oscillatory.*

Chatzarakis et al. [36] examined the oscillatory behavior for a class of nonlinear delta fractional difference equations with the damping term of the form:

$$\Delta\big(c_4(t)[\Delta(r_7(t) g_3((\Delta^\nu u)(t)))]^{\gamma_5}\big) + q_9(t)[\Delta(r_7(t) g_3((\Delta^\nu u)(t)))]^{\gamma_5}$$
$$+ f_{12}\left(t, \sum_{s=t_0}^{t-1+\nu} (t-s-1)^{(-\nu)} u(s) \right) = 0, \quad t \in \mathbb{N}_{t_0}, \quad (22)$$

where $0 < \nu \leq 1$; c_4, r_7, $q_9 : [t_0, \infty) \to \mathbb{R}^+$ are continuous sequences with $c_4(t) > q_9(t)$; $\gamma_5 \geq 1$ is a quotient of two odd positive integers; for the continuous function $f_{12} : [t_0, \infty) \times \mathbb{R} \to \mathbb{R}$, there exists a continuously differentiable function $q_{10} : [t_0, \infty) \to \mathbb{R}^+$ such that,

$$\frac{f_{12}\left(t, \sum_{s=t_0}^{t-1+\nu} (t-s-1)^{(-\nu)} u(s)\right)}{\left[\sum_{s=t_0}^{t-1+\nu} (t-s-1)^{(-\nu)} u(s)\right]^{\gamma_5}} \geq q_{10}(t),$$

for:

$$\sum_{s=t_0}^{t-1+\nu} (t-s-1)^{(-\nu)} u(s) \neq 0, \quad u \neq 0, \quad t \geq t_0.$$

Furthermore, g_3 is an increasing function, for which there exists a constant l_1 such that,

$$\frac{u}{g_3(u)} \geq l_1 > 0, \quad u g_3(u) \neq 0.$$

$g_3^{-1} : \mathbb{R} \to \mathbb{R}$ is a continuous function with:

$$u g_3^{-1}(u) > 0, \quad u \neq 0,$$

and for that function, there exists a positive constant l_2 such that,

$$g^{-1}(u_1 u_2) \leq l_2 u_1 g_3^{-1}(u_2), \quad u_1 u_2 \neq 0.$$

Theorem 28 ([36]). *Define:*

$$y(t) = \prod_{s=t_0}^{t-1} \frac{c_4(s)}{c_4(s) - q_9(s)}.$$

Assume that u is an eventually positive solution of Equation (22) *and:*

$$\lim_{t\to\infty} \sum_{s=t_0}^{t-1} \frac{1}{(y(s)c_4(s))^{\frac{1}{\gamma_5}}} = \infty, \quad (23)$$

$$\lim_{t\to\infty}\sum_{s=t_0}^{t-1} g_3^{-1}\left(\frac{1}{r_7(s)}\right)=\infty, \tag{24}$$

and:

$$\lim_{t\to\infty}\sum_{\xi=t_0}^{t-1} g_3^{-1}\left(\frac{1}{r_7(\xi)}\sum_{\tau=\xi}^{\infty}\left[\frac{1}{c_4(\tau)y(\tau)}\sum_{s=\tau}^{\infty}y(s+1)q_{10}(s)\right]^{\frac{1}{\gamma_5}}\right)=\infty, \tag{25}$$

then there exists a sufficiently large $T\in\mathbb{N}_{t_0}$ such that,

$$[\Delta(r_7(t)g_3((\Delta^\nu u)(t)))]>0,\quad t\in[T,\infty),$$

and one of the following two conditions holds: (i) $(\Delta^\nu u)(t)>0$ on $[T,\infty)$ or (ii) $(\Delta^\nu u)(t)<0$ on $[T,\infty)$ and,

$$\lim_{t\to\infty}\left[\sum_{s=t_0}^{t-1+\nu}(t-s-1)^{(-\nu)}u(s)\right]=0.$$

Theorem 29 ([36]). *Assume that u is an eventually positive solution of Equation* (22) *such that,*

$$[\Delta(r_7(t)g_3((\Delta^\nu u)(t)))]>0,\quad (\Delta^\nu u)(t)>0,\quad t\in[t_1,\infty),$$

where t_1 is sufficiently large and $t_1\geq t_0$. Then:

$$\Delta\left[\sum_{s=t_0}^{t-1+\nu}(t-s-1)^{(-\nu)}u(s)\right]$$
$$\geq\frac{l_1\Gamma(1-\nu)(y(t)c_4(t))^{\frac{1}{\gamma_5}}[\Delta(r_7(t)g_3((\Delta^\nu u)(t)))]}{r_7(t)}\sum_{s=t_1}^{t-1}\frac{1}{(y(s)c_4(s))^{\frac{1}{\gamma_5}}}.$$

Theorem 30 ([36]). *Assume that* (23)–(25) *hold. If:*

$$\limsup_{t\to\infty}\sum_{s=t_2}^{t-1}\left[q_{10}(s)-\frac{q_9^2(s)}{4c_4^2(s)R_2(s)y(s)}\right]=\infty,$$

where t_2 is sufficiently large,

$$R_2(t)=\left[\frac{l_1\Gamma(1-\nu)}{r_7(t)}\sum_{s=t_1}^{t-1}\frac{1}{(y(s)c_4(s))^{\frac{1}{\gamma_5}}}\right]^{\gamma_5},$$

then Equation (22) *is oscillatory or satisfies:*

$$\lim_{t\to\infty}\left[\sum_{s=t_0}^{t-1+\nu}(t-s-1)^{(-\nu)}u(s)\right]=0.$$

Theorem 31 ([36]). *Assume that* (23)–(25) *hold. If:*

$$\limsup_{t\to\infty}\sum_{s=t_2}^{t-1}\left[q_{10}(s)y(s)-\frac{[(\Delta y)(s)]^2}{4R_2(s)y(s)y(s+1)}\right]=\infty,$$

where t_2 is sufficiently large, then Equation (22) *is oscillatory or satisfies:*

$$\lim_{t\to\infty}\left[\sum_{s=t_0}^{t-1+\nu}(t-s-1)^{(-\nu)}u(s)\right]=0.$$

Theorem 32 ([36]). *Assume that* (23)–(25) *hold. Furthermore, we assume that there exists a double sequence such that:*

$$H(t,t) = 0 \text{ for } t \geq 0, \quad H(t,s) > 0 \text{ for } t > s \geq 0,$$
$$\Delta_2 H(t,s) = H(t,s+1) - H(t,s) \leq 0 \text{ for } t > s \geq 0.$$

If:

$$\limsup_{t\to\infty} \frac{1}{H(t,t_0)} \sum_{s=t_0}^{t-1} \left[H(t,s)q_{10}(s) - \frac{h_4^2(t,s)}{4H(t,s)R_2(s)y(s)} \right] = \infty,$$

where,

$$h_4(t,s) = \Delta_2 H(t,s) - H(t,s)\frac{q_9(s)}{c_4(s)},$$

then Equation (22) *is oscillatory or satisfies:*

$$\lim_{t\to\infty} \left[\sum_{s=t_0}^{t-1+\nu} (t-s-1)^{(-\nu)} u(s) \right] = 0.$$

Theorem 33 ([36]). *Assume that* (23)–(25) *hold. Furthermore, we assume that there exists a double sequence such that:*

$$H(t,t) = 0 \text{ for } t \geq 0, \quad H(t,s) > 0 \text{ for } t > s \geq 0,$$
$$\Delta_2 H(t,s) = H(t,s+1) - H(t,s) \leq 0 \text{ for } t > s \geq 0.$$

If:

$$\limsup_{t\to\infty} \frac{1}{H(t,t_0)} \sum_{s=t_0}^{t-1} \left[H(t,s)q_{10}(s)y(s) - \frac{h_5^2(t,s)}{4H(t,s)R_2(s)} \right] = \infty,$$

where,

$$h_5(t,s) = \Delta_2 H(t,s) + H(t,s)\frac{(\Delta y)(s)}{y(s+1)},$$

then Equation (22) *is oscillatory or satisfies:*

$$\lim_{t\to\infty} \left[\sum_{s=t_0}^{t-1+\nu} (t-s-1)^{(-\nu)} u(s) \right] = 0.$$

Grace et al. [37] investigated the non-oscillatory solutions of the delta fractional difference equations of the following form:

$$\begin{cases} (\Delta_*^\nu v)(t) = e(t+\nu) + f(t+\nu, u(t+\nu)), & t \in \mathbb{N}_{1-\nu}, \\ v(0) = c_0, \end{cases} \tag{26}$$

where $0 < \nu \leq 1$; $f : \mathbb{N}_1 \times \mathbb{R} \to \mathbb{R}$ is continuous and satisfies $uf(t,u) > 0$ for $u \neq 0$, and e is a positive sequence. Grace at al. carried out the investigation for the following particular cases of (26):

$$v(t) = \Delta\Big(r(t)\left|(\Delta u)(t)\right|^{\delta-1}(\Delta u)(t)\Big), \quad \delta \geq 1, \tag{27}$$
$$v(t) = (\Delta u)(t), \tag{28}$$
$$v(t) = u(t). \tag{29}$$

where r is a positive sequence.

Theorem 34 ([37]). *Consider (26) with (27). Assume that the function f satisfies:*

$$uf(t,u) \leq t^{(\gamma-1)}h(t)|u|^{\beta+1}, \quad u \neq 0,$$

for some function $h : (t_1, \infty) \to \mathbb{R}^+$ and real numbers $\gamma > 0$ and $0 < \beta < \delta$. For the sake of simplification, define:

$$R(t) = \sum_{s=1}^{t-1} r^{-1/\delta}(s),$$

and,

$$g_1(t) = \sum_{s=t_1-\nu}^{t-\nu} (t-s-1)^{(\nu-1)}(s+\nu)^{(\gamma-1)} m^{\beta/(\beta-\delta)}(s+\nu) h^{\delta/(\delta-\beta)}(s+\nu),$$

where $t_1 \in \mathbb{N}_1$ and m is a positive sequence. Let q be a conjugate number of $p > 1$, $p(\nu-1)+1 > 0$, and $\gamma = 2 - \nu - \frac{1}{p}$. Suppose that for any positive integer t_1, we have:

$$\sum_{s=t_1-\nu}^{\infty} (s+\nu)^q R^{q\delta}(s+\nu) m^q(s+\nu) < \infty, \quad \limsup_{t\to\infty} \frac{1}{t} \sum_{s=t_1}^{t-1} g_1(s) < \infty,$$

$$\liminf_{t\to\infty} \frac{1}{t} \sum_{\tau=t_1}^{t-1} \sum_{s=1-\nu}^{\tau-\nu} (\tau-s-1)^{(\nu-1)} e(s+\nu) > -\infty,$$

$$\limsup_{t\to\infty} \frac{1}{t} \sum_{\tau=t_1}^{t-1} \sum_{s=1-\nu}^{\tau-\nu} (\tau-s-1)^{(\nu-1)} e(s+\nu) < \infty.$$

Then, every non-oscillatory solution u satisfies:

$$|u(t)| = O\left(t^{1/\delta} R(t)\right), \quad t \to \infty.$$

Theorem 35 ([37]). *Consider (26) with (28). Assume that the function f satisfies:*

$$uf(t,u) \leq t^{(\gamma-1)}h(t)|u|^{\lambda+1}, \quad u \neq 0,$$

for some function $h : (t_1, \infty) \to \mathbb{R}^+$ and real numbers $\gamma > 0$ and $0 < \lambda < 1$. For the sake of simplification, define:

$$g_2(t) = \sum_{s=t_1-\nu}^{t-\nu} (t-s-1)^{(\nu-1)}(s+\nu)^{(\gamma-1)} m^{\lambda/(\lambda-1)}(s+\nu) h^{1/(1-\lambda)}(s+\nu),$$

where $t_1 \in \mathbb{N}_1$ and m is a positive sequence. Let q be a conjugate number of $p > 1$, $p(\nu-1)+1 > 0$, and $\gamma = 2 - \nu - \frac{1}{p}$. Suppose that for any positive integer t_1, we have:

$$\sum_{s=t_1-\nu}^{\infty} (s+\nu)^q m^q(s+\nu) < \infty, \quad \limsup_{t\to\infty} g_2(t) < \infty,$$

$$\liminf_{t\to\infty} \sum_{s=1-\nu}^{t-\nu} (t-s-1)^{(\nu-1)} e(s+\nu) > -\infty, \quad \limsup_{t\to\infty} \sum_{s=1-\nu}^{t-\nu} (t-s-1)^{(\nu-1)} e(s+\nu) < \infty.$$

Then, every non-oscillatory solution u satisfies:

$$|u(t)| = O(t), \quad t \to \infty.$$

Theorem 36 ([37]). *Consider (26) with (29). Let q be a conjugate number of $p > 1$, $p(\nu - 1) + 1 > 0$ and $\gamma = 2 - \nu - \frac{1}{p}$. Suppose that for any positive integer t_1, we have:*

$$\sum_{s=t_1-\nu}^{\infty} m^q(s+\nu) < \infty, \quad \limsup_{t\to\infty} g_2(t) < \infty,$$

$$\liminf_{t\to\infty} \sum_{s=1-\nu}^{t-\nu} (t-s-1)^{(\nu-1)} e(s+\nu) > -\infty, \quad \limsup_{t\to\infty} \sum_{s=1-\nu}^{t-\nu} (t-s-1)^{(\nu-1)} e(s+\nu) < \infty.$$

Then, every non-oscillatory solution u is bounded.

3.2. Oscillatory Behavior of Nabla Fractional Difference Equations

Let $\nu > 0$, and choose $N \in \mathbb{N}_1$ such that $N - 1 < \nu < N$. Take $p, q_i, r : \mathbb{N}_{a+N-1} \to \mathbb{R}$, $i = 1, 2, \cdots n$; $f_1, f_2 : \mathbb{N}_{a+N-1} \times \mathbb{R} \to \mathbb{R}$; $f : \mathbb{R} \to \mathbb{R}$; $p_1, p_2 : \mathbb{N}_{a+N-1} \to \mathbb{R}^+$; $w, h : \mathbb{N}_a \to \mathbb{R}$; $q, g : \mathbb{N}_{a+1} \to \mathbb{R}$; $x, z : \mathbb{N}_1 \to \mathbb{R}$; $w_2 : \mathbb{N}_1 \to \mathbb{R}^+$; y is a positive function defined on $\mathbb{N}_1$; β, γ are positive real numbers; λ_i $(1 \le i \le n)$ are the ratios of odd positive integers with $\lambda_1 > \cdots > \lambda_l > 1 > \lambda_{l+1} > \cdots > \lambda_n$.

We make the following assumptions:

(H1). *The functions f_i satisfy the sign condition $uf_i(t,u) > 0$, $i = 1, 2$, $u \neq 0$, $t \in \mathbb{N}_{a+N-1}$;*

(H2). $|f_1(t, u(t)| \ge p_1(t)|u|^\beta$ and $|f_2(t, u(t)| \le p_2(t)|u|^\gamma$, $u \neq 0$, $t \in \mathbb{N}_{a+N-1}$;

(H3). $|f_1(t, u(t)| \le p_1(t)|u|^\beta$ and $|f_2(t, u(t)| \ge p_2(t)|u|^\gamma$, $u \neq 0$, $t \in \mathbb{N}_{a+N-1}$;

(H4). *$\frac{f(t)}{t} > 0$ for all $t \neq 0$ and $x(t) < 1$ for all $t \in \mathbb{N}_1$;*

(H5). *$uf(u) > 0$ for $u \neq 0$ and $q(t) \ge 0$ for all $t \in \mathbb{N}_{a+1}$;*

(H6). *$uf(u) > 0$ for $u \neq 0$ and $w(t) \ge 0$ for all $t \in \mathbb{N}_a$.*

Alzabut et al. [38] initiated the study of the oscillation of solutions of nabla fractional difference equations. In [38], the authors established several oscillation criteria for the following nonlinear nabla fractional difference equations involving the Riemann–Liouville and Caputo operators of arbitrary order.

$$\begin{cases} (\nabla^{\nu}_{a+N-2} u)(t) + f_1(t, u(t)) = r(t) + f_2(t, u(t)), & t \in \mathbb{N}_{a+N-1}, \\ (\nabla^{-(1-\nu)}_{a+N-2} u)(t)\Big|_{t=a+N-1} = u(a+N-1) = c, & c \in \mathbb{R}, \end{cases} \tag{30}$$

and:

$$\begin{cases} (\nabla^{\nu}_{a+N-1*} u)(t) + f_1(t, u(t)) = r(t) + f_2(t, u(t)), & t \in \mathbb{N}_{a+N-1}, \\ (\nabla^{k} u(a+N-1) = b_k, \quad b_k \in \mathbb{R}, \quad k = 0, 1, 2, \cdots, N-1. \end{cases} \tag{31}$$

A solution u of (30) (or (31)) is said to be oscillatory if for every natural number M, there exists $t \ge M$ such that $u(t)u(t+1) \le 0$; otherwise, it is called non-oscillatory. An equation is said to be oscillatory if all of its solutions are oscillatory.

Theorem 37 ([38]). *Let $f_2 = 0$ and Condition (H1) hold. If:*

$$\liminf_{t\to\infty} t^{1-\nu} \sum_{s=a+N-1}^{t} (t-s+1)^{\overline{\nu-1}} r(s) = -\infty,$$

and:

$$\limsup_{t\to\infty} t^{1-\nu} \sum_{s=a+N-1}^{t} (t-s+1)^{\overline{\nu-1}} r(s) = \infty,$$

then Equation (30) *is oscillatory.*

Theorem 38 ([38]). *Let Conditions (H1) and (H2) hold with $\beta > 1$ and $\gamma = 1$. If:*

$$\liminf_{t\to\infty} t^{1-\nu} \sum_{s=a+N-1}^{t} (t-s+1)^{\overline{\nu-1}} \big[r(s) + H_\beta(s)\big] = -\infty,$$

and:

$$\limsup_{t\to\infty} t^{1-\nu} \sum_{s=a+N-1}^{t} (t-s+1)^{\overline{\nu-1}} \big[r(s) + H_\beta(s)\big] = \infty,$$

where,

$$H_\beta(s) = (\beta-1)\beta^{\frac{\beta}{1-\beta}} p_1^{\frac{1}{1-\beta}}(s) p_2^{\frac{\beta}{\beta-1}}(s),$$

then Equation (30) *is oscillatory.*

Theorem 39 ([38]). *Let Conditions (H1) and (H2) hold with $\beta = 1$ and $\gamma < 1$. If:*

$$\liminf_{t\to\infty} t^{1-\nu} \sum_{s=a+N-1}^{t} (t-s+1)^{\overline{\nu-1}} [r(s) + H_\gamma(s)] = -\infty,$$

and:

$$\limsup_{t\to\infty} t^{1-\nu} \sum_{s=a+N-1}^{t} (t-s+1)^{\overline{\nu-1}} [r(s) + H_\gamma(s)] = \infty,$$

where,

$$H_\gamma(s) = (1-\gamma)\gamma^{\frac{\gamma}{1-\gamma}} p_1^{\frac{\gamma}{\gamma-1}}(s) p_2^{\frac{1}{1-\gamma}}(s),$$

then Equation (30) *is oscillatory.*

Theorem 40 ([38]). *Let Conditions (H1) and (H2) hold with $\beta > 1$ and $\gamma < 1$. If:*

$$\liminf_{t\to\infty} t^{1-\nu} \sum_{s=a+N-1}^{t} (t-s+1)^{\overline{\nu-1}} \big[r(s) + H_{\beta,\gamma}(s)\big] = -\infty,$$

and:

$$\limsup_{t\to\infty} t^{1-\nu} \sum_{s=a+N-1}^{t} (t-s+1)^{\overline{\nu-1}} \big[r(s) + H_{\beta,\gamma}(s)\big] = \infty,$$

where,

$$H_{\beta,\gamma}(s) = (\beta-1)\beta^{\frac{\beta}{1-\beta}} p_1^{\frac{1}{1-\beta}}(s) \xi^{\frac{\beta}{\beta-1}}(s) + (1-\gamma)\gamma^{\frac{\gamma}{1-\gamma}} \xi^{\frac{\gamma}{\gamma-1}}(s) p_2^{\frac{1}{1-\gamma}}(s),$$

with $\xi : \mathbb{N}_{a+N-1} \to \mathbb{R}^+$, then Equation (30) *is oscillatory.*

Theorem 41 ([38]). *Let $f_2 = 0$ and Condition (H1) hold. If:*

$$\liminf_{t\to\infty} t^{1-N} \sum_{s=a+N-1}^{t} (t-s+1)^{\overline{\nu-1}} r(s) = -\infty,$$

and:

$$\limsup_{t\to\infty} t^{1-N} \sum_{s=a+N-1}^{t} (t-s+1)^{\overline{\nu-1}} r(s) = \infty,$$

then Equation (31) *is oscillatory.*

Theorem 42 ([38]). *Let Conditions (H1) and (H2) hold with $\beta > 1$ and $\gamma = 1$. If:*

$$\liminf_{t\to\infty} t^{1-N} \sum_{s=a+N-1}^{t} (t-s+1)^{\overline{\nu-1}}\left[r(s) + H_\beta(s)\right] = -\infty,$$

and:

$$\limsup_{t\to\infty} t^{1-N} \sum_{s=a+N-1}^{t} (t-s+1)^{\overline{\nu-1}}\left[r(s) + H_\beta(s)\right] = \infty,$$

where,

$$H_\beta(s) = (\beta-1)\beta^{\frac{\beta}{1-\beta}} p_1^{\frac{1}{1-\beta}}(s) p_2^{\frac{\beta}{\beta-1}}(s),$$

then Equation (31) *is oscillatory.*

Theorem 43 ([38]). *Let Conditions (H1) and (H2) hold with $\beta = 1$ and $\gamma < 1$. If:*

$$\liminf_{t\to\infty} t^{1-N} \sum_{s=a+N-1}^{t} (t-s+1)^{\overline{\nu-1}}\left[r(s) + H_\gamma(s)\right] = -\infty,$$

and:

$$\limsup_{t\to\infty} t^{1-N} \sum_{s=a+N-1}^{t} (t-s+1)^{\overline{\nu-1}}\left[r(s) + H_\gamma(s)\right] = \infty,$$

where,

$$H_\gamma(s) = (1-\gamma)\gamma^{\frac{\gamma}{1-\gamma}} p_1^{\frac{\gamma}{\gamma-1}}(s) p_2^{\frac{1}{1-\gamma}}(s),$$

then Equation (31) *is oscillatory.*

Theorem 44 ([38]). *Let Conditions (H1) and (H2) hold with $\beta > 1$ and $\gamma < 1$. If:*

$$\liminf_{t\to\infty} t^{1-N} \sum_{s=a+N-1}^{t} (t-s+1)^{\overline{\nu-1}}\left[r(s) + H_{\beta,\gamma}(s)\right] = -\infty,$$

and:

$$\limsup_{t\to\infty} t^{1-N} \sum_{s=a+N-1}^{t} (t-s+1)^{\overline{\nu-1}}\left[r(s) + H_{\beta,\gamma}(s)\right] = \infty,$$

where,

$$H_{\beta,\gamma}(s) = (\beta-1)\beta^{\frac{\beta}{1-\beta}} p_1^{\frac{1}{1-\beta}}(s)\xi^{\frac{\beta}{\beta-1}}(s) + (1-\gamma)\gamma^{\frac{\gamma}{1-\gamma}} \xi^{\frac{\gamma}{\gamma-1}}(s) p_2^{\frac{1}{1-\gamma}}(s),$$

with $\xi : \mathbb{N}_{a+N-1} \to \mathbb{R}^+$, then Equation (31) *is oscillatory.*

Following the work in [38], Abdalla et al. [39] established new oscillation criteria for (30) and (31) using the fractional Volterra sum equations and Young's inequalities. The authors in [39] observed that the cases $\beta > \gamma > 1$ and $\gamma > \beta > 1$ were not considered for (30) in [38]. The purpose of the paper [39] was to cover this gap and establish new oscillation criteria that improve the results in [38].

Theorem 45 ([39]). *Let Condition (H2) hold with $\beta > \gamma > 0$. If:*

$$\liminf_{t\to\infty} t^{1-\nu} \sum_{s=T+1}^{t} (t-s+1)^{\overline{\nu-1}}\left[r(s) + H(s)\right] = -\infty,$$

and:

$$\limsup_{t\to\infty} t^{1-\nu} \sum_{s=T+1}^{t} (t-s+1)^{\overline{\nu-1}}[r(s)-H(s)] = \infty,$$

for sufficiently large T, where,

$$H(s) = \left(\frac{\beta}{\gamma}-1\right)\left[\frac{\gamma p_2(s)}{\beta}\right]^{\frac{\beta}{\beta-\gamma}} p_1^{\frac{\gamma}{\gamma-\beta}}(s),$$

then Equation (30) is oscillatory.

Theorem 46 ([39]). *Let $\nu \geq 1$ and Condition (H3) hold with $\gamma > \beta > 0$. If:*

$$\liminf_{t\to\infty} t^{1-\nu} \sum_{s=T+1}^{t} (t-s+1)^{\overline{\nu-1}}[r(s)-H(s)] = -\infty,$$

and:

$$\limsup_{t\to\infty} t^{1-\nu} \sum_{s=T+1}^{t} (t-s+1)^{\overline{\nu-1}}[r(s)+H(s)] = \infty,$$

for sufficiently large T, where H is defined in Theorem 45, then every bounded solution of Equation (30) is oscillatory.

Theorem 47 ([39]). *Let Condition (H2) hold with $\beta > \gamma > 0$. If:*

$$\liminf_{t\to\infty} t^{1-N} \sum_{s=T+1}^{t} (t-s+1)^{\overline{\nu-1}}[r(s)+H(s)] = -\infty,$$

and:

$$\limsup_{t\to\infty} t^{1-N} \sum_{s=T+1}^{t} (t-s+1)^{\overline{\nu-1}}[r(s)-H(s)] = \infty,$$

for sufficiently large T, where H is defined in Theorem 45, then Equation (31) is oscillatory.

Theorem 48 ([39]). *Let $\nu \geq 1$ and Condition (H3) hold with $\gamma > \beta > 0$. If:*

$$\liminf_{t\to\infty} t^{1-N} \sum_{s=T+1}^{t} (t-s+1)^{\overline{\nu-1}}[r(s)-H(s)] = -\infty,$$

and:

$$\limsup_{t\to\infty} t^{1-N} \sum_{s=T+1}^{t} (t-s+1)^{\overline{\nu-1}}[r(s)+H(s)] = \infty,$$

for sufficiently large T, where H is defined in Theorem 45, then every bounded solution of Equation (31) is oscillatory.

In alignment with the above works, Abdalla et al. [40] investigated the oscillation of solutions for nabla fractional difference equations with mixed nonlinearities of the forms:

$$\begin{cases} (\nabla^{\nu}_{a+N-2}u)(t) - p(t)u(t) + \sum_{i=1}^{n} q_i(t)|u(t)|^{\lambda_i-1} = r(t), & t \in \mathbb{N}_{a+N}, \\ (\nabla^{-(N-\nu)}_{a+N-2}u)(t)\Big|_{t=a+N-1} = u(a+N-1) = c, & c \in \mathbb{R}, \end{cases} \quad (32)$$

and:

$$\begin{cases} (\nabla^{\nu}_{a+N-1*}u)(t) - p(t)u(t) + \sum_{i=1}^{n} q_i(t)|u(t)|^{\lambda_i - 1} = r(t), & t \in \mathbb{N}_{a+N-1}, \\ (\nabla^k u(a+N-1) = b_k, \quad b_k \in \mathbb{R}, & k = 0,1,2,\cdots,N-1. \end{cases} \tag{33}$$

Theorem 49 ([40]). *Let:*

$$p(t) > 0 \text{ and } q_i(t) \begin{cases} \geq 0, & 1 \leq i \leq l; \\ \leq 0, & l+1 \leq i \leq n. \end{cases} \tag{34}$$

If for some constant $K > 0$, we have:

$$\liminf_{t\to\infty} t^{1-\nu} \sum_{s=a+N}^{t} (t-s+1)^{\overline{\nu-1}} \left[r(s) + K \sum_{i=1}^{n} p^{\frac{\lambda_i}{\lambda_i - 1}}(s) |q_i(s)|^{\frac{1}{1-\lambda_i}} \right] = -\infty, \tag{35}$$

and:

$$\limsup_{t\to\infty} t^{1-\nu} \sum_{s=a+N}^{t} (t-s+1)^{\overline{\nu-1}} \left[r(s) + K \sum_{i=1}^{n} p^{\frac{\lambda_i}{\lambda_i - 1}}(s) |q_i(s)|^{\frac{1}{1-\lambda_i}} \right] = \infty, \tag{36}$$

then Equation (32) is oscillatory.

Corollary 3 ([40]). *Let $l = n$ in (32), then $\lambda_1 > \lambda_2 > \cdots \lambda_n > 1$. Suppose $p(t) > 0$, $q_i(t) \geq 0$, $i = 1,2,\cdots n$. If (35) and (36) hold for some constant $K_1 > 0$, then Equation (32) is oscillatory.*

Corollary 4 ([40]). *Let $l = 0$ in (32), then $1 > \lambda_1 > \lambda_2 > \cdots \lambda_n$. Suppose $p(t) < 0$, $q_i(t) \leq 0$, $i = 1,2,\cdots n$. If (35) and (36) hold for some constant $K_2 > 0$, then Equation (32) is oscillatory.*

Corollary 5 ([40]). *Let:*

$$p(t) \equiv 0 \text{ and } q_i(t) \begin{cases} \geq 0, & 1 \leq i \leq l; \\ \leq 0, & l+1 \leq i \leq n. \end{cases} \tag{37}$$

If there exists a positive function v on $\mathbb{N}_{a+N-1}$ such that for some constant $K_3 > 0$, we have:

$$\liminf_{t\to\infty} t^{1-\nu} \sum_{s=a+N}^{t} (t-s+1)^{\overline{\nu-1}} \left[r(s) + K \sum_{i=1}^{n} v^{\frac{\lambda_i}{\lambda_i - 1}}(s) |q_i(s)|^{\frac{1}{1-\lambda_i}} \right] = -\infty,$$

and:

$$\limsup_{t\to\infty} t^{1-\nu} \sum_{s=a+N}^{t} (t-s+1)^{\overline{\nu-1}} \left[r(s) + K \sum_{i=1}^{n} v^{\frac{\lambda_i}{\lambda_i - 1}}(s) |q_i(s)|^{\frac{1}{1-\lambda_i}} \right] = \infty,$$

then Equation (32) is oscillatory.

Theorem 50 ([40]). *Assume that Condition (34) holds. If:*

$$\liminf_{t\to\infty} t^{1-N} \sum_{s=a+N}^{t} (t-s+1)^{\overline{\nu-1}} \left[r(s) + K \sum_{i=1}^{n} p^{\frac{\lambda_i}{\lambda_i - 1}}(s) |q_i(s)|^{\frac{1}{1-\lambda_i}} \right] = -\infty, \tag{38}$$

and:

$$\limsup_{t\to\infty} t^{1-N} \sum_{s=a+N}^{t} (t-s+1)^{\overline{\nu-1}} \left[r(s) + K \sum_{i=1}^{n} p^{\frac{\lambda_i}{\lambda_i - 1}}(s) |q_i(s)|^{\frac{1}{1-\lambda_i}} \right] = \infty, \tag{39}$$

for some constant $K > 0$, then Equation (33) is oscillatory.

Corollary 6 ([40]). *Suppose $p(t) > 0$, $q_i(t) \geq 0$, $i = 1,2,\cdots n$. If (38) and (39) hold for some constant $K_1 > 0$, then Equation (33) is oscillatory.*

Corollary 7 ([40]). *Suppose $p(t) < 0$, $q_i(t) \leq 0$, $i = 1, 2, \cdots n$. If* (38) *and* (39) *hold for some constant $K_2 > 0$, then Equation* (33) *is oscillatory.*

Corollary 8 ([40]). *Let* (37) *hold. If there exists a positive function v on $\mathbb{N}_{a+N-1}$ such that for some constant $K_3 > 0$, we have:*

$$\liminf_{t\to\infty} t^{1-N} \sum_{s=a+N}^{t} (t-s+1)^{\overline{\nu-1}} \left[r(s) + K \sum_{i=1}^{n} v^{\frac{\lambda_i}{\lambda_i - 1}}(s) |q_i(s)|^{\frac{1}{1-\lambda_i}} \right] = -\infty,$$

and:

$$\limsup_{t\to\infty} t^{1-N} \sum_{s=a+N}^{t} (t-s+1)^{\overline{\nu-1}} \left[r(s) + K \sum_{i=1}^{n} v^{\frac{\lambda_i}{\lambda_i - 1}}(s) |q_i(s)|^{\frac{1}{1-\lambda_i}} \right] = \infty,$$

then Equation (32) *is oscillatory.*

Following the above trend, in [41], Alzabut et al. considered the following forced and damped nabla fractional difference equation:

$$\begin{cases} (1-x(t))(\nabla \nabla_0^{\nu} u)(t) + x(t)(\nabla_0^{\nu} u)(t) + w_2(t) f(u(t)) = z(t), & t \in \mathbb{N}_1, \\ (\nabla_0^{-(1-\nu)} u)(t)\Big|_{t=1} = u(1) = c, \quad c \in \mathbb{R}, \end{cases} \tag{40}$$

where $0 < \nu < 1$, and established sufficient conditions for the oscillation of the solutions of Equation (40).

Theorem 51 ([41]). *Let Assumption (H5) and the following conditions hold:*

$$\liminf_{t\to\infty} \sum_{s=1}^{t} \frac{(t-s+1)^{\overline{\nu-1}}}{P(s)} \left[A + \sum_{\tau=t_0+1}^{s} z(\tau) P(\tau) \right] < 0,$$

and:

$$\limsup_{t\to\infty} \sum_{s=1}^{t} \frac{(t-s+1)^{\overline{\nu-1}}}{P(s)} \left[A + \sum_{\tau=t_0+1}^{s} z(\tau) P(\tau) \right] > 0,$$

where A is a constant and,

$$P(t) = \prod_{s=t_0}^{t} \left(\frac{1}{1-x(s)} \right), \quad t_0 \in \mathbb{N}_1.$$

Then, Equation (40) *is oscillatory.*

Theorem 52 ([41]). *Let Assumption (H5) and the following conditions hold:*

$$\liminf_{t\to\infty} \sum_{s=1}^{t} \frac{1}{P(s)} \left[A + \sum_{\tau=t_0+1}^{s} z(\tau) P(\tau) \right] = -\infty,$$

and:

$$\limsup_{t\to\infty} \sum_{s=1}^{t} \frac{(t-s+1)^{\overline{\nu-1}}}{P(s)} \left[A + \sum_{\tau=t_0+1}^{s} z(\tau) P(\tau) \right] = \infty,$$

where A is a constant and,

$$P(t) = \prod_{s=t_0}^{t} \left(\frac{1}{1-x(s)} \right), \quad t_0 \in \mathbb{N}_1.$$

Then, Equation (40) *is oscillatory.*

Motivated by the paper [38], the authors [42] investigated the oscillation of a nonlinear fractional nabla difference system of the form:

$$\begin{cases} (\nabla_a^{\nu} u)(t) + q(t) f(u(t)) = g(t), & t \in \mathbb{N}_{a+1}, \\ (\nabla_a^{-(1-\nu)} u)(t)\Big|_{t=a} = u(a) = c, & c \in \mathbb{R}, \end{cases} \tag{41}$$

where $0 < \nu < 1$, and obtained some sufficient conditions for oscillation.

Theorem 53 ([42]). *Let Condition (H5) hold. If:*

$$\liminf_{t\to\infty} (t-a)^{1-\nu} \sum_{s=a+1}^{t} (t-s+1)^{\overline{\nu-1}} g(s) = -\infty,$$

and:

$$\limsup_{t\to\infty} (t-a)^{1-\nu} \sum_{s=a+1}^{t} (t-s+1)^{\overline{\nu-1}} g(s) = \infty,$$

then Equation (41) *is oscillatory.*

Theorem 54 ([42]). *Let Condition (H5) hold. Assume that there exists $t_0 \in \mathbb{N}_{a+1}$ such that:*

$$\liminf_{t\to\infty} \sum_{s=t_0+1}^{t} g(s) = -\infty,$$

and:

$$\limsup_{t\to\infty} \sum_{s=t_0+1}^{t} g(s) = \infty,$$

then Equation (41) *is oscillatory.*

In [43], the authors investigated the oscillation of fractional nabla difference equations of the form:

$$\begin{cases} (\nabla \nabla_a^{\nu} u)(t) + w(t) f(u(t)) = h(t), & t \in \mathbb{N}_a, \\ (\nabla_a^{-(1-\nu)} u)(t)\Big|_{t=a} = u(a) = c, & c \in \mathbb{R}, \end{cases} \tag{42}$$

where $0 < \nu < 1$.

Theorem 55 ([43]). *Let Condition (H6) hold. If the inequality:*

$$(\nabla \nabla_a^{\nu} u)(t) \le h(t), \quad t \in \mathbb{N}_a,$$

has no eventually positive solutions and the inequality:

$$(\nabla \nabla_a^{\nu} u)(t) \ge h(t), \quad t \in \mathbb{N}_a,$$

has no eventually negative solutions, then every solution u of Equation (42) *is oscillatory.*

Theorem 56 ([43]). *Let condition (H6) be hold. Assume that u is a solution of* (42) *and there exists $t_0 \in \mathbb{N}_a$ such that $(\nabla_a^{\nu} u)(t)\Big|_{t=t_0} = C$ exists. If:*

$$\liminf_{t\to\infty} (t-a)^{1-\nu} \sum_{s=a+1}^{t} (t-s+1)^{\overline{\nu-1}} \left[C + \sum_{\tau=t_0+1}^{s} h(\tau) \right] = -\infty,$$

and:

$$\limsup_{t\to\infty}(t-a)^{1-\nu}\sum_{s=a+1}^{t}(t-s+1)^{\overline{\nu-1}}\left[C+\sum_{\tau=t_0+1}^{s}h(\tau)\right]=\infty,$$

then, Equation (42) *is oscillatory.*

Theorem 57 ([42])**.** *Let condition (H6) be hold. Assume that u is a solution of* (42) *and there exists* $t_0 \in \mathbb{N}_a$ *such that* $\left(\nabla_a^{\nu}u\right)(t)\Big|_{t=t_0} = C$ *exists. If:*

$$\liminf_{t\to\infty}\sum_{s=t_0+1}^{t}\left(1-\frac{s-1}{t}\right)h(s)=-\infty,$$

and:

$$\limsup_{t\to\infty}\sum_{s=t_0+1}^{t}\left(1-\frac{s-1}{t}\right)h(s)=\infty,$$

then, Equation (42) *is oscillatory.*

4. Conclusions

The oscillation of difference equations has been a considerable topic due to its widespread applications in science and engineering. For this purpose, many researchers have contributed to this topic by studying several types of equations. With the rise of fractional calculus, the oscillation of fractional difference equations has become the object of an extensive investigation, and consequently, distinguishable results have been elaborated during the recent years.

In this paper, we presented a scientific platform that provided a comprehensive survey on the recent developments for the oscillation results of fractional difference equations. Different types of equations were investigated and presented by using both the nabla and delta operators. We believe that the results presented in this paper will provide a cornerstone literature for the relevant audience that is interested in the investigation of oscillation theory. The theoretical presentation in this paper is promising in the sense that it can be used to develop results for the oscillation of solutions for other types of equations such as the functional dynamic equations and fuzzy dynamic equations.

Author Contributions: Formal analysis and writing—review and editing, J.A.; supervision and validation, R.P.A.; project administration and methodology, S.R.G.; writing—original draft and resources, J.M.J.; investigation and data curation, A.G.M.S.; validation and writing—review and editing, C.W. All authors have read and agreed to the published version of the manuscript.

Funding: J. Alzabut is thankful to Prince Sultan University for funding this work.

Data Availability Statement: Data sharing is not applicable to this paper as no datasets were generated nor analyzed during the current study.

Institutional Review Board Statement: Not applicable.

Informed Consent Statement: Not applicable.

Acknowledgments: J. Alzabut is thankful to OSTİM Technical University for their endless support.

Conflicts of Interest: The authors declares no conflict of interest.

References

1. Diethelm, K. *The Analysis of Fractional Differential Equations*; Lecture Notes in Mathematics; Springer: Berlin, Germany, 2010; Volume 2004.
2. Miller, K.S.; Ross, B. *An Introduction to the Fractional Calculus and Fractional Differential Equations*; A Wiley-Interscience Publication; John Wiley & Sons, Inc.: New York, NY, USA, 1993.
3. Podlubny, I. Fractional Differential Equations. In *Mathematics in Science and Engineering*; Academic Press, Inc.: San Diego, CA, USA, 1999; Volume 198.

4. Debnath, L. Recent Applications of Fractional Calculus to Science and Engineering. *Int. J. Math. Math. Sci.* **2003**, *2003*, 753601. [CrossRef]
5. Holm, M. The Theory of Discrete Fractional Calculus, Development and Application. Ph.D. Dissertation, Nebraska University, Lincoln, NE, USA, 2011.
6. Agarwal, R.P. Certain fractional q-integrals and q-derivatives. *Math. Camb. Philos. Soc.* **1969**, *66*, 365–370. [CrossRef]
7. Atici, F.M.; Eloe, P.W. A transform method in discrete fractional calculus. *Int. J. Differ. Equ.* **2007**, *2*, 165–176.
8. Atici, F.M.; Eloe, P.W. Initial value problems in discrete fractional calculus. *Proc. Am. Math. Soc.* **2009**, *137*, 981–989. [CrossRef]
9. Anastassiou, G.A. Discrete fractional Calculus and Inequalities. *arXiv* **2009**, arXiv:0911.3370.
10. Atici, F.M.; Eloe, P.W. Discrete fractional calculus with the nabla operator. *Electron. J. Qual. Theory Differ. Equ.* **2009**, *3*, 1–12. [CrossRef]
11. Goodrich, C.; Peterson, A.C. Discrete Fractional Calculus; Springer International Publishing: Berlin/Heidelberg, Germany, 2018.
12. Gyori, I.; Ladas, G. *Oscillation Theory of Delay Differential Equations with Applications;* Clarendon Press: Oxford, UK, 1991.
13. Agarwal, R.P.; Bohner, M.; Grace, S.R.; O'Regan, D. *Discrete Oscillation Theory;* Hindawi Publishing Corporation: New York, NY, USA, 2005.
14. Grace, S.R.; Agarwal, R.P.; Wong, P.J.Y.; Zafer, A. On the oscillation of fractional differential equations. *Fract. Calc. Appl. Anal.* **2012**, *15*, 222–231. [CrossRef]
15. Tunc, E.; Tunc, O. On the oscillation of a class of damped fractional differential equations. *Miskolc. Math. Notes* **2016**, *17*, 647–656. [CrossRef]
16. Zhou, Y.; Alsaedi, A.; Ahmad, B. Oscillation for fractional neutral functional differential systems. *J. Comput. Anal. Appl.* **2018**, *25*, 965–974.
17. Sudsutad, W.; Alzabut, J.; Tearnbucha, C.; Thaiprayoon, C. On the oscillation of differential equations in frame of generalized proportional fractional derivatives. *AIMS Math.* **2020**, *5*, 856–871. [CrossRef]
18. Yang, J.; Liu, A.; Liu, T. Forced oscillation of nonlinear fractional differential equations with damping term. *Adv. Differ. Equ.* **2015**, *2015*, 1. [CrossRef]
19. Kilbas, A.A.; Srivastava, H.M.; Trujillo, J.J. *Theory and Applications of Fractional Differential Equations;* North-Holland Mathematics Studies; Elsevier Science B.V.: Amsterdam, The Netherlands, 2006.
20. Podlubny, I. Fractional differential equations. An introduction to fractional derivatives, fractional differential equations, to methods of their solution and some of their applications. In *Mathematics in Science and Engineering;* Academic Press, Inc.: San Diego, CA, USA, 1999.
21. Goodrich, C.; Peterson, A.C. Discrete Fractional Calculus; Springer: Cham, Switzerland, 2015.
22. Bohner, M.; Peterson, A. *Dynamic Equations on Time Scales. An Introduction with Applications;* Birkhäuser Boston, Inc.: Boston, MA, USA, 2001.
23. Abdeljawad, T. On Riemann and Caputo fractional differences. *Comput. Math. Appl.* **2011**, *62*, 1602–1611. [CrossRef]
24. Anastassiou, G.A. Nabla discrete fractional calculus and nabla inequalities. *Math. Comput. Model.* **2010**, *51*, 562–571. [CrossRef]
25. Kısalar, S.; Yıldız, M.K.; Aktoprak, E. Oscillation of higher order fractional nonlinear difference equations. *Int. J. Differ. Equ.* **2015**, *10*, 201–212.
26. Li, W.N. Oscillation results for certain forced fractional difference equations with damping term. *Adv. Differ. Equ.* **2016**, *2016*, 70. [CrossRef]
27. Secer, A.; Adiguzel, H. Oscillation of solutions for a class of nonlinear fractional difference equations. *J. Nonlinear Sci. Appl.* **2016**, *9*, 5862–5869. [CrossRef]
28. Chatzarakis, G.E.; Gokulraj, P.; Kalaimani, T.; Sadhasivam, V. Oscillatory solutions of nonlinear fractional difference equations. *Int. Differ. Equ.* **2018**, *13*, 19–31.
29. Adiguzel, H. Oscillation theorems for nonlinear fractional difference equations. *Bound. Value Probl.* **2018**, *2018*, 178. [CrossRef]
30. Adiguzel, H. Oscillatory behavior of solutions of certain fractional difference equations. *Adv. Differ. Equ.* **2018**, *2018*, 445. [CrossRef]
31. Bai, Z.H.; Xu, R. The asymptotic behavior of solutions for a class of nonlinear fractional difference equations with damping term. *Discrete Dyn. Nat. Soc.* **2018**, *2018*, 5232147. [CrossRef]
32. Chatzarakis, G.E.; Gokulraj, P.; Kalaimani, T. Oscillation tests for fractional difference equations. *Tatra Mt. Math. Publ.* **2018**, *71*, 53–64. [CrossRef]
33. Alzabut, J.; Muthulakshmi, V.; Özbekler, A.; Adıgüzel, H. On the Oscillation of Non-Linear Fractional Difference Equations with Damping. *Mathematics* **2019**, *7*, 687. [CrossRef]
34. Selvam, A.G.M.; Janagaraj, R. New oscillation criteria for discrete fractional order forced nonlinear equations. *J. Phys. Conf. Ser.* **2020**, *1597*, 012057. [CrossRef]
35. Selvam, A.G.M.; Janagaraj, R. Oscillation theorems for damped fractional order difference equations. *AIP Conf. Proc.* **2019**, *2095*, 030007.
36. Chatzarakis, G.E.; Selvam, G.M.; Janagaraj, R.; Miliaras, G.N. Oscillation criteria for a class of nonlinear discrete fractional order equations with damping term. *Math. Slovaca* **2020**, *70*, 1165–1182. [CrossRef]
37. Grace, S.R.; Alzabut, J.; Punitha, S.; Muthulakshmi, V.; Adıgüzel, H. On the Non-oscillatory Behavior of Solutions of Three Classes of Fractional Difference Equations. *Opuscula Math.* **2020**, *40*, 549–568. [CrossRef]

38. Alzabut, J.O.; Abdeljawad, T. Sufficient conditions for the oscillation of nonlinear fractional difference equations. *J. Fract. Calc. Appl.* **2014**, *5*, 177–187.
39. Abdalla, B.; Abodayeh, K.; Abdeljawad, T.; Alzabut, J. New oscillation criteria for forced nonlinear fractional difference equations. *Vietnam. J. Math.* **2017**, *45*, 609–618. [CrossRef]
40. Abdalla, B.; Alzabut, J.; Abdeljawad, T. On the oscillation of higher order fractional difference equations with mixed nonlinearities. *Hacet. J. Math. Stat.* **2018**, *47*, 207–217. [CrossRef]
41. Alzabut, J.; Abdeljawad, T.; Alrabaiah, H. Oscillation criteria for forced and damped nabla fractional difference equations. *J. Comput. Anal. Appl.* **2018**, *24*, 1387–1394.
42. Li, W.N.; Sheng, W. Sufficient conditions for oscillation of a nonlinear fractional nabla difference system. *Springer Plus* **2016**, *5*, 1178. [CrossRef] [PubMed]
43. Li, W.; Sheng, W.; Zhang, P. Oscillatory properties of certain nonlinear fractional nabla difference equations. *J. Appl. Anal. Comput.* **2018**, *8*, 1910–1918.

mathematics

MDPI

Article

Existence and Uniqueness Results for Fractional (p,q)-Difference Equations with Separated Boundary Conditions

Pheak Neang [1], Kamsing Nonlaopon [1,*], Jessada Tariboon [2], Sotiris K. Ntouyas [3,4] and Bashir Ahmad [4]

[1] Department of Mathematics, Faculty of Science, Khon Kaen University, Khon Kaen 40002, Thailand; pheakne@kkumail.com
[2] Department of Mathematics, Faculty of Applied Science, King Mongkut's University of Technology North Bangkok, Bangkok 10800, Thailand; jessada.t@sci.kmutnb.ac.th
[3] Department of Mathematics, University of Ioannina, 451 10 Ioannina, Greece; sntouyas@uoi.gr
[4] Nonlinear Analysis and Applied Mathematics (NAAM)-Research Group, Department of Mathematics, Faculty of Science, King Abdulaziz University, Jeddah 21589, Saudi Arabia; bashir_qau@yahoo.com
* Correspondence: nkamsi@kku.ac.th; Tel.: +66-8-6642-1582

Abstract: In this paper, we study the existence of solutions to a fractional (p,q)-difference equation equipped with separate local boundary value conditions. The uniqueness of solutions is established by means of Banach's contraction mapping principle, while the existence results of solutions are obtained by applying Krasnoselskii's fixed-point theorem and the Leary–Schauder alternative. Some examples illustrating the main results are also presented.

Keywords: Caputo fractional (p,q)-difference equations; boundary conditions; existence and uniqueness; Leray–Schauder alternative; fixed-point theory

MSC: 05A30; 26A51; 26D10; 26D15

1. Introduction

Fractional calculus, dealing with the integrals and derivatives of arbitrary order, constitutes an important area of investigation in view of its extensive theoretical development and applications during the last few decades. For some interesting results on fractional differential equations ranging from the existence and uniqueness of solutions to the analytic and numerical methods for finding solutions, we refer the reader to the following articles: [1–5]. Concerning the applications of fractional differential equations in engineering, clinical disciplines, biology, physics, chemistry, economics, signal and image processing, and control theory, for example, see [6–10] for more details.

The study of q-calculus was introduced by Jackson in 1910, see [11,12] for more details. As one of the major driving forces behind the modern mathematical analysis, q-calculus has played important roles in both mathematical and physical problems. For instance, Fock [13] has studied the symmetry of hydrogen atoms using the q-difference equation. The concepts of q-calculus found numerous applications in a variety of fields, such as combinatorics, orthogonal polynomials, basic hypergeometric functions, number theory, quantum theory, quantum mechanics, and theory of relativity for details, see [14–16], and the references cited therein. One can find the basic concepts of q-calculus in the text by Kac and Cheung [17], while some details about fractional q-difference calculus can be found in [14,18–21].

The subject of (p,q)-calculus is known as the extension of q-calculus to its two-parameter (p,q) variant and has efficient applications in many fields. One can find some useful information about the (p,q)-calculus in [22–30].

In 2021, Neang et al. [31] considered the nonlocal boundary value problem of nonlinear fractional (p,q)-difference equations with taking care of solutions of existence and uniqueness results obtained by

$$ {}^{c}D^{\alpha}_{p,q}u(t) = f(t, u(p^{\alpha}t)),\ t \in [0, T/p^{\alpha}], 1 < \alpha \leq 2, \tag{1} $$

$$ \beta_1 u(0) + \gamma_1 D_{p,q}u(0) = \zeta_1 u(\eta_1), \quad \beta_2 u(T) + \gamma_2 D_{p,q}u(T/p) = \zeta_2 u(\eta_2), \tag{2} $$

where $f \in C([0, T/p^{\alpha}] \times \mathbb{R}, \mathbb{R})$, $\beta_i, \gamma_i, \eta_i$ $(i = 1,2)$ are constants, ${}^{c}D^{\alpha}_{p,q}$ denoted by Caputo fractional (p,q) type, while $D_{p,q}$ denoted by first-order (p,q)-derivative.

Qin and Sun [32] studied on a nonlinear fractional (p,q)-difference Schrödinger equation in 2021, given by the following:

$$ D^{\alpha}_{p,q}u(x) + \alpha h(p^{\alpha}x) f(u(p^{\alpha}x)) = 0,\ x \in (0,1), \tag{3} $$

$$ u(0) = D_{p,q}u(0) = D_{p,q}u(1) = 0, \tag{4} $$

where $0 < q < p \leq 1, 2 < \alpha \leq 3, D^{\alpha}_{p,q}$ is a Riemann–Liouville-type fractional (p,q)-difference operator, and $f \in C([0,1], (0,\infty)), h \in C([0,1], (0,\infty))$.

Moreover, Qin and Sun [33] studied positive solutions for fractional (p,q)-difference boundary value problems given by the following:

$$ D^{\alpha}_{p,q}u(x) + f(p^{\alpha}x, u(p^{\alpha}x)) = 0,\ x \in (0,1), \tag{5} $$

$$ u(0) = u(1) = 0, \tag{6} $$

where $0 < q < p \leq 1, 1 < \alpha \leq 2$, $D^{\alpha}_{p,q}$ is a Riemann–Liouville-type fractional (p,q)-difference operator, and $f : [0,1] \times \mathbb{R} \to \mathbb{R}$ is a non-negative continuous function.

However, even though Neang et al. [31] investigated and proved the nonlocal boundary value problems by considering on existence results of a class of fractional (p,q)-difference equations, it still was a bit complicated with the domain of a function when the authors applied the fractional (p,q)-integral operators. In this paper, to make this paper more smooth and convenient, we have investigated the existence and uniqueness of solutions for the local boundary value problem of fractional (p,q)-difference equation with a new function obtained $g \in \mathscr{C}([0,b] \times \mathbb{R}, \mathbb{R})$, given by the following:

$$ {}^{c}D^{\alpha}_{p,q}x(t) = g(p^{\alpha}t, x(p^{\alpha}t)),\ t \in [0,b], 1 < \alpha \leq 2, \tag{7} $$

$$ \alpha_1 x(0) + \beta_1 D_{p,q}x(0) = \gamma_1, \quad \alpha_2 x(b) + \beta_2 D_{p,q}x(pb) = \gamma_2, \tag{8} $$

where $\alpha_i, \beta_i, \gamma_i$ $(i = 1,2)$ are constants, ${}^{c}D^{\alpha}_{p,q}$ denoted by Caputo fractional (p,q) type, while $D_{p,q}$ denoted by the first-order (p,q)-derivative.

2. Preliminaries

In this part, some fundamental results and definitions of the (p,q)-calculus, which can be found in [14,23,25] are given.

Let $[a,b] \subset \mathbb{R}$ be an interval with $a < b$ and $0 < q < p \leq 1$ be constants,

$$ [k]_{p,q} = \frac{p^k - q^k}{p - q}, \quad k \in \mathbb{N}, \tag{9} $$

$$ [k]_{p,q}! = \begin{cases} [k]_{p,q}[k-1]_{p,q} \cdots [1]_{p,q} = \prod_{i=1}^{k} \frac{p^i - q^i}{p - q}, & k \in \mathbb{N}, \\ 1, & k = 0. \end{cases} \tag{10} $$

For $n \in \mathbb{N}_0 := \{0, 1, 2, \ldots\}$, the q-analogue of the power function $(a-b)_q^{(n)}$ is given by

$$(a-b)_q^{(0)} = 1, \quad (a-b)_q^{(n)} := \prod_{k=0}^{n-1}(a - bq^k), \quad a, b \in \mathbb{R}.$$

For $n \in \mathbb{N}_0 := \{0, 1, 2, \ldots\}$, the (p, q)-analogue of the power function $(a-b)_{p,q}^{(n)}$ is given by

$$(a-b)_{p,q}^{(0)} = 1, \quad (a-b)_{p,q}^{(n)} := \prod_{k=0}^{n-1}(ap^k - bq^k), \quad a, b \in \mathbb{R}.$$

The generalization of q-gamma function is called (p, q)-gamma is given by

$$\begin{aligned} \Gamma_{p,q}(t) &= \frac{(p-q)_{p,q}^{(t-1)}}{(p-q)^{t-1}} \\ &= \frac{p^{\binom{t-1}{2}}}{(1-(q/p)^{t-1}} \prod_{k=0}^{\infty} \frac{1-(q/p)^{k+1}}{1-(q/p)^{k+t+1}}, \end{aligned} \tag{11}$$

For $t \in \mathbb{R} \setminus \{0, -1, -2, \ldots\}$, and an equivalent definition of (11) is given in [25] as

$$\Gamma_{p,q}(t) = p^{\frac{t(t-1)}{2}} \int_0^{\infty} x^{t-1} E_{p,q}^{-qx} d_{p,q}x \tag{12}$$

where

$$E_{p,q}^{-qx} = \sum_{n=0}^{\infty} \frac{q^{\binom{n}{2}}}{[n]_{p,q}!}(-qx)^n.$$

Remark 1. *$\Gamma_{p,q}(t+1) = [t]_{p,q}\Gamma_{p,q}(t)$ and $\Gamma_{p,q}(t) \le p^{\binom{t-1}{2}}\left(1-(q/p)_{p,q}^{1-t}\right)$.*

The definition of (p, q)-beta function for $s, t > 0$ is defined by

$$B_{p,q}(s,t) = \int_0^1 u^{s-1}(1-qu)_{p,q}^{(t-1)} d_{p,q}u, \tag{13}$$

and (13) can also be written as

$$B_{p,q}(s,t) = p^{(t-1)(2s+t-2)/2} \frac{\Gamma_{p,q}(s)\Gamma_{p,q}(t)}{\Gamma_{p,q}(s+t)}, \tag{14}$$

see [34,35] for more details.

Definition 1 ([23]). *Let $0 < q < p \le 1$. Then, the (p, q)-derivative of f is defined by*

$$D_{p,q}g(t) = \frac{g(pt) - g(qt)}{(p-q)t}, \; t \neq 0 \tag{15}$$

and $D_{p,q}g(0) = \lim_{t \to 0} D_{p,q}g(t)$, provided that g is differential at 0.

Definition 2 ([23]). *Let $0 < q < p \le 1$, g be an arbitrary function, and t be a real number. The (p, q)-integral of g is defined as*

$$\int_0^t g(s) d_{p,q}s = (p-q)t \sum_{n=0}^{\infty} \frac{q^n}{p^{n+1}} g\left(\frac{q^n}{p^{n+1}}t\right) \tag{16}$$

provided that the series of the right-hand side in (16) converges.

Theorem 1 ([23]). *Let g, h be differentiable on $[0, b]$ with a constant λ. Then,*

(i) $D_{p,q}(g(t) + h(t)) = D_{p,q}g(t) + D_{p,q}h(t)$;

(ii) $D_{p,q}\lambda g(s) = \lambda D_{p,q}g(s)$;

(iii) $D_{p,q}(gh)(t) = g(pt)D_{p,q}h(t) + h(qt)D_{p,q}g(t)$;

(iv) $D_{p,q}(g/h)(t) = \dfrac{h(qt)D_{p,q}g(t) - g(qt)D_{p,q}h(t)}{h(pt)h(qt)}$,

where $h(t) \neq 0$ for $t \in [0, b]$.

Theorem 2 ([30]). *Let g be a continuous function on $[0, b]$. Then,*

(i) $D_{p,q} \int_0^t g(s) d_{p,q}s = g(t)$;

(ii) $\int_0^t D_{p,q}g(s) d_{p,q}s = g(t) - g(0)$;

(iii) $\int_a^t D_{p,q}g(s) d_{p,q}s = g(t) - g(a)$, *for $a \in (0, t)$.*

Definition 3 ([34]). *Let g be a continuous function defined on $[0, b]$. Then, the Riemann–Liouville fractional (p, q)-integral type is stated by for $\alpha > 0$*

$$\begin{aligned}\left(I^{\alpha}_{p,q}g\right)(t) &= \frac{1}{p^{\binom{\alpha}{2}}\Gamma_{p,q}(\alpha)} \int_0^t (t - qs)_{p,q}^{(\alpha-1)} g\left(\frac{s}{p^{\alpha-1}}\right) d_{p,q}s \\ &= \frac{(p-q)t}{p^{\binom{\alpha}{2}}\Gamma_{p,q}(\alpha)} \sum_{n=0}^{\infty} \frac{q^n}{p^{n+1}} \left(t - \frac{q^{n+1}}{p^{n+1}}t\right)_{p,q}^{(\alpha-1)} g\left(\frac{q^n}{p^{\alpha+n}}t\right)\end{aligned} \tag{17}$$

where $t \in [0, p^{\alpha}b]$. Notice that if $\alpha = 0$,, then $\left(I^0_{p,q}g\right)(t) = g(t)$.

Definition 4 ([34]). *Let g be a continuous function defined on $[0, b]$. Then, the Riemann–Liouville fractional (p, q)-derivative type is stated by*

$$(D^{\alpha}_{p,q}g)(t) = \left(D^{\lceil\alpha\rceil}_{p,q} I^{\lceil\alpha\rceil-\alpha}_{p,q} g\right)(t), \text{ for } \alpha > 0 \tag{18}$$

where $\lceil\alpha\rceil$ is the smallest integer greater than or equal to α. Notice that if $\alpha = 0$,, then $(D^0_{p,q}h)(t) = g(t)$.

Definition 5 ([34]). *Let g be a continuous function defined on $[0, b]$. If $\alpha > 0$, then the Caputo fractional (p, q)-derivative is stated by*

$$({}^{c}D^{\alpha}_{p,q}g)(t) = \left(I^{\lceil\alpha\rceil-\alpha}_{p,q} D^{\lceil\alpha\rceil}_{p,q}g\right)(t), \tag{19}$$

where $\lceil\alpha\rceil$ is the smallest integer greater than or equal to α. Notice that if $\alpha = 0$, then $\left({}^{c}D^0_{p,q}g\right)(t) = g(t)$.

To obtain the sufficient condition of existence and uniqueness of solutions of (7)–(8), employing the following Lemmas of fractional (p, q)-calculus play an important role in those main results.

Lemma 1 ([34]). *Let g be a continuous function on $[0, b]$. Then,*

(i) $\left(I^{\beta}_{p,q}I^{\alpha}_{p,q}g\right)(t) = \left(I^{\alpha+\beta}_{p,q}g\right)(t)$;

(ii) $\left(D^{\alpha}_{p,q}I^{\alpha}_{p,q}g\right)(t) = g(t)$.

Lemma 2 ([34]). *Let g be a continuous function on* $[0, b]$. *If* $\alpha > 0$, *and* $n \in \mathbb{N}$, *then the following equality holds:*

$$\left(I_{p,q}^{\alpha} D_{p,q}^{n} g\right)(t) = \left(D_{p,q}^{n} I_{p,q}^{\alpha} g\right)(t) - \sum_{k=0}^{[\alpha]-1} \frac{t^{\alpha-n+k}}{p^{\binom{\alpha}{2}} \Gamma_{p,q}(\alpha - n + k + 1)} \left(D_{p,q}^{k} g\right)(0).$$

Lemma 3 ([34]). *Let g be a continuous function on* $[0, b]$. *If* $\alpha > 0$ *and* $n \in \mathbb{N}$, *then*

$$\left(I_{p,q}^{\alpha}\, {}^{c}D_{p,q}^{\alpha} g\right)(t) = g(t) - \sum_{k=0}^{[\alpha]-1} \frac{t^{k}}{p^{\binom{\alpha}{2}} \Gamma_{p,q}(k+1)} \left(D_{p,q}^{k} g\right)(0).$$

Lemma 4. *In order to prove (7) and (8), we first give a useful Lemma, as follows:*

$$\begin{cases} {}^{c}D_{p,q}^{\alpha} x(t) = g(p^{\alpha} t), \ t \in [0, b], \\ \alpha_1 x(0) + \beta_1 D_{p,q} x(0) = \gamma_1, \\ \alpha_2 x(b) + \beta_2 D_{p,q} x(pb) = \gamma_2, \end{cases} \tag{20}$$

is defined by

$$\begin{aligned} x(t) = {} & \eta_1 + \eta_2 t + \int_0^t \frac{(t - qs)_{p,q}^{(\alpha-1)}}{p^{\binom{\alpha}{2}} \Gamma_{p,q}(\alpha)} g(ps)\, d_{p,q}s \\ & + \frac{1}{\Delta}[\alpha_1 \alpha_2 t - \beta_1 \alpha_2] \int_0^b \frac{(b - qs)_{p,q}^{(\alpha-1)}}{p^{\binom{\alpha}{2}} \Gamma_{p,q}(\alpha)} g(ps)\, d_{p,q}s \\ & + \frac{1}{\Delta}[\alpha_1 \beta_2 t - \beta_1 \beta_2] \int_0^b \frac{(b - qs)_{p,q}^{(\alpha-2)}}{p^{\binom{\alpha-1}{2}} \Gamma_{p,q}(\alpha - 1)} g\left(p^2 s\right) d_{p,q}s, \end{aligned} \tag{21}$$

where

$$\eta_1 = \frac{\beta_1 \gamma_2 - \gamma_1(\alpha_2 b + \beta_2)}{\Delta}, \ \eta_2 = \frac{(\alpha_2 \gamma_1 - \alpha_1 \gamma_2)}{\Delta},$$

and it is supposed that

$$\Delta = \alpha_2 \beta_1 - \alpha_1(\alpha_2 b + \beta_2) \neq 0.$$

Proof. Applying fractional (p, q)-integral on (20), we obtain the following:

$$x(t) = \int_0^t \frac{(t - qs)^{(\alpha-1)}}{p^{\binom{\alpha}{2}} \Gamma_{p,q}(\alpha)} g(ps)\, d_{p,q}s + tc_0 + c_1, \tag{22}$$

where c_0, c_1 are constants and $t \in [0, b]$. Utilizing (20) again, we obtain

$$\begin{cases} \alpha_1 c_1 + \beta_1 c_0 = \gamma_1, \\ c_0(\alpha_2 b + \beta_2) + \alpha_2 c_1 = \gamma_2 - \alpha_2 \displaystyle\int_0^b \frac{(b - qs)^{(\alpha-1)}}{p^{\binom{\alpha}{2}} \Gamma_{p,q}(\alpha)} g(ps)\, d_{p,q}s \\ -\beta_2 \displaystyle\int_0^b \frac{(b - qs)^{(\alpha-2)}}{p^{\binom{\alpha-1}{2}} \Gamma_{p,q}(\alpha - 1)} g\left(p^2 s\right) d_{p,q}s. \end{cases} \tag{23}$$

Solving the above system of equations to find the constants c_0, c_1, we have

$$c_0 = \frac{1}{\Delta}\left[\alpha_2\gamma_1 + \alpha_1\alpha_2 \int_0^b \frac{(b-qs)^{(\alpha-1)}}{p^{\binom{\alpha}{2}}\Gamma_{p,q}(\alpha)} g(ps)\, d_{p,q}s \right.$$
$$\left. +\alpha_1\beta_2 \int_0^b \frac{(b-qs)^{(\alpha-1)}}{p^{\binom{\alpha}{2}}\Gamma_{p,q}(\alpha)} g\left(p^2 s\right) d_{p,q}s \right]$$

and

$$c_1 = \frac{1}{\Delta}\left[-\gamma_1(\alpha_2 b + \beta_1\alpha_2) \int_0^b \frac{(b-qs)^{(\alpha-1)}}{p^{\binom{\alpha}{2}}\Gamma_{p,q}(\alpha)} g(ps)\, d_{p,q}s \right.$$
$$\left. -\beta_1\beta_2 \int_0^b \frac{(b-qs)^{(\alpha-2)}}{p^{\binom{\alpha-1}{2}}\Gamma_{p,q}(\alpha-1)} g\left(p^2 s\right) d_{p,q}s \right].$$

Substituting the values of c_0, c_1 in (22), we derive (21). By direction computation, we obtain for the converse. Therefore, this completed the proof. □

3. Main Results

Let $C := \mathscr{C}([0,b],\mathbb{R})$ denote the Banach space of all continuous functions from $[0,b]$ to $\mathbb{R}$, endowed with norm, defined by

$$\|x\| = \sup\{|x(t)| : t \in [0,b]\}.$$

In view of Lemma 4, we define an operator $\mathcal{F} : C \to C$ as

$$(\mathcal{F}x)(t) = \eta_1 + \eta_2 t + \int_0^t \frac{(t-qs)^{(\alpha-1)}}{p^{\binom{\alpha}{2}}\Gamma_{p,q}(\alpha)} g(ps, x(ps))\, d_{p,q}s$$
$$+ \frac{1}{\Delta}[\alpha_1\alpha_2 t - \beta_1\alpha_2] \int_0^b \frac{(b-qs)_{p,q}^{(\alpha-1)}}{p^{\binom{\alpha}{2}}\Gamma_{p,q}(\alpha)} g(ps, x(ps))\, d_{p,q}s$$
$$+ \frac{1}{\Delta}[\alpha_1\beta_2 t - \beta_1\beta_2] \int_0^b \frac{(b-qs)_{p,q}^{(\alpha-2)}}{p^{\binom{\alpha-1}{2}}\Gamma_{p,q}(\alpha-1)} g(p^2 s, x(p^2 s))\, d_{p,q}s, \tag{24}$$

where $\Delta = \alpha_2\beta_1 - \alpha_1(\alpha_2 b + \beta_2) \neq 0$.

Observe that x is a solution to (7) and (8) if—and only if—x is a fixed-point of $\mathcal{F}$. For convenience, we denote

$$k = \int_0^b \frac{(b-qs)_{p,q}^{(\alpha-1)}}{p^{\binom{\alpha}{2}}\Gamma_{p,q}(\alpha)} L(ps)\, d_{p,q}s + \sigma_1(b) \int_0^b \frac{(b-qs)_{p,q}^{(\alpha-1)}}{p^{\binom{\alpha}{2}}\Gamma_{p,q}(\alpha)} L(ps)\, d_{p,q}s$$
$$+ \sigma_2(b) \int_0^b \frac{(b-qs)_{p,q}^{(\alpha-2)}}{p^{\binom{\alpha-1}{2}}\Gamma_{p,q}(\alpha-1)} L\left(p^2 s\right) d_{p,q}s, \tag{25}$$

where

$$\sigma_1(b) = \frac{1}{|\Delta|}(|\alpha_1||\alpha_2|b + |\beta_1||\alpha_2|),\ \sigma_2(b) = \frac{1}{|\Delta|}(|\alpha_1||\beta_2|b + |\beta_1||\beta_2|).$$

Theorem 3. *Let g be a continuous function on $[0,b] \times \mathbb{R}$ and there exists a integrable function $L : [0,b] \to \mathbb{R}$, such that*

(A_1) $|g(t,x) - g(t,y)| \leq L(t)|x-y|$, for each $t \in [0,b]$ and $x, y \in \mathbb{R}$.

If $k < 1$, then (7) and (8) has a unique solution.

Proof. We transform the problem (7) and (8) into a fixed-point problem $\mathcal{F}x = x$, where the operator $\mathcal{F}$ is given by (24). Applying Banach's contraction mapping principle, we will show that $\mathcal{F}$ has a unique fixed point. Define a ball, $B_r = \{x \in \mathcal{C} : \|x\| \leq r\}$, with the radius, r, satisfying

$$r \geq \frac{|\eta_1| + |\eta_2|b + MA}{1-k},$$

where

$$A = \frac{b^\alpha}{\Gamma_{p,q}(\alpha+1)} + \sigma_1(b)\frac{b^\alpha}{\Gamma_{p,q}(\alpha+1)} + \sigma_2(b)\frac{b^{\alpha-1}}{\Gamma_{p,q}(\alpha)}, \tag{26}$$

and $M = \sup_{t\in[0,b]} |f(t,0)|$. We have

$$\begin{aligned} |g(t,x(t))| &\leq |g(t,x(t)) - g(t,0)| + |g(t,0)| \\ &\leq L(t)r + M. \end{aligned}$$

Now, we shall show that $\mathcal{F} \subset B_r$. For any $x \in B_r$, consider

$$\begin{aligned} |(\mathcal{F}x)(t)| \leq{}& |\eta_1| + |\eta_2|t + \int_0^t \frac{(t-qs)^{(\alpha-1)}}{p^{\binom{\alpha}{2}}\Gamma_{p,q}(\alpha)}|g(ps,x(ps))|\,d_{p,q}s \\ &+ \frac{1}{|\Delta|}[|\alpha_1||\alpha_2|t + |\beta_1||\alpha_2|]\int_0^b \frac{(b-qs)_{p,q}^{(\alpha-1)}}{p^{\binom{\alpha}{2}}\Gamma_{p,q}(\alpha)}|g(ps,x(ps))|\,d_{p,q}s \\ &+ \frac{1}{|\Delta|}[\alpha_1\beta_2 t + |\beta_1||\beta_2|]\int_0^b \frac{(b-qs)_{p,q}^{(\alpha-2)}}{p^{\binom{\alpha-1}{2}}\Gamma_{p,q}(\alpha-1)}\left|g(p^2s,x(p^2s))\right|\,d_{p,q}s \\ \leq{}& |\eta_1| + |\eta_2|b + \int_0^b \frac{(b-qs)^{(\alpha-1)}}{p^{\binom{\alpha}{2}}\Gamma_{p,q}(\alpha)}|g(ps,x(ps))|\,d_{p,q}s \\ &+ \sigma_1(b)\int_0^b \frac{(b-qs)_{p,q}^{(\alpha-1)}}{p^{\binom{\alpha}{2}}\Gamma_{p,q}(\alpha)}|g(ps,x(ps))|\,d_{p,q}s \\ &+ \sigma_2(T)\int_0^b \frac{(b-qs)_{p,q}^{(\alpha-2)}}{p^{\binom{\alpha-1}{2}}\Gamma_{p,q}(\alpha-1)}\left|g(p^2s,x(p^2s))\right|\,d_{p,q}s, \\ \leq{}& |\eta_1| + |\eta_2|b + \int_0^b \frac{(b-qs)^{(\alpha-1)}}{p^{\binom{\alpha}{2}}\Gamma_{p,q}(\alpha)}(L(ps)r + M)\,d_{p,q}s \\ &+ \sigma_1(b)\int_0^b \frac{(b-qs)_{p,q}^{(\alpha-1)}}{p^{\binom{\alpha}{2}}\Gamma_{p,q}(\alpha)}(L(ps)r + M)\,d_{p,q}s \\ &+ \sigma_2(b)\int_0^b \frac{(b-qs)_{p,q}^{(\alpha-2)}}{p^{\binom{\alpha-1}{2}}\Gamma_{p,q}(\alpha-1)}\left(L\left(p^2s\right)r + M\right)\,d_{p,q}s \\ \leq{}& |\eta_1| + |\eta_2|b + M\left\{\frac{b^\alpha}{\Gamma_{p,q}(\alpha+1)} + \sigma_1(b)\frac{b^\alpha}{\Gamma_{p,q}(\alpha+1)} + \sigma_2(b)\frac{b^{\alpha-1}}{\Gamma_{p,q}(\alpha)}\right\} \\ &+ r\left\{\int_0^b \frac{(b-qs)_{p,q}^{(\alpha-1)}}{p^{\binom{\alpha}{2}}\Gamma_{p,q}(\alpha)}L(ps)\,d_{p,q}s\right. \\ &+\sigma_1(b)\int_0^b \frac{(b-qs)_{p,q}^{(\alpha-1)}}{p^{\binom{\alpha}{2}}\Gamma_{p,q}(\alpha)}L(ps)\,d_{p,q}s \end{aligned}$$

$$+\sigma_2(b)\int_0^b \frac{(b-qs)_{p,q}^{(\alpha-2)}}{p^{\binom{\alpha-1}{2}}\Gamma_{p,q}(\alpha-1)}L\left(p^2s\right)d_{p,q}s\Bigg\}$$

from (25) and (26), we obtain

$$\|\mathcal{F}x\| \le |\eta_1| + |\eta_2|b + MA + rk \le r.$$

This shows that $\mathcal{F}\mathcal{B}_r \subset \mathcal{B}_r$.
Now, for $x, y \in \mathcal{C}$, we obtain

$$\begin{aligned}
&\|\mathcal{F}x - \mathcal{F}y\| \\
&\le \sup_{t\in[0,b]}\Bigg\{\int_0^t \frac{(t-qs)_{p,q}^{(\alpha-1)}}{p^{\binom{\alpha}{2}}\Gamma_{p,q}(\alpha)}|g(ps,x(ps)) - g(ps,y(ps))|\,d_{p,q}s \\
&\quad +\sigma_1(b)\int_0^b \frac{(b-qs)_{p,q}^{(\alpha-1)}}{p^{\binom{\alpha}{2}}\Gamma_{p,q}(\alpha)}|g(ps,x(ps)) - g(ps,y(ps))|\,d_{p,q}s \\
&\quad +\sigma_2(b)\int_0^b \frac{(b-qs)_{p,q}^{(\alpha-2)}}{p^{\binom{\alpha}{2}}\Gamma_{p,q}(\alpha)}\left|g(p^2s,x(p^2s)) - g(p^2s,y(p^2s))\right|d_{p,q}s\Bigg\} \\
&\le \|x-y\|\Bigg\{\int_0^b \frac{(b-qs)_{p,q}^{(\alpha-1)}}{p^{\binom{\alpha}{2}}\Gamma_{p,q}(\alpha)}L(ps)\,d_{p,q}s \\
&\quad +\sigma_1(b)\int_0^b \frac{(b-qs)_{p,q}^{(\alpha-1)}}{p^{\binom{\alpha}{2}}\Gamma_{p,q}(\alpha)}L(ps)\,d_{p,q}s \\
&\quad +\sigma_2(b)\int_0^b \frac{(b-qs)_{p,q}^{(\alpha-2)}}{p^{\binom{\alpha-1}{2}}\Gamma_{p,q}(\alpha-1)}L\left(p^2s\right)d_{p,q}s\Bigg\},
\end{aligned}$$

which, in view of (25), we obtain

$$\|\mathcal{F}x - \mathcal{F}y\| \le k\|x-y\|.$$

This is because $k \in (0,1)$, $\mathcal{F}$ is a contraction. Therefore, (7) and (8) has a unique solution. The proof is completed. □

Remark 2. *If g is a continuous function on $[0,b] \times \mathbb{R}$, and there exists a constant $L > 0$ with*

$$|g(t,x) - g(t,y)| \le L|x-y|,$$

then (7) and (8) has a unique solution, if $k < 1$.

Lemma 5 (Kranoselskii's fixed-point theorem [36]**).** *Let M be a closed, bounded, convex, and non-empty subset of a Banach space X. Let A, B be two operators, such that:*

(i) $Ax + By \in M$, whenever $x, y \in M$;
(ii) A is compact and continuous;
(iii) B is a contraction mapping.

Then, there exists $z \in M$, such that $z = Az + Bz$.

Theorem 4. *Let g be a continuous functions on $[0,b] \times \mathbb{R}$, satisfying (A_1). Assume that*
(A_2) there exists a function, $\mu \in \mathscr{C}([0,b],\mathbb{R}^+)$, and a non-decreasing function, $\phi \in \mathscr{C}([0,b],\mathbb{R}^+)$, with

$$|g(t,x)| \le \mu(t)\phi(|x|),$$

where $(t,x) \in [0,b] \times [-b,b]$.

If

$$\sigma_1(b)\int_0^b \frac{(b-qs)_{p,q}^{(\alpha-1)}}{p^{\binom{\alpha}{2}}\Gamma_{p,q}(\alpha)}L(ps)\,d_{p,q}s + \sigma_2(b)\int_0^b \frac{(b-qs)_{p,q}^{(\alpha-2)}}{p^{\binom{\alpha-1}{2}}\Gamma_{p,q}(\alpha-1)}L\left(p^2s\right)d_{p,q}s < 1, \tag{27}$$

then (7) and (8) has at least one solution on $[0,b]$.

Proof. Define $\mathcal{B}_{\bar{r}} := \{x \in \mathcal{C} : \|x\| \le \bar{r}\}$, where

$$\bar{r} \ge \phi(\bar{r})\|\mu\|\left[\frac{b^\alpha}{\Gamma_{p,q}(\alpha+1)} + \sigma_1(b)\frac{b^\alpha}{\Gamma_{p,q}(\alpha+1)} + \sigma_2(b)\frac{b^{\alpha-1}}{\Gamma_{p,q}(\alpha)}\right],$$

where $\|\mu\| = \sup_{t\in[0,b]}|\mu(t)|$, and define the operators $\mathcal{P}$ and $\mathcal{Q}$ on $\mathcal{B}_{\bar{r}}$ as

$$(\mathcal{P}x)(t) = \frac{1}{\Delta}[\alpha_1\alpha_2 t - \beta_1\alpha_2]\int_0^b \frac{(b-qs)_{p,q}^{(\alpha-1)}}{p^{\binom{\alpha}{2}}\Gamma_{p,q}(\alpha)}g(ps,x(ps))\,d_{p,q}s + \frac{1}{\Delta}[\alpha_1\beta_2 t - \beta_1\beta_2]\int_0^b \frac{(b-qs)_{p,q}^{(\alpha-2)}}{p^{\binom{\alpha}{2}}\Gamma_{p,q}(\alpha-1)}g(p^2s,x(p^2s))\,d_{p,q}s$$

and

$$(\mathcal{Q}y)(t) = \eta_1 + \eta_2 t + \int_0^t \frac{(t-qs)^{(\alpha-1)}}{p^{\binom{\alpha}{2}}\Gamma_{p,q}(\alpha)}g(ps,y(ps))\,d_{p,q}s.$$

Observe that $\mathcal{P}x + \mathcal{Q}x = \mathcal{F}x$. For $x,y \in \mathcal{B}_{\bar{r}}$, we have

$$\begin{aligned}
|(\mathcal{P}x+\mathcal{Q}y)(t)| &\le |\eta_1| + |\eta_2|t + \int_0^t \frac{(t-qs)^{(\alpha-1)}}{p^{\binom{\alpha}{2}}\Gamma_{p,q}(\alpha)}|g(ps,y(ps))|\,d_{p,q}s \\
&\quad + \frac{1}{|\Delta|}(|\alpha_1||\alpha_2|t + |\beta_1||\alpha_2|)\int_0^b \frac{(b-qs)_{p,q}^{(\alpha-1)}}{p^{\binom{\alpha}{2}}\Gamma_{p,q}(\alpha)}|g(ps,x(ps))|\,d_{p,q}s \\
&\quad + \frac{1}{|\Delta|}(\alpha_1\beta_2 t + |\beta_1||\beta_2|)\int_0^b \frac{(b-qs)_{p,q}^{(\alpha-2)}}{p^{\binom{\alpha-1}{2}}\Gamma_{p,q}(\alpha-1)}\left|g(p^2s,x(p^2s))\right|d_{p,q}s \\
&\le |\eta_1| + |\eta_2|b + \int_0^b \frac{(b-qs)^{(\alpha-1)}}{p^{\binom{\alpha}{2}}\Gamma_{p,q}(\alpha)}\mu(t)\phi(|x|)\,d_{p,q}s \\
&\quad + \sigma_1(b)\int_0^b \frac{(b-qs)_{p,q}^{(\alpha-1)}}{p^{\binom{\alpha}{2}}\Gamma_{p,q}(\alpha)}\mu(t)\phi(|x|)\,d_{p,q}s \\
&\quad + \sigma_2(b)\int_0^b \frac{(b-qs)_{p,q}^{(\alpha-2)}}{p^{\binom{\alpha-1}{2}}\Gamma_{p,q}(\alpha-1)}\mu(t)\phi(|x|)\,d_{p,q}s, \\
&\le \phi(\bar{r})\|\mu\|\left[\frac{b^\alpha}{\Gamma_{p,q}(\alpha+1)} + \sigma_1(b)\frac{b^\alpha}{\Gamma_{p,q}(\alpha+1)} + \sigma_2(b)\frac{b^{\alpha-1}}{\Gamma_{p,q}(\alpha)}\right] \\
&\le \bar{r}.
\end{aligned}$$

Thus, $\mathcal{P}x + \mathcal{Q}y \in \mathcal{B}_{\bar{r}}$. By (A_1) and (27), $\mathcal{Q}$ is a contraction mapping. By continuity of f, we obtain that $\mathcal{P}$ is continuous. It is easy to see that

$$\|\mathcal{P}\| \leq \phi(\bar{r})\|\mu\|\left[\sigma_1(b)\frac{b^{\alpha}}{\Gamma_{p,q}(\alpha+1)} + \sigma_2(b)\frac{b^{\alpha-1}}{\Gamma_{p,q}(\alpha)}\right].$$

Thus, the set $\mathcal{P}(\mathcal{B}_{\bar{r}})$ is uniformly bounded. $\mathcal{P}$ is compact. First, Let

$$\bar{g} = \sup_{(t,x)\in[0,b]\times\mathcal{B}_{\bar{r}}} |g(t,x)| < \infty$$

and let $t_1, t_2 \in [0,b]$ with $t_1 < t_2$. Then, we obtain

$$\begin{aligned}
&|(\mathcal{P}x)(t_2) - (\mathcal{Q}x)(t_1)| \\
&\leq \frac{1}{|\Delta|}|\alpha_1||\alpha_2|(t_2-t_1)\int_0^b \frac{(b-qs)_{p,q}^{(\alpha-1)}}{p^{\binom{\alpha}{2}}\Gamma_{p,q}(\alpha)}|g(ps,x(ps))|\,d_{p,q}s \\
&+ \frac{1}{|\Delta|}\alpha_1\beta_2(t_2-t_1)\int_0^b \frac{(b-qs)_{p,q}^{(\alpha-2)}}{p^{\binom{\alpha-1}{2}}\Gamma_{p,q}(\alpha-1)}\left|g(p^2s,x(p^2s))\right|\,d_{p,q}s \\
&\leq \bar{g}\left\{\frac{|\alpha_1||\alpha_2|b^{\alpha}}{|\Delta|\Gamma_{p,q}(\alpha+1)} + \frac{|\alpha_1||\beta_2|b^{\alpha-1}}{|\Delta|\Gamma_{p,q}(\alpha)}\right\}(t_2-t_1),
\end{aligned}$$

which is independent of x, and tends to zero as $t_1 \to t_2$. So, the set $\mathcal{P}(B_{\bar{r}})$ is equicontinuous. By the Arzelá–Ascoli theorem, $\mathcal{P}$ is compact on $B_{\bar{r}}$. Thus, (7) and (8) has at least one solution on $[0,b]$. □

Remark 3. *Let g be a continuous function on $[0,b]\times\mathbb{R}$, satisfying (A_1). Assume that*

$$|g(t,x)| \leq \mu(t),\ \forall (t,x) \in [0,b]\times\mathbb{R} \text{ and } \mu \in \mathscr{C}([0,b],\mathbb{R}^+).$$

If (27) holds, then (7) and (8) has at least one solution on $[0,b]$.

Lemma 6 (Nonlinear alternative for single value maps [37]). *Let E be a Banach space, C a closed, convex subset of E and $\mathcal{U}$ an open subset of C with $u \in \mathcal{U}$. Suppose that $\mathcal{F}: \overline{\mathcal{U}} \to C$ is a continuous, compact function; that is, $\mathcal{F}(\overline{\mathcal{U}})$ is a relatively compact subset of C map. Then, either*

(i) $\mathcal{F}$ has a fixed point in $\overline{\mathcal{U}}$, or
(ii) there is a $u \in \partial\mathcal{U}$ (the boundary of $\mathcal{U}$ in C) and $\lambda \in (0,1)$ with $u = \lambda\mathcal{F}u$.

Theorem 5. *Let g be a continuous function on $[0,b]\times\mathbb{R}$. Assume that*

(A_3) there exists functions $u_1, u_2 \in \mathscr{C}([0,b],\mathbb{R}^+)$, and a non-decreasing function, $\Psi: \mathbb{R}^+ \to \mathbb{R}^+$, such that

$$|g(t,x)| \leq u_1(t)\Psi(|x|) + u_2(t), t,x \in [0,b]\times\mathbb{R};$$

(A_4) there exists a number, $M > 0$, such that

$$\frac{M}{|\eta_1| + |\eta_2|b + \Psi(M)\omega_1 + \omega_2} > 1, \tag{28}$$

where

$$
\begin{aligned}
\omega_i := &\int_0^b \frac{(b-qs)^{(\alpha-1)}}{p^{\binom{\alpha}{2}}\Gamma_{p,q}(\alpha)} u_i(ps)\, d_{p,q}s \\
&+ \sigma_1(b) \int_0^b \frac{(b-qs)_{p,q}^{(\alpha-1)}}{p^{\binom{\alpha}{2}}\Gamma_{p,q}(\alpha)} u_i(ps)\, d_{p,q}s \\
&+ \sigma_2(b) \int_0^b \frac{(b-qs)_{p,q}^{(\alpha-2)}}{p^{\binom{\alpha-1}{2}}\Gamma_{p,q}(\alpha-1)} u_i(p^2 s)\, d_{p,q}s,\ i=1,2.
\end{aligned}
\tag{29}
$$

Then, (7) and (8) has at least one solution on $[0,b]$.

Proof. Notice that $\mathcal{F} : C \to C$ defined by (24). $\mathcal{F}$ is continuous. Let $\{x_n\}$ be a sequence of the function, such that $x_n \to x$ on $[0,b]$. Since

$$
g(p^\alpha t, x_n(p^\alpha t)) \to g(p^\alpha t, x(p^\alpha t)).
$$

Therefore, we obtain

$$
\begin{aligned}
&|(\mathcal{F}x_n)(t) - (\mathcal{F}x)(t)| \\
&\le \int_0^b \frac{(b-qs)^{(\alpha-1)}}{p^{\binom{\alpha}{2}}\Gamma_{p,q}(\alpha)} |g(ps, x_n(ps)) - g(ps, x(ps))|\, d_{p,q}s \\
&\quad + \sigma_1(b) \int_0^b \frac{(b-qs)_{p,q}^{(\alpha-1)}}{p^{\binom{\alpha}{2}}\Gamma_{p,q}(\alpha)} |g(ps, x_n(ps)) - g(ps, x(ps))|\, d_{p,q}s \\
&\quad + \sigma_2(b) \int_0^b \frac{(b-qs)_{p,q}^{(\alpha-2)}}{p^{\binom{\alpha-1}{2}}\Gamma_{p,q}(\alpha-1)} \left|g\left(p^2 s, x_n(p^2 s)\right) - g(p^2 s, x(p^2 s))\right|\, d_{p,q}s,
\end{aligned}
$$

which implies that

$$
\|\mathcal{F}x_n - \mathcal{F}x\| \to 0 \quad \text{as } n \to \infty.
$$

Thus, the operator $\mathcal{F}$ is continuous.

Next, we show that $\mathcal{F}$ maps a bounded set into a bounded set in $\mathscr{C}([0,b],\mathbb{R})$. For a positive number $r > 0$, let $B_r = \{x \in \mathscr{C}([0,b]) : \|x\| \le r\}$. Then, for any $x \in B_r$, we have

$$
\begin{aligned}
|(\mathcal{F}x)(t)| \le\ & |\eta_1| + |\eta_2| t + \int_0^t \frac{(t-qs)^{(\alpha-1)}}{p^{\binom{\alpha}{2}}\Gamma_{p,q}(\alpha)} \left|f(s, x(p^{\alpha-1}s))\right|\, d_{p,q}s \\
&+ \frac{1}{|\Delta|}[|\alpha_1||\alpha_2| t + |\beta_1||\alpha_2|] \int_0^b \frac{(b-qs)_{p,q}^{(\alpha-1)}}{p^{\binom{\alpha}{2}}\Gamma_{p,q}(\alpha)} |g(ps, x(ps))|\, d_{p,q}s \\
&+ \frac{1}{|\Delta|}[\alpha_1\beta_2 + |\beta_1||\beta_2|] \int_0^b \frac{(b-qs)_{p,q}^{(\alpha-2)}}{p^{\binom{\alpha-1}{2}}\Gamma_{p,q}(\alpha-1)} \left|g(p^2 s, x(p^2 s))\right|\, d_{p,q}s \\
\le\ & |\eta_1| + |\eta_2| b + \int_0^b \frac{(b-qs)^{(\alpha-1)}}{p^{\binom{\alpha}{2}}\Gamma_{p,q}(\alpha)} [u_1(ps)\Psi(\|x\|) + u_2(ps)]\, d_{p,q}s \\
&+ \sigma_1(b) \int_0^b \frac{(b-qs)_{p,q}^{(\alpha-1)}}{p^{\binom{\alpha}{2}}\Gamma_{p,q}(\alpha)} [u_1(ps)\Psi(\|x\|) + u_2(ps)]\, d_{p,q}s \\
&+ \sigma_2(b) \int_0^b \frac{(b-qs)_{p,q}^{(\alpha-2)}}{p^{\binom{\alpha-1}{2}}\Gamma_{p,q}(\alpha-1)} \left[u_1\left(p^2\right)\Psi(\|x\|) + u_2\left(p^2 s\right)\right]\, d_{p,q}s
\end{aligned}
$$

$$\leq |\eta_1| + |\eta_2|b + \Psi(\|r\|)\left\{ \int_0^b \frac{(b-qs)^{(\alpha-1)}}{p^{\binom{\alpha}{2}}\Gamma_{p,q}(\alpha)} u_1(ps)\, d_{p,q}s \right.$$
$$+\sigma_1(b) \int_0^b \frac{(b-qs)_{p,q}^{(\alpha-1)}}{p^{\binom{\alpha}{2}}\Gamma_{p,q}(\alpha)} u_1(ps)\, d_{p,q}s$$
$$\left. +\sigma_2(b) \int_0^b \frac{(b-qs)_{p,q}^{(\alpha-2)}}{p^{\binom{\alpha-1}{2}}\Gamma_{p,q}(\alpha-1)} u_1\left(p^2 s\right) d_{p,q}s \right\}$$
$$+ \left\{ \int_0^b \frac{(b-qs)^{(\alpha-1)}}{p^{\binom{\alpha}{2}}\Gamma_{p,q}(\alpha)} u_1(ps)\, d_{p,q}s \right.$$
$$+\sigma_1(b) \int_0^b \frac{(b-qs)_{p,q}^{(\alpha-1)}}{p^{\binom{\alpha}{2}}\Gamma_{p,q}(\alpha)} p_1(ps)\, d_{p,q}s$$
$$\left. +\sigma_2(b) \int_0^b \frac{(b-qs)_{p,q}^{(\alpha-2)}}{p^{\binom{\alpha-1}{2}}\Gamma_{p,q}(\alpha-1)} u_1\left(p^2 s\right) d_{p,q}s \right\}.$$

We have
$$\|\mathcal{F}x\| \leq |\eta_1| + |\eta_2|b + \Psi(r)\omega_1 + \omega_2 \leq M.$$

Next, $\mathcal{F}$ maps bounded sets into equicontinuous sets of $\mathscr{C}([0,b],\mathbb{R})$. Let $t_1, t_2 \in [0,b]$ with $t_1 < t_2$ be two points and B_r be a bounded ball in $\mathcal{F}$. For $x \in B_r$, we obtain

$$|(\mathcal{F}x)(t_2) - (\mathcal{F}x)(t_1)|$$
$$\leq |\eta_2|(t_2 - t_1) + \left| \int_0^{t_2} \frac{(t_2-qs)^{(\alpha-1)}}{p^{\binom{\alpha}{2}}\Gamma_{p,q}(\alpha)} |g(ps, x(ps))|\, d_{p,q}s \right.$$
$$\left. - \int_0^{t_1} \frac{(t_1-qs)^{(\alpha-1)}}{p^{\binom{\alpha}{2}}\Gamma_{p,q}(\alpha)} |g(ps, x(ps))|\, d_{p,q}s \right|$$
$$+ \frac{1}{|\Delta|}|\alpha_1||\alpha_2|(t_2 - t_1) \int_0^b \frac{(b-qs)_{p,q}^{(\alpha-1)}}{p^{\binom{\alpha}{2}}\Gamma_{p,q}(\alpha)} |g(ps, x(ps))|\, d_{p,q}s$$
$$+ \frac{1}{|\Delta|}|\alpha_1\beta_2|(t_2 - t_1) \int_0^b \frac{(b-qs)_{p,q}^{(\alpha-2)}}{p^{\binom{\alpha-1}{2}}\Gamma_{p,q}(\alpha-1)} \left|g(p^2 s, x(p^2 s))\right| d_{p,q}s$$
$$\leq |\eta_2|(t_2 - t_1) + \left| \int_0^{t_1} \left[\frac{(t_2-qs)^{(\alpha-1)}}{p^{\binom{\alpha}{2}}\Gamma_{p,q}(\alpha)} - \frac{(t_1-qs)^{(\alpha-1)}}{p^{\binom{\alpha}{2}}\Gamma_{p,q}(\alpha)} \right] [u_1(ps)\Psi(r) + u_2(ps)]\, d_{p,q}s \right.$$
$$\left. + \int_{t_1}^{t_2} \frac{(t_1-qs)^{(\alpha-1)}}{p^{\binom{\alpha}{2}}\Gamma_{p,q}(\alpha)} [u_1(ps)\Psi(r) + u_2(ps)]\, d_{p,q}s \right|$$
$$+ \frac{1}{|\Delta|}|\alpha_1||\alpha_2|(t_2 - t_1) \int_0^b \frac{(b-qs)_{p,q}^{(\alpha-1)}}{p^{\binom{\alpha}{2}}\Gamma_{p,q}(\alpha)} [u_1(ps)\Psi(r) + u_2(ps)]\, d_{p,q}s$$
$$+ \frac{1}{|\Delta|}|\alpha_1\beta_2|(t_2 - t_1) \int_0^b \frac{(b-qs)_{p,q}^{(\alpha-2)}}{p^{\binom{\alpha-1}{2}}\Gamma_{p,q}(\alpha-1)} \left[u_1\left(p^2 s\right)\Psi(r) + u_2\left(p^2 s\right)\right] d_{p,q}s.$$

Obviously, the right-hand side of the above inequality tends to zero independently of $x \in B_r$ as $t_2 \to t_1$. Thus, it follows by the Arzelá–Ascoli theorem that $\mathcal{F} : \mathscr{C}([0,b],\mathbb{R}) \to \mathscr{C}([0,b],\mathbb{R})$ is completely continuous. Now, the operator $\mathcal{F}$ satisfies all the conditions of Lemma 6; therefore, by its conclusion, either condition (i) or condition (ii) holds.

Now, we show that the conclusion (ii) is not possible. Let

$$\mathcal{U} = \{x \in \mathscr{C}([0,b],\mathbb{R}) : \|x\| \leq M\}$$

with $|\eta_1| + |\eta_2|b + \Psi(M)\omega_1 + \omega_2 < M$. Then, it can be shown that

$$
\begin{aligned}
|\mathcal{F}x| \leq & |\eta_1| + |\eta_2|b + \Psi(\|x\|)\Bigg\{ \int_0^b \frac{(b-qs)^{(\alpha-1)}}{p^{\binom{\alpha}{2}}\Gamma_{p,q}(\alpha)} u_1(ps)\, d_{p,q}s \\
& +\sigma_1(b) \int_0^b \frac{(b-qs)_{p,q}^{(\alpha-1)}}{p^{\binom{\alpha}{2}}\Gamma_{p,q}(\alpha)} u_1(ps)\, d_{p,q}s \\
& +\sigma_2(b) \int_0^b \frac{(b-qs)_{p,q}^{(\alpha-2)}}{p^{\binom{\alpha-1}{2}}\Gamma_{p,q}(\alpha-1)} u_2\left(p^2 s\right) d_{p,q}s \Bigg\} \\
& + \Bigg\{ \int_0^b \frac{(b-qs)^{(\alpha-1)}}{p^{\binom{\alpha}{2}}\Gamma_{p,q}(\alpha)} u_2(ps)\, d_{p,q}s \\
& +\sigma_1(b) \int_0^b \frac{(b-qs)_{p,q}^{(\alpha-1)}}{p^{\binom{\alpha}{2}}\Gamma_{p,q}(\alpha)} u_2(ps)\, d_{p,q}s \\
& +\sigma_2(b) \int_0^b \frac{(b-qs)_{p,q}^{(\alpha-2)}}{p^{\binom{\alpha-1}{2}}\Gamma_{p,q}(\alpha-1)} u_2\left(p^2 s\right) d_{p,q}s \Bigg\} \\
\leq & |\eta_1| + |\eta_2|b + \Psi(M)\omega_1 + \omega_2 \leq M.
\end{aligned}
$$

Suppose there exists $x \in \partial\mathcal{U}$ and $\lambda \in (0,1)$, such that $x = \lambda\mathcal{F}x$. Then, for such choices of x and λ, we have

$$
M = \|x\| = \lambda\|\mathcal{F}x\| < |\eta_1| + |\eta_2|b + \Psi(\|x\|)\omega_1 + \omega_2 < M.
$$

Thus, it leads to a contradiction. Accordingly, by Lemma 6, $x \in \overline{\mathcal{U}}$ is fixed point of $\mathcal{F}$. Therefore, x a solution of the problem (7) and (8). This completes the proof. □

Remark 4. *If u_1, u_2 in (A_4) are continuous, then $\omega_i \leq A\|u_i\|$, $i = 1,2$, where A is defined by (26).*

4. Examples

Example 1. *Let $p = 1/4, q = 1/5$, $\alpha = 1.5$, $\alpha_1 = 1$, $\alpha_2 = 1/2$, $\beta_1 = 1/4$, $\beta_2 = 3/2$, $t\gamma_1 = 1/3$, $\gamma_2 = 1$, $b = 1$. Given a non-negative function, $g(t,x) = |\sin(t)| + \frac{\Gamma_{p,q}(1.5)}{4}x$. Consider*

$$
{}^{c}D_{p,q}^{\alpha}x(t) = |\sin(p^{\alpha}t)| + \frac{\Gamma_{p,q}(1.5)}{4}x(p^{\alpha}t),\ t \in [0,1], \tag{30}
$$

$$
x(0) + \frac{1}{4}D_{p,q}x(0) = \frac{1}{3},\quad \frac{1}{2}x(1) + \frac{3}{2}D_{p,q}x(4) = 1. \tag{31}
$$

Since

$$
|g(t,x) - g(t,y)| = \left| \frac{\Gamma_{p,q}(1.5)}{4}x - \frac{\Gamma_{p,q}(1.5)}{4}y \right| = \frac{\Gamma_{p,q}(1.5)}{4}|x-y|,
$$

it follows that the condition (A_1) holds. Let $L = \frac{\Gamma_{p,q}(1.5)}{4}$. From (25), by direct computation, we obtain $\Delta = -15/8, \eta_1 = 2/9, \eta_2 = 4/9$ and $\sigma_1(1) = 1/3, \sigma_2(1) = 1$. It easy to see that

$$
k = (1 + \sigma_1(1))\frac{1}{4[\alpha]_{p,q}} + \frac{\sigma_2(1)}{4} \approx 0.7187272601 < 1.
$$

This satisfies Theorem 3. Accordingly, by Theorem 3, (30) and (31) has a unique solution.

Example 2. *Let* $p = 1/4$, $q = 1/5, \alpha = 3/2, \alpha_1 = 1, \alpha_2 = 1/2, \beta_1 = 1/4, \beta_2 = 3/2,$ $\gamma_1 = 1/3,\ \gamma_2 = 1$, *and* $b = 1$. *Given a non-negative function*

$$g(t,x) = \frac{1}{10}\frac{e^{-x^2}|\sin(|x|)|}{x^2+1} + \frac{e^{-x}(t^2+1)}{2+t^2} + \frac{1}{3}.$$

Consider

$$^{C}D^{\alpha}_{p,q}x(t) = \frac{1}{10}\frac{e^{-(x(p^{\alpha}t))^2}|\sin(|x(p^{\alpha}t)|)|}{(x(p^{\alpha}t))^2+1} + \frac{e^{-x(p^{\alpha}t)}((p^{\alpha}t)^2+1)}{2+(p^{\alpha}t)^2} + \frac{1}{3},\ t\in[0,1], \tag{32}$$

$$x(0) + \frac{1}{4}D_{p,q}x(0) = \frac{1}{3},\quad \frac{1}{2}x(1) + \frac{3}{2}D_{p,q}x(4) = 1. \tag{33}$$

By applying Theorem 5, through simple calculation, we have $\Delta = -15/8$, $\eta_1 = 2/9$, $\eta_2 = 4/9$ *and* $\sigma_1(1) = 1/3, \sigma_2(1) = 1$.

Since

$$|g(t,x)| = \left|\frac{1}{10}\frac{e^{-x^2}|\sin(|x|)|}{x^2+1} + \frac{e^{-x}(t^2+1)}{2+t^2} + \frac{1}{3}\right| \le \frac{1}{10}|x| + 1,$$

(A_3) *holds. In fact,* $u_1 = 1/10, u_2 = 1, \Psi(M) = M$. *By computation, we obtain* $\omega_1 \approx 0.1380279163$, $\omega_2 \approx 1.38027916$. *Furthermore, from the condition (28), it follows that* $M > 2.374724041$. *Thus, it satisfies Theorem 5. So, (32) and (33) has at least one solution.*

5. Conclusions

In this paper, we investigated the local separated boundary value problem of a class of fractional (p,q)-difference equations involving the Caputo fractional derivative. By applying some well-known tools in fixed-point theory, such as Banach's contraction mapping principle, Krasnoselskii's fixed-point theorem, and the Leary–Schauder nonlinear alternative, we derive the existence and uniqueness of solutions for the problem. Moreover, some illustrating examples were also presented.

Author Contributions: Conceptualization, P.N. and K.N.; investigation, P.N., K.N., J.T., S.K.N. and B.A.; methodology, P.N. and K.N.; validation, P.N., K.N., J.T., S.K.N. and B.A.; visualization, P.N., K.N., J.T., S.K.N. and B.A.; writing—original draft, P.N. and K.N.; writing—review and editing, P.N. and K.N. All authors have read and agreed to the published version of the manuscript.

Funding: This research received funding support from the National Science, Research and Innovation Fund (NSRF), Thailand.

Institutional Review Board Statement: Not applicable.

Informed Consent Statement: Not applicable.

Data Availability Statement: Not applicable.

Acknowledgments: We would like to thank anonymous referees for comments which are helpful for improvement in this paper.

Conflicts of Interest: The authors declare no conflict of interest.

References

1. Gopal, N.S.; Jagan M.J. Existence and uniqueness of solutions to a nabla fractional difference equation with dual nonlocal boundary conditions. *Foundations* **2022**, *2*, 151–166. [CrossRef]
2. Ahmad, B.; Agarwal. R.P. On nonlocal fractional boundary value problems. *Dyn. Contin. Discrete Impuls. Syst.* **2011**, *18*, 535–544.
3. Wang, Y.; Liu, L.; Wu, Y. Positive solutions for a nonlocal fractional differential equation. *Nonlinear. Anal.* **2011**, *74*, 3599–3605. [CrossRef]

4. Ford, N.J.; Morgado, M.L. Fractional boundary value problems: analysis and numerical methods. *Fract. Calc. Appl. Anal.* **2011**, *14*, 554–567. [CrossRef]
5. Ahmad, B.; Ntouyas, S.K. Nonlinear fractional differential equations and inclusions of arbitrary order and multi-strip boundary conditions. *Electron. J. Differ. Equ.* **2012**, *2012*, 1–22.
6. Diethelm, K. *The Analysis of Fractional Differential Equations*; Springer: New York, NY, USA, 2010.
7. Kilbas, A.A.; Srivastava, H.M.; Trujillo, J.J. *Theory and Application of the Fractional Differential Equations*; North-Holland Mathematics Studies; Elsevier Science: Amsterdam, The Netherlands, 2006.
8. Lakshmikantham, V.; Leela, S.; Devi., J.V. *Theory of Fractional Dynamic Systyms*; Cambridge Scientific Publishers: Cottenham, UK, 2009.
9. Miller, K.S.; Ross, B. *An Introduction to the Fractional Calculus and Differential Equations*; Wiley: New York, NY, USA, 1993.
10. Podlubny, I. *Fractional Differential Equations*; Accademic Press: New York, NY, USA, 1999.
11. Jackson, F.H. On a q-definite integrals. *Quart. J. Pure. Appl. Math.* **1910**, *41*, 193–203.
12. Jackson, F.H. q-Difference equations. *Amer. J. Math.* **1910**, *32*, 305–314. [CrossRef]
13. Fock, V. Zur Theorie des Wasserstoffatoms. *Z. Physik.* **1935**, *98*, 145–154. [CrossRef]
14. Ferreira, R. Nontrivial solutions for fractional q-difference boundary value problems. *Electron J. Qual. Theory Differ. Equ.* **2010**, *2010*, 1–10. [CrossRef]
15. Aral, A.; Gupta, V.; Agarwal, R.P. *Applications of q-calculus in Operator Theory*; Springer: New York, NY, USA, 2013.
16. Ahmad, B.; Alsaedi, A.; Ntouyas, S.K. A study of second-order q-difference equations with boundary conditions. *Adv. Differ. Equ.* **2012**, *2012*, 35. [CrossRef]
17. Kac,V.; Cheung, P. *Quantum Calculus*; Springer: New York, NY, USA, 2002.
18. Al-Salam, W.A. Some fractional q-integrals and q-derivatives. *Proc. Edinburgh Math. Soc.* **1967**, *15*, 135–140. [CrossRef]
19. Ahmad, B.; Ntouyas, S.K.; Purnaras, I.K. Existence results for nonlinear q-difference equations with nonlocal boundary conditions. *Comm. Appl. Nonlinear Anal.* **2012**, *19*, 59–72.
20. El-Shahed, M.; Al-Askar, F. Positive solutions for boundary value problem of nonlinear fractional q-difference equations. *ISRN Math. Anal.* **2011**, *2011*, 12. [CrossRef]
21. Ferreira, R.A.C. Positive solutions for a class of boundary value problems with fractional q-difference equations. *Comput. Math. Appl.* **2011**, *61*, 367–373. [CrossRef]
22. Aral, A.; Gupta, V. Applications of (p,q)-gamma function to Szász durrmeyer operators. *Publ. l'Inst. Math.* **2017**, *102*, 211–220. [CrossRef]
23. Sadjang, P.N. On the fundamental theorem of (p,q)-calculus and some (p,q)-taylor formulas. *Results Math.* **2018**, *73*, 39. [CrossRef]
24. Usman, T.; Saif, M.; Choi, J. Certain identities associated with (p,q)-binomial coefficients and (p,q)-Stirling polynomials of the second kind. *Symmetry* **2020**, *12*, 1436. [CrossRef]
25. Sadjang, P.N. On the (p,q)-gamma and the (p,q)-beta functions. *arXiv* **2015**, arXiv:1506.07394.
26. Mursaleen, M.; Ansari, K.J.; Khan, A. On (p,q)-analogues of Bernstein operators. *Appl. Math. Comput.* **2016**, *278*, 70–71. [CrossRef]
27. Prabseang, J.; Nonlaopon, K.; Tariboon, J. (p,q)-Hermite-Hadamard inequalities for double integral and (p,q)-differentiable convex functions. *Axioms* **2019**, *8*, 68. [CrossRef]
28. Kamsrisuk, N.; Promsakon, C.; Ntouyas, S.K.; Tariboon, J. Nonlocal boundary value problems for (p,q)-difference equations. *Differ. Equ. Appl.* **2018**, *10*, 183–195. [CrossRef]
29. Promsakon, C.; Kamsrisuk, N.; Ntouyas, S.K.; Tariboon, J. On the second-order (p,q)-difference equation with separated boundary conditions. *Adv. Math. Phys.* **2018**, *2018*. [CrossRef]
30. Tunç, M.; Göv, E. (p,q)-Integral inequalities. *RGMIA Res. Rep. Coll.* **2016**, *19*, 1–13.
31. Neang, P.; Nonlaopon, K.; Tariboon, J.; Ntouyas, S.K.; Ahmad, B. Nonlocal Boundary Value Problems of Nonlinear Fractional (p, q)-Difference Equations. *Fractal. Fract.* **2021**, *5*, 270. [CrossRef]
32. Qin, Z.; Sun, S. On a nonlinear fractional (p, q)-difference Schrödinger equation. *J. Appl. Math. Comput.* **2021**, 1–14. [CrossRef]
33. Qin, Z.; Sun, S. Positive solutions for fractional (p, q)-difference boundary value problems. *J. Appl. Math. Comput.* **2021**, 1–18. [CrossRef]
34. Soontharanon, J.; Sitthiwirattham, T. On fractional (p,q)-calculus. *Adv. Differ. Equ.* **2020**, *2020*, 1–18. [CrossRef]
35. Milovanović, G.V.; Gupta, V.; Malik, N. (p,q)-beta functions and applications in approximation. *Bol. Soc. Mat. Mex.* **2018**, *24*, 219–237. [CrossRef]
36. Krasnoselskii, M.A. Two remarks on the method of successive approximations. *Uspekhi. Mat. Nauk.* **1995**, *10*, 123–127.
37. Granas, A., Dugundji, J. *Fixed point Theory and Applications*; Springer: New York, NY, USA, 2003.

MDPI AG
Grosspeteranlage 5
4052 Basel
Switzerland
Tel.: +41 61 683 77 34

Mathematics Editorial Office
E-mail: mathematics@mdpi.com
www.mdpi.com/journal/mathematics

www.ingramcontent.com/pod-product-compliance
Lightning Source LLC
Chambersburg PA
CBHW041941260926
51850CB00018B/385
9783725870288